THE NPR® GUIDE TO
BUILDING A
CLASSICAL
CD
COLLECTION

By
TED LIBBEY

Introduction by
MSTISLAV ROSTROPOVICH

WORKMAN PUBLISHING·NEW YORK

To my parents, to my brothers Scott and Chase,
and to Molly

Library of Congress Cataloging-in-Publication Data

Libbey, Ted 1951–
The NPR Guide to Building a Classical CD Collection /
by Ted Libbey.
p.   cm
Includes index.
ISBN 1-56305-051-X (paper)
1. Compact Discs—Reviews.   2. Music—Discography.
I. National Public Radio (U.S.)   II. Title

ML 156.9.L5   1994
016.78026′6—dc20   92-50292
CIP
MN

Workman books are available at special discounts when purchased in bulk for premiums and sales promotions as well as for fundraising or educational use. Special editions can be created to specification. For details, contact the Special Sales Director at the address below.

Workman Publishing Company, Inc.
708 Broadway
New York, NY 10003

Manufactured in the U.S.
First printing March 1994
10 9 8 7 6 5 4

A C K N O W L E D G M E N T S

*I*n his preface to *The Path to Rome*, Hilaire Belloc makes light of the authorial duty of acknowledgment, assuring his reader that his avoidance of it "is but on account of the multitude and splendour of those who have attended at the production of this volume." The present writer differs. While the reader may wince at the list of names that follows, it is precisely because this multitude is so splendid that I wish to thank each one for the assistance I have received in writing this book.

I begin with Ruth Sullivan, my editor at Workman, who has earned my respect and devotion with her insistence on quality, and Kathy Ryan, her highly resourceful assistant. My thanks are also due to Anita Dickhuth, who did a splendid job with photo research, to Lisa Sloane, who presided so skillfully over the book's design, and to Mildred Camacho Richardson and Ken Richardson—Mildred for keying much of the original manuscript, Ken for fact-checking and copy-editing the manuscript and for providing many helpful suggestions along the way.

I am grateful as well to many friends for their advice and encouragement, among them Michelle Krisel and Steve Wassermann, with whom the idea for this book originated, Leon Dana, Bob Silverstein, Denis Stevens, and Tom Dixon. I am indebted to my colleagues at National Public Radio®, especially those on the staff of *Performance Today*, including host Martin Goldsmith, producer Laura Bertran, and senior producers Ben Roe and Don Lee. More than anything else, what has sustained me in the writing of this book has been their enthusiasm, and that of NPR® listeners from Alaska to Florida.

To my friends in the record industry—particularly Aimee Gautreau, Albert Imperato, Susan Schiffer, Marlisa Monroe, Marilyn Egol, Philicia Gilbert, Sarah Folger, and Ellen Schantz—I offer thanks for responding so cheerfully to the many requests for information and assistance this book occasioned. And to *Musical America*, my home for many years, I make grateful acknowledgment of the free use of its photo archive.

Lastly, I humbly thank those who, over the years, have been my best teachers—John Merrill, Leon Plantinga, George Houle, and Leonard Ratner.

F O R E W O R D

*T*he arrival of the digital audio Compact Disc on the American market about a decade ago has caused a revolution in home-listening habits comparable to the changeover from shellac 78s to vinyl LPs during the 1950s, and from mono to stereo in the 1960s. The most compelling reason for the popularity of the CD is its sound quality. As a playback medium, it offers wider dynamic range and much less distortion than either the LP or the cassette. CDs sound clear, warm, and alive, often with astonishing impact and presence. Another reason for the CD's success is practicality: read by a laser beam while rotating at speeds up to 400 rpm, a five-inch-diameter CD can carry a piece as long as Beethoven's Ninth Symphony (lasting approximately 70 minutes), and play it back without interruption. Add to that value: all nine of Beethoven's symphonies, along with assorted overtures, will fit on five or six CDs and can be purchased as a set for about $35, which is less than what it cost to buy the same recordings on seven "long-playing" records 25 years ago.

The popularity of the Compact Disc has, however, brought a dilemma for the classical music buyer. In ten years, the classical CD catalog has grown from 100 titles to approximately 50,000. With so many recordings available on CD, there is an overabundance of options, particularly when it comes to the most familiar works in the repertory. The current issue of the *Schwann* catalog lists 86 single-CD offerings of Beethoven's Fifth Symphony, with entries for another 24 sets containing the complete Beethoven symphonies. There are 81 CD versions of Vivaldi's *The Four Seasons,* 78 of Mozart's *Eine kleine Nachtmusik,* and an astonishing 39 of Antonín Dvořák's Cello Concerto. For the ordinary music lover, leafing through the catalog or flipping through discs at the local record store is daunting. Having to decide which recording to buy becomes an exercise in self-intimidation.

That is one problem facing the consumer, and the bulky tomes with hard-to-read type, offering comments on 20 or 30 versions of a particular piece, do little to help. Another problem, which affects many people who find classical music appealing on a visceral level, is the fear of inadequate knowledge. "I like it," these people will say, "but I just don't feel I know enough to really understand it." To them I always say that what matters is not what one *knows* about music, but how it makes one *feel.* Nonetheless, some guidance—a few signposts to follow as one hears a piece—can often make a big difference, and turn an hour spent listening to music from a diversion into an experience.

The purpose of this book is to help the music lover and consumer alike. It is intended to serve both as a companion to the "basic" classical repertory—by providing background and insight into the finest accomplishments of the great composers—and as a highly selective guide to the best recordings of those works on Compact Disc, by identifying the recordings that offer the most compelling realizations of the music and the most natural sound.

That there is a pressing need for this kind of book I realized some years ago when I began to contribute a weekly segment to National Public Radio's® *Performance Today* called "The *PT* Basic Record Library." The response of listeners all over the country was immediate and enthusiastic, and requests for a list of recommended recordings poured in by the thousands. Now entering its sixth year, the "BRL" (as we refer to it in the studio) remains the most popular segment on *Performance Today.* This book follows much the same format as the show. For each work (except operas), the coverage consists of a commentary on the music followed by a listing of recommended recordings and capsule reviews. Originally, I planned to discuss 100 works, but the book grew well beyond that. Even then, difficult choices had to be made. I wanted to write about all nine Beethoven symphonies, but the 40 pages it would have entailed seemed too much. So I limited my coverage of Beethoven's symphonies to the four I feel are most important, in order to leave room for such works as Shostakovich's Tenth and Prokofiev's Fifth—both near and dear to my heart—and for single symphonic scores by the likes of Franck, Janáček, Nielsen, and Vaughan Williams, whose importance does not compare with Beethoven's, to be sure, but whose music strikes me as unique, distinctive, and valuable. In making these decisions I was often guided by what my father said to me when I first started collecting records 25 years ago: "Catholicize your taste." I still think it is better to have an appreciation of the repertory's breadth than an in-depth knowledge of just a part of it.

Still, much as I love the music of Chabrier, Chausson, and Dukas, I do not consider any of it basic and have left it out of this book. And much as I respect that of Webern, not a single piece of his has found a place in my heart, or, I suspect, in the hearts of most of those who have been exposed to it during the past three quarters of a century. So it has not found a place here.

As Mozart once said of his aim in composing, my aim in writing this book has been "to please both the connoisseur and the amateur." For ease of use, I have divided the text into six chapters, each of which covers a single, large genre—orchestral works (including symphonies and suites), concertos, chamber works, keyboard works, sacred and choral works, and operas. Within each chapter the entries have been arranged alphabetically by composer. This approach permits the reader with a special interest—for instance, in music for the orchestra or the piano—to plunge right in, while still making it easy for another reader to navigate from work to work and composer to composer without knowing their chronology, or for yet another reader to find the works of a favorite composer in each section with a minimum of fuss. In the case of opera, I decided that a chronological overview, emphasizing the achievements of the five greatest masters the genre has known—Mozart, Wagner, Verdi, Puccini, and Strauss—would provide the best foundation for listening, while facilitating the reader's further exploration of the subject.

Aristotle devoted the final part of his *Politics* to a discussion of music and the way in which "man relates to man." In assigning to music such an important role in the functioning of the well-governed state, Aristotle was simply acknowledging what was known to him and his contemporaries, namely that music could have a beneficial influence over the character and the soul, and that it could show a person what was possible and becoming in life. "Innocent pleasures are not only in harmony with the perfect end of life, they also provide relaxation," the philosopher rightly observed. In our own time, Duke Ellington said much the same thing when he declared: "It don't mean a thing if it ain't got that swing." This book agrees.

—*Ted Libbey*

The Analog vs. Digital Debate

The Compact Disc is the capstone of the digital audio revolution—whose credo is that any sound, including the highly complex sounds of music, can be represented by numerical samples and stored and retrieved that way. By the mid-1980s, digital recording—whereby music is converted to a binary code at the time of the recording—had become standard. Prior to this, all recordings were analog, made by storing the sound of a musical performance as an "analogous" waveform—in the groove cut onto a transcription disc or as an arrangement of magnetized particles on tape.

Proponents of digital recording and playback believe that it is superior to analog because it adds no noise to the recording chain (such as the hiss from a master tape), and because it does a better job of reproducing high frequencies, loud dynamics, and sudden transients. Moreover, digital recordings can be played back without degradation and copied without loss of quality. Adherents of analog complain that digital recording takes the life out of music by failing to capture its most subtle nuances, and that compared with the warmer sound of LPs, CDs are cold, analytical, and harsh. Most of these vinyl aficionados can afford the $30,000 systems needed to buttress their opinions.

T.L.

C O N T E N T S

INTRODUCTION

ON LISTENING TO MUSIC

By Mstislav Rostropovich

Page xi

CHAPTER I

ORCHESTRAL WORKS

Page 1

Bach • Barber • Bartók • Beethoven •
Berlioz • Bernstein • Bizet • Brahms •
Britten • Bruckner • Copland •
Debussy • Dvořák • Elgar • Falla • Franck •
Gershwin • Grieg • Handel • Haydn •
Hindemith • Holst • Ives • Janáček •
Liszt • Mahler • Mendelssohn • Mozart •
Mussorgsky • Nielsen • Prokofiev •
Ravel • Respighi • Rimsky-Korsakov •
Saint-Saëns • Schubert • Schumann •
Shostakovich • Sibelius • Smetana •
The Strauss Family • Richard Strauss •
Stravinsky • Tchaikovsky •
Vaughan Williams

CHAPTER II

CONCERTOS

Page 197

Bach • Bartók • Beethoven • Berg •
Brahms • Bruch • Chopin • Dvořák • Elgar •
Falla • Grieg • Haydn • Liszt •
Mendelssohn • Mozart • Prokofiev •
Rachmaninoff • Ravel • Rodrigo •
Schumann • Sibelius •
Tchaikovsky • Vivaldi

CHAPTER III

CHAMBER MUSIC

Page 287

BACH • BARTÓK • BEETHOVEN • BORODIN •
BRAHMS • DEBUSSY • DVOŘÁK • FRANCK •
HAYDN • MENDELSSOHN • MOZART • RAVEL •
SCHOENBERG • SCHUBERT • SCHUMANN

CHAPTER IV

SOLO KEYBOARD WORKS

Page 353

BACH • BEETHOVEN • BRAHMS • CHOPIN •
DEBUSSY • LISZT • MOZART • RACHMANINOFF •
RAVEL • SCARLATTI • SCHUBERT • SCHUMANN

CHAPTER V

SACRED AND CHORAL MUSIC

Page 401

BACH • BEETHOVEN • BERLIOZ • BERNSTEIN •
BRAHMS • BRITTEN • FAURÉ • HANDEL •
HAYDN • JANÁČEK • MOZART • ORFF • VERDI

CHAPTER VI

OPERA

Page 441

MOZART • BEETHOVEN • WEBER • ROSSINI •
DONIZETTI • BELLINI • MEYERBEER • WAGNER •
VERDI • TCHAIKOVSKY • MUSSORGSKY • BIZET •
MASCAGNI • LEONCAVALLO • PUCCINI •
RICHARD STRAUSS • DEBUSSY • BERG •
GERSHWIN • BRITTEN • STRAVINSKY

INDEX

Page 485

O N   L I S T E N I N G   T O   M U S I C

*T*here is a philosophy which says that in order to feel God, you must begin to believe in Him, just as in order to feel the warmth of a stove, you must come close to it. This is also true with music. In order to feel its warmth, you must come close to it, and open your heart to it. Sometimes that can be awfully hard work. I know many people who come to concerts buttoned up to the last button, so to speak, and who *leave* buttoned as well.

But music is not so aggressive that it will come through to you without your help. In order to feel its warmth and beauty, you have to shed your emotional insulation, just as if it were a coat, and prepare to listen with your heart. The key to finding happiness in music and to understanding it is not knowledge, because the music itself will teach you whatever you need to know. The key is feeling. What a treasure chest that key unlocks! I have been lucky enough to spend my life in the world of music, making it and sharing it with some of

MSTISLAV ROSTROPOVICH

the giants of our time, and I know, with all my heart, that every hour spent with great music illuminates the rest of one's life.

Real, great music should never serve as a background for activities or chores not connected with it. Our world has been cursed with "elevator music." Waiting in an airport or visiting the doctor or dentist, we are so often beset with canned "classical music." I have even visited cafés, especially in Japan, that serve classical music as they serve your food. Many's the time that I would leave, paying my bill for food and drink I had neither eaten nor drunk, because my attention had been captured by the music playing in the background.

The very nature of music makes it a different art: you can't stand before it, studying and examining it until you understand it. Therefore, if you are doing anything else while listening to classical music, you are distracted and lose the thread of development of the composer's musical idea. Just as if you were reading a book and skipped every ten pages or so.

We are fortunate today that we can explore music in so many ways, through concerts, broadcasts, and recordings. Yet the very abundance of choices available can be quite confusing. That is why we readers are lucky that Ted Libbey has provided this guide to the complex and magnificent realm of music. I have known Ted for many years, and I can promise you that he will be your best possible friend in the discoveries that lie ahead. Ted is one of the world's greatest musicologists. He has enormous academic knowledge, which he acquired at Yale and as a doctoral student at Stanford, and he is certainly familiar with the world of recordings. But for me the most important thing is the way Ted engages with the music. He comes to each performance with "open ears," ready to hear whatever the music will teach him, and his writing reflects this. The suggestions he makes in this book— the way he talks about the pieces themselves and his choice of recordings—all convey this essential understanding.

Ted is also a talented musician. He has performed in various orchestras as a percussionist and he continues to conduct professionally. In one instance I remember well, he sang in the chorus when I conducted the Rachmaninoff *Vespers* at Carnegie Hall. In my experience, only a handful of critics are as insightful about what goes on in the performer's mind. On the rare occasion when I read a review of my performance (or have one translated for me), it will usually tell me what I did in a particular moment. But his is the rare review in which the critic tells me what I was *thinking* in that moment.

So I am especially happy that Ted has written this book. Once you begin to read it and experience the music he has written about, you will find yourself coming close to the stove and feeling its warmth—and also, I hope, sharing in the happiness that listening to music can provide.

C H A P T E R   I

ORCHESTRAL WORKS

The concept of the orchestra as a large body of diverse instru-ments sounding together dates back to antiquity. It is memorably preserved in the words of Psalm 150, which calls for the Lord to be praised "with the sound of the trumpet" as well as with the psaltery and harp, stringed instruments and organs, and loud and high-sounding cymbals. The symphony orchestra that we know is of more recent vintage, having developed out of the string con-sorts and court ensembles of the Renaissance and early Baroque.

The most important forerunner of this orchestra was the court "chapel" (in Italian, *cappella*, in German, *Kapelle*) maintained by princes and prelates during the Middle Ages and the Renaissance. At first, chapels were nothing more than choirs, since instruments other than the organ were banned from use in church owing to their association with dancing, dining, and secular pursuits. During the Renaissance, instruments began to appear in court chapels throughout Europe, and as the times grew more secular the number of instrumentalists employed at court grew as well. By the beginning of the 18th century, the court chapel had in fact become an orches-tra, especially in Germany, and the musician in charge of it—known there as a *Kapellmeister* and in Italy as a *maestro di cappella*—was likely to be occupied not with church services but with concerts, operas, and chamber performances.

In the 18th century, the orchestra became the star of a thriving court and public concert scene. Whether it was the enormous, regally liveried array of the Concert Spirituel in Paris, the virtuoso court bands of Carl Theodor in Mannheim and Munich, or the Collegium Musicum Bach conducted at Zimmermann's coffeehouse in Leipzig, an orchestra offered listeners a taste of the magnificent and the sublime. For ears unaccustomed to anything louder than hoof beats and church bells, hearing 50 or 60 instruments playing at once was a breathtaking experience, beyond comparison with anything in nature or the imagination.

The orchestra of the 18th century was dominated by the strings, which were usually divided into four groups: first violins, second violins, violas, and basses (consisting of cellos and string basses playing together). The most commonly encountered woodwinds were flutes, oboes, and bassoons; since the same musicians often played both flute and oboe, scores would usually call for one or the other. In all but the largest ensembles, the clarinet was a rarity until the end of the century. Most orchestras had a pair of horns, and could muster two trumpets and timpani for festive occasions. Trombones, a familiar presence in the opera house (their solemn tone symbolized the supernatural), had to wait until early in the 19th century to gain admission to the symphony orchestra.

Doubling in size during the Romantic era, the orchestra achieved its present disposition of approximately 100 players around the turn of the century. Instead of woodwinds in pairs, one could expect to find three or four of each variety, along with such auxiliary instruments as piccolo, English horn, bass clarinet, and contabassoon. A full brass section included not just two horns and two trumpets, but as many as eight or ten horns, four trumpets, three trombones, and tuba. In addition to timpani the percussion section routinely included cymbals, bass drum, and triangle, and on demand could produce such paraphernalia as tam-tam, snare drum, tubular bells, sleigh bells, cowbells, glockenspiel, castanets, tambourine, rute, ratchet, and wind machine. A large body of strings—on the order of 18 first and 16 second violins, 14 violas, 12 cellos, and 10 double basses—was needed to balance the sonic weight of all that hardware.

Just as the orchestra changed over time, the formal genres in which orchestral music was written changed with fashion. Among the most popular forms of the Baroque were the suite, a collection of dances often prefaced by a movement in the style of an overture, and the concerto grosso, a kind of chamber music writ large, usually consisting of three or four movements in alternating fast and slow tempos, sometimes with solo parts. Handel's *Water Music* is an instance of the former, while Bach's *Brandenburg* Concertos are a particularly elevated example of the latter.

The symphony, from the Latin *symphonia* meaning "sounding together," was shaped by many hands during the course of the 18th century, most ably by Mozart and Haydn, and became the dominant orchestral format of the 19th century thanks to Beethoven's visionary essays in the genre. The Classical symphony generally consisted of four movements: an opening movement in lively tempo, a lyrical slow movement, a minuet, and a brisk finale. Nearly always, the first movement was in sonata form, also known as key-area form—in which, during the first part of the movement (called the "exposition"), there is a departure from the home key to a closely related key (the dominant if the home key is major, or the relative major if it is minor); a series of more radical departures later on (in what is called the "development"); and a return to the home key, usually by means of a reprise of the movement's opening material (called the "recapitulation"), which serves to confirm the key and provide a sense of completion to the movement. Often, the slow movement and finale of a symphony are cast in key-area form as well.

Departures from the four-movement model of Mozart and Haydn began with Beethoven's *Pastorale* Symphony and continued through the 19th century and the 20th, yet the model remained viable in the works of Mahler, Sibelius, Shostakovich, and Prokofiev, the most important symphonists of the past 100 years. The 19th century saw the emergence of two genres related to the symphony and to each other, the concert overture and the symphonic poem. But as the 20th century nears its end, these forms, along with the symphony, appear to be in decline. What has supplanted them might best be characterized as suites and orchestral concertos, suggesting that music has come back full circle to the forms of the Baroque. The orchestra is still a magnificent vehicle for the expression of thought and feeling, and its literature remains unmatched in the annals of music for its power, scale, and emotional range.

M A J O R   M A E S T R O

JOHANN SEBASTIAN BACH

*A*sked on a final exam to sum up Bach's life and achievement, a student in a music history class began: "Bach was a master of the passion, and the father of 20 children." Both of which are true, though not in the way it sounds.

Bach was the master not only of the passion but of the cantata, the concerto, the sonata, the suite—in short, of an astounding variety of forms both sacred and secular, instrumental and vocal, ranging from the most intimate to the most magnificent. And not only was he a prolific sire who, at age 45, could boast that his family could form a complete vocal and instrumental ensemble, he was also one of the most prolific composers in history, with musical "children" numbering in the thousands.

Born in Eisenach, into the most musical family in German history, Bach received an unusually thorough humanistic education. As a child he was a good singer, but it was only in his teens that he developed into a capable instrumentalist. In composition he was largely self-taught. After completing his studies in Lüneburg, Bach held various positions as a church organist. In 1705 he made a pilgrimage to Lübeck to hear Dietrich Buxtehude, the greatest organist of the day and a composer whose music was to have a profound effect on him. Bach's own fame as a virtuoso was beginning to spread, and by the end of his decade of service as court organist and concertmaster in Weimar (1708–1717), he had secured a reputation as the greatest organist and improviser in Germany—a distinction confirmed by the aged J. A. Reincken, who, after hearing him extemporize on the chorale *An Wasserflüssen Babylon*, remarked, "I thought this art was dead, but I see it still lives in you."

1 6 8 5 – 1 7 5 0

Some of Bach's happiest years were spent at the court of Cöthen (1717–1723), where his young patron, Prince Leopold of Anhalt-Cöthen, a fine musician himself, showed great generosity to his Kapellmeister. Bach had devoted most of his time in Weimar to composing cantatas and works for the organ. Now, the bulk of his output consisted of chamber and instrumental scores for the prince's music-hungry court. In 1723 Bach was appointed Kantor at the Thomaskirche in Leipzig, that city's most important church and its musical center. He remained Kantor until his death in 1750, composing five complete annual cycles of cantatas and other sacred works—including the St. Matthew Passion and the B minor Mass. In April 1729, shortly after the first performance of the St. Matthew Passion, Bach was offered the directorship of the Leipzig Collegium Musicum, an association of professional and student musicians founded by Telemann that enjoyed an excellent reputation for the quality of its performances. After six years of writing sacred compositions and working with limited forces to get his music performed, Bach was eager for the chance to return to orchestral composition and to work with top-flight instrumentalists. He withdrew from the Collegium in 1741; during the next few years, he undertook two remarkable studies that summarized his knowledge of the art and theory of music: Musical Offering and The Art of Fugue.

It made no difference whether Bach wrote for the keyboard, the voice, or any of the wind, brass, and string instruments known to him: he understood the capabilities of all. Neither did it matter what style he chose to express himself in, for though he had thoroughly assimilated the practices of the high German Baroque and wrote formidably in the archaic mode, he was also conversant with the newer tastes and understood the conventions of Italian instrumental and vocal music. Bach's novel approach to musical form and ability to synthesize elements of different styles into a personal idiom set him apart from all his peers. His craft knew no limits.

BACH TRAVELED *widely in Germany but never set foot outside of it. In this respect he differed from his more cosmopolitan contemporaries, among them Handel and Telemann. His music differed from theirs, too, in that almost all of it was written for his own performance or for presentation by groups under his direction, rather than for broader public consumption. Its high executant standards appeal to today's performers.*

BRANDENBURG CONCERTOS

One of the ironies of music history is that Bach's *Brandenburg* Concertos are dedicated to a prince who never paid for them, never used them, and probably never even looked at them.

Christian Ludwig, the Margrave of Brandenburg, was the brother of King Frederick Wilhelm I of Prussia. He resided in Berlin, the Prussian capital. It is not certain when Bach first met him, but it is known that Bach was in Berlin between June 1718 and March 1719—his mission, to buy a harpsichord for the court at Cöthen, where he was Kapellmeister. Bach played for Ludwig while in Berlin. Upon taking leave of the prince, he was invited to send a few of his compositions back from Cöthen.

Ever mindful of the importance of patronage, Bach was quick to comply. He selected six concertos from those he had written for his ensemble at Cöthen, modified them to make them a bit more showy, and copied them into a presentation manuscript. This manuscript of what Bach described in French (the official language of the Prussian court) as six *"Concertos avec plusieurs instruments"* made its way to the Margrave in 1721. It bore a dedication, also in French, "begging Your Highness most humbly not to judge the concertos' imperfection with the rigor of that discriminating and sensitive taste which everyone knows him to have for musical works, but rather to take into benign consideration the profound respect and the most humble obedience which I thus attempt to show him."

The six *Brandenburg* Concertos stand as the supreme achievements in the concerto grosso literature of the Baroque. The variety of the instrumental combinations they exploit sets them apart from any other opus, as does the flexibility of Bach's writing—which allows each of the participants to play both leading and supporting roles

An evening of music-making at the Bach family home.

in a constantly changing pattern of give-and-take. The six works, no two of which sound alike, encompass an impressive range of style and topic, and manifest in combination the courtly elegance of the French suite, the exuberance of the Italian solo concerto, and the gravity of German counterpoint. Subtle and brilliant at the same time, they are a microcosm of Baroque music, one that contains an astonishingly vast sample of that era's emotional universe.

RECOMMENDED RECORDINGS

*B*ACH'S FOUR SONS *had music in the blood—and, of course, got lessons from Papa as well. Still, it is remarkable that all of them became important composers in their own right. Carl Philipp Emanuel— C.P.E.—was the most celebrated and influential, and the symphonies and overtures of Johann Christian (the London Bach) are still performed today.*

Academy of St. Martin-in-the-Fields/ Sir Neville Marriner.
Philips 400 076-2 [Nos. 1–3] and 400 077-2 [Nos. 4-6]

Amsterdam Baroque Orchestra/ Ton Koopman.
Erato 45373-2 [Nos. 1, 3, and 4] and 45374-2 [Nos. 2, 5, and 6]

Munich Bach Orchestra/Karl Richter.
Deutsche Grammophon Archiv 427 143-2 [2 CDs; with Concerto for Oboe d'amore and Strings (after BWV 1055) and Concerto for Violin, Oboe, and Strings (after BWV 1060)]

Marriner's 1980 digital remake of the concertos with a top-notch assembly of soloists represents the epitome of the "orchestral" approach to this music. The readings are distinguished by superb modern string playing and outstanding work from the soloists. Sir Neville's flowing tempos are well suited to this approach, but the readings do tend to be a little downbeat-heavy, and the tendency of the St. Martin strings to smooth out the texture limits the rhythmic interest of the performances. Still, the tonal beauty of these readings and the virtuosity of the soloists are strong compensation. Philips's recording offers a warm, plush sound but is a little woolly at times.

Conductor Karl Richter was an accomplished organist.

The 1983 readings of Koopman and the Amsterdam ensemble are vital and altogether more polished than several competing period-instrument versions. The accent in these elegant, flowing accounts is on variety—in texture, ornamentation, and matters of phrasing and articulation. The executants' voicing of the counterpoint is effective, while their pointing of rhythm underscores the fact that much of this music comes from the dance.

Better than most, Richter knew that the *Brandenburg* Concertos are serious fun and ought to be played that way. There is a sense of joy in these wiry readings—of something elevated but at the same time earthy and jaunty and not too pious—that still delights after a quarter of a century, and nowhere does one get a better feeling for the extraordinary efflorescence of Bach's genius. The accounts are briskly paced and soloistic in approach, with every participant freely involved. While the intonation is at times less than precise, the 1967 recordings scarcely show their age, and the overall effect is delightfully fresh.

ORCHESTRAL SUITES NOS. 1–4

At least a couple of these suites owe their existence to Bach's involvement with the Leipzig Collegium Musicum, and probably all of them were performed by that group at one time or another during his tenure as director. In their formal layout and musical substance, all four show the influence of the French style, particularly Nos. 1 and 4. It is likely that these two were composed during Bach's years in Cöthen (1717–1723), though some revisions to No. 4, including the addition of the trumpet parts, were made after Bach arrived in Leipzig. Suite No. 3 can be fairly closely dated to around 1730 and was almost certainly composed as "big band" music for the Collegium players, perhaps to mark some special occasion.

There is a chamber-music quality to the scoring in Suite No. 2, in B minor, which calls for strings and continuo and a single transverse flute, an instrument that enjoyed a considerable vogue in the 1730s. Bach is quick to seize on the instrument's virtuoso capabilities, and masterful in the way he sets it up against a modest complement of strings.

Suite No. 3, in D, was composed for a large ensemble consisting of strings and continuo, two oboes, three trumpets, and timpani. The presence of trumpets and drums always indicates a festive occasion in Bach's music, often one out-of-doors, and this is certainly the most outgoing of his essays in the genre. It opens with a French overture of symphonic scope—dense, weighty, brilliantly worked out. The ensuing Air often is referred to as the "Air on the G String" after the title of an arrangement made in 1871 by the violin virtuoso August Wilhelmj, which called for the melody to be played on the violin's lowest string. It is constructed over a chaconne bass, and has become the suite's most familiar movement, indeed one of the most familiar in all of Bach's music.

While it calls for an even larger ensemble than the Third Suite, at least in the form in which Bach left it—strings and continuo, three oboes, bassoon, three trumpets, and timpani—Suite No. 4, in D, began life as a slenderly scored work and retains a more courtly manner throughout. The opening French overture has a yearning tenderness in its *grave* section, and a wonderful liveliness in its *allegro*, which is full of the spirit of the gigue. The outer sections of the Bourrée keep the trumpets and drums, as do the Gavotte and the concluding Réjouissance. But the Minuet eschews them, reminding us that at the heart of this music, as historian Karl Geiringer has pointed out, are the qualities of "wit, grace, and charm."

Bach made use of the virtuoso capacities of the transverse flute, in vogue in the 1730s.

RECOMMENDED RECORDINGS

**English Baroque Soloists/
John Eliot Gardiner.**
Erato ECD 88048 [Nos. 1–2] and 88049 [Nos. 3–4]

**Academy of Ancient Music/
Christopher Hogwood.**
Oiseau-Lyre 417 834-2 [2 CDs]

The English Baroque Soloists are a virtuoso period band, and in this fine 1983 recording Gardiner elicits readings that are full of resilience, energy, and life. These are foot-tapping performances, as earthy as they are courtly, and unmatched in their richness and piquancy of sound. What is notable, in addition to the pointing of rhythm, is the expressiveness of the playing.

Hogwood's accounts are stylish and well recorded, if not quite so bracing in effect. Both he and Gardiner have the same soloist in the B minor Suite: Lisa Beznosiuk, today's leading exponent of the Baroque flute. Hers is an appealingly light and delicate tone, one that gives her an almost ghost-like presence in the tuttis. But she is able to hold her own in the solo passages, despite the difficulty of fingering, and in both accounts her playing is nicely ornamented, not overly affected. On the Erato disc, she goes without credit anywhere except in the general roster of English Baroque Soloists, a lamentable oversight.

SAMUEL BARBER

ADAGIO FOR STRINGS

*O*n the programs of American symphony orchestras, the American composer whose music is most frequently encountered is not Aaron Copland, Leonard Bernstein, or George Gershwin, but Samuel Barber (1910–1981). For many

---

Classics on Celluloid

*D*ressing up soundtracks with classical music has been standard practice since the makers of *Elvira Madigan* showcased the *Andante* to *Mozart's Piano Concerto No. 21*. Other films that feature classical music include: *10*—*Ravel's* Boléro, *Out of Africa*—*Mozart's Clarinet Concerto*, *Death in Venice*—*the Adagietto from Mahler's Symphony No. 5*, *Platoon*—*Barber's* Adagio for Strings, *Die Hard 2*—*Sibelius's* Finlandia.

Samuel Barber, c. 1938.

years, Barber's *Adagio for Strings* has been the most frequently performed concert work by an American composer. This intense, elegiac piece was originally the opening part of the second movement of Barber's String Quartet, Op. 11; the composer then scored it for string orchestra at the request of conductor Arturo Toscanini, who gave the first performance of the arrangement in 1938 with the NBC Symphony Orchestra. The music begins quietly with a feeling of subdued but deep sadness, builds to a searing climax of extreme poignancy, and subsides again into the stark, melancholy mood of its opening.

Though familiar from repeated playings (and from use in Oliver Stone's film *Platoon*), the *Adagio for Strings* remains one of the most moving and beautiful elegies ever conceived, an outstanding example of Barber's remarkable lyric gift.

 RECOMMENDED RECORDING

Saint Louis Symphony Orchestra/ Leonard Slatkin.

EMI CDC 49463 [with Overture to The School for Scandal, *Essays Nos. 1–3 for Orchestra, and* Medea's Meditation and Dance of Vengeance]

For the essential orchestral pieces of Barber, EMI's compilation with Slatkin and the Saint Louis Symphony is the best currently available. Slatkin's reading of the *Adagio* is beautifully built, exactly on the mark. The Essays—works of magnificent craftsmanship in which Barber unerringly balanced the sorrowful with the triumphant—are powerfully stated, and *Medea's Meditation and Dance of Vengeance* emerges as an orchestral tour de force. The recordings are full, spacious, superbly atmospheric.

BÉLA BARTÓK

MUSIC FOR STRINGS, PERCUSSION, AND CELESTA

*T*he *Music for Strings, Percussion, and Celesta* is the finest and most concentrated work of the Hungarian composer Bartók (1881–1945) and also one of the most difficult of his scores to perform. Composed in 1936, it calls for a full string ensemble divided into two main groups, each of which is further divided in the standard way into multiple sections, along with a percussion complement that includes timpani, xylophone, harp, and piano. The writing is extremely demanding and rhythmically complicated.

The piece's opening movement is a rigorously worked-out fugue that reverses itself at midpoint; following a long crescendo, the theme is played backwards and voices begin to drop out until only two are left. The second movement is an energetic Allegro, the third a hauntingly atmospheric Adagio that provides a foretaste of the *"Elegia"* of Bartók's *Concerto for Orchestra*. In the dance-like finale, Bartók's love of folk music comes to the fore, and the eerily modal harmonies of the work's opening give way to a more conventional assertion of A major.

CONCERTO FOR ORCHESTRA

*T*he *Concerto for Orchestra* was Bartók's last completed work; he did not live to finish either the Third Piano Concerto or the Viola Concerto that followed it, although both of these were completed after his death by his pupil Tibor Serly. In these last works, all composed in America, Bartók turned away from the thorny complexities of the music he had written during the 1920s and '30s in his native Hungary, and toward a more accessible language based on the rhythmic and melodic contours of folk music. Yet there is very little that sounds folkish in these pieces. The writing is still vigorous, still austere and biting in many places. But melody is indeed more prominent, and rhythmic patterns less complex—as though Bartók had decided to simplify his way of saying things without oversimplifying what he was trying to say.

Whether Bartók might have continued in this vein if he had lived into the 1950s and '60s is hard to say. What is certain is that the *Concerto for Orchestra* has proven to be Bartók's most popular work, due in large part to the directness of its language.

As its title suggests, the *Concerto for Orchestra* treats the various sections and solo instruments of the orchestra as if they were protagonists in a concerto. The idea goes back as far as the Baroque concerto grosso, but Bartók's idiom and scoring are entirely modern. Sooner or later every principal player is called upon to solo, yet all this virtuosity is integrated into a work of deep expressive content. Even the excitement of the finale is tempered by feelings of mystery and urgency conveyed via Bartók's tonal ambivalence (he uses modes other than the standard major and minor) and the acerbic quality of his orchestration.

The *Concerto for Orchestra* is in five movements, each titled in Italian: "*Introduzione*," "*Giuoco delle coppie*" ("Game of Pairs"), "*Elegia*," "*Intermezzo interrotto*" ("Interrupted Intermezzo"), and "*Finale*." In the "*Giuoco delle coppie*," the paired wind and brass instruments take turns playing their material in parallel at different intervals—the bassoons in sixths, the oboes in thirds, the clarinets in sevenths, the flutes in fifths, and the trumpets in seconds. The "interruption" in the "*Intermezzo*" also deserves special comment. Listeners familiar with Franz Lehár's opera *The Merry Widow* will recognize the tune "Going to Maxim's" here. Bartók was not pastiching Lehár, but satirizing Dmitri Shostakovich's *Leningrad* Symphony (No. 7), which quotes the Lehár tune in its first movement. At

MAXIM'S, on the Place de la Concorde, was Paris's most famous restaurant at the time Lehar immortalized it in song in The Merry Widow. *It is still the embodiment of* Art Nouveau *splendor, but in* "Going to Maxim's," *it seems more of a Moulin Rouge than a place to eat:* ". . . the champagne flows, and they dance the can-can." *One of the specialties on the menu at Maxim's is crêpes* Veuve Joyeuse.

the time Bartók wrote the *Concerto for Orchestra*, Shostakovich's symphony was being played to death in concerts and on the radio, and impressed some as a contemporary masterwork. Bartók thought it was trite, and didn't mind saying so.

RECOMMENDED RECORDINGS

Chicago Symphony Orchestra/Fritz Reiner.
RCA Living Stereo 61504-2 [Concerto for Orchestra *and* Music for Strings, Percussion, and Celesta, *with* Hungarian Sketches]

Detroit Symphony Orchestra/Antal Doráti.
London 411 894-2 [Music for Strings, Percussion, and Celesta, *with* The Miraculous Mandarin *(complete)*]

It was Reiner who, together with the violinist Joseph Szigeti, persuaded conductor Serge Koussevitsky to commission the *Concerto for Orchestra*, and after all these years Reiner's recording of the score is still the best. Reiner understood the world of this music—the poignant, brooding, mysterious, and exuberant moods it explores—and his interpretation speaks with an authority no one else has matched. The Chicago Symphony plays as if it has been set on fire, with panache and plenty of power in reserve. The recording, in spite of rather noticeable tape hiss, has been painstakingly remastered.

Doráti's 1983 recording of the *Music for Strings, Percussion, and Celesta* is one of the finest achievements from a prolific career in front of the microphone. There is nothing showy in the conductor's handling of the piece; rather, his account has a feeling of continuity and cumulative momentum that sets it apart. The Detroit Symphony plays impressively, and the recording is precisely imaged and gorgeously life-like in the way it reproduces the weight of the strings and the impact of the percussion.

Orchestral Personalities

The Chicago Symphony's *internal discipline and* esprit de corps *are shared by only a handful of other ensembles. It has a brass section of unsurpassed splendor, and its winds and strings are as fine as any in the world. Since its founding in 1891, its music directors—including Theodore Thomas, Fritz Reiner, and Sir Georg Solti—have cultivated a Central European style of playing and sound: weighty, robust, and firm in the bass.*

LUDWIG VAN BEETHOVEN

*B*eethoven, as he always took great pains to admit, was no Mozart. His father tried to turn him into one anyway, leaving emotional scars that would mark him for life. Beethoven spent his childhood years in his native Bonn, starving for affection but acquiring skills that would stand him in good stead as a composer, and developing a remarkably resilient character marked by a strong will and incredible endurance.

By 1792, when Beethoven made his way to Vienna to begin his career, Mozart was dead. As his patron, Count Ferdinand Waldstein, had put it, Beethoven's task was to "receive Mozart's spirit from Haydn's hands." In Vienna, Beethoven would find patrons and princes who supported him, and he would form an especially close relationship with Archduke Rudolph, the son of Emperor Leopold II, to whom he dedicated many of his most important works. But the closest thing he would have to a lifelong friend was the piano. He was already on intimate terms with it when he arrived in the Austrian capital, and in little time the instrument provided him with an entry into the salons of the Viennese nobility. Beethoven took lessons with Haydn, Salieri, and Albrechtsberger as part of a well-planned campaign to advance his art, one in which he attacked the most important musical forms—the string quartet and the symphony—not frontally but by laying siege to them. His first published works were sets of piano trios and piano sonatas, which served both to announce his arrival and as studies for the larger forms.

Throughout his life Beethoven led a solitary existence. The turn of the century brought deafness, and with middle age came ill health and a string of family and personal disappointments.

1 7 7 0 — 1 8 2 7

These experiences wrought a transformation in Beethoven, one that can be seen in his changing likeness: the darkly handsome, well-dressed, and socially active young man of the portraits painted c.1800 became the wild, unkempt, irascible, and isolated figure of the years 1815–27.

Beethoven's music changed as well, dramatically enough that it has become standard practice to identify three stylistic periods in his career. The early period, which ended around 1803–04 and was climaxed by the Third Symphony (*Eroica*), marked Beethoven's conquest of the Classic style as exemplified in the works of Mozart and Haydn.

During the middle period—which lasted from 1804 until roughly 1818, including a creative hiatus during the years 1812–17—Beethoven emerged from his deafness with a renewed sense of purpose. The works of this period are characterized by emotional directness, by heightened expressiveness wedded to a feeling of rhetorical urgency, and in most cases by the expansion of form to meet the requirements of content. There is a new emphasis on texture and sonority, and a conscious play upon the elements of contrast, surprise, and innovation. An element of struggle is expressed through conflicts in key and disruptive gestures. The emotional point of the most celebrated works of this period—for example, the Fifth Symphony, the First *Razumovsky* Quartet, the opera *Fidelio*, and the Fifth Piano Concerto (*Emperor*)—is the achievement of a feeling of triumph through transcendence of formal limits.

The music of the late period, from about 1818 until Beethoven's death, takes on an almost visionary quality. Unfettered by preconceptions regarding form or content, Beethoven allows himself a new freedom of utterance, which includes the freedom to treat form in a schematic way (the number of movements in his late sonatas and string quartets varies markedly, as does their length). Counterpoint and fugal procedure acquire a new importance—perhaps because the composer's total deafness was now forcing him to rely on what he had learned in youth—and the inner workings of the music at times become more important than the outward effect. In the outstanding works of this period, particularly the Ninth Symphony, the *Missa Solemnis*, and the final piano sonatas and string quartets, the frame of reference is elevated from the individual to the universal, from the subjective to the metaphysical.

SYMPHONY NO. 3, IN E FLAT, OP. 55
Eroica

*L*ike many of his generation, Beethoven initially thought of Napoleon Bonaparte as a champion of the ideals of the French Revolution and a hero to the common man. Beethoven intended his Symphony No. 3 as a tribute, and in August 1803 wrote Bonaparte's name across the title page of the score. Nine months later, when he learned that Napoleon had crowned himself Emperor, Beethoven angrily scratched out the word "Bonaparte" and tore up the page. When the symphony was published in 1806, it carried an inscription that said only this: "Heroic Symphony, composed to celebrate the memory of a great man."

The accepted view of the *Eroica*—that it was a revolutionary departure heralding the age of symphonic Romanticism—is only partially right. In many ways the symphony is not so much a departure as a culmination, a work that carries the 18th-century ideal of the symphony to its theoretical limit. In the *Eroica*, Beethoven still observes the formal protocols of Classicism—in the layout, disposition, and relative weight of the four movements, and in the process of argument by which harmonic goals are reached and expressive points are made. Indeed, the symphony's sonata-form first movement can rightly be described as the high-water mark of Classical tonality, even though it is larger and more eventful than any of the symphonic allegros of Mozart or Haydn.

The harmonic plan is complicated by lengthy and daring excursions into tonal areas remote from the main key, but the pull of E flat, the symphony's center of gravity, is strong enough to hold the first movement together. The thematic material of this Allegro is unusual in that it consists of nearly a dozen motives, which in and of themselves seem to be incomplete, less conclusive than "themes." Beethoven allows these motives to flow

ECHOES: Once Beethoven had associated the key of E flat with heroism, other composers were bound to follow. Among the symphonic works that view the key in this context are Schumann's Symphony No. 3 (the Rhenish, *in which E flat suggests optimism perhaps more than heroism), Bruckner's Symphony No. 4 and Richard Strauss's assertive* Ein Heldenleben, *where the composer himself is the hero.*

Search for the Heroic Ideal

When news was brought to him of Napoleon's death in 1821, and he was asked if he intended to compose anything on its account, Beethoven replied, "I have already composed the music for that." Although disappointed in Napoleon, Beethoven did not cease to look for ways to evoke the ideal of a common humanity in his later works. The best example is the finale to the Ninth Symphony, with its famous setting of Schiller's ode To Joy.

into one another and combine in a variety of ways, a process that enables him to create a universe of musical thought that is not closed or circumscribed by melody, but organic and alive, capable of breathtaking expansion. As one would expect in the portrayal of a heroic figure, the ideas are bracing, their expression powerful. A mood of optimism prevails, yet there are turbulent moments that suggest darker sentiments.

The *Eroica*'s second movement, cast as a funeral march, is full of the "big band" sounds of French Revolutionary music. The shattering blare of the brass, the solemn drum rolls, and the hair-raising musket volleys that were part of any decent military funeral are here evoked almost as colorfully as they would be a quarter of a century later by Berlioz. Beneath the overt theatricality, however, is a feeling hovering between pathos and terror.

Standing in utter contrast to this is the winged fleetness of the ensuing scherzo, where the thrill of the chase seems almost palpable. Running quarter notes pulse through the strings, which are kept to a whisper most of the time, while the oboe and flute add bits of a skipping tune, but in keys other than the tonic. Suddenly, like quarry crashing through a thicket, the whole orchestra erupts *fortissimo* with the tune, which is at last in E flat. The exhilarating trio for the three horns, a tour de force of part writing, echoes the music of the hunt.

The finale is a brilliant set of variations on two themes. The more tuneful one, which is actually the second to appear, began life as a lowly contredanse, was later used in the ballet *The Creatures of Prometheus*, and finally turns up here. The movement's climax comes with a tender, hymnlike statement in the winds of this Prometheus tune; almost miraculously, what had been just a singsong melody is clothed with sentiment, nobility, and a feeling of compassion. After such a moment, the joyousness of the symphony's conclusion seems all the more satisfying.

Inside the Musikvereinssaal, home of the Vienna Philharmonic.

 RECOMMENDED RECORDING

Vienna Philharmonic/Leonard Bernstein.
Deutsche Grammophon 413 778-2 [with Egmont *Overture]*
(See also complete cycles)

In 1979, a year after this recording was made, the principal violist of the Vienna Philharmonic— a distinguished, silver-haired gentleman from Bürgenland named Streng—complained that "When we play Beethoven with Bernstein, we do it Bernstein's way"—as opposed to Beethoven's way. But Bernstein's personal identification with the heroic reach of this score causes the Vienna strings to give their all in this performance; their playing, and that of their colleagues in the wind and brass, is pure guts and glory. After all, the conductor's affinity for the music, like the orchestra's, is beyond challenge, and the vivid recording brings it all home.

SYMPHONY NO. 5, IN C MINOR, OP. 67

*T*he "Grand" Symphony in C minor received its first performance on December 22, 1808, in Vienna's Theater an der Wien. After that night, symphonic music would never be the same. The Fifth broke expressive ground and overturned many of the formal concepts on which the Classical symphony had been based. For the first time, the end of a symphony was more important and had greater weight than the beginning. Moreover, the 18th-century concept of unity of key was willfully rejected: the work begins in C minor but ends, to what was for Beethoven's listeners quite an amazing expressive effect, in C major.

As familiar as it has become, the symphony's

To many of his contemporaries, Beethoven's inspiration seemed to come out of the blue.

first movement—with its flight through the dark and dramatic landscape of C minor—still arouses the feelings of "nameless foreboding" that Beethoven's contemporary E.T.A. Hoffmann noted in a review. There is the relentless reiteration of the famous four-note motive (heard at the opening of the symphony as three G's and an E flat), so threatening in its force. The scoring is lean and severe, and the music does not flow smoothly; it is constantly being stopped and held back, which adds to one's sense of unease. Even the lyrical second subject is taut, restrained, and affords but a brief glimpse of the peaceful horizon. Of the many strange and wonderful moments in this movement, perhaps the strangest is the subdued passage in the middle of the development section, in which a series of hushed chords alternates in the winds and strings, suggesting an eerie calm in the eye of the storm. But calm of any sort is short-lived in this, one of the most tightly wound and disturbing symphonic movements ever penned.

The ensuing Andante is a theme with variations, rather free in form. There is a decidedly French accent in the wind and brass sonorities that color the proceedings, and no mistaking the grand, marchlike treatment the theme receives at several points, which resounds with the pomp typical of the Revolutionary bands. But there are meditative pages as well that seem almost pastoral in feeling and are full of yearning. The tension between them and the outbreaks of fanfare give the second movement a unique urgency.

On its heels comes one of the most remarkable scherzos in all of Beethoven. The Italian word *scherzo* means "joke," but there is nothing light or jocular about this one—here certainly is more of Hoffmann's "nameless foreboding." The main subjects of both portions of this spectral dance sound from the depths of the cellos and basses, and the four-note motive is back, fiercer than ever. But the most extraordinary feature is the long, suspenseful bridge that leads from the utter darkness and motionlessness of the scherzo's end to the blaze of C major that opens the finale.

Here, with the added weight of trombones, piccolo, and contrabassoon contributing to its sublime effect, a grand march proclaims the triumph of the major mode over the minor. It is a powerful metaphor for transcendence, and with it Beethoven makes a point that will echo throughout the 19th century—that fear, uncertainty, and ultimately all human limitations, including death, can be overcome, that *this* is the artistic project. Such victories must be won, and to suggest how hard the struggle can be, Beethoven brings back the music of the scherzo, which gives him the opportunity to reprise that marvelous transition yet more urgently. Even with victory assured, Beethoven hammers home the tonality of C major with a lengthy coda, saving 29 measures of pure C for the end of the symphony.

 ## RECOMMENDED RECORDING

Vienna Philharmonic/Wilhelm Furtwängler.
EMI CDH 69803-2 [with Symphony No. 7]
(See also complete cycles)

Furtwängler's 1954 account of the Fifth, part of EMI's "Great Recordings of the Century" series, really is one of the great recordings of the century and remains the most compelling reading of this symphony on disc. Here the conductor is caught in the act of creation, at the height of his powers, in a performance that develops from measure to measure. The players themselves are on the edge of their seats, and it can be felt in the way they play: the accents mean something, the climaxes mean something, even the changes of key are important. No one has ever said more with the four notes of the first movement's motto theme, found greater nobility of sentiment in the Andante, made the transition from the scherzo to the final movement more suspenseful, or com-

Pen-and-ink sketch of Beethoven on a Vienna street, c. 1820.

municated the triumph of C major more overwhelmingly. Made in the Musikvereinssaal, the recording boasts rich monaural sound.

SYMPHONY NO. 6, IN F, OP. 68
Pastorale

Though not the first composer to depict scenes from nature, Beethoven created such a compelling new language of musical pictorialism in the *Pastorale* Symphony of 1808 that it inspired imitation from a long line of 19th-century composers, just as if he really had been the first to capture the cuckoo or a summer storm in music. In some ways, particularly in terms of orchestral color and texture, the *Pastorale* is the most forward-looking of Beethoven's scores. The way in which the composer treats sound (rather than relationships of key) as an organizing principle marks the beginning of musical impressionism.

Beethoven knew that music which tries too hard or too literally to depict a scene is bound to fail. He consequently avoided mere sound effect, except in a couple of instances, and concentrated on the evocation of states of mind that he associated with natural surroundings and with nature's own musicality—her rhythms of change, her richness, power, and capacity to surprise.

Beethoven did give each of the symphony's five movements a brief descriptive title: "Awakening of Cheerful Feelings on Arrival in the Country," "Scene by the Brook" (with the calls of nightingale, quail, and cuckoo), "Merry Gathering of Country Folk," "Thunderstorm," and "Shepherds' Song: Happy, Thankful Feelings After the Storm." But despite titles and references to natural sounds, the symphony doesn't tell a story; it simply conjures a series of moods.

The *Pastorale* Symphony adheres to the same basic premise as the Fifth, but the Fifth's theme of transcendence is replaced here by a sense of

✔ *BEETHOVEN'S recollection of happy thoughts on visiting the country exerted a profound influence on the development of the symphony, leaving its mark on many works, including the following: Berlioz's Symphonie fantastique, Harold in Italy; Mendelssohn's Hebrides Overture; Wagner's Overture to The Flying Dutchman, "Forest Murmurs" from Siegfried; Bruckner's Symphony No. 9; Mahler's Symphony No. 6.*

deliverance, achieved not through struggle but by submission to nature. Instead of the choppy eventfulness of the earlier work, here one finds a flowing musical discourse in which Beethoven seems willing to inhabit a series of tonal regions as if time were standing still. In the first movement's exposition, he visits three key areas rather than the customary two, which broadens the harmonic action and makes the relationship between keys less polar and more open. Here and in much of the rest of the symphony, Beethoven is concerned with Romantic contemplation, as opposed to the vigorous, goal-directed action of Classicism. And in the way he is able to expand the symphony's time frame, he opens the door to a new expressive realm in music.

RECOMMENDED RECORDINGS

Columbia Symphony Orchestra/ Bruno Walter.
CBS MYK 36720

Philharmonia Orchestra/ Vladimir Ashkenazy.
London 410 003-2
(See also complete cycles)

The Berlin-born Bruno Walter conducting in Europe, c. 1932.

Walter's is a youthfully fresh and exuberant performance, but with the glow of deep spiritual maturity. It is full of conviction and emotional involvement, though it never sounds overdriven or pulled apart. The orchestra plays well, even if the violas are perpetually behind the beat and the winds ever so slightly reticent (which may be the fault of the remixing engineer). In spite of an occasional missed note, there is a compelling intensity to the performance; the finale, in particular, radiates a feeling of joy that seems to come right out of the world of Beethoven's opera *Fidelio*. Though more than 30 years old, the recording— bright, vivid, bass-heavy, and closeup—sounds like it was made yesterday. It has been well transferred, with no attempt to attenuate tape hiss, yet no harshness to the sound.

The Ashkenazy is beautifully played, a sonorous, spacious, and seductive reading that is exceedingly well paced. The 1982 recording is first-rate digital.

SYMPHONY NO. 9, IN D MINOR, OP. 125
Choral

*W*ith the Ninth Symphony, Beethoven refought—on higher ground and for greater stakes—the battle he had waged in the Fifth, and in the process once again changed the face of symphonic music. Like the Fifth, the Ninth is concerned with the assertion of the major key over the minor, and with the attainment of a feeling of transcendence. Here, though, the struggle has far greater emotional and psychological complexity, and the resolution is lifted above the plane of the idealized self to embrace all of humanity.

Conceptually as well as technically, the Ninth is a work of revolutionary innovation. New ground is broken in all four of the symphony's movements: in the harmonic ambiguities of the opening Allegro, in the violent rhythmic energy of the scherzo, in the extraordinary suspension and prolongation of harmonic action of the Adagio, and especially in the finale, a setting of Schiller's celebrated ode *To Joy*. The poem celebrates joy and freedom, and the joyful music of this movement mirrors the meaning of the text by actually escaping the bonds of conventional form.

It is here as well that Beethoven transforms the symphony, for the first time in its history, into an act of philosophy and personal confession. The ode *To Joy* came as close as words could to summarizing Beethoven's own moral views. In the symphony's finale, it is prefaced by a dramatic

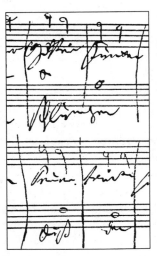

Beethoven's sketch for the Ninth's famous choral finale.

THE NINTH Symphony received its first performance on May 7, 1824, at the Kärntnerthor-Theater in Vienna. It was at this concert that Beethoven, by then totally deaf, had to be turned around to face the applauding audience (above). At least the appeal he had inscribed on the title page of the Missa Solemnis had been granted: "From the heart, may it go again to the heart."

prologue in which the principal themes of the three preceding movements are called up and rejected, and a new subject, first introduced in the cellos and basses, is proclaimed throughout the orchestra. *"O Freunde, nicht diese Töne!"* ("O friends, not these sounds!") the baritone soloist abruptly exhorts, as if declaring that the orchestral exposition of this theme, as beautiful as it is, were insufficient. He begins to sing the words of Schiller to the new melody, and his song is soon joined by the chorus.

The famous theme is plain in rhythm, plain even in its melodic outline. It is the kind of song a man might sing to himself off in the corner of a tavern, which is perhaps Beethoven's way of suggesting that the highest good is to be found in the commonplace. For Beethoven, common humanity comes first. The high moral truths—joy in the embrace of brotherhood, awe in the presence of the Creator of the universe—have to be felt on that level if they are to have any meaning at all. In setting the tenor solo *"Froh, wie seine Sonnen fliegen"* ("Happily, as His suns fly") as a march, with Turkish instruments (cymbals, bass drum, and triangle) prominently featured in the accompaniment, Beethoven makes an allusion to the cultural differences that have to be bridged by the concept of brotherhood. It is significant that these instruments return in the movement's ebullient coda, no longer alien but assimilated into the musical texture as part of a single, joyful shout of praise.

 RECOMMENDED RECORDING

**Vienna Philharmonic/
Leonard Bernstein.**
Deutsche Grammophon 410 859-2
(See also complete cycles)

By the time of his traversal of the Beethoven symphonies with the Vienna Philharmonic, a cycle

grandly capped by this rendition of the Ninth, Bernstein had decided to make recordings of live performances only. Under concert conditions, certain things occasionally do go awry, but there is often a feeling of cohesion to a performance that is difficult to duplicate in the studio. And when Lenny was conducting a concert, he almost always struck sparks with the musicians on stage. That is certainly the case with this account. It has an electrifying intensity throughout, together with a magnificent sense of sweep and rhetorical point. The 1979 recording is good, but somewhat veiled in climaxes.

 RECOMMENDED RECORDINGS

SYMPHONIES NOS. 1–9, COMPLETE CYCLES

Columbia Symphony Orchestra/ Bruno Walter.

Sony Classical SX6K 48099 [6 CDs; with Coriolan Overture *and* Leonore *Overture No. 2]*

Cleveland Orchestra/George Szell.

Sony Classical SB5K 48396 [5 CDs; with Overtures to Fidelio, Egmont, *and* King Stephen]

Walter recorded the Beethoven symphonies in stereo for CBS in 1958–59, taping No. 9 in New York and Nos. 1–8 in Los Angeles with orchestras of freelance and studio musicians who rose magnificently to the occasion. Walter was in his eighties, but that didn't stop him from grabbing these works by the throat; there is no mincing around, no effusive lingering over phrases, no ponderous trudging either. The even-numbered symphonies are sunny and outgoing, full of the warmth the conductor exuded during his Indian-summer years in the studio. Yet the drama of the odd-numbered works is not slighted. Walter's account of the Fifth, for example, is an intensely expressive one in

BEETHOVEN *was one of the first composers to put metronome markings in his scores to indicate tempo. He was acquainted with Johann Nepomuk Maelzel, the German inventor who perfected the mechanism around 1815, and he relied on it for tempo markings in his Ninth Symphony. Maelzel's metronome is one of the few precision instruments still manufactured according to original specifications, and composers honor the inventor every time they write "M.M." followed by a number.*

which lyricism and thrust are in perfect balance, an evocation of stormy Romanticism at its best. The recordings have held up extremely well; the sound on CD is spacious yet detailed, with amazing presence and solidity.

Between 1959 and 1964, CBS had tape rolling in Cleveland as well, and the label captured Szell and his orchestra at their peak in what remains a landmark cycle of the Beethoven symphonies. Rational rather than Romantic, Szell's approach was to view the canon as chamber music for symphony orchestra; the result was a traversal unsurpassed in its ensemble precision and tensile strength. The standouts are a thrilling *Eroica*— tight, dramatic, and clean—and a Fifth of rare cumulative power. The dryish sound of the original recordings seems to have been sweetened with some added reverb, but this has been very judiciously done.

Berlin Philharmonic/Herbert von Karajan.
Deutsche Grammophon 429 036-2 [5 CDs]

Berlin Philharmonic/Herbert von Karajan.
Deutsche Grammophon 429 089-2 [6 CDs; with assorted overtures; also available separately]

Karajan's electrifying performances earned him the nickname "The Wonder."

The first of these cycles, made in 1961–62, was conceived as an integral recording and released as such in 1963, rather than piecemeal. It is consistent sonically and interpretively, and its well-judged performances hold up to repeated hearing. Karajan may not have been as highly individualistic an interpreter as some in the generation that preceded him, but he possessed the same authority, as these readings show. They emphasize tautness of line, grip, and momentum, and convey exceptional energy. The highlight of the set is a suave, darkly handsome *Eroica*, the only disappointment a senselessly rushed *Pastorale*. The Berlin Philharmonic plays the music with exquisite polish and an understated but convincing sense of expression. The sound is good for the vintage, though it can be a bit grainy in the climaxes.

In contrast to his outlook in the early 1960s, Karajan's view of the canon in the mid-1970s might best be described as hedonistic. The later readings are typical of the "massaged" style of performance he cultivated at the time, which the critic Andrew Porter famously likened to Kobe beef. There *is* a certain softness under all that muscularity, though for the most part Karajan shows his usual strong grip and maintains a balance between lyrical and kinetic elements. The approach works best in the Eighth, which is imbued with a dynamism that clearly shows its connection to the Seventh. Symphonies Nos. 4, 5, and 9 are also extremely well done. The Philharmonic, at its peak when these recordings were made in 1975–77, is a marvel. Even if its playing rarely seems fiery, its sound is exhilaratingly rich. The recordings, made in Berlin's Philharmonie, are close-miked and firm.

THE "AUTHENTIC" *or period performance involves not just the use of period instruments or modern copies thereof, but also the original playing styles— tuning, articulation, orna- mentation, tempo, and phrasing. The performance of Baroque and Classical music has come a long way since 1953, when Pablo Casals led accounts of the* Brandenburg *Concertos featuring soprano saxophone in place of Baroque trumpet, flutes instead of recorders, and piano instead of harpsichord.*

 RECOMMENDED RECORDINGS

SYMPHONIES NOS. 1–9, COMPLETE CYCLES
ON PERIOD INSTRUMENTS

London Classical Players/Roger Norrington.
EMI A26-49852 [6 CDs; with Overtures to The Creatures of Prometheus, Coriolan, *and* Egmont; *also available separately]*

Academy of Ancient Music/ Christopher Hogwood.
Oiseau-Lyre 425 696-2 [6 CDs; also available separately]

The insights these groups of scholar-musicians bring to Beethoven are thought-provoking and often quite striking. In fact, these recordings are among the most important treatments of the symphonies committed to disc in the past quarter century.

Drawing distinctions between these two sets on period instruments may be a bit misleading, since both the approach and the players are largely the same. But there are differences nevertheless. Norrington's First and *Pastorale* are brilliant, his *Eroica* very good, though too fast in places. His account of the Ninth, however, is unsatisfactory; he misjudges some crucial tempos and has bad luck with soloists. Hogwood's *Eroica* and *Pastorale* are also outstanding—and his Ninth is possibly the finest period-instrument reading of *any* Beethoven symphony. In questions of style and musical judgment, Hogwood is often on firmer ground, but Norrington puts more personality and drama into the equation, allowing himself more interpretive and expressive involvement. With Norrington, textures generally sound fuller and heavier than with Hogwood, but where Norrington can be a bit harshly recorded, Hogwood has consistently good sound.

HECTOR BERLIOZ

SYMPHONIE FANTASTIQUE

Berlioz terrifies his audience with his "rowdy" music.

The French composer Berlioz (1803–1869) was a child of the Napoleonic era in more ways than just chronologically. Like the First Consul, he rose to prominence on a combination of brilliance, talent, and sheer willpower; like the Emperor, he had little tolerance for those he considered mediocrities, as well as an enormous appetite for grandiose projects that more common minds thought foolhardy.

Unable to play a single instrument well, Berlioz nonetheless developed into the supreme orchestrator of his time, and his Romantic imagination and extraordinary sensitivity to extramusical ideas helped him fashion works that would change the scope, content, and even the sound of orchestral music in the 19th century. His creativity was fired in particular by a love for great literature and an unquenchable passion for the feminine ideal, and in the best of his works these elements conspired to produce music of exquisite beauty and exceptional emotional power.

On September 11, 1827, Berlioz attended a performance of *Hamlet* at the Paris Odéon in which the Irish actress Harriet Smithson played the role of Ophelia. Overwhelmed by her beauty and charismatic stage presence, he fell desperately in love. Artist that he was, he found a way to channel the emotional upheaval of *l'affaire Smithson* into something he could control: a "fantastic symphony" that took as its subject the experiences of a young musician in love. A detailed program, written by Berlioz himself and published prior to the work's premiere, leaves no doubt that he conceived of the *Symphonie fantastique* as a romantically heightened self-portrait. In it Berlioz traces the infatuation of his hero through a series of scenes—a ball, a melancholy evening in the country, an opium dream of the artist witnessing his own execution, and finally a witches' sabbath, in which the hero's beloved appears as a hideous participant in the orgy.

Throughout the symphony, the beloved is represented by a brief melodic motif called an *idée fixe*. This device—which was to attain significance in the works of Franz Liszt and, later on, in the music of numerous Russian composers—is just one aspect of the revolutionary treatment of melody Berlioz introduces with this work. More remarkable still are the score's formal audacity and Berlioz's brilliantly innovative orchestration, as he makes groundbreaking use of multiple timpani, sponge sticks, orchestral bells, augmented brass, and unusual effects such as percussive *col legno* bowing, in which the string players bounce the wood of their bows off the strings. Together these innovations make the symphony one of the seminal works of Romanticism.

The *Symphonie fantastique* received its premiere on December 5, 1830, at the Paris Conservatoire, François-Antoine Habeneck conducting. Liszt was

Femme Fantastique

Harriet Smithson (above) was the inspiration for the Symphony Fantastique. About his infatuation Berlioz wrote to his friend Laforest: "[L]et me tell you what love is . . . For you, it's not that rage, that fury, that delirium which takes possession of all one's faculties, which renders one capable of anything . . . I would never want you to experience the unbearable suffering to which I have fallen prey since your departure."

among those in attendance. In the two years that followed, Berlioz made extensive revisions to the score, and his headstrong courtship of Smithson unfolded as if it had been scripted by Balzac. On October 3, 1833, the two were married.

 ## RECOMMENDED RECORDINGS

Royal Concertgebouw Orchestra/ Sir Colin Davis.
Philips 411 425-2

French National Radio Orchestra/ Sir Thomas Beecham.
EMI CDC 47863 [with Corsaire *Overture and "Royal Hunt and Storm" from* Les Troyens]

Davis's account has ranked among the best since the day it was made. Refined, sensitive, full of passionate reverie, it is a high-voltage performance that never seems to be overdriven. Avoiding the tendency of many conductors to treat the work in episodic terms, Davis brings to the reading a firm sense of structure and argument. He elicits fine playing from the Dutch orchestra, whose combination of chamberlike delicacy in the strings, characterful work in the winds, and brilliant brass is virtually ideal. The recording is superb; textures emerge clearly in a spacious setting, with good perspective.

Beecham got inside French music like no Frenchman of his day. His performance is a splendid one, full of nuance and rhythmic interest, truly magical in its evocative color. The only drawback is the recording, which sounds thin in places (especially the violins). The disc is well filled, with a stirring performance of the "Royal Hunt and Storm" and a *Corsaire* Overture that sounds like it was recorded yesterday; the latter is an absolute triumph, wonderfully played by the Royal Philharmonic Orchestra.

An effigy of Berlioz in the Parisian square named after him.

HECTOR BERLIOZ

1803-1869

LEONARD BERNSTEIN

SYMPHONIC DANCES FROM
WEST SIDE STORY
OVERTURE TO CANDIDE

*N*ew York in the 1940s was a wonderful
town, a vital place where the pulse of
life was strong and fast and where the identity of
postwar America was being forged even before
the war had come to an end. Everything that was
important in the arts was happening there, and
at the center of it all was the liveliest musical scene
in the world. On November 14, 1943, that scene
was transformed by the arrival of a *Wunderkind*
named Leonard Bernstein (1918–1990). Then 25
years old and the assistant conductor of the New
York Philharmonic, Bernstein leapt into the limelight when he substituted for Bruno Walter on
short notice at a Philharmonic concert.

The following year Bernstein made an equally
extraordinary debut as composer with the ballet
Fancy Free, to choreography by Jerome Robbins.
Fancy Free was so successful that Bernstein, with
the help of lyricists Adolph Green and Betty
Comden, expanded the scenario and used it as
the basis for his first musical, *On the Town*.

Bernstein later joined forces with Robbins on
another musical, this time with lyrics by an unknown newcomer named Stephen Sondheim. *West
Side Story*, first staged in 1957, proved to be Bernstein's masterpiece. A modern-day, big-city
adaptation of the story of Romeo and Juliet—in
which Tony, a former gang leader on the verge
of adulthood, and Maria, a girl newly arrived
from Puerto Rico, are the star-cross'd lovers, and
the rival streetgangs, the Jets and Sharks, are the
Montagues and Capulets—*West Side Story* transcends the limits of the musical genre without
attempting to be opera. The *Symphonic Dances*, a
continuous suite of eight orchestral excerpts from
the complete score, reflects its mix of dance
rhythms, cool jazz, soaring Broadway lyricism,

*Bernstein caught the pulse of
1950s New York City.*

and symphonic exuberance.

The bracing Overture to *Candide* contains the most enduring music from Bernstein's ill-fated 1956 Broadway musical (in which the composer collaborated with Lillian Hellman, Dorothy Parker, Richard Wilbur, and John Latouche). Familiar from concert performances, this brilliantly scored curtain-raiser is a tour de force of imagination and one of the 20th century's finest parodies of opera buffa. Melodies from the musical are seamlessly woven in, and the concluding canon really does end things with a bang.

BERNSTEIN *was not the first to write music inspired by Shakespeare's* Romeo and Juliet. *The tale of the star-crossed lovers had moved Berlioz to compose his "dramatic symphony"* Roméo et Juliette *in 1839. Tchaikovsky wrote his Fantasy Overture* Romeo and Juliet *in 1869, and Prokofiev fashioned a ballet on the subject in 1935–36. Delius transposed the story to Switzerland for his 1907 opera* A Village Romeo and Juliet.

 RECOMMENDED RECORDING

New York Philharmonic/Leonard Bernstein.
Sony Classical SMK 47529 [with Gershwin: Rhapsody in Blue *and* An American in Paris]

Almost nothing can compare with Bernstein's own accounts of his music. The best recordings are still the ones he made in 1958–60 with the New York Philharmonic for Columbia (now Sony Classical), when scores such as *Candide* and *West Side Story* were brave "new" music. Originally produced by John McClure (and remixed by him for CD), these recordings of the *Candide* Overture and the *Symphonic Dances* from *West Side Story* have never been bettered, not even by Bernstein himself.

GEORGES BIZET
L'ARLÉSIENNE SUITES NOS. 1 AND 2

Bizet found the idea of fatal infatuation interesting enough to have twice fashioned scores around it—the first his incidental music to the play *L'Arlésienne* (by Alphonse Daudet), the second his final work for the stage, the opera *Carmen*. The commission to write the music for the Daudet play—which deals with unrequited

Bizet at 22, after winning the Prix de Rome.

THE TOWN OF ARLES in Provence, famous for its sun-drenched climate, has attracted poets, painters, and musicians for centuries. To judge from the tragic denouement of Daudet's L'Arlésienne or the surreal canvases that Van Gogh painted in Arles, however, artists during the late 19th century saw the region in a different light. Sunny and starry, perhaps, but not all love and games.

love and suicide in sunny Provence—came from the impresario Léon Carvalho, who had already commissioned several operas from Bizet. Ever the professional, Bizet turned out the score in short order, apparently stimulated rather than impeded by the requirement that he write for an ensemble of just 26 players. At the first performance of the play, on October 1, 1872, at the Théâtre du Vaudeville in Paris, Bizet's music went more or less unnoticed by the critics and actually irritated many in the audience, who resented any musical intrusion in their theatrical reveries.

Bizet quickly extracted from the score and arranged for full orchestra a suite of four numbers, which he gave to the conductor Jules-Étienne Pasdeloup. Premiered on November 10, 1872, it was an instant hit. A second suite, consisting of four more numbers (one of which, the "*Minuet*," is actually from Bizet's opera *La jolie fille de Perth*), was compiled following the composer's death by his friend and colleague Ernest Guiraud.

The movements of Suite No. 1 are entitled "*Prélude*," "*Minuet*," "*Adagietto*," and "*Carillon*." The "*Prélude*" gets under way with a swift series of variations on the "March of the Kings," a Provençal song dating from the 18th century, and concludes with a beautiful *andante* section that features a sweetly melancholy solo on the alto saxophone. The C minor "*Minuet*," originally the intermezzo between Acts II and III of the play, sounds much like a waltz by Shostakovich and comes with a hurdy-gurdy-style trio in A flat. The expressive "*Adagietto*" spins out a tender melody in muted strings. As its name implies, the vigorous "*Carillon*" evokes the chiming of church bells.

Suite No. 2 consists of a "*Pastorale*," "*Intermezzo*," "*Minuet*," and "*Farandole*." The "*Pastorale*" combines rustic vitality with gentle lyricism in its outer sections and introduces a sprightly dance tune accompanied by tambourine in the middle section. There is almost a *verismo* quality to the "*Intermezzo*," and a suggestion of intense feeling in its long-breathed melody over pizzicato accompaniment. The *"Minuet,"* though not from the music Bizet wrote for Daudet's play, fits right in until the arrival of its trio, which sounds more like an echo of the waltz from Berlioz's *Symphonie fantastique*. In the rousing *"Farandole,"* the "March of the Kings" is combined with a Provençal folk tune called the *"Danse dei chivau-frus."*

THOMAS BEECHAM was the son of Sir Joseph Beecham, a manufacturer of pharmaceuticals (Beecham's Liver Pills) and one of England's wealthiest men. It was the elder Beecham's money that paid for the orchestras young Tommy engaged in his early years on the podium. Thanks to the many ills Beecham's pills were supposed to cure, Sir Thomas was also able to found both the London Philharmonic and the Royal Philharmonic Orchestras.

🎵 RECOMMENDED RECORDINGS

Royal Philharmonic Orchestra/ Sir Thomas Beecham.
EMI CDC 47794

National Philharmonic Orchestra/ Leopold Stokowski.
CBS MYK 37260 [with Carmen *Suites Nos. 1 and 2]*

A holiday in the South of France, and what better guide than Beecham? Sir Thomas loved French ballets and the music of Bizet, and it shows in this EMI recording. One finds less-than-perfect ensemble here, and the intonation is at times a bit piquant, but the spirit is exactly right—buoyant, sunny, and energetic, never driven or ponderous. The accounts are perfectly proportioned, and suffused with a radiant lyricism. The recording, however, is too dry and almost mono in its narrow spread.

If Beecham had a rival in his repertory, it was Stokowski. In this, one of the last of his recordings, Stokie waved his wand as magically as ever, drawing a rapturous expressiveness from the strings and painting every measure in the most glowing of orchestral colors. The occasional liberties with dynamics and tempo are turned into convincing touches by the conductor's extraordinary sense of rhythm and his unrivaled ear for sound. The recording, made in 1977, is richly atmospheric and detailed.

M A J O R   M A E S T R O

J O H A N N E S   B R A H M S

*B*arely 20 when he was discovered by Robert Schumann, Brahms struggled for years to live up to the great expectations of his elder colleague. Although dubbed a "young eagle" by Schumann, Brahms was by nature conservative, and eagle-like in one thing only: his lifelong determination to be a loner. By not aligning himself with the radicalism of Wagner and Liszt, he opened himself to the partisan musical politics of the day. Pundits on both sides sought to paint him as the champion of the anti-modern faction in German music, and he was unwillingly drawn into a maelstrom of controversy from which he did not escape until the death of Wagner in 1883, when Brahms himself was 50.

Though slow to mature, Brahms clung tenaciously to the idea that he should carry on the great tradition of Classicism. His extraordinary craftsmanship and severe self-criticism helped secure his reputation as the greatest instrumental composer of his day, and eventually he came to be seen as one of the most potent and original voices of Romanticism as well—for in the final analysis, his works are not as conservative as they seem. The composer Arnold Schoenberg drew attention to this in an essay entitled "Brahms the Progressive," praising him as the agent of "great innovations in musical language." Brahms was indeed progressive in his understanding of harmony, as he was in his predilection for rich, freely organized polyphonic textures—where the constituent lines are treated not as counterpoint in the traditional sense, but as parts of a living tissue of independent melodic elements. Perhaps most progressive of all was Brahms's acceptance of rhythm as an element of musical language on the same plane as melody

1 8 3 3 – 1 8 9 7

and harmony, a view whose implications have been felt throughout the music of the 20th century.

The most consistent characteristic of Brahms's music is its gravity: it is thoughtful, serious stuff. And it was as a center of gravity, in a time of heady Romantic expressionism, that Brahms had the greatest impact on his own era and on the history of music. For while his language was certainly inventive *and* expressive, his real achievement was the renovation of music as an abstract art and the resuscitation of its traditional forms.

Brahms's four symphonies form a family in which the clear resemblance between members does not lessen the remarkable differences in their personalities. The First is dramatic, with meditative middle movements; the Fourth tragic, with an ebullient interlude; the Second bucolic and spirited; and the Third, the hardest to pin down, an extraordinary amalgam of lyricism and nostalgia tinged with despair. The four express themselves differently, too, each in its own distinctive voice, with a syntax that runs from the almost Gothic constructions of the First to the taut line of the Fourth.

George Bernard Shaw once claimed that Brahms was "the most wanton of composers," one who delighted in dressing himself up as Handel and Beethoven. In some ways Brahms's symphonies do follow the Beethoven model—in their attempt to develop the bulk of their material from a few basic motives, in their quest for concentration and organic coherence, and in their avoidance of program and scene-painting. But there are important differences between the two as well. While Brahms successfully tried the transcendental approach in his First Symphony, the dynamic of struggle and victory meant less to him than it did to Beethoven. In the remaining symphonies Brahms was more interested in achieving a sense of emotional integrity, even if it meant accepting ambivalence, as was the case in the Third. In all of his symphonies but the Fourth, he eschewed the third-movement scherzo in favor of the intermezzo, and only rarely did he try to emulate the dynamism of Beethoven, preferring instead a more lyrical manner of speaking—a quality that Schumann would have appreciated.

THE REAL BRAHMS is not as well known today as he was a century ago, despite being more admired. Today's audiences esteem him primarily for his symphonies and concertos, which represent a relatively small portion of his output. The rest of his oeuvre includes two dozen chamber pieces, another two dozen works for piano solo, and about 200 songs.

SYMPHONY NO. 1, IN C MINOR, OP. 68

*B*rahms began work on his First Symphony in 1855, when he was 22. By the time he finished the score, he was 43. "You have no idea," he later wrote to the conductor Hermann Levi, "how people like me feel when we hear the steps of a giant like him behind us." The "him," of course, was Beethoven.

Brahms felt such keen respect for Beethoven's symphonies that he allowed the first movement of this symphony—completed in 1862, though without its remarkable introduction—to sit in a drawer for 12 years before he mustered the confidence to proceed. And when the work was finally presented to the public, first in Karlsruhe on November 4, 1876, and then in Vienna, it was precisely the connection with Beethoven that the critics noticed.

Like Beethoven's Fifth and Ninth, Brahms's First is concerned with the conflict of key, and also like them, it aims to achieve transcendence through the triumph of the major mode over the minor in the final movement. True to the model, the symphony's first movement is stormy and dramatic, full of portents of the great struggle that is to ensue. But Brahms relaxes his grip—something Beethoven was loath to do—in the ensuing Andante and Allegretto, establishing the pattern of intermezzo-like movements that would characterize his next two symphonies as well. In the finale, the battle is rejoined. Prefacing the movement with an extended slow introduction that begins in the mists of C minor, Brahms delays the arrival of the major key until the suspense is palpable. Then, following the lead of Beethoven's Ninth, he allows it to be ushered in gently, eschewing a dramatic proclamation in favor of a measured, hymnlike theme. The rest of the movement carries this idea forward, and Brahms creates a mounting sense of triumph in the score's final pages.

SYMPHONY No. 2, IN D, OP. 73

*F*or Brahms, whose Symphony No. 1 had taken 21 years from inception to first performance, it was clearly a relief to be able to start fresh on a second symphony. With his successful completion of the First, the floodgates of symphonic thought were opened to him, and ideas that had been dammed up for years poured out in a torrent. Symphony No. 2 was finished in a mere four months and received its premiere in 1877, only a year after the First.

The Second is the most serene and reflective of Brahms's symphonies. Some have called it "sunny," although it has its moments of turbulence. Pastoral at times, dramatic at others, it is also Brahms's most powerfully orchestrated symphony—the only one with a tuba anchoring the brass section. Its finale contains the most unashamedly brilliant music Brahms ever wrote, though the opening measures of the movement give no hint of what is to come.

Perhaps because he *was* so serious, Brahms constantly made light of his own works. Inviting his boyhood friend Julius Otto Grimm to attend a performance of the Second Symphony in Leipzig, he said, "You must not expect anything special. Nothing but a tiny, innocent piece!"

Despite this disclaimer, the Second Symphony is remarkably sophisticated. The thematic content, much of which is based on the three-note motive (D, C sharp, D) heard at the beginning of the work, is unusually rich and well developed throughout all four movements. The scoring is skillful, and the counterpoint, particularly in certain pages of the first movement, reveals extraordinary subtlety.

IF YOU LIKE THIS WORK, you might also enjoy listening to Robert Schumann's Symphony No. 2, in C and Sibelius's Symphony No. 2, in D. Among Brahms's own works, the early Serenade No. 1 and the Violin Concerto share the sunny expression of this symphony. For the closest match of all, listen to Dvořák's Symphony No. 6, in D; not only is the key the same, but the formal outline is similar.

Primo Dons

Brahms's popularity has never been universal. One of his most celebrated contemporaries, Tchaikovsky, wrote this in his diary: "I have played over the music of that scoundrel Brahms. What a giftless bastard! It annoys me that this self-inflated mediocrity is hailed as a genius."

SYMPHONY NO. 3, IN F, OP. 90

*I*n some ways the black sheep of Brahms's four symphonies, the Third, dating from 1883, is also the one that repays repeated listening with the greatest dividends—in much the same way Beethoven's Sixth (the *Pastorale*) does. Paradoxically, the Third is the symphony where Brahms strays farthest from the model of Beethoven. Here there is no heated argument, no transcendent victory of major key over minor, no Romantic heroism. The Third is Brahms's most personal symphonic canvas—no less emotionally intense for being basically lyrical and inward-looking—and the only one of his four symphonies to end quietly (in fact, all four of its movements end quietly).

Much has been made of the work's opening motto, the melodic outline of the notes F, A flat, and F—which supposedly represented the words *"Frei aber froh"* ("Free but happy"), Brahms's answer to the motto of his friend, the violinist Joseph Joachim, *"Frei aber einsam"* ("Free but lonely"). More interesting than what, if anything, these notes mean is how Brahms uses them as a motivic cell of remarkable generative power, developing virtually the whole of the first movement out of them. Not only does the theme appear frequently as a melody, it is often present as a background voice in the texture of fully scored passages, usually in the bass.

As in the two preceding symphonies, Brahms follows this expansive but tightly argued first movement with a pair of lighter, intermezzo-like movements. The first, an Andante in C major, begins graciously but contains a melancholy passage midway through that will prompt Brahms to further reflections on it in the finale. The intimate Allegretto has a memorable opening tune and seems to straddle the fence between yearning romanticism and bittersweet lament. Brahms does the unusual by starting the finale in the key of F minor. When, after much turbulence, the major key finally is embraced in the movement's closing pages, it occurs not with a triumphant blaze but quietly, with a sunset glow.

SYMPHONY NO. 4, IN E MINOR, OP. 98

"*T*he cherries are not sweet here, and you certainly wouldn't want to eat them!" So Brahms confided to the conductor Hans von Bülow in 1885 as he neared the completion of his Fourth Symphony while summering in rural Austria. Brahms had given similar warnings about the Second, intending to throw friends off the scent of his most expansive symphony, but the suggestion that the Fourth might be hard to swallow proved entirely correct.

On hearing a piano run-through prior to the first public performance, the critic Eduard Hanslick confessed that the experience had given him the sensation of being beaten up "by two terribly clever men." Several of Brahms's other intimates wondered aloud whether he might not have miscalculated in composing a finale characterized by such rigorous, joyless sobriety. The suggestion was made that Brahms strike the movement, a passacaglia consisting of 30 variations plus coda, and substitute another.

Brahms wisely declined the advice, leaving the symphony as it stood. He realized that the specific gravity of the work as a whole necessitated a weighty finale. For he had departed from his custom of placing a pair of slender inner movements between two large outer ones, choosing instead to answer the dramatic opening E minor exordium with a long-breathed, equally dramatic Andante and a true scherzo of extended proportions and great brilliance. With these two as the middle movements, rather than two intermezzos, the passacaglia was needed both as a counterweight to balance the structure and as a closing

Brahms on the podium as sketched by his friend Willy von Beckerath.

peroration that would allow the symphony's pent-up tide of emotion to break fully upon the listener.

The character of the Fourth Symphony has been described as autumnal. Even if it were not the last of Brahms's symphonies, the description would fit, for surely none of the others presents the same pathos, austerity, and unblinking seriousness encountered here. The first movement is particularly somber, and full of what Yeats, in an entirely different vein, would later call "passionate intensity." Brahms sustains this mood through the second movement as well, with its opening in the tonally ambivalent Phrygian mode (based on E, but neither major nor minor) and subsequent wanderings in harmonic regions both lighter and darker. The agitation of the first two movements yields to an earthy ruggedness in the scherzo, which possesses an exuberant energy unique in all of Brahms's output. Equally unique is the towering drama of the finale, a masterwork of scoring, architecture, and argument, and the most profound symphonic utterance Brahms produced. Incorporating elements of a full-blown sonata scheme within a single, all-encompassing arch, it stands as a fitting conclusion to Brahms's greatest achievement as a symphonist.

BRAHMS PURSUED *his interest in "old" music in a variety of ways. He owned the manuscripts to Mozart's G minor Symphony and Haydn's Opus 20 String Quartets, as well as Beethoven's sketchbook for the* Hammerklavier *Sonata. As editor, Brahms was responsible for Mozart's Requiem, in the first complete edition of that composer's works, and for the symphonies of Schubert, published by Breitkopf & Härtel.*

 RECOMMENDED RECORDINGS

Berlin Philharmonic/Claudio Abbado.
Deutsche Grammophon 431 790-2 [Symphony No. 1, with Gesang der Parzen*], 427 643-2 [No. 2, with* Alto Rhapsody*], 429 765-2 [No. 3, with* Tragic Overture *and* Schicksalslied*], and 435 349-2 [No. 4, with* Variations on a Theme by Haydn *and* Nänie*]*

Vienna Philharmonic/Leonard Bernstein.
Deutsche Grammophon 415 570-2 [4 CDs; Symphonies Nos. 1–4, with Variations on a Theme by Haydn *and the* Academic Festival *and* Tragic Overtures*; also available separately]*

CLAUDIO ABBADO *was born in Milan in 1933, the son of the violinist and theorist Michelangelo Abbado. Trained as a pianist, he went to Vienna to take the course in conducting taught by Hans Swarowsky at the Academy of Music. In 1990, he became only the fourth man this century to be named music director of the Berlin Philharmonic.*

Abbado's cycle, completed in the spring of 1992 with the release of the Fourth Symphony, is an impressive contribution to the catalog. These are big, passionate, sure-footed readings, notable both for their magnificence of tone and for their unimpeded sense of flow. In addition to his clear grasp of each symphony's line of action, Abbado has a generous feel for the expressive content, and he exhibits loving, though not excessive, attention to detail. The playing of the Berlin juggernaut is beautiful; the power of old is still evident, but there is now more of an inner glow. Deutsche Grammophon's engineers are to be commended for the recordings, especially that of the Fourth, which was made in the former East Berlin's Schauspielhaus—a hall that seems to echo the sound of the old Philharmonie.

Bernstein's recordings with the Vienna Philharmonic show Brahms through the lens of Wagner's *Tristan und Isolde*. The conductor's flowing, almost achingly prolonged interpretations emphasize the lyrical aspect of the music. At times he brings a rather fruity expressiveness to the music, but for the most part he achieves quite lovely results. The recordings on this 1983 release are fairly distant, and the Vienna strings come out sounding a bit more wiry than they really are.

BENJAMIN BRITTEN

THE YOUNG PERSON'S GUIDE TO THE ORCHESTRA

*V*ariations and Fugue on a Theme of Purcell *may not sound like the title of one of the 20th century's most popular symphonic works, but by its other name—*The Young Person's Guide to the Orchestra*—this 1946 score by Britten (1913–1976) has made more friends than any other work of English music, with the exception of Handel's* Messiah.

The theme Britten chose for his variations was

YOUNG LISTENERS *who have enjoyed this portrait of the orchestra may also enjoy Prokofiev's* Peter and the Wolf, *Copland's* Billy the Kid, *and Saint-Saëns's* The Carnival of the Animals. *Also very appealing is Respighi's ballet* La boutique fantasque, *a breezily scored arrangement of tunes by Rossini.*

from Purcell's incidental music for a drama entitled *Abdelazer, or The Moor's Revenge,* written in the last year of Purcell's life. The theme is stated by the full orchestra—with each section momentarily out front—as a kind of prologue to the main event, Britten's virtuosic treatment of the theme in successive variations through each division of the orchestra. The instruments appear from the highest in each group to the lowest. The winds are first, with the focus moving from flutes to oboes, clarinets, and bassoons, each receiving a variation uniquely well suited to it. The strings are given their turn, again from the highest to the lowest, and then the brass—horns, trumpets, and the trombones and tuba. Finally, the percussion gets a chance to show what it can do.

In the concluding fugue, the instruments again enter from highest to lowest, but this time the sequence is much more rapid, as the fugue subject—itself a variation of the theme—is tossed to and fro. In a concluding gesture, Britten brings back the original theme in the full brass to end the work in a flash of glory.

 RECOMMENDED RECORDINGS

London Symphony Orchestra/ Benjamin Britten.
London 425 659-2 [*with "Four Sea Interludes" from* Peter Grimes]

Royal Philharmonic Orchestra/André Previn.
Telarc CD 80126 [*with* Courtly Dances *from* Gloriana, *and Prokofiev:* Peter and the Wolf]

Many of the more subtle details of the writing emerge in the composer's own version, which for all the felicities of expression nonetheless moves forward smartly. The London Symphony clearly has great fun with the score and gives a thoroughly good account of itself. The 1963 recording has a touch of glare and brittleness at the high end, and the balances suggest some rather questionable miking—a bit surprising, since the accompanying "Four Sea Interludes," recorded five years earlier, sound breathtaking.

Previn's account of the *Young Person's Guide* is not quite as intense or evocative as Britten's, but it is potent and both better played and better recorded.

ANTON BRUCKNER

SYMPHONY NO. 7, IN E

From village organist to Viennese icon: Anton Bruckner at 36.

*S*INCE EARLY in the Baroque period, the key of E major has been regarded as the "celestial" key because its signature of four sharps places it about as far up the circle of fifths from C, the center, as one could go while remaining in tune.

*W*hen he wrote that Bruckner (1824–1896) was the first symphonic composer to take up the "metaphysical challenge" of Beethoven's Ninth—a challenge that had largely been ignored by Mendelssohn, Schumann, and Brahms—musicologist Deryck Cooke put his finger on what makes this Austrian composer such a significant figure in the history of the genre. The renewal of the symphony as an act of transcendence and an expression of personal ideology was a lifelong labor for Bruckner, a devout Roman Catholic whose faith permeated his work. Indeed, the very compositional process Bruckner adopted—which involves the contemplation, ordering, and unraveling of materials until the essential feeling of a movement or a work stands revealed—has been described as an attempt to clear away obstacles on the path to spiritual certainty. The mystical tranquility and visionary ecstasy Bruckner expressed in his last three symphonies (Nos. 7–9) are unique in the history of music.

Composed from 1881 to 1883, the Seventh Symphony has a soaring opening theme, carried by the cellos, that offers a glimpse of the vistas ahead and marks the beginning of a momentous journey from light into darkness and back. Much of the first movement is derived from this opening subject, but Bruckner's treatment is so inventive as to make every idea seem spontaneous. The music touches on moods from the mysterious to the exultant, and ventures into myriad tonal regions before returning to the key of E major and a majestic closing statement of the initial subject.

Throughout the 22 minutes of the dirge-like Adagio in C sharp minor, Bruckner sustains a feeling of great poignancy, which is heightened by outbursts from the brass and climaxed by a long crescendo and a victorious C major statement of the formerly mournful principal theme. In the movement's closing pages, which the composer said he had written in memory of Wagner, funereal gravity gives way to desolation and, in the last moments, an elevated calm.

The A minor scherzo opens with a shadowy unison figure in the strings that serves both as a motive in its own right and as accompaniment to a festive trumpet theme, said to have been suggested by a cock's crow. The treatment gets a bit fierce in the movement's climaxes, but as a counterbalance Bruckner offers an idyllic trio in the pastoral key of F major. The symphony's tumultuous finale is launched by a jaunty melody outlining the E major triad and resembling the opening subject of the first movement. As before, Bruckner introduces material of sharply contrasting character and establishes competing key areas in the course of the movement's development. But in a coda of great majesty, the key of E is once again confirmed, and the symphony ends with the brass proclaiming, in succession, both the main subject of the finale *and* that of the first movement.

"ONE DAY I CAME home and felt quite sad," *Bruckner wrote to conductor Felix Mottl. "The thought had occurred to me that the Master would soon die, and at that moment the C sharp minor theme of the Adagio came to me." The "Master" was Wagner, who died on February 13, 1883, just three weeks after Bruckner finished his first sketch of the Adagio. When the news reached him, Bruckner added a short, elegiac closing.*

 RECOMMENDED RECORDING

Vienna Philharmonic/Herbert von Karajan.
Deutsche Grammophon 429 226-2

This version of the Seventh, taped in April 1989, was the last recording Karajan made. His

HANS RICHTER *apprenticed himself to Richard Wagner in 1866 at the age of 23. Ten years later, Richter conducted the first performance of the* Ring *cycle at Bayreuth. He went on to champion the music of Brahms, Dvořák, and especially Bruckner. In 1881, during rehearsals for the Fourth Symphony, the well-meaning Bruckner tipped Richter a thaler. Richter thereafter kept the coin on his watch chain.*

powers were never greater than here, at the end of an astonishing 50-year recording career—when he deserted Berlin for Vienna and an orchestra that was ready to give him everything he wanted. The performance grows as one listens, accumulating extraordinary power. It is personal and visionary, far more urgent than Karajan's prior rendition with the Berlin Philharmonic, at times almost incandescent. The recording has good presence, though not enough firmness in the bass.

SYMPHONY NO. 8, IN C MINOR

*C*omposing the Eighth Symphony was an ordeal for Bruckner. In September 1887, after three years of work, he sent the score to Hermann Levi, the conductor who had led the first Munich performance of the Seventh. Levi was utterly baffled, a reaction that plunged the composer into despair and prompted him to begin a radical revision of the work that ultimately took another three years. Fortunately, the symphony's first performance, given by the Vienna Philharmonic under the direction of Hans Richter on December 18, 1892, was an unqualified success.

The first movement begins over a suspenseful tremolo, with a terse motive in the lower strings and a cryptic answer from the clarinet. These early passages center on B flat minor, not the home key of C minor, and the tension this establishes will not be resolved until the end of the symphony. The exposition is built on three main subject groups, the second of which, in G major, employs the composer's rhythmic hallmark of two quarter notes followed by a triplet. The harmonic plan of the rest of the movement is extraordinarily far-reaching, and Bruckner shows remarkable resourcefulness in his use of motive—at one point inverting the opening subject, recasting it in the major, and making a luminously beautiful digres-

Bruckner takes a bow.

sion out of it. After a series of elemental climaxes and hushed interludes, the movement ends with a bleak coda in which the clarinet and the violins recall its opening subject, accompanied by deathly quiet rolls on the timpani.

The scherzo, as Bruckner described it, evokes the legendary folk figure Michel—who typified "the Austrian folk spirit, the idealistic dreamer." Its opening subject, heralded by an arresting tremolo figure in the violins, is a Ländler that seems both earthbound and ecstatic—qualities that prompted music critic Richard Osborne to characterize the scherzo as "a movement in which the very mountains seem to dance." The trio offers just the sort of idyll a folk figure might dream of, especially the passage in which three horns and three harps cavort in the blissful key of E major.

With its intense climaxes, charged silences, and extraordinary radiance of tone, the Adagio of the Eighth seems chamber music writ large. The sense of space is immense and the feeling of motion cosmic as this meditation unfolds; in it, Bruckner comes as close to conveying spiritual elation as in any music he would write. As in the Seventh, the Wagner tubas lend their glow, joining horns and strings for a tender leave-taking in the coda.

The symphony's finale opens with a fanfare-like proclamation in the wind and brass over galloping quarter notes in the strings. Bruckner sustains the momentum of this idea through all the ensuing material, which includes a chorale-like subject in the strings, marches both shadowy and festive, and numerous returns of the opening fanfare. With the arrival of the movement's broad coda, which rises from a *pianissimo* beginning in C minor to a stupendous conclusion in C major, the battle for the home key is at last won. As a crowning gesture, the main themes from all four movements are sounded simultaneously in the final two pages of the score, a feat comparable to the quintuple juxtaposition of motives at the end of Mozart's *Jupiter* Symphony.

RECOMMENDED RECORDING

Vienna Philharmonic/Herbert von Karajan.
Deutsche Grammophon 427 611-2 [2 CDs]

Karajan recorded the Eighth three times, but this 1988 account is the clear choice. He sustains the reading magnificently: his deliberate tempos and careful pacing give the symphony time to unfurl, allowing the mystery and tenderness of Bruckner's vision to radiate from deep within a paroxysmal intensity. The large passages have a rolling grandeur that is breathtaking—yet by maintaining a sense of scale and coherence, Karajan enables the symphony to be perceived as a single utterance. The Viennese play beyond their limits, and the cumulative effect is breathtaking. The recorded sound is vivid and of very wide dynamic range.

AARON COPLAND
ORCHESTRAL WORKS

Aaron Copland puts the spring in Appalachian Spring, *1973.*

*A*merica has produced many gifted composers during the 20th century, but only one whose music speaks so naturally and is so recognizably American. Whether expressing the emotions of life on the streets of New York City or in the hills of Appalachia, whether depicting the Southwestern desert or just being itself, the music of Copland (1900–1990) embodies the rough-and-ready spirit and brisk optimism of America at mid-century. Like that spirit, it is outwardly confident, energetic, assertive . . . and on the inside, tender, nostalgic, occasionally sentimental.

Copland's greatest achievement was the creation of an idiom that was at once original and familiar, contemporary yet comprehensible, and capable of conveying a wide range of emotion.

"THROUGHOUT *the American Southwest," Agnes de Mille wrote, "the Saturday afternoon rodeo is a tradition. On the remote ranches, as well as in the trading centers and the towns, the 'hands' get together to show off their skills. . . . The theme of the ballet* [Rodeo] *is basic. It deals with the problem confronting pioneer women: how to get a suitable man."*

The works he composed in this style during the 1930s and '40s, while no less modern than the edgy, eclectic scores of his youth, are formally more accomplished and far easier to follow. Their language is instantly recognizable, their feeling genuine and compelling.

Copland's American idiom proved brilliantly successful in his ballet *Rodeo*, commissioned by the late Agnes de Mille, who choreographed the work and performed the lead role at its premiere in 1942. With small excisions, the four sections of *Rodeo* constitute the movements of the popular suite, entitled *Four Dance Episodes*, by which the work is best known on the concert stage. "Buckaroo Holiday" is a razzle-dazzle Allegro that in some ways follows the sonata-form structure typical of the first movement of a symphony. "Corral Nocturne" is an atmospheric slow movement in Copland's most pensive style. "Saturday Night Waltz" opens with a passage reminiscent of string instruments being tuned, and its loping waltz includes a couple of references to "Goodbye, Old Paint." The concluding "Hoe-Down," based on the square-dance tunes "Bonyparte" and "McLeod's Reel," is a kick-up-your-feet display of rhythmic verve and orchestral boldness.

The finest of the works Copland composed in his American vein is the ballet *Appalachian Spring*, written in 1943–44 for Martha Graham. Because the work was to receive its premiere in the Coolidge Auditorium of the Library of Congress, Copland found himself limited to just 13 instrumentalists, the maximum number that would fit there and still leave room for the dance. The enforced economy helped him produce a score of remarkable tenderness and austere beauty—precisely the qualities of the human spirit that Graham's ballet sought to evoke. It also encouraged Copland to emphasize variety of texture and timbre within the ensemble, and to make greater use of counterpoint and irregular meter than he had in previous essays, further contributing to the liveliness of the score. These traits

Martha Graham and Bertram Ross dancing Appalachian Spring.

were preserved when Copland, in 1945, devised a suite from the ballet scored for full orchestra, the form in which the music is best known today.

In the final part of the ballet, Copland uses a well-known folk tune, the Shaker song "The Gift to Be Simple," as the basis for a brief set of variations. Copland's own melodic style had by now acquired the gift of simplicity as well, so the rest of the ballet's thematic material, which is original, still sounds of a piece with folk music.

Copland's most familiar work by far is his *Fanfare for the Common Man*, which resulted from an unusual initiative taken by Eugene Goossens, the British-born conductor of the Cincinnati Symphony Orchestra. In the summer of 1942 he invited a number of American composers to write patriotic fanfares. Ten of the fanfares were written for brass and percussion and were published in a single volume, with Copland's as the first. A mere 46 bars long, *Fanfare for the Common Man* has become a part of America's national consciousness and makes as strong an impression today as it must have when it was first heard against the dark background of the country's entrance into World War II.

 RECOMMENDED RECORDINGS

New York Philharmonic/Leonard Bernstein.
Sony Classical MYK 37257 [Appalachian Spring *Suite and* Fanfare for the Common Man, *with* El Salón Mexico *and* Danzón Cubano] *and MYK 36727* [Four Dance Episodes *from* Rodeo, *with* Billy the Kid *Suite]*

Saint Louis Symphony Orchestra/ Leonard Slatkin.
EMI CDC 47382 [Rodeo, *with* Billy the Kid]

Bernstein's accounts with the New York Philharmonic, recorded by CBS in the late 1950s and early '60s, are incomparable in their vitality and impetus. Bernstein had the ability to move between delicacy and brashness, always getting the gestures right, and his versions of the *Rodeo* and *Billy the Kid* suites are exuberantly persuasive. The Philharmonic's playing, while sometimes a bit raw, is confident and rhythmically secure. There is also a wonderful immediacy to Bernstein's reading of the *Appalachian Spring* Suite, in which the New Yorkers give a virtuosic performance. Both of these CDs have been wonderfully remastered by their original producer, John McClure, with excellent presence and a palpable sense of atmosphere in the quiet passages.

Slatkin does both *Rodeo* and *Billy the Kid* complete, restoring some delightful music that is missed in the suites. In *Rodeo*, for example, it comes as a delicious surprise to hear the saloon-piano interlude before "Saturday Night Waltz"— and Slatkin insists on an out-of-tune upright, just the right touch. These are idiomatic, persuasive interpretations, thrilling in their buildups and visceral in the climaxes. The recordings have a wonderful ambience and dynamic range.

CLAUDE DEBUSSY

PRÉLUDE À L'APRÈS-MIDI D'UN FAUNE

At the piano, Debussy saw color in black and white.

*D*eeply influenced by literature, the French composer Debussy (1862–1918) was keenly attuned to poetic imagery and symbolism, and he had a remarkable ability to evoke through music the emotions they stirred in a sensitive reader—a skill he showed not only in this score but in the *Three Nocturnes* and the opera *Pelléas et Mélisande* as well. This talent was recognized by Stéphane Mallarmé himself, author of the poem *L'après-midi d'un faune*, for whom Debussy played this prelude shortly after composing it in 1894. "I had not expected anything like that," Mallarmé remarked. "The music prolongs the emotion of the poem and fixes the scene more vividly than colors could have done."

Nijinsky choreographed an erotic L'après-midi d'un faune.

COMPOSERS MAY owe their inspiration to the muse, but Debussy and Fauré went further: they had the same mistress, though not at the same time. Emma Bardac became involved with Debussy in 1903. She gave birth to Claude-Emma Debussy ("Chouchou," for whom Debussy wrote Children's Corner) in 1905, and three years later became the second Mrs. Debussy. Prior to meeting Debussy, Emma had a liaison with Fauré, who dedicated to her his song cycle La bonne chanson.

Debussy's orchestral palette in the *Prelude to the Afternoon of a Faun* is indeed more subtle and vivid than any painter's. The drowsy, suffocating warmth alluded to early in the poem is superbly rendered by the languorous flute solo as it unfolds against a dappled background of muted strings and feathery tremolos, and by the near-absence of pulse through the score's early pages. The feelings of desire and passion barely suppressed at the climax of the poem are expressed in the music's gradually intensifying lyricism. And the dreamy oblivion into which the faun sinks at its end is conveyed by the gradual fragmentation and overlapping of melodic motifs from earlier in the piece. The result is a score of haunting suggestiveness in which, just as in Mallarmé's poem, time seems to stand still and the senses take on an animation of their own.

THREE NOCTURNES

Debussy owed his inspiration for the *Three Nocturnes* about equally to several lines from the poetry of Henri de Régnier, a friend whose aesthetic views influenced him, and to the paintings of James McNeill Whistler. It was Whistler's *Nocturnes* that Debussy had in mind when he described his own tone pictures, completed in 1899, as "an experiment in the different arrangements of a single color, like a study in gray in painting."

Certainly the first of them, "*Nuages*" ("Clouds"), fits that description. Wispy chords in the strings oscillate without going anywhere, and fragments of a melancholy solo in the English horn, set in a different meter, are repeated aimlessly against the vague background. The music seems to float without any harmonic goal, and the cancellation of one meter by another seems to remove the work from the realm of time as well—just as clouds at dusk appear to pass without moving, eventually blending into darkness.

"*Fêtes*" ("Celebrations") drew its inspiration from lines in a couple of Régnier poems, in particular from one mentioning the "brilliance of angry tambourines and sharp trumpet calls." But it may also be the depiction of an event Debussy witnessed around the time he was working on the score, a festive procession that took place when Czar Nicholas II visited Paris to seal the Franco-Russian Alliance of 1896. The middle section of this scherzo-like movement is a spectral march that begins as if from afar and becomes louder and more insistent as it draws near. The outer portions, Bacchanalian in their frenzy, contain some of the most animated and vividly scored pages in Debussy's oeuvre.

The point of departure for the third *Nocturne*, "*Sirènes*" ("Sirens"), may have been a Régnier poem describing the image of mermaids seen in a dreamlike vision. The wordless vocalizing of Debussy's sirens—an eight-part women's choir behind the scene—is surrounded by a shimmering musical seascape that is among the composer's most evocative examples of tone painting, though surely in more than a single color.

LA MER

Debussy rides above La Mer's *swirling waves of sound.*

*D*ebussy's most concentrated and brilliant orchestral work, *La Mer* is one of the supreme achievements in the symphonic literature. A score whose refinement and expressiveness are typically French, it is nevertheless a work of such imagination that it stands apart from traditions and influences. Its modernity can still be felt today, 90 years after it was composed.

The sea fascinated Debussy: "You may not know that I was destined for a sailor's life," he wrote to the composer André Messager in 1903, the year he started work on *La Mer*. "It was only quite by chance that fate led me in another di-

THE IMAGE THAT seems to have exercised the greatest influence on Debussy as he sought to convey the sheer power of the sea was the Japanese print "Hollow of the Deep-Sea Wave Off Kanagawa," (above) by Katsushika Hokusai. In it the wave seems about to swallow up a boat and its passengers. The wave dwarfs Mt. Fuji itself, seen in the distance, and the crest divides into numerous sprays of foam, each in the shape of a claw.

rection. . . . But I have an endless store of memories [of the sea], and to my mind, they are worth more than reality, whose beauty often deadens thought."

The sea Debussy remembered, from his childhood visits to Cannes and later travels in Italy, was of course the Mediterranean. It is a civilized sea, whose moods Debussy caught in all their richness. For Debussy truly had the ability to see images with an impressionist's eye, and to work with the color and mass of instrumental combinations much as a painter worked with pigments. He subtitled *La Mer* "Three Symphonic Sketches," and the names of the movements provide us with verbal suggestions to stimulate our own sense of imagery.

"From Dawn to Midday on the Sea" explores the sometimes subtle, sometimes dramatic changes of atmosphere and lighting that accompany the progress of morning on the water. The music suggests a gradual coming to life, from calm grayness to almost blinding brightness, ending with brass and percussion breaking over the full sonority of the orchestra.

The second movement, "Play of Waves," draws the imagination equally to the spheres of light and motion. One senses the rocking of the waves, the unexpected shifts of current, the glint of sunlight on the surface of the water, and the mysterious depths teeming with life. Of the three movements, this is the most "impressionistic" in its scoring, and perhaps the most musically engaging as well.

"Dialog of the Wind and the Sea" is more ominous, more urgent than anything that has gone before. One feels close to the sea's danger, as the orchestra heaves and swells in great washes of sound. A moment of suspenseful calm is reached before a final great buildup shows the sea in stormy triumph, the violent rhythms and dazzling clash of sonorities conveying at last the fullness of its elemental force.

Stylistic versatility distinguishes the Concertgebouw Orchestra.

 RECOMMENDED RECORDINGS

Montreal Symphony Orchestra/ Charles Dutoit.

London 425 502-2 [Three Nocturnes, *with* Images pour orchestre*] and 430 240-2* [La Mer *and* Prélude à l'après-midi d'un faune, *with* Jeux *and orchestral excerpts from* Le martyre de Saint Sébastien]

Royal Concertgebouw Orchestra/ Bernard Haitink.

Philips 400 023-2 [Three Nocturnes, *with* Jeux] *and 416 444-2* [La Mer *and* Prélude à l'après-midi d'un faune, *with* "Ibéria" *from* Images]

Boston Symphony Orchestra/Charles Munch.

RCA Living Stereo 61500-2 [La Mer, *with Saint-Saëns:* Organ *Symphony, and Ibert:* Escales]

Several years after their landmark recordings of Ravel's orchestral music, Dutoit and the Montreal Symphony have finally gotten around to Debussy, with results that are certainly worth the wait. The *Nocturnes* are impeccably rendered, with extreme refinement in *"Nuages,"* color and energy aplenty in *"Fêtes,"* and languor and mystery in *"Sirènes."* More of an outdoorsman than a hedonist when it comes to *La Mer,* Dutoit emphasizes body and voluptuousness of sound over atmosphere, striving for an effect of photographic realism rather than impressionism. Ultimately, it is the score of *La Mer,* not the sea itself, that the conductor is interested in projecting, but what a glorious noise he makes. These are perhaps the best recorded performances of Debussy's music in the catalog, close-miked but with ample space, vivid, and well balanced.

Haitink's versions from the late 1970s still rank among his most impressive discographic achievements, a tribute both to his skills as an interpreter and to the stylistic flexibility of the Concertgebouw Orchestra. The account of the *Nocturnes* is one of the finest—poetic, gorgeously played, and brilliantly detailed. In *La Mer*, there is poise, flow, and high suspense, and the response of the orchestra is similarly far-reaching. The work comes across precisely as intended, a set of three "symphonic sketches" rather than a kaleidoscope with one picture jerkily falling upon the next. Although the Concertgebouw is a difficult venue in which to record, the Philips team manages to achieve excellent balances on both CDs, with a nearly ideal sense of distance.

Munch was an excitable, spontaneous musician, one who gave everything to his performances and never conducted a piece the same way twice. There is an organic quality to his 1956 interpretation of *La Mer*—it is "live," urgent, and quite passionate (especially in the finale), but not overstated. RCA's recording is excellent; the new "Living Stereo" remastering wonderfully captures the presence, balance, and spaciousness of the original.

ANTONÍN DVOŘÁK

SYMPHONY NO. 7, IN D MINOR, OP. 70

The "discovery" of Dvořák (1841–1904) was largely the work of Brahms, who in the 1870s arranged three Austrian state stipends for his Czech counterpart and even went to the trouble of recommending Dvořák to his own publisher, the firm of Simrock in Berlin. By the mid-1880s, Dvořák's fame had spread throughout Europe, and in 1884 the composer accepted an invitation from the Philharmonic Society of London to visit England and conduct several of his works there. The success of his Symphony No. 6 at its London premiere that spring prompted the society to commission a new symphony, which Dvořák began in December of 1884 and completed in March.

The powerful new work, in the dark key of D minor, attested to the impact of Brahms's mel-

Dvořák mined his native Bohemia for folk themes.

THE FIRST GROUP of Slavonic Dances, composed in 1878 for piano four hands, catapulted Dvořák to fame and made a fortune for his publisher Simrock. For many years thereafter, a tug of war existed between the composer, who wanted to devote himself to large-scale works, and Simrock, who wanted more Slavonic Dances. In 1886, Dvořák orchestrated both sets of dances himself, and this is how these lively works are best known today.

ancholy Third, which had just been published and had deeply impressed Dvořák. The Seventh Symphony's moody first movement is as remarkable for the concentration of its argument as for the energetic treatment its ideas receive. Particularly impressive is the wealth of content Dvořák mines from the first subject, a dramatic, brooding theme in violas and cellos that apparently came to him as he watched a train carrying anti-Hapsburg demonstrators pull into Prague.

The Adagio, among the greatest of Dvořák's slow movements, begins with a lyrical subject in the winds over a delicate pizzicato accompaniment. This is followed by a somber idea in violins and cellos that is answered by hushed diminished-seventh chords in the clarinets, bassoons, and trombones (a direct and unapologetic paraphrase of a haunting passage in Brahms's Third). An idyllic second subject is intoned by the solo horn, after which the movement builds to a heated climax. A gentle coda brings a poignant reprise of the movement's opening theme, played by the oboe over shimmering tremolo strings, along with echoes of the second subject in the flute and violins.

The tightly wound scherzo is a cross between a waltz and a *furiant*, a Czech dance whose name aptly conveys its character. The symphony's finale is determinedly, even a bit self-consciously, tragic in its emphasis on the minor key and its seething, tremolo-laden textures. With typical melodic fecundity, Dvořák offers a first subject group of two ideas: a convulsive theme in cellos, horns, and clarinets, and a subsidiary theme in the strings, prefaced by a stark, *forte* stroke in the timpani. The second group, in A major, has the character of a Slavonic dance. The recapitulation touches off a final struggle for supremacy between D minor and D major—which the minor key shows every sign of winning until, in the final ten bars, it is overthrown by the major. There is no transcendence or catharsis, only the feeling of heavy suffering stoically endured.

Symphony No. 9, in E minor, Op. 95
From the New World

*I*n 1892, on an invitation from Jeanette Thurber, the wife of a wealthy New York businessman, Dvořák arrived in the city to head the newly established National Conservatory of Music. The composer spent the next three years in America, homesick for Bohemia but busy, and sufficiently stimulated to write some of his most enduring works. The Symphony in E minor, subtitled *From the New World*, was the first work he composed entirely in the United States. Dvořák claimed that "everyone who has a nose must smell America in this symphony," having developed his own ideas in an intentionally rustic fashion so as to give the symphony the flavor of what he perceived to be American Indian music, American folk music, and the Negro spiritual. Literary impressions also played a part; it is clear from the sketches that the symphony's second movement was originally based on the scene of Minnehaha's forest funeral in "The Famine" from Longfellow's *The Song of Hiawatha*, while the third movement was to depict "a feast in the wood where the Indians dance."

It is not hard, however, to hear echoes of Bohemia—look twice, and the Indians turn into Czech farmers and peasants. Rather than being a musical postcard from abroad, Dvořák's Symphony *From the New World* is ultimately more of a fond look back toward home. On a technical level, it is what Dvořák wanted it to be: a demonstration piece to show American composers how to transform native American material into a grand symphonic gesture in the best European manner. The symphony succeeds in spite of the fact that Dvořák's material is original, not borrowed. In contriving to make it seem "American," the Czech composer may have surrendered some of his native eloquence, and in developing it in

*D*VOŘÁK *found a home away from home in Spillville, Iowa, a tiny farm community of Czech immigrants who preserved the language and culture of their homeland. In 1893, the composer spent a blissful and productive summer there with his wife and six children.*

an occasionally four-square manner he may have sacrificed a measure of subtlety to prove a point. But the very directness and tunefulness of the ideas themselves, and the energy with which they are worked, are precisely what have made this the most popular of Dvořák's symphonies. The music has a ruggedness, an openness, and a brassy confidence that are American in the best sense— together with a heartfelt lyricism that even Dvořák could hardly disguise.

RECOMMENDED RECORDING

London Symphony Orchestra/István Kertész.
London Weekend Classics 433 091-2 [Symphony No. 7, with No. 8] and London Jubilee 417 724-2 [Symphony No. 9, with Carnival *Overture and* Scherzo capriccioso]

Among the finest recorded achievements of the tragically short-lived Hungarian conductor István Kertész is his landmark stereo cycle of the Dvořák symphonies with the London Symphony, recorded from 1963 to 1966. This remains the best traversal of the symphonies. Kertész's readings are notable for their grasp of architecture and idiomatic good sense, as well as for their many fine interpretive touches. The London Symphony plays with polish and vigor, and the sound, after more than a quarter of a century, is still ravishing.

Conductor István Kertész—
a throwback to the Romantics.

EDWARD ELGAR

VARIATIONS ON AN ORIGINAL THEME,
OP. 36
Enigma

*T*he *Enigma* Variations were not commissioned, and Elgar (1857–1934) seems to have composed them as much for the discipline of writing in variation form as for anything else. The process brought an unforeseen benefit, for

ELGAR'S MASTERY of the orchestra leaps off every page of the Enigma Variations. One of the finest descriptive passages is the opening of Variation XI ("G.R.S."), whose subject is not George Robertson Sinclair but his bulldog Dan. In the first five measures, the music shows Dan falling into the river Wye (strings), waddling up the bank (basses and bassoons), reaching the top (full orchestra), and letting out a triumphant bark (horns, lower strings, and winds).

with this score Sir Edward found not only maturity as a composer but fame as well—though the latter never really mattered much to him.

The melancholy theme in G minor on which the variations are based is the "enigma" of the title. Elgar never revealed its source, but years later he confided that the theme "expressed when written [in 1898] my sense of the loneliness of the artist . . . and to me, it still embodies that sense." Each of the 14 variations is a portrait of someone known to the composer (the connection almost always musical), identified in the form of initials, codewords, or, in one case, a mysterious cipher. For a long time the names of the "friends pictured within" to whom Elgar dedicated the score remained an enigma as well, but the composer eventually revealed them in the notes he wrote to accompany a set of player-piano rolls of the piece.

Three of the variations are particularly important. Variation I ("C.A.E.") is an affectionate portrait of Elgar's wife, Alice, treated as a continuation of the theme itself. Variation IX ("Nimrod") is an emotional tribute to August Jaeger of the music publishers Novello and Co.—according to the composer's note, "the record of a long summer evening talk, when my friend discoursed eloquently on the slow movements of Beethoven." And the finale ("E.D.U.") is a vigorous portrait of Elgar himself that includes references to "C.A.E." and "Nimrod" and ends the work on a note of unreserved triumph.

The *Enigma* Variations are among the finest free-standing variations in the repertory, revealing a technique on the same level as that of Brahms in the *Variations on a Theme by Haydn* and Richard Strauss in *Don Quixote*. But they offer an even richer emotional experience, for in portraying the salient qualities of each of his friends—whether melancholy or tenderness, bluster or coy reserve—Elgar was actually characterizing himself.

Hans Richter, the great champion of Brahms, Dvořák, and Wagner, conducted the first performance of the *Enigma* Variations in London on

June 19, 1899. Rarely if ever had a composer's new work been a more perfect embodiment of its moment in history.

POMP AND CIRCUMSTANCE MARCHES

*T*he word "circumstance" as used in Shakespeare's famous lines means pageantry, and there is certainly plenty of that in these wonderful marches. Elgar composed the first four betweeen 1901 and 1907; the fifth came in 1930, though almost certainly it had been started many years earlier. Elgar did not intend these works as patriotic potboilers, nor in any way to glorify war. Rather, he hoped they would serve as reminders of England's greatness and as gestures of support for tradition in the midst of change.

Pomp and Circumstance March No. 1, in D major, opens boisterously and has the tune familiar from so many high school commencement ceremonies. (Colleges, with their larger classes, tend to graduate seniors to the more ample strains of William Walton's *Crown Imperial* or *Orb and Sceptre*—both modeled on Elgar, of course.) March No. 2, in A minor, with its reliance on the strings, is the most symphonic of the set; one would scarcely expect to *march* to this music, though it is martial enough in its swagger. The shadowy No. 3, in C minor, has been likened to a scherzo, while No. 4, in G major, the best processional after No. 1, is the most rhapsodic. The Fifth March, in C major, completes the circle in a light-hearted, almost nostalgic fashion.

All five marches are rich in sentiment and steeped in the rather dignified variety of nostalgia to which Elgar frequently gave voice. Sir Edward was no enemy of modernity (he was one of the first composers to record his own music), but he regretted the pace of change and the loss of so much that was good and human in scale about the past.

RECOMMENDED RECORDINGS

**London Symphony Orchestra,
London Philharmonic Orchestra/
Sir Adrian Boult.**
EMI CDM 64015 [Enigma *Variations and* Pomp and
Circumstance Marches]

Royal Philharmonic Orchestra/André Previn.
Philips 416 813-2 [Enigma *Variations and* Pomp and
Circumstance Marches]

**Royal Philharmonic Orchestra/
Sir Yehudi Menuhin.**
Virgin Classics VC 91175-2 [Pomp and Circumstance
Marches, *with* Cockaigne *Overture and other marches]*

Boult's recording of the *Enigma* Variations with
the London Symphony was made in the early
1970s, when both he and the orchestra were at
their peak. It reflects an extraordinary blend of
spontaneity and the grand manner. Smooth, flowing, majestic yet animated, it is a finely molded
account in which every variation counts toward
the whole. Boult's understated readings of the
Pomp and Circumstance Marches with the London
Philharmonic are, like the music itself, the epitome of Englishness. The sound in the variations,
closely miked and remastered at a very high level,
is a little on the bright side; the marches have
exemplary sonics.

Previn elicits beautiful playing from the Royal
Philharmonic in his account of the *Enigma* Variations, while projecting a darker, more subdued
view of the score than Boult. This is a reading of
substantial cumulative power, distinguished by
the orchestra's velvety sound. Previn's treatment
of the marches, while not exactly fiery, is genial
and warm. Rhythms are nicely sprung, contributing to a relaxed, almost playful mood, though
the readings take on plenty of gravity where
appropriate. The wide-range digital sound of the

*The Royal Philharmonic
Orchestra, founded by Beecham
in 1947.*

1985–86 recordings is excellent.

Menuhin's 1989 interpretations of the marches offer a glimpse into the inner world of Elgar. Wonderfully spirited, they are put across with an affection born of personal acquaintance and a deep and lifelong devotion to the composer. There are many loving touches: in the first march, for example, there is an unexpected expressive emphasis in the percussion in one crescendo, the violins are kept *under* the solo horn in the trio, and the organ is brought in magnificently for the final reprise of the trio. Menuhin makes the marches sound more like the music of Elgar's two symphonies than a pleasantly rousing parade; more than any other interpreter on disc, he endows them with a deserved sense of nuance and complexity. They are impressively recorded.

MANUEL DE FALLA

EL SOMBRERO DE TRES PICOS

*F*alla (1876–1946) moved freely in several currents of 20th-century musical thought. Both a colorist and a classicist, he endowed his ballet scores with a subtle sensuality and a feel for the exotic that invariably rang true, yet he achieved a formal rigor that frequently eluded others. Much like Bartók, he had the gift for assimilating the patterns and the personality of folk music into his own highly developed language, so that the ideas he explored were at the same time original and derivative; their connection to the musical roots of his Spanish culture endowed them with immense vitality.

Falla's most substantial orchestral work, *El sombrero de tres picos* (*The Three-Cornered Hat*), originated as a quasi-balletic pantomime—a setting for chamber orchestra and vocalist based on Alarcón's novel. Following a commission from Sergei Diaghilev, whose Ballets Russes had premiered such works as Stravinsky's *The Rite of Spring* and Ravel's

Picasso's drawing of Manuel de Falla, 1920.

THE MUSIC OF SPAIN
reached a golden age in
the works of Falla and his
contemporaries Isaac Albéniz
and Enrique Granados. All
were students of the musicologist Felipe Pedrell, himself a
composer by training. It was
Pedrell who turned the attention of Spanish musicians
toward Spain and showed
his countrymen the way to
their heritage.

Daphnis and Chloé, Falla revised the first part of
the pantomime and expanded the instrumental
palette to create a vivid ballet score. The work
debuted in London in 1919 with designs by Picasso. The writing is virtuosic and warmly lyrical,
spiced with extraordinary rhythmic and instrumental touches. There are also a few musical "in
jokes," including a quote from Beethoven's Fifth
Symphony. Throughout the score, the sultry,
changing moods and the dynamic tempos of life
and love under the Spanish sun are evoked with
genuine flair. The concluding jota, in particular,
transmits the dizzying, coloristic whirl of an Iberian
festival with authentically visceral intensity.

 RECOMMENDED RECORDINGS

Montreal Symphony Orchestra/ Charles Dutoit.
London 410 008-2 [*with* El amor brujo]

London Symphony Orchestra/ Gerard Schwarz.
Delos DCD 3060 [with Nights in the Gardens of Spain]

London's 1981 pairing of the two Falla ballets
with Dutoit and the Montreal Symphony is a
recording to prize. The interpretations are suave
and finely crafted, seductive rather than incandescent, but nonetheless very appealing. The
recorded sound is good, although the acoustic of
Montreal's Church of St. Eustache comes across
as, in fact, too "churchy," causing Falla's colors to
run just a bit (London's engineers have since done
better there). Unfortunately, the individual scenes
of the ballets are not given separate index or track
numbers.

The Delos offering, from 1987, is stunningly
well recorded, and both scores are virtuosically
played by the London Symphony (with Carol
Rosenberger as piano soloist in *Nights*). These
are big, bold, colorful interpretations. *The Three-*

Cornered Hat receives a particularly rousing performance under the baton of Gerard Schwarz, brilliantly paced and wonderfully detailed.

CÉSAR FRANCK

SYMPHONY IN D MINOR

*T*HE ORGAN's rich sonority was certainly in Franck's mind when he composed his Symphony in D minor. Using chorale-like voicings, close chordal spacing, and frequent doublings and mixtures of the flutes and reeds, he created a luminous blend of sound much like that which the best French organs of his time were designed to produce.

*F*ranck (1822–1890) was one of the 19th century's most potent musicians—a thinker, teacher, and craggy individualist idolized by his students and beyond the comprehension of most of his tradition-bound colleagues. But while he was strongly sympathetic to the musical futurism that emanated from Wagner and Liszt, Franck was also solidly rooted in the organ music of Bach. Like Brahms, he was conservative and progressive at the same time. His greatest works are nearly all late ones, and to such important forms as the symphony and the string quartet he contributed but a single effort.

The Symphony in D minor, completed in 1888, is arguably the greatest symphony composed in France after Berlioz. It remains in the repertory while works by Bizet, Saint-Saëns, Gounod, Chausson, D'Indy, and other contemporaries drift in and out, testimony both to Franck's rigorous craftsmanship and to the power of his musical thought. The symphony *has* such a strong effect not only because of the dark intensity of its opening movement and the exultant energy of its finale, but because so much comes out of so little. As Brahms might have done, Franck develops an extended argument out of the three-note motivic cell heard right at the symphony's start. Not that the results sound Brahmsian. The harmony, with its chromatic complexity and yearning ambiguity, points, if anywhere, toward Wagner.

In this symphony, Franck eschews both the Beethovenian scherzo and the Brahmsian intermezzo. The score consists of three movements, the second of which is an Allegretto that owes something of its character, perhaps, to the corresponding movement of Beethoven's Seventh. Together, the Allegretto and the finale are just about as long as the turbulent opening Allegro. They also represent an emotional counterbalance to the almost unrelieved urgency of that glowering meditation.

The symphony presents what amounts to a theological argument: the foreboding of the first movement is transcended in the rapturous pages that come midway through the Allegretto, then vanquished altogether in the finale, where transcendence and transformation go hand-in-hand. As the themes of the preceding movements are recalled and superimposed upon one another, the symphony's brooding germinal motive is subjected to a series of mysterious rising modulations that culminate in the triumphant blaze of D major.

 RECOMMENDED RECORDINGS

Chicago Symphony Orchestra/ Pierre Monteux.

RCA Gold Seal 6805-2 [with D'Indy: Symphony on a French Mountain Air, *and Berlioz: Overture to* Béatrice et Bénédict]

Berlin Radio Symphony Orchestra/ Vladimir Ashkenazy.

London 425 432-2 [with Psyché *and* Les Djinns]

Monteux was 85 when he made this recording in 1961, and the opening pages are very deliberate, almost groping; the ensemble is not good in places, as though the beat were somewhat imprecise. But once the long buildup begins, remarkable things start to happen. The Allegro takes off at a fierce clip, and from there on the performance simply cooks. Part of Monteux's secret is the way he animates the tremolos and ostinatos that fill the score (and which can sound like so much wallpaper unless they are brought

The transition to conducting has been smooth for pianist Ashkenazy.

to life). The sound is remarkably fine except for some tape saturation in the loudest passages. There is good presence and atmosphere on the remastered CD, and the couplings are excellent.

Ashkenazy's ear for tone color and texture is a plus in Franck's music, and while his reading of the symphony just misses going over the top, it succeeds remarkably in conveying the emotions behind the music without false sentimentality. Although this is among the quickest readings in all three movements, there is no sense of haste. The Berlin Radio ensemble plays with an appealing transparency, producing lighter colors than are usually associated with Franck. The recording, made in Berlin's Jesus Christus Kirche in 1988, is well balanced and solid, and the inclusion of the symphonic poem *Psyché* is a real bonus.

GEORGE GERSHWIN

RHAPSODY IN BLUE
AN AMERICAN IN PARIS

Gershwin composes at the piano.

Rhapsody in Blue, the first "serious" composition of Gershwin (1898–1937), is likely to remain his most popular work in any form, owing to its prodigious melodic richness rather than to any deeper expressiveness or structural brilliance. In the hands of another composer, *Rhapsody in Blue* could easily have turned into a disjointed exercise in symphonically dressing up jazz rhythms, melodic figures, and quasi-improvisatory instrumental licks. Gershwin's uncanny sense of timing, and a gift for memorable melody unparalleled in the 20th century, turn the *Rhapsody* into an embodiment of the Jazz Age's upbeat lyricism and dance-driven vitality. The Roaring Twenties had a soul, and this was it.

The piece was composed in considerable haste for a concert on February 12, 1924, organized by jazz bandleader Paul Whiteman at New York's Aeolian Hall and billed as an "Experiment in

*Leslie Caron and Gene Kelly in
An American in Paris.*

Modern Music." Whiteman's arranger, the multi-talented Ferde Grofé, scored the piece for jazz band, and Gershwin himself played the piano solo, which at the time of the premiere he had not yet written out. Grofé also scored the work's orchestral version.

An American in Paris, Gershwin's second most popular score, is a brilliant orchestral showpiece and a nonstop experience in melodic invention. For all the color introduced at the start by the use of four taxi horns (which Gershwin had brought back from Paris), the tone of the score is really more American than French, with allusions to the blues and even the insertion of a Charleston. Far better than in *Rhapsody in Blue*, Gershwin succeeds not only in maintaining the flow of the work from one section to the next, but also in building a convincing overall structure out of his song and dance forms.

The work received its premiere in New York on December 13, 1928. It was scored by Gershwin himself, although the version commonly heard today omits many changes Gershwin later made.

 RECOMMENDED RECORDINGS

Columbia Symphony Orchestra, New York Philharmonic/Leonard Bernstein.
CBS Masterworks MK 42264 [with Grofé: Grand Canyon Suite]

Cleveland Orchestra/Lorin Maazel.
London 417 716-2 [with Cuban Overture, *and Copland:* Appalachian Spring Suite *and* Fanfare for the Common Man]

The Bernstein is a disc for the ages. Here is American music performed with mid-century flair, a moment never to be recaptured. Bernstein had the feel for *Rhapsody in Blue*, and he does full justice to the still racy and spontaneous score. His performance of the piano solo has a smoky, sultry

---

THE SUCCESS OF Rhapsody in Blue *prompted Gershwin to fashion another rhapsody for piano and orchestra in 1931. The* Second Rhapsody *is equally energetic; its driving rhythms and glossy, jazz-inspired scoring are as unmistakably urban as a New York accent. The piece might be better known today had Gershwin stuck with an original title:* Manhattan Rhapsody.

jazziness to it, along with a brash exuberance; there is touching tenderness in the lullaby, riveting dynamism in the fast pages. The performance of *An American in Paris* is bracing and energetic, and strikes a deft balance between intimacy and grandeur. The old New York Philharmonic incandescence comes through in every bar, and the sound has excellent presence and impact despite some breakup in the extreme high range.

The 1974 account of *Rhapsody in Blue* from Maazel and the Cleveland Orchestra is brisk, full of "big band" bravura. And at the start of *An American in Paris*, you feel like you're right in the street. The virtuosic playing of the Clevelanders is a delight from start to finish. The analog sound is outstanding, too, and this disc receives kudos for repertory and budget.

EDVARD GRIEG

PEER GYNT

Grieg at home in 1907.

In 1874, the Norwegian composer Grieg (1843–1907) was asked by his countryman Henrik Ibsen to compose incidental music for the first production of the play *Peer Gynt*, slated for Oslo in 1875. The project turned out to be a mammoth undertaking, occupying most of the composer's time during 1874–75. The finished score, amounting to well over an hour of music, probably had more to do with the play's success than the lavish decor or even the story itself.

Ibsen's *Peer Gynt* offers a rather cynical commentary on the Scandinavian character. Its central figure is an amalgam of Don Juan (in his misdirected sexuality) and Don Quixote (living a parody of the old heroism) whose exploits echo those of the heroes of *The Odyssey* and Voltaire's *Candide*. After years of searching, Peer goes home and finds Solveig—the woman who was right for him all along—waiting on the doorstep.

Grieg understood both the idealism and the

The grandeur of Norway's fjords left its mark on Grieg's music.

irony at the play's heart, but chose to let his music set the mood of various scenes rather than expose the flaws in the characters and their motives— wisely leaving that to Ibsen. While the music for *Peer Gynt* is softer in tone than Ibsen might have wanted, it shows insight nonetheless. There is plenty of profile in the dramatic segments such as "Scene with the Boyg" and "In the Hall of the Mountain King," along with affecting emotion in "Aase's Death" and an almost cinematic atmosphere in such numbers as "Morning Mood" and "Night Scene." The liveliness of the dances and the pastoral quality of Grieg's scoring give the music remarkable appeal.

 RECOMMENDED RECORDINGS

San Francisco Symphony Orchestra/ Herbert Blomstedt.

London 425 448-2

Gothenburg Symphony Orchestra/ Neeme Järvi.

Deutsche Grammophon 423 079-2 [2 CDs; with incidental music for Sigurd Jorsalfar]

Blomstedt and the San Francisco Symphony uncork an account that is unmatched in its richness and dramatic fervor. Here is a conductor with a real feel for the music, and in his hands Grieg's multi-movement score shows all its emotional depth. The performance is well paced and brilliantly played, and London's crew provides a high-impact recording, very forward and with excellent detail.

Järvi's recording is marked by good instinct for pacing and color, and excellent contributions from the soloists. This account is melodramatic in the good sense, particularly in the confrontation with the Boyg. The sound is excellent.

IBSEN WROTE Peer Gynt *in 1867 while he was living in Italy. He had left Norway three years earlier, impoverished and embittered by his failure as an author. The success of* Peer Gynt *probably had more to do with Grieg's music than Ibsen's story.*

GEORGE FRIDERIC HANDEL

*L*et us second Beethoven's famous remark and "bend the knee to Handel." It was Handel's prowess as a composer of vocal music that impressed Beethoven, and more than any other aspect of Handel's art it compels admiration even today. But though Handel was by temperament and training inclined to the theater, he created works of lasting value in every important musical genre of his day. Indeed, among all other composers of the 18th century, only Mozart achieved similar success in so many fields.

In his youth, Handel absorbed the elements of the German, French, and Italian styles of the mid-Baroque. His knowledge of Italian music came first-hand, during a three-year sojourn in Italy that amounted to a master class in composition. His exposure to the music of the Venetian masters, especially Antonio Caldara and Giovanni Legrenzi, freshened his correct but rather stolid native German counterpoint, softening its edges and giving its lines allure and fluidity. While in Rome, Handel witnessed how his Italian colleagues evaded the papal ban on opera by composing oratorios and cantatas in the theatrical style, and he followed their lead. Later in life, facing up to the demise of Italian opera in England, he would use the same trick again and produce a magnificent array of English oratorios.

In 1710, Handel was appointed Kapellmeister to the Elector of Hanover—the future King George I of England—and was granted an immediate leave of absence to spend the better part of a year in London. He returned to Hanover the next summer, but found it rather dull compared with the English capital. In the fall of 1712 he again asked to be temporarily relieved of his duties,

1 6 8 5 – 1 7 5 9

and permission was granted on the condition that he return "within a reasonable time."

Back in London, Handel found it easy to forget his obligations in Hanover. It was a long, long way away. He plunged into the composition of Italian operas, then in vogue, and also wrote some of his finest ceremonial music. He had been in London a little over a year when Queen Anne died, leaving the throne to George I, Handel's boss. Following the coronation, Handel prepared himself to face the sort of music no one likes to hear, but George, benevolent monarch that he was, continued to favor him—and pay him, even doubling his salary.

Handel spent the next two decades pumping out operas and solidifying his reputation as England's leading composer. But the old style of opera was doomed. A lighter, more comic vein was gaining favor, and the public eventually grew indifferent to the monumental style of Handel's creations. People still enjoyed good singing, however, and Handel saw that by writing oratorios, he could give them what they wanted. From the mid-1730s, when he switched to the oratorio genre, until 1750, when he composed *Theodora*, he enjoyed a dazzling string of successes. One of them was *Messiah*, premiered in Dublin in 1742.

Handel was himself a pleasure-lover, and he always made certain his music gave pleasure to those who heard it. This most professionally accomplished of musicians possessed a lively wit, penetrating intelligence, rare cultivation, unshakeable integrity, and both good humor and good sense. More than that, he was an artist of the highest rank, the most cosmopolitan and eclectic of his age. His range as a composer—his mastery of a variety of forms and techniques and his ability to draw on them at will—has never been surpassed.

(image caption area)

KING GEORGE *was
not the only monarch to
enjoy "table music," of which
the* Water Music *is a particularly grand example.
Louis XIV dined to the
strains of Michel-Richard de
Lalande's* Sinfonies pour
les soupers du Roi. *Georg
Philipp Telemann brought
table music within the means
of the bourgeoisie—his three
"productions" of* Musique
de table *could be had by
anyone for eight reichsthal-
ers—and now, thanks to
recordings, we can all eat
like kings.*

WATER MUSIC

*T*he popular story that Handel wrote the
Water Music as a means of restoring himself to the good graces of King George I is now
generally regarded as myth. In fact, it was the
king, not Handel, who was in need of some good
PR. His subjects were beginning to regard him as
a bit of a blockhead, owing in part to the fact that
he spoke no English. Much as a public figure
today might do, he decided to go on the offensive
with a determined show of magnificence. In the
summer of 1717, he had his adviser, Baron Kielmansegge, arrange for a musical entertainment
on the Thames followed by a nighttime cruise up
the river to Chelsea for supper. Naturally enough,
Kielmansegge commissioned Handel, the court
composer, to write the music for this spectacle.
The king and his favorites listened from the royal
barge as an ensemble of 50 musicians played from
another, while boats "beyond counting" crowded
alongside.

Though the original scores have been lost, it is
clear from the instrumentation and keys that Handel composed the *Water Music* in three suites: a
large one in F with ten movements, featuring two
horns in addition to oboes, bassoon, and strings;
one in D with five movements (among them the
celebrated "Alla Hornpipe"), including parts for
trumpets and timpani as well as horns, oboes,
bassoon, and strings; and one in G with seven
movements (some of which are often linked in
performance), for a "softer" complement of flute,
recorders, oboes, bassoon, and strings. While the
suites in F and D are clearly open-air music, meant
to be played on the barge, the G major grouping
was intended perhaps to accompany the king's
meal at Chelsea.

Well suited to its purpose—as both divertissement and advertisement for the king—the *Water
Music* is memorably tuneful and makes fashionable use of the dance forms typically found in the

Baroque suite, such as the minuet, bourrée, gavotte, and gigue. In his resourceful scoring, designed to keep the royal ear from tiring, Handel combines festivity and finesse in perfect measure.

MUSIC FOR THE ROYAL FIREWORKS

✔ *IF YOU LIKE THIS WORK: you might also enjoy two early 20th-century pieces meant not to accompany fireworks but to actually portray them: Stravinsky's* Fireworks, *Op. 4, and the Debussy Prelude for piano, Book II, entitled* Feux d'artifice.

*T*he War of the Austrian Succession ended in 1748 with the signing of the Treaty of Aix-la-Chapelle. To show that he was on the winning side, even though Britain's gains were negligible, the king—this time George II—ordered the construction of an enormous victory pavilion in London's Green Park. Modeled on a Greek temple, with figures of the gods and a bas-relief of the king himself, the 410-foot-long edifice was to serve as the site of a spectacular fireworks display. Music for the occasion had to be the very best, so the king asked Handel, at the height of his fame, to compose it.

The monarch not only expected Handel to use as many martial instruments as possible, but also let it be known that he hoped there would be no fiddles. Handel nearly balked at that suggestion, but ultimately gave the king what he wanted: an enormous French overture in D scored for nine trumpets, nine horns, 24 oboes, 12 bassoons, contrabassoon and serpent (later cut), three pairs of timpani, and assorted side drums—along with four companion movements. A note in the score indicated that strings should double the oboe and bassoon parts; like his king, Handel knew that making peace and surrendering were not the same thing.

The actual fireworks display, on April 27, 1749, was a dismal failure, made up for only by the grandeur of Handel's music. With or without strings—and these days it is almost always performed with them—the overture stands as one of the greatest instrumental movements of its age, a brilliant showpiece marked by jubilant fanfares

AT A PUBLIC *rehearsal six days before the official celebration, more than 12,000 people crowded into Vauxhall Gardens (above) to hear Handel's music, creating a three-hour traffic jam on London Bridge.*

and wonderful interplay between groups of wind and brass instruments. Though much smaller in scale, the remaining movements—a bourrée, a siciliana (entitled "*La Paix*"), an Allegro ("*La Réjouissance*"), and a minuet—appropriately convey the "pomp and circumstance of glorious war" but suggest, in their lyricism and elegance, the more gracious passions of peacetime as well.

 RECOMMENDED RECORDINGS

Philharmonia Baroque Orchestra/ Nicholas McGegan.
Harmonia Mundi USA HMU 907010 [Water Music]

Academy of St. Martin-in-the-Fields/ Sir Neville Marriner.
Argo 414 596-2 [Water Music *and* Music for the Royal Fireworks]

McGegan's period-instrument account of the *Water Music*, taped in 1987–88, is informed, vibrant, and brilliantly recorded—a wonderful argument for authenticity. As an interpretation it ranks second to none, conveying the dances in an ideally vivacious manner. The Philharmonia, consisting mostly of American players, is not quite as accomplished as the London bands that have dominated the period-instrument scene. But while the execution in places is a bit under par (the oboes, for example, get a little scrappy), there can be no complaints about Lowell Greer's superb work as first horn.

Marriner thins out the usual textures of St. Martin's Academy to lead vigorous, stately accounts of both the *Water Music* and the *Music for the Royal Fireworks*. The playing is snappy, the feeling of dance-inspired animation just right. This is the ideal compilation, presenting both scores complete, and the sound of the 1971 recording is open, well balanced, and extremely well defined.

JOSEPH HAYDN

*I*n 1761, the 29-year-old Austrian composer Haydn accepted an offer of employment from Prince Paul Anton Esterházy. When the prince died the following year and was succeeded by his brother Nikolaus, Haydn stayed on—and worked for Nikolaus for almost 30 years, first in Eisenstadt and then at the newly built residence called Esterháza, in what is now Hungary. All that time, Haydn presided over the flowering of the Classical style, in effect making it up as he went along. And after 1790, when he was released from further service to the Esterházy family, he penned a brilliant series of culminating essays in the forms of symphony, string quartet, and piano sonata. With these, he finished the job of developing the Classical style out of the Baroque and the Rococo and bringing it to the threshold of Romanticism.

The musicians in the orchestra at Esterháza affectionately called Haydn "Papa" because he looked after their well-being as a parent might have. But posterity has tended to derive from that nickname the image of an old-fashioned and slightly doddering composer, which the prolifically innovative Haydn assuredly was not. A better connotation for this term of endearment might be that of paternity. For while he was not alone, Haydn in effect "fathered" the symphony and the string quartet.

Haydn's work as a symphonist was particularly crucial to the evolution of musical thought. At the time he began, around 1760, there were several types of symphony. The most popular was the Italian symphony, basically a glorified opera overture with a fast-slow-fast arrangement of movements using short, binary forms. A four-movement symphony, with a minuet as the second or third

1 7 3 2 — 1 8 0 9

part, had begun to catch on among German and Austrian composers and would become Haydn's model. Usually with a sonata-form first movement, it had its origins in chamber music rather than opera, and often partook of the instrumental dialog common to the concerto grosso. Haydn was constantly experimenting with orchestration and the arrangement of movements. His relative isolation at Esterháza, plus the requirement of a steady output of music for immediate consumption, no doubt helped him develop an original style, while the fact that he had an orchestra at his disposal created a laboratory atmosphere in which he felt free to try out new ideas and perfect his craft.

One finds an enormous variety of formal and expressive currents in Haydn's symphonies of the 1760s and 1770s, but certain personal hallmarks begin to manifest themselves. Underlying the originality and fine craftsmanship of these works there is often humor, expressed in surprising gestures and unexpected juxtapositions of styles, as well as in striking harmonic modulations. Most important, though, is the manner in which Haydn develops his thematic material, by carrying over the imitative counterpoint of the Baroque to create a texture based on the contours of a subject. It was on this principle of thematic development that the music of the next two centuries would be based.

In 1779 Haydn signed a contract with Prince Nikolaus that freed him to accept outside commissions, and he took advantage of this in 1785 to compose a set of six symphonies (Nos. 82–87). By this time, the four-movement form was firmly established as Haydn's model. In variety of effect and expressive profile, these *Paris* Symphonies are among his finest works. Haydn followed them with five further essays in which the diversity of material and the cogency of the argument set a new standard. But one last, huge proof of Haydn's ability remained. Following the death of Prince Nikolaus in 1790, Haydn was commissioned to write a set of six symphonies for London, the success of which prompted a contract three years later for another six. At the time he wrote the 12 *London* Symphonies (Nos. 93–104), Haydn's command of form and rhetoric was absolute, his reputation secure. Yet not once in them does he come close to exhausting his imagination. In their stylistic sophistication and richness of ideas, the *London* Symphonies stand among the highest peaks of symphonic art.

SYMPHONY NO. 88, IN G
SYMPHONY NO. 92, IN G
Oxford

*H*aydn composed five symphonies (Nos. 88–92) between 1787 and 1789, the same period during which Mozart penned his last four, and greatest, works in the genre. Taken together, these composers' nine essays may well constitute the high-water mark of Classical symphonic writing—though the 12 works Haydn would complete in London after Mozart's death can certainly be said to reach the same exalted level.

Falling between those better-known *London* Symphonies and the half-dozen he wrote for Paris, the five scores are sometimes humorously referred to as Haydn's "Channel" Symphonies. Two works in G major form the bookends to this extraordinary set, which marked the climax of Haydn's years as court composer at Eszterháza. They possess in full measure the vitality and thematic invention that distinguish his mature idiom, while revealing a still greater depth of thought and formal elegance.

Symphony No. 88 is one of Haydn's most buoyant symphonies, a work more infectiously cheerful than festive or grand, and one in which Haydn indulges his sense of symphonic levity to particularly good effect. As he frequently did, Haydn provides a slow introduction to the first movement, a highly charged Allegro that looks forward to the opening movement of Beethoven's Eighth Symphony. In the theme-and-variations second movement, each variation is more elaborate and richly scored than its predecessor. A typically witty minuet follows, and a finale borrowing the jaunty rhythmic character of a country dance brings the symphony to a close on a note of light-hearted good cheer.

The *Oxford* Symphony was actually intended for Paris and bears a dedication to the same Comte

H*AYDN'S CONTRACT when he entered the service of the Esterházy family stated that he should dress "as befits an honest house officer of a princely court" and provide an example to his musicians. Haydn was to take his meals with them, but was to "avoid undue familiarity in eating and drinking or in his relations with them, lest he lose the respect due him" as Kapellmeister.*

Prince Nikolaus Esterházy,
Haydn's patron for 30 years.

d'Ogny who had commissioned the *Paris* Symphonies. It got its name in July 1791, when Haydn was awarded an honorary doctorate by Oxford University and pressed the score into service as his thesis. It contains occasional references to the learned style—in the form of brief fugal passages—but while the fugues may justify a doctorate, Haydn's heart remains with the peasant, particularly in the simple clockwork motif concluding the first movement. In one important way, his habits are still those of the servant, too: throughout the symphony, he often uses the back door to get where he is going harmonically. The mix of refinement and rusticity that characterizes the opening movement is echoed both in the minuet and in the Presto finale, a perfect romp with motoric themes and bouncing, off-the-string accompaniments. Yet the beautifully spun-out theme of the Adagio has the melodic curve and expressive grace of an opera aria; here, Haydn's serenade-like writing for the winds is pure elegance.

 RECOMMENDED RECORDINGS

Vienna Philharmonic/Leonard Bernstein.
Deutsche Grammophon 413 777-2

Vienna Philharmonic/Karl Böhm.
Deutsche Grammophon Resonance 429 523-2
[with Symphony No. 89]

Royal Concertgebouw Orchestra/
Sir Colin Davis.
Philips 410 390-2 [Symphony No. 92, with No. 91]

Bernstein's reading of the *Oxford* is a brilliant one. In Symphony No. 88, the intense string vibrato he encourages in the slow movement may be too much for some ears, though his jaunty treatment of the finale is right on the mark. One can appreciate the chemistry that enabled the Vienna Philharmonic, at one New York performance, to encore the finale while Bernstein kept his arms folded across his chest.

Böhm's accounts with the same orchestra are genial and straightforward. The Austrian conductor opts for rather stately tempos and a big-orchestra sound, which the Viennese willingly provide; their playing is beautifully polished and urbane. Unfortunately, the recording is a bit boomy. Still, three symphonies at a rock-bottom budget price is nothing to sniff at.

Davis is always at his best in Haydn, and his 1983 reading of the *Oxford* is no exception. Like Böhm, he prefers a big orchestra, exactly the kind of ensemble for which Haydn wrote the music. Davis draws brisk, assured, animated playing from the Dutch players, especially the winds, and the recording is outstanding.

SYMPHONIES NOS. 93–104
London

The London Symphonies *received their premieres in this Hanover Square Room.*

*H*aydn's last 12 symphonies, commissioned by the London impresario Johann Peter Salomon and composed between 1791 and 1795, are known as the *London* or *Salomon* Symphonies and are considered the composer's supreme achievements in the form. As the American musicologist Leonard Ratner has noted, the twelve mark "the culmination of a long period of growth in skill, fluency, and fantasy," growth that Haydn achieved through much trial, if little error, in the course of composing nearly 100 prior symphonies.

These are the grandest of Haydn's symphonies, in both proportion and orchestration. Haydn here offers a compendium of late 18th-century symphonic thought, embracing the full range of style and topic found in the music of the Classical period. Dance types such as the bourrée, gigue, gavotte, contredanse, and Ländler are evoked at every turn, and the vocabularies of the learned

THE VIENNESE fascination with Turkish music is a direct outgrowth of war. When the Ottoman armies swept up the Danube and laid siege to Vienna, Vienna's musicians went to the city walls and taunted the Turks by imitating the music of the Janissary bands. Once the threat of invasion had receded, Turkish-style music was all the rage, and Janissary instruments were incorporated into the orchestra.

and galant styles—touching on everything from fugal imitation to pastoral musettes, Turkish marches, and the music of the hunt—are employed with consummate skill. While the ideas themselves are not new, they are expressed with a new directness and a heightened sense of profile. Also new are the freedom and flexibility evident in Haydn's treatment of harmony and phrase structure, plus the richness of texture he creates in the scoring, which is comparable to that of Mozart's last symphonies. Most remarkable of all, perhaps, is how each of these works exhibits its own character while remaining unmistakably the work of one mind.

When he wrote *"Fine Laus Deo"* ("The End, Praise God") at the bottom of the score of Symphony No. 104, Haydn was 63 years old—an old man by the standards of his day. He had said everything he had to say about the symphony and was ready to pass the torch to the only one worthy of receiving it, Beethoven. Yet still ahead for Haydn were his oratorios *The Creation* and *The Seasons*, as well as the six great masses of his last years in Vienna.

Symphony No. 94, in G (*Surprise*)—The most famous nickname in the symphonic repertory belongs to this work, the second of the *London* set. One can imagine a sizable number of the audience in the Hanover Square Rooms on March 23, 1792, literally jumping out of their seats at the "surprise," an explosive *fortissimo* punctuated by a timpani stroke, which Haydn drops like a bomb 16 bars into the mildest of Andantes—certainly one of the composer's best jokes. But then the whole symphony is a delight. After a slow introduction, the Vivace first movement offers up a laughing first subject and a second group that almost titters for a few measures, then brays outright. The waltzlike minuet is equally full of high spirits, and the finale, one of Haydn's most exuberant, shows that music with a light heart can also be virtuosic.

Symphony No. 100, in G (*Military*)—Haydn's flamboyant allusion to Turkish march music in the second movement gave this symphony its nickname. The work begins with one of Haydn's most imaginative Allegros, a movement whose two wonderfully characterized subjects—the first an innocent little ditty for the winds, the second a graceful bourrée in the strings—are treated with spectacular inventiveness. The romance-like opening of the Allegretto gives no hint of the noise in store, but soon enough the "Turkish" instruments—cymbals, triangle, and bass drum—make their incursion. Rather remarkably, Haydn manages to weave them in and out of the texture, as though their presence were not the extraordinary thing it is, and he even throws in a bugle call for good measure. The minuet sounds like something that village musicians might play, were it not for the trumpets and drums, while the finale is dashing and deliciously digressive. At the end, the Turks return to boost the celebration.

Symphony No. 101, in D (*The Clock*)—The nickname was inspired by the tick-tock pulse—in bassoons and plucked strings—that accompanies the charming principal tune of the symphony's second movement. This is only one of many inspired touches in Haydn's orchestration; throughout, he uses the winds to exceptional effect. While the minuet has a peasant roughness that nearly disguises the finesse in the scoring, the musette-style trio, in which the flute cavorts over a cleverly activated drone, exudes pastoral charm. The opening movement is a gigue that might seem to belong to the end of the symphony—but here it is at the start, all irrepressible exuberance and inner delicacy. The real finale, a rondo, begins with a long-breathed string melody that provides plenty of material for racy treatment, including a remarkable fugato episode prior to the final reprise.

A tick-tock pulse gives the Clock Symphony *its name.*

HAYDN'S SKULL *(below)—an unusually large one—was of great interest to phrenologists of his day, who believed that clues to intelligence and character could be read in a skull's topography. After Haydn's death, his body was clandestinely disinterred and the skull removed for study. Its absence was discovered in 1820 when Haydn's remains were transferred from Vienna to his home town.*

Symphony No. 102, in B flat—One of Haydn's greatest instrumental works, this score exhibits an unusual symmetry of design, as well as striking melodic richness and harmonic invention. Energy crackles through the two outer movements, both of which are assigned exceptionally lively tempos. The dance is never far away, though Haydn plays the game of starting the symphony with a slow introduction shrouded in mystery and shadow— and does so more effectively than in any of his other symphonies. Just as he begins with a joke, he ends with one: nearly everybody in the orchestra, one by one, has a go at the main theme, but each gets only as far as the third note, as if what comes next somehow escapes the players. Eventually, as always in Haydn, matters are righted. The violins break through, and even the timpanist gets a chance to proclaim the three-note figure, in triumph.

Symphony No. 103, in E flat (*Drumroll*)—The soft roll on the timpani that gives this symphony its nickname occurs in the first measure of the slow introduction, which foreshadows the mysterious world of Romanticism. In this work, things are not always what they seem. As lyrical as much of the Andante sounds, its music never strays from the march. In the minuet, made to sound like a peasant dance, horn calls lend a touch of nobility, even if later on they are rather mawkishly echoed by flute and oboe. More horn calls, this time suggestive of the hunt, open the symphony's finale, while the strings introduce a vivacious subject with a strong off-the-beat rhythm. Haydn's treatment of this pithy material has an élan suggesting the work of a young master, but his scoring anticipates the tonal palette of the mid-19th century.

Symphony No. 104, in D (*London*)—The last of Haydn's *London* Symphonies is a work of summation whose nickname attests to its pride of place in the group. It begins with a weighty introduction in the style of a French overture, full of pathos

The Wisdom of Salomon

After Haydn's retirement, concert manager Johann Peter Salomon (above) engaged him to compose half a dozen new symphonies for a series of concerts in London. Haydn's first London sojourn, in 1791, was so successful that he was invited back two years later to compose six more symphonies. The whole affair resulted in some of the most exquisite music ever written and also gave birth to Haydn's inventive and robust late style—a tribute to the wisdom of Salomon—Johann Peter, in this case.

and without a hint of D major. Tables are turned in an instant by the Allegro, where Haydn ingeniously works out a tune that combines affectionate lyricism with the vitality of the march. In the Andante, a theme-and-variations movement, there is a strong element of fantasy, and the manipulation of the theme shows an inventiveness that is extraordinary even for Haydn. The minuet is a brilliant country dance with a hint of the hurdy-gurdy, its trio a witty affair in which winds and strings tinker with a modest two-note motif while spinning out a little make-believe counterpoint. The sonata-form finale opens with an exuberant treatment of a Croatian folk tune over a musette-style drone bass. Its joyous conclusion combines the folk song and a second idea in a heady affirmation of D major.

 RECOMMENDED RECORDINGS

Royal Concertgebouw Orchestra/ Sir Colin Davis.

Philips Silver Line 432 286-2 [4 CDs; Symphonies Nos. 93, 94, and 96 (Philips 412 871-2) and Nos. 100 and 104 (411 449-2) also available separately]

London Philharmonic Orchestra/ Sir Georg Solti.

London 411 897-2 [Symphonies Nos. 94 and 100], 417 330-2 [Nos. 95 and 104], and 414 673-2 [Nos. 102 and 103]

Academy of Ancient Music/ Christopher Hogwood.

Oiseau-Lyre 414 330-2 [Symphonies Nos. 94 and 96] and 411 833-2 [Nos. 100 and 104]

The *London* Symphonies have been interpreted in different ways by many different conductors, and picking the best recordings is a difficult task. That said, the laurel goes to Davis, whose 1975–81 accounts with the Concertgebouw Orchestra stand among the most impressive recorded accomplishments of recent years. These are exceptionally personable interpretations, with wit and warmth in every measure. All 12 symphonies are wonderfully well played, and very well recorded. At full price, these CDs would be a top choice; at midprice, with three symphonies to a disc (averaging more than 75 minutes of music each), they're a steal.

Solti's are big-boned readings, very much in the Romantic mold. While the playing of the London Philharmonic might have struck Haydn as a bit brash (especially in the strings, which sound more steely than anything he ever heard), chances are he would have been bowled over by the weight and firmness of tone Solti and this band produce. Though a certain unsmiling quality occasionally emerges, these are for the most part animated performances. The sound of the 1983–87 recordings ranges from excellent to superb.

So far, Hogwood and his Academy of Ancient Music have brought out just four of the *London* Symphonies, but their success makes one impatient for the rest. These are period-instrument performances of the most elegant and informed cast, yet they possess plenty of panache as well. Hogwood uses a bigger ensemble than in his groundbreaking traversal of the Mozart symphonies, with a string complement of eight first violins, eight seconds, four violas, three cellos, and two basses. They make an impressive noise, as do the wind players. These accounts, from 1983–84, stand out for their tasteful ornamentation, crisp articulation, and excellent tempos. Symphony No. 104 seems to have been less brilliantly recorded than the rest, though all sound quite good.

Christopher Hogwood gave period performance its cachet.

"The Concert of Angels" from Grünewald's altarpiece.

PAUL HINDEMITH

SYMPHONY MATHIS DER MALER

Mathis der Maler began as an opera inspired by the altarpiece of the Church of St. Anthony at Isenheim, which was painted by Matthias Grünewald between 1512 and 1515. But Hindemith (1895–1963), in his own libretto, went beyond mere biography to comment on the artist's role in times of social upheaval. Set against the background of the Reformation and the Peasants' War of 1524–25, the opera depicts Grünewald's struggle to act conscientiously in the face of cruelty and repression.

The analogy with Hindemith's own situation—that of an artist in Nazi Germany in the mid-1930s—did not escape those in power there, and the opera's planned premiere in Berlin during the 1934–35 season was blocked, in spite of conductor Wilhelm Furtwängler's staunch defense of the work and its composer. Hindemith out-maneuvered the authorities by extracting a three-movement suite, which he entitled Symphony *Mathis der Maler* and which Furtwängler premiered in 1934 with the Berlin Philharmonic. The public's response was enthusiastic, but the officials were predictably hostile; shortly after the full opera's premiere in 1938 (in Zurich), Hindemith was forced to leave Germany.

The movements of the symphony are named after panels in the Isenheim altarpiece: "The Concert of Angels," "The Entombment," and "The Temptation of St. Anthony," a finale that concludes with a majestic, chorale-like peroration representing the Alleluiah duet of St. Anthony and St. Paul. Though removed from its operatic context, the music retains a remarkable eloquence and dramatic urgency. Hindemith's radiant scoring for the strings and magnificent use of the brass make it one of the most impressive of modern orchestral showpieces.

HINDEMITH taught at Yale from 1940 to 1953, where he proved a formidable pedagogue. His exams, which from time to time go on display, still strike fear into the hearts of music students. One sight-reading test calls for the victim, seated at the piano, to play from bass and alto clefs, while simultaneously singing from the tenor clef.

RECOMMENDED RECORDING

**San Francisco Symphony Orchestra/
Herbert Blomstedt.**
London 421 523-2 [*with* Symphonic Metamorphosis on
Themes of Carl Maria von Weber *and* Trauermusik]

This first recorded collaboration (from 1987)
of Blomstedt and the San Francisco Symphony is
powerful, deeply felt, and thrilling to the ear.
Blomstedt is notably successful with the score's
difficult concluding movement; because he makes
each of its episodes substantive, the whole seems
less episodic than usual. Both here and in the
Symphonic Metamorphosis, there is beautiful wind
and brass playing from the San Franciscans. The
recording is of demonstration quality, impressive
in its sense of space and visceral impact.

GUSTAV HOLST

THE PLANETS, OP. 32

*T*he English composer Gustav Holst (1874–
1934) is known to most music lovers by
this one piece, which is a little bit as if Prokofiev
were known only for his *Peter and the Wolf*. The
real Holst was a more "serious" composer than
one might think from a first acquaintance with
this all-stops-out essay in orchestral showmanship.
Yet even here, one encounters characteristics of
that deeper musician—in the remarkable gift for
melody exhibited on nearly every page of the
score, and in the mysticism that pervades much
of the writing. They are in perfect equilibrium
here, strengthening a piece that is firmly within
the orbit of comprehension.

Holst's treatment of the planets focuses not on
their celestial nature but on the astrological aspects long associated with them and their
mythological namesakes. The suite opens with a

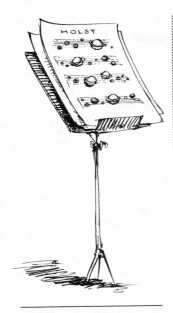

THE EXISTENCE
*of a ninth planet had
been theorized, but astrono-
mers had not yet actually
discovered Pluto when Holst
began* The Planets *in
1914. Thus the score consists
of seven rather than eight
movements—the one known
planet not written about
being Earth.*

portrait of "Mars, the Bringer of War." The ensuing movements are "Venus, the Bringer of
Peace," "Mercury, the Winged Messenger," "Jupiter, the Bringer of Jollity," "Saturn, the Bringer
of Old Age," "Uranus, the Magician," and "Neptune, the Mystic."

It was Holst's friend Clifford Bax who had given
him the idea of attempting a piece on the planets—
and the imagery this suggested led Holst to compose a work unlike any other he had written. At
its first performance in 1918, the listeners assumed "Mars" to be a depiction of World War I,
then still raging—but Holst had actually written
the movement before the August 1914 outbreak
of hostilities. The final pages of "Neptune," with
the offstage female chorus, made the strongest
impression on the audience, but Holst himself
rightly judged "Saturn" to be the finest movement.

With audiences today, it is "Jupiter" that usually
makes the biggest impression—and the whole
score has become a modern classic, as likely as
not to be performed in a Pops setting. Interest-
ingly enough, today's master of extraterrestrial
music, John Williams, has borrowed freely from
The Planets in his film scores, most notably in his
depiction of the Empire forces in *Star Wars*, which
echoes the sinister martial rhythm heard at the
beginning of "Mars, the Bringer of War."

 RECOMMENDED RECORDINGS

**Montreal Symphony Orchestra/
Charles Dutoit.**
London 417 553-2

**London Philharmonic Orchestra/
Sir Adrian Boult.**
EMI Studio Plus CDM 64748 [*with Elgar:*
Enigma *Variations*]

Even with the score's profligate effects, it takes
a special talent to bring off *The Planets*. Dutoit

goes straight to the point and elicits a stirring performance from his Canadian forces. Every gesture, every nuance, is surely realized and breathtakingly vivid. The sound of the 1986 recording is still state-of-the-art.

It was Boult who conducted the 1918 debut of *The Planets*, winning Holst's undying gratitude for making the score "shine" under his baton. Sixty years later, Boult recorded the piece for the last time. Then in his 90th year, he was still capable of making it shine, and brightly. Boult has the measure of each movement, bringing out expressive details no one else has found in the music. The London Philharmonic follows the venerable maestro right over the top, and the sound is remarkably full-bodied.

CHARLES IVES

THREE PLACES IN NEW ENGLAND

Mr. and Mrs. Charles Ives at their pastoral Connecticut home.

The son of a Connecticut Yankee bandmaster, Ives (1874–1954) grew up in Danbury, in the rich musical soil of late 19th-century New England. He was exposed to every available musical stimulus, from the European classics to Protestant hymnody and popular song, with a considerable amount of municipal band music thrown in. Heated in the crucible of his father's nonconformist attitudes about serious music, and tempered by his own carefully considered rejection of mainstream teachings at Yale, these ingredients produced in Ives an idiosyncratic musical alloy, a language utterly unlike anyone else's.

But as anarchistic as Ives got in his composing, he never strayed from his roots in the American experience. And in nearly every work, the imagery is extraordinarily vivid, as though each score were really a motion picture in sound. Ives's homespun "movies" have waited many years to be received by a comprehending audience—and they still have an uphill battle ahead of them—but no music is more American in its freedom of thought and rugged individualism.

The *First Orchestral Set*, better known as *Three Places in New England*, shows the Ivesian amalgam at its best. Composed between 1908 and 1914, it received its premiere in 1931 at one of the few performances of his own music Ives ever attended. The first movement of the triptych is entitled "The Saint-Gaudens in Boston Common (Col. Shaw and his Colored Regiment)," the reference being to the Shaw Memorial created in 1897 by the Irish-born American sculptor Augustus Saint-Gaudens. Out of a nebulous opening, strains of Stephen Foster's "Old Black Joe" begin to crystallize, dreamily overlapped by fragments of Civil War marching tunes. The mood is broken by a single forceful outburst, and the restless meditation concludes.

"Putnam's Camp, Redding, Connecticut" refers to the Revolutionary War encampment of Israel Putnam, the Continental Army general. Snatches of several familiar patriotic tunes are heard in this wild mix of ragtime and martial fantasy.

The final movement, "The Housatonic at Stockbridge," is named after a poem by Robert Underwood Johnson. Ives revealed that the piece is a reminiscence of "a Sunday morning walk that Mrs. Ives and I took near Stockbridge [Massachusetts] the summer after we were married. We walked in the meadows . . . and heard the distant singing from the church across the river. The mists had not entirely left the river bed, and the colors, the running water, the banks and elm trees were something that one would always remember." The piece is one of Ives's most remarkable creations. Water and mist are evoked by the muted strings, while English horn and French horn quote hymns. This impressionistic collage builds to a chaotic climax before the scene vanishes into memory.

IVES WAS A MAN OF many talents. As a right-handed pitcher for the Hopkins Grammar School varsity baseball team, he defeated Yale's freshman team in 1894. As a student at Yale, Ives continued to be more interested in baseball than in academics and received gentleman's C's. After graduating, he went into business, eventually making a sizeable fortune in the insurance industry.

RECOMMENDED RECORDINGS

Orchestra New England/James Sinclair.
Koch Classics 3-7025-2 [with Country Band *March and other works]*

**Boston Symphony Orchestra/
Michael Tilson Thomas.**
Deutsche Grammophon 423 243-2 [with Symphony No. 4 and Central Park in the Dark]

Sinclair's 1990 recording of *Three Places in New England,* the first to use the Charles Ives Society critical edition of the score, presents the piece in the small-orchestra instrumentation Ives prepared in 1929. The performance and sound are immaculate; the rest of the disc, containing numerous first recordings of smaller pieces, is well worth investigating.

Thomas is one of our best Ivesians, in the mold of Bernstein and equally devoted to the cause. His 1970 account of *Three Places* is passionate, sure-footed, and penetrating, and the Boston Symphony brings plenty of polish to the reading. The recording is warm and well balanced. Seiji Ozawa conducts the couplings.

LEOŠ JANÁČEK

SINFONIETTA

*J*anáček (1854–1928) composed some of the most beautiful and compelling operas of the 20th century and will go down as one of its most original musical thinkers. He is also music's greatest late bloomer, not finding his mature idiom until after the turn of the century, when he was in his late forties. Janáček's lifelong interest in the folk music of his native Moravia, as well as his training in the choir school of the

Brno as it looked at the time of Janáček's Sinfonietta.

✓ *IF YOU LIKE THIS WORK, you might also enjoy Janáček's symphonic rhapsody* Taras Bulba, *based on Gogol's tale of the Cossack headman who rose up against the Poles and paid with his life. Janáček saw the Russian people as the hope and salvation of Slavs everywhere. In the heroic figure of Taras Bulba he found an embodiment of the nationalistic ideals to which he was devoted.*

Augustinian monastery in Brno, contributed some eclectic strands to his unorthodox musical language; so, too, did his open ear for new music. But for the most part his style was *sui generis*, based on an instinctive feel for rhythm, harmony, and tone color and given refreshing edge by the terseness of his melody and exuberant orchestration.

In 1926, the year he wrote *Sinfonietta*, Janáček was 72 and in the midst of a brilliant Indian summer of creativity, spurred on by his platonic but passionate attachment to Kamila Stösslová— who was 38 years younger and married. The score, Janáček's largest purely orchestral composition, is really more of a suite than the "little symphony" its title implies. Each of the five movements showcases a different combination of instruments, and the orchestration of most of the work is bold, colorful, and in spite of the expanded wind and brass sections, characteristically lean.

Janáček's editors at the newspaper *Lidové noviny*, for which he wrote occasional articles, had requested "some fanfares" for the Sokol gymnastic festival of 1926, a national celebration of the newly forged Czechoslovak Republic. A fervent patriot, Janáček took advantage of the commission to write a work that conveyed his feelings of optimism and pride in country, dedicating it "To the Czechoslovak Armed Forces." As the work took shape, it also became a tribute to Brno, which had been under German domination until the founding of the republic in 1918. Each movement after the first was meant to portray a landmark or an aspect of the Moravian capital's character.

The first movement, which Janáček originally intended to call "Fanfares" (he later dropped all titles), is scored for brass and timpani and features a fanfare theme played by nine trumpets. It is followed by "The Castle" (a reference to the Špilberk Castle overlooking Brno), a movement full of the bustle of shifting meters and displaced accents that presents an almost kaleidoscopic succession of ideas and moods. The elegiac third movement, "The Queen's Monastery," builds to an impassioned, *prestissimo* climax before the tide of emotion subsides.

Similar in feeling to a scherzo, the fourth movement, "The Street," is brisk and lively. The energetic ringing of a bell provokes a moment's reflection before the active pace is resumed. The *Sinfonietta*'s final movement, to which Janáček had given the title "City Hall," opens mysteriously and gradually gains momentum. At its end, the music of the opening fanfare returns, this time recapitulated with a full orchestral accompaniment accented by trills throughout the winds and strings.

RECOMMENDED RECORDING

Vienna Philharmonic/Sir Charles Mackerras.
London Jubilee 430 727-2 [with Taras Bulba, *and* Shostakovich: Age of Gold *Suite]*

Mackerras conveys the extraordinary color and spirit of this score better than anyone, and the 1980 recording, with an inspired Vienna Philharmonic playing on the edge of their seats, is electrifying. One of London's earliest digital efforts, this is also one of the label's best-sounding recordings from any era and any venue.

Mackerras mastered the Czech repertory in Prague.

FRANZ LISZT

LES PRÉLUDES

*L*iszt (1811–1886) is remembered as perhaps the greatest virtuoso pianist the world has known. The Hungarian's technique was legendary, and he had a stage presence to match it. But he retired from the concert platform at the age of 35, thereafter playing only in private or for charity. During the last 40 years of his life, Liszt devoted himself to composing, teaching, and

L ISZT SETTLED in
Weimar in 1848 with
Princess Carolyne von Sayn-
Wittgenstein and over the
next decade enjoyed his most
productive years as a com-
poser. While Liszt wrote
music, Carolyne wrote
words—a lot of them, in-
cluding many like the ones
that found their way into the
preface to Les Préludes.

furthering the cause of other composers, chief among them Wagner. But his own achievements as a composer are often overlooked.

Liszt's ideas concerning harmony, motivic treatment, and large-scale structure were novel and advanced, and they were to prove highly influential during the 19th century. He also possessed an exceptionally poetic imagination. In combination, these factors spurred him to create a new musical genre, the symphonic poem, in which a literary or pictorial idea serves as the point of departure for an orchestral meditation touching on a variety of moods. While Liszt's symphonic poems tend to be more loosely organized than the programmatic symphonies from which they descend, they avoid the pitfall of mere scene-painting, focusing instead on the evocation of psychological states.

Les Préludes, the most effective and popular of Liszt's 13 symphonic poems, was originally drafted in 1848 as the preface to a choral composition based on the poet Joseph Autran's *Les quatre élémens*. In the early 1850s, after deciding to recast the score as an independent work, Liszt revised it and looked for a suitable program to which he could say he had fashioned the music. He found one among the *Méditations poétiques* of Alphonse de Lamartine, France's first Romantic poet and, for a brief period after the revolution of 1848, the head of its government.

The score is in four broad sections, corresponding to the four elements of Autran's text and, fortuitously, to the divisions of Lamartine's poem. The music of the first section supposedly suggests, in the verse of Lamartine, "moods of spring and love," that of the second the "storms of life." There is a long "peaceful idyll," followed by a militant celebration of "strife and victory." Two recurrent melodic ideas dominate the work, appearing in several different guises, each with a different expressive character, a process Liszt called thematic transformation.

The music of *Les Préludes* is tremendously effective; in this century, several passages became Hollywood stock-in-trade, turning up in everything from Flash Gordon serials to Bugs Bunny cartoons. Liszt's treatment of the orchestra is nearly as inventive as his manipulation of the thematic material, and the work's blazingly scored concluding pages, where "victory" is won, are among the most triumphant in the Romantic literature.

RECOMMENDED RECORDINGS

Berlin Philharmonic/Herbert von Karajan.
Deutsche Grammophon Galleria 427 222-2 [with Sibelius: Finlandia, *and Tchaikovsky:* Capriccio italien *and* 1812 *Overture]*

Philadelphia Orchestra/Riccardo Muti.
EMI Studio CDD 63899 [with Brahms: Piano Concerto No. 1]

"WHAT IS OUR *life but a series of Preludes to that unknown song, the first solemn note of which is sounded by Death? The enchanted dawn of every existence is heralded by Love. . . . Yet, no sooner does the trumpet sound the alarm, than he runs to the post of danger, be the war what it may that summons him to its ranks. For there in the struggle he will find complete self-realization and the full possession of his forces."*
—Franz Liszt, Preface to *Les Préludes*

Karajan's 1967 account of *Les Préludes* has never been bettered for its gung-ho martial fervor, hothouse Romanticism, and symphonic sweep. The Berlin ensemble is at fever pitch throughout, and the sound is remarkably good. *Finlandia* and the *Capriccio italien* receive equally fine performances (though the latter suffers a little from glary sound). The *1812* Overture cannot be recommended because of some unfortunate singing by the Don Cossack Choir, but three out of four isn't bad.

Muti's version of *Les Préludes*, from the early 1980s, is more reserved and poetic than Karajan's, but still trashy where it needs to be. The Philadelphia Orchestra plays with immense polish and lyric beauty, the brass most impressive in the climaxes.

Mahler in 1907, his final year as Vienna Court Opera director.

GUSTAV MAHLER

Symphony No. 2, in C minor
Resurrection

*M*ahler (1860–1911), not long after completing this work, said: "The term 'symphony' means creating a world with all the technical means available." The *Resurrection* Symphony *is* an all-embracing work, the first of the Austrian composer's symphonies to make use of voices and words as well as the orchestra, and the piece that set the composer decisively on the path toward the grandly scaled, highly individualistic and confessional style of symphony that was to become his legacy. It was also the composition that brought Mahler his first fame, and its premiere in Berlin on the night of December 13, 1895 (staged with the help of Richard Strauss), marked the real beginning of Mahler's career as a composer.

The symphony was written between 1888 and 1894, mostly while Mahler was serving as chief conductor of the opera in Hamburg. It consists of five movements, the first three purely instrumental, the last two also calling for vocal forces. The opening movement is an emotionally charged essay that spans an enormous range of feeling. It begins in dramatic fashion with a funeral march in C minor, offering up a consolingly lyrical second subject in C major before proceeding to a lengthy development where there are passages full of mystery, and some terrifying climaxes as well. Mahler saves the most forceful treatment for the recapitulation, bringing back the funeral march with an almost hysterical intensity.

After this extraordinary introduction, Mahler felt it necessary to call for a pause of at least five minutes before the start of the second movement, a gentle minuet. The composer described this Andante as the evocation of "a memory, a ray of sunlight, pure and cloudless. . . ." The following movement, based on Mahler's setting of the song

M*AHLER FOUND something comical, almost macabre, in St. Anthony's preaching to the fish, mainly because the fish went on leading exactly the same mischievous lives as before. For a more devout view of this line of evangelism, try the first of Liszt's two Légendes for piano, entitled* St. François d'Assise: la prédication aux oiseaux *(St. Francis of Assisi Preaching to the Birds).*

"*Des Antonius von Padua Fischpredigt*" ("St. Anthony of Padua's Sermon to the Fish") from *Des Knaben Wunderhorn*, serves as a sort of scherzo. Mahler's original program suggested that the music should have a fantastic, nightmarish quality, and indeed there may be a suggestion here of the temptation of the other St. Anthony in the desert. Still, one senses more a macabre humor in the music than outright anguish, for which Mahler would eventually find more powerful expression.

The fourth movement is a setting for alto solo and reduced orchestra of another *Wunderhorn* song, "*Urlicht*" ("Primeval Light"), and the music sounds as if it were indeed suffused with a gentle light. Mahler noted that the text should be sung as if by a child who imagines he is in heaven.

Heaven, however, has yet to be stormed. That is the task of the symphony's final movement, among the greatest transcendental utterances in 19th-century music. After a dramatic opening and a series of imaginative episodes—marches, fanfares, and processionals suggesting the bizarre preliminaries to judgment—what Mahler refers to as "the great call" is sounded. From opposite sides of the stage, horns and trumpets proclaim their fanfares, while between them, flute and piccolo answer with birdcalls, suggesting nature stilled to near-silence. Out of this, a voice emerges: the unaccompanied chorus, softly intoning the command "*Aufersteh'n*" ("Arise"). Soprano and alto soloists join the chorus in Klopstock's ode *The Resurrection*, and the setting gradually builds in majesty until the final stanza is hurled out "with the greatest force" in E flat major, over a concluding *fortissimo* in the orchestra supplemented by organ, deep bells, and ten horns.

 RECOMMENDED RECORDINGS

Columbia Symphony Orchestra/ Bruno Walter.
CBS Masterworks M2K 42032 [2 CDs]

**Saint Louis Symphony Orchestra/
Leonard Slatkin.**
Telarc CD 80081/82 [2 CDs]

New York Philharmonic/Leonard Bernstein.
Deutsche Grammophon 423 395-2 [2 CDs]

For generosity of spirit and insight, Walter's account with the Columbia Symphony is still unmatched. It is a reading of breadth and scope, deeply committed and thoroughly uplifting in the finale. There is some noticeable tape hiss on the remastered CDs, along with a bit of constriction in the loudest passages, but the sound is excellent for its late-1950s vintage.

Slatkin's 1982 recording was one of Telarc's early digital triumphs, an outstanding achievement both technically and musically. The interpretation is noteworthy for the powerful, disciplined playing of the Saint Louis Symphony, as well as for Slatkin's clear, intelligent presentation of the score. And the vocal soloists, Kathleen Battle and Maureen Forrester, are exceptional; 25 years after Forrester made the recording with Walter, here she is again, singing as beautifully as ever.

Bernstein's is an apocalyptic vision. This is the *Resurrection* taken to the limit, and then well beyond. It may not be a reading to everyone's liking, but it is certainly an experience, and there is no question of the performers' commitment. The sound of this 1987 live recording is extraordinarily good for Avery Fisher Hall, vivid, ample, and quite detailed.

Soprano Kathleen Battle soars in Mahler's Resurrection.

SYMPHONY NO. 5, IN C SHARP MINOR

*M*ahler completed the Fifth Symphony in 1902, the year of his marriage to Alma Schindler. The marriage marked a turning point in his life, and the symphony the beginning of his full maturity as a composer. In its melodic content and mood, the Fifth has clear connections to Mahler's earlier, song-based symphonies, but it marks an important advance toward a more organic concept of structure and a greater reliance on thematic linkages between movements. At times, the development of the melodic material is overtly, even ironically, "Classical" in its rigor. Yet the emotional trajectory—from the funereal weight and violence of the first two movements, through the dreamlike digressions of the scherzo, to the almost giddy optimism of the finale—is intensely subjective and Romantic.

The symphony begins in a solemn vein with a funeral march in C sharp minor, alternately lugubrious and hysterical. The ensuing A minor Allegro, with its heaving string passages and outbursts in the brass, is frightening in its wildness. The climax of this stormy movement, carefully marked "High Point" by Mahler, is an abortive bid for transcendence: a radiant chorale issues from the full brass, only to disintegrate into a reprise of the shadowy opening material.

The third movement is the keystone, an 819-measure scherzo opening up a world of vast expanse and almost manic energy. Yet behind its exuberance and waltzlike gaiety there is contemplation, and a certain nervousness as well, clearly evoked by the haunting horn and wind solos in the middle section of the movement.

In the final two movements, Mahler turns to a revelation of more intimate feelings. First comes an Adagietto in F major for strings and harp, which is at once tender and searing. Recent research has shown that Mahler conceived of this movement as a "love letter" to Alma; its pages, among the most beautiful in all of his music, build to a passionate climax in which the tragic energy of the symphony's opening movements undergoes a glowing metamorphosis.

A rondo finale in D major brings the Fifth Symphony to an unambiguously optimistic close. Amid torrents of eighth-note counterpoint rem-

ALMA SCHINDLER, the daughter of Austrian landscape painter Anton Schindler, was an outstanding composer in her own right before she married Mahler in 1902. She also possessed one of the most magnetic personalities of her time. As the song by Tom Lehrer tells it, she married the greatest minds in Europe: first Mahler, then architect Walter Gropius, then the novelist Franz Werfel.

Bronze bust of Mahler by Rodin.

iniscent of Bach at his most inventive, Mahler releases the pent-up emotion of the preceding hour in a 15-minute display of orchestral fireworks. For the climax, he brings back the chorale that had been cut short in the second movement, this time allowing it to lead to a joyous, breathlessly accelerating coda.

 RECOMMENDED RECORDINGS

Vienna Philharmonic/Leonard Bernstein.
Deutsche Grammophon 423 608-2

Royal Concertgebouw Orchestra/ Bernard Haitink.
Philips 416 469-2

New Philharmonia Orchestra/ Sir John Barbirolli.
EMI Studio Plus CDM 64749

The Mahler Fifth was one of the pieces Lenny owned. He and the Vienna Philharmonic give a telling performance, transmitting the impetuous energy of the score to the fullest. Bernstein's sureness of touch enables him to realize the many little expressive gestures that add up to something miraculous. The players, with him all the way, contribute some wonderful touches of their own, especially the strings. The recording, made live in 1987 in Frankfurt's Alte Oper, is solid and has remarkable impact.

Haitink's is the Apollonian counterpart to Bernstein's reading, a lucid, clearly thought-through account that nonetheless has plenty of emotional grip. The Concertgebouw—an orchestra with a great Mahler tradition going back to the time this symphony was written—takes the bit in its teeth and plays impressively, imparting many felicities. With just the slightest tape hiss, the 1970 recording is outstanding.

Barbirolli offers a hyper-Romantic and in-

IF YOU LIKE THIS WORK, listen to Mahler's Symphony No. 7. After its lugubrious opening movement, the three middle movements are mysterious and nocturnal. The buoyant C major finale has puzzled both listeners and conductors. It can seem oddly insincere unless the glorious cacophony of its closing pages is treated as a last evocation of fin de siècle optimism amid the ruins of Romanticism.

tensely personal interpretation. There is a seat-of-the-pants feel to much of it, and one can readily hear Sir John exhorting his colleagues with grunts and groans from the podium. This 1969 account is not without moments of peril—tempos are broad, especially in the finale, and rubato and rhetorical point are sometimes stretched to the limit—but one suspects that this is how the piece was played when it was new. The sound is warm and spacious, with natural weight and excellent definition.

DAS LIED VON DER ERDE

*T*he summation of Mahler's work as a song symphonist, and the most intimate and profound linkage he ever achieved between the two modes of expression, came with *Das Lied von der Erde* (*The Song of the Earth*). This six-movement score, composed in 1908–9, is based on texts from a collection of Chinese poetry that had been translated into German by the writer Hans Bethge and given the title *Die chinesische Flöte* (*The Chinese Flute*). The poems, with their exotic imagery evoking an unencountered world, opened a spiritual door for the composer and served as the starting point for an extraordinarily intense meditation on the passing of life.

Each of the six songs of *Das Lied von der Erde* is set for a single solo voice and orchestra. The first movement, entitled "*Das Trinklied vom Jammer der Erde*" ("The Drinking Song of Earth's Sorrow"), is a ferocious A minor Allegro that moves restlessly through three verses of Li-Tai-Po, the most famous of all Chinese poets. The prevailing mood is tragic and impassioned, which makes the otherworldly treatment of parts of the text unusually poignant, particularly at "*Das Firmament blaut ewig . . .*" ("The heavens are ever blue . . .").

"*Der Einsame im Herbst*" ("The Lonely One in Autumn") mirrors the loneliness Mahler said had

*O*NE OF HISTORY'S *most interesting face-to-face encounters between composers took place in 1907 when Sibelius and Mahler met in Helsinki. Mahler told Sibelius that a symphony "must be like the world. It must embrace everything." Sibelius differed. To him, a symphony was not like the world, but a world unto itself: "Its style and severity of form and profound logic create an inner connection between all the motives."*

Mahler's intensity terrified players and electrified audiences.

descended upon him as he contemplated his own end. The scoring of this song, in which the contralto's lines seem to come one at a time, is gentle and surprisingly spare until the poem reaches its emotional crux in the last two lines, which are treated rhapsodically.

The next two movements, "Of Youth" and "Of Beauty," deal with some of the more pleasant experiences of life, but are tinged with melancholy, while *"Der Trunkene im Frühling"* ("The Drunkard in Spring") has a lurching grandiloquence that is eventually transmuted into light-headed joy.

"Der Abschied" ("The Farewell"), among the most heartbreaking finales in the symphonic literature, is also the most expertly realized of Mahler's creations. In its translucent beauty and sheer "otherness" of sound, the scoring opens entirely new regions of expression and color—new to Mahler, new to music itself. Like brushstrokes in a Chinese landscape, touches of celesta, harp, and mandolin are applied to pages almost bare of sound to create a fragile, haunting backdrop for the solo voice. The final section, in which the Earth's eternal cycle of self-renewal is observed and embraced, brings a feeling of spiritual release unprecedented in music.

 RECOMMENDED RECORDINGS

Vienna Philharmonic/Bruno Walter.
London 414 194-2

Philharmonia Orchestra/Otto Klemperer.
EMI Classics CDC 47231

Walter conducted the premiere of *Das Lied von der Erde* in Munich in 1911, six months after Mahler's death, and he made the first recording of the score 25 years later in Vienna. After World War II, Walter renewed his ties with the Vienna Philharmonic, leading to this 1952 account of *Das*

*The English contralto
Kathleen Ferrier, c. 1950.*

Lied, one of the treasures of the pre-stereo era. The conception and execution are on the highest level, and the singing of Kathleen Ferrier—who knew she was dying of cancer at the time the recording was made—imparts a radiance to the final song that has never been approached by any other performance.

The account from Klemperer has in Fritz Wunderlich the greatest tenor who has ever recorded the music, and in Christa Ludwig a mezzo soprano scarcely less impressive. Sonics are glorious, and the conductor's measured direction imparts a striking sense of grandeur.

SYMPHONY NO. 9, IN D

*W*ritten in 1909, two years before his death, Mahler's Ninth Symphony is the greatest valedictory work in the orchestral literature. In certain ways, particularly in its four-movement layout, it represents a return to more conventional notions after the formal departures of the Seventh and Eighth Symphonies and *Das Lied von der Erde*. But it is also a work of striking innovation, most notably in the scheme of its first movement—which is based on the idea of a recurring crescendo rather than the harmonic patterns of conventional sonata form—and in the disintegration and collage-like reassembly of the thematic material in all four movements. Deep pathos and satirical rage seem to share the stage in this, the most paradoxical of Mahler's works. In the end, a poignant farewell wins out over the warring emotions of anger, hysteria, and nostalgia that are prominent in the preceding movements.

The symphony's opening Andante is a succession of powerful buildups to increasingly violent outbursts. It was the composer Alban Berg who referred to this movement as "the most glorious" Mahler ever produced, and who succeeded in penetrating its secret when he wrote: "The whole movement is based on a premonition of death which constantly recurs. That is why the tenderest passages are followed by climaxes like new eruptions of a volcano." Not for the first time, Mahler's life had invaded his music, laying down the very laws by which it could function. The result—an entire symphonic movement constructed on a dynamic process, rather than conventional harmonic logic—was to influence not only Berg but many other 20th-century composers.

Mahler steps away from the brink in the second movement, an affectionate, almost comical Ländler full of high spirits and remembrance. The tone is hinted at in his tempo marking, which specifies that the expression should be "somewhat clumsy and very coarse." But chaos is never far away, and what began humorously veers repeatedly toward the frenzied and grotesque until the opening idea returns, now aimless and disoriented. The movement ends by literally unraveling itself in fragmentary reminiscences of its own material.

The ensuing, oddly named Rondo-Burleske is a tug-of-war between anger, exuberance, and innocence, with anger winning out in the end. The dance of death—here no longer a dance but a march, with snarling brass and hammered bow strokes—advances inexorably until it becomes a bacchanalian revel in the movement's final pages.

In closing with an Adagio, as Tchaikovsky had done in his *Pathétique*, Mahler most likely had in mind not that symphony nor his own Third but the conclusion of *Das Lied von der Erde*. Here, in instrumental form, is the same expression, though more pained; the wordless song of parting passes from heavy melancholy through several dreamlike interludes, reaching a climax that screams out not from fear but with the sadness of one who has an all-consuming love for life and is about to die. Gradually, the emotion subsides and the tone of the movement turns elegiac. Fragments of motives pass like memories, until all that is left is a calm acceptance of the end.

MAHLER CANCELED three appointments with Sigmund Freud before he finally went to see the doctor in the summer of 1910. Freud later wrote: "If I may believe reports, I achieved much with [Mahler]. . . . [In the course of] a highly interesting journey through his life history, we discovered his personal conditions for love, particularly his Holy Mary complex (mother fixation). I had much opportunity to admire the capability for psychological understanding in this man of genius."

MAHLER *came to New York in 1907 to take up the post of conductor at the Metropolitan Opera. He left after two seasons of bickering with the management and sharing the limelight with Toscanini. Mahler's tenure at the New York Philharmonic proved similarly tumultuous. Yet Mahler retained warm feelings for America and Americans, and particularly liked riding the New York subway.*

 RECOMMENDED RECORDINGS

Berlin Philharmonic/Herbert von Karajan.
Deutsche Grammophon 410 726-2 [2 CDs]

Vienna Philharmonic/Bruno Walter.
EMI CDH 63029

Columbia Symphony Orchestra/ Bruno Walter.
CBS Masterworks M2K 42033 [2 CDs]

Karajan made a studio recording of the Ninth with the Berlin Philharmonic in the late 1970s, but he was apparently dissatisfied and pressed for this remake, recorded at a concert during the Berlin Festival Weeks of 1982. The result is riveting, with visionary intensity from first bar to last. There is unshakable control over Mahler's vast canvas here, but also an extraordinary "of the moment" quality that is unusual in Karajan's discography. The sound is excellent.

It was to Walter that Mahler entrusted the score of his Ninth Symphony in the autumn of 1910, knowing that he himself would not live to conduct the premiere. Walter also presided over the first recording of the work, and it remains one of the most remarkable documents of this century. With an incandescent Vienna Philharmonic on stage, the recording was made at a concert in the Musikvereinssaal on January 16, 1938, just prior to the Anschluss. Walter, then 61, and his colleagues, some of whom had played under Mahler, give an overwhelming reading inspired not only by the memory of the composer but by the grim situation in Austria and Europe at that moment. Listening to the account is like stepping back in time, and it can be a chilling experience. The sound is magnificent for a recording more than 50 years old.

Walter's 1961 traversal takes a more philosophical view and is suffused with deep sentiment. In making this recording, one of his last, Walter still carried inside him the physical memories of 50 years earlier: despite repeated pleas from the control room, he could not keep himself from stamping his foot on the upbeat to the string entrance at the beginning of the Ländler. It is after all a dance—and Walter felt it that way, just as Mahler would have.

FELIX MENDELSSOHN

A Midsummer Night's Dream: Overture, Op. 21
Incidental Music, Op. 61

Land of the fairies in A Midsummer Night's Dream.

*T*here are prodigies, and then there is Mendelssohn (1809–1847). Not even Mozart demonstrated as a 17-year-old anything quite like the level of inspiration that marks this German composer's Overture to *A Midsummer Night's Dream.* True, Mendelssohn possessed one of the most cultivated sensibilities in the history of arts and letters, but his feeling for Shakespeare (whose works he knew in Schlegel's translations) nevertheless bordered on the miraculous for one so young. In the vast number of musical works inspired by Shakespeare, there is hardly another as perfect as this overture. Yet when asked years later to describe what he had attempted to depict, Mendelssohn could only say that the music follows the play rather closely in mood and imagery.

With the first soft woodwind chords in E major, a spell of enchantment is cast, and the listener is translated (as Bottom might say) to the domain of Oberon and Titania, king and queen of the fairies. In a quick-march tempo, the strings scurry along at the extreme of *pianissimo,* staccato, their eighth notes flying by so quickly that when the melody comes to rest on a single note, it becomes a suspenseful tremolo. Fanfares in the brass announce that a celebration is in store, and here and there woodwinds pop out of the texture like

MENDELSSOHN'S influence on his 19th-century contemporaries and successors was second only to that of Beethoven. The effervescent brilliance of the Overture to A Midsummer Night's Dream *left its mark on every composer of atmospheric music from Berlioz (the "Queen Mab" scherzo in* Roméo et Juliette) *to Richard Strauss (the second section of* Ein Heldenleben*), while the more festive style of the last three symphonies and the concert overtures influenced Saint-Saëns, Bruch, Brahms, Strauss and Elgar who goes so far as to quote the clarinet theme from his* Enigma Variations.

forest sounds, conjuring up a mysterious world in which even the shadows are animated. Mendelssohn uses the ophicleide (a descendant of the medieval serpent, a wind instrument with a brass mouthpiece) to color the bass line a weirdly supernatural shade, and he depicts the braying of Bottom, who wears the head of an ass, with a raucous *fortissimo* plunge of a ninth—from D sharp down to C sharp—in the violins and clarinets.

But Mendelssohn's romance with *A Midsummer Night's Dream* was not over. In 1842, he was commissioned by Friedrich Wilhelm IV to compose incidental music for a production of the play in Potsdam the following year. Rather remarkably, the 33-year-old was able to rekindle the flame of genius that had burned so brightly in the overture, so that the 13 additional numbers seem of a piece with the earlier work.

In addition to several songs, the incidental music includes four larger movements that are often grouped with the overture to form a suite. These are a scherzo (more feather-light fairy music, led by the winds), an intermezzo (in the minor, with a turbulent undercurrent evoking the darker side of the forest), a nocturne (love music, with a gentle chorale played by the horns and bassoons), and the most beloved of all wedding marches, to celebrate the triple marriage at the heart of the play's concluding revels.

Symphony No. 4, in A, Op. 90
Italian

*T*he inspiration for the *Italian* Symphony came from a journey Mendelssohn made to Italy during 1830–31. Few tourists have ever been so well equipped to appreciate the splendors of that country as Mendelssohn or so expert at capturing its many moods for others to enjoy. Here was a composer well acquainted with Italy's

The Spanish Steps, sketched by Mendelssohn.

musical tradition, and his ear must have delighted in the daily stimulus it received, not just in churches and opera houses but in the streets as well.

Following his return to Berlin in 1832, he set to work fleshing out the sketches he had made in Rome of a symphony intended to evoke the spirit of Italy and the warmth and vitality of its people. The essay that resulted a year later, so full of color, lyricism, and energy, is an extraordinary example of musical portraiture and remains the most popular of Mendelssohn's symphonies.

The ebullient first movement, in the bright key of A major, conveys at once the giddy feeling that seems to come upon all true lovers of life the moment they set foot in Italy. Its upthrusting main theme and racing eighth-note pulse are the embodiment of joy. Other sides of the country's varied personality are reflected in the remainder of the symphony. The brief second movement, in a penitent-sounding D minor, suggests a pilgrims' processional with its walking bass line and chorale-like inner voices, while the third movement, ostensibly a scherzo, has the easy flow and ornamental grace of a moonlight serenade. Passions seethe and erupt with Vesuvian force in the finale, a saltarello (a dance in rapid triple meter) in the fierce key of A minor. The inspiration is clearly Neapolitan, though the tune is Mendelssohn's own.

 ## RECOMMENDED RECORDINGS

Berlin Philharmonic/Herbert von Karajan.
Deutsche Grammophon Galleria 415 848-2 [Symphony No. 4, with Schubert: Symphony No. 8]

Boston Symphony Orchestra/Sir Colin Davis.
Philips 420 653-2 [Symphony No. 4 and Overture and selected Incidental Music for A Midsummer Night's Dream]

Vienna Philharmonic/André Previn.
Philips 420 161-2 [Overture and complete Incidental Music for A Midsummer Night's Dream]

The account of the *Italian* Symphony from Karajan and the Berlin Philharmonic is pretty near ideal—potent yet elegant, with a polish to the playing that exemplifies the Mendelssohnian virtue of smoothness. Strings dominate winds here, producing an operatic sound which suggests that Mendelssohn's impressions of Italy were of a Verdian sort, just what one would expect from Karajan. In the finale the sobriety of the minor mode outweighs the excitement of the dance, leaving things a bit more civilized than they need be. Sound is good but a bit glassy by today's standards, and detail is somewhat reduced by close miking. The coupling of Schubert's *Unfinished* Symphony, in an outstanding account, is perfect for those building a collection.

The 1976 performance of the *Italian* Symphony by Davis and the Boston Symphony is marked by a light touch and lots of finesse, yet there is plenty of power in the finale. Overall, this is one of the most satisfying readings of the symphony in the catalog, and it is coupled to an excellent account of the overture, scherzo, nocturne, and wedding march from *A Midsummer Night's Dream*. The sound is outstandingly good analog—natural, warm, and well balanced.

Previn's reading of the complete *Midsummer Night's Dream* music is highly profiled and Romantic, as the Viennese strings immediately make clear by the way they dig into their parts. The performance reflects an interesting balance between Previn's reflective approach and the Philharmonic's high-voltage playing; Previn gets his way, but occasionally one wishes the Viennese would get theirs, because they certainly know how to play expressively, witness their glorious showing in the nocturne. The sound of the 1986 recording is somewhat drier than is customary of the Musikvereinssaal.

Karajan was no stranger to Italy; he hid there after World War II.

M A J O R   M A E S T R O

WOLFGANG AMADEUS MOZART

From the time he was seven until he was 23, Mozart spent more than half of his life traveling and performing away from his home in Salzburg. His father put aside his own duties as composer and violin instructor in order to mastermind every move of his phenomenally talented son, who in turn absorbed everything he could in hopes of eventually commanding an appointment at a major court.

The three journeys to Italy father and son made between 1769 and 1773 gave Wolfgang a thorough exposure to Italian church music and opera. They also enabled him to assimilate the Italian symphonic style, which he mastered brilliantly while still in his teens. An extended trip to Mannheim and Paris with his mother in 1777–78 further broadened Mozart's symphonic horizons and brought him into contact with some of the best ensembles in Europe. The orchestra of Elector Carl Theodor in Mannheim was unequaled in its virtuosity and power—and was also the repository of one of the strongest symphonic traditions on the continent. There, Johann Stamitz had founded a style of symphonic composition that emphasized bold tuttis, breathtakingly long crescendos (the famous "Mannheim steamroller"), and brilliant effects in the strings and winds. While he was in Mannheim, Mozart fell in love with this grand idiom, and he also formed a lasting attachment to the sound of clarinets.

Mozart's symphonies from the 1770s are cosmopolitan in the best sense, incorporating elements of the Italian and German traditions, the latest styles from Paris, and the occasional usage from Salzburg. Mozart's ear for color and keen understanding of the woodwinds helped him produce potent effects; indeed, by the

1756 – 1791

time of the *Paris* Symphony in 1778, his scoring had become more muscular, and at the same time more subtly nuanced, than that of any other composer of the 18th century.

In 1781 Mozart settled in Vienna. Along with the uncertainty of life as a freelance musician in the big city came the freedom to create as he wished, and Mozart responded with an outpouring of brilliant works. The availability of a pool of topflight musicians enabled Mozart to write virtuosically in his Viennese symphonies, especially for the wind players.

It was long thought that some mysterious inner urge prompted Mozart to compose his last three symphonies, Nos. 39–41, which were completed in the short span of six weeks during the summer of 1788. Mozart's financial situation—which had begun to grow uncomfortable early in 1787, around the time he started work on *Don Giovanni*—had worsened during the winter and spring of 1788. By that summer, he had started writing letters to Michael Puchberg, a fellow Freemason, begging for loans. It is unlikely that during such a strained period, Mozart would have composed solely out of artistic necessity. Rather, he would have been especially careful to use his time profitably; his pattern, after all, was to work on commission, for publication or performance.

The keys of the final three symphonies—E flat, G minor, and C major—are strikingly contrasted, and each work has its own sound and plays up different elements of expression. But the stylistic consistency of these symphonies is just as remarkable, and together with their predecessor, the *Prague* Symphony of 1786, they not only stand among Mozart's highest achievements but also represent the pinnacle of musical Classicism. Only Haydn's *London* Symphonies can compare with them among orchestral works of the 18th century, though nothing Haydn or anyone else has written quite matches the intense emotional expression and contrapuntal brilliance Mozart achieved in these scores. They remain a profoundly satisfying part of the concert repertory, as meaningful today as they were 200 years ago.

*Mozart's birthplace at
Getreidegasse #9 in Salzburg.*

> **"M**OZART *possessed an aston-
> ishing wealth of ideas. He
> does not allow the listener to
> draw breath; for if one
> wants to think about an at-
> tractive idea, it has already
> been followed by another
> which makes one forget the
> first and which then leads on
> to another, and this contin-
> ues at such a rate that in the
> end one can retain none of
> these beautiful themes in
> one's memory."*
> —Carl Ditters von
> Dittersdorf

SYMPHONY NO. 29, IN A, K. 201

A combination of elegance, intimate yet intense expression, and supreme craftsmanship characterizes Symphony No. 29. More ornamental in style than the other Salzburg symphonies, it is paradoxically more substantial as well. Its moods are not easy to pin down, but that is part of what makes it so fascinating. For a moment, Mozart steps outside of conventions to bare his soul.

Later, when he was working in Vienna, the key of A major would become one of Mozart's favorites, in large part because it was good for the clarinet—an instrument he was among the first to use in the symphony orchestra. There were no clarinets in Salzburg, however, only oboes, and the A major of the present symphony is not the radiant, strangely poignant key of works like the Piano Concerto No. 23, K. 488, but a more austere, plangent tonality. Its quality is well suited to the surprisingly urgent expression we encounter in this work.

The opening Allegro is remarkable for the sureness of its line of action, as well as for the balance struck between gentleness and charged emotion—both products of the same melodic material. Much of the effect comes from repetition and imitation, but the process is so subtle as to almost escape notice, and the result is the most assured and well-integrated symphonic movement Mozart had yet penned.

The fact that violins are muted in the Andante only serves to heighten the intensity of the sharply profiled principal theme. The writing for strings here is exceptionally intricate, the scoring (particularly the use of the oboes) of a delicacy previously unencountered in Mozart's music. And this permits the movement's final four bars—when the mutes come off and the first oboe wails out the dotted theme in *forte*, over the horns—to have a telling effect.

Mozart during the Salzburg years.

A dotted rhythm figures in the ensuing minuet as well, but here it imparts energy as much as elegance. The trio introduces the kind of suave string melody that will mark much of Mozart's later work; on the other hand, the dotted calls to attention on oboes and horns are pure Salzburg. The hunting motif is unmistakable in the finale, but it is the string players who are the quarry here—dashing along, trying not to trip over their treacherous exposed runs, hoping to escape into the thicket of notes. There is time for rest in an ornamented, singsong second subject, but the chase continues, with a tallyho from the horns at the very end that still brings a shiver of excitement to this listener every time he hears it.

The Symphony in A was completed on April 6, 1774. Mozart would write symphonies for another 14 years, during which time his material would get stronger, his treatment would become surer, and the structural seams would disappear altogether. But he would never again quite touch the gallantry of this work.

 RECOMMENDED RECORDINGS

**Prague Chamber Orchestra/
Sir Charles Mackerras.**
Telarc CD 80165 [with Symphonies Nos. 25 and 28]

**English Baroque Soloists/
John Eliot Gardiner.**
Philips 412 736-2 [with Symphony No. 33]

Mackerras has perfect pitch when it comes to Mozart, and his high-voltage performances of these pre-Viennese symphonies are stylistically informed and splendidly musical. He gives a passionate reading of Symphony No. 29. The playing is exciting—and clean, too, with the Prague musicians showing excellent ensemble, often at breakneck tempos. The recording was made in

1987 at Prague's House of Artists, and it sounds superb.

Gardiner's period-instrument Mozart cycle with the English Baroque Soloists impresses with its interpretive acumen and polished execution; the accounts are as interesting and well played as any in the catalog, showing just how far "authenticity" has come in 15 years. Gardiner paces his readings superbly, and the expressiveness he draws from the players is welcome and always appropriate. The recording, from 1984, is open and detailed, with thrilling presence and solid impact.

SYMPHONY NO. 38, IN D, K. 504
Prague

*M*ozart's final years in Vienna were a period of intense musical creativity, intermittent financial worries, and waning celebrity. Yet even as the Viennese were losing interest in the virtuoso and his music, which was growing too profound for their tastes, Mozart was finding solace (and some much-needed patronage) in Prague. In January of 1787, he spent a month in the Bohemian capital, where he conducted a performance of *The Marriage of Figaro* and premiered a new symphony in three movements that he had just completed. The score has been known ever since as the *Prague* Symphony.

In its conciseness and dramatic thrust, the *Prague* is without equal in Mozart's work. In the first movement, following a slow introduction that is the most imaginative and powerful in all of Classical music, the learned, brilliant, storm-and-stress, and singing styles are all embraced, with dazzling virtuosity and seamless connections from topic to topic. The writing displays a contrapuntal severity exceeding anything that had been tried in a symphony before, particularly in the development section; it is the same kind of writing one encounters in Mozart's finest chamber music (which,

*O*N THE OCCASION of the Prague premiere on January 19, 1787, Mozart treated the audience to an improvisation on his own piano (below). Said Mozart's friend Franz Niemetschek, who attended: "Never had there been such unanimous enthusiasm as that awakened by his heavenly playing."

with a string complement of no more than fourteen in the Prague orchestra, may have been just what the work sounded like at the first performance). Yet there is a symphonic richness to the scoring that makes the overall effect grand indeed.

The G major Andante opens in the strings with what in other hands might have been a simple, aria-like subject. But in Mozart's, it quickly takes on a chromatic inflection and is spun out almost in the manner of a fantasy, through a series of highly profiled episodes in which sharp pathos and pastoral gentleness succeed one another with surprising swiftness. It has been suggested that Mozart's decision to omit the minuet and proceed straight to the finale was a concession to Bohemian taste; whatever the reason, the music of the effervescent concluding Presto was itself most certainly a nod to the audience. The opera-buffa brilliance of the writing must have delighted those who already knew *Figaro*, while sending those who didn't—if any there were—scurrying out of the concert eager for tickets to the opera.

 RECOMMENDED RECORDING

**Prague Chamber Orchestra/
Sir Charles Mackerras.**
Telarc CD 80148 [with Symphony No. 36]

Fittingly enough, Mackerras and the Prague Chamber Orchestra do a magnificent job with the *Prague* Symphony. The account reveals a thorough acceptance of scholarly performance-practice notions with regard to accents, tempos, articulation, repeats, and orchestral seating, yet it is achieved without the use of original instruments—a decent compromise, and one that permits virtuoso results. Mackerras brings to the podium a sure grasp of tempo and fresh interpretive insights, and the Czech musicians respond with playing of the utmost polish. What stands out is the way they suit the action to the idea; the violin

Mackerras's interpretation of the Prague is "mostly Mozart."

What's the "K" in Mozart's Works?

The works of most composers are identified by opus numbers, usually indicating the order in which they were published. Those of Mozart come with "K" numbers, which were given to them by Ludwig Ritter von Köchel (1800–1877), an Austrian botanist whose real life work was the creation of a catalog of Mozart's works.

figures in the introduction are splendidly caressed, while the scale passages in the Allegro are boldly dashed off. Sir Charles and the band revel in the complexities of the music, just as they delight in the panache of its climaxes. In this regard, the best is saved for last: the finale of the *Prague* would have made Mozart stand up and cheer.

SYMPHONY NO. 39, IN E FLAT, K. 543

From Mozart's entry in his catalog of works, we know that Symphony No. 39 was completed on June 26, 1788, and that it calls for his beloved clarinets. Their presence here, and the absence of oboes, lends the work a certain gentleness that its siblings in G minor and C major lack.

The symphony also comes closer than either of those to the sunny lyricism of opera buffa, particularly in its overture-like first movement and racy finale. The opening movement is prefaced by a grand Adagio in the style of a French overture, with double-dotted fanfare figures in the winds and brass and sweeping scale passages in the strings. The main part of the movement, an Allegro in 3/4 time, avoids the marchlike expression typical of many of Mozart's openers, offering instead flowing first and second subjects set off by much brilliant working-out of material borrowed from the introduction.

The Andante steers a suspenseful course between pastoral innocence and pathos. There is a highly charged poignancy to the harmony, and the movement's drama is all the more impressive for the thematic economy Mozart observes in it, deriving nearly everything from the initial four-measure subject.

What follows is perhaps the stateliest minuet Mozart ever composed, one that combines courtly elegance and full-voiced élan. It is graced with a

T WAS the clarinet's sound—round, luminous, and poignant—that appealed to Mozart. He often used clarinets to suggest the love element in his instrumental music.

beautiful Ländler-like trio that features the two clarinets, one taking the melody, the other accompanying in the resonant low register, called the *chalumeau* after a 17th-century precursor to the clarinet. The spirited closing movement is a virtual *moto perpetuo* (a type of piece featuring the sustained flow of rapid notes) that bubbles along like an operatic finale. As in the Andante, Mozart shows a remarkable economy here, weaving the entire fabric of the movement from the insouciant opening tune.

SYMPHONY NO. 40, IN G MINOR, K. 550

*I*n his 1945 biography of Mozart, musicologist Alfred Einstein, the physicist's cousin, characterized the G minor Symphony as a "fatalistic piece of chamber music"—a description that still holds up under the scrutiny of recent investigations into 18th-century performance practice. By any measure, this is Mozart's most emotional and rigorously argued symphony. The minor mode had special significance for Mozart, almost always compelling him to give vent to feelings of extraordinary turbulence and passion. On that plane, the G minor Symphony stands alone—not only among Mozart's works, but among all works of the 18th century.

The feeling of restlessness of the opening Allegro is immediately apparent in the first measures, as divided violas accompany the principal subject in quiet agitation. The tone of this subject is both poignant and tense, and Mozart's ensuing treatment of it ranges from anxious to nearly manic. A chromatically inflected second subject in B flat introduces a gentler kind of melancholy, but offers little respite. During the recapitulation, the return of this second subject, now in G minor, seals the prophecy of doom with which the movement began.

After such a harrowing look into the abyss, it

is necessary to withdraw—yet the second movement, an Andante in E flat, offers at best a temporary reprieve. Though the mood here is pastoral, there is something shadowy and bizarre about the surroundings, almost as though one were looking at a Venetian landscape with an approaching storm in the background. In this largely restrained movement, Mozart is unusually insistent in his emphasis of the underlying eighth-note pulse. This imparts a feeling of restlessness to the proceedings, which is given haunting elegance by the use of a two-note figure known as the "Lombard snap," named for the region in Italy where it originated.

The minuet and its trio contrast sharply, the one poignant and heavy, the other pastoral and light. The symphony's finale brings a return of the passionate sentiment of the opening movement, only now more fierce and demonic. A tightly wound sonata, it begins with a "rocket" theme that vehemently shoots up the G minor triad. The seething drama of the first key area suggests nothing so much as terror and flight, though the arrival of the second subject brings a fleeting sense of consolation. When, in the recapitulation, this subject returns in the minor, the feeling is funereal. With this cry from his soul, Mozart closes the most unflinchingly grim symphony of the 18th century.

Mozart dashes off what was to be his last symphony.

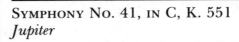

SYMPHONY NO. 41, IN C, K. 551
Jupiter

On August 10, 1788, a mere 16 days after completing Symphony No. 40, Mozart entered in the catalog of his works the four opening measures of another new symphony, his third of the summer. This one, in C major, would eventually come to be known as the *Jupiter* Symphony in recognition of its grandeur and its pride of place among symphonies of the 18th century.

W.A. MOZART

Did Salieri do it?

As one of the most highly placed musicians in Vienna in the 1780s, Salieri probably aroused more envy in Mozart than Mozart did in him—indeed, the Italian was often generous in his praise and arranged for first performances of some of Mozart's works. In their modern interpretations of Mozart's life, Peter Shaffer and Milos Forman embellished the rumor that Salieri poisoned Mozart. We owe it to Salieri to set the record straight. Mozart died of heart failure brought on by rheumatic fever. Nobody poisoned him.

For while Mozart could not have known that it would be his last, this was his summa, a glorious proof of his mastery of both musical style and the compositional craft.

In the opening measures, a phrase alluding to the march topic is answered by one in the singing style. These are the two fundamental poles of 18th-century musical expression, and what makes Mozart's treatment so remarkable—here and throughout the rest of the first movement—is that they are not contrasted but fused into a single idea. The whole movement is a tour de force of sparkling invention and symphonic drama, marked by a seamless connection of material. The brilliant style predominates, but Mozart includes a storm-and-stress episode, elements of the fantasy style, and a little cadential tune in the rhythm of a gavotte.

The Andante second movement of the *Jupiter* is a sarabande, the most passionate of Baroque dance forms, here made painfully intense by the extraordinary chromaticism of the writing and the many wrenching turns of phrase introduced along the way. Mozart mutes the violins for added effect, and he makes pointed use of the winds. The melodic and rhythmic complications of this movement are remarkable even for him, the pathos unparalleled in music of the 18th century. For the minuet Mozart climbs back down the stylistic ladder to a countrified setting with an unusually colorful complexion. The outer parts of the movement are festive and easygoing, but the trio manifests a heated virulence in the midst of its bucolic simplicity.

Mozart brings things full circle with the finale, a sonata-form Allegro in the brilliant style whose scope, variety, and contrapuntal inventiveness are astonishing. The whole movement is an example of the *ars combinatoria*, the process of finding the maximum number of different arrangements possible with a set of musical figures. In the coda, five of the movement's six principal motives are gradually superimposed until all five are going at once—not only that, but over the span of 20 measures the counterpoint is inverted five times, so that each of the five string groups (first violins, second violins, violas, cellos, and basses) carries a different motive in succession. It is a matchless summation of musical technique, one whose exuberance and freedom seem to reflect the very qualities Mozart prized most in life and art, and whose harmonious complexity shows him doing what he loved most: holding up the mirror to the richness of creation.

 RECOMMENDED RECORDINGS

Columbia Symphony Orchestra/ Bruno Walter.
Sony Classical SM3K 46511 [3 CDs; Symphonies Nos. 39–41, with Nos. 35, 36, and 38]

Chamber Orchestra of Europe/ Nikolaus Harnoncourt.
Teldec 9031-74858-2 [2 CDs; Symphonies Nos. 39–41]

There is a narrative quality to Walter's interpretations, almost as though the symphonies were operas without words. The phrasing is highly vocal, and while the tempos are nearly always broad, there is a deftly "sprung" feeling to the rhythm that prevents the accounts from sounding stodgy. The winds have greater prominence than in many readings, and the bass line is markedly emphasized. These are graceful, sweet, lyrical renditions, reflecting the qualities attributed to the "sublime" Mozart by the 19th century. Walter's account of Symphony No. 40 remains the great one, unmatched in emotional depth and dramatic expressiveness. The 1959–61 recordings are close-miked and very pleasant, with a "live" air around the orchestral body. Previously available on CBS CDs, the recordings have been freshly and superbly remastered for Sony Classical.

Bruno Walter makes Mozart dance as well as sing.

Notoriously erratic as an interpreter of Mozart, Harnoncourt scores big with his latest offering of the last three symphonies, recorded in concert at Vienna's Musikvereinssaal on December 5, 1991, the 200th anniversary of Mozart's death. The approach is authentic, yet highly idiosyncratic, the ensemble a conventional one whose young players have been thoroughly coached to play in period style. Harnoncourt's performance of Symphony No. 40 is tight and dramatic, while his *Jupiter* is simply outstanding, particularly in the brilliantly realized finale. The recording is reasonably well balanced and detailed for a live pickup, though one might wish to hear a little more atmosphere.

EINE KLEINE NACHTMUSIK, K. 525

*M*ozart wrote *Eine kleine Nachtmusik* in the summer of 1787, while he was at work on the second act of *Don Giovanni*. The forces for which *A Little Night Music* is scored— a "serenade quartet" consisting of string quartet with added double bass—are modest, as is the musical content, if one compares it to what Mozart was putting into his string quintets at the time. But while the ideas themselves are generic by Mozart's standards—rhythmically square, harmonically uncomplicated, neutral in expression— the craftsmanship and part-writing are exquisite.

Better than most musicians of his day, Mozart knew that the important events of life took place either on the battlefield or in the boudoir. So there is a certain appropriateness to the fact that the opening Allegro of *Eine kleine Nachtmusik*, with its fanfares and quick-march brilliance, is followed by a gentle Romance—not by the minuet referred to in Mozart's catalog of works but removed from the score at an early date (by whom and for what reason, no one knows). The Romance's aria-like tranquility is only momentarily troubled by a shadowy, canonic episode in the minor. *Now* comes a

A little night music.

minuet, contrasting its courtly pomp with a flowing trio. In the serenade's finale, a giddy tune in bourrée rhythm and its pulsating inner-voice accompaniment conspire to produce the musical equivalent of euphoria—Mozart's way of suggesting, perhaps, that the night is still young.

RECOMMENDED RECORDINGS

"Big band" Mozart was a Karajan specialty.

Prague Chamber Orchestra/ Sir Charles Mackerras.

Telarc CD 80108 [with Posthorn *Serenade, No. 9, K. 320]*

Berlin Philharmonic/Herbert von Karajan.

Deutsche Grammophon 423 610-2 [with Divertimento No. 15, in B flat, K. 287]

Academy of St. Martin-in-the-Fields Chamber Ensemble.

Philips 412 269-2 [with Divertimento in D, K. 136, and A Musical Joke, K. 522]

The strings of the Prague Chamber Orchestra contribute admirably to the Mackerras reading. The approach is modern but well informed, the resulting account clean, agile, luminous. Mackerras observes the repeats (including that of the first-movement recapitulation) and chooses excellent tempos; the Romance is especially lovely. Telarc's 1984 recording yields a fairly realistic concert-hall perspective, but the distant pickup tends to muddy the texture a little. The coupled *Posthorn* Serenade is superb.

If you like a full string ensemble in this music—with smooth legatos, polished tone, unaccented ornaments, almost decadent opulence, and lots of vibrato—the 1981 recording by Karajan and the Berlin Philharmonic is the one to have. In the immortal words of music critic Alan Rich, Karajan's Mozart had a way of being powerful and prissy at the same time; yet there is an athleticism to this reading of *Eine kleine Nachtmusik* that is quite impressive. The sound is bright, with a good sense of space around the ensemble.

The Academy of St. Martin-in-the-Fields Chamber Ensemble plays the piece as Mozart intended, with a string quartet and added bass. It is a fine reading, though some ornaments and figures are smoothed over in modern fashion rather than clearly articulated. The sound of the 1984 recording, close-miked and naturally balanced, is excellent.

MODEST MUSSORGSKY

A NIGHT ON BALD MOUNTAIN

*A*lthough fiscally and emotionally unstable for much of his adult life, Mussorgsky (1839–1881) was beyond question the most talented member of the group of 19th-century Russian composers known as "The Mighty Handful," or "The Five" (the others being Mily Balakirev, Alexander Borodin, César Cui, and Nicolai Rimsky-Korsakov). He had a remarkably fertile imagination but found it difficult seeing projects through to completion; barely 42 when he died from alcoholism, he left important scores unfinished. As a result, many of his works are familiar to the public in orchestrations and arrangements by other composers, especially Rimsky-Korsakov.

That was long the case with *St. John's Night on the Bare Mountain* (1867), commonly called *A Night on Bald Mountain*—and known in the thoroughly revised and reorchestrated version Rimsky-Korsakov produced after Mussorgsky's death, with the aim of correcting the "unsuccessful scoring" and "artistic transgressions" he felt had marred his friend's work. Today, Mussorgsky's spartan original (not published until 1968), with its rough-hewn orchestration and brutal transitions, is gain-

*M*USSORGSKY *spent the last month of his life in a hospital in St. Petersburg, dying from the effects of alcoholism just a week after his 42nd birthday. Shortly before the end, this portrait was painted by Ilya Efimovich Repin. It shows Mussorgsky in his dressing gown, hair disheveled, nose reddened, the look of a madman in his eyes.*

Strange Deaths of Composers

Musical composition is not normally thought of as a dangerous activity, but throughout history composers have suffered their share of strange deaths. One of the first was Jean-Baptiste Lully, who stubbed his toe with the point of the cane he was using to beat time at a performance, and died of gangrene. Ernest Chausson drove his bicycle into a wall, and Anton Webern was shot by a jumpy American soldier during the final weeks of World War II, after he lit up a cigar on the darkened porch of his country house in Austria.

Hartmann's Gate of Kiev, one of the Pictures at the Exhibition.

ing a place for itself alongside the more colorful and polished—but unnecessarily lavish—version left by Rimsky-Korsakov.

St. John's Eve, which occurs around the time of the summer solstice, is traditionally the night in northern climes when witches gather and hold their sabbath on the slopes of the local mountain. Mussorgsky's terrifyingly elemental vision of this ritual—with its menacing crescendos, shrieking wind and brass passages, and vivid evocation of the witches dancing (which sounds like Cossack reveling on a particularly wild night)—makes this score a classic of the musical macabre.

PICTURES AT AN EXHIBITION

*A*s an orchestral showpiece—the form in which it is familiar to most listeners—*Pictures at an Exhibition* is two times over a work of enlargement. Mussorgsky's original suite for piano, composed in 1874 as a memorial to the painter Victor Hartmann, took as its point of departure ten pictures displayed at a posthumous exhibition of the artist's work. Though pianistically crude, Mussorgsky's renderings of his friend's images convey their rich fantasy with sincerity and great imaginative force. Ravel's celebrated orchestration of *Pictures at an Exhibition*, undertaken in 1922 at the request of conductor Serge Koussevitzky, in turn faithfully amplifies both the wit and deep feeling of Mussorgsky's tribute.

One is surprised, listening to the orchestral version, to discover that Hartmann's originals were modest little sketches and watercolors. For example, the "Ballet of Chicks in Their Shells" was inspired by a whimsical costume sketch for a children's ballet. Mussorgsky had turned that into a lively scene painting, and Ravel's scoring, with its clucking oboes and scurrying scale passages in the bassoon and strings, transforms the children in their eggshell costumes into real chicks.

IN HIS 22 YEARS behind the wheel (1969–91), Sir Georg Solti drove the Chicago Symphony Orchestra to the pole position among America's "top five" orchestras—traditionally those of Chicago, Cleveland, New York, Boston, and Philadelphia. Known for his dynamic, all-stops-out music-making, this native of Budapest has won more Grammys (30 at last count) than any other musician, including Stevie Wonder, Paul Simon, and Michael Jackson.

The inspiration for "The Hut on Fowl's Legs" came from a quaint design for a clock in the shape of a cabin built on chicken's feet—the unlikely abode of the witch Baba Yaga. Mussorgsky decided to portray the legendary hag's frightful ride through the air. Ravel marshals the heavy brass and a businesslike array of percussion to create a thunderous chase.

In "The Great Gate of Kiev," the most breathtaking and at the same time most touching part of the suite, Mussorgsky apostrophized his departed friend with a monumental realization of Hartmann's lopsided, ornately decorated drawing of a city gate in the old Russian style, with a cupola in the shape of a helmet surmounting the gatehouse. Based on the theme Mussorgsky called "Promenade"—which opens *Pictures at an Exhibition* and is meant to depict the viewer's passing from one work to the next—this finale was the composer's way of saying farewell and, at least in music, giving substance to one of his friend's fondest dreams. In Ravel's hands, Mussorgsky's vision of a gate that was never built becomes one of the architectural wonders of the world, magnificently brought to life by full brass, pulsing strings, pealing bells, and triumphant cymbals.

 RECOMMENDED RECORDINGS

Chicago Symphony Orchestra/ Sir Georg Solti.

London 430 446-2 [Pictures at an Exhibition, *with Prokofiev: Symphony No. 1, and Tchaikovsky:* 1812 *Overture*]

Montreal Symphony Orchestra/ Charles Dutoit.

London 417 299-2 [Pictures at an Exhibition *and* A Night on Bald Mountain, *with Khovanshchina* Prelude, *and Rimsky-Korsakov:* Russian Easter Overture]

Thunder is impressive, but lightning gets the work done. There's plenty of both in Solti's 1980 account of *Pictures*, a piece that has long been one of the cornerstones of the conductor's repertoire. This is an over-the-top performance—brash, brilliant, and virtuosic in the big movements, yet remarkably delicate in the right places ("Tuileries," for example, is marvelous). The recording is early London digital, dry and fierce, with string tone that's a little abrasive, but solid and suitably atmospheric in the quiet pages.

If Solti comes at *Pictures* from the percussive standpoint of Mussorgsky's original for piano, Dutoit sees the music through the lens of Ravel. The Montreal Symphony gives a beautifully finished performance—though as is often the case with Dutoit, this 1985 reading is fairly matter-of-fact, not as epic or highly charged as one might wish in this music. The stars here are the Montreal orchestra's solid American brass and supple French winds. The recording is London digital at its best: warm and richly detailed.

CARL NIELSEN

SYMPHONY NO. 4, OP. 29
The Inextinguishable

Poster for a Nielsen Festival in Copenhagen, 1953.

*W*hereas the Finnish composer Sibelius sought to compress, to make his symphonies as organic as possible, Denmark's Carl Nielsen (1865–1931) was interested in liberating the centrifugal elements of musical expression. With roots in the music of Brahms, Schumann, and his countryman Niels Gade, he was among the most natural, least orthodox composers of his time—a man who had experienced life to the fullest, reflected upon it intently, and translated it all into a unique species of communication. Nielsen was extremely close to nature, both elemental and human. His emotions about the latter

NIELSEN AS A BOY *became a regimental bugler (above) in the Danish army. He did not see action, though 15 years earlier the Danes had taken a beating from the Prussians, and the memory of combat was still fresh among his elders. When Nielsen's battalion went on maneuvers, the young bugler learned to keep up with his commander by twisting the tail of the officer's horse around his left hand and letting the horse drag him along.*

were bittersweet; in his music, particularly his Symphony No. 4, he gave voice to the conflict of negative and positive forces that he saw at the core of human experience. Nielsen was not a great melodist—his melodies are rhythms, textures, arabesques—and in any case he was against making things too easy on the listener. In fact, his scores have a rather sharp edge to them, often jabbing with irony and sarcasm. Yet for all this, his works virtually shout with life.

That love of life was sorely tested by World War I. Nielsen found the experience of being on the sidelines both disheartening and cathartic. "The whole world's disintegrating," he wrote at the time. "National feeling, which hitherto was regarded as something lofty and beautiful, has become like a spiritual syphilis that has devoured the brains, and it grins out through the empty eye sockets with moronic hate." Nielsen's answer to that diseased time was his Fourth Symphony (1916), where he aimed to show that amid the terror, the life-seeking force could be as strong. In that regard, the symphony is a great success, for it holds the listener for the better part of 40 minutes. This is especially so toward the end, where Nielsen portrays the struggle quite literally in a battle involving two groups of timpani, placed on opposing sides of the orchestra, and the orchestra itself.

The symphony, in four continuous movements, draws much of its effect from the towering contrasts of sound Nielsen builds up. The outbursts are violent, rhythmically insistent; the moments of tranquility, with their echoes of folk song, seem almost to come from another world. In the end, harmony triumphs. Nielsen's own note to the score says in part: "By using the title *The Inextinguishable*, the composer has endeavored to indicate in one word what the music alone is capable of expressing to the full: the elemental Will to Life. Music *is* Life and, like it, is inextinguishable."

RECOMMENDED RECORDING

**San Francisco Symphony Orchestra/
Herbert Blomstedt.**
London 421 524-2 [with Symphony No. 5]

Blomstedt has the full measure of Nielsen's music, and his 1987 coupling of the Fourth and Fifth Symphonies, impossible before the advent of CD, is the ideal program. These are excellent performances, knowingly shaped and magnificently played. London provides a state-of-the-art recording, in a living, breathing, spacious ambience.

SERGEI PROKOFIEV

SYMPHONY NO. 1, IN D, OP. 25
Classical

Prokofiev at the time he composed his best-known symphony, the Classical.

*T*he idea of writing a symphony that was intentionally "Classical" in spirit and layout yet modern in phraseology, instrumentation, and harmonic language appealed to the iconoclast in Prokofiev (1891–1953). Even as a student, he had felt the urge to distance himself from the excesses of Russian Romanticism, and as his style developed he became increasingly hostile to sentimentality for its own sake. Owing to the peculiarly ironic temperament through which his musical thoughts were usually filtered, Prokofiev's striving for directness of effect and economy of means could at times take on the air of sarcasm. In the *Classical* Symphony, however, wit and charm have the upper hand from the start, and the mood of the piece is naturally exuberant.

Prokofiev aptly characterized the spirit of the symphony when he later wrote, "If Haydn had lived to our era, he would have retained his compositional style but would also have absorbed something from what was new." While the *Classical* Symphony's proportions are more slender than

THE CONCEPT *of mimicking the Classical style in a symphony can be traced back to Beethoven, whose Eighth was the first in a long line of such purposefully retrospective works. Others include Mendelssohn's* Italian *Symphony, Bizet's* Symphony in C, *Mahler's Fourth, Sibelius's Sixth, Stravinsky's* Symphony in C, *and Shostakovich's Ninth.*

one would find in a work by Haydn, the structural plan of its opening Allegro comes reasonably close to the model—though with typical playfulness, Prokofiev recapitulates in the wrong key and then, after eight measures, ratchets up the harmony to where it belongs. The expression is a bit racy for a Classical first movement, however, and the scoring is altogether modern in its bite.

In the second movement, a Larghetto, Prokofiev mimics the ornamental melodic style of a Classical Andante. Then again, the melody itself, beginning on a high A in the first violins, soars well above what would have been safe territory in Haydn's day. Where Haydn would have put the minuet, Prokofiev inserts a gavotte, an anachronism by Classical standards. With ungainly octave leaps in the melodic line and graceless grace notes in the bassoon's low register, the treatment is intentionally rude but wonderful fun. The finale is a joyous romp in which the harmony virtually jumps through hoops to avoid the minor mode, a challenge Prokofiev set himself while composing the movement. Prokofiev completed the *Classical* Symphony during the eventful year of 1917. He conducted the premiere himself, in St. Petersburg (then called Petrograd), on April 21, 1918.

SYMPHONY NO. 5, IN B FLAT, OP. 100

*T*he tide of World War II had turned by 1944, the year Prokofiev set to work on the composition of his Fifth Symphony, which he described as "the culmination of a long period of my creative life." During that period, Prokofiev had undergone a metamorphosis. The *enfant terrible* whose iconoclastic creations had left audiences electrified and confused through the 1920s had been replaced by a new composer—one who, in his own words, had "gone down into the deeper realms of music" in search of a more direct and simpler style, with emphasis on emotional expression rather than novelty of syntax.

At the outbreak of the war, Prokofiev, like many Soviet artists, had been evacuated from Moscow. Yet the war's grim presence can be felt in many parts of this symphony, most graphically in the concluding pages of the first movement, where the thunder of heavy guns is evoked in a towering, percussive climax. Here and elsewhere one senses a disquieting ambivalence of mood: triumph and tragedy seem interlinked in such a way that neither clearly predominates.

Tension permeates the opening Andante, where broad, rhapsodic passages based on the warmly diatonic principal subject clash with rhythmically edgy material, much of it derived from a persistent repeated-note figure first heard in the violins. The quasi-balletic third movement, like the first, is predominantly lyrical and again strikingly ambivalent. The funereal tread of its opening measures gives way to a gentle theme in the clarinets; as the first violins soar aloft with it, they uncover a waltz hidden within. The uneasy yet elegiac quality of the writing conveys a dreamlike melancholy— but a subsidiary theme in violas and horns, over lurching pizzicato cellos and basses, introduces a darker sentiment, and the waltz ultimately undergoes a brutal transformation before the earlier mood is recaptured.

Prokofiev may have taken a page out of Shostakovich's book in composing these two uncharacteristically meditative but powerful movements. The symphony's second movement, however, shows a familiar side of Prokofiev; it is a toccata that touches on the macabre and the comical while giving every section of the orchestra a virtuoso workout. The rondo finale is irrepressibly exuberant, an *Allegro giocoso* animated by a stream of bantering solos for the woodwinds.

Because of the way it successfully dispels the tensions of the preceding three movements without seeming artificially tacked on, the finale must be considered one of Prokofiev's most extraordinary achievements. The symphony as a whole,

S.S. PROKOFIEV

RUSSIAN *that he was, Prokofiev was an exceptionally clever and competitive chess player. Games were as much of a daily ritual as composing or practicing the piano, and Prokofiev even won a tournament at sea during an Atlantic crossing on the* Aquitania *in 1921.*

PROKOFIEV *(above)*
*conducted the premiere
of the Fifth in the Great
Hall of the Moscow Con-
servatory, on January 13,
1945, with victory over Germany in sight. Fittingly, as
he stood on the podium about
to begin the piece, the Moscow garrison touched off an
artillery salvo to salute the
Red Army, which at that
moment was crossing the
Vistula on its final advance
into Germany.*

with its rugged grandeur and wealth of material,
its strong motivic connections between movements and supple orchestration, remains one of
the great works in the literature. Prokofiev rightly
considered it his finest creation.

 RECOMMENDED RECORDINGS

Berlin Philharmonic/Herbert von Karajan.
Deutsche Grammophon 437 235-2 [Symphonies Nos. 1
and 5]

**Montreal Symphony Orchestra/
Charles Dutoit.**
London 421 813-2 [Symphonies Nos. 1 and 5]

**Chicago Symphony Orchestra/
Sir Georg Solti.**
London 430 446-2 [Symphony No. 1, with Mussorgsky:
Pictures at an Exhibition, *and Tchaikovsky:*
1812 *Overture]*

Karajan's 1968 account of the Fifth has been a
classic since the day it appeared. Remarkable for
its tensile strength and lyric sweep, the traversal
has the power of the conductor's best recordings
with the Berlin Philharmonic. Tempos are well
chosen, the performance moving inexorably forward without seeming to be pushed. The playing
is assured throughout and rich in atmosphere.
The *Classical* Symphony, recorded 13 years later,
comes off sounding just a bit heavy; it is brilliantly
played but not quite light-hearted enough. The
recorded sound is somewhat glary in the Fifth
but has adequate weight and detail.

Dutoit and the Montreal Symphony pick up the
Gallic element in Prokofiev's language with readings that are sensuous and suave. In a leisurely
stroll through the *Classical*, there is no effort to
portray the bad-boy side of Prokofiev, so the result
is a little soft. The version of the Fifth places a
premium on beauty of tone and line—and pro-

vides as voluptuous an experience of the score as can be imagined. The 1988 recording is warm, spacious, and nicely balanced, with real bass and lovely string tone.

Solti, as could be expected, delivers a virtuosic if rather fierce *Classical* Symphony. Even though this 1982 account is one of the fleetest on disc, there is nothing cut-and-dried about the playing, which is polished to perfection. The recording, made in Orchestra Hall, is on the reverberant side, but still quite satisfactory in its detail.

PETER AND THE WOLF, OP. 67

Each character is whimsically cast as a particular instrument.

As an adult, Prokofiev had a marked aversion to sentimentality. Reserved and cool by nature, he avoided openly showing his affection for others, and he tended to be uncomfortable in his relationships with children—including his own two sons, from whom he remained fairly distant. But Prokofiev never lost the ability to look at the world through a child's eyes. He loved fairy tales, delighted in the imaginative aspects of play, and believed in happy endings.

As a composer, Prokofiev realized that children often bring more to the act of listening than adults do, and he wrote a substantial number of pieces for them, including his Seventh Symphony. By far the most engaging of his works for youthful listeners is the tale for narrator and orchestra *Peter and the Wolf*, commissioned by the Children's Theatre Center of Moscow. Prokofiev himself composed the text, in collaboration with Natalia Satz, and the work received its premiere on May 2, 1936.

With his keen understanding of how children think, the composer packs the narrative with events and characters, each one represented by a memorable melody. The scoring clearly delineates the "personalities": the bird is represented by excited, flighty runs on the flute; the duck, its music in a minor key, by the plaintive sound of the oboe; the cat, whose sultry, gliding steps are to be articulated *con eleganza*, by the clarinet; Peter's crusty grandfather by lurching figures in the bassoon; the wolf, its music also in the minor, by snarling brass; the not-so-smart hunters by their errant gunfire in the timpani and bass drum; and Peter himself by the string section, with its warmth and added expressive dimension.

As the characters interact, the repetition of their melodic tags creates a sense of satisfaction in the young listener, while the suspense of Peter's confrontation with the wolf is resolved in a happy march that brings all the characters back together again. For the adult listener, it is the combination of Prokofiev's fetching melodies and readily recognizable idiom that brings delight, along with the thought that Peter's challenge to authority and willingness to take risks are what save the day. The outcome of such behavior in the composer's own life, as Stalin's 1948 purge of the Union of Soviet Composers was to show, would be different. Prokofiev would never recover from the censure he endured on that occasion, though the thought that the composer of *Peter and the Wolf* could be branded an extremely decadent formalist remains one of the supreme ironies of 20th-century art.

RECOMMENDED RECORDINGS

Royal Philharmonic Orchestra/André Previn.
Telarc CD 80126 [with Britten: The Young Person's Guide to the Orchestra *and* Courtly Dances *from* Gloriana]

The New London Orchestra/Ronald Corp.
Hyperion CDA 66499 [with Winter Bonfire, Summer Day, *and* The Ugly Duckling]

Previn wears two hats, as narrator and conductor of Peter.

Previn does a deft job of both narrating and conducting a lush, symphonically scaled performance from 1985. His helpful introduction to the score, giving musical cues, is ideal for young listeners. Telarc's sonics are breathtaking, and the coupling with Britten is highly desirable.

The Hyperion CD brings together four of Prokofiev's major works for children in very well-recorded performances from 1991. As for the narration by Oleg and Gabriel Prokofiev, the composer's son and grandson, it would have been better if Gabriel had done the whole thing.

MAURICE RAVEL

BOLÉRO

The diminutive Ravel was a superb miniaturist.

The French composer Ravel (1875–1937) enjoyed great success converting pieces originally intended for the piano into orchestral music, and then passing off the orchestral works as ballets when the occasion suited. But his most popular score, *Boléro*, was intended as a ballet from the start, commissioned by Ida Rubinstein and premiered in 1928 at the Paris Opéra.

Indeed, without the orchestra, *Boléro* never would have worked. The entire score is one long crescendo over a recurring harmonic sequence, with a constant rhythmic obbligato—the first notes heard, played throughout by the snare drum. Only on the last pages of the score does the harmony shift briefly from C to E, creating an exhilarating high before slamming back into C for the exuberant closing. What gives *Boléro* its vitality and color is the subtle shifting of the orchestration, the deployment of one instrument or instrumental combination after another, borne on the inexorable buildup from opening whisper to concluding roar. The erotic undertones are clear, and witnesses report that the way Rubinstein danced it, *Boléro* was the hottest thing in Paris.

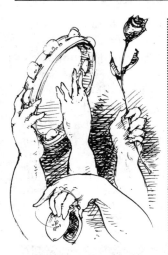

Tambourines and castanets create a whirl of Spanish color.

RAPSODIE ESPAGNOLE

*M*uch of Ravel's music looks in one way or another toward Spain, which for him represented not only the remote, colorful, fascinating world of dreams the real world would like to be, but an inexhaustible source of exotic musical ideas. Spain's specific appeal to Ravel was the rhythmic and melodic richness of its dance forms. In the *Rapsodie espagnole*, his first published work for full orchestra (1907), these dances became the building blocks for a four-movement suite that clearly shows the composer's talent for transforming suggestive ideas into viscerally exciting music.

Ravel's resourceful scoring—particularly his virtuosic use of percussion (including such distinctively "Spanish" instruments as castanets and tambourine) and deft touches with muted strings and brass—helps make the *Rapsodie espagnole* one of his most appealing works. And his skillful incorporation of dance forms such as the malagueña and the habanera, which preserves their exotic character while imparting to them a symphonic suppleness and open-endedness, won the approval of Ravel's contemporary Manuel de Falla, who praised the score for its authentic Spanish character.

The four movements create a sequence much like that of a short symphony. The opening *"Prélude à la nuit"* ("Prelude to the Night") is a hypnotic evocation of the Iberian evening, almost fragrant with color. As a descending four-note motive (F, E, D, C sharp) repeats itself in the background, this song of the night blooms briefly, like a nocturnal flower, in two passionate phrases for the strings, before closing with cadenzas for paired clarinets and bassoons. Punctuated by flashes of tambourine, the shadowy *"Malagueña"* fills the role of a scherzo, vanishing into the night as quickly as it had come. With the ensuing *"Habanera,"* a piece originally composed for two pianos,

Ravel shows the subtle side of his craft as an orchestrator, creating a mosaic of the most delicate color. The finale, entitled *"Feria"* ("Festival"), is a brilliantly scored showpiece with dizzily shifting rhythms in its outer sections and a sultry central section featuring serpentine solos by the English horn and clarinet. Amid echoes of the "night" motive from the first movement, the festivities become increasingly lively until, with his sure sense of climax, Ravel brings things to a dazzling conclusion.

AT THE TIME *Ravel wrote* Daphnis et Chloé—*just one year before the debut of Stravinsky's* Rite of Spring—*his musical language was considered quite advanced. And his use of the 5/4 meter throughout the concluding* "Danse générale" *gave the dancers of the Ballets Russes no end of trouble. In order to keep the pulse, they had to resort to a trick: repeating in their heads the five-syllable name of their impresario,* Ser-gei Dia-ghi-lev, *over and over so as not to get lost.*

DAPHNIS ET CHLOÉ, SUITE NO. 2

*I*t occasionally happens that a great work is better known by excerpts. Such has been the fate of Ravel's *Daphnis et Chloé* ever since its creation. While occasionally performed as a ballet, it is usually heard in concert, represented by its final three numbers: *"Lever du jour"* ("Daybreak"), *"Pantomime,"* and *"Danse générale"* ("General Dance"). Ravel himself designated these excerpts as Suite No. 2 following the score's completion in 1912.

Based on a pastoral drama by the Greek poet Longus, the scenario for the ballet was devised by Mikhail Fokine, a classically trained dancer and choreographer for Sergei Diaghilev's Ballets Russes. The first two scenes of the ballet portray the courtship of Daphnis and Chloé and the latter's abduction by, and miraculous escape from, a band of pirates. The third scene, comprising the three numbers of Suite No. 2, takes place in a grove sacred to the god Pan. Ravel portrays the murmuring of a nearby brook at daybreak with undulating figures in the winds, harps, celesta, and later the strings. In the foreground, birdcalls are sounded by the piccolo and three solo violins. As the shades of dawn give way to the colors of day (violins, cellos, and basses are instructed to gradually remove their mutes), a luxuriant mel-

Laughter in Music

There is much in music that can make us laugh, and on occasion composers have even tried to make their music laugh by itself. In Daphnis et Chloé, during the "Grotesque Dance of Dorcon," Ravel's brass and winds guffaw in short bursts of eighth notes over flashes of string tremolo. Bartók succeeded in the fourth movement of his Concerto for Orchestra with bouts of raucous trilling in strings, winds, and brass, followed by descending streaks of tittering eighth notes.

ody builds in the orchestra. Daphnis awakes, anxiously looks for Chloé, and sees her among a group of shepherdesses. The two throw themselves into each other's arms, the melody reaching an impassioned climax.

In gratitude to Pan, whose intervention saved Chloé from the pirates, Daphnis and Chloé mime the story of the god and his beloved Syrinx, to a sultry flute accompaniment. Marked "expressive and supple," the solo is actually shared by the four members of the flute section—piccolo, two flutes, and alto flute—but played as if written for a single instrument. Over a gentle pizzicato accompaniment colored by horns, harps, celesta, and percussion, the dance becomes increasingly animated, until with a last whirl Chloé falls languorously into Daphnis's arms.

In a brief but passionate epilogue, young women dressed as bacchantes enter, shaking their tambourines, followed by a group of young men. Setting the bacchanal against a dizzying 5/4 meter, intoxicating in itself, Ravel deploys the full resources of the orchestra to create an exhilarating orgy of sound.

 RECOMMENDED RECORDINGS

Montreal Symphony Orchestra/ Charles Dutoit.
London 421 458-2 [4 CDs; Boléro, Rapsodie espagnole, *and* Daphnis et Chloé *(complete), with other orchestral works]*

Boston Symphony Orchestra/Charles Munch.
RCA Living Stereo 61846-2 [Daphnis et Chloé *(complete)]*

Berlin Philharmonic/Herbert von Karajan.
Deutsche Grammophon 427 250-2 [Boléro *and* Daphnis et Chloé, *Suite No. 2, with Debussy:* Prélude à l'après-midi d'un faune *and* La Mer]

Not too loud . . . Munch cautions his cohorts during a rehearsal.

*R*AVEL RECORDED Boléro *with the La-moureux Orchestra in January of 1930, a little over a year after the work's premiere. Ravel's tempo is on the slow and steady side, but the performance is in no way stodgy. Indeed, some of the solos are remarkably free, especially the one for first trombone, which is played with numerous jazzlike slides between notes.*

Dutoit's may not be the most pointed interpretations of this music, or the most subtly nuanced, but they are deftly characterized, dashingly played, and brilliantly recorded—which places them among the jewels of the CD catalog. London's engineering puts the listener right inside the orchestra, which is really what Ravel's scoring is after. While there is more detail than one would hear in a live performance, the balance and perspective of these early-1980s recordings are perfectly natural. Dutoit's *Boléro* and *Rapsodie espagnole* have a sultry warmth. The polished, opulent account of *Daphnis et Chloé* is what put Dutoit and the Montreal Symphony—a better French orchestra than any in France—on the map. The only drawback on this CD is that the scenes of the ballet are not given separate track or index numbers.

Munch's performance of *Daphnis* is full of commitment, painted in blazing colors with the sure strokes of a master. While the tempos occasionally seem idiosyncratic, there is always an underlying logic. At the time the recording was made, the Boston Symphony—with its refined winds and luminous strings—was indisputably the best French orchestra in the world, and it plays the music with a consummate sense of style. RCA's early stereo recording, newly remastered, has a "live" quality and wonderful impact.

Karajan's 1966 *Boléro* ranks with the finest accounts ever recorded: polished, suave, remarkable for its hypnotic control and splendid cumulative effect. At 16:09, it comes out at precisely the same timing as Ravel's own recording—for like the composer, Karajan knew that the piece cannot go as fast as the score *says* it should go. Among the virtues here are the wonderful solos by the Berlin winds and the magnificent tonal sheen of the full band. The 1964 performance of the Suite No. 2 from *Daphnis et Chloé* is powerful. For a recording more than 25 years old, *Boléro* sounds superb; the *Daphnis* suite is nearly as vivid, though clouded by a too-diffuse reverberation.

BERNINI'S FONTANA del Tritone *was commissioned by Pope Urban VIII (born Maffeo Barberini) in 1643. Standing in the middle of the Piazza Barberini, it is a masterpiece of design. Four dolphins at its base draw water in through their open mouths. Atop their raised tails is a giant scallop shell, upon which is seated the figure of Triton, who blows water out through an upraised conch shell.*

OTTORINO RESPIGHI

FOUNTAINS OF ROME
PINES OF ROME

ountains of Rome, completed in 1916, is the first of three symphonic poems by Respighi (1879–1936) inspired by the Eternal City. The works portray not so much the city's architecture or flora but the mood of particular scenes—and the sense of atmosphere and history that makes Rome unique among cities of the world.

In *Fountains of Rome*, each of four fountains is rendered at a different time of day. The work opens with a gently atmospheric portrayal of the Fountain of the Valle Giulia at dawn, during which one can almost see the mists rising over a pastoral landscape. The bucolic reverie is broken by a unison blast on the horns, and the scene shifts to the Triton Fountain in the morning. Here, Respighi's imagination proves more than equal to the task of depicting the mythological demigod of Bernini's splendid fountain, who blows on his conch shell in the middle of what is today one of Rome's busiest intersections. All manner of musical sea-beings answer to his call; as their play subsides we are brought face to face with the power of the sea itself, by the Trevi Fountain in all its midday splendor. Neptune's chariot, heard here in the trumpets and trombones, passes triumphantly over the strings' waves, followed by tritons on their sea horses and cavorting Nereids. This one movement, like the fountain, is certainly worth a coin or three. Dusk arrives and we find ourselves at the Fountain of the Villa Medici, looking out over the Castel Sant'Angelo, the Vatican, and all of central Rome. The air is soft, and as the light fades the tolling of bells brings an end to the day, and to this lush symphonic poem.

Sequels in music are dangerous things—only rarely do they match or surpass the originals. But eight years after completing *Fountains of Rome*,

IF YOU LIKE *Respighi's Rome,* *you might also want to visit Elgar's and Vaughan Williams's London (as portrayed in the* Cockaigne *Overture and* A London Symphony, *respectively),* Gershwin's Paris (An American in Paris), *Ibert's Valencia (Escales), Bernstein's and Copland's New York (Fancy Free and Quiet City), and Ravel's Vienna (La Valse).*

Respighi outdid himself with *Pines of Rome.* Conceived on a larger scale and with even more brilliant orchestral effects, it portrays four Roman settings where pine trees flourish.

Again the scenes are viewed at characteristic times of day. "The Pines of the Villa Borghese" finds children at play in the midday sun. "Pines Near a Catacomb" is a twilit affair, the work's first look at Rome's ancient past. With "The Pines of the Janiculum," Respighi paints a shimmering nocturne in which, conscious of effect as always, he introduces the recorded call of a nightingale as the final touch. And "The Pines of the Appian Way" summons up a full-blown Roman triumphal march that begins almost imperceptibly out of the mists of dawn before building to a thunderous conclusion. The score was first performed in Rome in 1924, and it is one of the few works of the past 70 years to have attained the status of warhorse.

RECOMMENDED RECORDINGS

London Symphony Orchestra/István Kertész.
London Weekend Classics 425 507-2 [with The Birds]

Montreal Symphony Orchestra/ Charles Dutoit.
London 410 145-2 [with Roman Festivals]

With an incandescent London Symphony spread out in front of him, and the best engineering team of the 1960s at his back, Kertész had merely to pick up a baton to make memorable recordings. His performances here are superlative in every way: warm, imaginative, and Italianate to the core (Kertész had studied at the Accademia di Santa Cecilia in Rome). They are also stunningly played and recorded, which makes this disc, at budget price, the best choice for this repertory. Instead of offering *Roman Festivals,* the third part of Respighi's trilogy, the coupling here is *The Birds—*

Respighi captured Rome's grandeur and shimmering beauty.

even better, because as a piece of music, *Roman Festivals* is, well, for the birds.

As an interpreter, Dutoit may be a touch refined for Respighi, but the 1982 accounts of *Pines* and *Fountains* he leads with the Montreal Symphony are among the best. The latter work is vivid and sprightly in the middle sections and wonderfully atmospheric at the end. *Pines* moves along briskly as well—perhaps a little too much so in the finale, which lacks the gaudy grandeur of some other accounts. The sound is typically fine, somewhat distanced but solidly imaged.

NIKOLAI RIMSKY-KORSAKOV
SCHEHERAZADE, OP. 35

*W*hat the Wild West was to the American imagination in the 19th century, the near East was to the Russian. These lands were full of intriguing cultures, wondrous sights, striking beauty, and heroic deeds—at least that was the impression a literate Russian of the day probably had. As a lieutenant in the Czarist navy and later as the inspector of naval bands, Rimsky-Korsakov (1844–1908) had traveled the length and breadth of the empire and seen much of the world beyond by the time he reached middle age. In 1888, with some of his finest work already behind him, he composed a large orchestral suite inspired by *The Thousand and One Nights*—intended, as he later said, to leave listeners with the impression of "an Oriental narrative of some numerous and varied fairy-tale wonders."

Named for its storytelling heroine, Rimsky's *Scheherazade* resembles a symphony in structure. The four movements, each of which carries a descriptive title, share much thematic material—including a sinuous melody portraying Scheherazade herself, played by the solo violin, and a stern motive representing the Sultan Shahriar, forcefully hurled out by strings and full brass at

Rimsky-Korsakov amid the birches on his estate, in 1905.

"WE SAILED FROM
city to city, island
to island, and sea to sea,
until one day we encountered
a nasty wind. Then we all
began to pray, and as we
were doing this a furious
squall hit the ship and tore
the sails to tatters. The ship
whirled around three times
and was driven backward.
Then the rudder broke and
the ship headed toward a
cliff. . . ."
—"The Tale of Sinbad
the Seaman" in the
Arabian Nights

the start of the piece. Each of these two motives is subjected to numerous transformations, so that the whole work is, as he claimed, "closely knit by the community of its themes and motives, yet presenting a kaleidoscope of images and designs. . . ."

The imagery of the opening movement, "The Sea and Sinbad's Ship," is easy to discern. The undulating lower strings beneath Shahriar's motive, here doing double duty as a theme for Sinbad, immediately show the gallant sailor on the deck of his ship, riding out the timpani swells. "The Tale of the Kalendar Prince," with galloping rhythms, warlike fanfares, and cymbals that glint like scimitars, tells of land-based adventure and takes the place of a conventional scherzo, while "The Young Prince and the Young Princess" is a tender romance with hints of arabesques and a processional. Wild revels and an undercurrent of urgency mark the finale, "The Festival at Baghdad—The Sea—Shipwreck on a Rock Surmounted by a Bronze Warrior." Toward the end there is a cyclical return of the music depicting the sea and Sinbad's ship, only this time a storm rages. Woodwinds, strings, and percussion portray the billowing waves in all their terrifying magnificence, as the brass proclaim the theme of Shahriar/Sinbad. The ship crashes against the rocks and is destroyed . . . but it is only a story, and gentle Scheherazade has the last word, bringing comfort to the wise king who has spared her life.

 RECOMMENDED RECORDINGS

**Royal Concertgebouw Orchestra/
Kirill Kondrashin.**
Philips 400 021-2

**Royal Philharmonic Orchestra/
Sir Thomas Beecham.**
EMI CDC 47717 [with Borodin: Polovtsian Dances
from Prince Igor]

Kondrashin fled the Soviet Union, but never forgot his Russian roots.

Kondrashin sensitively balances the masculine and the feminine in his account of *Scheherazade*, which is notable for both its sonic opulence and Oriental splendor. The conductor leads a performance in the grand manner but maintains firm orchestral discipline. The whole thing is a riot of color, and the excellent analog recording from 1979 has been beautifully transferred.

Beecham loved a colorful score, and he came up with a gloriously vivid account of this one in 1957, during his later years with the Royal Philharmonic. There is a sense of spontaneity in this performance, of the orchestra literally sitting on the edges of their seats. The stereo recording has a bit of edge, too, causing brass and strings to sound glassy on occasion. But the image is firm and has remarkable depth.

CAMILLE SAINT-SAËNS

SYMPHONY NO. 3, IN C MINOR, OP. 78
Organ

One of the great masters of French music, Saint-Saëns (1835–1921) has been judged by posterity as a reactionary. In fact, he was one of the most astute and eclectic musicians of his day. A pianist and organist of unsurpassed abilities who possessed a prodigious memory and a legendary gift for sight-reading, he was thoroughly acquainted with the works of Liszt and Wagner, yet was also on familiar terms with the music of the Baroque. While he was more of a consolidator than a pioneer, Saint-Saëns nonetheless remained true to the spirit and traditions of French music by fusing the best of the new and old, and by exhibiting consummate craftsmanship and a sensitive ear for sonority.

Saint-Saëns composed five symphonies, two of them early works that remained unpublished for many years. His most important work in the form is his Symphony No. 3, in C minor, completed in

1886. Conceived on the grandest scale, and clearly influenced by the innovative compositional techniques of Liszt (to whose memory the score is dedicated), it is known as the *Organ* Symphony because of the important role that instrument plays in the work—not in a solo capacity, but as a complement to the orchestra.

Within the symphony's unorthodox two-part layout can be found the conventional division of material into four movements: the first part consists of an Allegro (prefaced by a brief slow introduction) and an Adagio, while the second part combines a scherzo and a Presto finale. A striking feature of the music is the degree to which Saint-Saëns makes use of the process of thematic transformation, a technique developed by Berlioz and Liszt in which a melodic cell from one movement is modified to produce a new subject in a subsequent movement. There are two motto themes in the *Organ* Symphony. One is an ascending four-note motive first heard in the slow introduction, voiced by the oboe over a plaintive harmonization in the strings; it later appears in expanded form as the consoling theme of the Adagio and as the grand, chorale-like subject of the finale. The other motto theme first launches the Allegro in the guise of an accompaniment, a scurrying sixteenth-note line in the violins. It reappears in altered form at many points—in two different transformations within the Adagio, as both the opening and a subsequent theme in the scherzo, and as a subsidiary theme in the finale.

The organ's majestic full voice is saved for the closing portion of the symphony, where it sounds triumphant chords amid the orchestra's bracing proclamation of the first motto theme. But its most beautiful moment comes at the beginning of the Adagio, where its pedal tones support a hushed, lyrical treatment of the same subject in the strings.

Saint-Saëns in 1910, the gray eminence of French music.

THE CARNIVAL OF THE ANIMALS

*E*ven though he was born before the invention of the telegraph, Saint-Saëns lived long enough to become the first major composer to write film music. The same gift for characterization that makes a good film score is evident in the highly cinematic musical entertainment known as *The Carnival of the Animals,* which Saint-Saëns humorously described as a *"Grande fantaisie zoologique."*

Scored for two pianos and an ensemble of two violins, viola, cello, string bass, flute, clarinet, glockenspiel, and xylophone, *The Carnival of the Animals* pokes fun at Offenbach, Berlioz, Mendelssohn, Rossini, and not least, Saint-Saëns himself. The tortoises dance Offenbach's famous cancan in the slowest of tempos, and the elephant cavorts to the strains of both the "Dance of the Sylphs" from Berlioz's *La damnation de Faust* and the scherzo from Mendelssohn's music for *A Midsummer Night's Dream.* Pianists are considered animals in this menagerie, and their incessant finger exercises and scales are parodied with merciful good humor. Saint-Saëns targets himself in "Fossils," where the xylophone plinks out his *Danse macabre.* "Twinkle Twinkle Little Star" and the aria *"Una voce poco fa"* from Rossini's *The Barber of Seville* also gain admission to this select group of animal remains. It's all concluded with a mirthful finale.

Fearing that this divertissement might direct attention away from his more important works, Saint-Saëns forbade publication during his lifetime. He was right; the popularity of this carnival has eclipsed that of his other compositions.

Some participants in Saint-Saëns's grand zoological fantasy.

RECOMMENDED RECORDINGS

Boston Symphony Orchestra/Charles Munch.
RCA Living Stereo 61500-2 [Organ *Symphony*, with *Debussy:* La Mer, *and Ibert:* Escales]

Berlin Philharmonic/James Levine.
Deutsche Grammophon 419 617-2 [Organ *Symphony, with Dukas:* The Sorcerer's Apprentice]

Montreal Symphony Orchestra, London Sinfonietta/Charles Dutoit.
London 430 720-2 [Organ *Symphony and* The Carnival of the Animals]

Academy of London/Richard Stamp.
Virgin Classics VC 90786-2 [The Carnival of the Animals, *with Prokofiev:* Peter and the Wolf *and Mozart:* Eine kleine Nachtmusik]

The account of the *Organ* Symphony from Munch and the Boston Symphony is another example of how this conductor could take a warhorse and turn it back into a serious piece of music. Serious, but not dull. The Allegro is impassioned, the Adagio is intensely poetic, and the finale generates real edge-of-the-seat excitement. The new "Living Stereo" remastering has restored the 1959 recording's life-like presence and minimized the effects of tape saturation in the loudest passages. The glorious tone of the orchestra comes through loud and clear, along with a thrilling sense of Symphony Hall ambience. The couplings are generous and every bit as impressively performed.

Levine and the Berlin Philharmonic raise the roof with their spacious 1986 rendition of the symphony, combining virtuosity with finesse and an engaging sense of color. Under Levine's baton the momentum never flags, and while the Berlin trumpets aren't quite up to some of the notes, the

Orchestral Personalities

Founded in 1881, the Boston Symphony is one of America's most versatile orchestras. Since the days of Serge Koussevitzky (above), it has possessed the warm string tone and well-defined timbres that are the essence of Russian sound, as well as the gleaming brass and rhythmic precision favored in American music. A generation of American composers wrote with the sound of the Boston Symphony in mind—Copland, Bernstein, and Walter Piston.

strings and winds play with extraordinary polish. The recording is vivid and well balanced.

Dutoit and the Montrealers give a well-played if rather straightforward reading of the symphony. The music emerges with an authentic Gallic accent, and the coupling of *The Carnival of the Animals* (performed by the London Sinfonietta) makes sense for collectors in search of a single-disc sampler of Saint-Saëns's most popular works.

The 1987–88 *Carnival* from Virgin is lively and exceptionally well recorded. It also has the best coupling of works for young listeners.

FRANZ SCHUBERT

SYMPHONY NO. 8, IN B MINOR, D. 759
Unfinished

*A*fter the Venus de Milo, this score may well be the most celebrated torso in Western art. The Austrian composer Schubert (1797–1828) undoubtedly intended to fashion a four-movement symphony that would depart dramatically from the models of Mozart and Haydn and open up a vast and strikingly subjective realm of expression. From the start he goes in a direction quite different from that of his preceding six symphonies (there is no Symphony No. 7). Woodwinds and brass—which for the first time in any symphony are allowed a sonic presence equal to that of the strings—lend a poignant coloration to the texture, heightened by unusual doublings (for example, clarinet and oboe playing the first movement's main subject in unison). The trombones, which Beethoven had saved for his most climactic moments, are part of this orchestra from the beginning and are used with great skill to deepen its sonority and add a cutting edge to the outbursts.

The music of the opening Allegro seems fraught with premonition. A lugubrious introductory passage in the cellos and basses, which Schubert later

Near-sighted, pudgy, and touched with genius, Schubert c. 1825.

Unfinished Works

Schubert's Symphony No.8 was aborted in the Third movement (above). Other unfinished works popular in the repertory are: Schubert's own Quartettsatz in C minor, the first movement of a projected four-movement string quartet, and Bruckner's Symphony No. 9, in D minor, which lacks its final movement but is quite effective without it.

expands upon in the movement's development section, prefaces the true main theme from clarinet and oboe—an urgent, melancholy subject in B minor over a feverish sixteenth-note accompaniment in the violins. Only one other melody is offered, and it is the famous one, almost but not quite a waltz. Schubert's scoring, for cellos over pizzicato basses, with an off-the-beat accompaniment in clarinets and violas, is a tour de force of understatement. In this haunting movement's entirely new world of orchestral color and expression, Romanticism appears in symphonic music for the first time.

The ensuing Andante, in the idyllic key of E major, continues the exploration. Once again the music is set in a flowing triple meter (though this time in 3/8 rather than 3/4), and once again the woodwinds and brass are used with exceptional finesse. As the clarinet intones the movement's desolate second subject in C sharp minor, Schubert again uses an off-the-beat accompaniment to lend a sense of fragility to the expression. But on this occasion, the magic goes even further: midway through, Schubert changes the harmony from minor to major, and with that the melody, now taken up by the oboe, changes from poignant to consoling.

The two movements were penned in the autumn of 1822, but during the winter of 1822–23 Schubert became desperately ill. He may have left the symphony incomplete because of the association it bore with such a traumatic experience. But the piece had also become problematic in a purely formal sense. By developing his material forcefully in the manner of Beethoven, Schubert had gone against the grain of his own thinking, for the material itself is notably "closed" (that is, melodic)—as opposed to being "open" (motivic) and capable of the kind of expansion and reconfiguration that typified Beethoven's procedures in sonata form. Schubert would find the solution to this problem in his Ninth Symphony.

Taking the score by the throat, Bernstein urges the cellos to sing.

RECOMMENDED RECORDINGS

**Royal Concertgebouw Orchestra/
Leonard Bernstein.**
Deutsche Grammophon 427 645-2 [with Symphony No. 5]

London Classical Players/Roger Norrington.
EMI CDC 49968 [with Symphony No. 5]

Boston Symphony Orchestra/Eugen Jochum.
*Deutsche Grammophon Resonance 427 195-2
[with Beethoven: Symphony No. 5]*

Bernstein's highly personal 1987 account of the *Unfinished* yields some remarkable insights into the score's troubled expressiveness. The first movement reveals a tonal darkness, with a feverish, trembling quality to the viola accompaniment of the big tune. The Andante is leisurely, but there is a fragile tension to the argument, together with a sense of motionlessness, breathlessness, and far-off distance. The symphony's climaxes are unerringly judged, but the ending is not as radiant as others have it; Bernstein instead makes it quietly, tenderly detached. The Concertgebouw strings play magnificently throughout, and the winds are striking in their excellence. For a realization based on live takes in a difficult hall, the recording is very well engineered.

Norrington's period-instrument treatments of the Fifth and the *Unfinished* are a delight. Here, "authentic" means brisk, with textural details emerging in absolute clarity. There is a feathery lightness of touch in the strings, great delicacy in the winds, glistening tone in the horns. The playing often has a decidedly vocal quality, just as it should, and the accounts of both works sail along without ever seeming to be in haste. EMI's 1989 recording is outstanding.

In his sincere, powerfully emotional account of the *Unfinished*, Jochum is gentle in the lyrical pages but fills the climaxes with visionary intensity and edge-of-the-seat drama. The first movement's development section is especially hair-raising, while the Andante has never sounded lovelier. Jochum was unsurpassed in his ability to move between extremes while holding everything together, and here the elements of mood, pacing, color, weight, and expression are in perfect adjustment. The Boston Symphony plays radiantly, and the account is exceptionally well recorded.

SYMPHONY NO. 9, IN C, D. 944

*S*chubert began work on the Ninth Symphony in 1825 and put the finishing touches on the score in March of 1828, hoping to get a performance from the Gesellschaft der Musikfreunde in Vienna. The society found the piece too long and the writing too difficult. Following Schubert's death later that year, the manuscript of the Ninth passed to Schubert's brother. It remained in his possession until it was discovered in 1839 by Schumann, who was instrumental in arranging the work's premiere that same year by the Gewandhaus Orchestra in Leipzig.

In spite of its belated appearance, the Ninth proved to be among the most important scores of the 19th century, strongly influencing Schumann himself, tangentially affecting Brahms, and in the vastness of its design—the quality Schumann referred to as "heavenly length"—boldly pointing the way for Bruckner and Mahler. Many of the stylistic and formal approaches Schubert had pioneered in the unfinished Eighth Symphony are carried forward in the Ninth. Still, in one crucial respect, the concept is different: here, Schubert contains the impulse to spin out melody and instead bases each movement on pithy, readily malleable motives.

The subtlety of Schubert's orchestral palette in

"Here has music entombed a rich treasure, but far fairer hopes"—epitaph on Schubert's grave.

all four movements is breathtaking. As he had in the *Unfinished* Symphony, he lays the colors of winds and brass over the strings in a warm, lustrous fashion that places the symphony firmly in the sonic realm of Romanticism. Equally important is the way he uses these instruments in solo capacities—the two horns in unison, but *piano*, on the symphony's noble opening fanfare, or the oboe, again *piano*, with string accompaniment, sounding like a distant trumpet in the Andante's first theme.

The most remarkable feature of the Ninth is its rhythmic vitality, and the way in which two specific cells—the dotted quarter (or lesser value) followed by an eighth note (or its equivalent), and the triplet—gain strength through the course of the work. These two rhythms, joined by an insistent four-note figure first heard in the horns, become the chief substantive element in the finale, a movement of enormous length that goes like a shot because of the rhythmic material's horsepower.

The poetry and imagination of Schubert's later music are present in the Ninth to the utmost degree. At least one passage in the symphony's Andante deserves special mention. Schubert sets up the arrival of the recapitulation with chorale-like sequences in the trombones, winds, and strings, all marked *pianissimo*, out of which the two horns emerge, playing a softly repeated high G. In the intervals between the notes on the horns, the strings offer a hushed, slowly changing harmonization—first the cellos and basses, then violas and violins—which gradually intensifies until strings and horns together emerge in the movement's home key of A minor. It is a passage of absolute genius—and it is echoed more than once in the music of both Schumann and Brahms.

 RECOMMENDED RECORDINGS

Vienna Philharmonic/Sir Georg Solti.
London 400 082-2

THE HORN HAS
traditionally been the instrument of the nobility, used in battle and in the chase. In The Song of Roland, *written 900 years ago, the ambushed Count Roland blows on it to summon Charlemagne and his army; its tone, at first forceful, then despairing, and finally feeble, tells the Franks how the battle is going. Since then, in music of every period, the horn has been used to evoke sentiments of nobility, images of the hunt, or a mood of heroism.*

Supremely confident Schubert from Sir Georg Solti.

Orchestra of the Age of Enlightenment/ Sir Charles Mackerras.

Virgin Classics VC 90708-2

Coaches of champion teams talk about chemistry, and that is precisely what Solti and the Vienna Philharmonic bring to this winning performance. The conductor provides just the edge and sense of impulse needed to help make the players come alive. Tempos are near-ideal as the piece settles into those wonderful regions of tone color Schubert alone seemed to inhabit. Solti observes the repeats in the first and last movements, the latter particularly important if the finale is to have the weight it requires. The Philharmonic contributes many fine touches along the way; what could be more apt, to mention one, than the sound of the Viennese oboe to begin the second movement? London captures the 1981 performance in bright early digital sound.

Mackerras's period-instrument recording is a joy, full of life, excitement, and intensity—but *not* period prissiness. The transition from the first movement's Andante introduction to the Allegro is very tricky—conductors always seem to be shifting gears—but here it goes off splendidly. In fact, Sir Charles exhibits a sure grasp of tempo throughout the performance along with a fine ear for balance, and he provides plenty of fresh interpretive insights. The 1987 recording has extraordinary realism.

ROBERT SCHUMANN

SYMPHONY NO. 3, IN E FLAT, OP. 97
Rhenish

Although identified as No. 3, the *Rhenish* Symphony of Schumann (1810–1856) was actually the fourth and last of his completed works in the form. It was written at breakneck speed during five weeks in the autumn

Robert and Clara Schumann moved to the Rhineland in 1850.

of 1850, shortly after the German composer had moved to Düsseldorf, where he assumed the post of municipal music director.

The optimism with which Schumann greeted this move can be felt in many parts of the five-movement score, especially in the festive opening, marked *lebhaft* ("lively"). In a mood of sunny ebullience, passages of chorale-like majesty and breathless animation are juxtaposed in such a way that an almost giddy tension results. The second movement, called a scherzo, is actually a free-wheeling Ländler that was originally to have borne the title "Morning on the Rhine." An intermezzo follows, reflecting the tranquility in which Schumann wrote the symphony. The only outright allusion to the symphony's "Rhenish" origins comes with the penultimate movement, which was supposedly inspired by a scene Schumann witnessed at the cathedral in nearby Cologne—a ceremony marking the elevation of an archbishop to the rank of Cardinal. The music here, unlike that of the rest of the symphony, is solemn and grave, suitably evoking a processional in the immense interior spaces of a Gothic nave. The finale, a brisk march, brings the symphony to a close on a note of energetic confidence.

The idyll that gave birth to the *Rhenish* was unfortunately a brief one. Schumann ultimately ran into difficulty with the critics and the orchestra in Düsseldorf. And within four years of the symphony's completion, he succumbed to the effects of syphilis and was committed to an asylum—after an unsuccessful attempt to drown himself by jumping into the waters of his beloved Rhine.

SOME OF HISTORY'S *best composers earned part of their living as music critics, among them Schumann, Berlioz, Fauré, Debussy, and the American Virgil Thomson. Though Schumann's intuition was at times stronger than his analysis, his work was especially important; thanks to him, Chopin, Mendelssohn, Berlioz, and Brahms got needed boosts.*

 RECOMMENDED RECORDINGS

Berlin Philharmonic/Herbert von Karajan.
Deutsche Grammophon 429 672-2 [2 CDs; with Symphonies Nos. 1, 2, and 4]

The Cologne cathedral inspired the fourth movement of the Rhenish.

New York Philharmonic/Leonard Bernstein.
Sony Classical SMK 47612 [with Symphony No. 4 and Manfred *Overture]*

Karajan's integral recording of the four Schumann symphonies, available at midprice on two CDs, is hard to resist. The account of the *Rhenish* is hedonistic, extroverted, full of panache. Even though Karajan takes off with an unusually frenzied opening, more hyper than noble, every bar is purposeful, the playing passionate and committed. The 1971 recording is distant but warmly atmospheric.

No one has more fully conveyed the exuberance of the score than Bernstein did in this 1960 recording, the capstone of a Schumann symphony cycle he and a fired-up New York Philharmonic taped for CBS in just three weeks. The performance scales the heights of Romantic ardor, and the sound is amazingly vibrant.

DMITRI SHOSTAKOVICH
SYMPHONY NO. 5, IN D MINOR, OP. 47

A native of St. Petersburg who at the age of 19 had dazzled teachers and public alike with his First Symphony, Shostakovich (1906–1975) flourished in the permissive atmosphere of post-Revolutionary artistic ferment that lingered in the Soviet Union through the 1920s. As the deadly 1930s unfolded, he continued on his course as the fearless boy wonder of Soviet music with the full-length opera *Lady Macbeth of the Mtsensk District* and the dissonant, sprawling Symphony No. 4. Nothing he had done so far had been as daring as these two scores, and he paid the price. When Stalin heard *Lady Macbeth* in 1936, he personally demanded a scathing review be published in *Pravda*. The next morning, Shostakovich woke to a state of disgrace.

The composer turned his energies to a new

SHOSTAKOVICH *was often cheeky with his teachers. On one occasion it proved too much for conductor Nikolai Malko. The year was 1928, and* No, No, Nanette, *the Broadway musical, was the rage all over Europe. "OK," Malko challenged his pupil, "if you're so great, go into that room and orchestrate 'Tea for Two,' and have it ready in an hour." Forty-five minutes later, Shostakovich emerged with a finished score entitled* Tahiti Trot. *Malko conducted the piece at his next concert.*

work, a conventionally styled and structured symphony in four movements, with an easy-to-follow argument beginning on a tragic note and leading to a heroic conclusion. The Fifth would be different, characterized in the famous remark by an unknown commentator as "a Soviet artist's response to just criticism."

Completed in 1937, Symphony No. 5 works brilliantly as pure music, and it has justifiably become Shostakovich's most frequently performed symphonic work. While the archlike plan of its charged first movement may have been borrowed from the corresponding movement in Tchaikovsky's *Pathétique* Symphony, the treatment is nonetheless devastatingly effective (so much so that Shostakovich adopted the same layout again in his Eighth Symphony). Here, after a portentous introduction, the strings begin a tense climb from the bleakness toward a rapt, almost visionary lyricism. But there is a grim coloration to even the most consoling moments, and soon enough the reverie is shattered by a brutally mechanical march. A relentless buildup ensues, until the march is trumpeted out in all its garish magnificence. After a climax of nearly hysterical force, the first movement uneasily settles back into the desolate mood of its start.

The symphony's second movement, a scherzo-like Allegretto, is not as light-hearted as it seems. The heavy, burlesque tread of its outer portions and the mawkish delicacy of its trio, while humorous, have a lugubrious point that elicits, at best, a grim smile. The following Largo is altogether serious; by turns searing and elegiac, it is the expressive heart of the symphony. The almost dreamlike melancholy of the music transcends any autobiographical interpretations, as its pathos is universal—and for that reason all the more touching. In the remarkable finale, Shostakovich achieves one of the greatest coups of his symphonic career: a "victorious" closer that manages to drive home the expected message and at the same time make an entirely different point, the real one. The resounding march that ends the movement represents the triumph of *evil* over *good*. The apparent optimism of the concluding pages is, as one colleague of the composer put it, no more than the forced smile of a torture victim as he is being stretched on the rack.

 RECOMMENDED RECORDINGS

**Royal Concertgebouw Orchestra/
Bernard Haitink.**
London 410 017-2

Scottish National Orchestra/Neeme Järvi.
*Chandos CHAN 8650 [with Ballet Suite No. 5 from
The Bolt]*

Haitink's 1981 account of the Fifth is a stunning realization. Plumbing the full depth of the music's desolation, it also rises to towering heights in the climactic pages of the opening and closing movements. The Concertgebouw Orchestra plays magnificently and is powerfully recorded.

The Estonian conductor Järvi brings an authentic accent to his interpretation, which is spontaneous in the best sense and suitably brazen in its splendor. The Scots are taken to the limit, and their ensemble playing occasionally shows it, but they deliver some real fireworks along the way. The 1988 recording is vivid and thrillingly natural in atmosphere.

*Haitink has recorded all 15
Shostakovich symphonies.*

SYMPHONY NO. 10, IN E MINOR, OP. 93

*T*he Tenth is one of Shostakovich's most personal utterances. From the brooding first movement to the march-gone-mad finale, it is a grippingly communicative work. It is also one of the handful of indisputable masterpieces penned in the second half of this century, a creation that summons up the ambivalence, complexity, and turbulence of the world into which many of us were born.

The symphony begins with a Moderato of tremendous breadth, an ominous exordium in E minor. Its long-breathed opening subject, gropingly announced in the lower strings, is treated at length before a halting, waltzlike second subject is introduced in the flute; together, these ideas conspire to evoke a mood of nightmarish desolation. There is a long buildup to a terrifying climax at midpoint, after which the fabric unravels in a fantasy of haunting despondency.

The ensuing scherzo is one of Shostakovich's most violent. Despite its brevity it manages to convey an impression of polished brutality—which is just as it should be, since Shostakovich later revealed that the music was a portrait of Stalin. The Allegretto, reminiscent of the Ländler-like movements Mahler used in some of his symphonies, introduces a mysterious solo horn call in the midst of its energetic celebration of the dance. It also introduces Shostakovich's motto theme— D, E flat, C, B natural—whose German spelling (D-Es-C-H), when pronounced phonetically, yields the composer's monogram "D. Sch."

Shostakovich makes much of this subject both here and in the finale, which begins with a meditative Andante introduction, then rather whimsically takes off into realms of exuberance that could scarcely have been imagined at the symphony's start. By movement's end, with the timpani hammering out the motto theme, the emotional landscape of the piece has changed. There is, however, nothing false about the festivity of this conclusion: the joy has been hard-earned, and it is even offset by anguish recollected from earlier in the symphony. It is the perfect balance of these competing tendencies—the lack of finality in this finale—that makes the movement so giddy and yet so convincing.

It is not hard to find the reason for this approach in Shostakovich's personal experiences of

Shostakovich served as a fireman in World War II.

Stalin as culture vulture.

the preceding five years. In 1948, again on orders from Stalin, he had been condemned even more viciously than in 1936. The composer was forced into a musical cocoon—pressured to shelve his more serious projects for fear of further reprisal—and driven out of his professorship at the Moscow Conservatory. Not until Stalin's death, in the winter of 1953, did the darkness in Shostakovich's spirit begin to lift.

So the Tenth, composed in the summer and autumn of 1953, was a score meant to settle a score. It received its first performance on December 17, 1953, in Leningrad with the Leningrad Philharmonic under the baton of Yevgeny Mravinsky. The American premiere was given on October 15, 1954, in New York by Dimitri Mitropoulos and the New York Philharmonic.

 RECOMMENDED RECORDINGS

Royal Concertgebouw Orchestra/ Claus Peter Flor.
RCA Red Seal 60448-2

Scottish National Orchestra/Neeme Järvi.
Chandos CHAN 8630 [with Ballet Suite No. 4]

Flor's 1990 reading with the Concertgebouw Orchestra is incandescent in its inspiration. The young German conductor paces the work superbly, allowing the music plenty of time to unfold, always to extraordinary effect. The Dutch orchestra plays spectacularly, and the recording brings a burnished splendor to the whole affair.

The Tenth is obviously a work close to Järvi's heart, and this account is one of the conductor's most successful. His approach is poignantly lyrical and comes close to the spirit of the piece. The Scottish orchestra produces a massive sound, but one that possesses plenty of intensity. The recording, made in 1988 in Caird Hall, Dundee, is superbly atmospheric and well engineered.

JEAN SIBELIUS

THE SWAN OF TUONELA

*S*ibelius (1865–1957) found the inspiration for a number of his earlier works in the *Kalevala*, the national epic of his native Finland. The hero of the *Kalevala* is Lemminkäinen, upon whose exploits Sibelius based a suite of symphonic poems, which he called *Four Legends*.

The Swan of Tuonela (1893), the second of these legends, depicts a scene that Sibelius described as follows: "Tuonela, the land of death, the Hades of Finnish mythology, is surrounded by a large river with black waters and a rapid current, on which the singing Swan of Tuonela floats majestically." Sibelius's scoring is appropriately somber: no flutes or trumpets are used, and of the clarinets, only the bass. The swan is personified by the solo English horn, which intones a haunting solo against the sustained harmonies of the strings.

This is a masterpiece of orchestral colorism, not kaleidoscopic but nocturnal—much like the canvasses James McNeill Whistler painted in black and gray. In its austerity and darkness, it foreshadows Sibelius's last major symphonic scores, the Seventh Symphony and the tone poem *Tapiola*.

SYMPHONY NO. 2, IN D, OP. 43

*W*hen it came to the symphony, Sibelius, like Brahms, hesitated before plunging into the arena where he would eventually win widespread and lasting acclaim. He was 32 before he began work on his First Symphony, in 1898, though by that time his technique as an orchestrator was highly developed, thanks to two large-scale symphonic scores inspired by the Finnish national epic, the *Kalevala*.

Sibelius completed his Second Symphony in 1902. Although its antecedents certainly included

Brahms's own Second Symphony (also in D, and nearly identical in instrumentation) and Beethoven's Fifth, Sibelius's already quite individualistic tonal language, particularly his penchant for stepwise melodic contours and modal harmony, gives the music a distinctive austerity. On an emotional level, the Second stands apart from any model. The volatile Finnish spirit, capable of moving so quickly between the poles of optimism and pessimism, can be felt on every page.

The pastoral mood of the first movement soon grows troubled. Melodic utterances, some of them mere gestures of a few notes rather than full-fledged themes, seem to arise at random and trail off inconsequentially. Behind this apparent shapelessness is a subtle coherence: all of the movement's material emerges either from the two repeated-note subjects heard in the strings and winds at the start, or from a brooding idea first presented by the winds and brass. There is a climax of rugged grandeur before the gentleness of the beginning is recaptured.

In the Andante, Sibelius sets up a titanic confrontation between subjects in two competing keys. The first, a dirge-like melody in D minor, marked "lugubrious," is intoned by the bassoons in octaves over a stalking pizzicato bass and slowly builds to a towering culmination in winds and brass; the second, played by divided strings in the ethereal key of F sharp major, conveys a gentle, faltering spirituality, full of pain but offering the hope of salvation. In his manuscript, Sibelius had originally penned the inscriptions "Death" and "Christ" over these two themes. The movement, full of turbulence and without consolation at its end, seems to make Death the victor.

The scherzo, with its machine-gun figures in the strings, generates remarkable energy. The bucolic woodwind motif of the trio stands in sharp contrast, though it too is based on the repetition of a single note. Following the precedent of Beethoven's Fifth Symphony, Sibelius leads directly into the finale via a bridge of grand rhetorical

Sibelius in 1894, tormented by debts and alcohol.

thrust. The movement itself is a throwback to the Romantic tradition: with a broad melody that verges on the singsong, it makes a triumphant assertion of D major amid the heavy weather of D minor. And again like Beethoven, Sibelius brings back the transitional material a second time so that the victory of the major key can be savored anew, after which he concludes the work with a hymnlike peroration. This is the last time Sibelius would wear the mantle of his predecessors; in subsequent works, he would single-mindedly pursue the formal concision and searching self-expression that characterize the first two movements of this symphony.

SYMPHONY NO. 5, IN E FLAT, OP. 82

*A*fter his first two symphonies, each of them a broadly proportioned four-movement essay calling for a large orchestra and spectacular effects, Sibelius turned his back on the Romantic tradition and the mainstream of contemporary symphonic thinking. His next two symphonies were boldly experimental. The idyllic, aphoristic Third sounds neo-Classical in spirit, while the grimly pessimistic Fourth embraces a dissonant language that brings it to the very edge of harmonic dysfunction. With the Symphony No. 5, first performed on December 8, 1915, at a concert marking his 50th birthday, Sibelius reconciled these seemingly disparate directions in a work of stark beauty, economy, and affirmation.

If one work could be said to characterize Sibelius's mature style, it is the Fifth Symphony. The organic growth of the first movement—from nebulous beginnings and the majestic emergence of a theme of compelling grandeur, through music of scherzo-like momentum surging with life and growing ever more fleet, to a final, exhilarating rush of energy—offers a stunning example of

*P*HOTOGRAPHS OF *Sibelius taken after about 1925 show an austere-looking man whose most striking feature is his complete baldness. As his hair had started to turn gray, Sibelius sacrificed it to the razor rather than let others see that he was aging.*

*S*IBELIUS *recorded in his diary the inspiration for the "swan theme" in his Fifth Symphony: "At ten to eleven today saw 16 swans. God, what beauty! They circled over me for a long time. Disappeared in the solar haze like a silver ribbon. Their call the same woodwind type as that of cranes, but without tremolo. That of swans closer to trumpet . . . a low refrain, reminiscent of a child sobbing. Nature's mysticism and life's lament."*

Sibelius's ability to build a symphonic movement on the dynamic development of a single idea, in this case the first four notes of the horn theme that opens the work. Rather than using relationships among keys to drive the argument, the composer uses tempo, creating an *accellerando* across 401 measures, a vast span of musical time that becomes dramatically compressed as the tempo increases. The effect is incandescent: out of the mists, Sibelius fashions a blazing sun, in music that seems to illustrate the very process of creation.

The remaining two movements fill out the cosmos brought into being by this extraordinary opening essay. The Andante in G is a set of variations on a wistful pizzicato subject delicately introduced by the violas and cellos. Except for a brief passage toward the end of the movement, where the brass let loose with a couple of snarling outbursts, the variations are warmly rhapsodic. In the symphony's breathless *moto perpetuo* finale, Sibelius introduces one of his most memorable ideas, a bell-like tolling of chords among the four horns that is said to have come to him after he watched a flight of swans pass overhead. This "swan theme," which emerges from the giddy rush of the tremolo strings, is the soul of the movement, and it is accompanied by a poignant, singing subject given out in octaves by the woodwinds and cellos.

Sibelius brings the finale to climax by means of a grand slow-down, the reverse of the method he had used in the first movement. The last pages of the symphony offer a mighty apotheosis of the "swan theme," capped by six isolated, powerful chords, so slow in cadence they seem removed from any temporal framework. The world that had been summoned out of the ether ends as a succession of huge, monolithic shouts of Amen.

Colin Davis rehearsing with the Boston Symphony in 1975.

 RECOMMENDED RECORDINGS

Boston Symphony Orchestra/Sir Colin Davis.
Philips 416 600-2 [4 CDs; Symphonies Nos. 1–7 and The Swan of Tuonela, *with* Finlandia *and* Tapiola]

Royal Philharmonic Orchestra/ Sir John Barbirolli.
Chesky CD 3 [Symphony No. 2]

Berlin Philharmonic/Herbert von Karajan.
Deutsche Grammophon 415 107-2 [Symphony No. 5, with No. 7] and 413 755-2 [The Swan of Tuonela, *with* Finlandia, Tapiola, *and* Valse triste]

Davis and the Bostonians are still the choice for a complete set of the symphonies. Sir Colin's approach is a Classicizing one, at times even impressionistic, as opposed to the Romanticism favored by a good many other interpreters (and represented best by Karajan). But while these accounts lean to the objective side of the emotional ledger, they are illuminating and unfailingly expressive. The recordings are good mid-1970s analog, quite well remastered, though the sonic picture is still a little dense in places owing to Symphony Hall's ample reverberation. Davis's intimate treatment of *The Swan of Tuonela* conveys not so much a sense of great space as one of an interior world coming momentarily into view.

Barbirolli's magnificent account of the Second Symphony with the Royal Philharmonic is one of the greatest interpretations of the score on disc. It is a broad, burnished, heart-on-sleeve reading, wonderfully somber in the Andante but neither self-conscious nor overly sentimental. The splendid original recording, with excellent atmosphere and presence, has been brilliantly transferred by the Chesky brothers.

Karajan's mid-1960s reading of the Fifth Symphony is remarkable for its pacing and pointing of detail—and almost frightening in the way it conveys a feeling of power held in reserve. The account dates from a period when Deutsche Grammophon was making excellent recordings in Berlin—although the remastering could have been more painstaking. On a 1984 CD, Karajan tackles the tone poems for the last time, and does so in arresting fashion. *The Swan of Tuonela*, with strings brought to the fore, is urgent and atmospheric, while the subdued English horn solo lends the performance a desolate cast. The sound of this CD exhibits the typical high-gloss effect of mid-1980s DG digital, and at less than 44 minutes the disc is not really a bargain—but those performances are compelling.

BEDŘICH SMETANA

VLTAVA (THE MOLDAU)

*E*ven though German was his first language, the Czech composer Smetana (1824–1884) saw it as his primary duty to create a national operatic repertory for his countrymen. But his desire to celebrate the history, legends, and landscape of Bohemia carried over into symphonic composition as well, motivating an epic cycle of six tone poems that Smetana patriotically called *Má Vlast* (*My Country*).

Today only a few of Smetana's operas are known or performed outside of the Czech Republic, but concert audiences everywhere are familiar with the second part of *Má Vlast*. Entitled *Vltava* (known to English-speaking listeners as *The Moldau*), this symphonic poem from 1874 depicts Bohemia's most important river in a series of deftly connected vignettes, and is a masterpiece of atmospheric orchestration.

As described in Smetana's explanatory notes, the score begins at the source of the river, where two springs flow together. The undulating line heard here is one of music's most effective portrayals of water; starting in the flutes, it spreads

Patriot and patriarch of Czech music, Smetana c. 1880.

to the clarinets and on through the strings, suggesting the ever-gathering flow. The river courses through the forest (we hear horn and trumpet calls, sounds of the hunt), past a village in the countryside (wedding participants dance a polka), and into a moonlit glade (muted strings), where water nymphs delicately cavort. Reaching the Rapids of St. John—heard in heavy brass, turbulent strings, and percussion—the river sweeps majestically past Vyšehrad Castle and through the city of Prague, finally passing out of sight on the way toward its confluence with the Elbe.

 RECOMMENDED RECORDING

Berlin Philharmonic/Herbert von Karajan.
Deutsche Grammophon 427 808-2 [with Liszt:
Les Préludes, *Grieg:* Holberg Suite, *and Sibelius:*
Finlandia]

Nothing compares with the sensuous textures and luminous sonorities of Karajan's cruise along the Moldau. The piece was one of his favorites, and he made several recordings of it. This midprice CD offers the best available couplings.

THE REPERTORY *abounds in music associated with rivers. Smetana's* The Moldau *is a portrait of the Vltava in Prague (above); the water in Handel's* Water Music *is that of the Thames, while the Rhine runs through Schumann's* Symphony No. 3. *But the most beloved of all musical tributes to a river is Johann Strauss's waltz* An der schönen, blauen Donau *(By the Beautiful, Blue Danube).*

THE STRAUSS FAMILY

*T*he music of Johann Strauss II, his brothers Josef and Eduard, and their illustrious father has long been one of the mainstays of the light classical repertory. While the intoxicating potency these scores once had as dance music may have faded—along with notions that a man looked best in the uniform of a hussar—they have lost none of their charm or popularity.

For the better part of a century, from about 1830 to 1900, the Strauss family dominated the Viennese social scene. In 1846 the title of *Hofballmusikdirektor* (director of music for court balls) was created for Johann Strauss I, and between 1863 and 1901 it was borne by either Johann II or Eduard. The family's origins were Jewish, a fact Johann Strauss did his best to hide from the intolerant Viennese. The senior Johann became an accomplished violinist and violist before joining the dance band of Josef Lanner in 1819. Following his marriage in 1825, Strauss struck out on his own. His rise to fame was quick: in four years, he was already a celebrity in Vienna, and by 1833 he was touring with his orchestra to other countries. His career was unfortunately short, however. After catching scarlet fever from one of his children, he died in 1849 at the age of 45. Although he wrote many waltzes that were popular in his time, Johann I is best known today for a single work—the *Radetzky* March, Op. 228, composed in 1848—still the finest musical embodiment of the once great military might of the Hapsburg monarchy.

Strauss's oldest son, Johann Strauss II, became known as "The Waltz King" during the heyday of that dance in the mid-19th century. Born in 1825, he entered the waltz business officially in 1844, requiring a special permit to give concerts, as he was still underage. His success quickly started to rival that of his father, and upon the elder's death, the two Strauss orchestras were merged and Johann II took over as leader. During the next five decades, until his death in 1899, Strauss conducted and toured with the family orchestra and on his own, meanwhile turning out hundreds of waltzes, polkas, and quadrilles in a stream that reached its peak in the 1850s and '60s. The best of his waltzes—*Emperor, Blue Danube, Roses from the South, Tales from the Vienna Woods, Vienna Blood, Artist's Life,* and *Wine, Women, and Song*—stand among the triumphs of 19th-century Viennese music, perfect crystallizations of the cultural milieu in which they were written.

Josef Strauss, two years younger than Johann II, was perhaps an even more formidable composer than his famous brother. Melancholy and

JOHANN STRAUSS II became the Waltz King based on both the quantity and the quality of his work. His vast musical output, which runs to 498 opus numbers, includes 18 stage works and nearly 200 each of waltzes and polkas.

STRAUSS'S WALTZ By the Beautiful, Blue Danube, *was first heard in 1867—not in the shimmering orchestral colors familiar today but in a more folksy setting for band and men's chorus. With its patriotic text,* The Blue Danube *was intended to raise Austria's spirits after its defeat by Prussia in 1866. But it was not until Strauss created the orchestral version, for the World Exposition in Paris, that the piece conquered Europe and the rest of the world.*

introverted by nature, he revealed in his works a profound musicality and a sophisticated imagination. His best waltzes, which include *Music of the Spheres* and *Delirium,* combine poetic beauty with an almost neurotic expressiveness. Josef may well have ghost-written some of the waltzes credited to Johann II, and the two brothers also teamed up on several occasions, most notably for the popular *Pizzicato* Polka.

Eduard Strauss, born in 1835, turned to music after receiving a classical education; the family waltz business was going so well that his participation was virtually required. He was only a fair violinist, but he became the best conductor of the three brothers. Not as compelling a composer as his two siblings, he nonetheless contributed more than 300 works to the canon.

 RECOMMENDED RECORDINGS

Berlin Philharmonic/Herbert von Karajan.

Deutsche Grammophon 400 026-2 [Johann Strauss II: Blue Danube *and* Artist's Life, *with other works], 410 022-2 [Johann Strauss II:* Emperor, Roses from the South, *and* Wine, Women, and Song, *with other works], and 410 027-2 [Josef Strauss:* Music of the Spheres *and* Delirium, *Johann Strauss II:* Tales from the Vienna Woods *and* Vienna Blood, *and Johann Strauss I:* Radetzky *March, with other works]*

Vienna Philharmonic/Herbert von Karajan.

Deutsche Grammophon 419 616-2 [Josef Strauss: Music of the Spheres *and* Delirium, *Johann Strauss II:* Blue Danube, *and Johann Strauss I:* Radetzky *March, with other works]*

The three discs with the Berlin Philharmonic feature the better-known waltzes, polkas, and overtures of Johann Strauss II and two of the best waltzes by his brother Josef. With the wind of *Gemütlichkeit* blowing at their backs, Karajan and the Berliners go at these works under full sail, possessed of all the carefree elegance—if not always the lightness or lilt—that one generally associates with the Viennese temperament. The orchestra plays the music with an ensemble homogeneity that is simply breathtaking, and the fabled silken string tone suits the music to perfection. Biggest successes are the performances of Johann II's *Artist's Life*, as Viennese as the pastry at Demels, and Josef's *Music of the Spheres*. The recorded sound is remarkably fine, with plenty of atmosphere and an ideal, not-too-heavy resonance.

For the lightness and lilt, there's Karajan's offering with the Vienna Philharmonic, recorded live on January 1, 1987. Playing to the manner born, the Viennese summon every nuance out of the music. Kathleen Battle sings Johann II's *Voices of Spring* exquisitely.

RICHARD STRAUSS

Don Juan, Op. 20

The German composer Strauss (1864–1949) portrayed a different Don Juan from the one Mozart characterized in *Don Giovanni*—not the lusty, high-living rake but the idealist eternally in search of feminine perfection. Strauss's Don is more akin to Wagner's Flying Dutchman, and closest of all to Goethe's Faust.

It was not Mozart or his sources for the Don Juan character (going back to Tirso de Molina) or even George Bernard Shaw who provided the original inspiration for Strauss, but a poem by Nikolaus Lenau (which Strauss quotes on the score's title page). One of the unusual elements of Lenau's portrayal is that it is Don Juan himself—the seducer rather than the seduced—who suffers most from his ultimately fruitless quest.

Strauss wisely does not overplay that card. The most his 1888 tone poem suggests is that things end uncertainly for Don Juan; he is unfulfilled, but perhaps not yet disillusioned. The elements

Hero–to–be: Richard Strauss at the time he composed Don Juan.

The Oboe

Defined as "a treble woodwind instrument with a double reed and conical bore," the oboe is better known to musicians as "the ill wind that nobody blows good." The instrument's name comes from the French hautbois, meaning "high wood"—but high in the sense of "loud" rather than high-pitched. There are theories about what happens to those who play it: insanity, baldness, etc. Still, real oboists wouldn't think of playing anything else.

of longing and heroic pursuit are much more significant to Strauss. As in so many of his "heroic" scores, the opening motif is an ascending one—symbolic, many a university professor has noted, of the male libido. In this opening rush, it is not difficult to detect the seeds of similar figures that will begin *Ein Heldenleben, Der Rosenkavalier,* and the *Symphonia Domestica.* The orchestral writing in *Don Juan* is astoundingly brilliant and complex for a 24-year-old composer—strings, winds, and especially the brass are required to play passages virtuosic enough to belong in concertos—and the control of form is remarkably sure. A lyrical reprieve is provided by one of the most extraordinary oboe solos in the symphonic literature, before a reprise of the heroic opening material gives way to the ambivalent ending.

TILL EULENSPIEGEL, OP. 28

"**C**omposed for large orchestra after the old roguish manner—in rondeau form" is how Strauss describes his 1895 symphonic poem *Till Eulenspiegels lustige Streiche* (*Till Eulenspiegel's Merry Pranks*) on the title page of the score. The orchestra calls for triple winds, eight horns, and an unusually large battery that includes a ratchet. And the musical illustration is certainly roguish enough for the old days, or for any other time one might happen to choose.

Till Eulenspiegel (the last name means "Owl-glass," a type of mirror that distorts an image) is a character out of German folklore, supposedly a real-life practical joker and miscreant who died near Lübeck around 1350—in bed, not on the gallows as Strauss has it. Tales of his exploits began to enter the folk literature around 1500, and he came to symbolize the qualities of defiance and farcical lightness that are latent in the German temperament. His high-spirited pranks included riding through the marketplace and upsetting the

A surprised Till Eulenspiegel at the gallows.

stalls, dressing up as a priest, chasing after girls, and mocking the good townspeople, all of which Strauss characterizes here in the most vivid manner.

In the end, at least according to the composer, Till is caught and tried. The full orchestra, with the snare drum rolling ominously, indicts him. He at first answers cavalierly, then whimpers for mercy. His judges, the trombones, condemn him to death with the fierce proclamation of a descending seventh—taken from the scene in Mozart's *Don Giovanni* where Donna Anna and the other characters, having just captured Leporello, sing "*morrà!*" ("He dies!"). Unlike Leporello, who gets off, Till is hanged. But in a sweet epilogue, Strauss confirms that the rogue's spirit lives on, with an echo of his theme in the violins.

Whereas *Don Quixote* marks Strauss's apotheosis of the variation form, and *Ein Heldenleben* and *Don Juan* represent boldly stretched sonatas, *Till* is the ultimate rondeau, in which the hero's theme returns after each contrasting episode according to the scheme A-B-A-C-A-D-A-E. *Till Eulenspiegel* was completed in 1895 and premiered in Cologne that November, with Franz Wüllner conducting.

 RECOMMENDED RECORDING

Cleveland Orchestra/George Szell.

CBS MYK 36721 [Don Juan *and* Till Eulenspiegel, *with* Death and Transfiguration]

The listener enjoys a privileged moment sitting in on Szell and his Clevelanders at the peak of their game. Szell exhibits sovereign command of the music, and the recording is extraordinary for its late-1950s vintage, naturally balanced on this CD transfer. These are fired-up performances, full of tension, and distinguished by standout work from the winds and brass. The treatment is bracingly unsentimental, though Szell's hortatory grunts come right through in the background of the climaxes.

STANLEY KUBRICK *appropriated not only the opening of* Also sprach Zarathustra *for* 2001, *but also the music of Johann Strauss, memorably juxtaposing the* Blue Danube *Waltz with the leisurely wheeling of a space station in orbit. Kubrick's film also popularized the eerie sounds of Swedish composer Karl-Birger Blomdahl's "space opera"* Aniara, *written in 1957–58.*

The bourgeois gentleman: Strauss with wife and son.

ALSO SPRACH ZARATHUSTRA, OP. 30

The spirit of Liszt hovers over *Also sprach Zarathustra*, along with that of Friedrich Nietzsche, yet the music could only have been written by Strauss. Like his close contemporary Mahler and his predecessor Wagner, Strauss was fascinated with Nietzsche . . . for a while.

Zarathustra is Nietzsche's most powerful tract, though not his most important one. Strauss took it with a grain of salt, happy to receive the inspiration of Nietzsche's heady prose but smart enough to sidestep the more serious philosophical convolutions. His own note on the score's title page says that the music is only "freely based on Nietzsche." He is known to have said that he would have preferred, as a subtitle to his tone poem, the legend: "Symphonic optimism and *fin-de-siècle* form, dedicated to the Twentieth Century."

Although the opening pages of the score have now acquired a life of their own thanks to the Stanley Kubrick film *2001: A Space Odyssey*, they are but the prelude to one of Strauss's most profligate orchestral tapestries, full of large effects and clever tone-painting. Examples of the latter are Strauss's incorporation of a thunderous fugue in the section entitled "Of Science" (the fugue being music's most "learned" form), the use of an opulently scored Viennese waltz to evoke the "Dance Song," and the tolling of the midnight bell to introduce the "Song of the Night Wanderer" near the end of the piece.

Strauss saves one of the most striking effects for last. To suggest the enduring riddle of the cosmos, and the antithetical relationship between Zarathustra's enlightenment of Man and the continuing, mysterious presence of Nature in the background, Strauss juxtaposes the keys of C and B, leaving the end, and the resolution of all this Nietzschean philosophy, uncertain.

DON QUIXOTE, OP. 35

*S*trauss is supposed to have boasted once
that he could depict anything in music,
even a glass of beer. Fortunately, this penchant
for musical portraiture was balanced by a keen
sense of architecture, so that in the best of his
pieces, structure and imagery complement each
other so closely that one cannot imagine another
composer attempting the same subject. Strauss's
supreme achievement in this regard is the 1897
tone poem *Don Quixote*, based on the famous
romance by Miguel de Cervantes and subtitled
"Fantastic variations on a theme of knightly
character."

The key word here is "variations," for in *Don
Quixote*, Strauss subtly takes over an established
form and turns it to programmatic ends. Each of
the quixotic escapades in the score—from the
hero's tilting at windmills to his attacking a flock
of sheep in the belief that they are an enemy
army, and his final combat with the Knight of the
White Moon—is cast as a variation on Don Quixote's own theme. There are ten variations in all,
prefaced by an introduction and the theme itself
and followed by an epilogue-style finale. To further link structure and imagery, Strauss added a
bit of the *sinfonia concertante* to the scheme: a
major and a lesser solo part are created for the
cello and viola, the former instrument representing Don Quixote himself and the latter his squire,
Sancho Panza.

With these elements in place, Strauss was free
to lavish his attention on the sonic realization of
Cervantes's tale. Nowhere is his skill as an orchestrator more evident than when he depicts the
bleating sheep (Variation II) by having the muted
brass flutter-tongue a series of dissonant intervals.
Strauss is even able to conjure a vision with the
glory of a full orchestra and deny it with a single
note. He does this in his portrayal of Don Quixote's flight through the air (Variation VII), using

a host of atmospheric effects in the strings, whooshing figures in the winds, and even a wind machine. But does the Knight of the Sorrowful Countenance ever really leave the ground? The persistent low D in the basses tells the listener that this is only a flight of fancy.

Don Quixote is one of Strauss's surest scores, as well as one of his most touching, especially in the finale's portrayal of the Don's death. As the old man's sanity returns, the music grows hymnlike and calm; the solo cello, marked *molto espressivo* for the first time since Quixote's rapturous discourse on the meaning of chivalry (Variation III), soars one last time in an ecstatic embrace of the ideal, then gives up the ghost with an octave glissando to the low D.

EIN HELDENLEBEN, OP. 40

*T*he title is *A Hero's Life*—and the hero, but thinly disguised, is Strauss himself. By 1898, when he completed *Ein Heldenleben*, Strauss was only 34. Yet in the ten years he had been writing tone poems, he had become adept at characterizing the heroic temperament, whether in Don Juan, Superman, or Don Quixote.

Strauss devised an intriguing narrative framework for *Ein Heldenleben*, found an effective formal scheme to accommodate it, and put some of his most unabashedly heroic music into the effort. The score, although in a single continuous movement, falls into six distinct parts with descriptive titles. Underlying the sprawling pictorialism of the music is a masterfully erected sonata form, expansive in its dimensions and with a fantasy-like development. Strauss's portrayal of the Hero's struggles, triumphs, and reveries is bolstered by the harmonic action fundamental to the form.

The opening section is simply called "The Hero," and his theme—full of vitality, glowing with self-confidence—is proclaimed by strings and first

✓ *IF YOU LIKE THIS WORK, you might sample Strauss's last two symphonic poems,* Symphonia domestica *and* Eine Alpensinfonie (An Alpine Symphony). *In the former, the hero of* Ein Heldenleben *has fully embraced a bourgeois existence; the piece is a rollicking portrait of a day in the life of composer, wife, and child.* Eine Alpensinfonie *celebrates a day spent amid nature, complete with sheep bells and a wind machine.*

Strauss's profligate scoring inspired this caricature of him atop a gigantic orchestra.

horn, with punctuation from the rest of the horns, the bassoons, and the heavy brass. The key is E flat major, the heroic key since Beethoven's *Eroica*. This may have been Strauss's ideal view of himself, but the parodist does not let it stand for long.

In "The Hero's Adversaries," music critics are depicted by series of mawkish, strident, querulous solos in the winds and brass. Under the din, the name of the ponderous Doktor Dehring, one of Strauss's real-life nemeses, is repeatedly intoned by the tubas ("Dok-tor DEH-ring . . ."). Strauss adds insult to injury by having the tubas move in parallel fifths, a voice-leading error of the most elementary kind. The scene shifts to a portrayal of "The Hero's Companion," represented by the solo violin—a fitting choice, since in real life Strauss was married to the soprano Pauline de Ahna. For a while, the Hero seems a bit henpecked, so frequently does his own theme get interrupted by the violin. Love triumphs eventually, and the music grows passionate.

The idyll is broken off by the sound of offstage trumpets, a distant call to arms. The Hero and his adversaries clash mightily on "The Hero's Battlefield," which ultimately is littered with the corpses of the critics. The music of the opening returns as the Hero parades in victory, but it soon gives way to contemplation. Motives from a number of Strauss's previous compositions are interwoven in "The Hero's Works of Peace," in which the Hero revels not only in his past triumphs but in his ongoing, absolute mastery of the orchestra.

In "The Hero's Withdrawal from the World," Strauss allows the bourgeois side of himself, the *real* Richard Strauss, to have the final word. Life's battles have been fought and won, freeing the Hero to seek tranquility at home and inner peace. He and his companion, now cast in the role of friend and comforter, find harmony at last, a harmony that transcends the final, briefly flickering memory of heroism.

Performing Personalities

Famous for his small beat, sparing gestures, hawk-like gaze, and fiery temper, Fritz Reiner was a stern taskmaster but also a brilliantly gifted musician. His recordings with the Chicago Symphony (where he was music director from 1953–62) have almost acquired cult status. Yet Reiner's most important contribution to the CSO survives in the nucleus of principal players he engaged; if Reiner were to step up to the podium today he would still recognize his band.

RECOMMENDED RECORDINGS

Chicago Symphony Orchestra/Fritz Reiner.
RCA Living Stereo 61494-2 [Also sprach Zarathustra *and* Ein Heldenleben]

Berlin Philharmonic/Herbert von Karajan.
EMI CDC 49308 [Don Quixote]

Berlin Philharmonic/Herbert von Karajan.
Deutsche Grammophon Galleria 429 184-2
[Don Quixote, *with* Death and Transfiguration]

Ein Heldenleben can occasionally sound like 30 minutes of symphonic poetry interrupted by a 15-minute violin concerto; it requires an interpreter with grip and a long view of the score to hold the piece together. Reiner does just this in his 1954 account. It is a formidable reading—massive, yet with an Old World expressiveness in the strings and gloriously transparent textures. The richness of sound in RCA's remastering is staggering for a document nearly 40 years old. Reiner's interpretation of *Also sprach Zarathustra*, recorded at the same time, is equally impressive.

In 1975, cellist Mstislav Rostropovich and Karajan recorded for EMI what is still the consummate *Don Quixote*. Rostropovich's command of the solo part is overwhelming, but even more impressive is the imagination he brings, particularly his identification with the poignant, crazed side of the Don. The Berliners give a richly characterized reading and produce a rainbow of orchestral color, though the sound lacks visceral impact.

Rostropovich himself often hailed Pierre Fournier as the greatest cellist of his day, and on the Berlin/Karajan disc from Deutsche Grammophon, Fournier portrays a more delicate, soulful, and capricious Don than Rostropovich would a decade later. This Don is a gentleman of the old school and a true Romantic—and the dreaminess of Fournier's conception is echoed in a reading that sounds impressively fresh. The coupling here is the gripping *Death and Transfiguration* from 1972, which makes this budget-price CD an out-and-out winner.

IGOR STRAVINSKY

THE FIREBIRD

Czarevich and Firebird, in George Balanchine's Firebird.

*B*ut for the impatience of the impresario Sergei Diaghilev, the brilliant first ballet of Stravinsky (1882–1971) might never have been written. Diaghilev first commissioned Anatoly Liadov to compose the score for his Ballets Russes, but when the older composer took too long on the project, Diaghilev turned to the all-but-unknown Stravinsky, still in his twenties and fresh from studies with Rimsky-Korsakov.

Stravinsky rose to the challenge, creating a ballet score that, while padded and discursive in some sections, contained effects of such incandescence and power that it set the musical establishment of 1910 on its ear. The scenario, by Mikhail Fokine, offered some spectacular opportunities for pictorialism, of which the young composer took full advantage: Ivan, the Czarevich, captures the Firebird but spares its life in return for one of its magic plumes, which will summon the creature if the Czarevich is ever in jeopardy. In the enchanted palace of the monster Katschei, 13 princesses are being held captive; Ivan himself is captured, and he summons the Firebird, which casts a spell over the guards. The Firebird then guides Ivan to a treasure chest where the egg containing Katschei's soul is hidden; the egg is smashed, Katschei's sorcery evaporates, and Ivan and the 13 princesses rejoice.

Stravinsky shows complete mastery of the exotic orchestral colorism Rimsky-Korsakov had used in works like *The Golden Cockerel*, and he carries even further the practice of characterizing the supernatural world by means of chromaticism and the

Stravinsky by Picasso.

human protagonists by diatonic harmonies. He also makes use of Russian folk music, the most prominent example being the main subject of the final tableau.

In scoring *The Firebird*, Stravinsky drew on the resources of a gigantic orchestra, including triple winds—with additional parts for two piccolos, English horn, clarinet in D, bass clarinet, and two contrabassoons—as well as full brass and string sections, three harps, and an enormous array of percussion. Yet these forces are used with economy and specificity. For instance, to set the introduction's mood of dark enchantment, Stravinsky begins with a stalking subject in the lowest range of the double basses, cellos, and violas, intoned *pianissimo* over a bass drum roll. But the score instructs two unmuted basses to double the subject pizzicato, creating a sepulchral thump on each note.

The Firebird debuted at the Paris Opéra on June 25, 1910, and was the hit of the season for the Ballets Russes. Stravinsky extracted a suite from the ballet in 1911, which he subsequently revised twice. All three versions of the suite are recorded, but the 1919 version, which reduces the size of the orchestra, is preferred for its balance and concision. The most satisfying listening experience comes with the full ballet.

PETRUSHKA

*H*aving discovered Stravinsky and given him his first break, Sergei Diaghilev, like a good Hollywood producer, wasted no time in putting together a sequel to *The Firebird*. The new creation, *Petrushka*, emerged in 1911, a ballet in four scenes set during Mardi Gras in St. Petersburg of the 1830s. The plot revolves around a fatal *ménage à trois*, with a wrinkle: the three principal characters—Petrushka, a Ballerina, and a Moor—are puppets.

Petrushka's *ménage à trois*.

Petrushka had its origins in a concert piece for piano and orchestra that Stravinsky sketched after being inspired by the image of a puppet "suddenly endowed with life, exasperating the patience of the orchestra with diabolical cascades of arpeggios. The orchestra in turn retaliates with menacing trumpet blasts. The outcome is a terrific noise which reaches its climax and ends in the sorrowful and querulous collapse of the poor puppet." Stravinsky played his sketches for Diaghilev in the summer of 1910. The impresario saw the theatrical potential and persuaded Stravinsky to transform the piece into a ballet.

The musical language of *Petrushka*, compared with that of *The Firebird*, is audaciously iconoclastic. The score does indeed make a terrific noise, partly because the strings are dominated by winds, brass, and percussion, producing a harder, edgier sonority. Even more important is the composer's revolutionary treatment of rhythm and harmony. The frequent shifting and mixing of meter, as well as the use of asymmetrical phrases and disruptive syncopations, goes far beyond anything previously attempted in orchestral music. Already on the fifth page of the score, where the hustle and bustle of the Shrovetide fair are marvelously evoked, two bars of superimposed 3/4 and 7/8 are followed by two bars of 2/4 and 5/8 and one of 3/4 and 8/8. While all seems to be clash and clatter on the surface, the complexity of rhythm produces extraordinary animation and an irresistible drive.

The result is that for the first time in modern Western music, rhythm rather than harmony becomes the primary force in the development of a line of action, freeing harmony to be used in new ways. And Stravinsky's new methods are startling, particularly so in his superimposition of chords of different keys at several points in the score, an effect known as polytonality. While this effect had been anticipated by Mussorgsky and Rimsky-Korsakov, it was Stravinsky who gave it currency and brought it into the vocabulary of 20th-century

THE PREMIERE
of Petrushka *took place
in the Théâtre du Châtelet
on the night of June 13,
1911, with Pierre Monteux
conducting. Tamara Karsa-
vina was the Ballerina, and
Vaslav Nijinsky (above) the
Petrushka.*

music. He later wrote that he had devised the juxtaposition of triads in C major and F sharp major that permeates the score as a means of representing Petrushka's insults to the audience at the Shrovetide fair. The sound is so distinctive it has been called the "Petrushka chord."

In keeping with his maxim that "a good composer steals," Stravinsky appropriates melodies from Russian folk songs, and the French tune *"Elle avait un' jambe en bois,"* and makes them his own. But in the third tableau, the transformation of tunes from Joseph Lanner's *Die Schönbrunner Waltz* and *Steyrische Tänze* into a waltz for the Ballerina and the awkward Moor is conscious parody. Here, Stravinsky hits upon a process that will mark his idiom for the rest of his life.

THE RITE OF SPRING

*T*hat *The Rite of Spring* sparked the most famous riot in music history when it was premiered at the Théâtre des Champs-Elysées on May 29, 1913, has long been the stuff of performing-arts lore. But it says something for the Parisian listeners that they knew when to be shocked, for the ballet was calculated to do just that. Never before had a symphonic work so completely violated the conventional notion that meaning resided in an orderly interrelationship between melody, harmony, and form. Never before had subsidiary elements of expression—most notably texture, dynamics, and rhythm—been brought so boldly to the fore. What could be felt intuitively in 1913 has become clear in retrospect: more than any work before it, *The Rite of Spring* challenges the concept that music has its basis either in rational thought or in the higher emotions. For as complex as it is from a technical standpoint, *The Rite of Spring* comes across as a visceral experience of the most elemental kind.

Subtitled "Pictures from Pagan Russia," the ballet was composed to a two-part scenario drawn up during the summer of 1910 by the Russian painter and archaeologist Nicolas Roerich, to whom the score is dedicated. Where *The Firebird* and *Petrushka* had emerged from fairly specific narrative frameworks, *The Rite of Spring* grew out of an essentially scenic one, with a great deal of action centering around primitive springtime fertility rites (the focus of the ballet's first part, "Adoration of the Earth") and human sacrifice (a concession to sensationalism with no basis in anthropological fact, but nonetheless the culmination of the ballet's second part, "The Sacrifice"). Folklore was one of the hottest fashions in pre-World War I art, particularly in Russia, but while others were interested in it primarily for decorative purposes, Stravinsky tapped into the very essence of the primitive in *The Rite of Spring*. Much of the melodic material is derived from folk song (at least nine specific songs), and the mysticism and animalistic vitality of the score seem to have been dredged directly from the barbaric past.

Stravinsky anticipated a good deal of the *Rite* in *Petrushka*, especially its preoccupation with rhythm as both a structural and an expressive device. Indeed, rather than marking a total break with his past, as has often been claimed (even by the composer), the score represents a continuation of Stravinsky's development, although here the accumulation of dissonance reaches an all-time high, and metric complexity is pushed almost as far as it can go.

For example, in the 17 measures on the very first page of the score, there are nine changes of meter. And in the explosive final section of the piece, the "Sacrificial Dance," there is a passage where the meter changes every measure for 15 measures in a row. Here, the listener is forced to abandon himself to the physical rush of the music—an experience that reaches down to the most primitive levels of perception. Elsewhere, as in the introduction to the second part of the score (where the stage is set for the ritual of the sacri-

Stravinsky, master of modernism, constructed his scores at the piano.

Stravinsky discusses interpretation at a 1962 recording session.

fice), constant metrical changes, syncopation, asymmetrical phrase groupings, and nebulous harmonies reminiscent of Debussy's *Nuages* erase the sense of pulse altogether, creating a mood of portent and mystery. In every case, the effect is precisely tailored to the aims of the scenario.

The orchestra employed in *The Rite of Spring* is huge, generating moments of unprecedented loudness. Stravinsky also calls for many instruments to play at the extremes of their range, producing the strangeness of sound that is one of the score's hallmarks. The opening bassoon solo—which begins on a high C, includes several high D's, and stays entirely above middle C—is a notable example, and the first of many surprises contained in the score, some subtle, some truly shocking.

 RECOMMENDED RECORDINGS

Royal Concertgebouw Orchestra/ Sir Colin Davis.
Philips 400 074-2 [The Firebird *(complete)*] and *416 498-2* [Petrushka *and* The Rite of Spring]

Montreal Symphony Orchestra/ Charles Dutoit.
London 414 409-2 [The Firebird *(complete), with* Scherzo fantastique *and* Fireworks]

New York Philharmonic, Cleveland Orchestra/Pierre Boulez.
CBS Masterworks MK 42395 [Petrushka *and* The Rite of Spring]

Davis gets the mystery of the opening pages of *The Firebird* exactly right. He gives the score time to unfold, drawing superlative playing from the Dutch orchestra. The interpretation is gentle and expressive, but momentum never flags, and there is energy aplenty in the score's flashier scenes. Philips's 1978 recording is warm and nicely atmospheric. On another disc, recorded in 1976–77, Davis brings the same beautiful pacing to *Petrushka*. The account has jewel-like clarity and watch-like precision; this is chamber music on the grandest scale. The recording imparts a natural concert-hall perspective to the piece, yielding excellent ambience but plenty of detail. With *The Rite of Spring*, which gets so much of its effect from the savagery of rhythm and the loudness of climaxes, it is difficult to evoke chaos without succumbing to it. But in Davis's account, the piece is played as music, not noise. Again and again, new details in harmony, texture, and voicing emerge; rhythm is not the only important element. The recording, closely miked for clarity, retains a firm bass and lots of impact.

Dutoit's 1984 recording of *The Firebird* is a marvel of atmospheric impressionism: shimmering, seductive, beautifully played by the Montreal Symphony. The sound is spacious and detailed, and the couplings are ideal.

With the New York Philharmonic on its best behavior, Boulez uncorks a *Petrushka* that is vibrant and full-voiced, with razor-sharp rhythm and ensemble, and with solos illuminatingly played by the likes of flutist Julius Baker and pianist Paul Jacobs. The sizzling sonics are typical of CBS's late-1960s multi-track heyday, offering a closeup of the score in this excellent remastering. Boulez's interpretation of *The Rite of Spring* emphasizes structure, clarity, and texture over raw energy and visceral excitement, but is potent nonetheless in the "Glorification of the Chosen One" and the "Sacrificial Dance." Boulez and the Cleveland Orchestra established here a new standard for ensemble virtuosity and idiomatic execution of the music (a standard they themselves fail to meet in their remake for Deutsche Grammophon), and this *Rite* remains one of the great achievements of the stereo era. The sound is rather dry, as one would expect from Severance Hall, and it lacks the impact a digital recording might have provided.

As big as you can make it . . . Pierre Boulez calls for more.

PIOTR ILYICH TCHAIKOVSKY

*I*t is still fashionable for critics to dismiss Tchaikovsky as one of two things: a superficial manipulator or a self-absorbed borderline hysteric wallowing in his own emotions. He was neither.

Tchaikovsky's preternaturally sensitive nature and his talent for self-expression were apparent early on. As he grew older, his music became increasingly emotional, but it rarely raged out of control. For Tchaikovsky was more than an artist with intense and often painful feelings to bare. He was also the most professional Russian composer of his day—conservatory trained, literate, astutely critical of both his own work and that of others, and highly disciplined. He kept a rigorous daily schedule that enabled him to sketch and score his works quickly, though he resisted the temptation to rush them to completion, polishing and revising those that did not initially satisfy him (in the case of Symphonies Nos. 1 and 2 and the fantasy overture *Romeo and Juliet,* several times).

Tchaikovsky created a sizeable body of songs and chamber compositions, many of them quite lovely. But it was in the larger forms that he excelled. Here his output was evenly balanced between dramatic works—operas and ballets—and symphonic ones, the common denominator being the orchestra. Unlike many of his colleagues, who practiced orchestration as if it were a sartorial exercise, Tchaikovsky thought directly in terms of orchestral color. And though his resourcefulness with individual instruments was unsurpassed, for him it was the full orchestra that had a sound—which is why all of his orchestral scores have a lustrous sonority that can be immediately identified.

Among the most beautifully scored of his works are the three

1 8 4 0 – 1 8 9 3

ballets, *Swan Lake*, *The Sleeping Beauty*, and *The Nutcracker*. Tchaikovsky was able to evoke a specific atmosphere in each and draw listeners into an enchanted world. But while the stories are fanciful, the emotions in the music are profoundly human. And in seeking to transform the music of the ballet from a grand decorative gesture into an essential component of the drama on stage, Tchaikovsky revolutionized the art of composing for the dance.

As a symphonist, Tchaikovsky enriched the repertory and exerted a vital influence on composers as diverse as Sibelius, Prokofiev, and Shostakovich. Yet it was not until he set to work on his Fourth Symphony that Tchaikovsky discovered—in the expression of heated emotion—the key to both melodic inspiration and mastery of form. Had it not been for momentous changes in his personal life at the time he was writing the Fourth, Tchaikovsky might well have developed into a different composer, one less trusting of his talent and less inclined to deal with his feelings in an overtly confessional manner. But fate, that mysterious force whose nature he would seek to elucidate in several of his works, intervened directly in Tchaikovsky's life.

First, in the winter of 1876–77, had come the unforeseen appearance of a benefactress, the elusive Nadezhda von Meck, who was to provide much-needed financial and emotional support—and an outlet for Tchaikovsky's communicative urge. Then, in the spring of 1877, he proposed marriage to a young woman he barely knew, Antonina Milyukova, despite the facts that he was homosexual and she emotionally unstable. He hoped the union might bring at least a semblance of stability into his life. Instead, the short-lived marriage was disastrous and Tchaikovsky tried to kill himself.

Inevitably, Tchaikovsky's music became the chief outlet for the strong emotions that could not be expressed physically. Listeners recognize that the sentiment arises from a profound awareness of vulnerability and loss. Significantly, in his most emotional music—in scores like *Romeo and Juliet*, the Fourth Symphony, and the *Pathétique*—Tchaikovsky also shows his greatest originality in structure. Like Mozart, whose music he admired, Tchaikovsky was responsive to the challenge of characterization in both stage and symphonic music. He tried to get inside the characters of his operas and to create worlds of feeling in his symphonies. In the act of composition, Tchaikovsky found the freedom to emote, and the means to control it, that he sorely missed in his personal life.

Fatal infatuation.

ROMEO AND JULIET

*I*n 1869, the composer Mily Balakirev suggested to Tchaikovsky the idea of writing a work based on Shakespeare's *Romeo and Juliet*. When the project stalled, Balakirev sent to Tchaikovsky a proposed outline of the score's harmonic organization, even writing out four opening bars of his own. Tchaikovsky finished the fantasy overture six weeks later. But Balakirev had some criticisms, and after the March 1870 debut of the work, Tchaikovsky realized that the comments were on the mark and thoroughly rewrote the work. Ten years later, still dissatisfied with the piece's ending, he revised *Romeo and Juliet* again. It is this third version that usually is performed.

Romeo and Juliet was Tchaikovsky's first masterpiece. In its tightly wound argument and insightful handling of the story, it reveals the balance between symphonic logic and expressive power that would mark Tchaikovsky's finest efforts and set him apart from his Russian contemporaries. The slow introduction is rich in thematic material, and the characterization is sharply drawn: the somber chorale in modal F sharp, its phrasing reminiscent of plainchant, does double duty by establishing the tragic atmosphere of the story while evoking the religious presence behind the scene, that of the long-suffering Friar Laurence. Other motives suggest the enmity and passion that will draw the star-cross'd lovers to their doom. There is a buildup to the main Allegro, culminating in a repeated B minor chord that grows more intense with each reiteration. The martial theme depicting the strife of the Montagues and Capulets erupts in full fury, to be followed, inevitably, by the music representing Romeo and Juliet in the intentionally remote key of D flat major.

The idea of putting the young couple in a world of their own, harmonically distant from the warring families, had been Balakirev's, but Tchaikovsky does his would-be mentor one better by forging a link between the strife theme and that of the two lovers, allowing the fatal nature of the relationship to be felt on a subliminal level from the start. Tchaikovsky's development of the material is assured, and he builds the overture to a climax made devastatingly effective in the revision of 1880: after the music of the feud overwhelms that of Romeo and Juliet, a pained echo of the love theme, now wrenchingly recast in B minor, issues from the strings. The tragic feeling foreshadows the end of the *Pathétique* Symphony, also in B minor, though Tchaikovsky does not allow his lovers a quiet end. Instead, he summons a series of tumultuous *fortissimo* chords and closes the overture with a reminiscence of the pitiless violence that had driven Romeo and Juliet to their deaths.

 RECOMMENDED RECORDING

Royal Philharmonic Orchestra/ Vladimir Ashkenazy.

London 421 715-2 [*with* Italian Capriccio, Francesca da Rimini, *and* Elegy]

Ashkenazy's 1987–88 interpretations are solid and superbly recorded. There is suavity in the playing, rather than all-out intensity, and polish in the conducting, rather than passion. The performers are a little slow getting off the mark in *Romeo and Juliet*, but the piece is well played. The vivid imagery and Rachmaninoff-like orchestration of *Francesca da Rimini* bring out Ashkenazy's Russianness in a way the more lucidly argued *Romeo and Juliet* does not. In *Francesca*, the Royal Philharmonic shows itself for what it is: a youthful orchestra of great ability, enjoying the ride up.

Tchaikovsky's home in Klin, 50 miles from Moscow.

SYMPHONY NO. 4, IN F MINOR, OP. 36

*T*he powerful currents that run through the Fourth Symphony, especially its first movement, make it not only one of the great works of Romanticism but the first truly great symphony by a Russian composer. In a letter to his patroness Nadezhda von Meck, written after completion of the score in 1878, Tchaikovsky confided the supposedly secret program: the subject was Fate, "that tragic power which prevents the yearning for happiness from reaching its goal." The symphony's motto theme—the implacable fanfare in the horns with which the work so arrestingly opens, and which returns at several important junctures—is indeed a musical embodiment of this concept of Fate.

With that in mind, one can see the first movement as a psychological drama of escape, of reveries cut short and hope crushed by the weight of destiny, borne out musically by the use of a progressive key scheme that creates mounting harmonic tension. Specifically, the movement seems a succession of attempts to try to move away from the oppressive F minor of the Fate motto. There is momentary escape in a delicate waltz in B major—a key as far removed from F as you can get. The waltz reappears in F major, only to be crushed by the return of F minor, and any hope of transcendence is dashed.

The second movement begins with an oboe solo consisting of 80 consecutive eighth notes, extended by the cellos for another 83—the longest rhythmically undifferentiated subject in any symphony. The bleakness is meant, said Tchaikovsky, to portray loneliness and nostalgia. Once again, escape is momentarily achieved in a climax of emotional ardor and balletic opulence before the dream vanishes and the plaintive solo returns. The third movement, a scherzo played pizzicato, is just "elusive figures that flit past the imagination when one has drunk a little wine and feels

TCHAIKOVSKY'S bene-factor, Mme. von Meck (above), expressed the wish to never meet the composer. Yet during the 14 years of their curious, arm's-length relationship he frequently found himself in close proximity to her. This could be exasperating for the composer; in 1878, during a joint but separate sojourn in Florence, he noted that she stopped in front of his villa every morning. "How should I behave?" he wrote his brother Anatoly. "Should I go to the window and bow?"

Tchaikovsky in 1863.

exuberant," the composer noted. In a good performance, the drunkenness can be delightful, if the insouciant little wind solos that open the trio are adequately characterized, along with their reeling chromatic accompaniments.

In the symphony's finale, Tchaikovsky makes use of the Russian folk song "In the Fields, There Stood a Birch" and, as his second subject, a giddily trimphant march tune. The writing is virtuosic in the extreme, and the contest between F major, now the home key, and the F minor of Fate continues to the very end. The composer had suggested that one could discern in the movement's tumult a scene of popular merrymaking, but the joyful end is not easily won. The Fate motto returns again; its reappearance unifies the symphony but also gives Tchaikovsky the opportunity to exorcise his demon. This time, joy, in the form of the triumphant march tune, at last overcomes despair.

SYMPHONY NO. 6, IN B MINOR, OP. 74
Pathétique

*I*n his biography of Tchaikovsky, the English musicologist David Brown characterizes the *Pathétique* as "the most truly original symphony to have been composed in the 70 years since Beethoven's Ninth." That is an accurate assessment, though it may not go far enough. For the *Pathétique* is also, in emotional terms, the contrapositive of Beethoven's Ninth. As the first truly tragic symphony, concerned with loss, isolation, and despair, it projects a negative image of Beethoven's triumphant aspiration; in place of spiritual transcendence, it seeks annihilation. From the standpoint of aesthetics, this represents a fundamental turning point in the history of the symphony. Psychologically, the *Pathétique* marks the beginning of modernism.

The title was suggested to Tchaikovsky by his

eg. Tschaikovsky.

TCHAIKOVSKY'S
last symphony was com-
posed between February 16
and April 5, 1893, and
scored in August of that
year. The premiere took place
in St. Petersburg on October
28, 1893, with Tchaikovsky
conducting. Nine days later,
he was dead.

brother Modest after the score's completion in 1893—and it is indeed fitting if one considers that the primary meaning of "pathetic" in Russian, as in Greek, corresponds to the word's secondary meaning in English, usually rendered as "affecting or moving the feelings." This symphony, especially in its outer movements, assuredly does that. It also embodies some remarkable formal innovations, most notably the choice of an Adagio as the concluding movement and the radical transformation of sonata structure in the first movement.

In both its material and structure, this first movement is a departure from the rhetorical succession of ideas characteristic of Classicism and Romanticism. There is an extreme contrast between the exposition's first subject, a skittish utterance in the violas and cellos that conveys agitation and dread, and its second subject, a keenly poignant melody in the strings scored over three octaves—but what is especially unusual is the almost dreamlike way in which the latter evolves out of the former. The transition is seamless, yet there is a complete disconnection between the ideas themselves.

The convulsive beginning of the first movement's development section still comes as one of the great shocks in symphonic music, exploding out of the extraordinary *pppppp* dynamic of the exposition's final moments. The violence of this nightmarish episode, along with its breathlessly fast tempo, make it, too, seem to be disconnected from what has come before, even though it is based on the exposition's first subject. Acknowledging that behind these pages are thoughts of death, Tchaikovsky has the trombones quote a phrase of the chant "With thy saints, O Christ, give peace to the soul of thy servant," drawn from the Russian Orthodox Requiem. The recapitulation is also unconventional; far from restoring the mood and material of the exposition, it extends the development and intensifies its drama in a searing climax set over an ominous timpani roll. All energy spent, the first movement ends with a quiet coda that again seems eerily removed from the reality of what has just happened.

One encounters a surreal detachment in the second movement, a waltz subtly disfigured by its 5/4 meter, and in the ensuing scherzo as well, a movement that, with its fleeting images and manic energy, amounts to a march gone over the edge. The illusory lightness of these interludes makes the weight of desolation in the symphony's finale all the more oppressive. Marked *adagio lamentoso*, this crushing valedictory opens with Tchaikovsky's favorite motive, a descending scale figure representing Fate. The finale's second subject, a hymnlike lament in D major that at first offers hope of consolation, builds to an impassioned climax that is soon stifled. Instead of a development, the first subject returns out of the fragments of the lament. Anguish mounts in a feverish second climax, there is a solemn cadence, and Fate's final blow is delivered by a single, chillingly soft stroke on the tam-tam. The second subject—now in the minor and nothing but an echo—sinks lower and lower, offering no escape but into oblivion.

This finale, as simple as its message, and the symphony's first movement, virtually a new species, reflect Tchaikovsky's absolute control of the musical process and were to have a profound effect on the likes of Sibelius, Mahler, and Shostakovich. Just as important, the *Pathétique*'s unflinching truthfulness of expression, including its rejection of spiritual transcendence, changed forever the metaphysical framework of the symphony.

TCHAIKOVSKY'S death *was not caused by cholera, but by poisoning. The catalyst was a letter written by Duke Stenbok-Fermor to the Czar, complaining about the attention Tchaikovsky was paying to his nephew. The letter was entrusted to Nikolai Jacobi, one of Tchaikovsky's classmates. Knowing its contents would disgrace Tchaikovsky and the school, Jacobi convened a tribunal of classmates and friends, before which Tchaikovsky was brought. They ruled that Tchaikovsky should kill himself.*

 RECOMMENDED RECORDINGS

Leningrad Philharmonic/Evgeny Mravinsky.
Deutsche Grammophon 419 745-2 [2 CDs; Symphonies Nos. 4 and 6, with No. 5]

Berlin Philharmonic/Herbert von Karajan.
Deutsche Grammophon 429 675-2 [4 CDs; Symphonies Nos. 1–6]

The recordings by Mravinsky and his Leningrad Philharmonic, taped in the autumn of 1960 in London while on tour, are among the absolute classics of the catalog. They are readings of hair-raising intensity; no one else has had the nerve, or ability, to play the music this way. The treatment is *very* Russian: the passions more feverish, the melancholy darker, the climaxes louder. It has been said that the string musicians played as if their lives depended on it—and given the nature of those days and that Soviet regime, it was probably true. Equally distinctive are the wind and brass timbres; those who heard the Leningrad Philharmonic in performance under Mravinsky say that no other ensemble sounded remotely like it in *pianissimo* or *fortissimo*. These accounts leap out of the speakers as if they were being played in the here and now. The sonics are remarkably good for the time, though a little edgy in the loudest pages.

The mid-1970s accounts from Karajan and the Berlin Philharmonic are red-hot. There is grip in these interpretations, creating a feeling of undertow. The Fourth has both menace and suavity; Karajan exhibits masterful control of pacing, and the climaxes are superbly judged. The *Pathétique* was always a Karajan specialty; on balance, this is his best recording of it. The sound for the Fourth and Sixth Symphonies is closeup, a little hard in the treble and soft in the bass, but with good ambience. The well-done remastering preserves a wide dynamic range with excellent clarity.

Tchaikovsky's most famous work, the 1812 Overture, *was composed to consecrate this Moscow church.*

IN THE NUTCRACKER *Tchaikovsky was determined to prove that as a colorist he was capable of outdoing even Rimsky-Korsakov. Having come across the celesta in Paris, he immediately wrote to his publisher about its "divinely wonderful" sound, asking that one be bought and sent to St. Petersburg. Tchaikovsky warned that the instrument should be kept under wraps, lest Rimsky find out about it and "use it for unusual effects before I can."*

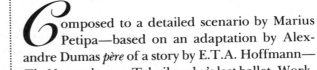

THE NUTCRACKER SUITE, OP. 71A

Composed to a detailed scenario by Marius Petipa—based on an adaptation by Alexandre Dumas *père* of a story by E.T.A. Hoffmann—*The Nutcracker* was Tchaikovsky's last ballet. Working with a trite story in which there is no real human drama, and following some almost measure-by-measure instructions from Petipa, Tchaikovsky was freed from having to worry about content, which allowed him to indulge his gift for memorable melody and ignited his imagination as an orchestrator. While the feeling of the ballet can at times seem rather shallow—a child's Christmastime vision of the Kingdom of Sweets—the skill with which Tchaikovsky dresses up individual numbers in the most evocative orchestral colors still delights the ear.

Even where his melody is not extraordinary, Tchaikovsky's treatment is. The main motive of the Act II pas de deux is nothing but a simple descending scale, yet the way it is harmonized and phrased, and clothed in the warmest of string colors, endows it with powerful sentiment. Tchaikovsky's orchestration transcends the material in the overture as well; scored without cellos and basses, and with violins and violas divided into six parts, it conjures up the sound of a Classical orchestra with just a triangle and a piccolo added. A silvery, child-like, "play" overture, small in scale but full of glittering tinsel, it is just the thing for Christmas eve.

The Nutcracker is typical of Tchaikovsky's later music in its delicate use of the strings, which provide shimmering backdrops to many of the scenes. But it shows a literalism unusual for the composer, especially in the children's voices in the "Waltz of the Snowflakes" and the children's instruments for several other numbers in Act I. The writing for standard instruments is marvelously inventive, particularly in the Act II divertissement, where chocolate is represented by a Spanish Dance, coffee by an Arabian Dance, and tea by a Chinese Dance. But the most wonderful touch of all is the solo celesta in the "Dance of the Sugar-Plum Fairy," which so charmingly suggests the drops of water "spurting from fountains" called for in the scenario.

Nine months prior to the ballet's debut, Tchaikovsky extracted a suite from the score, which he premiered in St. Petersburg on March 19, 1892. It is in this form that the most characterful numbers of *The Nutcracker* have attained universal popularity. The suite begins with the overture to the ballet, followed by the march from Act I and the "Dance of the Sugar-Plum Fairy" from the Act II pas de deux. Next are four numbers from the Act II divertissement: the Russian Dance, the Arabian Dance, the Chinese Dance, and the Dance of the Mirlitons. The suite concludes with the "Waltz of the Flowers" from Act II, one of the best known of Tchaikovsky's waltzes.

 RECOMMENDED RECORDING

Berlin Philharmonic/Mstislav Rostropovich.
Deutsche Grammophon Galleria 429 097-2
[The Nutcracker *Suite, with Suites from* Swan Lake *and* The Sleeping Beauty]

Russian to the core: Rostropovich on the podium.

Around the time he recorded the three ballet suites in 1978, Rostropovich likened conducting the Berlin Philharmonic to driving a locomotive. You get on, and you go where it takes you, he said—but in this case, the orchestra went where *he* wanted. The playing is magnificent, but what makes these accounts so memorable is the characterization, the things Rostropovich gets the players to do that they wouldn't otherwise do. In the *Nutcracker*, for example, the liberties they take with phrasing and expression are telling: the way the bass clarinet stretches its roulades in the "Dance of the Sugar-Plum Fairy," or the way the flutes seem to hang in midair in the "Dance of the Mirlitons." The analog recording captures it all in outstanding fashion.

RALPH VAUGHAN WILLIAMS

A LONDON SYMPHONY

Piccadilly Circus at the time of A London Symphony.

*E*ngland's Vaughan Williams (1872–1958) was 40 when he began work on *A London Symphony*—no youngster, to be sure, but still at the beginning of a real career as a symphonist. For the notorious slow starter who in 1908 had taken lessons with Ravel (three years younger than he), this second symphony marked a turning point. It confirmed his greatness as an orchestral composer and revealed for the first time his remarkable gift for investing deeply personal, even visionary expression in conventional forms.

But while the four-movement layout is conventional, the treatment is highly innovative, particularly in the addition of an epilogue that echoes the mood and substance of the introduction. There is an especially nice touch as Vaughan Williams, using the harp, quotes the half-hour chime of Big Ben in the introduction, then the third quarter-hour in the epilogue, suggesting that the intervening 45 minutes of music have filled only 15 minutes of real time.

There is no actual written program to *A London Symphony*; it is purely impressionistic, seeking to convey something of the spirit of a great city. A motive in the first movement does go to the same rhythm as the word "Piccadilly"—proclaimed *fortissimo* in B flat major by the brass and winds, *"Pic-ca-dilly!"* The main body of the movement certainly suggests the hustle and bustle of Piccadilly Circus. The composer himself said that the melancholy second movement was intended to portray Bloomsbury Square on a November day, with all the somber grayness one would expect.

In the end, *A London Symphony* stands out for

its own musical strength, rather than for the associations it evokes. Though large in scale, it is wonderfully coherent, and its striking ideas are surely and energetically developed. Yet it remains a tribute to a place, as nobly emotive as Wordsworth's sonnet *Composed Upon Westminster Bridge.* "Earth has not anything to show more fair . . ." than London. Indeed.

 RECOMMENDED RECORDINGS

London Philharmonic Orchestra/ Bernard Haitink.
EMI CDC 49394 [*with* Fantasia on a Theme by Thomas Tallis]

London Philharmonic Orchestra/ Sir Adrian Boult.
EMI CDC 47213 [*with* Fantasia on a Theme by Thomas Tallis]

Haitink's 1986 reading of *A London Symphony* is thrilling in its play of color, and bracing—like the city itself—in its sudden, unexpected turnings. No stranger to London, Haitink insightfully evokes the pre-dawn stillness of the opening pages and the melancholy poetry of the second movement. Perhaps most remarkable is how successfully he conveys the symphony's modernity; much of the finale, in its intensity and sharply chiseled gestures, sounds surprisingly like Shostakovich. The London Philharmonic backs the Dutch conductor handsomely, and EMI's engineers get excellent sound from their familiar Abbey Road studio.

Boult's interpretation with the same orchestra, from the early 1970s, is lively and lyrical, a brisk view of London. If the approach is more fanciful and rhapsodic than that of Haitink there is no shortage of power in the big moments of the two outer movements. The orchestra plays with idiomatic fluency, and the recording is open and finely detailed.

Boult wielded his long baton with martial swagger.

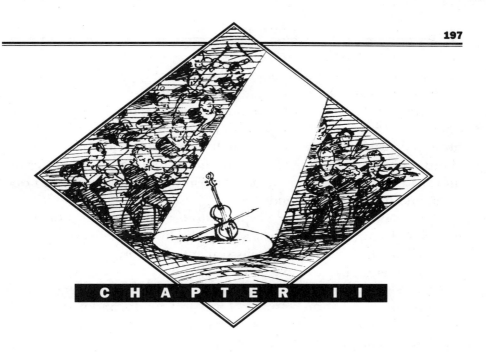

C H A P T E R   I I

CONCERTOS

*T*hough a child of the Baroque, the solo concerto did not come of age until the last decades of the 18th century, largely through the efforts of Mozart. As both an outstanding violinist and the preeminent pianist of his day, Mozart was able to shape the concerto to his own very exacting standards of musicianship. In his hands—and in the works of such contemporaries as Joseph and Michael Haydn, Giovanni Battista Viotti, Jan Ladislav Dussek, and Ignaz Pleyel—it became the form we know today, usually consisting of three movements (in a fast-slow-fast sequence) and combining serious content with virtuosic display.

In a Mozart concerto, the first movement is typically in sonata form, the same form found in the first movement of a Classical symphony, though in a concerto the structural demarcations are often less clear. The exposition, introducing the main thematic material (usually two subject groups), is generally the province of the orchestra. (A passage where the full orchestra plays is sometimes referred to as a tutti, from the Italian word meaning "all.") A transition passage prepares for the soloist's entrance; this corresponds to the beginning of the exposition repeat in a symphony's first movement. The solo instrument and orchestra then engage in a dialog that recasts the earlier material, with the solo instrument frequently adding new material tailored to its own use. In the development section and the recapitulation, ideas are further explored until the harmony comes to rest on an unstable version of the tonic chord (known as a cadential six-four chord), setting the stage for an improvised cadenza by the soloist. This in turn is followed by a brief coda, and the movement ends.

The second movement of a typical Mozart concerto has a slow tempo and is often laid out as an aria (usually in three-part song form). This showcases the solo instrument's capacity for intimate expression and gives the player an opportunity to inflect lines and improvise ornaments as a singer would. The third movement is usually a rondo or a hybrid of sonata form and rondo, and it is almost always fast, light, tuneful, and display-oriented. Mozart's finales, like his slow movements, often have an operatic quality; where the slow movements resemble arias of love, the finales have the rapid repartee and exciting shifts of mood of act-ending ensembles.

Beethoven built his concertos on this model, greatly expanding the scale and altering the relationship between solo instrument and orchestra. His first two piano concertos clearly follow Mozart, but with the subsequent concertos in C minor, G major, and E flat major, the balance between piano and orchestra is less the back-and-forth shifting of a seesaw than a dynamic process in which the two forces are set in motion toward the same goal and must jointly shape the musical material into a vast, overarching structure. Remarkably, this transformation of the concerto, one of the great achievements of Beethoven's middle period, took little more than ten years.

As his symphonies had done, Beethoven's concertos left the early Romantics with a dilemma: it was impossible to carry the same ideas further. So in the works of Chopin, Mendelssohn, Schumann, and Liszt, there is a new focus on virtuosity, with the soloist often being treated as a heroic protagonist. These composers were all preoccupied with conveying the impression that the concerto had emerged from a single inspiration—not from the topical stage-play of Mozart or the constructive struggles of Beethoven, but from an elevated, rhapsodic state of feeling within which the listener was free to wander. Still, Beethoven's example did force his successors to think about unity. The connected movements of his Fifth and Sixth Symphonies, the Triple Concerto, the Violin Concerto, and the *Emperor* Piano Concerto were emulated by Mendelssohn in his E minor Violin Concerto and by Schumann in his Piano Concerto. Liszt, in his First Piano Concerto, took the more daring step of conjuring a multi-movement structure from a sonata-form design. Only Brahms managed to equal Beethoven in the scale of his concerto structures and in his skill at casting their material into powerful symphonic arguments.

The 20th century has been a particularly rich period for the concerto. Composers have posited new relationships between soloist and orchestra, demanded a heightened virtuosity, and shown a new eclecticism in their choice of material. Among the ideas and procedures explored have been jazz (in Ravel's piano concertos), the 12-tone row (Berg's Violin Concerto), and folk-inspired rhythms and melodies (Bartók, Rodrigo). The three-movement form has survived as the norm, though multiple alternatives have been tried successfully. For all their variety, the best 20th-century concertos have been works of serious content and challenge that have remained true to the character of the solo instrument. Mozart would have been proud.

Cöthen, where Bach flowered as a composer of concertos.

JOHANN SEBASTIAN BACH

VIOLIN CONCERTOS

*M*ost of Bach's purely instrumental music dates from 1717–23, his years as Kapellmeister at Cöthen. A considerable quantity of Bach's music from this period is lost; nonetheless, what remains is extraordinarily rich in conception and accomplished in execution, and one can justifiably say that as a body of work it represents the apogee of Baroque instrumental composition.

The only concertos from Cöthen that have come down to us in their original form are the Violin Concertos in A minor and E major, BWV 1041–42, and the Concerto for Two Violins, in D minor, BWV 1043. (A number of others can be reconstructed, or at least guessed at, on the basis of Bach's later arrangements of them as keyboard concertos, or from his subsequent use of parts of them in transcription for various cantatas.) There is a strong Italian flavor to these concertos that bespeaks Bach's familiarity with and indebtedness to the concertos of Vivaldi. But Bach shows a sophistication far beyond the Italian model, both in structure and in his treatment of material. The line of action is smoother, less episodic, and more organic than with Vivaldi, and the writing for the violin more substantive, less effect-oriented, thus anticipating the Franco-Italian galant style of Mozart and Beethoven.

All three works are notable for their outstanding craftsmanship and expressiveness. The slow movements of the two solo concertos, composed in chaconne style (over a repeating bass line), are particularly impressive—that of the E major Concerto for its poignancy, that of the A minor for its richly ornamented cantilena (a singing-style melody). The Double Concerto has an equally remarkable slow movement, a deeply felt Largo in which the lines of the two solo violins intertwine almost vocally.

*B*ACH WAS NOT ONLY *the greatest organist and keyboard musician of his day, but an accomplished violinist and violist as well. He learned the string instruments from his father, Johann Ambrosius, and the keyboard from his older brother Johann Christoph. In composition he was entirely self-taught.*

RECOMMENDED RECORDINGS

Pinchas Zukerman, José Luis Garcia; English Chamber Orchestra.
RCA Red Seal 60718-2 [with Concerto in G minor, BWV 1056]

Simon Standage, Elizabeth Wilcock; English Concert/Trevor Pinnock.
Deutsche Grammophon Archiv 410 646-2

Monica Huggett, Alison Bury; Amsterdam Baroque Orchestra/ Ton Koopman.
Erato 2292-45283-2

Zukerman conducts and plays lead violin.

Zukerman's accounts are appealing for their emphasis on line and phrasing, as well as for their restraint. They are intelligently drawn, if a little drawn out (and Russianized, with un-idiomatic slides) in some of the slow tempos; there is also a tendency to hasten in the Allegros. But most of the time, Zukerman scales down his gestures to fit the music. The Largo of the Double Concerto is especially lovely. The 1990 recording is excellent, the soloists ever so slightly forward.

Textures are lighter with Standage and Pinnock, the playing drier and more articulate, though tonally less appealing if your focus is on the solo instrument. Pinnock provides the usual straight-ahead accompaniment; his tempos in the fast movements are bracing but well managed. The 1983 accounts are recorded in typically bright, closeup fashion, with ample detail.

The feathery delicacy of Huggett's playing throughout, and the intimacy of her tone and expression in the slow movements, make her renditions highly satisfying. These accounts have more of the glow of chamber music to them than the glare of the concert stage. Koopman and his ensemble provide lively yet discreet support, and the sound is excellent.

*Bartók in 1943, with his wife
Ditta Pásztory at the piano.*

IN APRIL OF 1942,
18 months after Bartók's
arrival to the United States,
Bartók's health began to deteriorate. His illness was
diagnosed as polycythemia, a
condition similar to leuke-
mia. Despite weakness and
long periods of convales-
cence, Bartók continued to
compose at a furious pace
until the very end. All of his
medical bills were paid by the
American Society of Composers, Authors, and Publishers.

BÉLA BARTÓK
PIANO CONCERTO NO. 3

*I*f Bartók's first two piano concertos were
shocking, exploratory, and decidedly percussive, the Third, composed in 1945 during the
final months of his life, has an almost Mozartean
tenderness. Here, even more than in the *Concerto
for Orchestra*, there is a sense of leave-taking as
the music unfolds. An unexpected simplicity of
line and a feeling of resignation, nostalgia, and
spiritual tranquility characterize the solo part, all
brought into relief by a softening of dynamics
and a lightness in the scoring of many pages of
the work. The melodic material itself is reminiscent of Mozart in its graceful, seamless integrity,
as is the free play of fantasy in Bartók's development of it.

For all that, Bartók's distinctive voice can be
heard throughout the work—in the modal character of the melodies (which often sound as if
they had been borrowed from folk music), in the
vigorous rhythmic accents of many passages, and
in the piquant counterpoint. The first movement
exhibits all of these elements. The sharply chiseled
main theme, given out in octaves by the piano
over a quivering tremolo in the strings, is certainly
folk-flavored, and as it is extended it becomes
punchier and more dance-like. The added piquancy comes as Bartók builds a crescendo by
means of a gradual accretion of instruments, creating a complex texture in which rhythms, accents,
and melodic intervals clash bracingly.

The most touching and fantastic pages of the
concerto are in the slow movement, an Adagio
that Bartók, a spiritual man but certainly no be-
liever, rather surprisingly marks *religioso*. The
style of the initial pages is indeed that of church
music, the feeling one of rigor and almost rapturous sadness. But the movement's central section
is a wonderfully animated nocturne—a shimmering evocation of the night chirping of insects and

birds, delightful in its freedom. It is almost as if Bartók is saying farewell to life and trying to hold it in his hands, all in the same movement. Philosophy is discarded in favor of the dance in the concerto's finale, a vigorous Allegro that draws energy from cross-rhythms and offbeat accents.

Knowing of his imminent death, Bartók composed the concerto for his second wife, the noted pianist Ditta Pásztory, probably in the hope that she could help support herself by performing it. Bartók finished all but the final 17 bars of the orchestration, which were filled in from his sketch by his student Tibor Serly.

 RECOMMENDED RECORDING

György Sándor;
Hungarian State Orchestra/Adam Fischer.
Sony Classical SK 45835 [with Concertos Nos. 1 and 2]

Sándor played the world premiere of this concerto in 1946, just a few months after Bartók's death. His deep knowledge of the composer's works and special insights into the style make this 1989 account indispensable, even if it is not as brilliantly played as some. The pianist is quite free with rhythm and accent, conveying not the otherworldly atmosphere that more than a few interpreters have found, but something very much of the moment. There is an astringent joy to the performance that is both refreshing and quite in keeping with the mood of the composer's other essays from the last years of his life. Fischer and the Hungarian orchestra do a superb job on their end, and the recording, while slightly distant and diffuse, is well balanced and satisfying.

BARTÓK FLED *Europe along with many other artists and intellectuals during the 1930s and '40s in response to the rise of fascism. As the Nazis took control in Germany and overran the continent, the United States became the destination for many, including Hindemith, Schoenberg, Stravinsky, Rachmaninoff, Bruno Walter, and Thomas Mann.*

VIOLIN CONCERTO NO. 2

*B*artók's two-movement Violin Concerto of 1907–8 had been a labor of love, composed for the violinist Stefi Geyer, with whom the 26-year-old composer was emotionally involved at the time. When the two parted company, the manuscript of the concerto went with Geyer. It was to be 30 years before Bartók, in full maturity, returned to the genre to compose what is now usually referred to as his Violin Concerto No. 2, though Bartók himself spoke of it without numerical designation.

The idea of a concerto may have been suggested to Bartók by his countryman, the violinist Zoltán Székely, to whom the composer dedicated the finished work. Originally, Bartók had wanted to compose a set of variations for violin and orchestra, but Székely pressed for a full-scale concerto. In the end, both got their way: Bartók composed a concerto in which the concept of variation serves as the guiding principle in all three movements. Throughout, the material is extremely engaging. The first movement's opening theme, given out by the violin over a warm accompaniment in the harp and pizzicato strings, is in the rhythm of a *verbunkos*, or recruiting march; the chromatic second subject, also introduced by the violin, is an eerily expressive 12-tone theme over a pedal A in horns and strings. The delicate second movement is an actual theme-and-variations, quite atmospheric in feeling, and the third movement is itself a grand variation of the first, converting the rather broad and rhapsodic themes of the concerto's opening pages into folk dances.

The concerto is brilliantly scored and requires almost as much virtuosity from the orchestra as it does from the soloist. So rich is the conception that at times the ideas almost run away with the piece; Bartók's energetic treatment, however, overcomes the inherently episodic nature of the form.

*O*N MARCH 23, 1939, *less than six months before the outbreak of World War II, Zoltán Székely gave the first performance of the concerto in Amsterdam, with Willem Mengelberg conducting the Concertgebouw Orchestra. The score is published with two endings for the finale: Bartók's original one with its striking brass glissandi, which Székely found too "symphonic," and the more violinistic ending Bartók wrote to replace it, which has become standard.*

THE KING OF SWING, *clarinetist Benny Good- man moved in classical circles as well. He commis- sioned a number of important works for his in- strument, including Bartók's* Contrasts *(for violin, piano, and clarinet) and concertos by Copland and Hindemith, and made several recordings as a classical artist.*

RECOMMENDED RECORDINGS

Kyung Wha Chung; London Philharmonic Orchestra/ Sir Georg Solti.
London Jubilee 425 015-2 [with Concerto No. 1]

Pinchas Zukerman; Saint Louis Symphony Orchestra/ Leonard Slatkin.
RCA Red Seal 60749-2 [with Viola Concerto]

Chung's performance blazes with energy and commitment and is brilliantly backed up by Solti and the London Philharmonic. If the violinist errs at all, it is in trying to put swagger into the opening subject of the first movement by leaning into its accents. The result sounds unduly Romanticized. But in the rapt second movement, Chung is ex- quisite, and she turns in an electrifying account of the finale, abetted by Solti's energetic prodding of the orchestra. The 1976 recording is very close- miked and a bit overbalanced in Chung's favor, though it enables one to hear every nuance of this high-octane reading.

Zukerman has been among this concerto's most capable interpreters for many years; in this 1990 recording, he emphasizes the lyricism of the solo part, playing it with a remarkable richness of tone. Slatkin and the Saint Louis are ideal partners in this interpretation, for they too have a burnished, deep sound and a knack for playing big scores as if they were chamber music. The recording is plush, though a little diffuse and lacking in depth— typical of this team in this venue. The tone is natural and the balance reasonably good—and as a bonus, the disc offers both the standard ending and Bartók's original one.

Mozart made the mold (Concerto No. 24) and Beethoven broke it.

LUDWIG VAN BEETHOVEN

PIANO CONCERTO NO. 3, IN C MINOR, OP. 37

*T*he opening bars of this concerto bear a much-noted resemblance to those of Mozart's Concerto No. 24, something Beethoven no doubt intended. At a performance of that work, Beethoven is reported to have told a composer-friend, referring to a haunting phrase at the end of the final movement, "We shall never have an idea to compare with that!" And this is precisely the point Beethoven makes at the beginning of his concerto, for in spite of the similarity, his subject is quite different from Mozart's. It is blunt, basic, unfinished—a gesture to be developed, rather than a fully realized theme. And develop it Beethoven does, starting with a tutti lasting 110 measures, the longest in any of his concertos. In this revolutionary opening, one can clearly see Beethoven's twin middle-period tendencies, toward the enlargement of form and the heightening of expression.

The extraordinary power and scope of this symphonic prologue do something else: they create an imbalance that the solo instrument must struggle mightily to restore. As the orchestra is brought to a halt on three *fortissimo* C's, the piano launches a bravura counterattack in blazing octave runs, *forte*, a chandelier-shaking entry. In this confrontation, the piano is cast as a Promethean protagonist, answering the orchestra's superior firepower with daring feints and brilliant virtuoso fusillades. Much of the flavor of the drama derives from the key of C minor, which for Beethoven was associated with harmonic turbulence and the utmost intensity of expression. It is in this movement that Beethoven, for the first time in his concertos, ceases to sound like Mozart, and here that the era of the Romantic concerto begins.

With the Largo, Beethoven goes about as far away from C minor and confrontation as is possible, to the ethereal key of E major and a meditative communion between piano and orchestra. The solo part still contains an element of fantasy and improvisatory brilliance, but the writing for orchestra is suffused with rapture right up to the surprising final chord, the only *fortissimo* in the entire movement. The main subject of the concluding C minor rondo has the feeling of a Turkish march, and for a while storm clouds seem to gather around it. But ensuing episodes are more jocular, and the weight of the minor key lessens. A *presto* coda in 6/8—skipping, dazzling, and unreservedly showy—brings the concerto to a close in jubilant C major.

PIANO CONCERTO NO. 4, IN G, OP. 58

"*G*od knows why my piano music still makes the poorest impression on me," Beethoven wrote in June of 1805. It was more than just another complaint from the dependably self-critical composer. Within months, however, he was putting the finishing touches on the *Appassionata* Sonata and had begun his Fourth Piano Concerto. The astonishing qualities of these works—their affective power and the way they seem to fit the keyboard—suggest that in spite of what Beethoven had already written for the piano, he *did* have more to say.

Even while he was being drawn to the extremes of pianistic expression, Beethoven was still concerned with lyricism and coherence, with thematic economy, and more than ever, with formal originality. In the G major Concerto, he achieved all of these objectives while bringing a new feeling of poetic elevation to his writing for both the orchestra and the piano. Although it is not a work of uprooting grandeur, the Fourth Piano Concerto *is* a work of unparalleled invention whose sustained flow of ideas makes it one of the masterpieces of Beethoven's oeuvre.

*B*EETHOVEN *himself played the Piano Concerto No. 4 at its premiere on April 5, 1803, in the Theater an der Wien. He had revised the solo parts shortly before the performance, to take advantage of the latest extensions in the range of the piano's keyboard, thus giving added brilliance to the passagework and extra weight to the bass.*

The piano has the first words here—and it speaks them *piano* and *dolce*, with sublime understatement. Just as surprising is the way the first movement unfolds not as a contest with the orchestra but as a partnership. The piano is almost constantly active, yet the ideas are so generous and the figuration so varied that it never seems to be in danger of wearing out its material. Indeed, the piano's tone is one of the unifying threads of the movement; Beethoven even keeps the trumpets and drums out of the orchestra here to give the solo instrument a weight more nearly equal to that of the tutti.

In the Andante, piano and strings (the rest of the orchestra is silent) turn in stark opposition to each other. They engage in a tense *recitativo* dialog that culminates with the piano spinning off a fierce, cadenza-like passage, leaving the strings spellbound and hushed. A recent study has proposed that this concerto—long thought to be associated with a program based on the myth of Orpheus—does in fact have an Orphic subtext from beginning to end, and that here the piano is Orpheus, the strings the Furies of Hades.

Few of Beethoven's finales are as giddy or energetic as this concerto's rondo, with its quick-march tempo and surprise introduction of trumpets and drums. There is a pair of episodes where the chorale-like writing in the winds and strings foreshadows the finale of the Ninth Symphony. Noteworthy, too, is a developmental passage beginning in E flat—scored for pizzicato strings with light wind chords sounding above, *pianissimo*—from which Mendelssohn almost surely derived the characteristic, elfin scoring of his scherzos. In its triumphant gestures and expression of profound joy, this movement is decidedly of a piece with the other great works of Beethoven's middle period.

"**Y**OUR FORTEPIANO *has turned out to be really excellent. . . . But I would be lying were I not to tell you that it is too good for me. Why? Because it takes away my freedom to create the tone for myself. Don't let this keep you from making all your pianos this way— there probably aren't that many people who have such whims."*
—Beethoven, letter to the piano builder Andreas Streicher

Beethoven beats the drum of war as Napoleon's army arrives at Schönbrunn Palace.

PIANO CONCERTO No. 5, in E FLAT, Op. 73
Emperor

*T*he year 1809 was a trying one for the citizens of Vienna. Napoleon's armies besieged the city and briefly occupied it. Joseph Haydn, 77 years old and ailing, died two weeks after the French came in—and Beethoven's friend, pupil, and patron, Archduke Rudolph, was forced to flee the city, along with the rest of the royal family, to avoid capture by Napoleon's agents. Beethoven himself, nearly deaf, spent hours in his brother Caspar's basement during the bombardment, hoping to protect the last vestiges of his hearing. "The whole course of events has affected me in both body and soul," he later wrote. "What a destructive and unruly life I see and hear around me; nothing but drums, cannon, and human misery in every form."

It was against this background that Beethoven completed his fifth and final piano concerto, yet there is little hint of turmoil in the music itself. He used the key of E flat, with its noble connotations, once again in this triumphant work, intended as a tribute and dedicated to Archduke Rudolph, though the piece would later become known as the *Emperor* Concerto and thus carry a title that outranked its dedicatee. The score epitomizes Beethoven's tendency at the height of his middle period to enlarge on the Classical model and portray the relationship between piano and orchestra less as a dialog than an epic of struggle and triumph. Beethoven achieves a synthesis of the heroic and the poetic that gives the *Emperor* a unique place in his own output and in the concerto literature as a whole.

The opening Allegro, 578 measures long, is one of the largest sonata-form movements Beethoven ever wrote. It takes roughly 20 minutes to perform—as long as some of Mozart's complete concertos—and in every respect its scale is monumental. Beethoven's extraordinary thematic invention turns the march topic, traditionally used to characterize nobility in music of the 18th century, into an engine of the Industrial Age. The movement's principal subject is sweeping yet graceful, qualities that are developed with consummate skill in the pages that follow, resulting in an exquisite balance between the projection of strength and festivity on one hand and the play of fantasy on the other. Through it all, the piano somehow stands firm against the sheer weight of the orchestra. It is a magnificent achievement, this assertion of the individual voice against a huge collective counterpart, and it fits well with Beethoven's personality.

Having thundered grandly, the composer rises above the fray for a wondrous moment of hymn-like introspection in the Adagio. Time virtually stands still during the meditative course of the movement, which is set in the lofty key of B major and so gently scored that the piano converses almost exclusively in the softest tones. If Apollo seems the soul of this slow movement, Dionysus is very much the spirit of the concerto's finale, a dance-driven rondo that hurtles impulsively along.

Szell (right) and Fleisher have great chemistry.

 RECOMMENDED RECORDINGS

Leon Fleisher;
Cleveland Orchestra/George Szell.
Sony Classical SB3K 48397 [3 CDs; complete piano concertos, with Triple Concerto; *Nos. 1 and 3 (SBK 47658), Nos. 2 and 4 (SBK 48165), and No. 5 (SBK 46549) also available separately]*

Murray Perahia;
Royal Concertgebouw Orchestra/
Bernard Haitink.
CBS Masterworks M3K 44575 [3 CDs; complete piano concertos; Nos. 3 and 4 (MK 39814) and No. 5 (MK 42330) also available separately]

A Word About Music

The words *"concerto"* and *"concert"* are both derived from the Italian concertare, *meaning "to agree."*

Steven Lubin; Academy of Ancient Music/ Christopher Hogwood.

Oiseau-Lyre 421 408-2 [3 CDs; complete piano concertos]

Fleisher's fiery accounts of these concertos are justly celebrated. The young pianist was at his peak when he made the recordings in 1959 and 1961, and while his part in them has been compared with the action of a Swiss watch—brilliant, but a little too tightly wound and mechanical—there was and still is something electrifying about the playing. In addition, Fleisher exhibits remarkable rhythmic flexibility and lyrical warmth, qualities that are utterly winning in this music. He is especially expressive in the slow movements of Nos. 3 and 5, where he conveys a sense of the gentleness and depth of feeling in the music. The chemistry between Fleisher and the leonine conductor Szell, in sovereign command of his Cleveland Orchestra, is something to marvel at. The recordings give a bold, closeup view, and the sound is at times a bit grainy, though appealing considering the vintage.

Perahia and Haitink provide a wonderful, stylish alternative to the high-intensity approach. Their readings are elegant yet full of panache, with the thoughtful voicings and balances typical of good period-style performance—achieved without any sacrifice of virtuosity. Perahia's approach to Concertos Nos. 1 and 2 is Mozartean in its elegance and jewel-like clarity, his playing a marvel of detail and deftness. In the bigger works he delivers the requisite power, yet never sounds harsh. The playing of the Concertgebouw Orchestra is glorious, and all five accounts are well recorded, with the piano very close but not overly prominent.

The acoustic limitations of the fortepiano make recording these concertos on period instruments highly problematic. Nonetheless, several attempts have been made, the most successful of which is the 1987 set from Lubin and Hogwood. In an attempt to get as close as possible to the right

Lubin used a replica of Beethoven's Graf piano (above) from 1824.

sound for each concerto, Lubin uses four different instruments, all modern reproductions of Viennese originals dating from 1795–1824. Lubin's playing is informed and expressive; with the help of sensitive conducting and engineering, he is able to hold his own against the accompaniment, which even on period instruments is often powerful.

VIOLIN CONCERTO IN D, OP. 61

*T*his concerto was written for Franz Clement, concertmaster of the orchestra of Vienna's Theater an der Wien. Clement was an extraordinary virtuoso, noted for his sweetly expressive tone, his skill as an improviser, and his phenomenal musical memory, faculties that were put to the test at the concerto's first performance on December 23, 1806. Beethoven, as was typical when he was working on a commission, had composed the piece in feverish haste, barely completing it in time for the premiere. Clement was forced to virtually sight-read the solo part—and did so with little apparent difficulty.

What sets the Violin Concerto apart from previous works in the genre is the integration of the solo part within the orchestral fabric, the fusion of violin and orchestra into something far beyond the conventional 18th-century notion of the concerto as a mere solo-tutti confrontation. The violin is still given the opportunity to do what it does best on a grand scale—namely, to sing. Yet the concerto's most telling moments are its quietest, where Beethoven speaks not as the thunderer, but as the "still, small voice," taking advantage of the solo instrument's marvelous expressiveness in soft dynamics—as when the violin emerges from the first-movement cadenza playing the gentle second subject on its two lower strings, over a hushed pizzicato accompaniment.

The opening movement is typical of Beethoven's festive style, as opposed to his more dramatic

BEETHOVEN *indulged his love of puns in mixed languages by inscribing on the manuscript of this work,* "Concerto par Clemenza pour Clement, primo Violino e Direttore al Theatro a Vienna, dal L. v. Bthvn., 1806" *["Concerto kindly meant for Clement, first violin and conductor at the theater in Vienna, by Ludwig van Beethoven, 1806"]. He might well have added* "e pour Clementi," *for in 1810 the concerto was published in London by his friend and colleague Muzio Clementi.*

*F*URTWÄNGLER'S
*decision to remain in
Germany during the Third
Reich was highly controver-
sial. Yet he defied the Nazis
at every opportunity, refus-
ing to conduct in occupied
countries, obtaining exit
visas for Jewish musicians,
and even insisting that one
musician who had been sent
to Dachau be assigned to
copy music, thereby saving
his life. When Furtwängler
was engaged as conductor of
the Chicago Symphony for
the 1949–50 season, a
smear campaign caused the
orchestra's board to withdraw
its offer.*

manner. There is an air of solemnity and mystery right from the start of this Allegro, in the soft drumbeats that open it so arrestingly, and in the answering chorale-like theme in the winds. Long stretches are devoted to soaring lyricism, and Beethoven is not afraid to take repose in seemingly remote tonal regions—where there is no hurry, no need to triumph, just a sublime expansiveness with the violin at the center.

The majestic eloquence of the first movement is followed by the soulful meditation of the Larghetto, among the most elevated and beautiful of Beethoven's slow movements. Written in the style of a Romance, the typical middle movement in a French concerto, it is a series of variations in which the violin traces a delicate embroidery around the theme. Having exhausted the lyric vein in the first two movements of the concerto, Beethoven allows the extrovert side of the violin's personality to emerge in a rondo finale that draws on the hunting style so beloved of Mozart and Haydn. Here, that style is given new boldness and sweep, and the work ends on a note of triumphant assertion.

 RECOMMENDED RECORDINGS

**Itzhak Perlman;
Philharmonia Orchestra/Carlo Maria Giulini.**
EMI CDC 47002

**Henryk Szeryng;
Royal Concertgebouw Orchestra/
Bernard Haitink.**
Philips 416 418-2 [with Romances, *Opp. 40 and 50]*

**Yehudi Menuhin;
Philharmonia Orchestra/
Wilhelm Furtwängler.**
*EMI CDH 69799 [with Mendelssohn: Concerto
in E minor]*

Giulini joins Perlman in a climb to the top of Parnassus.

The catalog contains no finer recording of this concerto than Perlman's early digital reading with Giulini and the Philharmonia. The soloist's playing is technically precise yet utterly free of mannerism, deeply felt and gripping from first page to last. With equal ease Perlman enters into the first movement's soaring lyricism, the Larghetto's gentle reverie, and the finale's spirited exaltation. Giulini, the steadiest of partners, is with him every step of the way and elicits a majestic reading from the orchestra. Very much like the performance, the sound is warm, spacious, and reassuringly natural.

Szeryng and Haitink offer an Olympian view, taking a broad tempo in the opening movement and building climaxes of enormous force. There is an urgency to Szeryng's playing that verges on the incendiary, but there is considerable delicacy and poetry as well. The Dutch orchestra plays with regal authority, and Philips's analog recording is immediate and full-bodied.

Menuhin and Furtwängler, born a generation apart and separated by a world at war, were nonetheless musical and philosophical soulmates. Their 1953 recording of the Beethoven concerto, made seven years after they first met, is one of the treasures of the EMI archive, a testament to a bygone era of spontaneous and subjective music making. There is a nobility to the reading that has never been equaled, an unforced passion that would be difficult for any of today's musicians to duplicate. The monaural recording is remarkably fine, with satisfying depth and abundant detail.

ALBAN BERG

VIOLIN CONCERTO

*I*n his early twenties the Austrian composer Berg (1885–1935) had become friends with Gustav Mahler and his wife, Alma, and he remained on good terms with Alma following

Mahler's death. Alma married the architect Walter Gropius in 1915, and in 1916 they had a daughter whom they named Manon. "Mutzi" Gropius was the darling of her parents and their many friends, a young woman full of charm, beauty, and intelligence who seemed, somehow, to have come from another world. Her death from polio in April 1935, at the age of 18, was a deep blow to Berg, who had watched her grow up, and it hastened him in the composition of what turned out to be his last finished work.

Earlier that year, Berg had been asked for a concerto in the 12-tone idiom by the American violinist Louis Krasner, whose interest in contemporary music had prompted him to seek out the composer. At first reluctant to interrupt work on his opera *Lulu*, Berg accepted Krasner's commission, though his progress on the concerto was initially slow. When he learned of Manon's death, Berg worked virtually nonstop, completing the piece on July 15, 1935, and inscribing it "To the Memory of an Angel."

The work's two movements are each subdivided into two parts whose music, while in different tempos, is seamlessly joined. The first movement begins with a gentle Andante; as it unfolds, the meditative expression becomes more rhapsodic, and the writing for the solo instrument shows increasing animation. With the arrival of the second part of the movement, a scherzo-like Allegretto in 6/8 meter, the pace of activity quickens. The clarinets introduce a lilting tune, which is taken up by the violin and transformed into a waltzing, macabre subject marked *wienerisch* ("Viennese") and a more innocent-sounding singsong marked *rustico* ("rustic"). From this point to the end of the movement, the motives appear in a kaleidoscopic array of juxtapositions—much as they might in a scherzo by Mahler. There is a brief, idyllic interlude as a Carinthian folk song is nostalgically quoted by the first horn and the two trumpets, after which the dance resumes more energetically than ever.

"THE GLASS DOORS of Alma's music room afforded a view of a beautiful terrace and of the garden beyond. I can still see the unearthly apparition we beheld when we sat there one day after luncheon. An angelically beautiful girl of about fifteen appeared in the door with a young deer at her side. Her hand on the animal's slender neck, she gave us an unembarrassed little smile and disappeared again."
—Bruno Walter, remembering Manon Gropius

"THE BERG *Concerto evolved . . . out of the climactic, onrushing events of Vienna and Austria in the 1930s. With the city's agitation, ferment, trepidation, and suffering interlocked to its spirituality, culture, idealism, and intellectuality, Karl Kraus called it 'The proving ground for world destruction.' "*
—Louis Krasner

The second movement begins with an agitated confrontation between violin and orchestra. A crescendo built on an insistent, sharply etched rhythm leads to the movement's first climax, out of which the solo instrument emerges to begin an extended cadenza-like passage. Gradually, the entire orchestra becomes involved, leading to a hysterical climax that subsides into exhaustion. The tempo changes to *adagio*, and the second part of the movement begins with the violin's quiet introduction of the chorale melody "*Es ist genug!*" from Bach's cantata *O Ewigkeit, du Donnerwort*—a melody whose opening ascent of three whole steps has been prefigured in the concerto's opening measures. The chorale is picked up by the clarinets in Bach's exact harmonization, the purity of which places an otherworldly halo around the rest of the movement's material. There are two variations followed by a transcendent coda in which the violin slowly ascends to the upper reaches and, in a passage marked *amoroso*, plays the final notes of the chorale tune. It retreats into silence and then ascends once more to an angelic high G, which it holds in poignant serenity as the orchestra sounds a bittersweet farewell.

One could listen to this concerto any number of times and never be aware that much of its thematic content is derived from a 12-tone row, so smoothly does Berg weave not only the 12-tone material but the piece's other quoted melodies into the evocative fabric of its sound. While that sound can occasionally be harsh—in keeping with the anguished feelings that gave rise to the music in the first place—it is also quite expressive. Berg uses it to create a powerful series of metaphors for life, struggle, and death, and what is, or may be, beyond it. Only days after finishing the Violin Concerto, Berg developed an infection that led to a fatal case of blood poisoning. He died before the premiere of the work, which became not only a memorial for Manon Gropius but his own requiem as well.

Alban Berg in 1934.

Perlman: expressive warmth and virtuoso technique.

RECOMMENDED RECORDINGS

Kyung Wha Chung;
Chicago Symphony Orchestra/
Sir Georg Solti.
London 411 804-2 [with Bartók: Concerto No. 1]

Itzhak Perlman;
Boston Symphony Orchestra/Seiji Ozawa.
Deutsche Grammophon 413 725-2 [with Stravinsky:
Violin Concerto]

Tenderness, spontaneity, and a certain fragility distinguish Chung's flowing account. Her playing is poetic and expressive, yet true to the music's intentions and not overly emotive; her tone, intense yet slightly attenuated, has an ideal singing quality. The orchestral sound is quite spectacular in its transparency and depth, and London's engineering gives weight and atmosphere to the 1983 recording.

Perlman is the more Romantic of these two interpreters, and here he is at his most virtuosic and commanding, playing in a way that will leave future generations agog, just as Jascha Heifetz did. Ozawa and the Boston Symphony provide solid support. This 1979 recording was one of the finest that Deutsche Grammophon made in Boston, and the impact, clarity, and close perspective on Perlman have been retained in the remastering for CD. The Stravinsky coupling is excellent.

JOHANNES BRAHMS

PIANO CONCERTO NO. 1, IN D MINOR, OP. 15
PIANO CONCERTO NO. 2, IN B FLAT, OP. 83

*I*n both of his piano concertos, Brahms sought to combine emotional profundity with rigorous formal logic, to explore the piano's

Brahms in 1854, at the time of the D minor Piano Concerto.

capabilities while engaging in serious symphonic argument, and to match the orchestra's weight and range of color in writing for the solo instrument. Clearly, Brahms had in mind bridging the gap between concerto and symphony. The First Concerto, completed in 1858, actually evolved out of thoughts for a symphony in D minor, retaining the sweep and proportions of the original conception. The Second Concerto, composed between 1878 and 1881, is even longer and is divided into four movements—conventional for a symphony, unusual for a concerto.

Unlike most of his generation of Romantics, Brahms had little interest in pianistic display for its own sake or in the concerto as a vehicle for the virtuoso. He wrote both of these concertos for himself, and they directly reflect his talents as a pianist. For Brahms, the piano was the most suggestive of solo instruments and a versatile and articulate partner in chamber music; both roles are encouraged in the two concertos. In the First, piano and orchestra are placed in classic opposition to one another—not to heighten the piano's profile, but to put in sharper relief the emotional contrasts of the music itself. By the time he composed the Second Concerto, Brahms had banked the fires somewhat but found deeper thoughts to express. In both works the writing for the piano is chordal, thick-textured, and occasionally ungrateful, calling for strength and stamina—qualities Brahms himself possessed as a pianist—in lieu of a fluid technique.

The First Concerto's titanic opening movement begins with a stormy orchestral prologue anchored by a series of long-held pedal tones in the bass. The fierce, sharply chiseled opening theme perfectly defines the storm-and-stress of Romanticism. The piano enters, meditative and gentle at first but soon growing agitated. After further thunderings and a brooding transition, the piano emerges from the mists with the movement's radiant second subject, a hymnlike idea that is treated at length here and in the recapitulation.

ACCORDING TO Joseph Joachim, the dramatic opening theme of the D minor Piano Concerto expressed the anguish Brahms had felt on hearing that Robert Schumann had thrown himself into the Rhine in a suicide attempt.

Brahms composed the second and third movements of the concerto following the death of Robert Schumann. In a letter to his widow, Clara, Brahms said of the D major Adagio, "I am painting a tender portrait of you." It *is* a movement of Schumannesque beauty and gentleness, as much a memorial for Robert as a portrayal of Clara, for whom Brahms, at the time and for the rest of his life, was to feel an abiding spiritual and emotional love. The main subject of the rondo finale is a turbulent D minor march with an overlay of Hungarian dance, and the coda, which contains two cadenzas, is graced by a lovely horn solo and some pastoral bagpiping before it winds up in a race between piano and orchestra to finish first.

Brahms began work on the Second Piano Concerto following one trip to Italy and finished it shortly after another. The music has a southern warmth and affability to match the Olympian grandeur of its conception. Yet despite the largeness of the score—it is longer than any of the four symphonies—much of it is in the realm of chamber music, with the orchestra and solo instrument in an intimate discourse usually marked *dolce.*

The concerto begins with what might best be called an invocation, a noble summons from the first horn that is graciously answered by chordal arpeggios in the piano. No sooner has a pastoral mood been established than the piano interrupts with a dramatic cadenza. This sets the stage for a grand statement of the opening horn subject by the full orchestra, and with that the vast symphonic canvas of the first movement unfolds. The D minor scherzo that follows, far more serious than playful, contains the concerto's most passionate music—yet it does have a jubilant trio in D major.

The piano is not the only solo instrument in this concerto. At the beginning and end of the third movement, Brahms gives a pair of extended solo passages to the cello. Two titanic outbursts lend drama to the movement's autumnal expres-

"I *HAVE JUST finished a tiny, tiny piano concerto with a tiny, tiny wisp of a scherzo."*
—Brahms to Elisabet von Herzogenberg, July 7, 1881, after completing the Piano Concerto No. 2

sion—but when the piano joins with 'the cello at movement's end, all is calm, and the listener is ushered into a world of the most sublime chamber music. The same gentleness of spirit informs the finale, which is breezy and ebullient in spite of its size.

 RECOMMENDED RECORDINGS

Emil Gilels;
Berlin Philharmonic/Eugen Jochum.
Deutsche Grammophon 419 158-2 [2 CDs; with Fantasias, *Op. 116]*

Rudolf Serkin;
Cleveland Orchestra/George Szell.
CBS Masterworks MK 42261 [No. 1, with R. Strauss: Burleske] *and MK 42262 [No. 2, with* Piano Pieces, *Op. 119]*

Gilels is magisterial in these concertos. Where the writing calls for poetry, he can be gentle and rhapsodic; where it demands passion, he erupts. Jochum and the Berlin Philharmonic manage to span Brahms's long developmental arches with convincing success, giving the musical argument the feeling of a single impulse. Gilels gets his share of wrong notes (especially in No. 2), but when he plays there is never any fooling around: no doldrums, no pushing or dragging. The orchestra, too, though not always immaculate, plays at fever pitch from first bar to last. The bottom line is that in spite of the flaws, one would look in vain to find more inspired accounts. The venue of these 1972 recordings, Berlin's Jesus Christus Kirche, lends a great deal of ambience, but there's enough definition and presence to hold onto. Deutsche Grammophon's engineers do a good job of capturing the pianist's astounding tone.

Serkin and Szell give an honest, rugged account of the First Concerto, emotionally somewhat understated yet very strong. It's a reading that wears

Performing Personalities

One of the greatest of Russian pianists, Emil Gilels was a magisterial interpreter of Beethoven, Brahms, and Tchaikovsky. His recordings are landmarks—bold, articulate, and compelling.

well, like good leather—and there's no question that both of these gentlemen were comfortable in this particular saddle in 1968. The Second Concerto, recorded two years earlier, is treated as a real symphony for piano and orchestra. Here, the Cleveland Orchestra is amazing, playing like a chamber ensemble on a grand scale, with details emphasized by an exceptionally dry recording. Though the violins still sound thin and the winds sometimes seem undernourished, the CDs are much better balanced than the LPs ever were.

VIOLIN CONCERTO IN D, OP. 77

*B*rahms often sought the advice of experts when writing for instruments other than the piano. He was particularly lucky when it came to the violin. From the Hungarian violinist Eduard Reményi, with whom he traveled through Europe as a teenager, Brahms learned about not only the violin but also the gypsy style, which was to play an important part in his later musical thinking.

Reményi performed an even more important function when he introduced Brahms to the talented and strong-willed Joseph Joachim, a fine composer in his own right and one of the greatest violinists of the 19th century. It was to him that Brahms turned for advice in the summer of 1878, several months after he had started writing this concerto. Joachim's generous assistance helped shape the solo part into one of the most challenging and satisfying in the literature, and contributed in no small measure to the concerto's overall success.

The first movement is in the warmly lit D major of the Second Symphony and is set in the same flowing 3/4 time. A full-scale orchestral introduction exposes the two subject groups and builds to a climax in D minor, at which point the violin enters with a dramatically arpeggiated treatment

THE CONCERTO'S premiere on New Year's Day, 1879, was unexpectedly entertaining. For in his haste to get to the Gewandhaus, Brahms forgot to fasten his suspenders. As he conducted, the trousers fell lower and lower—although, to quote Yehudi Menuhin, "the concerto ended before the anticipated sartorial denouement."

of the movement's main subject. Things take a dramatic turn in the development, which includes a passage marked *tranquillo* where the violin plays a haunting subject full of serpentine, Baroque turns. A convulsive climax in C sharp minor, which finds the violin wrenching itself by ninths across a three-octave chasm, eventually leads to D major and the recapitulation. Brahms nods to tradition by not writing out a cadenza. Joachim's great cadenza, still the one most frequently played today, was to fully justify the composer's confidence in his soloist.

The lovely F major Adagio has a feeling midway between folk song, lullaby, and hymn. It is prefaced by a lengthy introduction given entirely to the winds, the oboe taking the melody. When the violin enters, it does not repeat the tune, but rhapsodizes upon it. There is an interlude in F sharp minor, agitated yet subdued, in which the winds are tacit and the solo violin meditates with increasing urgency over interjections from the strings. A return to F major brings a reprise of the oboe melody, this time embellished from above by the violin and extended by both violin and solo horn.

The rondo finale has the character of a Hungarian dance. Not only was this a way for the composer to acknowledge the nationality of his intended soloist, but it assured a rollicking good end for what might otherwise have seemed a rather serious piece. The movement's robust main subject is announced in double stops by the solo instrument over volatile strings. There is a forceful second subject in dotted rhythm, a lyrical subject in which the hard-charging 2/4 meter is softened to a lilting 3/4, and an episode in mock-chorale style. In a final display of exuberance, Brahms appends a vigorous coda, which quiets at the end and almost seems to be slipping away until three D major chords, *forte*, bring the work to a joyous close.

BRAHMS SPENT the month of October 1853 in Düsseldorf, staying with Robert and Clara Schumann. While there, he joined Schumann and his pupil Albert Dietrich in composing a violin sonata for Joseph Joachim (above); it was based on a melodic motif consisting of the notes F, A, and E, representing Joachim's motto "Frei aber einsam" ("Free but lonely"). Dietrich wrote the first movement of the so-called F-A-E Sonata, Schumann composed the Intermezzo and Finale, and Brahms provided the scherzo.

BRAHMS'S *colleague Joseph Hellmesberger, among the foremost violinists of the day and a musician known for his wit, delivered a celebrated brickbat when he characterized Opus 77 as "a concerto* against *the violin."*

 RECOMMENDED RECORDINGS

Itzhak Perlman;
Chicago Symphony Orchestra/
Carlo Maria Giulini.
EMI CDC 47166

Anne-Sophie Mutter;
Berlin Philharmonic/Herbert von Karajan.
Deutsche Grammophon 400 064-2

No one comes close to Perlman in the broad, grand feeling he imparts to the music. His reading is Romantic, long on sentiment and sweetness of tone, and full of spirit. Giulini's accompaniment has a warm-blooded, meaty substantiality, and the Chicagoans make a glorious sound under his baton; their tremolos fairly quiver with excitement. The 1976 recording establishes an excellent balance between the participants, up close but true.

Mutter's account is filled with electricity and a devil-may-care vibrancy that conveys a real sense of occasion. Keeping textures lean, Karajan draws playing of hushed intensity from the Berliners. The chemistry makes for a suspenseful, ultimately thrilling performance. Deutsche Grammophon's engineering brings Mutter a little too close—her mike seems to be positioned right over the strings—and the sound has the analytic quality typical of the label in this 1982 vintage.

MAX BRUCH

VIOLIN CONCERTO No. 1, IN G MINOR, OP. 26

*B*ruch (1838–1920) was a melodist of the first rank. The popularity of the German composer's works for violin and orchestra, and of this concerto in particular, stems primarily from the fact that even though he did not play

Bruch didn't need glasses to find a melody. There was always one at his fingertips.

the violin himself, he knew how to get the instrument to sing. Bruch made his first sketches for the G minor Concerto in 1857, when he was just 19, and completed the score in 1866. Following the work's premiere that year, the composer sought out the violinist Joseph Joachim for advice on how the solo part might be improved. Joachim, as he was to do a decade later for Brahms, offered a number of suggestions that, without changing the character of the music, added an element of virtuosity to it. The revised version of the concerto premiered in Bremen, with Joachim as soloist, in 1868.

The rhapsodic character of the concerto is apparent not only in the unstinting lyricism of the solo part, but in the fantasy-like formal layout of the entire work. The first movement in particular is imaginative and unconventional, beginning with a slow introduction (the score refers to it as a Prelude) that sounds as if it belongs in an opera rather than a concerto; a somber timpani roll is answered by a few morose chords in the winds, after which the violin enters with a dramatic recitative. The main Allegro gets under way with an impassioned solo in the violin, set over urgent tremolos and a loping pizzicato bass. Even here, at its most virtuosic, the writing for the solo instrument is essentially lyrical; in the delicately sentimental second subject, that lyricism is carried to new heights. A brief echo of the wind chords from the Prelude sets up a cadenza, which leads directly into the slow movement and another tender melody for the solo instrument—at first halting, then increasingly radiant. There is a consoling second subject in the horns, bassoons, and lower strings, over which the violin weaves a series of florid embellishments. The movement builds in yearning to a rapturous climax, then softens, ending quietly.

The rondo finale opens with a short, suspenseful orchestral introduction, out of which the violin emerges with a springing tune. Soloist and ensemble cavort until a warmly lyrical second subject is announced by the full orchestra. This is taken over and elaborated upon by the violin, which steers a flamboyant course through the movement's remaining episodes and its coda.

RECOMMENDED RECORDINGS

Jascha Heifetz;
New Symphony Orchestra of London/
Sir Malcolm Sargent.
RCA 6214-2 [with Scottish Fantasy, *and Vieuxtemps: Concerto No. 5]*

Cho-Liang Lin;
Chicago Symphony Orchestra/
Leonard Slatkin.
CBS Masterworks MK 42315 [with Scottish Fantasy] *or* MDK 44902 [with Mendelssohn: Concerto in E minor; and various encore pieces]

Joshua Bell;
Academy of St. Martin-in-the-Fields/
Sir Neville Marriner.
London 421 145-2 [with Mendelssohn: Concerto in E minor]

Who Is *Neville* *Marriner?*

Known for his recordings with the Academy of St. Martin-in-the-Fields, which was named for the London church (above), the English conductor spent the early years of his career as a violinist with the Philharmonia Orchestra. Knighted in 1979, Marriner has interpreted and reinterpreted the great works of the 18th and 19th centuries with singular success.

The heart-on-sleeve emotions of this concerto, which some violinists are afraid to wear, benefit from the larger-than-life Heifetz treatment; the result is that a piece which often sounds uncomfortable, if not dull, emerges here as a glorious outpouring of Romantic sentiment. The violinist's approach is epic, virtuosic, and reassuringly free of mannerism. Sargent and the New Symphony Orchestra keep up with the soloist, and the 1962 recording puts it all in excellent perspective.

Lin's is a straightforward reading, warmly phrased and beautifully played. Slatkin and the Chicago Symphony provide outstanding support, and the 1986 performance is captured in a recording of ideal depth and spaciousness. Two versions of the account are now available; the choice for most buyers is the midprice recoupling that pairs the Bruch with Mendelssohn's Concerto in E minor and encore pieces by Fritz Kreisler and Pablo de Sarasate.

Bell's technique is outstanding, even if his interpretation at times seems studied rather than directly, convincingly musical. There are some lovely moments, especially in the Adagio, and there can be no question that Bell is solidly in the grand manner. Tonally, London offers a very satisfying recording from 1986, though the balance favors the soloist to an undesirable degree.

Chopin by Delacroix: equal parts passion and poetry.

FRÉDÉRIC CHOPIN

PIANO CONCERTO NO. 1, IN E MINOR, OP. 11
PIANO CONCERTO NO. 2, IN F MINOR, OP. 21

Chopin (1810–1849) composed his two piano concertos in 1829 and 1830, prior to leaving Poland on a tour of Europe that was to see him hailed as one of the preeminent virtuosos of his day. He never again returned to his native country, but Poland's loss was to become Paris's gain. During the final two decades of his life, in spite of emotional ups and downs and recurrent illness, Chopin produced a remarkable body of compositions for the piano, works unrivaled both in their poetic feeling and in their sensitive exploration of the instrument's tonal capacities.

Chopin identified with the piano more strongly than did any other composer in the history of the instrument, to the extent that he was uncomfortable writing for anything else, including the orchestra. And while his compositions for solo piano broke new ground both technically and formally, he tended to cling to established patterns when outside his element. Chopin wrote both of his piano concertos along conventional lines, using as his model the concertos of Johann Nepomuk

IT IS HARD to believe that a single ten-year span—the years 1803 to 1813—saw the births of Berlioz, Mendelssohn, Schumann, Chopin, Liszt, Wagner, and Verdi, the entire vanguard of the Romantic movement which profoundly affected the course of music history. The decade of their birth coincided exactly with that of Napoleon's quest for empire and the beginnings of the modern political age.

Hummel (he did not know those of Mozart and Beethoven at the time).

Although it is designated as the second of these works, the Piano Concerto in F minor was actually the first one Chopin composed; it owes its higher opus number to its later publication date. The concerto leaves no doubt where Chopin's sympathies lay: its heart is a poetic Larghetto in which everything of importance is said by the piano, and its outer movements provide the solo instrument with a series of opportunities to elaborate on ideas announced by the orchestra. Although dark passions are hinted at in the first movement's opening tutti, the writing for the piano has a rhapsodic brilliance that eludes the grip of pathos and invites the listener to soar. A feeling of elevated, almost escapist, reverie marks the Larghetto. Beginning like a nocturne, it has a dramatic middle section that erupts into great passion and subsides, ending in an almost dreamlike state. Chopin confided that this music had been inspired by fond memories of a young singer and fellow conservatory student with whom he had fallen in love, Konstancia Gladkowska. The concerto closes with an energetic rondo based on a melody associated with the *kujawiak*, a Polish folk dance. The piano, constantly occupied with flowing passages in eighth-note triplets, is once again the star. The concerto received its premiere at the National Theater in Warsaw on March 17, 1830, and Chopin made his Paris debut with it, at the Salle Pleyel, in the spring of 1832.

The Concerto in E minor utilizes the same template. The expansive first movement opens with a grim, urgent tutti momentarily softened by an aria-like second subject. The piano enters in a meditative vein, and immediately the orchestra becomes almost incidental to the further development of material. The solo part is discursive but rich in fantasy, and notable for its radiant treatment of the movement's second subject. Once again, the heart of the concerto is the second movement, a Romance probably also inspired by

Konstancia and described by Chopin as having "a romantic, calm, and partly melancholy character." There is a brief orchestral introduction, after which the piano takes up a nocturnal melody that it extends at rhapsodic length. The concerto's finale has a Slavic feeling from the start, partly as a result of the coloristic modal harmonies Chopin employs. The solo part combines etude-like energy with considerable elegance, while working up to a virtuosic conclusion. The concerto received its premiere on October 11, 1830, at Chopin's farewell Warsaw performance.

RECOMMENDED RECORDINGS

Artur Rubinstein;
New Symphony Orchestra of London/
Stanislaw Skrowaczewski.
Symphony of the Air/Alfred Wallenstein.
RCA Red Seal 5612-2

Tamás Vásáry;
Berlin Philharmonic/
Jerzy Semkow and Janos Kulka.
Deutsche Grammophon Musikfest 429 515-2

By the time he made these recordings in 1958 and 1961, Rubinstein had forgotten more about the Chopin concertos than most pianists ever know. The natural ease with which they emerge in these accounts, the sense of inevitability that attends every gesture, puts the readings in a class of their own. Rubinstein is the freest of pianists in this music, yet no phrase ever seems bent out of shape, no point too heavily made. Everywhere is that beautiful tone conjured from deep in the keys. Both conductors provide expert and sympathetic accompaniments, with fire and passion from Skrowaczewski in Concerto No. 1 and poetic nobility from Wallenstein in No. 2. The recordings have been exceptionally well remastered; the

First Concerto sounds pleasantly spacious, while the Second is somewhat drily recorded on the stage of Carnegie Hall.

Vásáry's interpretations are aristocratic and refined, exemplary in their blend of lyricism and keyboard brilliance. The accompaniments from the Berlin Philharmonic, under the direction of Semkow in the First Concerto and Kulka in the Second, are weighty and grandly symphonic. There is an excellent concert-hall perspective to the recordings, and the sound is vintage Deutsche Grammophon analog from the mid-1960s. At budget price, this disc is self-recommending.

ANTONÍN DVOŘÁK

CELLO CONCERTO IN B MINOR, OP. 104

Though its name is "violoncello"— "little viol"—the cello is actually a bass violin.

*T*he Cello Concerto was the last of the scores Dvořák composed during his three-year residence in the United States, when he served as the director of the National Conservatory in New York City. In more ways than one, Dvořák's experiences in the New World influenced this music. Early in 1894, he had attended a performance of Victor Herbert's Cello Concerto No. 2. Herbert himself had played the solo part, and Dvořák had come away inspired by the younger composer's skill in scoring the work so that the cello could be heard. As Dvořák wrote his own concerto, the homesickness he had been feeling so intensely during his last year in America emerged and contributed a bittersweetness to the character of the work.

From a formal standpoint, the Cello Concerto is among the most assured of Dvořák's compositions. There is a symphonic sweep to the outer movements, as well as a felicitous development and linkage of ideas throughout the piece. The melodic content of the score is astoundingly rich; in the first movement, for example, the second subject is a beautiful, expansive horn theme in D

DVOŘÁK ARRIVED at an ideal balance between orchestra and cello. He put the cello in its upper range and then made primary use of the winds in the orchestra, whose color differs enough from that of the cello that there is never any danger of the latter's being covered. Brahms, hiding his admiration behind a façade of irritation, is supposed to have exclaimed: "Why on earth didn't I realize that one could write a cello concerto like this? Had I only known, I would have composed one long ago!"

major, which even Dvořák said he could not hear without emotion. Clouds of melancholy more than occasionally pass over the concerto's landscape, echoes perhaps of the *dumka* style of Dvořák's homeland. Whether the rustic sentiment of the slow movement owes its inspiration to Iowa (where the composer spent the summer of 1893) or to the memory of Bohemia's meadows and fields would be impossible to say, but there *is* an "American" quality to some fairly simple, squarish rhythms and strongly diatonic themes, clearly linking this work to Dvořák's *American* Quartet and the Symphony *From the New World.*

There is also a good deal of Wagner's influence in the chromatic harmonies and long-breathed melodic lines, as though Dvořák could not help but think of *Tristan und Isolde* in a work where his thoughts turned to longings for home and to the recollection of the passions of yesteryear. For while he was at work on the Adagio, Dvořák received news of the illness of his sister-in-law Josefina Kaunitzová, with whom he had once been deeply in love and to whom he was still enormously devoted. As a tribute to her, he included in the middle section of the Adagio a reference to a song he had composed seven years earlier, "*Lasst mich allein*" ("Leave Me Alone"), which was one of her favorites. Josefina died shortly after Dvořák's return to Bohemia in 1895, and in memory of her he added a passage of about 60 measures at the end of the concerto's finale, this time literally quoting the song. It is as lovely an elegy as anyone has ever had.

 RECOMMENDED RECORDINGS

**Mstislav Rostropovich;
Berlin Philharmonic/Herbert von Karajan.**
Deutsche Grammophon 413 819-2 [with Tchaikovsky: Variations on a Rococo Theme]

AT THE SAME TIME *Dvořák was writing the Cello Concerto, Richard Strauss was working on* Till Eulenspiegel. *Mahler was composing his Third Symphony and Bruckner his Ninth. Debussy was finishing his opera* Pelléas et Mélisande, *and Puccini was beginning* La bohème.

Pierre Fournier;
Berlin Philharmonic/George Szell.

Deutsche Grammophon Musikfest 429 155-2 [with Bloch: Schelomo, *and Bruch:* Kol Nidrei]

Pablo Casals;
Czech Philharmonic/George Szell.

Pearl GEMM CD 9349 [with Bruch: Kol Nidrei, *and Boccherini: Concerto in B flat]*

Of the half-dozen accounts of this concerto played by Rostropovich that are currently on CD, this one is the best; indeed, it ranks with certainty among the greatest readings ever. It is a performance of heroic size and intensity, notable for the soloist's expressive range and awe-inspiring command of his instrument. Karajan sculpts a powerful, polished accompaniment from the Berlin Philharmonic. The recording has the "hot" analog sound typical of Deutsche Grammophon in the late 1960s: bright, a little light in the bass, but with good detail and reasonably clean textures.

Fournier's ardent tone—so wonderfully seamless from bottom to top—and the urgency of his playing still sound extraordinary in this 30-year-old recording. Szell, no stranger to the work, keeps the score moving along but gives Fournier all the space he needs; this approach lets the cello keep its place at the center of the concerto, rather than being muscled out by the climaxes in the orchestra. There is a certain Czech inflection in the playing that comes in the rhythmic interpretation of small notes, lending an exultant feeling to the whole. DG's recording is open and well balanced, with surprisingly solid bass. There is some graininess in the violin tone, but otherwise the sound is quite natural.

No wrapup of this concerto would be complete without mention of the hair-raising 1937 account by Casals and the Czech Philharmonic, conducted by the 39-year-old Szell. Here was the greatest cellist of the day, surrounded by an ensemble that had been trained by the peerless Václav Talich,

Rostropovich playing his trademark cello with bent endpin for extra power and more resonance.

some of whose musicians had actually played under the baton of Dvořák himself. On the podium, a brilliant young conductor—and in the back room, the legendary producer Fred Gaisberg. The sound is good considering the vintage, and Pearl's transfer and remastering are outstanding.

EDWARD ELGAR
CELLO CONCERTO IN E MINOR, OP. 85

*E*pics traditionally begin with an invocation of the Muse. In a gesture of striking originality, Elgar begins this four-movement concerto with an invocation of Bach, assigning the soloist a recitative that specifically conjures up the Bach of the six suites for unaccompanied cello. As this somber prologue dies away, the violas intone the main theme of the concerto's first movement, a world-weary lament in gently swaying 9/8 time, and with it the melancholy voice of Elgar himself takes up the tale.

Completed in 1919, the Cello Concerto was Elgar's last major work for orchestra, and his most confessional. In spite of fleeting moments of idyllic release, it is dominated by disillusionment, by a sense of suffering that at times cries out against life, yet more often speaks in quiet anguish. Elgar had been ill, and he was deeply depressed by the Great War's destruction of the world he had known. All of this he poured into the unlikely vessel of a concerto for the cello—but perhaps not so unlikely, considering the instrument's rich-toned yet brooding personality and its searing, dark timbre.

The four movements unfold from one another as if forming a single, rhapsodic thought—which in view of Elgar's masterful use of his thematic material, they actually do. After the almost funereal beginning of the first movement, the clarinets introduce a lyrical second theme in 12/8, which is treated in the graceful manner of a siciliana.

*E*LGAR, WHO HAD *a keen interest in science, was one of the first composers to use the phonograph to record his own music. He began recording for the Gramophone Company (owner of the label His Master's Voice) in 1914. Among his most celebrated achievements on disc is his Violin Concerto, captured in July 1932 with the 16-year-old Yehudi Menuhin as soloist.*

The second movement is prefaced by a pizzicato version of the cello's opening recitative; the main body of this movement is a scherzo-like *moto per-petuo* in G major. A meditative Adagio of great beauty reduces the orchestra to chamber size, and the cello sings through all but a single measure.

In the concerto's rondo finale, something of the pre–World War I Elgarian swagger can be detected, but only fleetingly. Fragments of melody from the concerto's earlier movements are hinted at before a climax of anguish and resignation is reached, with an accompanied cadenza quoting a phrase from the principal theme of the Adagio. It is as if Elgar were saying farewell to happier times and a world that could never be retrieved—but the elegy is cut short by a brief reappearance of the opening recitative, and with one last statement of the rondo theme, the work abruptly ends.

 RECOMMENDED RECORDINGS

Heinrich Schiff;
Staatskapelle Dresden/Sir Neville Marriner.
Philips 412 880-2 [with Dvořák: Cello Concerto]

Jacqueline Du Pré;
London Symphony Orchestra/
Sir John Barbirolli.
EMI CDC 47329 [with Sea Pictures]

Schiff possesses a superior technique, an outstanding musical intelligence, and a rich, powerful tone. His tendency to internalize the music he interprets, to put its every phrase and nuance under the microscope, suits this music particularly well. Marriner and the Dresden orchestra provide an opulent, dark-hued accompaniment, and the 1982 recording is superbly spacious and vivid. The coupling is an excellent account of the Dvořák Cello Concerto.

Recorded in 1965, the passionate reading from Du Pré and Barbirolli is one of the classics of the

Cellist Heinrich Schiff strolls through the Elgar Concerto.

catalog. Both the pain and the tenderness of this valedictory work are captured in full by the performance—and fittingly, there is always gentleness in the pain, always an edge to the tenderness. The sound, while somewhat grainy, has remarkable presence and weight, and the balances are ideal.

MANUEL DE FALLA
NIGHTS IN THE GARDENS OF SPAIN

Falla (left) with choreographer Leonide Massine in Granada.

*A*lthough he went through several changes of style in his career, Falla always kept a connection to the music of his native Spain. He did not find it necessary to borrow actual folk melodies—he simply produced original material in the style, material that by its very nature seemed to be derived from popular sources. His music wears its Spanish costume very comfortably, and never seems contrived.

Falla's works get their vitality as much from vibrant imagery and direct emotional expression as from the composer's admittedly well-developed craftsmanship. Among his greatest successes in the sphere of non-theatrical music is *Nights in the Gardens of Spain*, a concerto-like set of three symphonic impressions for piano and orchestra, completed in 1915. In this suite, which captures the nocturnal essence of Andalusia, Falla's colorism is softened almost to the point where it becomes perfume. That is as it should be, for in Granada—whose Generalife is one of the settings depicted by the piece—the scent of flowers is truly the color of the night.

The piano takes a role halfway between foreground and background in all three movements, often playing material that is more coloristic than substantive. The result is a uniquely satisfying integration of the pianistic and orchestral personalities, almost as if the two were engaged in a love scene—which is just what one would expect to find at night in the gardens of Spain. While this

NDALUSIA, *where Falla was born, has long held a special place in the hearts of composers. Exotically set apart from Europe, it was the preferred locale for opera: Mozart's* The Marriage of Figaro *and* Don Giovanni, *Beethoven's* Fidelio, *and Bizet's* Carmen *are all set there. Spanish composers, like Falla, have reveled in the colorful mix of European and Arabic elements that marks Andalusian music to this day.*

may be a rather romantic notion, Falla himself indicates that it is the correct one when, at the climax of the first movement, he quotes the four-note motive of the love potion from Wagner's *Tristan und Isolde.*

 RECOMMENDED RECORDINGS

Alicia de Larrocha;
London Philharmonic Orchestra/
Rafael Frühbeck de Burgos.
London 430 703-2 [with El amor brujo, *and Rodrigo:* Concierto de Aranjuez]

Carol Rosenberger;
London Symphony Orchestra/
Gerard Schwarz.
Delos DCD 3060 [with El sombrero de tres picos]

De Larrocha's latest account of this work is also her best, fully capturing the score's Andalusian atmosphere. After all, it's not really a work about landscapes and flowers; it's about *love.* Frühbeck does a superb job of drawing color out of an English orchestra. The 1983 recording is vivid.

The American pianist Rosenberger is featured in a fine account led by Schwarz on Delos's 1987 CD, which is generously filled and splendidly recorded.

EDVARD GRIEG

Piano Concerto in A minor, Op. 16

O nly Grieg could have composed a work as tuneful and as pianistic as his Concerto in A minor. Yet somehow, one gets a feeling that the piece was destined to exist, as it so perfectly sums up the Romantic notion of the concerto as a duality, a vehicle for virtuosic display and heart-melting sentiment. For Grieg, who was just 25

"WHY HAVE *songs*
played such a
prominent role in my music?
Quite simply because I, like
other mortals, was (to use
Goethe's phrase) once en-
dowed with genius. And that
flash of genius was: love. I
loved a young woman with a
marvelous voice and an
equally marvelous gift as an
interpreter. This woman be-
came my wife and has
remained my life's compan-
ion to this day."
—Grieg in a letter about
his wife, Nina Hagerup
(above)

when he wrote it in 1868, the score was a special triumph, establishing him on the international scene and, for the remainder of his life, winning acclaim as the most successful of his large-scale concert works. Part of the reason for its success is that Grieg never betrays his essentially lyrical genius. He was first and foremost a composer of songs, and he keeps the melodic flame alive on every page of this score.

In concept, the piece follows the lead of Robert Schumann's Piano Concerto in A minor. It has a youthful vitality that makes its melodic generosity seem spontaneous rather than contrived. And just as the warmth of Grieg's passion keeps the music moving ever forward, the brilliance of his pianistic technique—reflected in some of the most wonderfully idiomatic writing for the piano ever penned—makes the journey a challenging and ultimately rewarding one for the performer.

With the impetuous solo passage that opens the work, Grieg establishes a mood of headlong urgency that is sustained throughout the first movement. There are several distinct thematic ideas in this spacious Allegro, and while some of them are related to one another, the movement as a whole offers ample variety and contrast. An intermezzo-like Adagio, in the remote key of D flat major, provides a reprieve from the tempestuous passions of the opening movement. But this is swept aside by the energetic arrival of the finale, based on the *halling,* a characteristic Norwegian dance. Here, Grieg holds in reserve one of his best melodies for use as the second subject. It is first heard in the flute, and just before the end of the work it returns in brassy splendor to set up the requisite triumphant conclusion—a glorious unison between piano and full orchestra in sunlit A major.

The concerto is dedicated to Edmund Neupert, who was the soloist at its premiere in Copenhagen on April 3, 1869. Grieg frequently performed the work himself. He revised the score prior to its publication in 1872 and continued to make changes in both the solo part and the orchestration up to the time of his death. The orchestral complement, large even by 19th-century standards, calls for four horns and three trombones in addition to paired winds, trumpets, timpani, and strings.

RECOMMENDED RECORDINGS

**Murray Perahia;
Bavarian Radio Symphony Orchestra/
Sir Colin Davis.**
CBS Masterworks MK 44899 [with Schumann: Piano Concerto]

**Stephen Bishop-Kovacevich;
BBC Symphony Orchestra/Sir Colin Davis.**
Philips 412 923-2 [with Schumann: Piano Concerto]

Perahia's account is utterly absorbing. The playing is brilliant, but the pianist's approach—essentially lyrical rather than dramatic—keeps that brilliance at the service of larger expressive goals. The result is a performance aglow with understated intensity, one in which the prevalent feeling is often melancholy, at times even bleak. Davis draws a wonderfully refined accompaniment from the Bavarian orchestra in this live reading from 1988 in Munich's Philharmonic Hall. The recording is excellent and effectively captures the beautiful tone Perahia coaxes from his piano.

Although his pianism is not as refined as Perahia's, nor his technique quite as secure, Bishop evokes a dreamy repose in his account. Here, too, the conductor is Davis—and once again he proves to be a superb partner. The BBC Symphony plays well, though it has a peculiar-sounding solo oboe and its violins get somewhat edgy up high. On the recording, which is excellent for 1971, the orchestra sound is slightly grainy and the piano tone not as true as with CBS's digital offering.

Colin Davis has the Grieg concerto in his hip pocket.

JOSEPH HAYDN

TRUMPET CONCERTO IN E FLAT

*H*aydn composed this concerto in 1796 for his associate and friend Anton Weidinger, the trumpet soloist of the Vienna Court Opera. Weidinger had been working since 1793 on an experimental keyed trumpet capable of playing notes other than those in the natural harmonic series, to which the standard instrument of the day was limited. With typical ingenuity, Haydn took full advantage of the new instrument's capabilities; with typical good humor, he disguised the effort so that the novelty of what the trumpet was doing would dawn on the listener only gradually.

Thus the crisp fanfares that the trumpet interjects during the first movement's opening ritornello are entirely conventional, touching only on the notes of the harmonic series. The revelation begins at measure 37, when the trumpet launches into its first solo. It takes up the movement's marchlike subject—which contains all the notes of the E flat major scale—and does so in its middle range, where some of those notes ought not to be playable. Then, in the 11th measure of the solo, Haydn throws in a brief descending chromatic scale, another impossibility which to the judicious ear would have come as a splendid shock. By the end of the concerto, the soloist has been called upon to play every chromatic note across a two-octave compass, something that would have been utterly impracticable on the natural trumpet. This demand obliged Weidinger to make further improvements in his instrument's mechanism, and the concerto had to wait four years for its premiere, on March 28, 1800.

This is the only concerto Haydn composed in the final quarter century of his life, but it shows a master's hand in every detail. While the formal layout and proportions owe something to Mozart, the writing is full of the hallmarks of Haydn's late style. The festive and robust scoring of the opening movement, with flutes prominently doubling the violins and trumpets and with drums adding their weight to the tuttis, immediately evokes the world of the *London* Symphonies. So does the Andante; short, sweet, and songful, it is an exquisite example of the composer's pastoral vein. The finale is not a gigue, as would have been likely in one of Mozart's horn concertos, but a boisterous quick march, full of the bracing, unexpected modulations that are another of Haydn's characteristic touches.

 RECOMMENDED RECORDINGS

**Hakan Hardenberger;
Academy of St. Martin-in-the-Fields/
Sir Neville Marriner.**
Philips 420 203-2 [with concertos by Hertel, Hummel, and Stamitz]

**Wynton Marsalis;
National Philharmonic Orchestra/
Raymond Leppard.**
CBS Masterworks MK 39310 [with Violin Concerto in C and Cello Concerto in D]

Cool Haydn from Wynton Marsalis.

Hardenberger possesses a polished technique, a clear tone, and a smooth legato. A few examples of questionable artistry (such as the undue stress he puts on the resolution of trills) reveal he is not yet fully educated as a virtuoso. One might prefer a somewhat more mellow and burnished sound, but Hardenberger's technique and control are not to be faulted. He offers an excellent cadenza, true to the style of the period. Marriner and the Academy do a smashing job with the rest of the piece. Philips's engineering is excellent, though the trumpet is larger-sounding and closer than it should be, a small flaw.

Marsalis has an articulate style, a very tightly focused sound, and a natural way with this music—

a bit surprising considering his unbridled success as a jazz trumpeter. His tone, however, is rather lightweight and sharp-edged for a classical soloist, and he does show a certain abandon with the top notes, his specialty; here they're almost screamers. Marsalis also succumbs to the temptation to play a Romantic-style cadenza, though he does it very well. Under Leppard's direction the National Philharmonic proves ideally supportive. Its strings are notably good, but a diffuse recording robs the bass line of proper firmness.

FRANZ LISZT

PIANO CONCERTO NO. 1, IN E FLAT

*L*ike a number of his other works, Liszt's First Piano Concerto went through a long process of development before reaching its final form. First sketches were made in 1830, when the composer was not yet 20, and additional material was drafted in 1839–40. But it was not until 1849, following his retirement from active concertizing, that Liszt turned the sketches into a finished work. After that, he put the concerto aside for another four years, revising it in 1853 and finally performing it two years later. There were further revisions in 1856 prior to the score's publication.

Rather paradoxically, the result of Liszt's deliberate labor was a work of striking bravura. The brilliance of the solo part is apparent not only in the blazing octave runs and whirlwind passages of broken chords, but also in the variety of touch and expression called for in less showy moments. Remarkable as well is the originality of the concerto's construction, a format one can readily imagine *did* take Liszt a long time to figure out.

To begin with, a four-movement design is compressed into a three-movement layout, with the scherzo appended directly to the slow movement (and bridged to the finale as in Beethoven's Fifth

Liszt c. 1848, during the composition of his First Piano Concerto.

Symphony). And the linkages are thematic as well. The scherzo and finale recapitulate material from each of the concerto's preceding movements, so that the whole work resembles a sonata form writ large, exhibiting the thematic unity of a single movement. Liszt pioneered this cyclical approach to form and gave it ultimate expression in his Piano Sonata in B minor. While the concerto is not as tightly argued, it succeeds nonetheless—as a showcase for pianistic virtuosity, as an exploration of thematic material, and as a large-scale structure.

The opening measures are pompous in the best sense. Flamboyant and assertive, they leave no doubt that both orchestra and piano will have something to say, while giving the misleading impression that their relationship will be antagonistic. After the piano has wrestled the orchestra into submission—with a cadenza that comes just ten bars into the piece—the two in fact work hand in glove. The remainder of the first movement is by turns dramatic and rhapsodic, drawing a gallant display of athleticism and delicacy from the solo instrument.

The B major Adagio opens with a gentle, aria-like melody. The reverie is shattered by a dramatic piano recitative over tremolo strings, but the end of the movement is even more beautiful than the beginning, foreshadowing Liszt's late style and the delicate effects of his solo piano piece *Les jeux d'eau à la villa d'Este*. The scherzo portion of the second movement steals upon the scene to the impish tinkling of the triangle. Here the mood is one of scintillating diablerie, with the piano an active participant throughout. As the scherzo nears its end, there is a reprise of the first movement's grandiose call to action.

Grand, rambunctious, and decidedly virtuosic, this last movement is based on a metamorphosis of earlier material, the Lisztian process of thematic transformation. The march theme announced by the winds is a sped-up version of the second-movement aria, and themes from the first movement and the scherzo appear in new guises as the finale progresses. One other thing happens as well: Liszt cranks up the tempo to a vertiginous *presto*, guaranteeing that the work's final double octaves will astonish and delight.

The premiere of the E flat Concerto took place in Weimar on February 17, 1855, with Liszt playing the solo part and Berlioz, having had just five days to learn the score, conducting.

 ## RECOMMENDED RECORDINGS

Santiago Rodriguez;
Sofia Philharmonic Orchestra/Emil Tabakov.
Elan CD 2228 [with Grieg: Piano Concerto, and Tchaikovsky: Concerto No. 1]

Krystian Zimerman;
Boston Symphony Orchestra/Seiji Ozawa.
Deutsche Grammophon 423 571-2 [with Concerto No. 2 and Totentanz]

Zoltán Kocsis;
Budapest Festival Orchestra/Iván Fischer.
Philips 422 380-2 [with Concerto No. 2, and Dohnányi: Variations on a Nursery Song]

The American pianist Rodriguez puts his breathtaking technique to good use in an articulate and exhilarating performance of the concerto. The rhythmic liveliness he brings to the solo part and his detailing of inner voices are a tribute not only to extraordinary fingers, but to an equally extraordinary musicality. He is well partnered by Tabakov and the Bulgarians, although there are minor blemishes in tuning and ensemble. The 1990 recording leaves the orchestra sounding a bit recessed and is overly bright and reverberant. The coupling of Grieg and Tchaikovsky concertos, both exceptionally well played, is the most generous in the catalog.

Zimerman's is a controlled reading rather than

THE TRIANGLE'S prominence in the scherzo and finale caused such consternation among critics that Liszt felt it necessary to warn the pianist Alfred Jaëll, who was planning a performance of the work, to "take care that the triangle has not too vulgar a vibration and that the triangle player does his job delicately, precisely, and intelligently." The solo is but one example of Liszt's imaginative scoring, in which the emphasis is more often on chamber-like delicacy than power.

Polish pianist Krystian Zimerman.

a spontaneous one. He emphasizes lightness of touch and accuracy, taking aim at the filigree in the writing, of which there is certainly enough to occupy any pianist. He is superbly accompanied by Ozawa and the Boston Symphony, whose contribution is highlighted by some very fine solos in the winds. The 1987 recording is typically over-miked and dry; the tone is reasonably natural, though shy in the bass.

In a recording from the following year, Kocsis is a bit grandiose in the opening of the concerto, and a bit *larmoyant* in the meditations, but impulsive nonetheless. The Hungarian pianist enjoys the athleticism of the score, and his performance of the finale really sweeps one along. The Budapest orchestra does a solid job in the tuttis, and the sound is rather good.

FELIX MENDELSSOHN
VIOLIN CONCERTO IN E MINOR, OP. 64

*A*mong the most frequently performed concertos in the literature, this work owes its existence to the friendship between Mendelssohn and the violinist Ferdinand David, whom Mendelssohn engaged as concertmaster of the Leipzig Gewandhaus Orchestra after becoming its director in 1835. The fact that the composer was willing to entrust so much of the concerto's expressive content to his soloist suggests that David was not only a first-rate virtuoso but a sensitive artist as well.

That he was definitely the former is obvious from the solo part itself. Here, the full range of a violinist's technique is challenged by writing that calls for lyricism and agility in equal measure, as well as an ability to project nuance and emotion in the softest dynamics. Mendelssohn's fabled skill as an orchestrator is also apparent, in the lucid textures that allow the solo instrument to be heard at all times and in the felicitous use of the winds

The Gewandhaus in Leipzig, painted by Mendelssohn.

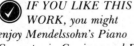

IF YOU LIKE THIS WORK, you might enjoy Mendelssohn's Piano Concertos in G minor and D minor, composed in 1831 and 1837, respectively. In spite of their minor-key tonality, both are scintillating, vivacious works that place a premium on fleet-fingered virtuosity.

to color the tutti passages. But the concerto is most impressive for its coherence—the way the three movements unfold as if informed by a single thought, and the way the solo part and the orchestra intertwine. To achieve this degree of symphonic integration, Mendelssohn resorted to some rather daring formal innovations, including a linkage of the first two movements, the insertion of the first-movement cadenza not at the end of the movement but as part of the development, and the use of a transitional passage between the second movement and the finale that recalls the thematic material of the opening movement.

The idea for the concerto came to Mendelssohn in 1838. "It is running through my head," the composer wrote to David. "The beginning of it gives me no peace." Mendelssohn's description was apt, for the opening bars are among the most haunting in music. They are also an ingenious way to begin a concerto. There is no extended orchestral tutti, no preamble, no flourish from the soloist—instead, just a measure and a half of restless accompaniment before the violin announces the movement's principal subject, a soft cry from the heart. One of the concerto's loveliest moments comes with the arrival of the second subject, as the violin drops to a low G and holds it for eight measures while the clarinets and flutes sound the tranquil chordal melody above it. Only then does the violin itself take up the theme, and the effect is rhapsodic. The high point of the development is the cadenza—and when the violin finishes it and launches into the recapitulation, *it* is playing the restless accompaniment and the orchestra has the opening theme, a clever reversal of roles.

A sustained B in the bassoon provides a link to the Andante, a radiant "song without words" in C major with a turbulent middle section in the minor. A transitional recitative in E minor, recalling the concerto's opening subject, sets up the vivacious E major finale, whose opening fanfares and capricious main subject, marked *pianissimo* and *leggiero*, recapture the spirit of *A Midsummer Night's Dream*. The writing for the solo instrument is unabashedly virtuosic, a virtually unbroken stream of flowing eighths and racing sixteenths. The orchestra provides soft-spoken fireworks before erupting at movement's end.

RECOMMENDED RECORDINGS

Kyung Wha Chung;
Montreal Symphony Orchestra/
Charles Dutoit.
London 410 011-2 *[with Tchaikovsky: Violin Concerto]*

Nathan Milstein;
Vienna Philharmonic/Claudio Abbado.
Deutsche Grammophon Galleria 419 067-2
[with Tchaikovsky: Violin Concerto]

Jascha Heifetz;
Boston Symphony Orchestra/
Charles Munch.
RCA Red Seal 5933-2 *[with Tchaikovsky: Violin Concerto,* Sérénade mélancolique, *and Waltz from Serenade for Strings]*

Chung's radiant lyricism and ardent virtuosity make her recording of the concerto especially appealing. Dutoit and the Montreal orchestra provide exquisite support, and the 1981 recording is transparent in its detail and superbly balanced. With an outstanding account of the Tchaikovsky concerto as the coupling, this disc is a winner.

Ever the patrician in his phrasing, tone, and manner, Milstein brings warm sentiment to the music. There is a continuity to his interpretation that allows the piece to unfold almost rhapsodically, as if it were taking shape spontaneously under his fingers. Abbado and the Vienna Philharmonic create a dark, burnished background against which Milstein glows in this fine recording.

In Mendelssohn as in everything else, Heifetz

Performing Personalities

Where Jascha Heifetz dazzled, Nathan Milstein delighted, probing for meaning and emotion without ever losing sight of musical architecture. A virtuoso who had something more—call it warmth or finesse—he was the consummate stylist among the 20th century's great violinists.

plays with an edgy intensity that gives urgency to the music even in its most poetic moments. He also brings dazzling technique and heart-on-sleeve Romanticism, and he is brilliantly backed up by Munch and the Bostonians. The 1959 recording is spacious, clean, and tonally quite accurate, though Heifetz is a bit closely miked.

WOLFGANG AMADEUS MOZART

Piano Concerto No. 9, in E flat, K. 271

"I live in a country where music leads a struggling existence," Mozart wrote to his friend and mentor Padre Martini on September 4, 1776. The 20-year-old composer was already finding it difficult to conceal his contempt for Salzburg and the ordinariness of its musical life. Suddenly, a touring French pianist by the name of Jeunehomme burst onto the scene. Not much is known about her—not even her first name—but her appearance in Salzburg in January 1777 elicited from Mozart one of the most remarkable works he was ever to compose. The brilliance, boldness, and emotional maturity of the Piano Concerto in E flat, K. 271, are without precedent in Mozart's oeuvre up to that point and establish the piece as a prototype, delivered well ahead of schedule, for his sublime Viennese essays of the mid-1780s.

One can only marvel at the ideas and workmanship Mozart brought to this concerto. Pianist Alfred Brendel has called it a "wonder of the world," and even in the august world of Mozart's piano concertos it is certainly that. Conceived on a much larger scale than any of Mozart's previous works in the form, it is also far more subtle and sophisticated. The writing is full of colorful, felicitous turns that manage without the slightest hint of self-consciousness to lift the piece out of the ordinary.

THOUGH HE FELT confined in Salzburg, Mozart wrote several symphonic works there during his last years in the Archbishop's service that are unusually festive and outgoing, similar in spirit to the E flat Piano Concerto. Two of the finest are the powerfully scored Posthorn Serenade, K. 320, and the Symphony No. 34, in C, K. 338. Both might be subtitled "How I Spent My Summer Vacation."

The concerto opens with a delightfully cheeky gesture, as the piano interrupts the orchestra's fanfare-like opening phrase in the second bar. From here Mozart develops a rich dialog between solo instrument and orchestra that hinges on the piano's newly established freedom of action. The Andantino, in C minor, begins with a somber passage in the violins' dark lower register. The entrance of the piano precipitates a shift to the major, leading the listener on a journey into the heart of 18th-century sensibility. Here, as the piano floats a delicately ornamented singing line above it, the attenuated passion of the orchestra's pleading—with poignant, muted violins and plaintive oboes—looks far, far ahead toward Romanticism.

A mood of festivity returns in the finale, which begins with a brilliant exposition of the movement's rondo subject by the soloist. But as the orchestra is trying to work out *its* material, the piano pounces on that idea as well, snatching it away. The most striking break with protocol comes a little later with the introduction of a minuet as the rondo's second episode. Each strain of the minuet is repeated with florid ornamentation before orchestra and soloist resume their dash to the finish line, this time at a full *presto.*

PIANO CONCERTO NO. 20, IN D MINOR, K. 466

Of all Mozart's concertos, this one, finished on February 10, 1785, was the favorite of the Romantics. Its turbulence and lyricism appealed to the 19th-century view of Mozart as a pre-Romantic revolutionary and a forerunner of Beethoven and the other titans of self-expression. While Mozart's music is no longer viewed in terms of what came later, but rather as a uniquely adept and insightful synthesis of what was going on at the time, this work does seem revolutionary; its

THE "MANNHEIM
rocket" was a favorite
musical device of the late
18th century. It refers to a
theme built on the notes of a
major or minor triad that ascends rapidly (i.e., "rockets")
from its the lowest note to its
highest. This theme has an
arrestingly bold effect, and it
was frequently used by the
composers of the Mannheim
school. Mozart used a rocket
theme to launch the finale of
his Symphony in G minor,
K. 550, and Beethoven
touched one off at the start
of his first piano sonata,
Op. 2, No. 1.

music is unlike that of any concerto Mozart had
written before, in both its gravity and its subjectivity. With this concerto, the first of six supreme
works in the form that he would write in just
under two years, Mozart reached a new plateau
in his development as an instrumental composer.

The first movement begins with a foreboding
subject that is as much accompaniment as melody.
At its heart is a subdued, syncopated figure in the
violins and violas that seems an embodiment of
fear. From this uneasy beginning, the opening
tutti builds to a ferocious climax, in which there
is a hint of the furious D minor yet to come in
the opera *Don Giovanni*. As the storm clears, the
piano makes its entrance—and it is an extraordinary one, conveying deep agitation in the midst
of lyricism. The melody's wide jumps signify intense feeling, and Mozart expands on this during
the course of the movement. The subtle play of
major and minor helps create a mood of restlessness and tension to the very end.

A contrasting mood of innocence characterizes
the start of the Romance, where a songlike subject
is heard first in the piano, then in the orchestra.
The simplicity of the melody itself and the gentleness of Mozart's scoring, which favors the winds,
conspire to provide a welcome respite. The idyll
is disturbed as the piano enters a maelstrom of
swirling triplet figures, but the return of the opening melody brings the movement to a placid close.

The lightning bolt with which the rondo finale
begins—actually a "Mannheim rocket" launched
by the piano and answered by the orchestra—
signals a return of the emotionally charged atmosphere of the first movement. Fiery passages
in the strings anticipate the demonic penultimate
scene of *Don Giovanni*, and even the piano's lyrical
second subject is wrenched across wide intervals.
In the final pages, Mozart allows the key of D
major to supplant D minor—a sudden and satisfying relaxation of tension. Even so, the end of
the concerto is explosive and abrupt.

Piano Concerto No. 21, in C, K. 467

*T*his work, completed on March 9, 1785, stands out as one of the most elegant and imaginative of Mozart's Viennese piano concertos. Its opening Allegro makes much of the march topic and the trumpets and drums that go with it, and while that in itself is hardly remarkable, what *is* remarkable is Mozart's ability to fashion such a tightly constructed symphonic argument around a solo part so rich in fantasy. Indeed, from its appearance—no straightforward pronouncement of the movement's main theme, but a series of flourishes followed by a long trill that hovers impatiently while the orchestra restates the tune—the piano is in constant motion, on what seems a flight of pure fancy. Here and there it alights, hummingbird-like, on a melody; elsewhere, its part is an exuberant play of bravura passagework and ornamental figuration.

The celebrated Andante offers what may well be Mozart's most ethereal aria—even though there are no words to go with it. Indeed, with its heartbeat of soft triplets, the tune is so lovely that Mozart cannot resist having the orchestra sing it right at the start. The piano then takes it up in an improvisatory manner, spinning out an embellished extension full of stirring leaps and plunges that no coloratura soprano could ever hope to match. The luminous accompaniment of muted violins and plangent woodwinds, over a gentle pizzicato bass, lends tender emotion to the treatment, while the bittersweet dissonances and subtle shifts of harmony and tone color anticipate the language of Romanticism.

The finale, a light-hearted romp full of operatic gaiety, begins with a mischievous subject that shoots partway up the scale and right back down again. By phrasing it so that it is always off balance—the rhythmic emphasis falls at the beginning of the *second* measure rather than the first—Mozart gives this idea a headlong thrust that animates

ELVIRA MADIGAN, *the Swedish film, made prominent use of this composition's Andante in its soundtrack, thereby attaching to the concerto the nickname by which it is now widely known.*

the entire movement. He further energizes the proceedings by introducing a subsidiary subject with prominent offbeat accents. Throughout the movement, the piano keeps challenging the orchestra to follow it into new melodic territory, and the orchestra keeps trying to get back on a familiar track. The conversation becomes fairly argumentative in the central episode, where the first six notes of the main subject are tossed back and forth, each time in a different key, but the movement ends in the brightest of spirits.

Piano Concerto No. 24, in C minor, K. 491

*M*ozart finished this concerto on March 24, 1786, and played the premiere two weeks later at a subscription concert in Vienna's Burgtheater. A look at the manuscript shows it was written in great haste: The solo part is sketchy in a number of places, with many details of figuration either missing or furtively encoded on empty staves above it. Also absent are cadenzas for the first and third movements. We will never know precisely how Mozart realized these things in performance.

Even so, this is the most compelling of his piano concertos. Here Mozart uses the largest wind complement in any of his concertos—flute, two oboes, two clarinets, two bassoons, and two horns—plus trumpets and drums, giving the tuttis unprecedented power and richness of tone while opening up a world of nuance within the orchestra. The atmosphere is tragic, pathetic, hauntingly grim—already apparent in the opening theme of the first movement, which combines anxiety (in unsettling chromatic tinges and poignant leaps of a diminished seventh) with severity (the rigorous dotted rhythm). Later, there are echoes of the church and fantasy styles in the winds. The piano

BEHIND BOTH *the potent feeling and unbridled fantasy of this concerto's first movement is the weight of grim foreboding. Mozart himself must have felt it: he filled in an empty bar of the manuscript, just before the movement's coda, with a drawing of a grotesque face (above).*

Mozart's concert piano in Salzburg.

makes a quiet entrance with a new theme that is rhythmically related to both of the main themes. The writing for the solo instrument is remarkable not only for its varied figuration but for its invention and seamless connection of ideas.

The second movement, marked *Larghetto* by an anonymous hand but written in the style of a Romance, has all the trappings of an aria of love, featuring serenade-style woodwind writing in sonorous thirds. The main subject is introduced by the piano alone, answered by strings and winds, and then jointly embellished by all.

In the third movement, Mozart turns to the variation form for the last time in his piano concertos. The theme is funereal and marchlike, but Mozart's treatment explores a wide range of textures and emotional shadings. Two of the variations are in the major and find the winds taking the lead: the fourth, in A flat, is pastoral, while the sixth, in C, subjects the theme to playful canonic treatment. Mozart returns to C minor for the shadowy seventh variation and stays there for the final one as well, which because it plays against the supposed lightness of its own rhythm, a gigue-like 6/8, is especially chilling.

RECOMMENDED RECORDINGS

**Murray Perahia;
English Chamber Orchestra.**
CBS Masterworks MK 34562 [Concertos Nos. 9 and 21] and MK 42242 [No. 24, with No. 22]

**Robert Casadesus;
Cleveland Orchestra and
Columbia Symphony Orchestra/
George Szell.**
Sony Classical SM3K 46519 [3 CDs; Concertos Nos. 21 and 24, with Nos. 22, 23, 26, and 27 and Concerto for Two Pianos, K. 365; Nos. 21 and 24 also available separately on CBS MYK 38523]

"**W**E DID NOT know what to admire most, whether the extraordinary compositions or his extraordinary playing. . . . [H]is improvisations exceeded anything that can be imagined in the way of piano playing, as the highest degree of the composer's art was combined with perfection of playing."
—Czech music critic Franz Niemetschek, on Mozart's playing

Sir Clifford Curzon;
London Symphony Orchestra/
István Kertész.
London Weekend Classics 433 086-2 [Concertos No. 24, with No. 23, and Schubert: Impromptus, Op. 90, Nos. 3 and 4]

Sir Clifford Curzon;
English Chamber Orchestra/
Sir Benjamin Britten.
London 417 288-2 [Concerto No. 20, with No. 27]

Perahia has recorded all of the Mozart piano concertos, and his effortlessly brilliant accounts can be recommended across the board. The playing is on the highest level: vibrant, unfailingly beautiful, wonderfully acute in its grasp of style and expression. Equally outstanding is the English Chamber Orchestra, which Perahia leads from the keyboard. The recorded sound, while not as radiant as the music making, is consistently good and well balanced from disc to disc.

The energetic readings of Casadesus and Szell set a standard for this repertory that has yet to be surpassed. Dramatic and tightly wound but never unsmiling, the accounts combine grace and lucidity with an almost operatic lyricism. The sound is dry but firm and detailed, and Sony has done an excellent job of remastering these recordings from 1959–62.

Curzon was a very special Mozartean, a pianist of exceptional ability who communicated profound insights into the music and played with the utmost refinement. These readings of four of Mozart's greatest concertos, recorded under ideal circumstances in 1968 near the end of Curzon's life, are among the most impressive in the catalog. For this a share of the credit must go to Kertész and Britten, whose sensitivity to Mozart made them extraordinary accomplices. The playing of both orchestras is at a high level throughout, and the recordings sound wonderfully alive, as if they were made yesterday.

Performing
Personalities

There was no better pianist of Mozart and no finer chamber musician in any repertory than Clifford Curzon. He was an artist of patrician taste and flawless technique, and in the few recordings he made, the depth of his musical and spiritual insights are readily sensed.

MOZART PLAYED *his Violin Concerto in G, K. 216, at performances in Munich and Augsburg in October 1777. "I played as though I were the finest fiddler in Europe," he wrote his father from Augsburg. "It went like oil, and everybody praised my beautiful, pure tone." And Leopold Mozart could certainly relate. As a young man Leopold had been one of the finest fiddlers in Europe.*

VIOLIN CONCERTO NO. 3, IN G, K. 216
VIOLIN CONCERTO NO. 5, IN A, K. 219

"*Y*ou yourself do not know how well you play the violin," Leopold Mozart wrote to his son in 1777. "If only you would do yourself justice and play with energy, with your whole heart and mind, you could be the best violinist in Europe." It was a candid assessment from the man who had written the most important treatise of the day on violin playing. Nor was Leopold alone in thinking so, for while Wolfgang was undoubtedly among the best pianists in Europe, he was also a good enough violinist to be appointed concertmaster of the court orchestra in Salzburg when he was 16.

Traditionally, the date 1775 has been assigned to all five of Mozart's authenticated violin concertos. Recent scholarship has suggested that the first of these may have been written in 1773, just after Mozart became Salzburg concertmaster. Four concertos in a single year is still an impressive tally, but it is only half the story. During the years 1773–76, Mozart also incorporated a number of concerted movements for violin into his serenades—sometimes, as is the case with the *Haffner* Serenade, K. 250, embedding an entire three-movement concerto within the score. Thus, Mozart's real output during this four-year span was an impressive 37 movements for solo violin and orchestra. It is almost as if the composer had decided to occupy himself, between the ages of 17 and 20, with a master's degree in the violin concerto. Just why he did this is not known.

The most popular of Mozart's violin concertos are those in G major, K. 216, and A major, K. 219, which date from September and December of 1775. In each, the variety of material and the assurance with which it is treated seem utterly remarkable for a composer in his teens.

The Concerto in G opens with a cheery march borrowed from Mozart's own musical play *Il rè*

BAROQUE DANCES *such as the bourrée,* *gavotte (above), sarabande,* *minuet, and gigue permeated* *the instrumental music of the* *18th century. The gavotte* *and other lively dances lent* *elegance and vitality to* *music in fast tempos, while* *more courtly dances such* *as the sarabande brought* *heightened expressiveness to* *slow movements. The typical* *Baroque suite consisted of* *an overture or prelude fol-* *lowed by a string of dances,* *and by 1770 the minuet* *had been adopted as the* *standard third movement of* *the four-movement Classical* *symphony.*

pastore, completed earlier in the year. The topic is colored with a vibrant athleticism here, a coquettish daintiness there, producing a series of animated exchanges between soloist and orchestra that could almost be described as sexual encounters. A whole new world opens up in the beautiful Adagio, with its tender pastoral sentiment and delicate scoring. Here Mozart offers one of the most ethereal melodies for the violin, spun out with an elevated feeling that takes one's breath away. He brings things back to earth in the lively rondo finale, where he inserts an unexpected episode. It begins with the solo violin serving up an elegantly ornamented gavotte, then transforms itself into a musette-style quotation of a popular tune known as "The Strassburger." The original material then returns with a sheepish grin on its face, and the concerto ends in bashful delight.

The Concerto in A has a broad opening movement (Mozart designates it an *Allegro aperto,* literally an "open" or "spacious" Allegro) where material is treated in an especially felicitous and confident manner. In a departure from convention, the solo violin introduces itself not with a reprise of the opening theme, but with an arrestingly poetic sixbar Adagio, as though it had been awakened from a dream. The second movement, also unusually large, is one of Mozart's most inspired Adagios; nevertheless, Antonio Brunetti, Mozart's successor as Salzburg concertmaster, thought the movement too "studied" and asked for a replacement, which Mozart generously supplied (now numbered separately as K. 261). The concerto's rondo finale is a celebrated movement where Mozart inserts one of his most memorable allusions to Turkish music. Cellos and basses use the backs of their bows to suggest the snap of drums that accompanied Turkish marches, while the violin takes off like a whirling dervish in a spicy solo. Once the episode is played out, the rondo's minuet-like subject returns and brings the concerto to a gentle conclusion.

RECOMMENDED RECORDINGS

Cho-Liang Lin;
English Chamber Orchestra/
Raymond Leppard.
CBS Masterworks MK 42364 [with Adagio, K. 261]

Arthur Grumiaux;
London Symphony Orchestra/
Sir Colin Davis.
Philips 412 250-2

Anne-Sophie Mutter;
Berlin Philharmonic/Herbert von Karajan.
Deutsche Grammophon 429 814-2

Lin's combination of understated virtuosity and solid musicality is the perfect one for Mozart. His accounts are superbly wrought, and they show remarkable insight and grace for a 26-year-old. Leppard and orchestra back their soloist in superb fashion, with playing that is alert and deftly balanced. Leppard's stylish cadenzas are a joy. The 1986 recording is clean and natural, like the performances themselves.

Grumiaux's approach to this youthful music is polished, patrician, elegant. At times there is just a hint of the grand manner, but no violinist has ever phrased a singing line more beautifully. With Davis and the London Symphony providing outstanding support, these accounts are full of rewards for the connoisseur. The sound is excellent for its 1961 vintage.

Barely in her teens, Mutter made her recording debut with these miraculous readings. The playing is angelic in its beauty and sweetness, and full of warmth and spontaneity. Karajan's accompaniment is, as usual in Mozart, like a suit of armor: highly polished if a bit heavy. The sound is bright and close-miked, but balances are suitable and there is ample detail.

Mutter and Karajan discuss interpretations of a concerto.

OR MOZART the key of E flat had a dual nature. Because of its suitability for the woodwinds, especially the clarinet, he often used it for amorous music; in Le nozze di Figaro, *for example, the first arias of Cherubino and the Countess are both in E flat. At other times the key carried a festive connotation, as in the first movements of the* Sinfonia concertante, K. 364, *and the* Symphony in E flat, *K. 543.*

SINFONIA CONCERTANTE IN E FLAT FOR VIOLIN AND VIOLA, K. 364

As used in the latter part of the 18th century, the term *sinfonia concertante* meant any concerto-like work with more than one solo instrument. Mozart's *Sinfonia concertante* for Violin and Viola dates from 1779, a miraculous time of turning in the composer's life. He had recently completed his ear-opening 16-month journey to Mannheim and Paris, where the *concertante* genre was popular. Even though this concerto was conceived for the smaller forces available in Salzburg, its polished orchestral writing reflects the cosmopolitan influence and suggests that he had reached a new height of stylistic and technical assurance.

Mozart's abilities as violinist and violist are evident in the challenging yet idiomatic writing for the solo instruments. And he shows his knowledge of the tricks of the trade in his clever instruction to tune the viola a half-step sharp to help the softer-toned instrument achieve a balance with the solo violin.

In the long first movement, the march topic predominates, and the influence of Mannheim is apparent in the richness and warmth of the scoring and the prominent use of the "Mannheim steamroller" crescendo. Mozart has the two solo instruments trading off with one another and weaving their way in and out of the orchestral fabric with supreme ease. The written-out cadenza provides one of the best examples of how a Classical cadenza should be constructed, using motifs and passagework rather than complete themes.

The aria-like second movement is a somber C minor Andante tinged with poignant dissonances. An ornamented melody is taken up in responsory fashion by the two soloists, then duetted. Following a brief transition, there is a buildup to a radiantly scored climax in the major, which rounds

Mozart got the most out of the Mannheim steamroller.

The viola (lower) is the alto member of the violin family.

out the first part of the aria. When the opening material returns toward the end of the movement, Mozart does not allow it to escape the grip of the minor mode.

Festive spirits return in the finale, a giddily animated rondo that offers plenty of opportunity for plain old virtuoso fiddling. In his treatment of the material, Mozart shows much variety and freshness, as well as that remarkable, seamless sense of connection between ideas he alone seemed to possess. The climax comes as the soloists rocket up to a pair of show-off high E flats—first the viola, then the violin—to close the piece with a last surge of voltage.

 RECOMMENDED RECORDINGS

**Cho-Liang Lin, Jaime Laredo;
English Chamber Orchestra/
Raymond Leppard.**
Sony Classical SK 47693 [with Concertone *in C for Two Violins and Orchestra, K. 190]*

**Iona Brown, Josef Suk;
Academy of St. Martin-in-the-Fields.**
London Jubilee 433 171-2 [with Violin Concertos No. 2, K. 211, and No. 4, K. 218]

**Thomas Brandis, Giusto Cappone;
Berlin Philharmonic/Karl Böhm.**
Deutsche Grammophon 429 813-2 [with Sinfonia concertante *in E flat for Winds, K. 297b]*

For sheer exuberance—to say nothing of their warmth and elegance—violinist Lin and violist Laredo have the field nearly to themselves. Theirs is an unusually close partnership of two strong, outgoing musicians. The detail-work is exceptionally fine, the ensemble breathtakingly clean. Leppard and orchestra support the effort with playing of real symphonic weight, giving a big-boned, muscular account of the score, yet one

IF YOU LIKE THIS WORK, *you may enjoy other multi-instrument concertos that have won a place in the repertory, including* Haydn's Sinfonia concertante *for Oboe, Bassoon, Violin, Cello, and Orchestra,* Beethoven's Triple Concerto, *and Brahms's Concerto in A minor for Violin, Cello, and Orchestra, Op. 102.*

that is wonderfully suave. The 1991 recording packs a punch, even if it is a little bass-heavy.

Brown and Suk take a similar approach, offering a stylish account with plenty of gung-ho fiddling. Tempos are excellent: There is a vigorous yet relaxed feeling to the Allegro, room to breathe in the Andante, and plenty of life in the Presto. The St. Martin players accompany with remarkable dash and power, and the 1983 recording is spacious and beautifully detailed. Coupled with two of Mozart's violin concertos, this midprice disc has plenty to recommend it.

With Böhm presiding, Berlin Philharmonic principals Brandis and Cappone turn in a fluent interpretation. Their playing is polished and persuasive and is generously supported by their colleagues. The tempo of the first movement is broad, but as usual with Böhm the music moves with Apollonian grace. Deutsche Grammophon's recording is excellent for its mid-1960s vintage, with ample presence and good depth.

HORN CONCERTO NO. 3, IN E FLAT, K. 447

*T*his concerto was composed in 1787 or 1788, around the time Mozart was working on *Don Giovanni*. Like all of Mozart's horn concertos, it was written for the virtuoso Joseph Leutgeb, whom the composer had known from his youth. The scoring, which calls for clarinets and bassoons rather than oboes and horns, is warmer and darker than that of Mozart's other horn concertos, the harmonic language richer and noticeably more chromatic. At times, the concerto's thematic material is almost melancholy.

The first movement is remarkable both for its sustained lyricism and for its seamless line of action, particularly through the development section, where Mozart traverses some rather tricky harmonic ground in extraordinary fashion. The ensuing Romance is an amoroso aria of considerable charm that briefly touches on pathos, which

Look, ma, no valves!
Natural horn with crook.

Performing Personalities

Dennis Brain is the supreme horn virtuoso of this century. No one has ever possessed a comparable tone or dexterity, and when he perished in an auto accident in 1957, at the age of 36, the music world was left in despair. He had made only a handful of recordings to document his artistry, and was serving as the principal horn in two of London's top orchestras, the Royal Philharmonic and the Philharmonia.

in its sophistication gives prima facie evidence that Leutgeb could not have been the "ass, ox, and fool" Mozart had dubbed him in the dedication to the Second Horn Concerto. The hunt figures as the main topic of the concluding rondo, but the treatment is gentler and more restrained than previously, and the pathetic accents that crop up near the end suggest that a deeper feeling has begun to enter into the merriment.

 RECOMMENDED RECORDING

**Dennis Brain;
Philharmonia Orchestra/
Herbert von Karajan.**
EMI CDH 61013 [with Concertos Nos. 1, 2, and 4]

Pride of place in this repertory will always belong to Brain, the greatest virtuoso the horn has ever known. Here his legendary agility, fluidity, evenness of tone, and musicality are readily apparent, undimmed by the haze of a 40-year-old monaural recording. Karajan draws elegant work from the Philharmonia strings, though the recording boxes them in somewhat and leaves the basses sounding a bit light. In this remastering, EMI's engineers seem to have shaved something off the top in order to limit tape hiss; even so, the disc is a must.

CLARINET CONCERTO IN A, K. 622

*M*ozart's love affair with the clarinet began in Mannheim when he was 21, but it would be several more years before he met Anton Stadler, the clarinetist whose playing would inspire what many say is the most beautiful music ever written for a wind instrument. Anton, second clarinet to his younger brother Johann at the court opera in Vienna, had a keen interest in the instrument's lower register and played an

ANTON STADLER *was in debt to Mozart for 500 gulden at the time of the composer's death. He also was responsible for the loss of several Mozart manuscripts. Stadler's acquaintances claimed he had pawned them. Stadler must have played like an angel, for in spite of his behavior Mozart loved him like a brother; the music of this concerto and the Clarinet Quintet show what the composer thought of his artistry.*

important part in the development of the basset clarinet, which had an extended lower joint that enabled it to reach A, a major third below the low C sharp of the standard clarinet in A. The basset clarinet was the instrument Mozart had in mind when he composed his two most important works for the elder Stadler, the Quintet in A, K. 581, and the Concerto in A, K. 622.

The concerto was to be Mozart's last completed instrumental composition, and it shows all the hallmarks of his late style. There is an impressive range of topical allusion, particularly in the first movement, where church-style counterpoint, operatic lyricism, and symphonic brilliance coexist amid aspects of the storm-and-stress and sensibility styles, and where the most songlike melody can be transformed into a march or a gavotte in the blink of an eye. The scoring—for two flutes, two bassoons, two horns, and strings—is uncannily refined, and the solo writing is without parallel anywhere in the woodwind literature for the way it remains substantive even in the most virtuosic passages.

Like the quintet, the concerto inhabits a realm where fantasy and gentle pathos prevail. The fusing of these elements produces extraordinary richness and ambivalence of feeling. The opening movement, because of its kaleidoscopic variety of topic and affect, is especially hard to pin down, but it has a bittersweet sadness that haunts the memory long after the music has ended. The Adagio in D, written as if it were an embellished aria for the clarinet, is ineffably tender, while the finale, a hunting rondo on an exalted plane, has a wistful quality that belies its surface gaiety.

While it is a masterpiece on every level, the Clarinet Concerto is perhaps most remarkable for its sheer lyrical invention. One could listen to the opening melody of the first movement a thousand times and never notice that the rhythm in each of its eight measures is different. Here, as in so much of the music of Mozart's final years, the means are subtle, the end simplicity itself.

RECOMMENDED RECORDINGS

Antony Pay;
Academy of Ancient Music/
Christopher Hogwood.
Oiseau-Lyre 414 339-2 [with Oboe Concerto, K. 314]

Alfred Prinz;
Vienna Philharmonic/Karl Böhm.
Deutsche Grammophon 429 816-2 [with Oboe Concerto, K. 314, and Bassoon Concerto, K. 191]

Playing a basset clarinet (a copy, made in 1984, of a period instrument), Pay gives a splendid account of Mozart's most beautiful concerto. He is right on the mark in terms of tempo, expression, and accent, and his tone is exquisite, with that watery, plangent sound that immediately distinguishes the basset clarinet from its higher-pitched siblings. Pay's shadings are soft and natural, his embellishments and passagework simply marvelous. Hogwood and the Academy give a bold, dance-like reading of the score, full of verve in the tuttis and wonderfully transparent in the quiet pages. The 1984 recording captures it all with excellent fidelity.

Prinz and Böhm take leisurely tempos in the concerto's outer movements, offering a ripe reading of the piece. With the Vienna Philharmonic providing lovely support in the tuttis, this account still stands very near the top of the list. The remastering of the original 1974 release is excellent, and with three of Mozart's wind concertos packed onto the disc, all in first-rate performances, this midprice CD is an outstanding value.

MOZART MAY NOT *have been the laughing hyena portrayed by Tom Hulce in the film* Amadeus, *but he certainly had a lighter side. He was fond of inventing foolish words and phrases and enjoyed a good joke, especially if it was obscene or scatological. He had a special genius for pranks—as when he fooled around with the glockenspiel part at a performance of* Die Zauberflöte, *forcing the singer Emanuel Schikaneder to ad-lib. His passion for dancing and billiards knew no bounds, and he loved good wine and pipe smoking.*

A pensive Prokofiev by Matisse.

SERGEI PROKOFIEV
Piano Concerto No. 3, in C, Op. 26

The summer of 1921, which he spent in the village of St. Brevin-les-Pins in Brittany, was a productive one for Prokofiev. Though only 30, he had acquired an international reputation and could afford to write music that pleased rather than shocked. The major work of the summer was this concerto, in which Prokofiev embraces a conventional three-movement design, writes in an unabashedly melodic style, and strives for many of the effects traditionally associated with the concerto as a bravura vehicle. The work strikes quite a balance: on one hand, ethereal lyricism and an almost nostalgic sentimentality, and on the other hand, the humor—alternately wry, blustery, and caustic—and the athleticism that Prokofiev the *enfant terrible* was known for. He wrote the piano part for himself, and it is not easy, demanding fleet-fingered agility as well as raw power. The nonstop activity means that a player must have tremendous endurance just to achieve an even draw with the orchestra.

The first movement opens *andante*, with a warm yet melancholy theme played by the clarinet. A heady transition to *allegro* (heralded by flying scale runs in the strings) leads to the piano's introduction of the main theme—an exuberant, motoric idea that is then tossed back and forth between orchestra and solo instrument. Out of nowhere, a burlesque second subject appears in the oboe and pizzicato violins, over a salty accompaniment of winds, strings, and castanet. This is taken up by the piano and subjected to a bravura treatment until the tempo reverts to *andante* and the orchestra gives out the solo clarinet theme *fortissimo*. Soon we're back to *allegro*, and now the piano has the scale runs. In a recapitulation of the first and second subjects, the elements of grotesquerie and flamboyance are heightened, and the movement ends with a dashing crescendo.

The second movement offers five variations on a theme whose piquant character comes partly from the way Prokofiev keeps it from settling firmly into either the major or the minor mode. After the theme is announced by flute and clarinet in a stalking rhythm, the piano applies itself to the chromatic first part of the theme (variation 1) and then distributes decorative figuration around snatches of the theme in the orchestra (variations 2 and 3). The fourth variation is meditative, and the fifth, at first energetic and brassy, fades magically into a restatement of the theme, now delicately ornamented in chordal filigree by the piano.

The finale opens with a galumphing theme in the bassoons and pizzicato strings. This is interrupted by the piano—which, as the composer Francis Poulenc aptly put it, "literally slaps the strings in the face." The piano's cheeky behavior leads to what Prokofiev characterized as "frequent differences of opinion as regards key" between orchestra and soloist. There is a climax, after which a yearning, melancholy theme is introduced by the woodwinds and tenderly taken up by the strings. The piano responds with an acerbic little tune, and is mocked in turn by the winds. Piano and orchestra settle down with the first of these tunes and build it to a potent climax. Stealing onto the scene one last time is the movement's opening theme, but the piano changes the galumphery into a coda of pyrotechnics.

PROKOFIEV *himself recorded the Third Concerto in 1932 with the London Symphony Orchestra and conductor Piero Coppola. It was the composer's first encounter with the recording microphone, and he wrote to fellow composer Nicolai Miaskovsky, "Just think . . . I can't sneeze or miss any notes!"*

RECOMMENDED RECORDINGS

Santiago Rodriguez;
Sofia Philharmonic Orchestra/Emil Tabakov.
Elan CD 2220 [with Rachmaninoff: Concerto No. 3]

Vladimir Ashkenazy;
London Symphony Orchestra/André Previn.
London 425 570-2 [2 CDs; complete piano concertos]

*The intrepid Cuban-born
virtuoso Santiago Rodriguez.*

The small Elan label went to Bulgaria in 1989 to record the Prokofiev Third with Rodriguez and came back with perhaps the most brilliant and impudent account ever captured on disc. Heartfelt lyricism and high-voltage virtuosity are what the piece demands, and Rodriguez delivers on both counts with electrifying, seat-of-the-pants élan (no pun intended). Tabakov and the Sofia Philharmonic respond with some highly charged playing of their own—witness the piece's magical opening pages—even if they are occasionally taxed by the writing. The recording is well balanced and warm, though the ambience is reverberant enough to put some murkiness into the climaxes. Coupled with an outstanding performance of the Rachmaninoff Third, this is a disc to seek out.

Ashkenazy and Previn project a far more debonair image of the composer in their polished account—a vibrant and inviting treatment even if Ashkenazy's playing lacks the hair-raising intensity and visceral thrills of Rodriguez's. The London Symphony is at its scintillating best under Previn's expert direction. The recording is excellent.

IF YOU LIKE Prokofiev's First Violin Concerto, you will probably find his Second, in G minor, appealing as well. Cast in the conventional three movements, it seems to hover between the shimmering, graceful lyricism of Romeo and Juliet *and the acerbic grotesqueries of* Love for Three Oranges. *The piece was written in 1935 on a commission from friends of the French violinist Robert Soetens.*

VIOLIN CONCERTO NO. 1, IN D, OP. 19

*A*t the outbreak of the Russian Revolution in 1917, the most talked-about musical revolutionary in Russia was Prokofiev, a recent graduate of the St. Petersburg Conservatory still in his mid-twenties. Like most of his colleagues, Prokofiev welcomed the revolution with open arms; he even took to the streets himself (hiding behind house corners when the shooting came too close).

But Prokofiev was not to be used. After the Bolsheviks seized power, he made up his mind to leave Russia; save for a brief concert tour in 1927,

IN A LETTER written to Natalia Koussevitzky, wife of conductor Serge Koussevitzky, Prokofiev offered these reassurances prior to the concerto's Paris premiere: "Tell the maestro to calm down. This is not a Stravinsky symphony—there are no complicated meters and no dirty tricks. It can be conducted without special preparation; it is hard for the orchestra, not for the conductor."

it would be 15 years before he returned. During his time abroad, mainly in Paris, Prokofiev continued to perform and compose, and the conductor Serge Koussevitzky became his publisher and commissioned several works from him for concerts in Paris and Boston. It was at one of Koussevitzky's Paris concerts that the First Violin Concerto—actually completed before Prokofiev left Russia—received its premiere in 1923.

The work's blend of traditional and modern elements left both halves of the Parisian audience cold. After all, it was ten years since Stravinsky's *The Rite of Spring* had created a scandal, and the avant-garde wanted something *really* shocking. The conservatives, on the other hand, were put off by the concerto's unorthodox manner and unconventional structure, with a quiet beginning and ending, a fast movement in the middle, and no cadenza. Neither camp fully appreciated the extraordinary imagination Prokofiev had brought to the effort or the striking quality of his ideas, evident in the dreamy opening melody, the quicksilver scherzo, and the ethereal tenderness of the pages that close both the first movement and the ostinato finale. Prokofiev's light tone and other self-named "Mendelssohnisms" *were* noted by the critics—"not without malice," according to Prokofiev's autobiography.

In spite of the chill that accompanied its premiere, the work quickly caught on, and over the years it has come to be recognized as one of the finest—and arguably the most lyrically enchanting—of all violin concertos of the 20th century.

 RECOMMENDED RECORDINGS

Kyung Wha Chung;
London Symphony Orchestra/André Previn.
London Jubilee 425 003-2 [with Concerto No. 2, and Stravinsky: Violin Concerto]

Dmitry Sitkovetsky;
London Symphony Orchestra/
Sir Colin Davis.
Virgin Classics VC 90734-2 [with Concerto No. 2]

Shlomo Mintz;
Chicago Symphony Orchestra/
Claudio Abbado.
Deutsche Grammophon 410 524-2 [with Concerto No. 2]

Even if it were not available on a generously filled midprice CD, the account from Chung and Previn would be a clear first choice in this repertory. Chung not only has the requisite dramatic spark, but conveys the fragility and mystery behind much of the writing. She displays a rhapsodic legato, laser-sharp tonal focus, and precise intonation. Previn is the most knowledgeable of accompanists, capturing the piece's mercurial shifts of mood with extraordinary aplomb. The 1975 analog recording is excellent, affording a natural image with good depth and balance.

Sitkovetsky sees a darker side to the concerto, drawing at times an almost painful melancholy out of its lyricism. His is a probing performance, soulful and rapt in the more atmospheric pages but sneering and suggestive in the athletic ones. Davis and the London Symphony are impressive if restrained partners. The 1988 digital recording is spacious and extremely solid.

The fantasy of Chung and the macabre vision of Sitkovetsky may be missing from Mintz's reading, but there is no lack of brilliance or bite to his interpretation. The playing is confident and colorful, and the accompaniment from Abbado and the Chicagoans is virtuosic, if perhaps a bit too assertive for the performance's own good. The recording has remarkable presence and impact.

The prodigy Kyung Wha Chung remains one of the world's top violinists.

Even at rest, Rachmaninoff remained a coiled spring.

RACHMANINOFF'S *obsession as a pianist was to make the musical architecture convincing. He believed that in every piece— his own works included— there was a culminating musical and emotional moment called "the point." It might come at the end of a piece or in the middle, but wherever it came, the performer's job was to arrive at it in the same compelling way that a runner breaks the finish-line tape at the end of a race.*

SERGEI RACHMANINOFF

PIANO CONCERTO NO. 2, IN C MINOR, OP. 18

*F*ollowing the disastrous premiere of his First Symphony in 1897—a drunken Alexander Glazunov had conducted and critics raked the piece over the coals—Rachmaninoff (1873–1943) became so severely depressed that he was unable to compose for the next three years. In despair, friends took him to see Dr. Nikolai Dahl, a specialist in hypnotism and a skilled amateur musician, whose efforts to restore the Russian composer's confidence and creative urge soon had phenomenal results. In the summer of 1900, Rachmaninoff began the composition of what was to become his most popular work, the Piano Concerto in C minor.

The second and third movements stood complete by the end of 1900; Rachmaninoff performed them in Moscow that December and, spurred by their success, added the first movement the following spring. The completed work, dedicated to Dr. Dahl, received its premiere on November 9, 1901. In its progression from somber introspection to triumphant celebration, the concerto surely reflects something of its composer's journey out of depression. The opening movement is prefaced by eight stark chords in the piano, and Rachmaninoff adroitly builds on the tension between the movement's grim principal subject and a soaring second theme in E flat, using as intermediary a nervous repeated-note motif related to both of them.

The word "romantic" is overused, but it is the only way to describe the concerto's second movement, set in the idyllic key of E major. Here, accompanied by muted strings and delicate arabesques from the piano, the flute and clarinet spin out a wistful, long-breathed melody full of attenuated passion. Rachmaninoff treats the idea with rhapsodic freedom, building to a fantasy-like climax and ending with a serenely beautiful coda. The athletic writing for both piano and orchestra in the concerto's finale echoes Tchaikovsky at his most exuberant, though only Rachmaninoff could have conceived the "Oriental" tint of the movement's famous second subject, popularized by the song "Full Moon and Empty Arms." From the restless excitability of its opening pages, the finale builds to a powerful conclusion, sweeping away all trace of C minor in a rush of C major.

RHAPSODY ON A THEME OF PAGANINI, OP. 43

*R*ACHMANINOFF *made a substantial number of recordings of his own music. His hands— which were powerful and large, with long, beautifully tapered fingers—were invariably cool, so during recordings he would keep them warm in a specially-designed electric muff until the moment he was to play. Then out they would come in a flash, and as soon as the passage was over, back in they went.*

*N*icolò Paganini was the prototype of the Romantic virtuoso, a glamorous, charismatic violinist with such extraordinary talent that legends grew up about his having made a pact with the Devil to attain it. His 24 Caprices (c. 1805) are still considered the touchstone of the solo violin repertory for their sheer technical difficulty. The last of them, in A minor, has had an impact on the piano repertory as well: Schumann, Liszt, Brahms, and Rachmaninoff were all struck by its suitability for a set of piano variations. Part of the reason is that the 24th Caprice is itself a set of 12 variations, on a tune whose bass line (marked by the notes that fall on the beat) establishes a simple harmonic progression—the perfect foundation upon which to build.

The *Rhapsody on a Theme of Paganini*—Rachmaninoff's last work for piano and orchestra, dating from 1934—holds pride of place among all compositions inspired by this diabolically difficult caprice. There are 24 variations in the *Rhapsody*, no doubt a tribute to the numbering of Paganini's original piece. The actual "theme" is not stated until *after* an introduction and the first variation have been played—and it appears, of course, in the violins. The ensuing variations ex-

IN VARIATIONS 7, 10, and 24 of his Rhapsody, *Rachmaninoff quotes the theme of the* Dies irae *from the Latin mass for the dead—a favorite compositional quirk of his (it also appears in the* Symphonic Dances *and the tone poem* The Isle of the Dead) *and in this instance a gesture that may acknowledge Paganini's reputed ties to the Devil.*

plore a scintillating range of pianistic and orchestral textures. The composer's sense of *diablerie* is palpable in the driving energy of variations 8 and 9; elsewhere, particularly in the cavalry charge of variation 14, one recognizes the grand Romantic sweep of the piano concertos. With the 18th variation comes one of Rachmaninoff's most celebrated melodies; wistful, yearning, it is no more than the theme played upside down with a slightly altered rhythm. The final variations build in momentum to a conclusion that would have left even Paganini a bit breathless, and an excuse-me ending that undoubtedly would have given him delight.

 RECOMMENDED RECORDINGS

Vladimir Ashkenazy;
London Symphony Orchestra/André Previn.
London Jubilee 417 702-2 [Concerto No. 2 and
Rhapsody on a Theme of Paganini]

Van Cliburn;
Chicago Symphony Orchestra/Fritz Reiner.
RCA 5912-2 [Concerto No. 2, with Tchaikovsky:
Concerto No. 1]

Ashkenazy's 1970–71 performances of the Second Concerto and the *Rhapsody* are bold and impassioned. Previn, also at his best, leads a fired-up London Symphony through accounts notable for their freshness and sweep. The analog sound is excellent, and the combination of engineering by two old pros (Kenneth Wilkinson and James Lock) and a Kingsway Hall venue yields superb balance and perspective. The pairing of these works is ideal; at midprice it's hard to do better.

Cliburn was on the cusp of fame in 1958 when he recorded the Second Concerto with Reiner and the Chicago Symphony, having just won the first International Tchaikovsky Competition in Moscow. His technique is electrifying, almost hair-raising, yet his interpretation goes well beyond the notes and leaves the listener in no doubt whatsoever that at 23 the lanky Texan was already a master of the grand manner. Reiner and orchestra are rock-solid, and the coupling is *still* the best recording available of Tchaikovsky's Piano Concerto No. 1 (with Kirill Kondrashin and the RCA Symphony). For 35 years this disc has never been out of the catalog, for reasons that are evident in both performances.

MAURICE RAVEL

PIANO CONCERTO IN G
PIANO CONCERTO IN D

*R*avel worked simultaneously on his two piano concertos during the years 1929–31. The G major Concerto was intended for his own use. Of it, he said, "[It] is a concerto in the strict sense, written in the spirit of Mozart and Saint-Saëns. I believe that a concerto can be both gay and brilliant, without necessarily being profound or aiming at dramatic effect. It has been said that the concertos of some great classical composers, far from being written *for* the piano, have been written *against* it. And I think that this criticism is quite justified." Ravel's writing for the instrument shows him to be as good as his word. The G major is a pianist's piano concerto, a succession of dazzling but not overpowering pages that display the full range of pianistic keyboard invention. The scoring is colorful, with a jazz flavor to much of it that lends an especially sultry feeling to some of the quieter pages and a wonderful sense of vibrancy to the climaxes.

The Concerto in D, for the left hand, is cast in a single movement, with a more subtle internal division into three parts. The mood here is substantially different from that of the G major. This concerto's solemnity and power, and its predominantly dark orchestral textures, are in striking

Maurice Ravel dressed as elegantly as he wrote.

"WE WERE HAPPY, *cultivated, and aggressive. . . . I can see Ravel now, like some debonair wizard, sitting in his corner at* Le boeuf sur le toit *telling endless stories that had the same elegance, richness, and clarity as his compositions. He could tell a story as well as he could write a waltz or an Adagio."*
—Léon-Paul Fargue, who with Ravel belonged to a group of artists called *Les Apaches*

FOLLOWING *World War I, the one-armed pianist Paul Wittgenstein rebuilt his career by commissioning a number of composers to write works for the left hand. In addition to Ravel's concerto, there were pieces by Prokofiev, Britten, Richard Strauss, and Franz Schmidt, not all of which Wittgenstein liked or played.*

contrast to the other work's airy, almost neoclassical grace.

Prior to Ravel, composers such as Chopin and Scriabin had written music for the left hand as a challenge to pianists of conventional ability; the purpose was to train the left hand to match the "dexterity" of the right. But in composing this concerto, Ravel was writing for a pianist who had no choice. Paul Wittgenstein, brother of the philosopher Ludwig Wittgenstein and scion of one of Vienna's finest families, had lost his right arm in World War I, fighting on the other side from Ravel. The piano part of this work is so complex that one can hear the concerto and be entirely unaware that only the left hand is being used. The spans of large intervals, the use of thumb melody, and the frequent arpeggiation certainly don't give it away. What's more, the orchestration is gauged so that it both supports the piano's sonority and allows its melodic passages to sound through. All this for a musician who, like Ravel himself, had been deeply scarred by the experience of war.

 RECOMMENDED RECORDING

**Pascal Rogé;
Montreal Symphony Orchestra/
Charles Dutoit.**
London Jubilee 421 458-2 [4 CDs; with collected orchestral works]

Ravel's concertos are not easy to bring off in concert or on disc. They require considerable finesse from soloist and orchestra alike, yet each work makes entirely different demands in style and technique. All the more reason to admire what Rogé and Dutoit achieved in 1982 in this idiomatic, appealing account, played with sensitive bravura and recorded in state-of-the-art sound.

JOAQUÍN RODRIGO

CONCIERTO DE ARANJUEZ

*O*ver the years, Spain has given the world more than its share of prodigiously talented individuals, including a few who have had to struggle with severe disabilities. In fact, it sometimes seems that adversity is necessary to bring out the best in the Spanish temperament. One thinks of the deaf painter Francisco Goya, and of this composer, blind since the age of three, whose *Concierto de Aranjuez* is the most popular work in the history of the guitar.

Born in 1901, Rodrigo is not only the last of the great Spanish nationalists, but the last representative of the wonderful creative axis that linked France and Spain during the 70 years between Isaac Albéniz's arrival in Paris and the death of Ravel. Rodrigo has never attempted, as Falla did, to tap the emotive core of Spanish folk and popular idioms. Instead, he has tried to endow his works with a picturesque quality—something that would give his music, which is essentially neoclassical in cast, a Spanish flavor. His style mixes some elements of folk music with the rhythms of Renaissance and Baroque dances and a French-influenced orchestral colorism.

In the *Concierto de Aranjuez*, which was completed in 1940, Rodrigo weaves a particularly effective fantasy out of these materials. The jaunty opening movement, marked *Allegro con spirito*, retains a chivalrous grace amid dance-like exuberance, a delicate balance between the guitar's relaxed, almost improvisatory solos and the orchestra's often ebullient commentary. The Adagio starts with a poignant English horn solo over gentle strumming in the guitar. The song draws nostalgia to the heights of passion before quieting to stillness. A lightly scored, vivacious Allegro concludes the work.

"CONCIERTO DE ARANJUEZ *evokes a vast array of colorful imagery and feelings. Being a history lover, especially Spanish history, when I created this concerto I had in mind the courts of Charles IV, a Bourbon king of 18th-century Spain, whose summer residence was the palace of Aranjuez [above]."*
—Joaquín Rodrigo

PARKENING *is a man of many talents. In addition to being one of the world's preeminent classical guitarists, he is also a casting and fly-fishing champion, having won the International Gold Cup Tarpon Tournament, the Wimbledon of fly-fishing, in Islamorada, Florida.*

 RECOMMENDED RECORDINGS

Carlos Bonell;
Montreal Symphony Orchestra/
Charles Dutoit.
London 430 703-2 [with Falla: El amor brujo *and* Nights in the Gardens of Spain]

Christopher Parkening;
Royal Philharmonic Orchestra/
Andrew Litton.
EMI Classics CDC 54665 [with Fantasia para un gentilhombre *and Walton: Five Bagatelles for Guitar and Orchestra]*

Bonell's 1980 account is deft and characterful, despite a few small problems with the fingering of rapid scale passages. In fact, these blemishes make the performance seem more alive. Dutoit and his charges are superb accompanists, with the Montreal winds providing some wonderful solos. London's sound, while a little bright, is well focused and atmospheric, almost in the demonstration class. The coupling with Falla's *El amor brujo* and *Nights in the Gardens of Spain* is ideal.

Lovers of the *Concierto de Aranjuez* breathed a sigh of relief when Parkening made this recording of it, his first, in 1992. The American guitarist delivers an interpretation rich in feeling and nuance; his playing, remarkable for its elegance, the astonishing evenness of the fingerwork, and above all for beauty and variety of tone, freshly illuminates a justly familiar work. Parkening brings the flamenco elements of the conception to the fore and ornaments the concerto's slow movement in an especially appealing manner, and is backed by a wonderfully alert reading of the score from Litton and the RPO. The sound is excellent.

ROBERT SCHUMANN

PIANO CONCERTO IN A MINOR, OP. 54

*T*wice while still a teenager, Schumann attempted to compose a piano concerto, but both essays were left unfinished. He tried again in 1839, a turbulent year filled with litigation as Schumann and his fiancée, Clara Wieck, sought to circumvent the opposition of Clara's father to their marriage. The attempt at a concerto again proved fruitless, but the couple's legal efforts succeeded, and Robert and Clara were married in 1840.

This union resulted in an enormous creative outpouring. Already in 1840—the composer's "year of song"—Schumann had anticipated marriage in a decidedly lyrical state of mind, focusing all his pent-up emotion on vocal music. Now, in a mood of outright celebration, he turned to the orchestra. The works of 1841 included two symphonies—No. 1, in B flat (known as the *Spring Symphony*), and No. 4, in D minor—as well as the *Overture, Scherzo, and Finale* and a *Fantasie* in in A minor for Piano and Orchestra.

Composed in little more than a single week in May of 1841, the *Fantasie* was played by Clara Schumann on August 13 at a rehearsal of the Gewandhaus Orchestra in Leipzig. Two weeks after that read-through, Clara gave birth to the first of the Schumanns' eight children. The *Fantasie* stood alone until the summer of 1845, when Robert decided it should become the first movement of a full-fledged piano concerto. He composed the second and third movements—a delicately expressive intermezzo in F major and a dashing rondo in A major—in the span of about five weeks. The concerto received its premiere in Dresden on December 4, 1845, with Clara again as soloist.

This concerto is a marvelous example of a composite work that doesn't sound like a com-

Clara Schumann was an ideal interpreter of Robert's works.

I N THE EXCITEMENT of a live performance, conductor Zubin Mehta launched into the opening of the Schumann Piano Concerto before soloist Daniel Barenboim had adjusted his bench. With only one beat to react, the pianist shot his hands out, and missed the first two chords. Before the second movement Barenboim beckoned Mehta over to him. Looking Mehta dead in the eye, Barenboim played the movement's opening phrase as Mehta bounded back to the podium to bring the orchestra in with the answer.

posite. Because the two concluding movements are cut from the same cloth as the original *Fantasie* in both thematic material and pianistic style, the work enjoys a unity that is rare even in concertos composed at a single stroke. The score's appeal resides largely in its combination of drama, lyricism, and dreamlike imagery—elements not simply contrasted with one another but brought into a fragile, almost ephemeral, ever-changing balance. Schumann's writing imparts a surprisingly troubled quality to the yearning of certain passages in the first movement, yet produces a glowing rapture in the intermezzo and an ardent fire in the finale.

 RECOMMENDED RECORDINGS

Eugene Istomin;
Columbia Symphony Orchestra/
Bruno Walter.
CBS Masterworks MK 42024 [with Brahms: Double Concerto]

Murray Perahia;
Bavarian Radio Symphony Orchestra/
Sir Colin Davis.
CBS Masterworks MK 44899 [with Grieg: Piano Concerto]

Stephen Bishop-Kovacevich;
BBC Symphony Orchestra/Sir Colin Davis.
Philips 412 923-2 [with Grieg: Piano Concerto]

It takes quite a musician—actually two of them, one at the keyboard and one on the podium—to bring off the heady mix of elements in this concerto. Istomin and Walter succeeded in 1960. Istomin is incandescent in all three movements, and his performance crackles with life; every note is treated as music, and every emotion rings true.

Walter and the Columbia Symphony show a wonderful rapport with the soloist, breathing with him, rejoicing with him. The sound is dry yet thrillingly alive. Interpretations like this don't come along very often, and when they do it's nice to have them recorded so successfully.

Perahia is one of the best at making this difficult score seem effortlessly appealing. His superb pianism and energetic engagement allow the work's greatness to show through; his playing conveys affection for the music without a single trace of affectation. Transitions are smoothly managed in this live recording from 1988, and Davis and the Bavarians provide warm support.

Bishop's treatment is more volatile than Perahia's in the outer movements—equally lovely, but more passionate than affectionate. In the intermezzo, he seems a little more delicate, though less spontaneous. Still, there are plenty of subtle stirrings and shadings here, in both the piano and the orchestra, and Davis presides in masterful fashion over this 1970 recording.

Pianist Murray Perahia, an adept at Schumann.

JEAN SIBELIUS

VIOLIN CONCERTO IN D MINOR, OP. 47

*O*f all the works in the repertory, this one comes closest to being the violinist's violin concerto. As a first-rate player himself, Sibelius knew the instrument's capabilities and how to draw from it the most idiomatic and expressive effects. As a first-rate composer, he also knew how to introduce elements of virtuosic display into a work of serious content. Moreover, he was an original thinker who could conceive of fresh ideas within a conventional context. All of these elements are evident in the Violin Concerto, Sibelius's only essay in the concerto form.

The composition did not come easily. Sibelius's heavy drinking took its toll on his creative capac-

Sibelius personified a rugged Nordic individuality.

SIBELIUS TOOK *up the violin as a boy and started formal lessons at 14. Later, he would write: "The violin took me by storm, and for the next ten years it was my greatest ambition to become a great virtuoso." The young man's dream died hard: At age 26, he was still auditioning for a spot in the Vienna Philharmonic. But by 1903, the year Sibelius started writing his own violin concerto, his hopes of becoming a concert artist had long been abandoned.*

ities. Financial difficulties caused domestic strain as well, forcing Sibelius to schedule the premiere earlier than he would have liked. The concerto's debut, on February 8, 1904, was a near-disaster, and in a fit of self-criticism Sibelius embarked on a drastic revision. The first movement was thoroughly rewritten: certain purely virtuosic passages in the violin part were discarded, a rhythmically fussy subordinate subject was transformed into a far more potent motive, and the loose-limbed, episodic development was abandoned for a more symphonic and tightly integrated structure. The new version of the concerto received its premiere in Berlin on October 19, 1905, with Richard Strauss as conductor and Czech violinist Karel Halíř as soloist.

One of this concerto's most striking features is the bleakness of its first movement, where Sibelius's starkly suggestive orchestration calls to mind, as one of the Berlin reviews noted, "the Nordic winter landscape painters who through the distinctive interplay of white on white secure rare, sometimes hypnotic and sometimes powerful, effects." This is certainly true of the opening pages (carried over from the original version), where the haunting principal subject is announced by the violin against a muted, slowly oscillating backdrop in the orchestral violins, as though emerging from the mists. In contrast, the Adagio possesses an ardent lyricism, while the finale exudes optimism. The final version of the concerto thoroughly justifies Sibelius's decision to revise the original, and it exhibits the same formal mastery and classical balance that were to mark the Third Symphony, begun at roughly the same time. With these two works, Sibelius departed forever the world of late Romanticism and began the lonely quest for self-expression that was to culminate in the later symphonies and the tone poem *Tapiola*.

RECOMMENDED RECORDINGS

Cho-Liang Lin;
Philharmonia Orchestra/Esa-Pekka Salonen.
CBS Masterworks MK 44548 [with Nielsen:
Violin Concerto]

Jascha Heifetz;
Chicago Symphony Orchestra/Walter Hendl.
RCA RCD 1-7019 [with Prokofiev: Violin Concerto No. 2,
and Glazunov: Violin Concerto]

Cho-Liang Lin, master of many styles.

Lin and Salonen make a marvelous team in this evocative, powerful rendition of the concerto, which fully conveys the emotional compass of the music. Lin's playing is immaculate, and Salonen and the Philharmonia bring just the right sense of desolation and visionary expanse to their reading. The 1987 recording is excellent, with a solid image and an exceptionally live atmosphere.

Heifetz shows blazing speed in all three movements and goes in for a bit of circus virtuosity, perhaps too much for some tastes. Hendl and his players are almost hard pressed to keep up. The interpretation is hyper-Romantic; particularly remarkable are Heifetz's tone and control, and his warm vibrato in the Adagio. The stereo recording from the 1950s is coarse in tone, and there is some breakup in the loudest parts.

PIOTR ILYICH TCHAIKOVSKY
PIANO CONCERTO NO. 1, IN B FLAT MINOR, OP. 23

*A*lthough hypersensitive by nature, Tchaikovsky was nonetheless an astute judge of his own work. He was understandably shaken when in 1875 he brought the manuscript of his First Piano Concerto to his colleague, the pianist Nikolai Rubinstein, who pronounced it

Tchaikovsky's Concerto No. 1 placed him among the greats of the keyboard.

unperformable and in need of wholesale revision.

Yet Tchaikovsky refused to alter a single note—and no decision ever proved more sensible. From the day of its premiere (which curiously enough took place not in Russia but in Boston), the Concerto in B flat minor has in fact become the standard against which all virtuosos must measure themselves. The grand flourishes of its opening, the gossamer passagework of its Andantino, and the pyrotechnics of its finale are to pianists what Everest is to the climber.

While the soloist gets little rest, the listener never wearies, as interesting things are always happening in this concerto, thanks not only to the profusion of melodic material but to Tchaikovsky's skills as an orchestrator. The approach to form is also quite inventive. From the sixth measure, the piano takes part in the grand opening tutti of the first movement. Yet the entire passage—107 measures of majestic symphonism in D flat—is nothing but a prologue to the main body of the movement, whose proper key of B flat minor is finally asserted at measure 114. The soaring melody in first violins and cellos never returns, though there are plenty of new melodies to take its place. The structure of the second movement, in which a scintillating, scherzo-like interlude is embedded in a songful Andantino, imaginatively departs from the norm as well.

Tchaikovsky wrote a second piano concerto and left a third unfinished, but he never equaled the range of expression of this one, which by itself places him among the greats of the keyboard for all time. Eventually, even Nikolai Rubinstein recognized this and became an eminent performer of the B flat minor Concerto.

RECOMMENDED RECORDINGS

Van Cliburn;
RCA Symphony Orchestra/Kirill Kondrashin.
RCA Red Seal 5912-2 [with Rachmaninoff:
Concerto No. 2]

Santiago Rodriguez;
Sofia Philharmonic Orchestra/Emil Tabakov.
Elan CD 2228 [with Grieg: Piano Concerto, and Liszt:
Concerto No. 1]

With this 1958 recording made in Carnegie Hall just weeks after he had won the first International Tchaikovsky Competition in Moscow, Cliburn established himself overnight as one of the great interpreters of the piece. The account is played from the heart, with a spellbinding virtuosity that seems almost effortless—a reminder that the concerto is genuine music after all, not merely some flashy showpiece of fast octaves. Kondrashin draws committed playing from the RCA Symphony, and while the recording shows its age, it also conveys every nuance of a thrilling occasion.

Rodriguez, a silver medalist at the 1981 Van Cliburn International Competition in Fort Worth, also approaches the concerto as music rather than fireworks. The outer movements are taken at blazing tempos, yet the playing is magisterially cool. Indeed, this is one of the most arrestingly dramatic readings of the concerto since the celebrated 1943 account by Vladimir Horowitz and Arturo Toscanini. And they are far better recorded. The inclusion of brilliant accounts of both the Liszt E flat and Grieg A minor concertos makes the disc a decided bargain.

Performing Personalities

One of the greatest pianists America has produced, Van Cliburn was catapulted to fame in 1958 by his victory in the first International Tchaikovsky Competition in Moscow (above). His recordings, which have sold in formidable numbers, are lasting reminders of playing that combined technical brilliance and emotional warmth in unique fashion, as well as power, sensitivity, and insight.

Tchaikovsky's marriage to Antonina—over before it began.

VIOLIN CONCERTO IN D, OP. 35

*A*fter Tchaikovsky's disastrous marriage to Antonina Milyukova in 1877, his younger brother Anatoly hustled him off to Clarens, Switzerland, where it was hoped the composer could work in peace and recover his emotional equilibrium. During the months that followed, Tchaikovsky journeyed to Paris and Vienna and traveled widely in Italy. He completed his Fourth Symphony and the opera *Eugene Onegin* and learned that his newfound patroness, Nadezhda von Meck, was willing to provide him with an annual stipend of 6,000 rubles.

While in Vienna, Tchaikovsky renewed contacts with Yosif Kotek, an accomplished violinist and former composition student of his, who had been responsible for bringing his work to the attention of Mme. von Meck. Stimulated by a visit from Kotek, Tchaikovsky embarked on the composition of a violin concerto. The work, begun on March 17, 1878, was fully scored by April 11.

Although Kotek had helped him with the solo part, Tchaikovsky offered the new work and its dedication to the well-known virtuoso Leopold Auer—who promptly spurned the piece because he thought it unplayable. Kotek, whom Tchaikovsky had managed to appease with the dedication to his *Valse-scherzo*, was then to present the concerto in St. Petersburg, but he got cold feet and abandoned his plans. So it was not until December 4, 1881, that the Violin Concerto had its debut, when Adolf Brodsky rather rashly played it in Vienna at a concert of the Philharmonic conducted by Hans Richter. The audience demonstrated vociferously against it, and the critic Eduard Hanslick scornfully dismissed the work as an example of "stinking music."

The concerto nonetheless made headway with performers and the public. Brodsky continued to champion it—and Auer soon took it up as well, eventually introducing it to his pupils (who would include Mischa Elman and Jascha Heifetz). The work was published in 1888, by which time it was being played all over Europe. It has been a staple of the repertory ever since.

The Violin Concerto is indeed among Tchaikovsky's freshest inspirations. It is also quite masterfully constructed, with a wealth of material ideally suited to the violin's lyrical nature. The first movement—by turns tender, capricious, and festive—is unfailingly lyrical. The aptly named Canzonetta follows, where a characteristically gentle Tchaikovskian melancholy is pierced by ardor. This second movement was fashioned as a replacement for the original slow movement; since he had already composed the concerto's finale, Tchaikovsky was able to provide the new second movement with a custom fit transition passage. The finale, thus anticipated, proves all the more satisfying. Propelled by a heady mixture of folkish exuberance and dance-like energy, it builds to a breathless conclusion.

 RECOMMENDED RECORDINGS

**Kyung Wha Chung;
Montreal Symphony Orchestra/
Charles Dutoit.**
London 410 011-2 [with Mendelssohn: Concerto in E minor]

**Nathan Milstein;
Vienna Philharmonic/Claudio Abbado.**
*Deutsche Grammophon Galleria 419 067-2
[with Mendelssohn: Concerto in E minor]*

**Jascha Heifetz;
Chicago Symphony Orchestra/Fritz Reiner.**
*RCA Living Stereo 61495-2 [with Brahms:
Violin Concerto]*

*Dutoit: sparkling accompaniments
to the Tchaikovsky.*

Chung gives a beautiful, communicative performance of this concerto, her playing marked by an exquisite sense of detail. She is glowingly partnered by Dutoit and the Montreal Symphony, and the 1981 recording is brilliant.

Milstein's interpretation is reserved, but still very warm in its expressiveness, and the Viennese provide a sensitive accompaniment. The recording sounds slightly distanced but is detailed and well balanced.

The "Living Stereo" reissue of Heifetz's 1957 account captures his high-voltage playing in all its incandescence. Anyone familiar with the grainy sonics of RCA's earlier CD release is in for a surprise: Heifetz actually sounds sweet at the top, and the Chicago Symphony produces succulent, full-bodied textures behind him.

ANTONIO VIVALDI

CONCERTOS FOR VIOLIN, STRINGS, AND CONTINUO, OP. 8, NOS. 1–4
The Four Seasons

Vivaldi: interesting figuration, arresting fantasy.

*K*nown as "the red priest" because of his hair color and his membership in the clergy, Vivaldi (1678–1741) was the most original and influential Italian composer of his generation. Though he spent most of his life in his native Venice, Vivaldi traveled widely outside of Italy. Thanks to this peripatetic tendency, and to his extraordinary fecundity, his music became known throughout Europe. Bach, Vivaldi's junior by seven years, had a high regard for it.

Vivaldi wrote in a number of forms, but it is the concertos—of which he composed more than 500—that make up the bulk of his output. More than anyone else, Vivaldi established the three-movement form as the standard for concertos. The techniques he used to keep these works interesting and lively—deftly varying the texture and figuration, and favoring angular, energetic rhythms that packed extra punch—were adopted by composers all over the continent, but some-

Vivaldi's strings signal the coming summer storm.

thing in the sound of Vivaldi's music remained unique and impossible to imitate. No two of his concertos are alike.

Vivaldi's Opus 8 is entitled *Il Cimento dell'Armonia e dell'Inventione* (*The Contest Between Harmony and Invention*), and the 12 concertos it contains are meant to illustrate the simultaneous workings of the rational and imaginative aspects of music: form and fantasy. The first four concertos of the collection depict the different seasons of the year, beginning with spring and ending with winter. Published in 1725, these concertos are among roughly 230 that Vivaldi wrote for violin and string ensemble. The wealth of effect and the quality of diversion that Vivaldi was able to achieve in *The Four Seasons*, using nothing more than string instruments, still compels the greatest admiration. Their imagery—of birds in spring, storms in summer, huntsmen in autumn, and icy landscapes in winter—is as vivid today as on the day the notes were penned.

Vivaldi wrote an "illustrative sonnet" as a guide to each of the concertos. Accordingly, *Spring*, in the bright key of E major, celebrates the sounds of "joyful bird song," briefly interrupted as "gentle breezes give way to a passing storm." In the slow movement, a shepherd sleeps in "the pleasant flowering meadow" while a dog (the solo viola) barks. Nymphs dance a graceful gigue through the finale as the sun emerges from behind the clouds.

Summer comes in with the brutal heat of the midday sun, whose rays "sear the pine" in the menacing key of G minor. The calls of cuckoo, turtle dove, and finch are heard, and soft breezes stir the air—until the north wind sweeps in. The second movement finds the shepherd in fear of "lightning's flash and thunder's roar," as insects of all sizes are "stirred to a frenzy" by the turbulent air. The effects here are marvelous. The thunder is depicted by tremolos in the low strings, played threateningly close to the bridge, while the shepherd's trembling is suggested by the halting rhythm in the violins as they accompany the solo. In the finale, the storm breaks (descending scales and strings of violent tremolos suggest the downpour) and hailstones pound the fields of ripened corn.

Autumn is set in the pastoral key of F major. In its opening movement, a farmer sings and dances in celebration of the harvest. Wine flows, and soon the peasant revelers are fast asleep, their "sweet repose" suggested by the concerto's second movement. The finale depicts hunters at the break of day; we hear their horn calls and dogs and tallyhos, and the din of gunfire as they give chase.

Winter brings a shift to the desolate key of F minor. According to the composer's sonnet, the opening movement depicts our shivering against the wind (as the strings' edgy repeated notes clash dissonantly with one another) and the stamping of our feet (a more forceful passage with sharply accented notes). In the Largo, we "muse contentedly by the fire" while those outside are drenched by the rain. We cautiously tread the icy path in the finale, then slip and fall, get up, and are battered by the wind. "This," Vivaldi tells us, "is Winter, and such are its delights."

Performing Personalities

In spite of his ebullient personality, Salvatore Accardo exhibits maturity, thoughtfulness, and self-control in his playing. He is at his best in the poetic pages of the repertory, though few violinists can rival his sureness in display passages. Accardo renders the major works of the 18th century as capably as he does those of the 19th and 20th, and he is a convincing exponent of contemporary music as well.

 RECOMMENDED RECORDINGS

Alan Loveday;
Academy of St. Martin-in-the-Fields/
Sir Neville Marriner.
Argo 414 486-2

Salvatore Accardo;
Soloists of the International Festival
of Naples.
Philips 422 065-2 [with Concertos in F and B minor for Three and Four Violins, RV 551 and 580]

Nils-Erik Sparf;
Drottningholm Baroque Ensemble.
BIS CD-275

Loveday's sweet tone and unmistakable finesse give his account the understated elegance of a Saville Row suit, while the intimate accompaniment of Marriner and the Academy is the epitome of English good manners. The 1970 recording is nicely balanced, with a slightly soft-focused and distant pickup that allows a little extra warmth into the proceedings.

Accardo and the Neapolitans offer Romantic, suave, full-toned accounts, notable for their lovely textures and dashing style. Accardo's playing is fiery but never merely flashy, and he produces an even, exquisite tone on four different Stradivari instruments; here truly is a violinist for all seasons. The accompaniment is no less impressive, and Bruno Canino keeps up a remarkable commentary from the keyboard, ingeniously filling things out. The 1987 recording is outstanding, with excellent definition and imaging.

Sparf and his Stockholm-based cohorts give vital, sharply characterized readings. Sparf is a versatile fiddler; although not a "specialist" in the field of early music, he uses a Dutch violin (c. 1680) and a period bow in these accounts, and he plays in a way that demonstrates remarkable sensitivity to the style. The Drottningholm players achieve articulations and tonal effects that modern instrumentalists find difficult, and in doing so also manage to project the "contest" that the music is supposed to represent. The continuo work is excellent, and the spacious, full-bodied recording from 1984 does a good job of capturing the fabulous tone of those Baroque strings.

Vivaldi—a man for all seasons.

CHAPTER III

CHAMBER MUSIC

*C*hamber music—meant to be played in rooms rather than in a church, theater, or large public space—is the bedrock of the classical literature. As a genre it embraces everything from simple pieces for solo instruments to multi-movement compositions for ensembles of a dozen or more, easily forming the largest and the most diverse segment of the repertory.

Nearly every major composer from the 17th century to the beginning of the 19th produced some chamber music. Many of the most important contributions to the repertory—the works of Bach and Haydn are the first that come to mind—were the result of princely patronage. Indeed, hundreds of composers had court positions and composed serviceable music for a variety of occasions. What set Bach and Haydn apart was the thought they put into their music, and the way they challenged themselves to be formally inventive and emotionally daring when their noble employers would surely have been satisfied with something merely pretty.

It was Haydn who, more or less single-handedly, established the string quartet as the supreme chamber music form. The Italians had been the first to explore this medium for two violins, viola, and cello, and their idiomatic feel for string writing quickly made it viable. The pioneering efforts of Giuseppe Tartini and Giovanni Battista Sammartini, dating from the mid-18th century, were elegant and well crafted if fairly lightweight works, while the quartets of Luigi Boccherini, composed in the late 1760s and early 1770s, show more finesse than Haydn's from the same period. Haydn soon outstripped his Italian colleagues in the contrapuntal animation of his quartet textures, as well as in the depth of expression he achieved within the form. By the beginning of the 1780s, with his Opus 33 set of six quartets, he had perfected a model that would serve him and subsequent generations admirably, one in which all four instruments had melodically substantive parts and were free to engage in a rich, conversational repartee.

The homogeneity of sound that could be achieved by instruments of the same family and similar tonal character playing without a continuo, together with the contrapuntal possibilities inherent in a four-part texture, was what made the quartet the ideal vehicle for serious instrumental composition. In addition to a refined blend of sound, the quartet afforded composers unprecedented flexibility owing to the virtuosic capabilities of the instruments themselves and to their five-octave aggregate range. Despite changes in construction and playing technique, the tonal qualities of string instruments today are relatively close to what they were in the 18th century, so the brilliance of Haydn's quartets (and Mozart's and Beethoven's, for that matter) can still be fully appreciated when the works are played on modern instruments.

As the 18th century gave way to the 19th, composers wrote less for the privileged few, more for the music-loving multitude. Then as now, music was the most stimulating form of entertainment, and the enthusiasm of the bourgeois public for opera and symphonic music carried over to chamber music as well. Mozart and Beethoven, who preferred patronage when they could get it, adjusted to the changing reality and aimed the bulk of their chamber music at the paying public.

Mozart refined and improved on Haydn's string quartet style in his six famous essays dedicated to the elder master, but he preferred the rich texture and more complex part-writing possible in the quintet medium (which added a second viola or cello), and it was here that he achieved his greatest successes in the field of chamber music.

Beethoven, on the other hand, chose to stretch the string quartet toward symphonic dimensions, while enriching its expressive context through the use of parody and a breathtaking range of textures.

As with the symphony, so in chamber music: composers of the Romantic era and in our own century have had to acknowledge Haydn's invention, Mozart's perfection, and Beethoven's vastness in one way or another, and most have done so by trying not to follow too closely in any one set of footsteps. Schubert, Mendelssohn, and Schumann were most successful when they applied themselves to unusual instrumental combinations in their chamber music. Brahms, too, while dutifully composing the piano trios (for piano, violin, and cello) and string quartets that were expected of Beethoven's successor, found other forms more congenial—particularly that of the sonata with keyboard accompaniment. With Debussy, Ravel, and Bartók, the quest for new sounds and formal approaches reinvigorated the string quartet and carried over to works for other chamber complements as well.

Today, chamber music is still the busiest classical genre. And today's composers and performers are drawn to it for the same reasons Bach and Haydn were drawn to it in their day: a love of pure music, a delight in conversational discourse among players, and a desire for intimate communication with an audience.

JOHANN SEBASTIAN BACH

VIOLIN SONATAS AND PARTITAS,
BWV 1001–6

*T*hese solo works, the touchstone of every violinist's art, have come down to us in an immaculately copied presentation manuscript in Bach's hand, dated 1720. The sonatas and partitas appear in alternating order, though it is not known in what order Bach composed them or intended them to be performed.

The three sonatas conform to the model of the church sonata, consisting of four movements in a slow-fast-slow-fast sequence. The opening movements of the first two sonatas have the character of a slow prelude, with an upper-voice melody supported by chordal textures; in contrast, the Adagio of the third sonata is a study in imitative counterpoint. The fast second movements of all three sonatas are fugues, the slow third movements have an aria-like quality, and the concluding movements tend to be lively and unfold in an even rhythm.

The strength and meditative depth of Sonata No. 1, in G minor, are apparent from the beginning of the improvisatory opening Adagio and throughout the fugue, though the music of the following siciliana is almost Romantic in its lyrical warmth. The more passionate character of Sonata No. 2, in A minor, is reflected in the unrelenting drive of its fugue and in the throbbing melancholy of its Andante. Sonata No. 3, in C, grand and imposing, is the most rigorously argued of the three essays, particularly in its ten-minute fugue on the chorale *Komm, heiliger Geist.* The formal plan of this fugue, which consists of four sections and features concerto-like passages as interludes, is especially impressive, and the music itself is a challenge to play.

In Bach's day, the term "partita" could be used to designate any work constructed along the lines of a suite—that is, with multiple movements, some

Care for a canon? Bach with a 6-part round, 1746.

The bourrée was the most vigorous and earthy of the old dance forms.

THE CHACONNE *from the Partita in D minor is such a magnificent feat of musical architecture that it has elicited numerous arrangements for other instruments. Particularly notable are those for piano by Ferruccio Busoni (dating from around 1897) and Brahms (1877), in which the contrapuntal gauntlet is run on ivory rather than gut, but to great effect nonetheless.*

or all derived from dance types. Because of the differing characters of the dances incorporated in these three partitas for solo violin, the pieces are more diverse in expression than the sonatas. Within them, Bach employs a remarkable variety of playing styles and formal schemes; whereas the sonatas are exercises in concentration, the partitas, in their encyclopedic survey of violinistic capabilities, reflect Bach's urge to catholicize.

Partita No. 1, in B minor, consists of an allemande, courante, sarabande, and bourrée. Each is followed by its *Double*, a flowing, etude-like variation in fast notes. The writing throughout is extremely demanding and places a premium on the performer's sense of rhythm and articulation. By contrast, Partita No. 3, in E, is almost a divertissement, offering a wealth of melodically engaging material. The vibrant aerialism of its *moto perpetuo* prelude, the brilliance of its "Gavotte en Rondeau" (whose familiar melody is embellished with five sparkling interludes), the charming echo effects of its bourrée, and the exuberance of its concluding gigue make this the most dazzling of the three partitas.

The most daunting, however, is Partita No. 2, in D minor. As if to obscure its true stature, the partita opens with the traditional sequence of dances: allemande, courante, sarabande, and gigue. Only then does the mountaintop come into view. The chaconne with which the D minor Partita concludes is the most challenging single movement written for a solo string instrument. Almost 260 measures long and taking about 15 minutes to play, this variation movement is by itself virtually as long as the four previous movements put together. Its expression ranges from the declamatory to the awestruck. To build a satisfying climax, the soloist must be able to sustain a grand line of development through to the piece's end. In a performance where this happens, the world outside melts away, and the world of the spirit is played out on four strings.

The Russian emigré Milstein entranced with his eloquence.

RECOMMENDED RECORDINGS

Nathan Milstein.
Deutsche Grammophon 423 294-2 [2 CDs]

Shlomo Mintz.
Deutsche Grammophon 413 810-2 [3 CDs]

There is a patrician elegance to Milstein's renditions, in which the all-but-insurmountable difficulties of the music are overcome with deceptive ease. His burnished tone has a warmth like that of mahogany, and his fine fingerwork and flawless bowing make for an assured connection of ideas. In the chaconne to Partita No. 2, Milstein zeros in with the concentration of a chess champion.

Mintz's recording offers the set on three discs rather than two, each disc pairing a sonata with a partita. These are commanding accounts, showing exceptional musicality and depth (and lacking, if anything, just a touch of lightness and variety of color). The control of tone, amplitude, and intonation is extraordinary, and the approach is never showy or self-conscious. Judging from differences in ambience and image, the readings may have been recorded at several different sessions, though the takes are nicely joined in the final mix. The recording has a striking immediacy.

CELLO SUITES, BWV 1007–12

*T*here are no known works for solo cello before these six suites, which were composed between 1717 and 1723 while Bach was Kapellmeister at Cöthen. Together with the sonatas and partitas for solo violin, the cello suites show Bach's enormous powers of invention and counterpoint in a special light. Never before and never since have the elements of rhythm, harmony, and motive been so impressively integrated

The courtly allemande, a regal dance in slow tempo.

in music for a single string instrument.

Each suite begins with a flowing, quasi-improvisatory prelude (except for the Suite in C minor, whose prelude is cast in the rigorous mold of a French overture), and each work incorporates the standard dances of allemande, courante, sarabande, and gigue within a scheme of six superbly crafted movements. The interpolation of optional dances are also standard, and include gavottes, bourrées, and minuets. What is unconventional about the suites is that such a wealth of content and treatment could be worked into the "standard" forms.

Four of the six suites are in the major mode, an unusual proportion for Bach, who preferred the more intense expression customarily afforded by minor keys. But the C major tonality of Suite No. 3 enables Bach to write numerous four-part chords for the cello, taking advantage of the lower pair of open strings, C and G, as anchors for the tonic and dominant harmonies. The resultant richness of texture and timbre is a distinguishing feature of this piece. Suites Nos. 1 and 6, in G and D, similarly exploit the middle pair of open strings, G and D, and the upper pair, D and A. The character of the former is reserved and elegant, that of the latter outgoing and dramatic.

The two minor-key works, whose souls are to be found in their sarabandes, are among Bach's most profound creations. The sarabande of Suite No. 2, in D minor, exudes a feeling of heartbreaking loss, which the work as a whole amplifies with immense gravity. For Suite No. 5, in C minor, Bach instructs the soloist to tune the cello's A string to G, a whole step lower, darkening the instrument's color. The grim character of the suite is at its most pronounced in the sarabande, where the theme descends from the upper to the lower reaches of the cello's voice like a metaphysical sigh.

Fournier's playing was a paragon of style and subtlety.

RECOMMENDED RECORDING

Pierre Fournier.
Deutsche Grammophon 419 359-2 [2 CDs]

With his meditative yet confident approach, Fournier opens up an emotional realm that mere mortals have the good fortune to inhabit only on very rare occasions. He plays the low C at the end of the C minor Suite as if it were the alpha and omega of all music ever written for the cello—which in a way it is. Such insights abound in this midprice set. The 1960 recording is gorgeous.

BÉLA BARTÓK
STRING QUARTETS

*B*artók's six string quartets are among the most important contributions to the chamber music literature after those of Beethoven. Like Beethoven's quartets, Bartók's reflect their composer's growth and stylistic development over a period of three decades—and ultimately they served as the vehicle for his deepest, most intimate expression, revealing in microcosm the essence of his musical thinking.

The six quartets embrace a wealth of styles and folk idioms and make use of an extraordinary range of advanced techniques, including fierce "snap" pizzicatos in which the plucked string rebounds off the fingerboard (also called "Bartók pizzicatos"), haunting glissandos, dramatic mutings, and extended passages in multiple stops. While all six works share these hallmarks of Bartók's sound, each quartet creates its own world of expression, in itself a remarkable achievement. The lush textures and tonal vagueness of late Romanticism can be found in the First Quartet (1908) alongside driving ostinatos and energetic rhythms derived from folk music. An almost im-

BARTÓK *was one of the 20th century's finest ethnomusicologists. Aided by his colleague Zoltan Kodály, Bartók made a systematic study of Hungarian, Slovak, and Romanian folk music. He scoured the eastern European countryside carrying a portable Edison phonograph, with which he dutifully captured the voices and melodies of incredulous peasants. By 1918, he had gathered more than 9,000 folk songs.*

Bartók spices up the Fourth Quartet with "snap" pizzicatos in which a violin string is plucked.

pressionistic play of texture takes place just beneath the surface of the highly episodic Second Quartet (1915–17), which sounds alternately impassioned and macabre in its opening two movements before ending in a nightmarishly ethereal turbulence.

The Quartet No. 3 (1927) marks a forceful move away from conventional tonality toward an austere and sharply dissonant idiom, at the same time reflecting Bartók's growing preoccupation with formal compression and the rigorous, almost molecular, analysis of his material. Bartók would alter his course again with the Fifth Quartet (1934), a dynamic work that makes heavy use of the overlapping meters, complex dance rhythms, and unusual modes and scales of Hungarian and Bulgarian folk music. In the Quartet No. 6 (1939), he returns to a constant in Beethoven's late quartets, the idea of variation on a theme, and closes out the cycle with a work whose four-movement design and relatively strong embrace of tonality suggest a reconciliation with the Classical ideal.

But we must go back to the Fourth Quartet (1928) to find what composer Halsey Stevens said "comes close to being . . . Bartók's greatest and most profound achievement." Particularly impressive for its compression of highly complex material into the tightest possible framework, the Fourth Quartet is also a work of great expressive beauty, characterized by sheer rhythmic exuberance and a sensuous profusion of sonorities, most notably in the swirling ecstasies of the second movement.

One of the most striking aspects of the Fourth Quartet is its formal plan: a palindrome. The quartet must therefore be perceived not only as a succession of five movements, but also as a work that grows outward from a central kernel. This kernel is a nocturnal Lento that employs sustained tone clusters as a backdrop to recitative-like solos by the cello and first violin. Around this core are wrapped two related scherzos: the second movement, a mercurial tour de force calling for mutes on all instruments and spiced by glissandos and *sul ponticello* harmonics, and the fourth movement, played entirely pizzicato and full of offbeat accents. These movements are in turn surrounded by angular Allegros that share the same germinal motive, an ascent of three half-steps (from B to D flat) followed by a snappy descent of three (from C to B flat), which is first given out by the cello in the seventh bar of the quartet. The energetic canonic writing of the first movement is mirrored in the driving virtuosity of the finale.

 RECOMMENDED RECORDING

Emerson Quartet.
Deutsche Grammophon 423 657-2 [2 CDs]

These quartets have been well represented on LP; the choice on CD, however, is limited to one. The Emerson players show the kind of ensemble polish that caused one European critic to label their performances as "too smooth. . . . I like my Bartók rougher." But awkwardness and rhythmic uncertainty, which have made many another group sound rough in this music, should not be confused with expressive edge, which the Emersons bring to the music in full measure. They get all six essays onto two CDs, the odd-numbered quartets on one, the even on the other. The sound quality is excellent throughout.

Named for the 19th-century poet, the Emerson String Quartet gives transcendent accounts of Bartók's 20th-century masterpieces.

LUDWIG VAN BEETHOVEN

VIOLIN SONATA IN A MINOR, OP. 47
Kreutzer

*B*eethoven's penultimate violin sonata was composed in 1803 for George Polgreen Bridgetower, a noted interpreter of Giovanni Viotti's music who happened to be visiting Vienna at the time. In one of his sketchbooks, Beethoven described the work as "a sonata written in a very

Kreutzer turned his back on Beethoven's sonata.

concertante style—almost a concerto," and the composition's huge scale and virtuosic violin part certainly bear him out.

The Adagio introduction to the first movement begins with an arresting gesture: a hymnlike, four-measure proclamation by the solo violin, played in euphonious double stops. The main body of the movement, a blazing Presto, is launched by a vigorous staccato subject in A minor. The mood is scarcely lightened by the appearance of a serene second subject, for as soon as the violin has presented it, the piano takes it over and turns it to the minor as well. The F major Andante is a grand variation movement that fills a quarter of an hour with music of rhapsodic beauty. The long-breathed theme is the height of suavity, and while its treatment in the ensuing four variations is more decorative than probing, Beethoven's mastery of the lyric utterance is everywhere apparent. An impetuous tarantella finale caps the work with nonstop theatrics.

Bridgetower gave the first performance of the sonata, with Beethoven at the keyboard, on May 24, 1803, in Vienna. There was a subsequent falling out between the two, apparently over a woman, and Beethoven decided to dedicate the work to the French violinist Rodolphe Kreutzer— who according to Berlioz found the piece "outrageously unintelligible." Kreutzer never played it or acknowledged the dedication.

HE SON of an African father and a Polish mother, George Bridgetower was brought to England as a child and entered the service of the Prince of Wales at the age of ten. A year later, he played in the violin section for Haydn's London concerts of 1791. He was an old man of 23 when he premiered the Kreutzer Sonata.

RECOMMENDED RECORDINGS

Itzhak Perlman, violin; Vladimir Ashkenazy, piano.
London 410 554-2 [with Sonata in F, Op. 24]

Yehudi Menuhin, violin; Wilhelm Kempff, piano.
Deutsche Grammophon Galleria 427 251-2 [with Sonata in F, Op. 24]

Performing Personalities

Perhaps the greatest American-born violinist, Yehudi Menuhin astounded the world with prodigious accomplishments as a child. A mystical personality and deep moral convictions have made him one of the great spirits and consciences in the field of music today. He has recorded prolifically since the 1930s and remains active as a teacher and writer.

Perlman and Ashkenazy give an account of unrelenting virtuosity and symphonic scale. The fingers and bow fly, yet Perlman never loses command of his tone. Recorded in 1973, the reading is closely miked—so closely, in fact, that one can literally hear the hair on Perlman's bow. The sound is weighty but clear, with excellent presence.

In 1970, Menuhin no longer had the control of the bow he exhibited in his youth, and occasionally some rawness of tone and awkwardness were the result. The approach here is nonetheless highly musical, and the reading testifies to a wonderful partnership that fuses Kempff's insight and elegance with Menuhin's expressiveness and lyricism. The midprice CD retains the live feel of the original analog recording, and the overall sonic detail is exemplary.

CELLO SONATA IN A, OP. 69

*T*he best known and most appealing of Beethoven's cello sonatas, this work was composed during the years 1807–8, the same period that saw the completion of the Fifth and Sixth Symphonies. It bears a dedication to Beethoven's friend Ignaz von Gleichenstein, an amateur cellist of exceptional skill who served as a planner at the Imperial war council in Vienna.

The sonata opens with a poignant yet noble statement by the cello, setting the stage for an impassioned first-movement dialog between cello and piano. The material is brilliantly worked out, and the movement culminates with a sublimely theatrical unison reprise of the opening theme. The scherzo—lengthy and almost symphonic in character—is built on a syncopated rhythmic figure and has a magnificent trio foreshadowing that of the Seventh Symphony. A short Adagio serves as prelude to the finale, where both lyricism and kinetic energy propel the movement headlong toward an almost giddy conclusion.

THE STRADIVARI *cello on which Pierre Duport played the premiere of Beethoven's Sonata in A, Op. 69, is one of the finest instruments in existence. Napoleon admired its perfection the same way he admired most things— jealously. He seized the instrument from its owner's hands and gouged it down one side with his spur, scarring it but failing to change its sound in the slightest. Today, the Duport Strad belongs to Mstislav Rostropovich (below).*

 RECOMMENDED RECORDING

Mstislav Rostropovich, cello; Sviatoslav Richter, piano.

Philips 412 256-2 [2 CDs; complete cello sonatas]

One encounters a partnership of equals in the accounts of Rostropovich and Richter. The cellist's approach is rhapsodic, his aim very much an illumination of the inner spirit of the music. Richter is utterly amazing, tossing off runs and passagework with supreme elegance, conversing with Rostropovich in the most intimate manner, surrounding and supporting the sound of the cello the way a crystal vase holds a bouquet of roses, so that both can be appreciated. The sound on this 1961 recording may lack immediacy, but it matches the warmth of the performances.

PIANO TRIO IN B FLAT, OP. 97
Archduke

Completed in 1811, this work—dedicated to Beethoven's friend and patron, Archduke Rudolph—still stands as the pinnacle of the literature for piano trio, a composition of unparalleled richness and imagination that exemplifies Beethoven's middle-period manner at its best.

The spacious opening movement begins with a flowing subject announced by the piano—a march, in fact, though conceived in the gentlest terms. The nobility of this idea is counterbalanced by an animated second subject, which despite its jaunty rhythm is also a march. The grand development section takes as its point of departure the initial subject's division into two clearly marked phrases, each of which serves as grist for the mill. A beautifully ornamented restatement of the opening subject ushers in the recapitulation, and a brilliant coda rounds off the movement.

Archduke Rudolph, Beethoven's father confessor and patron.

The ensuing scherzo, with its shadowy trio section, is a splendid demonstration of technique and imagination. The bantering of the instruments as they snatch phrases away from one another, together with Beethoven's side-slipping modulations, keep the listener guessing as to the direction things will go. The play of high style (in the guise of fugal writing) against low (represented by the waltz) is heady and exuberant in a way only Beethoven can make it.

An ambitious variation movement follows, in the distant key of D major. The opening theme is broad and consoling, and the variations, each one progressively more decorative, are masterfully sustained. From the quiet, almost motionless stirrings of the movement's final bars, Beethoven jumps directly into the finale, a dance-like rondo that makes a game to the very end of avoiding the home key of B flat. The exhilaration mounts to an almost unbearable pitch before the coda carries everything off at a gallop.

The *Archduke* Trio was first performed on April 11, 1814, with Beethoven—who by then was nearly deaf—at the keyboard. Ignaz Moscheles, one of the composer's young followers, wrote of the premiere: "In the case of how many compositions is the word 'new' misapplied! But never in Beethoven's, and least of all in this."

 RECOMMENDED RECORDINGS

Itzhak Perlman, violin; Lynn Harrell, cello; Vladimir Ashkenazy, piano.
EMI CDC 47010 [with Trio in B flat, WoO 39]

Beaux Arts Trio.
Philips 412 891-2 [with Trio in D, Op. 70, No. 1]

Perlman, Harrell, and Ashkenazy combine majesty with a splendid sense of flow in the opening movement, and they treat the variations of the third movement in the manner of late Beetho-

IF YOU LIKE THIS WORK, you will probably find Beethoven's Trio in D, Op. 70, No. 1, appealing as well. The trio gets its nickname, the Ghost, *from its lugubrious D minor Largo, which is full of eerie trills and tremolos. You might also want to investigate the Trios in B flat and E flat, D. 898 and 929, by Schubert.*

The Beaux Arts Trio, with cellist Bernard Greenhouse (left), violinist Isidore Cohen, and pianist Menahem Pressler.

ven—with an emotive power that is all the more intense for being hushed. The digital recording from 1982 is fairly dry but quite acceptable.

The Beaux Arts Trio takes a contemplative view of the work in this 1981 recording, a reaction to the players' lighter reading from the 1960s. They bring almost *too* much finesse and refinement to the opening movement. The Andante holds the key to their interpretation: where Ashkenazy and company treat it as a reverie, the Beaux Artistes see it as a meditation, and take a full two minutes longer to play it. The early digital recording offers good atmosphere and excellent detail.

STRING QUARTETS, OP. 18

*B*y the time Beethoven appeared on the scene, the string quartet had become an established, refined genre, the only one whose expressive flexibility and tonal perfection could rival that of the human voice. Whereas in his orchestral and piano works Beethoven often fought against the limitations of the medium, his writing for string quartet is almost always idiomatic. He was drawn to the sound of the genre, and from the start he treated sound as a component of form, stretching out textures until they took on a value of their own. But the fact that Beethoven wrote idiomatically does not mean he was always graceful. In his quartets, as elsewhere, Beethoven was interested in difficulty.

Beethoven composed the six quartets of Opus 18 before he reached his 30th year. Considering their place in history—following close on the heels of the supreme achievements of Haydn and Mozart—and their place in Beethoven's output, they are works of tremendous accomplishment. Beethoven made certain the ground was carefully prepared, writing a pilot version of the Quartet in F, Op. 18, No. 1, before starting the set. Though these quartets thoroughly assimilate the formal accomplishments of Beethoven's predecessors, they subvert the expectations of those familiar with the Classical style.

For example, the Quartet in G, Op. 18, No. 2, opens with a near-parody of the galant style, the ornamental quality of the writing meaningfully excessive. Beethoven balances the superficial elegance of this posture by complicating the structure, by enriching the texture beyond that of the true galant, and by being already a little impertinent— which he is again in the *alla breve* Allegro that interrupts the quartet's slow movement. Beethoven's love of sharpening garden-variety contrast into something quite dangerous manifests itself throughout the six quartets. To cite one case, in the scherzo to the Quartet in B flat, Op. 18, No. 6, he lets the rhythmic scansion go wild, then "rights" the wrong by emphasizing the downbeats in the trio.

The three final members of Opus 18 are particularly impressive. The Quartet in C minor (No. 4) opens with a theatrical Allegro whose pulsating, agitated style is more akin to that of early 19th-century Romanticism than to anything the 18th century produced. As a counterpoise to this potent beginning, Beethoven offers two fairly brisk sequels, a scherzo (here parodying a waltz in its overplaying of the second beat) *and* a sentimental minuet, effectively banking the fires of passion. The concluding movement, a French-style "couplet rondo," pulls up short at a number of early cadences but concludes in a breathless coda.

The Quartet in A (No. 5) has a taut, smoothly argued first movement and a delightfully resourceful variation movement that explodes at the end with the panache of a military band. The tongue-in-cheek finale begins with a suggestion of the learned style, but moves quickly into the realm of the lowly contredanse. The Quartet in B flat, the final work in the set, begins with a *moto perpetuo* parody of comic-opera style that is both humorous and provocative, while the clockwork Adagio and schizophrenic scherzo explore motion

HUMOR, *arising from the unexpected juxtaposition of contrasting styles and topics, is fundamental to the music of Beethoven. But this is the humor of an angry man. It is expertly crude rather than unrefined. It upsets, hits hard, and holds tight. Were it to be expressed as a physical gesture, it would hurt.*

in two entirely different ways. Beethoven prefaces his flowing Allegretto finale with a fantasy introduction in the dark *ombra* style, building suspense before brilliantly relieving it.

The Smithson String Quartet at the Smithsonian.

 RECOMMENDED RECORDINGS

Alban Berg Quartet.
EMI Classics CDC 47126 [3 CDs]

Quartetto Italiano.
Philips 426 046-2 [3 CDs]

Smithson String Quartet.
Deutsche Harmonia Mundi 77029-2 [2 CDs]

The Alban Berg Quartet gives patrician accounts of the Opus 18 set, lean-textured and precise, with a characteristically Viennese blend of intensity and restraint. The 1981 recording was made at a low level and puts the ensemble at a slight distance, but it offers good balance and clarity.

If the Austrians appear at times to take these works too seriously, the Italians, full of peasant heartiness, are almost too exuberant. In tonally opulent performances, they make Beethoven less the bad boy, more the genial, avuncular successor to Haydn—which in some ways he was trying to be. Recorded between 1972 and 1975 and reissued in 1989 at midprice, these handsomely remastered accounts are close-miked and have vivid presence.

The Smithson String Quartet, resident at the Smithsonian Institution in Washington, D.C., performs the set on period instruments. These revelatory accounts combine insight into style with a wonderful spontaneity, and the group's articulate playing allows textures to emerge with luminous clarity. The 1987 recording is warm, full, and beautifully balanced.

Count Razumovsky maintained a resident quartet at his palace.

THE MIDDLE PERIOD *of Beethoven's output is marked by music whose simple ideas are put together according to complex plans. Often the commonplace is made substantive by being ever so slightly modified, as when a likeness is turned into a caricature by the exaggeration of a single feature.*

STRING QUARTETS, OP. 59
Razumovsky

*T*hese three quartets were written for Count Andreas Razumovsky, the Russian ambassador to the Hapsburg court and an amateur violinist of considerable merit. His substantial wealth enabled him to maintain a resident quartet that included among its members the outstanding violinist Ignaz Schuppanzigh and the cellist Joseph Linke. The *Razumovsky* Quartets were commissioned toward the end of 1805 and completed within a year. It is hard to imagine that their initial reception could have been so discouraging, yet the compositions provoked consternation and ridicule, even among Beethoven's musically literate friends. At least one perceptive critic reported of these works that "the conception is profound and the construction excellent, but they are not easily comprehended—with the possible exception of the third in C major, which cannot but appeal to intelligent lovers of music because of its originality, melody, and harmonic power."

The Quartet in C is indeed appealing. It opens, much as Mozart's *Dissonance* Quartet had, with an evocation of harmonic chaos. Out of this an Allegro emerges, at first unsure of its key; only after a few false starts does Beethoven land on C major, emphatically, with the jaunty march subject that begins the exposition proper. The ensuing Andante is a slow barcarolle in rondo form, the minuet a study in contrast between flowing and angular gestures. The quartet's finale takes off like a shot with an electrifying solo for viola. It is among the supreme showpieces for string quartet, with a pace that would bring even a dancing Russian to his knees.

As a tribute to Razumovsky, Beethoven weaves Russian themes into two of these quartets. In the scherzo to the Quartet in E minor, Op. 59, No. 2, he quotes a tune that Mussorgsky would later insert in the Coronation Scene of *Boris Godunov*. And in the finale to the Quartet in F, Op. 59, No. 1, he uses a Russian theme as the subject of what amounts to a monothematic sonata. The rhetorical energy and expansive view of form that make the F major Quartet the *Eroica* of Beethoven's string quartets are evident in the confident opening measures of the first movement, which set the trajectory of the entire piece. Through the first 19 bars the texture expands from three to eight voices, the dynamic increases from *piano* to *fortissimo*, and the melody rises from C in the cello to high F in the first violin. The remainder of the first movement follows a vast sonata plan, with a development that makes a long descent into the distant key of E flat minor, from which the climb back to F major is both eventful and exhilarating.

The ensuing scherzo is the most original of all Beethoven's inspirations. It begins with an eccentric gesture, a series of repeated B flats in the cello that have a definite rhythm but seem to go nowhere—an accompaniment without anything to accompany, and a wonderful example of Beethoven's love of the schematic. From here the movement unfolds as a meditation on the clockwork textures of the 18th century, but with harmonic and structural surprises on every page. The Adagio, marked *mesto* ("sad"), shows great refinement of texture in spite of the essential simplicity of its material. Time is stretched out to great length in this movement, without the slightest loss of continuity or intensity. In fact, the tonal glue is so strong here and in the transition to the concluding *"Thème Russe"* Allegro that the third movement's final cadence does not occur until 35 measures into the finale. With that finale, Beethoven sets an exuberant cap on one of the grandest quartets in the literature.

RAZUMOVSKY *Quartet No. 1 perplexed even the musicians for whom the work was written. When Ignaz Schuppanzigh and his quartet read through it the first time, Carl Czerny recalled, "they laughed and were convinced that Beethoven was playing a joke." A decade later, at an early performance in St. Petersburg, the assembled listeners burst into laughter when the cellist began the second movement with his solo on one note.*

RECOMMENDED RECORDINGS

Melos Quartet.

Deutsche Grammophon 427 305-2 [Op. 59, No. 1, with Quartet in E flat, Op. 74; complete middle-period quartets also available on 415 342-2, 3 CDs]

Smetana Quartet.

Denon C37-7025 [Op. 59, No. 1]

The Melos players turn in an impressively propulsive reading of the First *Razumovsky* Quartet. Their tempo in the opening movement may seem quite fast, but they play with such accuracy that nuances and articulations emerge more clearly than in any competing version. The 1985 digital recording sounds rather bright, and Deutsche Grammophon's close-miked pickup makes things seem louder and larger than they are, a frequent tactic in those years.

The Smetana Quartet's reading of the First *Razumovsky* is one of the highlights of the group's complete cycle for Denon. The playing is assured and wonderfully communicative, the sound excellent—naturally balanced and precisely imaged. The only drawback is the lack of a coupling, in this case easily outweighed by the warmth of the performance.

STRING QUARTET IN C SHARP MINOR, OP. 131

*D*uring his later years Beethoven's need to pose new challenges to his creativity was as great as it had been at any point in his life. He felt obliged, as the musicologist Maynard Solomon has put it, "to test his powers against the restraints of the Classic model." What Beethoven found in the process was a new means to communicate feeling and thought. It is this communi-

Still life with fiddle heads.

cativeness that lies at the heart of Beethoven's late works for string quartet.

As Beethoven had to rely more and more on what he remembered, he increasingly manipulated materials he had known in his youth: cadential harmony, 18th-century topics, the innate sound of the string quartet, and standard forms such as the sonata, the fugue, and theme and variations. As a group, the late quartets are marked by a tendency toward contraction; for example, there is not a single grandly scaled opening movement in any of the essays. And yet there is a paradoxical expansion—of expressive scope, of rhythm, harmony, and color, and of time itself, which even in short movements can stand still.

Composed in 1826, the Quartet in C sharp minor, Op. 131, was Beethoven's favorite. It has the most involved road map of any work in the chamber literature, and it is arguably *the* monumental work for string quartet. With its seven movements and 14 tempo changes, all played without pause, the score presents a massive challenge to any who attempt it. The connection between the movements is not just circumstantial but organic, established through motivic relationships and also by a remarkable key scheme: all seven movements are in sharp keys, and there is no final cadence on C sharp minor anywhere in the piece. In effect, there is no arrival, just a continuous, mind-boggling journey. The score also has a hidden plan: the seven movements follow the operatic scheme of an overture, a number of arias and recitatives, and an ensemble finale—though because of the fugue in the first movement, the closest model is probably that of an act from an oratorio. It is an act in which the participants play out the progression from fantasy to reality.

The opening fugue is noticeably ecclesiastical, almost as if patterned after a Renaissance motet. In this contemplative mood, Beethoven seeks to achieve a vocal richness. The ensuing Allegro is

BEETHOVEN *embraced the principle of theme-and-variations in his late music. For him, there was an important difference between variation and embroidery, as his contemporary Jérôme-Joseph de Momigny made clear: "Variation is scientific, embroidery is tasteful." Applying the science of variation to his material was a way for Beethoven to sail off wherever his imagination took him, without losing sight of land. For a composer who had lost his hearing, having a musical compass was important.*

Op. 131 quartet was influenced by operatic styles of the day.

an aria in the Italian style. The content, far from being elevated, is made frivolous in a parody of the low-style pastorale. A *recitative obligé* follows as the third movement; only 11 measures long, it is a brilliantly compressed play of texture in which the tradeoffs between first and second violin have to be seen, like the wheels of a ticking watch, rather than merely heard.

The central movement of the quartet is a set of six variations on an Andante contredanse, pointedly marked *molto cantabile* ("very lyrical"). Each variation represents a short aria in a different style; at one point, Beethoven even parodies the strummed guitar chords of an Italian serenade. The following scherzo has a singsong quality, but its melody keeps disappearing . . . fragmenting itself . . . and being reassembled in new ways. Ultimately the wheels fall off—and it is only then that Beethoven allows the tune a last, glorious dash straight into the next movement, an Adagio whose harmonies take on a Romantic pregnancy.

The quartet's concluding Allegro, like a good operatic finale, makes much of unison performance. The layout is that of a sonata, and the driving rhythm of the opening subject bears a family resemblance to that of the finale of the Second *Razumovsky* Quartet. Meanwhile, the emphasis on incision counterbalances the concern for flow that marked the opening movement. And it is worth noting that in the heart of the development, Beethoven inserts an ascending scale in whole notes, sustaining it for 23 measures as countersubject and running it through all four instruments, as though he were going back 30-odd years to his counterpoint lessons. In more ways than one, then, Beethoven has come full circle by the end of this extraordinary piece.

 RECOMMENDED RECORDINGS

Guarneri Quartet.
Philips 422 341-2 [with Quartèt in E flat, Op. 74]

EVEN WITH *as serious a work as the Quartet in C sharp minor, Beethoven was not above making a joke. His publisher, B. Schott's Söhne in Mainz, had told him that the quartet must be an "original" one, so Beethoven wrote on the manuscript, "put together from pilferings from one thing and another."*

Talich Quartet.

Calliope CAL 9638 [with Razumovsky *Quartet No. 3]*

The Guarneri players understand the profound lyrical impulse behind this quartet, and they manage the paradoxical feat of imparting a sense of inevitability to the music and achieving spontaneity at the same time. The recording for Philips, made in 1988, puts the pathos and whimsy of Beethoven's writing in clear relief and conveys a crystalline clarity and richness of sound.

The Talich Quartet takes a dark, foreboding view of the fugue, bringing it close to the world of Schoenberg and post-Romanticism—which is indeed the next place one finds such writing. The remainder of this performance sustains the remarkable tension of the opening, yet the playing is full of old-world warmth and relaxation, deftly understated and distinguished by the luminous tone to which Czech ensembles alone seem to have the key. The account is captured in a very fine, naturally balanced analog recording.

The Guarneri Quartet, one of America's premier ensembles.

ALEXANDER BORODIN

STRING QUARTET NO. 2, IN D

*T*he illegitimate son of a Russian prince, Borodin (1833–1887) devoted his life to the service of two muses. The first was chemistry, a field in which he achieved distinction for his research into acids and aldehydes. At the age of 31 he was appointed to a full professorship at the Medico-Surgical Academy in St. Petersburg, where he spent the rest of his life teaching and living adjacent to his laboratory. Borodin's second love was music, and on the strength of his talent he became a leading figure in Russian musical life, taking his place in the St. Petersburg group of composers known as "The Mighty Handful."

Borodin excelled all of his peers in melodic

gift—and his String Quartet No. 2 possesses a lyricism unparalleled in the repertory. Although he usually worked slowly, Borodin raced this score to completion in just two months during the summer of 1881, intending it as a present to mark the 20th anniversary of his courtship of and engagement to the pianist Ekaterina Protopopova. Rarely has a romantic idyll been more beautifully remembered.

The quartet's first movement opens with one of those long-breathed cantilenas Borodin was so good at, a warm, tender melody started by the cello, taken over by the first violin, and spun out ravishingly over a gently sighing accompaniment. It is the sort of melody that would traditionally appear as a second subject; coming first it casts the entire movement in a lyrical vein. Borodin mines that vein with an arabesque-like second subject in the minor, introduced by first violin over a pizzicato accompaniment.

Both the second and third movements contain melodies that have since been popularized by the Broadway show *Kismet*. The breezy scherzo holds its tune in reserve for a few moments, which only adds to listeners' delight when they recognize the waltzlike second subject as "Baubles, Bangles, and Beads." The ensuing *Notturno* opens with one of the greatest love songs ever penned, the soft yet passionate melody that was to become "And This Is My Beloved." It is sung by the cello, Borodin's own instrument, in its upper range—and proclaims clearly enough that the composer was still very much in love. The high point of the movement comes when the theme is treated canonically by cello and violin over a delicately shivering tremolo accompaniment.

The only weakness of the quartet is its finale, which attempts to mimic the dynamism of Beethoven's late quartets. Borodin, however, was not a dramatic composer. Still, the treatment holds interest, and three perfect and melodically memorable movements are more than enough to make this quartet one of the gems of the literature.

BORODIN *(above) was not the only member of "The Mighty Handful" with a career outside of music. In fact, only Mily Balakirev was a full-time composer. Rimsky-Korsakov was a naval officer and civil servant, Mussorgsky worked in the Czarist ministries of communications and forestry, and César Cui was a music critic and professor of military engineering.*

KISMET, *the Broadway musical, made a Top 40 tune out of "Stranger in Paradise," which was lifted from Borodin's* Polovtsian Dances, *as were the numbers "Not Since Nineveh" and "He's in Love." The song "Rhymes Have I" came from Borodin's Symphony No. 2. Thanks to* Kismet, *Borodin won the Tony award for best Broadway composer in 1954.*

 RECOMMENDED RECORDINGS

Borodin Quartet.
EMI CDC 47795 [with Quartet No. 1]

Cleveland Quartet.
Telarc CD 80178 [with Smetana: Quartet No. 1]

The Borodin Quartet plays the music of its namesake as to the manner born. Here is a beautiful, *lush* realization—polished, full of nuance, and well served by the 1980 analog recording. The coupling with Borodin's First Quartet is especially attractive.

Playing on a matched set of Stradivari instruments that once belonged to Paganini (and are now in the collection of the Corcoran Gallery of Washington, D.C.), the Cleveland Quartet shows that Americans can do the music proud, too. Their reading is well paced and thoughtfully phrased, and while their sound is lighter than that of the Borodin ensemble, it is handsomely captured in Telarc's 1988 recording. Smetana's E minor Quartet (*From My Life*) makes for a desirable coupling.

JOHANNES BRAHMS
VIOLIN SONATAS

*I*t is in his instrumental music that Brahms most clearly dominates his century, and no one approached his mastery in the field of chamber music. The major, and most successful, part of his chamber output involves the keyboard and includes the sonatas for violin and piano. Brahms's inflexible self-criticism resulted in the destruction of his first several attempts at a violin sonata, but the efforts that eventually followed produced three appealing works—the first two intimate essays intended for the salon, the third a public piece intended for the concert stage.

Lake Thun where Brahms spent some inspiring summers.

N THE SUMMER
Brahms would retreat to
the mountains or a lake. The
summers of 1877–79 found
him at Pörtschach on the
Wörthersee in Carinthia. In
1880 and again in 1882 he
went to Bad Ischl in the
Salzkammergut, and in
1884 and '85 he summered
at Mürzzuschlag in the Styr-
ian Alps. During all these
sojourns, Brahms composed
actively.

The Sonata in G, Op. 78, was composed during the summers of 1878 and 1879 at Pörtschach on the Wörthersee, near the Carinthian border with Italy. The countryside there was so thick with melodies, Brahms quipped in one of his letters, "that one has to be careful not to step on them." The songlike opening of the sonata's first movement certainly bears the composer out, as the violin soars over an accompaniment of softly voiced chords and gentle arpeggios. The Adagio that follows is dominated by a marchlike subject of funereal weight, and the sonata's finale is based on the melancholy melody of Brahms's song *Regenlied*, Op. 59, No. 3, whose three repeated D's also form a link to the opening subject of the first movement. The sense of yearning that builds as the finale unfolds is only partly satisfied by an ardent climax in E flat major. The real resolution comes when the movement finds its way back to G major, allowing the sonata to end in a mood of radiant tranquility.

The Sonata in A, Op. 100, composed during the summer of 1886 in the Swiss lakeside village of Hofstetten near Thun, takes after the G major Sonata in its understated manner and is among the gentlest of Brahms's chamber works. The placid opening Allegro begins with a consoling theme in the piano; the movement's even more tender second subject is derived from another of Brahms's songs, *Wie Melodien zieht es mir*, Op. 105, No. 1, written the same year for the young contralto Hermine Spies. Its presence is not accidental, for Spies was one of the summer's frequent visitors to Hofstetten. The sonata's Andante, part slow movement and part scherzo, begins as a meditation shared by violin and piano and proceeds to alternate this material with a Hungarian-flavored dance that becomes more schematic each time it appears, until it is no more than a wispy reminiscence of itself. The concluding Allegro opens with a noble subject announced by the violin and extended by the piano. Brahms's subsequent use of diminished seventh chords in the piano accompaniment undercuts the harmonic stability of the theme, but ambivalence eventually gives way to lyrical certainty as the violin warmly intones the subject for the last time.

The Sonata in D minor, Op. 108, finished during the summer of 1888 in Hofstetten, springs from a more symphonic conception than its siblings. Its four movements are tightly constructed, and its textures are unusually dense owing to the virtuosic piano part—which may have been what allowed Brahms to dedicate the score to Hans von Bülow, one of the great pianists of the day. After a restless first movement, the Adagio exudes heartfelt poignancy in a way that is unusual for Brahms. The movement reaches a searing climax in its closing measures, as the violin rises to deliver a fervent lament. The sonata's third movement finds the violin and piano darting in and out of the shadows of F sharp minor, though this game of hide-and-seek is more mysterious than playful. The finale begins with a tempestuous eruption and remains a turbulent, highly charged affair to the end. The heavy, chordal style of the piano part lends colossal force to the movement's unfolding, and no concessions are made to the violin, which must claw its way through the texture to be heard.

Violin and bow: the mystical union of wood, gut, and horsehair has charmed the ear for centuries.

 RECOMMENDED RECORDINGS

Itzhak Perlman, violin;
Vladimir Ashkenazy, piano.
EMI Classics CDC 47403

Josef Suk, violin; Julius Katchen, piano.
London 421 092-2

Perlman is the greatest living exponent of the Romantic style of violin playing, and he proves it in these intensely emotional accounts. It would be easy to guess the first two sonatas' relationship to songs from the way Perlman plays them in a

ON A LAKESIDE *stroll with Mahler during the last year of his life, Brahms complained that the directions composers were taking would lead to the end of music. Mahler grabbed him by the arm, pointed to the shoreline, and shouted, "Look, Doctor, there goes the last wave!" Wearily, Brahms replied, "Perhaps the real question is whether it's flowing into the lake, or into a swamp."*

single, seamless line, marked by soaring climaxes and tender, haunting *pianissimos.* In this 1983 recording (sonically superior to Perlman's recent remake for Sony Classical with pianist Daniel Barenboim), the violin sounds slightly forward, though not unpleasantly so. Supportive, lyrical playing from Ashkenazy rounds out a marvelous offering.

The Czech violinist Suk—grandson of the composer by that name and great-grandson of Dvořák—recorded the sonatas in London's Kingsway Hall in 1967, just two years before the untimely death at age 42 of his partner, the American pianist Katchen. Their account remains one of the unsung classics of the catalog, and an especially good value at midprice. Suk's tone may lack the opulence and glow of others who have championed this repertory, but his phrasing and projection of mood are masterly. He is wonderfully accompanied by Katchen in these rhapsodic, effectively understated readings. The sound is good, though somewhat grainy in the treble and a bit shallow in the piano.

CELLO SONATA IN E MINOR, OP. 38
CELLO SONATA IN F, OP. 99

Begun in 1862, the Sonata in E minor was not only Brahms's first for cello and piano, it was the first of all his sonatas for a solo instrument and piano. In its brooding pessimism, it is classic early Brahms. The long elegy of the opening movement verges on the lugubrious, its more agitated passages coming close to the stormy pathos of the Piano Concerto in D minor. Brahms's treatment of the cello part is curiously vocal throughout the sonata, and he keeps the instrument in its resonant lower register, surrendering brilliance for tonal richness. The weighty Romanticism of the first movement is lifted in the minuet-style Allegretto but returns in the sonata's fugal finale, where in spite of his preoccupation with demonstrating compositional technique, Brahms achieves a formidable urgency.

The Sonata in F was composed in 1886, by which time Brahms had the confidence to take the cello out of its lower range and allow it to balance the piano in a register better suited to lyrical projection. From the first bars, the sonata strikes a dramatic pose, sweeping the listener along with bold, soaring gestures and pages of spirited interplay between the two protagonists. While there are more intimate moments—in which the warmth and tenderness of Brahms's later music come to the fore—the writing favors the intense over the idyllic, impressing the listener again and again with its impassioned eloquence.

RECOMMENDED RECORDINGS

Jacqueline du Pré, cello; Daniel Barenboim, piano.
EMI Studio CDM 63298

Yo-Yo Ma, cello; Emanuel Ax, piano.
Sony Classical SK 48191 [with arrangement of Violin Sonata in D minor, Op. 108, for cello and piano]

English cellist Jacqueline du Pré, whose career and life were cut tragically short by multiple sclerosis.

Du Pré and Barenboim were married in 1967. One of the first things they did as a couple was make this recording of the Brahms sonatas (when it was finished, in 1968, Du Pré was only 23, Barenboim an old man of 25). Their collaboration is an intense one, both in the dark E minor work and in the passionate F major Sonata, which receives a fulminant performance here even if its scherzo sounds rather elephantine. Du Pré is quite rough much of the time, but her tone is huge and she wrings incredible expression out of every gesture; Barenboim is musically and sonically in the background, which under the circumstances is fine. Excellently remastered, the analog recording has striking immediacy and depth.

Ma and Ax are smoother and more lyrical in their approach and comparatively understated in their expression, though there are interesting interpretive touches from both. The recording establishes a concert-hall perspective with good balance and a solid, well-focused image.

CLARINET SONATAS, OP. 120

*I*n 1890, shortly after completing the String Quintet in G, Op. 111, Brahms decided to give up composition. On his 58th birthday the following year, he made out his will. Then, that very summer, he succumbed—not to illness or infirmity, but to a new onset of creative fervor, largely stemming from his friendship with Richard Mühlfeld, the first clarinetist of the renowned Meiningen Court Orchestra.

Mühlfeld's extraordinary virtuosity and exquisite tone inspired Brahms to write some of the most beautiful music of his career. Only once before had Brahms used a wind instrument in his chamber music (in the Trio in E flat for Violin, Horn, and Piano, Op. 40), but from 1891 the clarinet would figure in several works, including the Quintet in B minor for Clarinet and Strings, Op. 115, and the two Sonatas for Clarinet and Piano, Op. 120. The latter pieces, written in 1894 for *Fräulein Klarinette*, as Brahms had come to call the instrument, were the last sonatas he would write, and they also served as his farewell to instrumental composition.

The Sonata in F minor, Op. 120, No. 1, finds Brahms at his most rhapsodic. The opening Allegro, as its *appassionato* marking suggests, is an impassioned and turbulent essay, while the Andante is a subdued utterance in long-breathed phrases, almost inaudibly soft at the start. The Allegretto is a typical intermezzo in the restrained style Brahms favored in later years, while the

UNDER THE BATON *of Hans von Bülow, its music director from 1880 to 1885, the Meiningen Court Orchestra became perhaps the best band in all the German lands. Bülow trained the orchestra to play from memory, and he made a specialty of the music of Brahms.*

Clarinet in B flat with key system perfected in the late 19th century.

finale is a lively and virtuosic romp. Throughout the work, the piano plays an equal role with the clarinet.

The Sonata in E flat, Op. 120, No. 2, is among the gentlest and most ingratiating of Brahms's instrumental works. Once again, the opening Allegro lives up to its designation, which in this case is *amabile* ("amiable")—an unusual term for Brahms but aptly descriptive of the music's placid, warmly lyrical nature. Following the more heated lyricism of the second movement, Brahms's lifelong love of the variation form manifests itself for the last time in the sonata's finale, a set of six variations on a tender theme that sounds like a folk song, all capped by a stirring coda.

CLARINET QUINTET IN B MINOR, OP. 115

*I*t is hard to tell when listening to the late chamber music of Brahms, and to this work in particular, whether the composer should be thought of as the heir to Schumann or the forerunner of Schoenberg. For as much as Brahms admired Schumann's lightness of touch, it is the warm textures and hyperexpressive harmonies of Schoenberg's *Verklärte Nacht* that he anticipates in this autumnal essay, composed in 1891.

What is immediately noticeable is the resigned nature of the piece. It begins in a mood of darkness, glows fiercely with passion and nostalgia, and ends despairingly. The thematic connections of all four movements and the strong B minor/ D major harmonic scheme in three of them create an inner cohesion that contributes much to the emotional effect. The richness of the clarinet's sound and its vast array of tonal shadings are exploited to the fullest, as is the instrument's unique ability to fit with the strings or stand out from them.

The two opening movements are both quite

THE GYPSY STYLE was adapted by Brahms on a number of occasions. Prior to touching on it in the slow movement of his Clarinet Quintet, he had made use of it in the Hungarian Dances *and in the finales of the* Violin Concerto *and the* Piano Quartet in G minor, Op. 25. *The latter, a particularly flamboyant exercise, so intrigued Schoenberg that he rolled out a colorful arrangement of it for large orchestra.*

large. The first manages to express gentleness and longing amid deep gloom. Its writing allows an extraordinary play of color, with the clarinet at first soaring over the strings and later, to launch the development, sounding a mellow foundation beneath them. The serenely nocturnal world of the B major Adagio's opening and closing sections encapsulates a wild gypsy fantasy, in which the clarinet gets a rare opportunity to exhibit its virtuosity over passionate string tremolos redolent of a Hungarian cafe.

The serenade-like intermezzo also has a contrasting middle section, a slender scherzo that Brahms instructs the ensemble to play *con sentimento.* The quintet's finale is a set of five variations on a theme of near-Baroque formality; among them, the agitated second variation alludes once again to the gypsy style, the third opens a capricious dialog between clarinet and first violin, and the fifth unfolds as a shadowy waltz led by the viola, at the end of which Brahms slips effortlessly into his coda. With astonishing sureness and economy, he repeats the opening theme of the first movement and immediately recaptures the melancholy feeling with which the work began. The clarinet plays a last, poignant cadenza, then drops slowly to its somber final note. An intense B minor chord in the strings, played *forte,* is echoed by one marked *piano,* and the quintet ends in the depths of regret.

 RECOMMENDED RECORDINGS

**David Shifrin, clarinet;
Carol Rosenberger, piano.**
Delos DCD 3025 [Clarinet Sonatas, with Schumann: Fantasiestücke, *Op. 73]*

**David Shifrin, clarinet;
Chamber Music Northwest.**
Delos DE 3066 [Clarinet Quintet, with String Quintet in G, Op. 111]

Karl Leister, clarinet; Amadeus Quartet.
Deutsche Grammophon 419 875-2 [3 CDs;
Clarinet Quintet, with complete string quintets and sextets]

The account of the sonatas from Shifrin and Rosenberger brings unalloyed pleasure. Shifrin's limpid tone and unforced lyricism, together with his appealing gentleness, hint at the fragility that caused Brahms to describe Richard Mühlfeld's instrument as *Fräulein Klarinette*. Delos provides a closeup recording with a lovely salon ambience—in keeping with the theme of the disc, the re-creation of a musical soirée of November 13, 1894, at the home of Clara Schumann.

Despite its name, Chamber Music Northwest is an assembly of New York regulars. They offer a subdued rather than searing account of the Clarinet Quintet, with leisurely tempos and a feeling of point-to-point navigation through the score. The ensemble is excellent, with sisters Ani and Ida Kavafian remarkably well matched on violin, their unisons, octaves, and thirds uncannily together. The singing quality of Shifrin's playing is admirable, and he shows an interpretive restraint in keeping with his view that the clarinet should not be treated as a solo part, but as one strand among five. The 1989 recording is intimate and highly satisfying.

At the opposite expressive pole from Shifrin and company is the high-intensity reading from Berlin Philharmonic principal clarinetist Leister and the Amadeus Quartet, recorded in 1967 in a reverberant and dramatic acoustic that lends symphonic proportions to the account. Yet for all the hair-raising passion here, no performers have better conveyed the restraint, sadness, and surrender of the quintet's slow movement, or more fully captured the work's overall feeling of melancholy bordering on dejection.

David Shifrin takes a bow with clarinet and basset clarinet.

Claude Debussy at the time of the Quartet in G minor.

CLAUDE DEBUSSY

QUARTET IN G MINOR, OP. 10

*T*his is the only work of Debussy to be published with an opus number and a key designation. In view of the fact that the piece was composed in 1893 and is a relatively early work, its title can be taken as Debussy's nod to tradition. But it would be wrong to assume that the score is traditional, for here Debussy radically reinterprets the string quartet genre.

Structurally, the Quartet in G minor is based on the concept of cyclical form that had been articulated by César Franck in his Quartet in D, composed four years earlier. In Debussy's treatment, the work is in fact monothematic: the melodic material of all four movements is derived from a motto theme announced right at the start of the piece. A mosaic of repetition and variation takes the place of conventional thematic development, and a process of intensification—whereby climaxes are produced by "crescendos" of activity and pitch as well as loudness—often supplants the goal-oriented action of traditional harmony. Both procedures owe something to late 19th-century Russian music, with which Debussy was thoroughly conversant.

Throughout the quartet, the implications of traditional tonality are weakened by Debussy's use of archaic modes rather than conventional major and minor scales. The quartet's first movement, laid out as a sonata, opens in the Phrygian mode and offers subsidiary ideas in both that mode and the Dorian mode. The ensuing scherzo, with its guitarlike pizzicatos, subtle cross-rhythms, and rapid shifts of texture, is a hedonistic romp more concerned with aural effect than with matters of form or argument.

The slow movement contains the most rapturously beautiful music ever written for string quartet. The main theme, announced after a quiet preface from muted violin and viola, is almost religious

*T*HE PIZZICATO writing of the scherzo to the Quartet in G minor may well have been influenced by the scherzo to Tchaikovsky's Fourth Symphony, which Debussy knew from having played the piece with Tchaikovsky's patroness Nadezhda von Meck. Engaged by her to serve as pianist during the three summers of 1880–82, Debussy learned much Russian music at the keyboard.

in feeling and has a hushed tenderness reminiscent of the *Notturno* from Borodin's Second Quartet. Two chant-like interludes set off the more ardent second theme; introduced by the viola and taken up by the cello, it flares into a brief climax. At movement's end the first theme returns, ineffably gentle, conjuring up the warmth and sweetness of a starry night.

A recitative-style prologue sets the stage for the quartet's vigorous finale, a kaleidoscopic fantasy in which thematic ideas succeed one another with dizzying speed. Following a series of climactic buildups, the quartet's motto theme is dramatically reprised. A fast-moving coda brings the movement to an exhilarating conclusion.

RECOMMENDED RECORDINGS

Dutch-based and multinational (like Shell Oil), the Orlando Quartet specialized in delivering high-octane performances.

Orlando Quartet.
Philips 411 050-2 [with Ravel: Quartet in F]

Guarneri Quartet.
RCA Silver Seal 60909-2 [with Suite bergamasque, *and Ravel: Quartet in F]*

The Orlando Quartet came out of nowhere with this recording, and although the group never really hit the big time, its readings remain accounts of reference. The moods of both quartets are rightly gauged: the Debussy is hot-blooded, the Ravel languorous, reserved, *retenu.* Both are captured in a superb digital recording.

The Guarneri Quartet's 1973 recording, sounding a little woolly but nonetheless quite lovely on CD, conveys the music with endearing sweetness and warmth. No group has ever gotten closer to the spirit of Debussy's slow movement, or more beautifully captured its fragrant atmosphere and attenuated, almost heartbreaking sentiment. First violinist Arnold Steinhardt is exquisite here, and the group's playing overall is elegant.

Dvořák on a country walk, with avian inspiration.

✓ *IF YOU LIKE the easygoing tunefulness of Dvořák's* American *Quartet, you will probably find its companion piece, the Quintet in E flat, Op. 97, appealing as well. The quintet is cut from the same melodic cloth and is even more opulent in sound.*

ANTONÍN DVOŘÁK

STRING QUARTET IN F, OP. 96
American

*H*ere is an extraordinarily polished composition, generously endowed with memorable tunes and full of the animation that characterizes Dvořák's music, particularly the works from this period—his American sojourn of 1892–95. The melodic material is somewhat simplified and artificially rustic in character, similar to that of Dvořák's Symphony *From the New World.* But as in the symphony, the tunes themselves are original, not borrowed—except for a brief motivic cell in the scherzo derived from a bird call Dvořák had heard. The piece makes prominent use of the pentatonic scale, common to many folk musics and a feature Dvořák had noticed in both American Indian music and Negro spirituals. Yet in spite of his attempts to imbue his melodies with "Americanisms," the inflections are still Bohemian.

Dvořák composed the quartet while he was vacationing in Spillville, Iowa, home to a sizeable Czech community. Being among his countrymen kept him in high spirits, and work on the quartet proceeded at a rapid pace: the score was sketched and completed in 16 days, June 8–23, 1893.

PIANO QUINTET IN A, OP. 81

*T*he melodic and rhythmic vitality of this quintet are remarkable even for Dvořák, and few of his works exhibit more clearly his skill at fusing highly divergent ideas into a unified line of action. The element of contrast is central to the first two movements. At the beginning of the piece, over a gentle accompaniment in the piano, the cello introduces a warm melody that somehow can't keep from turning itself to the minor and a mood of pathos. Once the turn is made, the ensemble erupts in a fit of minor-key virulence. What follows sounds like a slew of new ideas but is really a series of different views of this subject, an alternately elegiac and stormy exposition that calms down just long enough for the viola to intone a plaintive second subject, again in the minor key. The development is turbulent, and after a dramatically telescoped recapitulation the movement ends with a fierce coda.

The second movement is a *dumka*, a Slavonic song form that Dvořák utilized in a number of his compositions. This one has the sectional layout (A-B-A-C-A-B-A) typical of the form, in which a minor-key lament alternates with dance-like material in the major. Here, the contrast is particularly striking, as the graceful but melancholy melody of the A section, stated by the piano against a countermelody in the viola, is answered in the B section by an ecstatic little duet in the violins that soars above a bubbling pizzicato accompaniment.

The ensuing *furiant* is really a fast waltz, exuberant in its outer sections and idyllic in its trio, where Dvořák utterly transforms the character of the main subject and modulates with delectable abandon. The finale is a breezy rondo in which the gruff initial stamp of the principal subject gives way to much good-natured fiddling and frolicking. The notes whiz by, especially during a fugato episode in the development, and the movement ends with all five parts engaging in a mad dash to the final chords.

Performing Personalities

A wizard of the keyboard, Artur Rubinstein was one of the most inspired musicians of the 20th century. Celebrated for his Chopin, as well as his glowing interpretations of other 19th- and 20th- century repertory (his scope was enormous by today's standards), Rubinstein concertized for more than 80 years.

 RECOMMENDED RECORDINGS

Artur Rubinstein, piano; Guarneri Quartet.
RCA Gold Seal 6263-2

Emerson Quartet.
Deutsche Grammophon 429 723-2
[American *Quartet*, with Smetana: *Quartet No. 1*]

All Aboard!

Dvořák was fascinated by railroads and locomotives. He was an enthusiastic train-watcher with a keen knowledge of engine types and a passion for memorizing timetables. His sojourn in America occasioned some of the grandest train rides of his life, carrying him to such rail centers as Buffalo, Boston, St. Paul, and Chicago.

Rubinstein was a youthful 84 when he sat down with the Guarneri players in the spring of 1971 for this recording of the Dvořák quintet. His lovely tone and lively phrasing, the clarity of the textures that emerged under his hands, and most of all the instinct he possessed for the singing line proved infectious and spurred his colleagues to one of their best efforts. A year later, the Guarneri musicians were back in the studio to record the *American* Quartet, turning in a smooth, animated performance notable for its light touch and elegant phrasing. These two old-fashioned, highly expressive readings make a wonderful coupling. The sound, while not the best, has good presence.

The Emersons offer what is hands down the best account of the *American* Quartet on disc. It is exuberant, persuasive, and right to the point—a well-paced reading full of ravishing details like the duetting of the violins in the slow movement. Beautifully recorded for the Book-of-the-Month Club in 1984, the account was picked up by Deutsche Grammophon and released in the U.S. in 1990.

CÉSAR FRANCK

VIOLIN SONATA IN A

*F*ranck was 63 and at the height of his powers when he completed this sonata in 1886. The breadth of its conception and the density of its textures, as well as the heated chromaticism of its harmony, remind many of Wagner. Spiritually and philosophically, however, Franck came closer to the orbits of Beethoven and Liszt. Though well acquainted with the revolutionary harmonic language of *Tristan und Isolde*, he remained more of an architect than a sensualist. As powerful as the emotional undercurrents of this sonata are, it is essentially the work of a thinker whose main concerns are with contrapuntal and formal matters.

Eugène Ysaÿe, a formidable virtuoso and fine composer in his own right.

Franck composed the sonata as a wedding present for his countryman, the Belgian violinist Eugène Ysaÿe, who received the manuscript on the day of his marriage and immediately set to work to learn the piece. Thanks to his championing of it, the sonata caught on quickly—and proved so successful with audiences and performers alike that it was soon appropriated by cellists and flutists, and today serves as one of the foundation works of their repertoires as well.

Like a number of Franck's other works, the sonata is cyclical, the thematic material of all four of its movements being derived from a single germinal motive. The opening measures of the first movement introduce the motive, a serene, arpeggio-based theme in the violin that crystallizes out of an ethereal four-bar meditation in the piano. Restrained, then increasingly intense in its lyricism, the subject is developed at poetic length. In contrast with this reverie, the passionate D minor movement that follows seems all the more turbulent—though it, too, contains passages of idyllic languor.

The third movement, designated *Recitativo-Fantasia*, opens with a somber preface in the piano answered by a brief violin cadenza. At first, the dialog recaptures the dreamy mood of the sonata's beginning, but soon the violin's improvisatory arabesques become more probing, the piano's flourishes more dramatic. The final Allegro, in A major, begins with the gentle canonic presentation of its main subject, a marchlike yet flowing version of the motto theme. During the course of the movement, the writing runs the gamut of emotions from beatific to cataclysmically troubled, but the sentiment at the end is resolute, heroic, and transcendent.

AS GIFTED *a teacher as he was an organist and a composer, Franck taught a whole generation of French composers (his organ class at the Paris Conservatoire was really an advanced seminar in composition), among them Vincent d'Indy, Henri Duparc, Ernest Chausson, Paul Dukas, Gabriel Pierné, and Albéric Magnard.*

 RECOMMENDED RECORDINGS

Kyung Wha Chung, violin; Radu Lupu, piano.
London 421 154-2 [with works by Debussy and Ravel]

Kyung Wha Chung brings a languorous elegance to Franck.

Shlomo Mintz, violin; Yefim Bronfman, piano.

Deutsche Grammophon 415 683-2 [with sonatas by Debussy and Ravel]

Chung and Lupu collaborate on the most musical account of the Franck sonata in the catalog, one that restores to the work its Gallic elegance, a quality that rarely survives the passion of most performances. In Chung's playing, the dreaminess of the score is beautifully evoked. Lupu, with his brilliant technique and sparing use of the pedal, manages a revelation of detail in the piano part. The 1977 recording is warm and approachable. At midprice and generously filled out, this is as desirable as a disc can get.

Mintz's brooding interpretation benefits from his powerful yet immaculately controlled playing and his remarkable purity of tone. At times almost Russian in its melancholy, the account generates considerable warmth, without ever sounding heart-on-the-sleeve. The partnership with Bronfman is a good one, based on a shared understanding of the music. Deutsche Grammophon's recording, from 1985, is very close and balances Mintz rather heavily against the piano.

JOSEPH HAYDN

STRING QUARTETS, OP. 33
Russian

*C*ompleted in 1781 and known as the *Russian* Quartets because of their dedication to Grand Duke Paul of Russia, the six works of Opus 33 show Haydn effectively bringing the Classical string quartet into its maturity. He composed the set after taking a ten-year sabbatical from the genre (his prior works were called "divertimentos"), and he noted at the time of their publication that the six pieces had been written in "an entirely new and special way." Themes tend to be constructed out of more highly contrasted elements than before, opening up new possibilities in their development. In addition, the balance of the part-writing is more even, with the four instruments engaging almost as equals in the unfolding of the musical argument. Haydn does not abandon the *concertante* manner of some of his earlier quartets; in Opus 33, No. 1, for example, there are many exposed passages for first violin. But his writing is marked by greater finesse, and by a sensitivity to sound that enables him to achieve effects of feathery delicacy in the most cheerful of the six essays, the Quartet in C, Op. 33, No. 3 (*The Bird*).

For the first time, Haydn substitutes the livelier scherzo for the conventional minuet. The Quartet in E flat, Op. 33, No. 2, even carries the new term as its nickname: *The Joke*. In this case, though, the "joke" comes at the conclusion of the rondo finale, when first a sentimental Adagio interlude and then a series of agonizing pauses interrupt the final statement of the main theme. The last bit of the theme makes it out, the quartet appears to end, and there is a long silence—until suddenly the first part of the tune comes one more time. And only *then*, up in the air, does Haydn really end the piece, leaving his listener with the funniest delayed double-take in all of music. There is nothing laughable about the quality of Haydn's craftsmanship in this work. The ideas of the opening movement are lucidly developed out of the material of the initial four measures, the third movement has a marvelous gravity, and the scherzo balances rusticity with grace in a most satisfying manner.

HAYDN WAS *the first composer to use "scherzo"—a fast, dance-like movement in triple time—in place of a minuet. Beethoven adopted the scherzo as the standard "dance" movement in his sonatas and symphonies. "Scherzo" does mean "joke," but not all scherzos are light-hearted or funny; some, like the scherzo in Beethoven's Fifth, are positively grim. Ives had some mischief with this in his Trio for Violin, Cello, and Piano, entitling the scherzo "TSIAJ," "This Scherzo Is a Joke."*

Haydn, at right, playing the viola in one of his own quartets.

STRING QUARTETS, OP. 76
Erdödy

The late quartets of Haydn, together with Mozart's quartets dedicated to Haydn, represent the ultimate achievement in the genre in the 18th century. The six quartets of Opus 76, written for Count Joseph Erdödy and dedicated to him when published in 1799, are works of freshness and subtlety. Haydn shows he is still willing to experiment, still capable of finding new ways to treat form and texture, and readier than ever to express personal feeling, in a way that frequently anticipates the music of Beethoven.

For example, in the Adagio of the Quartet in E flat, Op. 76, No. 6, Haydn's lyricism acquires the sustained intensity thought to belong to a much later period in music. Here the writing has a monumental tenderness—while in the quartet's finale, the modulations strike with a pungency that must have wrenched patrician ears and left listeners wondering if something strange had happened to Haydn in his old age. The Quartet in B flat, Op. 76, No. 4 (*Sunrise*), so nicknamed for the crescent-shaped profile of its opening melody, is without doubt one of Haydn's finest creations, though scarcely a more consoling work. Its astonishingly bleak Adagio plumbs emotional depths rarely sounded in the 18th (or for that matter, the 19th) century. But Haydn as always achieves a balance, and the warm opening movement, the rustic minuet with its musette trio, and the ever quickening finale lend a sense of completeness to the work that is well gauged.

The best known of the Opus 76 quartets is the third, in C major, nicknamed the *Emperor* because the theme of its second movement is that of the anthem Haydn wrote for Emperor Franz II (*Gott erhalte Franz den Kaiser*), which became the national anthem of both Austria and Germany and is also the tune to the hymn "Glorious Things of Thee Are Spoken, Zion City of Our God." The deeply

HAYDN IS ONE of the *few great composers who actually made his living as a street musician. Tossed out of the choir of St. Stephen's Cathedral in Vienna at the age of 17, when his voice changed, he joined a group of itinerant musicians who played serenades in the streets for pocket change. He continued to sing and play the violin and organ in various churches, and lived for several years in an unheated garret.*

touching theme is subjected to four variations, all of exquisite beauty. To compensate for the extra weight of this Adagio, Haydn gives the work a somewhat lighter than usual opening Allegro and a straightforward minuet. The powerful finale, which spends much of its time in the minor, serves as the quartet's other center of gravity and balances out the lofty sentiment of the Adagio with something close to dramatic angst.

 RECOMMENDED RECORDINGS

Tátrai Quartet.
Hungaroton HCD 11887/88 [2 CDs; Opus 33]

Takács Quartet.
*London 421 360-2 [Opus 76, Nos. 1–3] and 425 467-2
[Opus 76, Nos. 4–6]*

The Tátrai players address the Opus 33 quartets with a sense of long familiarity, yet their accounts are in no way routine. The effortless gathering of the lines at cadences, the dovetailing of the voices, and the complete absence of excessive rhetoric make for elegant, warmly persuasive readings. If one could distill the essence of Classicism, it would come out sounding much like this. The recorded sound is typical Eastern bloc—just somewhat better than radio quality.

By the time Haydn wrote his late string quartets, his mastery of convention had grown to the point where his imagination was utterly unfettered, illustrating Robert Frost's famous dictum that freedom is "when you're easy in your harness." The Takács Quartet, a flamboyant ensemble founded in 1975, plays the Opus 76 essays in that spirit. The highly profiled accounts are intense but never rowdy. These more public expressions of Haydn's genius have been captured in reverberant spaces—the Schubertsaal of Vienna's Konzerthaus and London's St. Barnabas'—and the recordings have striking presence.

The Takács Quartet gives exuberant accounts of Haydn.

*ANNY Mendelssohn, the
composer's sister and a
superb pianist, summed up
the effect of the octet's
scherzo: "The whole piece is
to be played* staccato *and*
pianissimo, *the isolated tre-
molandos coming here and
there, the trills flashing with
the quickness of lightning—
all is new, strange, and yet
so ingratiating, so pleasing:
one feels so close to the world
of spirits, so lightly carried
up into the air . . ."*

FELIX MENDELSSOHN
OCTET FOR STRINGS, IN E FLAT, OP. 20

*T*he boy wonder composed his Octet for
Strings in October 1825 at the age of 16.
As striking as it is, both for freshness of inspiration
and confidence of treatment, the piece is not quite
the spontaneous manifestation of genius some
have assumed it to be, but a natural successor to
the four string symphonies Mendelssohn had
written in 1823. It is a brilliant score, but one for
which the groundwork had been thoroughly laid.

The octet was penned as a 23rd birthday present for Eduard Rietz, a valued member of the
Mendelssohn family circle and an outstanding
violinist. It was probably first performed *en famille*,
at one of the Sunday morning musicales in the
Mendelssohn home in Berlin, with Felix himself
taking one of the viola parts.

At the head of each part in the score, Mendelssohn cautions: "This octet must be played in
the style of a symphony in all parts; the *pianos*
and *fortes* must be very precisely differentiated
and be more sharply accentuated than is ordi-
narily done in pieces of this type." The music of
the opening Allegro makes it clear that the composer meant his advice to be taken seriously, for
here is a sonata movement of truly symphonic
proportions, one that reveals a consummate command of form and argument. Marked *con fuoco*,
it is indeed full of Romantic fire, with a soaring
first subject that exudes optimism and a coda that
has all the fizz of a summery shot of seltzer. The
Andante, melancholy and sentimental, stands in
marked contrast, its decorative imitation early
testimony to Mendelssohn's delicate craftsmanship.

The scherzo is gold drawn from the purest
Mendelssohnian vein. Inspired by the procession
of spirits depicted in the *Walpurgisnacht* scene of
Goethe's *Faust*, it can be recognized as a precursor
to the Overture to *A Midsummer Night's Dream*.
With the finale, Mendelssohn's youthful study of

Baroque counterpoint pays off handsomely. The movement begins with a jubilant eight-part fugato that rumbles up from the bottom register of the two cellos and rockets aloft. From this point on, notes are spun off like showers of sparks in a tour de force of inner-part writing that must have made the work's first performers absolutely giddy. The scherzo theme steals back onto the stage for a quick bow midway through, and the movement ends full of life and fun with all eight players scrubbing away at the limits of sound and speed.

 RECOMMENDED RECORDING

Academy Chamber Ensemble.
Philips 420 400-2 [with Quintet in B flat, Op. 87]

The chamber group from the Academy of St. Martin-in-the-Fields gives a bracing account of the octet. The playing is polished, the ensemble tight—and the style and scope of the interpretation are genuinely symphonic, as Mendelssohn desired. The analog recording, from 1978, has a pleasing immediacy and freshness.

WOLFGANG AMADEUS MOZART

STRING QUARTET IN B FLAT, K. 458
Hunt
STRING QUARTET IN C, K. 465
Dissonance

Title page of Mozart's six finest quartets.

ozart composed more than a dozen string quartets in his youth, some of them quite excellent. With the six quartets dedicated to Haydn (K. 387, 421, 428, 458, 464, and 465), written between December 1782 and January 1785, Mozart addressed the form in full maturity—and in possession of much wisdom gained from the elder master's quartets, specifically their conversational quality and their variety of texture and topic. Here then are Mozart's finest quartets, characterized by a rich sense of melodic and harmonic invention and by a remarkable degree of contrapuntal sophistication. Two of the six pieces have proved especially popular and merit a close look.

The Quartet in B flat, K. 458, is known as the *Hunt* because its opening theme alludes to the 6/8 rhythm and paired-horn fanfares associated with the hunting topic in 18th-century music. The exuberant tone set at the beginning is kept throughout; indeed, this quartet as a whole, notwithstanding the poignancy of its slow movement, is the most extroverted of the six *Haydn* Quartets. The first movement's robustness owes much to Haydn, and at the end of the movement the hornlike writing is brought back over a drone bass, a favorite touch in Haydn's music that Mozart appropriates with his usual grace.

In the minuet Mozart introduces a rhythmic imbalance that makes the proceedings suddenly seem more serious than one might have supposed. But he brings things down to earth in the trio with a frothy, ebullient country dance. The slow movement, in E flat, is the only true Adagio in the *Haydn* Quartets. There is a touch of uncertainty in its opening phrases; as the discourse gradually finds its direction, the movement unfolds with striking melodic beauty. The harmony shifts from major to minor, changing the context in what for Mozart is an unusually troubling way, until a poignant leave-taking is reached. The bouncy mood of the quartet's opening is restored in the breakneck finale, over which the spirit of Haydn once again hovers. Yet even here, amidst the hustle and bustle, one finds the lyrical expressiveness that Mozart alone could command.

The 22 dissonant measures of slow introduction that give the Quartet in C, K. 465, its nickname also create harmonic and melodic tension on which the rest of the work will draw. Part of the tension results from the ambiguity of key that Mozart intentionally sustains through the first dozen or

WHEN THE SIX *quartets were published, Mozart attached a dedication to Haydn that read in part: "A father who had decided to send his sons out into the world at large thought it his duty to entrust them to the protection and guidance of a man who was very famous at the time and who, furthermore, happened to be his best friend. Similarly, I send my six sons to you. . . . Please receive them with kindness and be to them a father, guide, and friend!"*

AFTER HAYDN HAD *a second opportunity to hear three of these quartets, he paid the following compliment to Mozart's father: "I tell you before God and as an honest man, that your son is the greatest composer whom I know personally or by reputation. He has taste and, what is more, the greatest knowledge of the technique of composition."*

so bars, an ambiguity that makes the ultimate confirmation of C major all the more impressive. Having wound up the spring, Mozart lets fly in the Allegro with an impetuous opening subject in the first violin whose energy is reinforced by a steady rhythmic pulse in the second violin and viola. The restlessness of the movement intensifies to agitation in the development section, where the lines take on a jagged quality reminiscent of the sharp intervallic clashes of the introduction.

In the ardent yet graciously sustained lyricism of the Andante, Mozart hints at what is about to come in *The Marriage of Figaro*, building an almost operatic scene out of a duet between first violin and cello. There is a foretaste of Beethoven in the brusque, scherzo-like energy and stark contrasts of the minuet, with its bright C major outer sections and overcast C minor trio. In the finale, Mozart tips his hat again to Haydn, uncorking a heady mixture of virtuosic display and melodic razzle-dazzle, though the material is transformed by Mozart's unique sense of timing and complexity.

 RECOMMENDED RECORDINGS

Melos Quartet.
Deutsche Grammophon 429 818-2 [complete Haydn Quartets *also available on 415 870-2, 3 CDs, midprice]*

Salomon String Quartet.
Hyperion CDA 66170 [Dissonance *Quartet, with Quartet in D minor, K. 421]*

The Melos offering is the recording of choice for these quartets. The Stuttgart-based foursome offers informed readings, remarkable for the aptness of tempos and the smoothness of ensemble; the accounts are buoyant and delivered with the kind of polish that allows one to see beneath the surface into the expressive grain of the music. The recordings, made during 1976 and 1977, are close but well balanced, and dry enough to let the instruments sound as they do in a real chamber environment. This allows the substantial tonal differences between first and second violins to register, as though the two were different personalities.

The Salomon String Quartet, one of the best period-instrument groups on the scene, offers an excellent performance of the *Dissonance* Quartet. For this 1985 recording, the players used "real" authentic instruments as opposed to modern copies. The warm tone and satisfying blend that result are readily apparent.

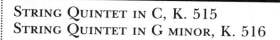

String Quintet in C, K. 515
String Quintet in G minor, K. 516

A view of Vienna's Graben district, where Mozart spent some melancholy years.

*W*ith these quintets for two violins, two violas, and cello, written during the spring of 1787, Mozart reached the pinnacle of his achievement as a chamber composer. One of their most noteworthy traits is the way they constantly introduce the unexpected and make it seem inevitable, testimony both to Mozart's command of argument and to the striking nature of his ideas.

The expansive opening subject of the C major Quintet's first movement finds the march topic and the singing style juxtaposed, much as they would be the following summer in the first movement of the *Jupiter* Symphony. The cello strides confidently upward three times, while the first violin sings delicately ornamented replies. After a measure of silence the violin begins to march, but unexpectedly in C minor. Now the cello answers with the singing figure, and the third reply is this time extended dramatically, by 23 measures. Through all of this, there is a subtle dislocation of the scansion, as the dialog is put into five- and six-bar phrases. The dynamic balance of uneven phrase groups and the surprising shifts in tonality that make this opening so exciting contribute to

THE AUTOGRAPH
of the C major Quintet is
part of the music collection
at the Library of Congress,
and when ensembles come to
perform the piece at the library's Coolidge Auditorium,
the staff leave the score by
the entrance for everyone to
see as they walk in. It is a
marvelous piece of hazing
for the players—and
humbling to listeners and
performers alike to realize
that Mozart tried desperately
to sell copies of this piece to
the public, without avail.

the movement's long-range effect as well; in its
breadth, symmetry, and sense of flow, this Allegro
is one of Mozart's grandest conceptions.

Because of the pagination in Mozart's manuscript, there is some question as to which movement
of the quintet comes next. Most performances
opt for the minuet, which seems to fit better than
the Andante after the long first movement. There
is a relaxed feeling to the minuet's beginning, but
soon a note of pathos creeps in; the trio, after
some questioning from the violin and a brief
chromatic excursion, breaks into a jaunty Ländler.
Both the counterpoint and the sentiment of the
Andante are remarkably complicated, and its melody twice experiences a rapturous, ornamental
flowering in the first violin answered with equal
expansiveness by the first viola. In an Allegro
finale full of brilliant fiddling, Mozart creates a
skipping lightheartedness not far from that of the
finale of *Eine kleine Nachtmusik*, though more complex in both texture and tone.

The description that musicologist Alfred Einstein gave Symphony No. 40, in G minor, is even
more apt to the second of these quintets, for if
ever there was a "fatalistic piece of chamber music,"
this is it. The unmistakable anguish of the first
movement may well reflect Mozart's state of mind
in May 1787, when the piece was written. He was
then beginning the composition of his darkest
opera, *Don Giovanni*, knowing full well that his
works were losing their hold on the Viennese
public. And as he wrote, his father lay dying in
Salzburg (Leopold's death on May 28 followed by
12 days Mozart's completion of the quintet). What
makes the Allegro of the G minor Quintet so
remarkable is that it seems to realize, in purely
musical terms, the anxiety these circumstances
must have caused.

The mood remains dark in the minuet, and the
angry, offbeat chords that pierce the opening
measures create new shocks that the trio cannot
dispel. The ensuing Adagio at first seems to retreat from the turmoil in search of consolation.

IN DECEMBER OF 1790, Joseph Haydn brought his viola to Vienna to participate in a reading of three of Mozart's string quintets—the two works from the spring of 1787 (K. 515 and 516), and the just-completed Quintet in D, K. 593. Mozart pulled out his viola as well, and the two friends took turns playing the first part.

The strings are muted, and there is an almost prayerful quality to the movement's opening. But shadows soon return—the music enters the key of B flat minor, as a poignant melody in the first violin is accompanied by agitated sixteenth notes in the other instruments—and the uneasiness eventually acquires a Beethoven-like intensity. One last surprise remains: after a slow introduction that suggests a baleful end is in store, the finale unfolds as a sunny rondo in G major—an unusual turn for Mozart, who normally kept his minor-key works in the minor. Although some have criticized this ending as implausible, there are sketches that show Mozart tried, and rejected, a finale in G minor. Clearly, he intended to take the listener out of the darkness and into the light.

 RECOMMENDED RECORDINGS

Franz Beyer, viola; Melos Quartet.
Deutsche Grammophon 419 773-2

Markus Wolf, viola; Alban Berg Quartet.
EMI Classics CDC 49085

One imagines Mozart would have been delighted by the winning performance both quintets receive from Beyer and the Melos Quartet. Tempos are apt, the ensemble crisp, the playing energetic and grandly sustained by a sense of the musical line. The technique of these musicians comes to the fore repeatedly in these 1986 accounts, particularly the superb intonation and elegant phrasing of first violinist Wilhelm Melcher. The recorded sound is a little analytic but pleasingly balanced. This is chamber music playing of the most glorious sort.

In a recording from the same year, the Berg ensemble gives perceptive accounts of both works, full of sweep and confidence in the C major Quintet and with an appealing mixture of lyricism and expressive understatement in the G minor.

Vienna's Alban Berg Quartet, founded in 1970.

Modern replica of a basset clarinet.

The sound is warm and resonant. Notwithstanding the track listings given in the booklet and on the back panel of the jewel box, the Quintet in C is played with the Andante as the second movement, a conjectural ordering that does not work as well in practice as it does in theory.

CLARINET QUINTET IN A, K. 581

*P*rior to this composition, Mozart's works for solo wind instrument and strings had been pieces of considerable charm but modest scope and intensity. With the Clarinet Quintet in A, however, Mozart revolutionized the genre for himself and for all who came later, writing a piece that not only requires real virtuosity from the solo instrument but also remains a true, substantive chamber work. The quintet was completed on September 29, 1789, as Mozart was composing his opera *Così fan tutte*, and the parallels between the two works in their melodic beauty and delicate scoring are worth remembering.

The Clarinet Quintet is characterized by a deft, almost imperceptible alternation between gentleness and pathos. It exhibits the highest degree of polish in its counterpoint, as well as Mozart's customary flair for *concertante* writing in the clarinet part and, to an almost equal degree, in the part for first violin. One of the most remarkable features of all is the utter transparency of the texture, which allows the clarinet to be absorbed into the harmony at certain points while subtly coloring the sound of the string ensemble. The first movement opens with a radiant though gently subdued series of singing lines in the strings, which the clarinet answers with trial flights of passagework that serve later as the basis for the development section. The second movement is a supremely tender Larghetto with the violins muted throughout, the third a lightly scored minuet with two trios. For the finale Mozart offers five variations on a sunny tune, to which he brings a touch of the rondo by allowing the theme to return, ebullient, at the end.

 RECOMMENDED RECORDING

Antony Pay, basset clarinet;
Academy of Ancient Music
Chamber Ensemble.
Oiseau-Lyre 421 429-2 [with Oboe Quartet, K. 370,
and Horn Quintet, K. 407]

Mozart composed this quintet, like the later Clarinet Concerto, for Anton Stadler. Both works were written for the basset clarinet and gain considerably from being played on that instrument. Here, Pay uses a period basset clarinet, and exhibits exceptional mastery of technique and expression. His cohorts, also playing period instruments, provide a rich, stylish contribution of their own; not long ago, one would have been hard pressed to characterize the tone of period strings as "silken," but the term is appropriate here, particularly for the first violin of Monica Huggett. This is a yearning, wistful account, full of character and life. The 1987 recording is immediate and beautifully balanced.

Antony Pay playing a basset clarinet in Mozart's Clarinet Quintet.

MAURICE RAVEL
STRING QUARTET IN F

*R*avel attended the Paris Conservatoire from 1889 to 1895, left briefly, and returned in 1897 as a member of Fauré's composition class. He wrote the Quartet in F, his sole essay in the genre, during the winter and spring of 1902–3 in his final months of study. But the work's fluency and consummate command of form mark it as a product of Ravel's early maturity, not a student effort.

RAVEL *and Debussy were acquainted with each other but were never close. Ravel held Debussy and his music in high regard, but Debussy's respect for Ravel was tempered by aloofness and a touch of irony. When, following the premiere of Ravel's quartet, some of the critics urged revisions, Debussy is supposed to have said to his younger colleague, "In the name of the gods of music, and in mine, do not touch a single note."*

The opening Allegro, in sonata form, begins with a broad subject played by the entire quartet. Ravel spins several ideas out of the theme, including one in the first violin over a feathery inner-voice accompaniment, before the arrival of the sultry second subject—a haunting melody played by the violin and viola two octaves apart, marked *pianissimo* and *très expressif*. Later, in a gesture testifying to the already remarkable sophistication of his technique, Ravel will recapitulate this subject at exactly the same pitches as before, but will write the cello's pizzicato accompaniment so that it shifts the harmonic context from D minor to F major.

The buoyant scherzo is in mixed meter and features a rich interplay of parts: the first violin and cello are written in 3/4, the second violin and viola in 6/8. There is a languorous central trio, calling for mutes, in which an expressive theme is announced by the cello in its highest register and taken over by the viola. Gradually, an idea emerges that sounds like a variation of the second subject of the first movement, and over whispered tremolos it is combined with the pizzicato subject from the opening of the scherzo.

A feeling of ecstatic yet melancholy meditation pervades the third movement, which again calls for mutes. Reminiscences of the first movement's opening theme are interspersed with ideas that pass like fleeting visions. The quartet's energetic finale opens with a violent passage in 5/8. A subsidiary idea in the first violin has a nervous fragility to it, and there is even an unsettled quality in the more lyrical second subject. Fragments of the work's opening theme are once more woven into the tapestry, and the movement ends with an exultant crescendo.

 RECOMMENDED RECORDINGS

Orlando Quartet.
Philips 411 050-2 [with Debussy: Quartet in G minor]

Guarneri Quartet.

RCA Silver Seal 60909-2 [with Debussy: Quartet in G minor and Suite bergamasque]

Quartetto Italiano.

Philips 420 894-2 [with Debussy: Quartet in G minor]

In this 1983 coupling of the Ravel and Debussy works, the Orlando Quartet made its debut with characterful, warmly atmospheric performances. The Ravel is imbued with a nostalgia and a passionate restraint that put it in the same world as Debussy's *Prélude à l'après-midi d'un faune*, and the recording is top-notch.

The Guarneri Quartet's 1973 recording has long been one of the outstanding accounts of the Ravel, notable both for the finesse of the playing and for the ardor of the interpretation. The colorful performance is a marvelous blend of polish and spontaneity. Although the ambience is dry, the sound itself is solid and well focused.

The Italian foursome responds to Ravel's atmospheric writing with some of its most galvanic playing in this 1965 account. The interpretation throws the languor and incandescence of the score into sharp relief, and is nearly symphonic in weight.

ARNOLD SCHOENBERG

VERKLÄRTE NACHT, OP. 4

Arnold Schoenberg, as sketched by Egon Schiele.

*T*he title *Transfigured Night* comes from a poem by Richard Dehmel that appears in the collection *Weib und Welt* (*Woman and World*). Dehmel's transcendent, intensely spiritual verse appealed to a number of German post-Romantic composers, among them Max Reger, Hans Pfitzner, and Richard Strauss, all of whom made vocal settings of it. And it deeply affected the Austrian composer Schoenberg (1874–1951), who in addition to setting eight other Dehmel poems as songs, used *Verklärte Nacht* as the basis for this

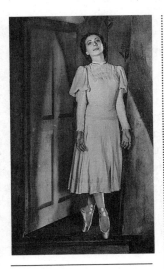

CHOENBERG made an arrangement of the score for full string orchestra in 1917 (which he revised in 1943). In 1942, for New York's Ballet Theater, choreographer Antony Tudor created the ballet Pillar of Fire (above) to the music of Verklärte Nacht.

work, his most enduring chamber composition.

Scored for string sextet—two violins, two violas, and two cellos—*Verklärte Nacht* combines the chromatic harmony of Wagner's *Tristan und Isolde* with the lush textures and painstaking motivic development of Brahms's late chamber works. It closely follows the expressive curve of the poem, in which, on a moonlit night among the trees, a woman confesses to her lover that she is pregnant by another man—and he reassures her that through their love for each other, the child will be as his. The first piece of program music in the chamber repertory, *Verklärte Nacht* is in essence a symphonic poem for six string instruments. Its five sections (corresponding to the stanzas of Dehmel's poem) form two large spans. The first, rooted in D minor, conveys the woman's despair and the turbulent emotion of her confession, while the second, in D major, evokes the transfiguration that the couple's love has brought to the night.

Schoenberg was an accomplished cellist with an insider's knowledge of the chamber repertory, and his writing for the strings here is idiomatic and colorfully effective. Nonetheless, following its completion in December of 1899, the sextet was rejected by the Vienna Tonkünstlerverein. On March 18, 1902, the first performance was given by the Rosé Quartet and two colleagues.

 RECOMMENDED RECORDINGS

Jiri Najnar, viola; Vaclav Bernasek, cello; Talich Quartet.
Calliope CAL 9217 [with Dvořák: Sextet in A, Op. 48]

The Raphael Ensemble.
Hyperion CDA 66425 [with Korngold: Sextet in D, Op. 10]

The Talich Quartet and their Czech colleagues play warmly throughout, in a brisk reading that sustains its tension to the end. The opening notes beat like a heavy heart, and the final pages glow with emotion. On this 1989 recording, the sound is close and extremely vivid. The work offered as the coupling, Dvořák's thoroughly enjoyable sextet, seems a bit ordinary next to *Verklärte Nacht*, but the musicians play it in the best Bohemian manner.

The playing of The Raphael Ensemble is wonderfully polished, and the account of *Verklärte Nacht* these young musicians deliver has lots of voltage behind it. The opening is extremely atmospheric—where the Czechs are almost voluptuous, the Raphael musicians are hauntingly stark and subdued—but the climactic pages that come later have rarely been as intensely presented. Hyperion's 1990 recording is outstanding, and the coupling, Korngold's excellent D major Sextet, receives a marvelous performance from the group that rediscovered it.

FRANZ SCHUBERT

PIANO QUINTET IN A, D. 667
The Trout

Schubert, in a rare moment when he wasn't making music.

*S*chubert's idea of partying was to play music with friends, and to that end he composed the *Trout* Quintet in 1819 while he and they were enjoying a summer vacation in the "inconceivably lovely" town of Steyr, in Upper Austria.

During that summer, musical evenings were spent at the home of Sylvester Paumgartner, an amateur cellist and chamber music enthusiast. For one of the gatherings, he commissioned Schubert to compose a quintet, specifying only that the instrumentation be the same as that of Johann Nepomuk Hummel's Quintet in E flat, Op. 87, and that it contain a set of variations on Schubert's song *Die Forelle* (*The Trout*), written in 1817. While conceived of as *Hausmusik*, intended entirely for pleasure, the resulting quintet shows remarkable resourcefulness in the way it handles the unusual

STEYR, *20 miles south-*
east of Linz, lies at the
junction of the Steyr and the
Enns rivers in scenic Upper
Austria. The weeks that he
spent here in 1819 with his
friend, the baritone Johann
Michael Vogl, were among
the happiest of Schubert's
life. Composer and singer
boarded at the home of Josef
von Koller, whose five
daughters considerably en-
livened the summer days
and evenings. One of them,
Josepha, kindled the flame of
love as well. She sang and
played the piano for Schu-
bert, and he dedicated a
sonata to her.

complement of string trio with added piano and double bass.

The quintet's serenade-like character is clearly reflected in its five-movement design, and its essential leisureliness underscored by the fact that two Andantes frame the lone dance movement, a reversal of the usual pattern. The opening Allegro begins with a bold chord from the full ensemble, rounded off by an arpeggiated flourish from the piano. The strings dreamily intone the movement's principal subject, which rapidly transforms itself from a meditation to a quick march over the galloping accompaniment of viola and cello. A songlike second subject is treated in duet fashion by the violin and cello, and briefly turned to the minor with telling effect. Schubert takes a shortcut, permissible in a work of such informality, by making the recapitulation a verbatim repeat of the exposition, transposed so that it begins on the subdominant and ends in the tonic.

He does something similar in the first Andante, cast in sonata form without development. The exposition takes up three distinct subjects: the first a placid theme in F major presented by the piano in octaves over a string accompaniment, the second a melancholy tune in F sharp minor played by viola and cello, and the third, emerging directly from it, a jaunty, offbeat caprice in D major from the piano over a pulsating bass. The second part of the movement repeats the first a minor third higher, cycling back to F by way of A flat major and A minor.

The energetic scherzo, with its upbeat opening subject, sets the stage for the hymnlike beginning of the fourth movement, where Schubert places the variations on *Die Forelle* requested by Paumgartner. Schubert's treatment is mostly decorative, clearly preserving the melody in four of the six variations. In the first three, the theme is taken up in turn by the piano, the viola and cello, and the double bass. The fourth variation starts as a tempestuous, minor-key rendition but is humorously gentled, while the fifth allows the cello a

truly speculative treatment, almost creating a new tune. In the final variation, Schubert has the piano finally play what everyone has been waiting to hear, the fluid accompaniment so familiar from the song, while the violin and cello alternate with the melody. An energetic finale in the Hungarian style, full of the highest spirits, brings the quintet to a boisterous close.

SCHUBERT composes at the piano while the baritone Johann Michael Vogl sings in a typical Schubertiade. The friendship between the two was close, and their artistic understanding even closer. "The way . . . in which Vogl sings and I accompany, so that we seem in such a moment to be one," wrote Schubert to his brother Ferdinand, "is something quite new and unheard of."

 RECOMMENDED RECORDING

Rudolf Serkin, piano; Jaime Laredo, violin; Philipp Naegele, viola; Leslie Parnas, cello; Julius Levine, bass.
Sony Classical SMK 46252 [with Mozart: Clarinet Quintet, K. 581]

The recording by Serkin and a contingent of his Marlboro Festival protégés, dating from 1967, is still a gem. Right off the bat the group settles on a perfect tempo for the Allegro, and the loving way they shape the music here holds up for the duration of the piece. The give-and-take is animated, the individual contributions brilliant. Serkin is masterly in the way he balances the piano part against the others. The glorious playing of Laredo, one of America's great violinists, is a continuous delight. The analog recording has been well transferred; at midprice this is a highly competitive offering, especially if you like your *Trout* with the spots played off it.

STRING QUINTET IN C, D. 956

*C*omposed in September of 1828, the Quintet in C for Two Violins, Viola, and Two Cellos was Schubert's last instrumental work and ranks among his greatest accomplishments. Schubert's decision to use a second cello, rather than the second viola characteristic of Mozart's quintets, permits him to explore the string trio texture in the middle of the ensemble while making embellishments with the "bookend" combination of first violin and second cello at the extremes of the quartet range. The presence of a second cello also adds to the overall richness of the piece, contributing a darker sound. Schubert's writing for the strings is symphonic, revealing in such details as the frequent fanfare rhythms and repeated-note patterns, touches of "orchestration" that would have been assigned to winds and brass in one of his symphonies.

The expansive first movement is in sonata form with an exposition touching on three key areas. The principal subject of the first one, in C major, grows out of the quintet's pregnant opening progression and gradually gains impetus with brisk calls to action. The second key area, E flat major, is announced with a memorable theme, poignantly duetted by the cellos in their upper register and full of desolate beauty. A warmer feeling marks the third key area, G major, which is introduced by a singing subject from the first violin.

Cast in ternary song form (A-B-A), the vast E major Adagio opens with a tender, almost motionless hymn in the three middle voices, ethereally ornamented by the first violin over a pizzicato foundation. The middle section of the movement, in the minor, comes with a sudden onslaught; the intense pain and darkness seem to belong to a world utterly removed from the movement's elegiac opening. The ensuing scherzo exults in joyous hunt-like figures in its outer sections—but with the movement's trio in D flat major, Schubert once again induces a change in the emotional current, and the listener hovers halfway between elegy and despair. Optimism regains the upper hand with the quintet's spirited finale. Twice during the movement's coda, Schubert ups the tempo, so that the strings are going at it hammer-and-tongs by the end. Even so, not all the demons are exorcised: the dramatic presence of D flat in the last moments of the quintet, darkens the final C.

Schubert enjoyed a joke and wrote this piece for violins using cats instead of notes.

RECOMMENDED RECORDINGS

Mstislav Rostropovich, cello; Melos Quartet.
Deutsche Grammophon Galleria 415 373-2

Heinrich Schiff, cello; Alban Berg Quartet.
EMI Classics CDC 47018

It would be difficult to imagine a finer account of this work than that of the Melos Quartet and its distinguished guest. There is a spontaneity to the playing that complements the profound whimsicality of Schubert's journeys to remote tonal regions, along with a sensitivity well suited to the meditative quality of the composer's lyricism. The recording is spacious, richly nuanced, and admirably balanced.

Schiff throws the considerable weight of his tone behind the Alban Berg Quartet in an impressive reading, notable for its energy and lyrical beauty. The recording is first-rate, except that the players omit the exposition repeat in the first movement, depriving it of the "heavenly length" it should have.

DIE SCHÖNE MÜLLERIN, D. 795
WINTERREISE, D. 911

Title page of an early edition of Die schöne Müllerin.

*S*chubert's known songs for solo voice with piano accompaniment total 634, of which nearly 400 were published after his death. Schubert revolutionized the Lied in a very real sense: he was among the first to exploit the possibilities of song cycles (within which a continuous narrative thread unifies the texts), and he brought a new level of sophistication and insight to the setting of poetry. The perfection with which melody and accompaniment suit the text in so many of his songs has rarely been approached.

Schubert was quick to capitalize on the new tonal and dynamic flexibility of the 19th-century

ALTHOUGH IT HAS been alleged that Schubert chose poetry by second-raters, it should be kept in mind that he set 55 poems by Goethe, 46 by Schiller, and six by his contemporary Heinrich Heine. His two most important song cycles, Die schöne Müllerin *and* Winterreise, *are indeed set to rather plain and sentimental texts by Wilhelm Müller, assuredly not a great poet. But the words offer plenty of imagery as grist for Schubert's very productive musical mill.*

Schubert and friends set off for the country—a Biedermeier-era outing.

piano as an instrument of accompaniment, making it an equal partner with the voice. He had a deep and innate understanding of poetry, along with the skill to achieve in music what a poem achieves in language. For him, writing a song was not a matter of setting the words *to* music, but of translating the poetry *into* music. His willingness to set poems of great emotional intensity was matched by his ability to conjure up harmonic twists and melodic turns that conveyed emotion with remarkable simplicity and force, so that without overextending his rhetoric he could in a few lines of music scale the heights of elation or probe the depths of suffering.

Die schöne Müllerin (*The Lovely Mill-Maid*), consisting of 20 songs composed during October and November of 1823, is a springlike idyll of unrequited love with a tragic ending, in which the brokenhearted young hero, spurned by the maid in favor of a hunter, drowns himself in the millstream. Schubert makes the sound of the stream a continuing motif of the cycle in the piano's rippling, arpeggiated figuration. The 24 songs of *Winterreise* (*Winter Journey*), which Schubert set between February and October of 1827, stand among his masterpieces in the art of song. In this desolate winter trek, the musical treatment is heavy with misery, particularly noticeable in the way melodic lines tend to drop at the ends of phrases. The more outwardly expressive nature of the songs in Book II of the cycle shows Schubert on a new plane of inspiration, capable of revealing, even in the gloom, marvelous emotional vistas.

The first song of Book II, "*Die Post*," illustrates Schubert's insight into lyrics, as well as the economy of his musical means. The arrival of the stagecoach carrying the day's mail is signaled by posthorn fanfares and a galloping figuration in the piano. But in the song's middle section, when the hero finds no letter from his beloved, a simple shift in the harmony from E flat major to E flat minor conveys with wonderful suddenness his plunge from anticipation to despair.

RECOMMENDED RECORDINGS

**Dietrich Fischer-Dieskau, baritone;
Gerald Moore, piano.**
Deutsche Grammophon 415 186-2 [Die schöne Müllerin]

Peter Schreier, tenor; András Schiff, piano.
London 430 414-2 [Die schöne Müllerin]

**Dietrich Fischer-Dieskau, baritone;
Alfred Brendel, piano.**
Philips 411 463-2 [Winterreise]

For more than 20 years, Fischer-Dieskau's *Die schöne Müllerin* with Moore has been a staple of the catalog. On balance the finest of the baritone's interpretations of the cycle, this is a reading of thrilling directness and impeccable balance between the partners. The excitement in the song *"Ungeduld"* ("Impatience") is palpable, and wherever Fischer-Dieskau soars, Moore soars right along with him. Originally released in 1972, the analog recording holds up well on CD, offering sharply focused sound.

Only a few other singers bring as much intelligence to Schubert's songs as Fischer-Dieskau, and one of them is the tenor Schreier. In this highly profiled reading, Schreier invests every phrase with emotion. The Saxon accent is sometimes a little hard on the ears, but each word comes across. At the piano, Schiff sings every bit as insightfully, illuminating the part in masterly fashion. The recording, made in Vienna's Konzerthaus in 1989, is wonderfully life-like.

In his 1985 recording of *Winterreise* with Brendel, Fischer-Dieskau can be heard utilizing all his art to overcome the erosion of his instrument— and bringing a theatricality to the cycle that makes this the most engaging of his interpretations. Even though there are signs of strain in his singing, his expression of sentiment is truly remarkable. The results here owe much to Brendel as well, who

*Dietrich Fischer-Dieskau, with
Gerald Moore at the piano.*

without ever reminding us that he is Brendel, never lets us forget that the piano part is by Schubert. The way the pianist presses the augmented sixth chord on the word *"drängst"* ("surge") in *"Die Post"* is just one example of his artistry.

ROBERT SCHUMANN
PIANO QUINTET IN E FLAT, OP. 44

Schumann, the quintessential Romantic, may have been a manic-depressive.

*T*his melodious, outgoing score, like so much of Schumann's chamber production, belongs to the year 1842. It is a seminal work, the first in a long line of Romantic piano quintets that includes essays by Brahms, Dvořák, and Franck. In its effective integration of the piano and string quartet, it set the standard that subsequent works in the genre have had to meet, while the lively interplay among its participants gives a perfect example of what any piece of chamber music should aspire to be.

Perhaps because he was a pianist and thought so often in pianistic terms, Schumann keeps his instrument at the forefront, establishing a balance of opposition between it and the quartet. After the ensemble has leapt into action with a forceful statement of the first movement's main subject, the piano softens the impetus and adds a warmly reflective quality to the discourse. Nothing if not a gracious partner, the piano defers to the cello and its companions in the second subject, a quintessential evocation of reverie. The development is stormy, but the passionate optimism of the opening pages is restored by movement's end.

The slow movement begins in the style of a funeral march but opens out to an elegiac second subject in which the string texture and the piano's rolling, arpeggiated patterns foreshadow Brahms at his most poetic. An agitated middle section that finds the piano exercising in brisk octaves leads to a reprise of the march, proclaimed in ghostly tones by the viola over a tremolo accompaniment.

> ✔ *IF YOU LIKE THIS WORK, you will probably enjoy listening to Schumann's Piano Quartet in E flat, Op. 44, and Brahms's Piano Quintet in F minor, Op. 34.*

The scherzo that follows has the animation one associates with similar movements by Mendelssohn, but it also possesses an athletic strength. The concluding Allegro begins vigorously in the minor key, a surprising touch, and ends with a spacious coda consisting of two fugal episodes, the second of which combines the main subjects of the first movement and the finale in a magisterial three-voice treatment.

*S*CHUMANN *dedicated the Piano Quintet to his wife Clara, but illness prevented her from participating in the work's first performance on December 6, 1842, in Leipzig. Her place at the keyboard was taken by Felix Mendelssohn, who had been invited to attend the unveiling, and gamely sight-read the piece.*

 RECOMMENDED RECORDINGS

Dolf Bettelheim, violin; Samuel Rhodes, viola; Beaux Arts Trio.
Philips 420 791-2 [with Piano Quartet, Op. 47]

Emanuel Ax, piano; Cleveland Quartet.
RCA 6498-2 [with Piano Quartet, Op. 47]

The approach of the Beaux Arts Trio and its associates is essentially reflective. The players are in perfect balance, giving a poised performance with a lovely dovetailing of voices. The analog recording, made in 1975, is warm and detailed and has been optimally transferred to CD.

Ax and the Clevelanders take a dramatic stance, making theirs a good counterpart to the interpretation of the Beaux Arts Trio. This is a high-contrast performance, in which the participants push the assertive element of Schumann's writing as far as it will go, and milk the sentimental. Ax is a fine chamber musician, but here he is still a soloist. The recording dates from 1986 and is almost symphonic in weight.

DICHTERLIEBE, OP. 48

*I*f Goethe represented the climax of Classicism and the arrival of Romanticism in German letters, much as Beethoven did in music,

"I *CAN HARDLY TELL you what a pleasure it is to write for the voice compared with instrumental composition—and how this rages and wells up within me when I sit down to work."*
—Robert Schumann

Heinrich Heine was the poet of choice for the later Romantics owing to the remarkable intensity and subjectivity of his work. Above all, Heine was direct—terse, yet rich in expressive content. This attracted composers from Schubert, who was his direct contemporary, to Grieg and Richard Strauss.

It is hardly surprising that Schumann also responded to Heine's poetry, for it embodied the turbulent emotions he himself felt. Schumann's *Dichterliebe* (the title literally means *Poet's Love*) is his best-known song cycle and a supreme achievement in the field of German Lieder. The music was penned in a single week at the end of May 1840, the "year of song" that saw Schumann's marriage to Clara Wieck over her father's objection. While the underlying theme of the cycle— love's joyous awakening and painful loss—had autobiographical connotations for Heine, Schumann's love for Clara scarcely went unrequited. But the sincerity of the composer's feelings and the agitation of this period in his life undoubtedly contributed to the musical intensity of the settings. The songs exhibit a tremendous compression of emotion into the tightest musical space. The piano is an active participant in the process, conveying much of the message and contributing considerable nuance as well in the astonishing variety of its figuration.

Most of the 16 songs of *Dichterliebe* are brief cameos, a few more thoroughly worked tableaux. *"Im wunderschönen Monat Mai"* ("In the Lovely Month of May"), which opens the cycle, creates an extraordinary impression with its rarified piano accompaniment and yearning harmonies. This is the moment in a man's soul when he becomes aware that something is happening to him, and Schumann, in a mere 26 measures, captures it perfectly. The scherzo-like third song, *"Die Rose, die Lilie, die Taube, die Sonne"* ("The Rose, the Lily, the Dove, the Sun"), has all the giddiness of puppy love, while the martial, angry seventh, *"Ich grolle nicht"* ("I bear no grudge"), seems to exult in the sadness of rejection. The downward course of the

The month of May—flowers, springtime, and song.

final song, "*Die alten, bösen Lieder*" ("The old, evil songs"), effectively recaps the final half of the cycle, from sarcastic rage to heartbreak. The piano has the last word, a tender envoy that seems to say, " 'Tis better to have loved and lost than never to have loved at all."

 RECOMMENDED RECORDINGS

Olaf Bär, baritone; Geoffrey Parsons, piano.
EMI Classics CDC 47397 [with Liederkreis, *Op. 39]*

Dietrich Fischer-Dieskau, baritone;
Alfred Brendel, piano.
Philips 416 352-2 [with Liederkreis, *Op. 39]*

Bär and Fischer-Dieskau recorded these cycles in the same month, July 1985, and the influence of the latter upon the former, stylistically and interpretively, is readily apparent. Bär not only sounds like the young Fischer-Dieskau, with a lustrous timbre and a velvety smoothness from bottom to top, he *sings* like Fischer-Dieskau, with a commanding yet intimate delivery and superb diction. Yet Bär has his own points to make—and he does so effectively, with outstanding support from Parsons in every song. The recording is ideally balanced and transmits the full impact of the voice in a natural ambience.

By the time of this recording, Fischer-Dieskau was well past his vocal prime. He is forced to croon many of the high notes, and a number of phrases are broken for breath, but his expressiveness is little diminished, his pointing of the text as sharp as ever. Brendel's playing is a revelation; the way he darkens the tone in the second phrase of the lead-in to "*Im wunderschönen Monat Mai*" foreshadows the direction the entire cycle is to take. It is artistry of a high order, joined to singing of profound insight.

Olaf Bär began his ascent to stardom with this recording.

SOLO KEYBOARD WORKS

*T*he literature for solo keyboard is surprisingly rich, particularly if one considers that both the organ and the harpsichord were originally regarded as foundation instruments whose main purpose was to accompany voices or other instruments. Until about the middle of the 17th century, few stylistic distinctions were made between one type of keyboard instrument and another. Players would use whatever was available or, if a choice existed, the instrument that best suited the music—the organ if the music was vocal, called for sustained notes, or needed a sonorous underpinning; the harpsichord if the music was instrumental or required a clear articulation of rhythm.

The emergence around 1600 of a new musical style, that of the early Baroque, brought a polarization of melody (in the upper voices) and harmony (in the lower ones) and established an important niche for the harpsichord. Alone or in combination with other instruments, it could sound the bass line and fill in the inner voices of the harmony, a function known as basso continuo. Because of its range the harpsichord was also well suited to playing melody and accompaniment simultaneously, which made it particularly attractive as a solo instrument. The full-size harpsichords made by Flemish and French builders, often magnificently decorated, were unexcelled for their sonority and tone and were prized by solo performers and music lovers throughout Europe.

The heyday of the solo harpsichord came during the 17th and early 18th centuries. Suites written for the instrument typically consisted of an improvisatory introduction (a prelude or allemande) followed by a variety of slow and fast dance movements (courantes, sarabandes, gigues, minuets, gavottes, and bourrées being the most popular). During the 17th century the literature for solo harpsichord grew rapidly, with major contributions from William Byrd, John Bull, and Thomas Tomkins in England, Jacques Champion de Chambonnières and Louis Couperin in France, Girolamo Frescobaldi and Bernardo Pasquini in Italy, and the German-born Johann Jacob Froberger in Austria. But the supreme works for the harpsichord date from the first half of the 18th century, when Bach, Handel, Jean-Philippe Rameau, François Couperin, and Domenico Scarlatti produced a matchless body of music ideally tailored to the instrument's capabilities.

Music for the organ also flourished during the Baroque era. It, too, often placed an emphasis on improvisation. But instead of dances, which required rhythmic accents not easily achieved on the organ, composers favored stricter forms such as the passacaglia and fugue, taking advantage of the instrument's remarkable ability to sustain a polyphonic texture. The Danish-born Dietrich Buxtehude, who served as organist at the Marienkirche in Lübeck from 1668 to his death in 1707, was the preeminent composer of organ music in the 17th century. He was also the single greatest influence on the most important master of the 18th century, Bach.

The piano was developed in Italy early in the 18th century, using a mechanism invented by Bartolomeo Cristofori. Its major advantage over the harpsichord was that it could produce dynamic gradations from soft to loud, hence its original name of *pianoforte*. The piano's rapid growth in popularity was a phenomenon of the late 18th and early 19th centuries, fueled both by social forces—the piano was the ideal instrument of the bourgeoisie because it stayed at home—and by the start of the Industrial Revolution, which permitted significant improvements in the construction of pianos, among them the development of a steel frame.

The efforts of Mozart, Beethoven, Muzio Clementi, and other pianists to provide themselves and their instrument with a repertory—which meant something quite apart from answering the enormous demand for music the piano-owning public could play—led to the piano's establishment as a vehicle for soloists as well as for the matrons and daughters of the middle class. About 1750, as the piano was replacing the harpsichord, the sonata supplanted the suite as the genre of choice for solo keyboard music. The typical Classical keyboard sonata, rather like a symphony for solo instrument, consisted of three or four movements in contrasting tempos, affording the performer a wide range of expression. The opening movement, the most substantial and rigorously argued, was in key-area form (also known as sonata form). It was followed by a slow movement in song or variation form and then a dance-like finale.

Whereas Mozart fashioned most of his sonatas for the home market, the composer-pianists of the 19th century—led by Schumann, Chopin, Mendelssohn, and most imposing of all, Liszt—intended nearly all of their keyboard music for public performance. For them the piano was the perfect extension of self: In the hands of Chopin and Schumann, it was the soul of poetry, though Liszt could make it roar with Promethean authority. The sonata, while still an important genre for these composers, shared the spotlight with a host of smaller forms or pieces patterned on dances. In the piano music of the Romantics, atmosphere and color are of prime importance, and the process begun by Beethoven of treating the piano as an orchestra is carried to breathtaking heights.

The 20th century has seen the literature enriched in a variety of ways. Debussy and Bartók, among others, imaginatively explored the piano's sonority and its status as a percussion instrument, while Rachmaninoff, Scriabin, Ravel, and Prokofiev expanded the virtuoso technique of 19th-century masters.

Clavier - Büchlein.

der

Wilhelm Friedemann Bach.
angefangen in
Cöthen den
22. Januar
Ao. 1720.

THE 24 PRELUDES *and fugues from each book of Bach's* The Well-Tempered Clavier *are considered so basic to the keyboard literature that among musicians and musicologists, especially in Europe, they are often referred to as simply "The Forty-Eight."*

JOHANN SEBASTIAN BACH

THE WELL-TEMPERED CLAVIER, BWV 846–893

*I*n 1722 Bach composed the 24 preludes and fugues of *The Well-Tempered Clavier*, Book I (some intended as instructional pieces for his son Wilhelm Friedemann), to prove the superiority for keyboard music of the tuning system known as equal temperament, which divides the octave into 12 exactly even half-steps. Under the irregular and mean-tone temperaments then widely in use, which called for unevenly tuned half-steps, keys with more than four sharps or flats—such as B major or E flat minor—could often sound out-of-tune, and they usually had to be avoided on organ or harpsichord because of the instrument's fixed tuning. In contrast, equal temperament made all keys sound equally good and allowed modulatory freedom of unimagined scope. While several composers before Bach had sought to investigate its possibilities, Bach's exploration in *The Well-Tempered Clavier* was of surpassing brilliance and thoroughness, with each of its two sets covering all 24 of the major and minor keys.

Bach's writing in Book I encompasses a huge variety of styles and contrapuntal techniques, and the expressive range of the material—considering that every piece is a prelude or a fugue—is remarkably vast. The justly celebrated opening piece, the Prelude in C major, uses a broken-chord figuration throughout that is reminiscent of lute style, while the Prelude in C minor has the character of a fantasy. Frequently the nature of a prelude contrasts markedly with that of the fugue in the same key, as when the ebullient D major Prelude gives way to a fugue with stately rhythms typical of a French overture. In the more remote tonalities, Bach shows beyond a doubt that at least *his* fingers knew their way around the back alleys of the keyboard. The fugues in Book I range in complexity from two to five parts, though most are three- or four-part settings. Several have chromatic subjects, and a number manage to work in melodic countersubjects. The Fugue in D sharp minor brings into play the theme, its inversion, its augmentation, and its double augmentation in a series of brilliant overlappings, while the final fugue of the collection, in B minor, has a theme that includes all 12 notes of the chromatic scale.

Book II of *The Well-Tempered Clavier* dates from the years 1738–42 and was assembled from both newly composed pieces and various existing preludes and fugues going back a number of years. There is even greater variety here: Bach expands some of the preludes to almost monumental proportions and writes others in binary form and aria style, neither of which had been utilized in the first book. In a few pieces, including the final fugue, he even tips his hat to the new galant style.

 RECOMMENDED RECORDINGS

Davitt Moroney.
Harmonia Mundi HMC 901285.88 [4 CDs]

András Schiff.
London 414 388-2 [2 CDs; Book I] and 417 236-2 [2 CDs; Book II]

Harmonia Mundi's larger-than-life 1988 recording makes it seem as if one is seated next to Moroney—not a bad way to hear the music. The instrument he plays, a John Phillips harpsichord built in 1980, has a stunningly bright sound and robust tone. At times it seems to project almost too forcefully, but it well suits Moroney's lively style of playing. His articulation is superb, his sense of shape wonderfully acute.

Schiff plays the *WTC* on the piano, with the utmost sensitivity to voicing and to the phrasing of counterpoint. He coaxes a lovely sound from his instrument (better captured in the 1985 recording of Book II than in the preceding year's

András Schiff's playing hardly puts the listener to sleep.

takes of Book I), and the experience of following him as he explores each piece is exceptionally rewarding.

GOLDBERG VARIATIONS, BWV 988

*C*ount Keyserlingk, the insomniac Russian ambassador to the Kingdom of Saxony for whom Bach may have written the *Goldberg* Variations, supposedly rewarded the composer with a golden goblet filled with 100 Louis d'ors. It was a small price to pay for the crowning achievement of Baroque keyboard music.

Johann Gottlieb Goldberg, thought to have been one of Bach's pupils, was in the service of Keyserlingk—presumably to play music during the small hours of the night, when his employer had difficulty getting to sleep. There remains some doubt about the connection between the music and the Count because Goldberg was only 14 years old when the variations were published, in 1741–42, as the fourth part of Bach's *Clavier-Übung* (literally, "keyboard practice"). Another paradox is that throughout his career, Bach showed relatively little interest in the variation form, this being the only large-scale set he wrote.

It is nonetheless an impressive one. Intended for a harpsichord with two manuals, it uses as its point of departure a two-part aria in G major from the second notebook Bach wrote (1725) for his second wife, Anna Magdalena. The theme's richly ornamented bass line gives solid harmonic support, and during the course of the variations the only changes Bach makes in the harmonization are changes of mode from major to minor. The piece is arranged as ten groupings of three variations; in each group, two variations are in free or characteristic style, one is a canon. Often an obbligato line in the bass accompanies the canon, producing a three-voice texture.

Fragonard's A Music Lesson.

QUODLIBET *means "whatever pleases." In music, a quodlibet is a piece in which different popular melodies are sounded either polyphonically or in succession. In the final variation of the* Goldberg Variations, *the tunes "Ich bin so lang nicht bei dir g'west" ("It's Been So Long Since I Saw You") and "Kraut und Rüben" ("Cabbage and Turnips") are played in counterpoint with the theme of the aria. Brahms's Academic Festival Overture trundles out one student song after another, ending with "Gaudeamus igitur" ("Let us therefore rejoice").*

The 30 variations function not only as a brilliant investigation of the theme, but as a masterly compendium of style and a study in how to write idiomatically for the keyboard. The fifth variation, for instance, calls for crossed hands, while the seventh is a siciliana and the tenth a fughetta. Variations Nos. 13 and 25 are both embellished arias, while No. 16 is a French overture. The final variation is a quodlibet in which Bach weaves two popular German songs into the texture. After this variation, he repeats the aria, going full circle; it is a wonderful touch, and the final demonstration of Bach's art. For try as one might, it is impossible to hear the aria the same way *after* the variations as before them.

 RECOMMENDED RECORDINGS

András Schiff.
London 417 116-2

Ton Koopman.
Erato 45326-2

Glenn Gould.
CBS MYK 38479

Schiff's playing is notable for its rhythmic flexibility and for the clarity it brings to the work's contrapuntal textures. His manner is sensitive, genial, and graceful—and while he has a tendency to be pretty where Glenn Gould would be piquant, he can also be remarkably insightful. Schiff brings spontaneity and animation to the faster variations, compelling directness to the slower ones, all in a performance of exceptional beauty and spirituality. The recording, made in London's Kingsway Hall in December of 1982, is excellent.

Playing on a wonderful harpsichord, Koopman takes the aria as a real sarabande. He emphasizes

Koopman captures the spirit of the dance in Bach's music.

the variations' rhythmic and contrapuntal elements and is masterly in phrasing, ornamentation, and articulation. At times the labor shows, as it should; this music was not meant to be easy. But to hear the dance-like spring that Koopman imparts to some of the variations is to know they can indeed be fun. Erato's 1987 recording is stunningly good, virtually ideal in its weight, presence, and ambience.

When it comes to Gould, one is either a great fan or not much of a fan at all. But the Canadian pianist's insights can be so valuable that his detractors will put up with his idiosyncrasies. This is the recording with which Gould made his debut in 1955. Where Schiff takes more than 72 minutes with the music, and Koopman more than 62, Gould gets through it in an astounding 38:25. The fast tempos are breathless, though cleanly negotiated. Gould does not bother with the repeats. In the end, in spite of its dryness, his is a Romantic view of the *Goldberg* Variations. It is instinctive, "pianistic," a communion of a very subjective sort—and valuable for that. The recording is close-miked, and one gets plenty of noise from Gould himself in his humming and foot tapping. There are a few tuning anomalies, as well as some tape hiss, but the piano tone is decent.

LUDWIG VAN BEETHOVEN

Piano Sonata in C minor, Op. 13
Pathétique

THE PATHÉTIQUE, among the most popular sonatas in Beethoven's entire oeuvre, has had a place in every pianist's repertory from the days of Ignaz Moscheles—who was seven when he first played it in 1801.

*N*owhere are Beethoven's gifts as a composer greater than in his sonatas for the piano. They contain what was, from the start, his most personal musical expression. The piano was *his* instrument, and he was constantly pushing its capacities—particularly its range and dynamic gradations—as far as they would go. Beethoven continued to do this even when he could no longer hear the results; had it not been for his deafness, he undoubtedly would also have remained the virtuoso interpreter of his own works that he was as a young man. It is ironic that Beethoven was both a brilliant improviser and a composer who habitually sketched and re-sketched his ideas before committing them to a work. But both elements—the spontaneous and the structured—are present in the sonatas, giving them strength and vitality unparalleled in the keyboard literature.

Even in his early pieces for the piano, the touch of a master can be heard. Among these works is the *Pathétique* Sonata, completed in 1798 and published the following year with a dedication to Prince Karl von Lichnowsky, with whom Beethoven had lodged upon arriving in Vienna in 1792, and at whose house his music was frequently played. Lichnowsky would become a formal patron in 1800, and the *Pathétique*, the most innovative of the composer's early sonatas, would decisively establish Beethoven's reputation in Vienna.

The integration of motivic elements from the sonata's slow introduction into the main body of its first movement, along with the daring modulations there and in the rondo finale, marked a bold departure from 18th-century norms. The gloomily dark tone and somber strength of Beethoven's writing lend the first movement an intensity that foreshadows some of his later treatments of the key of C minor, including the opening movement of the Fifth Symphony. The Adagio offers a reprieve of lyricism; melodic invention of serene beauty virtually conceals the rondo framework on which the movement is built. The turbulence of the first movement returns, somewhat muted, in the concluding Allegro.

THE C MINOR KEY had a special significance for Beethoven, conjuring up music of unusual vehemence and drama. Following the Pathétique *Sonata, he would further explore this vein in the String Quartet in C minor (Op. 18, No. 4), the Third Piano Concerto, and the Fifth Symphony. He visits the key a final time in the turbulent first movement of the Sonata in C minor, Op. 111, his last for the piano. No longer in need of exorcising its demon, he allows it to rage.*

PIANO SONATA IN C SHARP MINOR, OP. 27, NO. 2
Moonlight

A meditative Giulietta Guicciardi, dedicatee of the Moonlight *Sonata.*

*T*he two sonatas of Opus 27 were published in 1802 with the descriptive legend "*quasi una fantasia*" attached to each. The second of the pair, composed in 1801, bears a dedication to Countess Giulietta Guicciardi, who was then 17 and whom Beethoven somewhat furtively hoped he might marry. The work has been known since Beethoven's day as the *Moonlight* Sonata—a title bestowed on it by the poet Rellstab, who likened the first movement's eerie calm to a moonlit night on the Lake of Lucerne. But the simplicity of this opening Adagio is deceptive, for the sonata's concluding Allegretto and Presto movements are a musical Scylla and Charybdis.

In placing the slow movement first, following it with a scherzo, and concluding with the true sonata-form movement, Beethoven began an influential experiment in shifting emphasis toward the end of his works, one he would carry further in later compositions (and which would culminate in our own century in works by Mahler and Shostakovich, among others). So the opening movement of the *Moonlight* Sonata is really more of a prelude (whose repeated three-note figure most likely was inspired by the Act I trio of Mozart's *Don Giovanni*), while the movements that follow, more thoroughly worked out, present the composition's main argument—complete with treacherous tests of any performer's skill.

PIANO SONATA IN C, OP. 53
Waldstein

*I*n 1801, soon after completing what was to be the last of his four-movement *grandes sonates* for piano, the Opus 28 *Pastoral*, Beethoven remarked to the violinist Wenzel Krumpholtz that he was "only a little satisfied" with his previous works. "From today on," he said, "I will take a new path." The first of Beethoven's piano works to reflect his new thinking was the Sonata in C, Op. 53, completed in 1804 and dedicated to his good friend and patron Count Ferdinand Waldstein. The *Waldstein* Sonata comes as close to formal perfection and total mastery of materials as any in Beethoven's canon. Its harmonic daring and sheer energy make it a shining example of his middle-period style, as outstanding in its fashion as the First *Razumovsky* Quartet and the *Eroica* Symphony.

The first movement opens with a pulsating progression that approaches the home key by indirection, at the same time taking advantage of the strikingly resonant sound quality in the lower range of the early 19th-century fortepiano. Contrast and momentum are the essence of the movement; an enormous amount of energy is released as it unfolds, the impetus of C major gaining from each harmonic digression. Beethoven originally intended to place an Andante next—the celebrated *Andante favori*—but thought better of it, substituting an Adagio introduction to the finale. This brief prelude begins to spawn a melody in the warm middle range of the instrument, but its development is interrupted by a return of the Adagio's opening phrases, as Beethoven sets the stage for the work's conclusion. The rondo finale begins out of the mists, with the emergence of a consoling tune that builds by repetition into a paean of triumph. The intervening episodes set off the subject in a contrast of dark and light, until the movement ends, *prestissimo*, in an exultant delirium of sound.

"DEAR BEETHOVEN!* *You are going to Vienna in fulfillment of your long frustrated wishes. The Genius of Mozart is mourning and weeping over the death of her pupil. She found refuge but no occupation with the inexhaustible Haydn; through him she wishes to form a union with another. With the help of assiduous labor you shall receive Mozart's spirit from Haydn's hands."*
—Inscription in Beethoven's autograph album *(below)* by Count Ferdinand Ernst von Waldstein

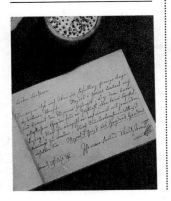

PIANO SONATA IN F MINOR, OP. 57
Appassionata

he F minor Sonata was completed in 1805 and published in 1807, with a dedication to Beethoven's close friend Count Franz von Brunsvik. Known as the *Appassionata*, it is among Beethoven's most popular and frequently played sonatas, in the same company as the *Pathétique*, the *Moonlight*, and the *Waldstein*. It is also one of the most immediately recognizable of his works for the piano, thanks to the sinister subject that issues *sotto voce* at the start of the work from the depths of the keyboard. In the opening Allegro there are precipitous changes of mood—from somber to elegiac to darkly furious—typical of Beethoven's minor-key expressiveness. Indeed, the accents and contrasts here are so intense that the piano itself sometimes seems to cringe from the task before it.

If the opening movement is as towering an essay as Beethoven ever penned, the ensuing Andante is tranquility itself: a masterful evocation of contemplative inaction, with four variations appended to a theme of surpassing gentleness. The finale breaks upon the conclusion of this movement with terrifying suddenness. Its irresistible onrush and pained intensity sweep the whole sonata toward an ending in near-hysteria, reminiscent of the howling of the shades in Dante's *Inferno*.

PIANO SONATA IN E FLAT, OP. 81a
Les Adieux

he "farewell" of the title refers to the forced parting of Beethoven from his patron and student the Archduke Rudolph in 1809. Although the score of the sonata, completed the following year, does not explain how Napoleon's

Beethoven bids a musical farewell to his patron.

Beethoven at the piano—work-shop, confessional, and soapbox.

THE ARCHDUKE
*Rudolph, son of the
Hapsburg emperor, became a
piano student of Beethoven
early in 1804. Despite the
vast difference in their social
standing, the bond between
student and teacher was a
strong one. The composer
dedicated many of his finest
scores to Rudolph, including
the Piano Sonata in E flat,
whose title refers to the
forced parting of Beethoven
and his patron.*

siege of Vienna had forced the Archduke and the rest of the royal family to flee the city while Beethoven stayed behind, the first page of the manuscript does show the syllables of the word *"Lebewohl"* ("Farewell") written over the three-note opening motive of the Adagio introduction. Grounded in Beethoven's noble and heroic key of E flat major, what follows is music of extraordinary power and imagination dealing with the emotions of separation and, ultimately, reunion—music meant to be listened to with the eyes and heart as well as the ears.

A sense of nostalgia pervades the opening measures, an effect achieved partly through Beethoven's use of deceptive rather than authentic cadences. The main body of the movement plays upon the "farewell" motive but in music of easy-going familiarity, suggesting perhaps something of the nature of the relationship between Beethoven and the Archduke. In the movement's final measures, as the motive is softly superimposed upon itself, one can almost picture the Archduke's coach disappearing around a bend.

The slow movement, subtitled *"Abwesenheit"* ("Absence"), is a study in subdued grief, with restlessly shifting sequences in the minor mode offset by a consoling section in the major. With characteristic suddenness, the finale, subtitled *"Das Wiedersehen"* ("The Return"), breaks the spell of sadness. In a flourish of excitement, the joyous music takes off at a tempo marked *Vivacissimamente*, replete with brilliant passagework that recalls the finale of the *Emperor* Concerto. At the movement's climax, one can easily imagine the Archduke's coach appearing at the same bend in the road where last it was seen, this time on a homeward course, and taking the curve on two wheels.

PIANO SONATA IN B FLAT, OP. 106
Hammerklavier

*A*lso dedicated to the Archduke Rudolph, this sonata was the first of the monumentally large works to occupy Beethoven in his final decade (the others being the *Missa Solemnis*, the Ninth Symphony, and the *Diabelli* Variations). Its composition, which took nearly a full year from the autumn of 1817 to the autumn of 1818, marked Beethoven's full recovery from several years of crisis.

The *Hammerklavier*'s exultant opening bars, in which fistfuls of notes are literally hurled at the keyboard, contain the chordal building blocks out of which this assertive work is constructed. They set in motion a brilliant study in contrast—between what Beethoven might have described as the "unbuttoned" manner and a more courtly, well-behaved style of playing. The potency of the various ideas, the unusual vehemence with which they are projected, and the linkage between them are all typical of Beethoven's late period.

The ensuing scherzo shows how Beethoven could create music of remarkable complexity out of quite simple material. Its subject, consisting of just a couple of notes, outlines the interval of a third, a pattern that links it to the opening of the sonata's first movement. Beethoven manipulates the figure with such skill and imagination that it seems utterly inexhaustible; it appears throughout the scherzo itself in dotted rhythm, and in the trio section it shows up in augmentation and in detached eighth notes. It is even hidden in the right-hand triplet figures that accompany a statement of the tune in the left hand. The violent disruptions of rhythm and harmony that happen during the course of the movement, including the hearty Bronx cheer that precedes the return of the scherzo, serve not to break the movement's flow but to energize it.

Now comes the Adagio, which has been de-

Beethoven's-eye view of his Graf piano.

"OF POWERFUL build, his face was a healthy red, his eyebrows very thick and his brow low. His nose was very big and broad, especially the nostrils, which were finely shaped. His bushy thick hair was already partly gray and stood up from his face. His hands were coarse and stout, his fingers short . . ."
—Carl Friedrich Hirsch, describing Beethoven's appearance in 1817

scribed as everything from a "manifestation of sublime beauty" (French composer Vincent d'Indy) to a "mausoleum of collective sorrow" (musicologist Wilhelm von Lenz). The marking *Adagio sostenuto, appasionato e con molto sentimento* serves as a warning to the performer, in pianist Alfred Brendel's words, "not to see the pain in the music from a position of calm, remote resignation." The movement opens in contemplation and builds like a great hymn; just when Beethoven seems to reach the limit of spirituality, he goes off still further, into a quite ethereal realm. An entire line of development in Romantic music—passing through Schubert, Chopin, Schumann, Brahms, and even Liszt—springs from this music.

The finale begins with a mysteriously schizophrenic introduction, a series of alternately meditative and violent asides. This sets the table for a three-voice fugue so elaborate and eventful it seems more like a fantasy, in which long arcs of invention are sustained by brilliant imitative writing. The marking *con alcune licenze* ("with occasional license") is a reminder from Beethoven that the academic strictures of the fugue are here relaxed. But the reason for the expansion—the almost volcanic expression underlying this musical outpouring—more than justifies the liberties that are taken.

FINAL PIANO SONATAS

*A*lthough they have separate opus numbers and were published individually, Beethoven likely conceived of his final three piano sonatas as a group, for they bear noticeable resemblances to one another—even though, as the pianist Denis Matthews has pointed out, each work remains "a law unto itself." The power of Beethoven's late style had been confirmed in the *Hammerklavier* Sonata, but now it found expression in even greater works.

The Sonata in E, Op. 109, was completed in 1820, and it exemplifies the increasingly private direction his music was seeking, along with the remarkable compression of idiom he had now attained. Although cast in three movements, the sonata is nonetheless highly original in form, partly because of the way its individual movements are constructed, also because it closes with an Andante rather than the expected rondo in lively tempo.

At this stage in his career, Beethoven's tendency was to compose movements that evolved organically from a basic, often simple, cell. But the first movement of Opus 109—in which sections marked *Vivace* and *Adagio* alternate with one another according to a freely adapted sonata form—is actually more Hegelian than Darwinian. Within its dialectic of contrast there is remarkable tension, which allows Beethoven a particularly wide range of expression. The second movement, a fierce Prestissimo in E minor, serves as a scherzo; the fact that its energy is compressed into a tightly wound sonata form makes it seem that much more vehement. The finale, with its potent aria-like theme, is not just an Andante but a set of variations. There are six of them, several of which are double variations, and they are followed rather exceptionally by a reprise of the original theme—a vanishing act through which the work ends.

The Sonata in A flat, Op. 110, was completed a year after its predecessor and shares with it a predilection toward intense drama within a lyrical framework. Its opening movement clings to Beethoven's designation *cantabile* ("singing"), what contrast there is coming not so much from the new ideas spawned by the opening subject as from differences in rhythm and figuration that are explored within them. The second movement, another substitute scherzo, plays extensively on the device of contrary motion, in which the hands move across the keyboard in opposite directions. And the finale follows a highly complex, subjective, even idiosyncratic plan. An Adagio in-

Out for a stroll: Beethoven in top hat, sketched by von Boehm.

THE PIANO'S SIZE, *sound, and construction changed dramatically during Beethoven's lifetime, turning what had been a soft-spoken drawing-room instrument into a thundering dreadnought of the concert stage. In 1817, Beethoven received as a gift a six-octave grand from John Broadwood and Sons, the finest instrument he was to own; its heavier action and powerful tone played a recognizable part in the genesis of the* Hammerklavier *Sonata.*

troduction consisting of a recitative and arioso (both conventions borrowed from opera) leads to a fugue that begins confidently in the tonic key of A flat. The exposition of the fugue is interrupted by a return of the arioso, now completely fragmented, a half-step lower—marked by Beethoven *perdendo le forze, dolente* ("wearily, lamenting"). There is a sudden resumption of the fugue, and from here the movement takes a triumphant new trajectory. A series of modulations leading back to A flat prepares the movement's ecstatic conclusion, a hymnlike passage in which Beethoven almost runs out of keys at the top end of the piano.

The two-movement Sonata in C minor, Op. 111, dates from 1822. The taut, fiery first movement is cast in a highly schematized sonata form. There is incredible compression of material here; connections are made with no wasted motion, yet the bonds that hold the movement's striking gestures together are absolutely sure. The finale, in which the searing C minor of the first movement is transmuted into an ethereal C major, was given the extraordinary designation *Arietta* by Beethoven. A set of variations of ineffable beauty and brilliant invention, it remains a touchstone for the interpreter of Beethoven and also foreshadows much that is to come in late Romanticism, especially in the works of Bruckner and Mahler. Thomas Mann was so taken with this visionary movement that he devoted a remarkable passage to it in *Dr. Faustus.* As Wendell Kretschmar says in that novel, this is an altogether extraordinary leave-taking on Beethoven's part, "an end without any return."

 RECOMMENDED RECORDINGS

Wilhelm Kempff.
Deutsche Grammophon 415 834-2 [Pathétique *and* Moonlight, *with* Pastoral *Sonata in D, Op. 28, and Sonata in F sharp, Op. 78]*

Gilels: Beethoven that was manly yet mannerly.

Emil Gilels.
Deutsche Grammophon 419 162-2 [Waldstein, Appassionata, *and* Les Adieux] *and 419 174-2 [Opp. 109 and 110]*

Maurizio Pollini.
Deutsche Grammophon 419 199-2 [2 CDs; Hammerklavier *and Opp. 109–111, with Sonata in A, Op. 101; also available separately on 429 569-2 and 429 570-2]*

Kempff was a wonderfully resourceful player, and he brought a marvelous sense of theater to these 1965 accounts. In the *Pathétique*, he uses a wide dynamic range, yet his playing is elegant and lyrical. Where others convey an almost funereal quality in the first movement of the *Moonlight*, Kempff suggests something more veiled and atmospheric; his reading of the finale is also less frenetic than what one tends to encounter. This is a gentleman's Beethoven, a philosopher's Beethoven, but also the Beethoven of a man of feeling. Kempff's integral recording of all 32 sonatas, on nine midprice CDs, could be recommended were it not for the extreme sonic glare from which the late works, recorded first, seem to suffer.

There is a percussive hardness to Gilels's tone that is fitting in Beethoven, as well as a softness that is amazing—qualities few other pianists have cultivated as skillfully. And there is always a feeling of power in reserve. As for technique, his rhythm is deadly accurate, his scales evenly weighted. But what is truly extraordinary is the lively, leonine quality of the playing. Gilels's account of the *Waldstein* has the appropriate energy and gruffness, and his rendition of *Les Adieux* is among the most imaginative ever captured. The analog recordings, from 1972–74, are solid, dry, and tightly focused. On a disc recorded in 1985—a fairly good digital effort with only a touch of glare—the Russian pianist is even more impressive in two of the late sonatas. Right from the start of Opus 109, one can tell that something remarkable is afoot. And indeed, the readings are

Olympian, with buildups, climaxes, and closings perfectly gauged. Even when Gilels opts for a slow tempo, his unerring sense of pulse and his shaping of line create a feeling of lift. In short, his readings are unmatched in profundity, humanity, and beauty of tone.

Pollini's accounts of the late sonatas are both heated and steely—outgoing interpretations with a sure grip of structure. In them, the pianist never seems to push his limits, which may be a drawback considering that Beethoven wanted to suggest that very effect. Still, Pollini leaves one deeply impressed, nowhere more so than in the finale of Opus 111: here is no great leave-taking, but a vision of Beethoven soaring beyond the bounds of song. In these recordings from 1975–77, the piano seems to have been miked from about six inches off the strings, yielding a clangorously aggressive sound.

JOHANNES BRAHMS

LATE PIANO WORKS

*L*ike nearly every important 19th-century composer, Brahms was a pianist—yet he focused on the piano as a solo instrument only intermittently. Three sonatas, the only ones he would write, were all finished before he was 20. Beethoven, Schumann, and Liszt are the models here, especially in the Sonata No. 3, in F minor, composed in 1853 and the most compelling of the three works.

Brahms next turned to the variation form as the one best suited to his pianistic ideas. Between 1854 and 1873 he wrote six sets, including the celebrated two-piano *Variations on a Theme by Haydn*, Op. 56b; two books of *Variations on a Theme by Paganini*, Op. 35, interpreting the same caprice that inspired Rachmaninoff's concerto-like *Rhapsody* but offering more technical challenge than musical reward; and the imaginative *Variations*

"HE LOOKED an old man," Florence May wrote of Brahms after visiting him in Vienna in 1888, the year of the D minor Sonata. "His hair was nearly white, and he had grown very stout. But he wore the happy, sunshiny look of one who had realized his purpose and was content with his share in life."

and Fugue on a Theme by Handel, Op. 24, the best of the sets. However, Brahms would ultimately discard the variation form, as he had the sonata.

Except for a couple of isolated instances, it wasn't until the last decade of his life that Brahms returned to composing for the solo piano—yet these works, in freer forms, are among the composer's most personal statements. The seven *Fantasias*, Op. 116, the *Three Intermezzos*, Op. 117, and the ten *Piano Pieces*, Opp. 118 and 119, all date from 1892. In their formal usage, harmonic function, and expression, they are intriguing—even progressive, as Schoenberg was right to point out. These last piano works are perhaps the purest sublimation of Brahms's melancholy and ambivalent genius, pieces in which passion glows in the midst of resignation, like the embers of a dying fire.

 RECOMMENDED RECORDINGS

Glenn Gould.

Sony Classical SM2K 52651 [2 CDs; Fantasia, Op. 116, No. 4; Three Intermezzos, *Op. 117; and* Piano Pieces, *Op. 118, Nos. 1, 2, and 6, and Op. 119, No. 1; with other works]*

*P*LAYING THE PIANO *was only a small part of what Glenn Gould was about, and after 1964— when, at the age of 32, he retired from concertizing—it became even smaller. Gould preferred the hermetic detachment of the recording studio and the elegance of the radio script to the concert stage. He lived his life as a recluse, keeping in touch with a few friends by phone and interviewing himself to avoid having to talk with someone else.*

Van Cliburn.

RCA Gold Seal 60419-2 [Fantasias, Op. 116, Nos. 3 and 6, and Piano Pieces, *Op. 118, Nos. 1–3, with* Two Rhapsodies, *Op. 79, and Beethoven: Piano Concerto No. 3] and 7942-2 [Intermezzos, Op. 117, Nos. 1 and 2, and* Piano Pieces, *Op. 119, Nos. 1–3, with Piano Concerto No. 2]*

Gould's accounts, recorded in 1960, are among his most affecting statements. He manages to balance the music on the edge of an almost unbearable emotional intensity, without falling into salon sentimentality. The result is downright depressing—but few pianists have so successfully distilled Brahms's late style as Gould has here, conveying painful passion held in check and maintaining a sense of fluidity within music that seems to be the embodiment of stasis. Sony's new 20-bit remastering has brought unexpected life and richness out of these analog recordings.

It is a pity that Cliburn's various recordings of this music have not been consolidated onto a single CD, for they are among his best efforts as well. There is warmth in his manner, which comes out in supple, graceful phrasing and remarkably beautiful tone. These are lyrical readings that project a deep sense of nostalgia, even if the melancholy is not as bleak as in Gould's utterly northern accounts.

FRÉDÉRIC CHOPIN

PIANO WORKS

*E*very one of Chopin's works was written either for solo piano or for a combination that included the piano. And of the virtuoso pianists of the day, it was Chopin who had the most improvisatory approach to performing, never playing a piece the same way twice.

It is hardly surprising that a taste for improvisation should lie at the heart of Chopin's compositional style as well. His long-breathed melodies are fluid and asymmetrical, and his forms are mostly derived from the improvisational principle of departing from set material and subsequently returning to it. Many of Chopin's compositions are in genres whose very titles underscore their improvisatory nature: ballades, nocturnes, and preludes.

Ballades—The four ballades of 1831–42, the most substantial single-movement pieces Chopin wrote, are also among his finest creations, notable for their wealth of content and their formal command. There is no precedent for Chopin's use of the term "ballade," and while the allusion to a

Chopin in 1829. He left Poland the following year.

specific kind of poetry is clear enough, there is nothing strophic about these works. On the contrary, in each of them Chopin fashions an episodic narrative from a pair of thematic ideas that are spun out and varied in an unbroken flow—so that while the mood is constantly changing, the line of action is continuous. The writing emphasizes variety of texture and is full of rhapsodic digressions through remote keys.

The first two ballades, in G minor, Op. 23, and in F, Op. 38, build from introspective beginnings to highly charged climaxes. The drama at the end of the former work is particularly savage; to achieve the same trajectory in the latter, Chopin casts the ending in A minor. The A flat major Ballade, Op. 47, is almost wholly lyrical, though Chopin creates a satisfying inner tension through its remarkably complex harmonic scheme. The most tightly constructed and gripping of the four ballades is the final one, in F minor, Op. 52, where Chopin masterfully uses a repeated-note figure from the opening melody as a unifying device throughout.

Nocturnes—The texture explored by Chopin in his nocturnes consists of an ornamentally decorated melody over a steady left-hand accompaniment, usually chordal or in broken figures. Chopin shows increasing resourcefulness in his later nocturnes, which on the whole are more speculative and elaborate. He does this by enriching the harmonic content, extending the left hand across the entire range of the keyboard (as in the Nocturne in C sharp minor, Op. 27, No. 1— dating from 1835 and a work of remarkable complexity and power—and the piece in E flat, Op. 55, No. 2, from 1843), even allowing the accompaniment to take on a melodic character itself. Elsewhere, as in the Nocturne in G, Op. 37, No. 2 (1839), he transforms the right-hand material into etude-like figures, saving the more conventional melody for the contrasting middle section.

The expression of most of these pieces is truly

IGHT MUSIC is a genre unto itself. The most prevalent form is the serenade from the Italian sera, *meaning "evening." The nocturne is a separate species, owing its origin to the Irish pianist John Field, who published his first nocturnes in 1814. Chopin took over the form and made it his own. Subsequent composers who have made a little night music include Liszt, Fauré, Tchaikovsky, Grieg, and Scriabin.*

"nocturnal": soft-spoken, meditative, sometimes sweet and caressing, more often melancholy. In a few, Chopin approaches the transcendent, only to pull back at the brink of ecstasy. And in a very few, particularly the Nocturne in C minor, Op. 48, No. 1 (1841), he shows an altogether more dramatic side of the genre—stormy, passionate, in a way that Liszt frequently is. Yet in all of them, the emotion is fleeting, which makes the music particularly precious and leaves the listener with a floating quality akin to Czech author Milan Kundera's "unbearable lightness of being."

Preludes—In their variety of form, figuration, and texture, the 24 Preludes, Op. 28 (1836–39), present a microcosm of Chopin's art. The idea of composing a set of preludes in each of the major and minor keys comes directly out of Bach's *The Well-Tempered Clavier*, and much as Bach did, Chopin uses individual preludes to explore the principle of building pieces out of specific textures or motifs. The resemblance ends there. Chopin makes no attempt to imitate an earlier keyboard style, sticking confidently to his own. And his preludes are quite specific in their expression. Though some are no more than a few measures long, they are all distillations of a particular mood, brief flights of Romantic fancy capable of standing on their own, no matter how evanescent.

Chopin's aim in writing the set was to produce not only contrast, but gradations within a continuous utterance, so that while each piece can be heard as a unique expression, it remains an integral part of the whole. The treatment ranges from the single-motif study of the Prelude No. 1, in C major, to the extended rhapsodizing of No. 15, in D flat. The effect can be compared to that of an exquisite necklace, strung from pearls remarkably different in size, shape, and color.

Waltzes—"The Viennese waltz is not for me." Chopin's remark should be understood in terms of what the waltz was at the time of his visit to

MAJORCA, *the largest of the Balearic Islands (hence its name), was home to Chopin and the novelist George Sand (above) in the fall and winter of 1838–39, the height of their stormy love affair. While on the island Chopin had a tubercular relapse, which so alarmed the locals that he and Sand were quarantined in an abandoned Carthusian monastery. Here, in a cozy little suite that opened on a garden, Chopin completed the Preludes, Op. 28.*

Chopin's waltzes: elegant, refined, and rhapsodic.

Vienna in 1830–31: not the elegant, sophisticated dance made memorable by Johann Strauss II (who was then five years old), but something closer to cafe music. In his own waltzes, Chopin sought to be both more elegant and expressive, and he was able to render the dance in a variety of moods. Few of his works are more gracious than the Waltz in E flat, Op. 18 (1831), or more dazzling than the Waltz in D flat, Op. 64, No. 1 (1846), the celebrated *Minute* Waltz. But some of Chopin's most convincing waltzes are less flamboyant. Of the other Opus 64 pieces, No. 3, in A flat, is wonderfully refined and rhapsodic, and No. 2, in C sharp minor—the greatest of Chopin's waltzes—conveys a sober resignation tinged with vulnerability.

Polonaises and Mazurkas—Although he was of pure French descent on his father's side and spent the latter part of his life in France, Chopin remained proud of his Polish birth and artistically true to the temperament of his homeland. Both the fiery and the melancholy aspects of the Polish character are reflected in his polonaises and mazurkas. The former are among his most direct works, though even their character ranges substantially, from almost pensive to utterly triumphant. The most famous of them is the Polonaise in A flat, Op. 53 (1842). Majestic, outgoing, and virtuosic, it is a quintessential example of the flamboyant approach to the genre. The middle section, with its grand crescendo built on demonically fast left-hand octaves, is a touchstone of technique and endurance.

The mazurkas are harder to characterize. Chopin wrote more than 50 of them; there are 13 sets, along with a number of separate pieces. Nearly all display the clear sectional layout characteristic of his dance pieces in general, and most exhibit the distinctive accent on the second or third beat of the measure, which produces the syncopated feeling typical of the mazurka as it is danced. Yet Chopin's subtle feeling for rhythm and harmony transforms the mazurka from a peasant dance into the most prescient and rarified of the genres in which he wrote. A number of his later mazurkas are deeply felt reflections of both the composer's nationalism and his febrile inner sensitivity. Among the best are two that Chopin wrote in 1842 and 1846 in his much-loved key of C sharp minor: Opus 50, No. 3, which is at once elegiac and troubled, and Opus 63, No. 3, which begins as if it were a waltz but grows increasingly questioning and surprising, with a remarkable concluding canon. Equally fine is the Mazurka in C minor, Op. 56, No. 3, which seems suspended between agitation and sultry yearning. A Polish pianist put it best when she said of Chopin's mazurkas: "This is our blood. We are up, down, volcanic—we have spleen, nostalgia."

 ## RECOMMENDED RECORDINGS

Artur Rubinstein.
RCA RCD 1-7156 [Ballades, with Scherzos], 5613-2 [2 CDs; 19 Nocturnes], 5615-2 [7 Polonaises], 5614-2 [2 CDs; 51 Mazurkas], RCD 1-5492 [14 Waltzes], and RCA Gold Seal 7725-2 [Chopin recital]

Krystian Zimerman.
Deutsche Grammophon 423 090-2 [Ballades, with Barcarolle *and* Fantasy *in F minor]*

Vladimir Ashkenazy.
London 414 564-2 [2 CDs; 21 Nocturnes]

Dmitri Alexeev.
EMI Eminence CDM 64117 [26 Preludes]

If there's one sure bet in this repertory, it's Rubinstein. His recordings of Chopin can be recommended without hesitation for their warmth, lyricism, and expressive point. Never overwrought, the music emerges with spontaneity and freshness. Rubinstein's fiery renditions of the bal-

Field of dreams: Ashkenazy scores in Chopin nocturnes.

lades and polonaises combine drama and poetry in mesmerizing fashion, while his readings of the nocturnes, mazurkas, and waltzes are notable for their Mediterranean color and unerring sense of mood. The sound of the 1960s stereo recordings may occasionally lack depth and seem slightly veiled, but it holds up well enough to convey unmistakably the tone and the touch that made Rubinstein one of the greatest pianists of all time. In addition to these separate CDs for each genre, there is the Rubinstein recital disc (a sampler drawn from the stereo recordings that are part of RCA's *The Chopin Collection*), offering everybody's favorite everything on one CD, except that there are no preludes or etudes. Well over 70 minutes of music, all of it ravishingly played.

With Zimerman's accounts of the ballades, nothing is thrown away, and the pianist brings energy and elegance to the music, along with an excellent sense of color and flow. Sometimes the touches seem applied rather than inevitable, but the interpretations are, on the whole, persuasive. The 1987 recording is solid and captures a good ambience, though the piano tone gets a little hard in the heavy going.

Ashkenazy recorded the nocturnes at various times in the 1970s and early 1980s. The accounts are long on virtuosity, and while the interpretations are straightforward, they go directly to the mood of the pieces. London's recordings—some analog, some digital—are uniformly good.

Though little encountered on the American concert circuit, the Russian pianist Alexeev is a remarkably astute interpreter of Chopin. His integral recording of the preludes, made in 1986, is thoroughly impressive, with performances that are as sensitive as they are brilliant. The sound is first-rate.

Rubinstein's Chopin recordings are gilt-edged securities in a crowded market.

CLAUDE DEBUSSY

IMAGES
PRELUDES

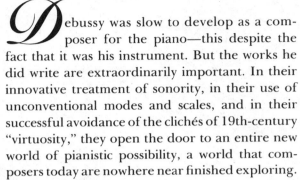

*D*ebussy was slow to develop as a composer for the piano—this despite the fact that it was his instrument. But the works he did write are extraordinarily important. In their innovative treatment of sonority, in their use of unconventional modes and scales, and in their successful avoidance of the clichés of 19th-century "virtuosity," they open the door to an entire new world of pianistic possibility, a world that composers today are nowhere near finished exploring.

From the time he was a conservatory student, a central element in Debussy's thinking about the piano was that it should be a sound resource—not, as in the Romantic era, an instrument for "singing" or a vehicle for the display of dazzling fingerwork, but a means to achieve tonal effects that are engaging to the ear. He wanted the piano to sound as if it had no hammers, and following the lead of Chopin and Liszt he sought to create the illusion of sustained tone, through pedaling, figuration, and the use of harmony saturated with non-chord tones. In 1889 his notions of how the piano could sound were profoundly expanded when he heard a Javanese gamelan at the World Exhibition in Paris.

The floating, elusive quality of much of Debussy's writing for the piano—derived from a constantly changing yet agreeably static texture of bell-like tones overlapped and gradually decaying—is but one characteristic of a very complex style. Equally important is the way these compositions are structured, not according to a process of argument but in a highly improvisatory fashion. At times Debussy resorts to a kind of cinematic cross-cutting in order to connect one idea to another, in a way that creates a profound *psycho*logical, as opposed to a purely logical, relationship between them. In one of the best examples of this

*T*HE TERM GAMELAN *refers to ensembles consisting of various tuned bronze gongs and other instruments, originally played in Java. The Indonesian influence of gamelan sound on Debussy's writing for the piano is apparent in a number of works, particularly in the pentatonic scales and bright, clanging chords of* "Pagodes," *the first piece in* Estampes, *and in the tolling sonorities of* "La cathédrale engloutie" *("The Sunken Cathedral").*

The Japanese lacquer panel that inspired Debussy's "Poissons d'or."

technique—the final pages of *"La soirée dans Granade"* (from the *Estampes* of 1903), where fragments of distant revelry cut into a sultry habanera—the effect is so atmospheric the music almost seems to levitate.

The two sets of *Images*, from 1905 and 1907, are Debussy's most substantial works for piano. Written at the height of his maturity, they show an astonishing mastery of technique and keyboard imagery. Each set contains three pieces, thus resembling a conventional sonata in layout if not in purpose or effect. The first series begins with *"Reflets dans l'eau"* ("Reflections in the Water"), one of the greatest pieces in the entire piano literature. These "reflections" are incomplete echoes or subtly distorted repetitions of thematic figures, just as Monet's paintings of water lilies show reflections as fragments of color and shape. The main theme consists of just three descending notes, around which Debussy creates an imaginative play of texture, at first gently dappled, later swirling, and then breathlessly still.

In *"Hommage à Rameau,"* the second piece in the first set of *Images*, Debussy sought not to sound like the great French composer of the 18th century but to offer a tribute written "in the style of a sarabande but without rigor." Graceful and dignified, but also very warm and nostalgic, it is a brilliant meditation on the austere melody given out in octaves at the start of the piece. The toccata-like *"Mouvement"* ends the first set of *Images* with a marvelous challenge to the performer's touch, as Debussy calls for notes to be sustained in the middle of a fluid sixteenth-note texture, and for a chorale to emerge from a pointillistic haze.

The second set of *Images* begins with one of the most aphoristic of Debussy's pianistic utterances, *"Cloches à travers les feuilles"* ("Bells Through the Leaves"). Here, the shimmering right-hand figuration and delicate middle-voice material are wonderfully set apart from each other, creating a tonal richness that is almost orchestral. The music of the ensuing piece, *"Et la lune descend sur le temple qui fût*" ("And the Moon Descends on the Temple That Was"), evokes the Oriental world of which Debussy was greatly enamored, with a dreamy stasis and the delicate use of parallel fourths and fifths. "*Poissons d'or*" ("Gold Fish"), inspired by a Japanese lacquer panel in Debussy's workroom showing two carp swimming beneath the branch of a tree, concludes the set with tonal smears that suggest rapid, darting movement, and with trills and arpeggios to depict the glint of light off the flowing water and the shiny forms underneath.

The sultry, almost tactile imagery of Debussy's preludes embraces everything from dancing fairies to sunken cathedrals. There are 12 preludes in each of two books, published in 1910 and 1913, respectively. Allusions to a variety of popular musical styles are a feature of the first book, and in the case of "Minstrels" and "*Les collines d'Anacapri*" ("The Hills of Anacapri"), they are brought off with particular aplomb. Debussy invests some of these settings with a pastel warmth, as in the first book's oft-played "*La fille aux cheveux de lin*" ("The Girl with the Flaxen Hair"). But others, notably Book II's "*Feux d'artifice*" ("Fireworks") and Book I's "*Ce qu'a vu le vent d'ouest*" ("What the West Wind Saw"), are among the most incandescent of his pieces.

Debussy's imagery evokes sunken cathedrals.

 RECOMMENDED RECORDINGS

Paul Jacobs.
Elektra/Nonesuch 71365-2 [Images, *with* Estampes *and the* Images *of 1894] and 73031-2 [2 CDs; Preludes]*

Claudio Arrau.
Philips 432 304-2 [2 CDs; Images *and Preludes, with* Estampes; *also available separately on 420 393-2 and 420 394-2]*

Jacobs was a specialist in the piano literature of the 20th century, which Debussy could be said to have influenced more than any other figure. These

Paul Jacobs was also principal keyboard player of the New York Philharmonic.

recordings of the composer's major works remain exemplary. The playing is technically fluent and musically imaginative, and the accounts are notable not only for their penetrating insight but also for a suavity that brings each piece to scintillating life. The piano sound is slightly veiled, but warm and resonant.

Arrau's 1979 readings find him in spectacular form. They may not be the last word in spontaneity or electricity, but they possess sincerity and beauty in full measure, along with an appealing tonal richness. *"Reflets dans l'eau"* is extraordinary water music, limpid and cooling, while *"La cathédrale engloutie"* emerges as a colossal sonic sculpture, full of nobility, sensitivity, sentiment . . . and heavy breathing that makes the experience of hearing it that much more immediate. The sound is vivid.

FRANZ LISZT

PIANO SONATA IN B MINOR

*I*f one looks at the Romantic period as the era of the soloist—of Prometheus unbound—then Liszt was its hero, and his Piano Sonata in B minor the greatest work of the age. In this vast, single-movement composition, Liszt achieved a synthesis of symphonic and sonata forms that has never been surpassed for its cogency, scope, and imagination. He managed this in a work that demands the utmost from the performer in *musical* as well as technical terms, a work that in the best of accounts can spark a transcendent emotional experience in the listener.

It is sometimes difficult to see the forest for the trees in this piece. The writing is so virtuosic that the long-range relationship of motives and harmonic regions to an overall plan tends to be indistinguishable. But the plan is there, and it is superbly well executed. On one level, the work is a single-movement sonata lasting half an hour, with an exposition in three broad key areas, a development, a recapitulation, and a coda. But it can also be perceived as a four-movement symphonic structure, with the standard features of an opening allegro, an andante, a scherzo (in the form of a fugato), and a finale. To make both of these schemes work, Liszt relies on the technique of thematic transformation upon which so much of his music is based, developing the work's entire thematic material from a constellation of cells presented in the opening measures. In the foreground at any given time, there is great diversity of texture and character—enough for a true multi-movement work—but in the background, there is tremendous unity.

The grand harmonic blueprint of the work places the keys of D major and F sharp major in opposition to the central key of B minor—central in spite of the fact that there is not a single clearly stated tonic triad in B minor in the entire piece. This is one of Liszt's most insightful touches, for it makes the *presence* of B minor stronger through implication than it would be from outright statement. In the recapitulatory pages, the material associated with D and F sharp returns in B major, setting up a compelling major/minor dialectic; this has led numerous observers to conclude that Liszt had a Faustian program in mind when he wrote the work. Liszt never suggested that such a program existed, but it is hard not to believe that a contest is being played out on a vast scale between diabolic menace and celestial consolation. The quiet ending, on the same descending scale with which the work opened, is one of the great envoys in music, a closing of the circle without a conclusion.

Liszt completed the Sonata in B minor on February 2, 1853, at the height of one of the most turbulent periods in his life. The score was published the following year with a dedication to Schumann, a gesture of appreciation for Schumann's dedication to Liszt, in 1839, of the *Phantasie* in C, Op. 17.

"**F**OR THE FIRST *time in my life I beheld real inspiration—for the first time I heard the true tones of the piano. He played one of his own compositions. . . . His manipulation of the instrument was quiet and easy, and his face was simply grand . . . . When the music expressed quiet rapture or devotion, a sweet smile flitted over his features; when it was triumphant, the nostrils dilated. There was nothing petty or egoistic to mar the picture."*
—George Eliot, describing Liszt (*above*) in Weimar, August 1854

RECOMMENDED RECORDINGS

Krystian Zimerman.
Deutsche Grammophon 431 780-2 [with other works]

Alfred Brendel.
Philips 434 078-2 [with other works]

Zimerman's powerful account makes an extraordinary impression, both in its overall sweep and in its fine resolution of detail. With excellent pacing, Zimerman gives an electrifyingly virtuosic yet disciplined performance; he can take the fugato at an unbelievable clip but render it with dazzling accuracy and effect. The recording, made in the concert hall of Copenhagen's Tivoli park in 1990, is outstanding in its balance of presence and ambience.

In his latest reading of the Liszt sonata, recorded in 1991, Brendel reveals his towering mastery of the piece's complex road map and a new depth of insight into its expressive concerns. His interpretation is notable for its grip and continuity, and it becomes especially affecting in the final pages as he draws the many emotional threads together in a transcendent reverie. The account is well recorded and nicely framed by several pensive selections.

Behind Alfred Brendel's reserve lurks a wry wit.

WOLFGANG AMADEUS MOZART

PIANO SONATAS

While Mozart wrote his piano concertos mainly for himself, he conceived his piano sonatas for the home entertainment market. They do not contain his most important music and were never intended as a personal testament, the way the sonatas of Beethoven would be. Rather, they are more in the spirit of Bach and his sons—works meant for the delight and enrichment of

THE SICILIANA, *frequently encountered in the instrumental music of the 18th and 19th centuries, is typically associated with an expression of reverie or melancholy. Its characteristic dotted rhythm, set in a duple meter with triplet subdivisions (either 6/8 or 12/8), gives it a gently rocking quality that is immediately recognizable.*

the player but outstanding examples of the composer's art nonetheless.

The Sonatas in C, A, and F, K. 330–332, were long thought to have been written during Mozart's Paris sojourn of 1778. All three are now known to date from a later period—possibly from early 1781, when Mozart was in Munich preparing his opera *Idomeneo* for its premiere, or more likely from the summer of 1783, which Mozart spent in Vienna and Salzburg. The three sonatas are among Mozart's most popular keyboard works, revealing an exceptionally skillful command of the medium along with a subtle mastery of topic and style.

The C major Sonata opens with a gracious Allegro in which a highly ornamented melody flows over a cleverly varied but consistent accompaniment. The Andante is on a par with some of the composer's finest concerto movements, particularly in the passages that descend into the minor mode. In the finale as well, Mozart the concerto stylist peeks out from behind the fairly conventional disposition of material, reveling in the contrast between lighter and heavier textures and bringing drama to the play of topic.

Mozart begins the celebrated Sonata in A with one of his most extraordinary slow movements: marked *Andante grazioso*, it is a set of variations on a siciliana of bewitching beauty. Only Mozart could treat such a lovely melody to a full range of variations without ever violating its simplicity. The German composer Max Reger was so impressed that he chose the theme for his massive orchestral *Variations and Fugue on a Theme of Mozart* in 1914. Mozart follows the slow movement with a minuet of unusual subjectivity. As music critic Eric Blom has noted, it has "a frail, wistful quality that makes it as haunting a piece of Romantic piano music as anything one can think of in Schumann or Chopin." The finale is Mozart's famous *Rondo alla Turca*, an astute takeoff on the then-current rage for Turkish military music—and a fine piece of pianism to boot.

The F major Sonata is an expansive and melodious work, extroverted in character and rich in contrast. Its centerpiece is a brief, beautifully fashioned Adagio in the singing style; significantly, when the sonata was published in 1784, the movement's simple melody appeared in richly embellished form at its recapitulation. The assumption is that this was Mozart's own addition.

Mozart intended several of his late piano sonatas for young players, probably because he needed the money such pieces would bring in. Even so, the works are quite engaging—and not all that easy to play. Mozart entered the charming Sonata in C, K. 545, into his catalog of works on June 26, 1788, as "a little piano sonata for beginners." It opens with an ornamented melody that has gained universal currency today as a result of a 1939 arrangement dubbed "In an Eighteenth-Century Drawing Room." The first movement is in standard key-area form, with a wonderful "false" recapitulation (was Mozart conspiring with the beginner to upset the experienced teacher?). The Andante offers a singing melody of seamless beauty over a standard broken-chord accompaniment known as an Alberti bass, while the finale is a miniature rondo with a theme in thirds, lest the beginner's fingers get too sure of themselves.

 RECOMMENDED RECORDINGS

Georges Pludermacher.
Harmonia Mundi HMC 901373.77 [5 CDs; complete piano sonatas]

András Schiff.
London 421 109-2 [K. 330, with other works] and 421 110-2 [K. 332, with other works]

The more popular Mozart sonatas tend to get split up when pianists record the cycle, so one must pick and choose. But if one is prepared to splurge, the five-disc set from Harmonia Mundi

Style and substance combine in Pludermacher's playing.

makes excellent sense. While not well known on this side of the Atlantic, the French pianist Pludermacher is highly regarded in Europe and ranks as one of the outstanding interpreters of this repertory. In these 1991 accounts, he is captivating from the first. His playing combines a refined sense of tone with a light and articulate touch; the phrasing is insightful, the treatment of ornaments excellent. And the recording is ideal, with presence, ambience, and tonal balance very much like that of a recital.

Schiff's accounts, without calling attention to themselves, prove eminently satisfying. The playing is sure-fingered and sensitively shaped—as in Bach, so in Mozart. Though the analog recordings are somewhat distant, they nicely capture the sound of the instrument.

SERGEI RACHMANINOFF

PIANO WORKS

Rachmaninoff with best friend in 1899.

*R*achmaninoff was among the foremost pianists of his era, and a brilliant composer whose concertos and solo works for piano have become more firmly established in the repertory than those of any other 20th-century figure. He wrote nearly all of his solo piano music before emigrating from Russia in 1917, when the need to start his life over in the West and secure a steady income forced him to devote increasing amounts of his time and energy to concertizing.

Rachmaninoff's keyboard technique was formidable, and his compositions for the piano capitalize on it, exploring the instrument's full range of dynamic and expressive effects. Invariably, there is a pronounced lyricism to his writing, sometimes tender, other times grand and soaring. There is also an underlying strength of sonority; indeed, no composer has ever drawn a more powerful sound from the piano. Just as the melodies call for great sensitivity to line and nuance,

RUSSIAN MUSIC
suffered doubly during
the years of Communist
rule—from intimidation
at the hands of rabid ap-
paratchiks, which inhibited
expression and destroyed ca-
reers, and from the exodus of
talent. In addition to Rach-
maninoff, who left in 1917,
the honor roll of Russian ex-
patriate musicians includes
Stravinsky, Rostropovich,
Nikolai Medtner, and
Feodor Chaliapin.

so the chordal textures and double-octave passages of Rachmaninoff's most demanding pieces call for unbridled virtuosity.

It took Rachmaninoff years to overcome the immense popularity of his Prelude in C sharp minor, Op. 3, No. 2. Written in 1892, it defined him in the minds of many as a composer of the most melancholic and lugubrious cast—leaving a long and deleterious shadow over works that showed other sides of his creative persona. Nonetheless, the intensity of this piece gave an early indication of what Rachmaninoff could achieve in a vignette, and its promise was largely realized with the ten preludes of his Opus 23, completed in 1903. Now the composer had in mind a scheme similar to that of the Chopin preludes: a cycle that would touch on all the major and minor keys and thereby pay homage to the preludes and fugues of Bach's *The Well-Tempered Clavier*. By the time of Opus 23, Rachmaninoff had composed his Second Piano Concerto, and aspects of the concerto's warm emotional ambience can be found in some of the preludes—in the Oriental lushness of the middle section of the Prelude in G minor (No. 5), for example, and in the flowing melodic figuration of the Preludes in D and E flat (Nos. 4 and 6).

With the 13 preludes of Opus 32, composed in 1910, Rachmaninoff completed the edifice he had begun to build, without knowing it, 18 years earlier. By now he had written his Third Piano Concerto, and once again reflections of the larger work's overall style can be found among the preludes: the expressive topography has great variety, and the structural divisions and formal seams are cleverly disguised. Compared with their predecessors, these preludes are more muscular, their harmonies less luxurious and their sonority more crystalline. Among the notable works of Opus 32 are the wonderfully gentle Prelude in G (No. 5), with its charged climax on an extended trill that turns the harmony from major to minor; the somber, grandly scaled Prelude in B minor (No.

10), which like a condensed version of Rachmaninoff's symphonic poem *The Isle of the Dead* builds to a paroxysm of passion; and the Prelude in G sharp minor (No. 12), with its scintillating right-hand ostinato and a haunting left-hand melody that looks forward in mood to his *Symphonic Dances*.

The *Moments musicaux* of Opus 16 (1896) and the *Etudes-tableaux* of Opus 33 (1911) and Opus 39 (1916–17) are, like most of the preludes, meditations on a particular mood or idea that develop into powerfully concentrated character pieces. The third of the six *Moments musicaux*, a dirge in B minor, is one of Rachmaninoff's most famous piano pieces; the fifth, in D flat, shows a pronounced similarity to the textures and figurations of Chopin's *Berceuse* in the same key. Some of the more dramatic of these works—such as the sixth *Moment musical*, in C, and the *Etude-tableau* in E flat minor, Op. 39, No. 5—are in effect miniature tone poems whose heaving textures can, in the hands of a first-rate pianist, take on a truly symphonic weight.

 RECOMMENDED RECORDINGS

Ian Hobson.
Arabesque Z 6616 [24 Preludes] and Z 6609 [17 Etudes-tableaux]

Dmitri Alexeev.
Virgin Classics VCD 59289-2 [2 CDs; 24 Preludes and 6 Moments musicaux, with other works]

Hobson offers complete traversals of the preludes and the *Etudes-tableaux*, each on a single disc. Not many pianists possess the technique to confront this music convincingly; Hobson does, though he never flaunts it. What sets his accounts apart is their delicacy of tone and limpid clarity of texture. The playing is thoughtful and often beautiful, and the sound is solid.

Alexeev makes short work of even the toughest

Ian Hobson won top honors at the 1981 Leeds Competition.

of these nuts, though his overall approach is introspective and rhapsodic rather than flamboyant. The recording, made in 1987 and 1989 but not released until 1993, is lightweight and slightly distant, yet ideally atmospheric.

MAURICE RAVEL

Gaspard de la nuit

*T*he piano music of Ravel is a synthesis of numerous elements, among them the flowing figurations of his teacher, Fauré, and the virtuosic technique of Chopin and Liszt. Ravel made much of Debussy's evocative harmony, but he also pioneered certain keyboard effects that Debussy later extended, most noticeably the shimmering textures of *Jeux d'eau*, written in 1901, which influenced Debussy's "*Reflets dans l'eau*" in the first set of *Images*, from 1905. Where Debussy's works are highly spontaneous in form, Ravel's pieces tend to gravitate toward standard layouts and to be more conventionally argued.

The three-movement suite *Gaspard de la nuit* (*Gaspard of the Night*) is Ravel's most challenging piano work and one of the supreme accomplishments of musical impressionism. Composed in 1908, it takes as its point of departure three texts from Aloysius Bertrand's *Histoires vermoulues et poudreuses du Moyen Age* (*Dusty and Wormeaten Tales from the Middle Ages*), a collection of lugubrious prose poems written in the mid-19th century. The imagery of these texts inhabits the dark world of Poe and Baudelaire, favorites of the Symbolist writers who shaped turn-of-the-century French aesthetics.

The first movement, entitled "Ondine" after the fatally alluring water nymph of numerous fairy tales, depicts the spirit beckoning to the poet at his window, "flecking with drops the sonorous pane illuminated by the pale moonlight." Ravel's

The seductive water nymph Ondine beckons the poet.

THE YEARS 1902–
1919 marked a golden
age in French piano music,
during which nearly all of
Debussy's and Ravel's most
important works for the instrument—from Debussy's
Pour le piano to Ravel's Le
tombeau de Couperin—
received their premieres.
Ricardo Viñes (above, left)
a favorite interpreter of both
composers, was involved in
many of these first performances.

strikingly effective translation of this image—into
a soft, repeated-note figure recast for full chords
in the right hand—creates a shimmering stasis
that is among the more haunting inventions of
the keyboard literature.

"*Le gibet*" ("The Gallows") is the second movement, inspired by a poem about a "bell that sounds
from the walls of a town on the horizon and a
corpse dangling from the gallows, red as the
setting sun." The influence of Debussy's "*Hommage à Rameau*" from the first set of *Images* can
be felt in the way the solemn opening melody is
worked out. Softly tolling B flats throughout the
piece chillingly suggest the funereal bell.

Concluding *Gaspard* is "Scarbo," a portrait of a
mean-spirited medieval dwarf. "How often," the
poem states, "have I seen him drop from the
ceiling, pirouette on one foot, and roll across the
room like the bobbin of a witch's distaff." With
its fiendish hand-crossings and wicked repeated-
note figures broken out into octaves, Ravel's texture aptly personifies the spinning dwarf. The
pianistic model is Russian composer Mily Balakirev's *Islamey*, then considered the most difficult
piece ever written for the instrument. In "Scarbo,"
Ravel made a conscious effort to write an even
more difficult piece, and succeeded.

 RECOMMENDED RECORDINGS

Ivo Pogorelich.
Deutsche Grammophon 413 363-2 [with Prokofiev:
Sonata No. 6]

André Laplante.
Elan CD 2232 [with other works]

Pogorelich's is the most nocturnal performance
of *Gaspard* on disc: demonic, haunting, full of the
malevolent night magic Ravel meant to depict. It
is the kind of performance Ravel would never

have heard from a French pianist—marked by an astonishing spontaneity, yet with an authority that suggests everything has been thought through. At certain points, especially in the phrasing and articulation of "Ondine," the pianist goes out on the most extreme of interpretive limbs. But his originality is unfailingly engaging, and his sensitivity to the music's imagery and mood is exquisite.

Coupling *Gaspard* with the *Valses nobles et sentimentales*, *Menuet antique*, and *Sonatine*, the Laplante CD is the best single-disc collection of Ravel's piano music in the catalog. Laplante's graceful playing, sensitive rubato, and expressive flair are great assets. The 1989 recording is intimate, yet it does not crowd in too closely, offering a satisfying concert-hall perspective.

DOMENICO SCARLATTI

KEYBOARD SONATAS

Domenico Scarlatti at the harpsichord.

Scarlatti (1685–1757), whose father, Alessandro Scarlatti, was one of the leading opera composers of the Baroque era, was born in Naples the same year as Bach and Handel. The younger Scarlatti was to find his own natural expression not in opera or chamber music but at the keyboard—and not in Italy but on the Iberian peninsula. He was 34 when he left Italy to take up duties in Lisbon as music master to the eldest daughter of King John V of Portugal, the Infanta María Bárbara de Braganza. When in 1728 María Bárbara married the heir to the Spanish throne, Scarlatti went with her—first to Seville, later to Madrid, where he spent the rest of his life.

The Palace of Aranjuéz, the primary residence of King Fernando VI and Queen María Bárbara, became the seat of a thriving musical establishment, at the center of which stood Scarlatti and the great Italian castrato Carlo Broschi, known as Farinelli. María Bárbara's interest in music, and her remarkable talent as both a harpsichordist

Musical Dynasties

The Scarlattis, father and son, reigned in turn over opera in Italy and keyboard music on the Iberian peninsula. Bach and his four composer sons were the culmination of the musical hegemony of the Bach family in Germany. In France, Louis Couperin and nephew François Couperin dominated keyboard music for nearly a century, while in Austria, three generations of Mozarts left their mark as composers.

and—judging from the instruments she owned—a pianist, was the stimulus that drew from Scarlatti the great work of his career, more than 500 single-movement keyboard sonatas. Under the queen's patronage, these were copied and bound, the collection eventually running to 15 volumes.

Though nearly all in two-part form, these sonatas show an extraordinary range of color, mood, and effect. There is an identifiably Spanish cast to many, whether from their dance rhythms, flamenco inflections, strummed-guitar like textures, or actual Spanish melodies. Some of the sonatas focus on striking, often peculiar harmonies, which Scarlatti found far more interesting than conventional counterpoint; other pieces rely on repeated rhythmic figures or ornaments, such as the persistent trilling and tolling of the Sonata in D minor, K. 516. Most important, while a few of the sonatas are technically easy, perhaps intended for María Bárbara's children, the majority often call for rapid hand-crossings, sudden jumps, and high-velocity fingerwork. These outward expressions of brio, along with the inner vitality of the musical ideas themselves, make Scarlatti's sonatas appealing to performers and listeners alike.

 RECOMMENDED RECORDINGS

Vladimir Horowitz.
CBS Masterworks MK 42410 [17 sonatas]

András Schiff.
London 421 422-2 [15 sonatas]

Rafael Puyana.
Harmonia Mundi HMC 901164.65 [2 CDs; 30 sonatas]

The Scarlatti sonatas were Horowitz's calling cards, and his recordings of them remain among his greatest contributions to the catalog. The playing is smooth and sensuous, the dynamic gradations remarkably delicate, highlighting the Italianate

With his lapidary touch, Horowitz made jewels of Scarlatti sonatas.

temperament of the pieces. Horowitz has no hesitation about using the sustaining pedal, but when he does, it is always to good effect. The sound of these 1962–68 recordings is dry, and there are some noticeable splices, but the overall quality is more than acceptable.

Where Horowitz revels in Scarlatti's lightness, Schiff draws attention to the composer's darker tones. His playing is big-boned and sonorous, yet rhythms are well sprung. The interpretive emphasis is on sentiment rather than surface appeal, and one finds a certain wistfulness, even a melancholy aspect, to some of the readings. London's 1987 recording has a nicely distant pickup that places the listener in seats midway back in an empty hall, rather than inside the lid of Schiff's piano, and there is good depth to the sound.

These sonatas acquire entirely different personalities on the harpsichord, and Puyana's treatment of them is supremely dignified. The Colombian-born virtuoso emphasizes sonority and color, exhibiting a preference for the more substantial sonatas and bringing a truly Spanish sultriness and swagger to his interpretations. He plays on a German three-manual instrument from 1740, a real battleship of a harpsichord, employing different manuals to achieve varied tone and weight. The analog recording, made in 1984, does full justice to these regal accounts of works written for a queen.

FRANZ SCHUBERT

Piano Sonatas

*I*n the piano literature of the 19th century, only the late sonatas of Schubert and the B minor Sonata of Liszt stand on the same exalted plane as the great sonatas of Beethoven. Schubert's interest in the genre, like Beethoven's, extended from the beginning of his career to the end—though in Schubert's case a mere 13 years separate his earliest essays, the unfinished works of 1815 in C and E, from the three sonatas of 1828 that bring the canon to a close. Viewed from this perspective, the formal mastery and emotional depth of the late sonatas become all the more remarkable.

The final two, in A and B flat, D. 959 and 960, represent the summit of Schubert's achievement as a composer for the piano. Both are four-movement sonatas of symphonic length, in the same manner as Beethoven's *Hammerklavier* though certainly not from the same mold. Their rhapsodic lines of action and their unique affective combination of turbulence and tranquility arise from a profoundly original concept of the purpose of the sonata—namely, the gradual revelation of an inner world, unfolded at "heavenly length" in an essentially intimate manner.

Both sonatas have broad opening movements characterized by an almost prodigal flow of ideas, frequent minor-key coloration, and a propensity for striking modulations. The two are distinctly different in mood, however; the A major Sonata's Allegro is upbeat, even restless, while the B flat Sonata's *Molto moderato* is haunting and otherworldly, at times bleak. And in their development sections, the former concerns itself almost entirely with a single two-measure subject that appears just before the end of the exposition, while the latter weaves a rich tapestry out of the exposition's two main themes, ultimately allowing them to dissolve away to nothing. The scale of both movements is immense; in performances where the exposition repeat is observed, the first movement of the Sonata in B flat can last more than 20 minutes.

The slow movements of the two works are extended, songlike structures with subdued opening and closing sections and more dramatic interludes. Of particular interest is the earlier sonata's melancholy Andantino in F sharp minor, where the outer pages enclose an exceptionally violent section marked by stabbing chordal screams.

AN UNFORGETTABLE *feat of musicianship occurred on August 11, 1978, when the Czech pianist Rudolph Firkusny played Schubert's Sonata in B flat to an audience that could hear him but not see him. A thunderstorm had knocked out power at the University of Maryland midway through the first half of the pianist's recital, but Firkusny had kept playing. After the intermission, he began the 40-minute sonata in complete blackness. He did not miss a note.*

The paws that refresh: Schubert gets moral support as he composes.

The other sonata's bittersweet Andante, in C sharp minor, opens and closes with a feeling between resignation and quiet desperation, though its tone becomes more urgent in its A major midsection. Both sonatas have vivid scherzos and well-developed rondo finales. The scherzo of the Sonata in A is particularly delightful in its Chopinesque grace, the finale of the B flat Sonata especially appealing for its ambiguous stance halfway between major and minor.

The "little" Sonata in A, D. 664, is the most gracious and lyrical of Schubert's piano sonatas. Traditionally dated to 1819, it may actually have been written in 1825. The opening movement, with its memorably sweet main theme, is entirely serene except for an outburst of strenuous octave scales in the development. The Andante has a mystical, yearning quality that looks ahead to Wagner's *Wesendonk Lieder*, while the finale seems to look toward Mozart in its lilting enthusiasm—though the dreamy pensiveness is entirely Schubert's.

 RECOMMENDED RECORDINGS

Murray Perahia.
CBS Masterworks MK 44569 [D. 959, with Schumann: Sonata in G minor, Op. 22]

Alfred Brendel.
Philips 422 229-2 [D. 959, with other works], 422 062-2 [D. 960, with Wanderer Fantasy], *and 410 605-2 [D. 664, with Sonata in A minor, D. 537]*

Wilhelm Kempff.
Deutsche Grammophon 423 496-2 [7 CDs; complete piano sonatas]

Perahia's interpretation of the Sonata in A is one of extraordinary tonal beauty, and it does justice to both the impetuosity and the gentleness of Schubert's writing. In the dramatic Andantino,

Perahia is particularly striking. The account, dating from 1987, is very well recorded.

In Brendel's most recent recordings of the sonatas, made in 1987–88, the relation of these works to both the sonatas of Beethoven and Schubert's own earlier works is clear enough, though one occasionally feels Brendel is more concerned with detail than with poetry and passion. In any case, the approach to the late sonatas is philosophical and solicitous; much like a doctor in a lab coat, Brendel listens to their heartbeat, takes their pulse, doesn't say much, and lets the music speak for itself. The sound is good. Meanwhile, in his early digital recording of the little A major Sonata, D. 664, Brendel is at his very best. There is a softness and a Biedermeier delicacy to the interpretation that provoke delight with every hearing.

Kempff's are flowing, magisterial readings of the sonatas, which sound as if he were making them up on the spot. Tone and phrasing take on the quality of song here as with no other interpreter—and while the approach is essentially meditative, there is always an extroversion to balance the introspection. The accounts of the late works are unsurpassed in their eloquence, and even in the little A major Sonata the dynamic shadings and phrasing are exquisite. Kempff's touch is lapidary, which the 1965 recordings of the late sonatas convey with uncanny fidelity; indeed, in the B flat, it sounds as if the piano is in your living room, somewhere behind your speakers. All of the sonatas were recorded at the Beethovensaal in Hanover, Germany, between 1965 and 1969, and it should be noted that some of the later sessions have rather shallow sonics. Even so, if one is willing to splurge on seven midprice CDs, this set is worth the investment.

A S AN INTERPRETER, *Wilhelm Kempff saw music in context. Raised in the rich cultural and intellectual soil of Wilhelmine Prussia, he studied philosophy and music history at the University of Berlin. He could relate the emotional world of a Schubert sonata to feelings expressed in Goethe's poetry, or explain its structure using analogies drawn from classical architecture, as easily and convincingly as he could phrase a singing line at the piano.*

ROBERT SCHUMANN

PIANO WORKS

*T*he piano was for Schumann, as for Chopin, an extension of himself, and Schumann wrote for the instrument with an innate sense of how it sounded and what it could do. The powerful chordal textures he loved were not an attempt to turn the piano into an orchestra, nor were they intended as demonstrations of pianistic brilliance, as Liszt's often were. Rather, they were meant to take full advantage of the sonority of the grand piano, to create a textural richness and a tonal weight that together, in Schumann's mind at least, represented an ideal.

Nearly all of Schumann's piano music is referential, an attempt to embody emotions aroused by the experience of literature or to characterize real or imaginary beings and their interaction in some ongoing novel or lyric poem of the mind. One of the composer's favorite conceits was the *Davidsbund* (The Society of David), peopled by imaginary characters who, like the Biblical David, had decided to stand up to the artistic Philistines of the day. The members of this society included the impetuous extrovert Florestan and the studious introvert Eusebius, reflecting two sides of Schumann's own character, as well as a figure called Meister Raro, who may have represented Schumann's teacher and future father-in-law, Friedrich Wieck. When writing music in the spirit of Eusebius, Schumann would affect a gentle lyricism seemingly scented with violets; when moved by the spirit of Florestan, he would create propulsive rhythms, brisk tempos, and bolts of pianistic lightning. Most of Schumann's compositions for the piano are emotional journeys with these two alter egos at the wheel.

The bold opening chords of *Carnaval*, Op. 9, are among the most famous in the piano literature. The piece, completed in 1835 and given the full name *Carnaval: Scènes mignonnes sur quatre*

Schumann's two alter egos emerge in his piano works.

SCHUMANN never became the virtuoso pianist he hoped to be, owing to a neuro-muscular dysfunction of the index and middle fingers of his right hand. It is not known whether the problem resulted from Schumann's use of a mechanical splint to try to strengthen the right hand, or from mercury poisoning related to treatment for syphilis, which he may have contracted in his teens.

notes (*Carnival: Pretty Scenes on Four Notes*), consists of 21 short numbers, all of which have titles. There are portraits of Florestan and Eusebius and of characters from the commedia dell'arte (Pierrot, Harlequin, Pantalon, and Colombine), as well as a pair of very appealing cameos devoted to two other composers, Chopin and Paganini, the former piece quite striking in the way it captures Chopin's nocturnal sound and style. Schumann also includes a characterization of the 15-year-old Clara Wieck ("Chiarina"), whom he would marry in 1840, as well as one of his current fiancée, then just 18, Ernestine von Fricken ("Estrella"). Ernestine is the key to the piece, for she had been born in the town of Asch in Bohemia, and the four notes on which *Carnaval* is based are the four whose German names spell that out: A, E flat, C, B natural (A, Es, C, H). The writing in *Carnaval* is brilliantly inventive, the character of individual numbers so artfully varied that the waltzlike feeling of the piece as a whole never grows monotonous.

The Symphonic Etudes, Op. 13, composed in 1834–37, are masterly variations on a square-cut funeral march in C sharp minor, a theme written by fiancée Ernestine's father, Baron von Fricken, an amateur flutist. Here is Schumann in one of his rare nonprogrammatic moods. His writing is of a high order throughout, fanciful and probing, much of it technically demanding. The mercurial shifts of mood between variations, from solemn to capricious, from fiery to sweetly lyrical, make the work one of Schumann's most engaging, while the score's archlike formal structure is indeed symphonic in its strength.

For his *Kreisleriana*, Op. 16, Schumann turned for inspiration to the music criticism of E.T.A. Hoffmann. The work gets its name from the Hoffmann character of Johannes Kreisler, a conductor who suffered from visions and in whom Schumann saw a reflection of himself. Cast as a set of eight fantasies and composed in just four days in April, 1838, the work is Schumann's most subjective piano piece. The opening vignette captures a mood of turbulent passion; subsequent fantasies touch on anxiety, despair, grotesquery, and Romantic longing, now and then escaping into soaring lyricism and a haunting meditative oblivion. The piece is dedicated to Chopin.

 RECOMMENDED RECORDINGS

Youri Egorov.
EMI Studio CDM 69537 [Kreisleriana, *with* Noveletten, *Op. 21, Nos. 1 and 8*]

Artur Rubinstein.
RCA Red Seal 5667-2 [Carnaval, *with other works*]

Maurizio Pollini.
Deutsche Grammophon 410 916-2 [Symphonic Etudes, with Arabeske, *Op. 18]*

Pianists who succeed at Schumann must possess a philosophical seriousness but also an ability to respond to emotions in the music, to let go when appropriate. And they must be masters of tone. Egorov, a drug addict who died of AIDS in 1988, was such a pianist. His *Kreisleriana* is an interpretation of profound sensitivity, fully thought through yet charged with spontaneity. The playing is powerful, but gentle at the same time. The 1978 recording captures the performance with optimal weight, warmth, and clarity.

Like his Chopin, Rubinstein's Schumann has an undeniable charm. The vignettes of *Carnaval* are sketched here with consummate skill, the pianist's flair for characterization apparent in every one. The 1962–63 recording is rather veiled, but Rubinstein's lovely tone manages to come through.

Pollini's account of the Symphonic Etudes offers an ideal balance of symphonic concentration and tonal allure. Architecture is confidently rendered, expression superbly gauged. The recording, from 1984, is sonorous and solidly imaged.

Pollini takes Schumann out of the hothouse and places him in the avant-garde of the 1830s.

SACRED AND CHORAL MUSIC

*T*he relationship between music and ritual has been close
throughout history and among all peoples. It has been
particularly close in the case of Western classical music, which
developed from the plainchant of the Roman Catholic Church. According to medieval legend, the chant melodies were miraculously
transmitted by the Holy Spirit to Pope Gregory the Great (540–
604), who in turn dictated them to a scribe; this is the reason Catholic plainchant is often referred to as Gregorian chant. In reality,
Gregory made decrees governing the use of chant which eventually
led to the development of a system of written notation by which the
chant melodies could be preserved. This style of notation, using
shaped notes called "neumes," was transformed during the supposedly dark Middle Ages into the staff-and-clef notation still in use
today, opening the door to the creation of a vast body of written
music whose complexity has spurred centuries of stylistic growth
and renewal.

Along with the invention of notation came a breakthrough of
equal importance in the way music was conceived. This was the advent, around 1200, of polyphony, the simultaneous sounding of

multiple melodic lines. Polyphony created a new dimension in music, a vertical one in which the relationship between separate strands of sound produced harmony and a sense of space. It was one of the great artistic achievements of the Middle Ages, and has been the basis of nearly all Western classical music.

By this time, skilled choirs had become a fixture of medieval worship, and composers had begun to make choral settings of the principal sections of the mass—called the "ordinary" and consisting of the Kyrie, Gloria, Credo, Sanctus, and Agnus Dei. The psalms and many other sacred texts received similar treatment. The chorus was among the most potent weapons of the Reformation and the Counter Reformation, ultimately a more persuasive one than gunpowder or the Inquisition.

The next major step in the development of choral music was taken during the Baroque era, when the orchestra, a secular body, joined forces with the chorus and added its weight and color to the vocal sonority. This brought a new flowering of choral composition and gave rise to such genres as the cantata and oratorio, usually calling for solo singers, chorus, and orchestra. The former, originally a secular genre, was eventually appropriated by the Lutheran Church; the latter, originally a sacred genre, reached its apogee outside the church as a substitute for opera.

In the 18th and 19th centuries, the mass underwent a process of secularization. Where earlier composers had sought to create a kind of spiritual reflection of its text, those of the Enlightenment and the Romantic era focused primarily on its implicit theatricality. This was particularly true of the Requiem, which in the hands of Berlioz and Verdi was fashioned into some of the most operatic pages in the literature of Romanticism. In this century, the need for belief has been strong and has produced sacred works of great intensity and power, such as Janáček's *Slavonic Mass* and Britten's *War Requiem*. Even in its questioning, much 20th-century choral music continues in the service of the ritual that gave it birth.

JOHANN SEBASTIAN BACH

CANTATAS NOS. 140 AND 147

BACH was surely the hardest-working composer who ever lived. In an average week during his years in Leipzig, he was expected to compose a 30-minute cantata, supervise the copying of its parts, rehearse it, and perform it on Sunday; to furnish music as required for feast days and special events such as weddings and funerals; and to attend to the musical training of 50-plus boarding students at the Thomasschule.

*O*ne of Bach's chief responsibilities as Kantor in Leipzig was to compose cantatas for the Sundays and feast days of the church calendar. During the years 1723–29 he composed four complete cycles of about 60 cantatas each, along with a number of individual settings for special occasions; it is believed he wrote a fifth cycle during the 1730s. While many of these cantatas have been lost, approximately 200 survive.

Bach's earliest cantatas date from his years as church organist in Mülhausen and include the celebrated cantata for Easter Sunday *Christ lag in Todes Banden* (*Christ Lay in the Bonds of Death*), composed around 1708. Another 20 cantatas survive from Bach's second period in Weimar (1708–17) and show the composer experimenting with a number of approaches to form and instrumentation. Bach concentrated on secular cantatas while in Cöthen (1717–23), but with his arrival in Leipzig he plunged into the composition of sacred cantatas with an energy that is remarkable even for him, averaging better than one a week for the first two years he was there. The Leipzig cantatas are the largest unified body of work by a major composer in the history of music, and they contain some of Bach's most inspired writing.

He wrote Cantata No. 140, *Wachet auf, ruft uns die Stimme* ("Awake," the Voice Calls Us), in 1731 for the 27th Sunday after Trinity, a date in the church calendar that occurs only if Easter falls extremely early. The chorale *Wachet auf* upon which the work is based was composed by the 16th-century German mystic poet Philipp Nicolai, whose text draws its imagery from the parable of the wise virgins and their heavenly bridegroom in the Gospel of Matthew.

Bach's treatment of the sumptuously scored opening chorus relies heavily on pictorialism and numerical symbolism. At the words *"sehr hoch"*

Cantata performance during Bach's era.

("high up"), Bach runs the tenors and basses to the top of their range; later, with the proclamation *"steht auf"* ("arise"), the vocal parts leap upward, and at the words *"wo, wo?"* ("where, where?") the chorus repeats itself uncertainly, as though lost—all typical of Bach's virtuosity at musical scene painting. Even more impressive is the way he transforms the underlying notion of "Trinity" into a pervasive element of the chorus's musical structure, inspired not only by the church season for which the cantata was intended, but also by the number of the specific Sunday involved, 27, which is 3 cubed. Bach casts the piece in the key of E flat (three flats) with a time signature of 3/4, utilizes a three-part form, and scores the setting for three groups with three parts in each group: two oboes and one oboe da caccia; first violins, second violins, and violas; and altos, tenors, and basses. (By design, the parts that have the *cantus firmus*, or "fixed melody"—the actual chorale tune as it appears in the composition—stand outside this scheme. They are the solo horn, employed here by Bach because it is the night watchman's traditional instrument, and the choral sopranos.)

It is the expressive beauty of the music here and in the remainder of the work that leaves the strongest impression. The most celebrated part of the cantata is the flowing chorale setting for tenors, *Zion hört die Wächter singen* (*Zion Hears the Watchmen Singing*), warmly accompanied by the three string parts playing in unison (another illustration of the Trinity). A real test piece for the choral tenors, it begins comfortably in the middle of their range but, as the watchmen's singing prompts "the heart to leap for joy," rises quickly to a high G.

Bach's Cantata No. 147, *Herz und Mund und Tat und Leben* (*Heart and Mouth and Deed and Life*), was composed in 1723 for the Feast of the Visitation. The scoring is especially rich, calling for obbligato solos from the trumpet, violin, cello, oboe d'amore, and two oboes da caccia. Four of the cantata's ten numbers are set to words by Salomo Franck,

Bach's favorite Weimar librettist, whose texts are among the finest and most penetrating of all those Bach employed.

Based on the Gospel of Luke, the cantata tells of Mary's visit to her cousin Elizabeth, who is soon to be the mother of John the Baptist. The highlight of the story comes when the unborn John kicks because he recognizes the presence of the unborn Jesus. Here Bach has the muffled sound of the oboes da caccia depict the unborn cousins. The use of the solo trumpet in the cantata's opening chorus and in the bass aria "*Ich will von Jesu Wunder singen*" ("I will sing of Jesus's miracles") is appropriate to the cantata's focus on John, who was to become "the voice crying in the wilderness" proclaiming the arrival of the Savior. The chorales ending the first and second parts of the cantata share the music known to English-speaking people as *Jesu, Joy of Man's Desiring*.

RECOMMENDED RECORDINGS

Ruth Holton, Michael Chance, Anthony Rolfe Johnson, Stephen Varcoe; Monteverdi Choir, English Baroque Soloists/ John Eliot Gardiner.
Deutsche Grammophon Archiv 431 809-2

Edith Mathis, Peter Schreier, Dietrich Fischer-Dieskau; Munich Bach Orchestra & Chorus/ Karl Richter.
Deutsche Grammophon Galleria 419 466-2
[Cantata No. 140, with Magnificat, BWV 243]

Gardiner's disc provides the perfect introduction to two of Bach's most frequently recorded cantatas. The interpretations are spirited and insightful, and the clarity of the orchestral texture allows the inner details of Bach's scoring to emerge. The solo vocalists in these 1990 accounts are stylish, the instrumental obbligatos beautifully

BACH COMPOSED *many cantatas for courtly or civic occasions. Among the most delightful of these is Cantata No. 211,* Schweigt stille, plaudert nicht (Be Quiet, Stop Chattering), *known as the* Coffee Cantata. *It takes up a standard comic-opera situation, but this time it's about a father and his coffee-crazed daughter—a reference to the then escalating drinking habit in Europe, recently adopted from the Turks.*

polished. It is all captured in naturally balanced digital sound.

In comparison with today's more scholarly practitioners, Richter reflects the grand manner, though his performances still convey a sense of elevation that few interpreters of any school have approached. His tempos are uniformly broader than Gardiner's in Cantata No. 140, his delivery far more weighty, but there remains much vitality to the reading, which was initially released in 1979 and sounds lovely on this budget-priced CD. The coupling is a vibrant though somewhat grainy 1962 account of the Magnificat.

Bach expected three or four heavenly singers to a part, as in this Memling triptych (detail).

St. Matthew Passion, BWV 244

*J*ust as there are Christian themes that have inspired frequent treatment in art—the Annunciation, the Nativity, the Last Supper, and the Crucifixion—there are key Christian texts that have received frequent settings in music. Those dealing with the Crucifixion and the events leading up to it are certainly the most common. Western composers have sought to dramatize this central moment in Christianity in a variety of ways, often by treating specific aspects of it, such as Christ's soul-searching on the Mount of Olives or His Seven Last Words from the Cross. When the whole story of Christ's final days is told, using the text of one of the four Gospels as the primary source, the setting is generally referred to as a passion.

The obituary notice published at the time of Bach's death credited him with having composed five passions, but only two have come down to us in their entirety. One is the *St. John Passion*, BWV 245. The other, fortunately, is the setting that members of Bach's own family called "the Great Passion": the *St. Matthew Passion*, composed in 1727 and probably first performed that year on Good Friday. It is gigantic in conception, calling

NUMEROLOGY *plays a significant part in the* St. Matthew Passion. *One celebrated example is the chorus* "Herr, bin ich's?" ("Lord, is it I?"), *which consists of 11 entries of the phrase, one for each of the disciples but Judas. On a larger scale, the score includes 14 solo arias and 14 chorales, an allusion to the 14 Stations of the Cross.*

One of Bach's organs.

for double orchestra, double chorus, and half a dozen soloists, and consisting of 68 separate numbers, many of them in several sections. Bach uses every manner of text-setting common to the sacred music of his day—including recitative, arioso, aria, chorus, and chorale—and treats each with extraordinary finesse. The structure operates on three levels simultaneously. The actual story of the passion is related in the recitatives and in many of the settings for chorus, with the choristers representing the bystanders of Biblical days. The emotional significance of the story is examined in a series of poetic meditations set as arias, from the viewpoint of the devout Christian of any age. And the participatory response of the Lutheran congregation of Bach's own day is conveyed in the chorales.

The actual words of the Evangelist (St. Matthew) and Jesus are set as recitative for tenor and bass soloists, respectively. Following a custom honored by both Heinrich Schütz and Georg Philipp Telemann, Bach places a "halo" of string sound around the words of Jesus—which is pointedly extinguished at the words *"Eli, Eli, lama asabthani?"* ("My God, my God, why hast Thou forsaken me?"). The score is full of such effects. When Jesus climbs the Mount of Olives, the bass line precedes him, and when He says *"Ich werde den Hirten schlagen, und die Schafe der Herde werden sich zerstreuen"* ("I will smite the shepherd, and the sheep of the flock shall be scattered abroad"), the strings are sent scurrying in all directions. Scene painting abounds in the arias as well. Teardrops are portrayed by repeated descending figures in the flutes in the alto's *"Buss und Reu"* ("Grief and remorse"), while in the tenor's *"Ich will bei meinem Jesu wachen"* (the disciple Peter's "I would stand watch beside my Lord") the oboe gives out an ornamented version of a town watchman's horn call, and the chorus answers *"So schlafen unsre Sünden ein"* ("So all our sins will fall asleep"), singing it ten times—once for each of the other disciples (except the absent Judas).

More than anything else, it is the diversity, emotional depth, and gentle yet precise point of the arias that place the *St. Matthew Passion* on the highest plane of sacred art. The pathos of the alto's *"Erbarme dich, mein Gott"* ("Have mercy, Lord"), in which a dignified sarabande rhythm and chaconne bass are fused with an intensely expressive obbligato violin solo, is unmatched anywhere in music. While none of the other arias surpasses it in feeling, each one is a masterpiece of design and content. Indeed, there is hardly a page of this score that does not contribute something to the sublime effect of the whole.

RECOMMENDED RECORDINGS

Peter Pears, Dietrich Fischer-Dieskau, Elisabeth Schwarzkopf, Christa Ludwig, Nicolai Gedda, Walter Berry; Philharmonia Orchestra & Choir/ Otto Klemperer.
EMI CDMC 63058 [3 CDs]

Anthony Rolfe Johnson, Andreas Schmidt, Barbara Bonney, Ann Monoyios, Anne Sofie von Otter, Michael Chance, Howard Crook, Olaf Bär, Cornelius Hauptmann; Monteverdi Choir, London Oratory Junior Choir, English Baroque Soloists/ John Eliot Gardiner.
Deutsche Grammophon Archiv 427 648-2 [3 CDs]

Peter Schreier, Theo Adam, Lucia Popp, Marjana Lipovšek, Eberhard Büchner, Robert Holl; Leipzig Radio Chorus, Staatskapelle Dresden/Peter Schreier.
Philips 412 527-2 [3 CDs]

6'4" Klemperer towered over others; his Bach interpretations have similar stature.

There is a quality to the Klemperer account that eludes description but has something to do with experience. When the recording was made

IN 1736, FOR WHAT *was probably the third performance of the* St. Matthew Passion, *Bach made an immaculate copy of the score (above) with ruler and compass, using red ink for the recitatives of the Evangelist to set off the divine gospel from the rest of the text. Bach's effort, an outstanding example of musical calligraphy, shows how important the piece was to him.*

in 1961, it had been 16 years since the end of World War II. The participants in this performance had an understanding of suffering, loss, deliverance, pity, and the acceptance of all things in faith—along with first-hand knowledge of the worst and the best in the human spirit. Klemperer's approach is heroic, yet suffused with tenderness and devotional sincerity. With its extraordinary lineup of soloists, inspired playing by the Philharmonia, and genuine participatory feeling of the choral numbers, this performance—from first note to last—gently blows one away. The recording shows some edits and contains some noise but is impressive nonetheless (as in the placement of the two choruses). At midprice, it is well worth having.

Gardiner's reading is conceived and executed on the highest level, an example of period practice that is unlikely to be bettered any time soon. The performance vibrates with life; soloists are first-rate, and wonderfully well chosen for their respective parts, and the choristers and orchestra are exemplary. The recording, made in 1988 in the spacious ambience of The Maltings, Snape, is well balanced and exceptionally vivid.

The 1984 account from Schreier and his German forces is a triumph. Beautifully performed and impressively recorded, it exemplifies an enlightened approach to interpretation in which the lessons of scholarship are judiciously applied to performance on modern instruments. Tempos are dance-like, and textures are lighter, less stately. Schreier is superb not only as the Evangelist but as conductor, presiding over an intimate performance that is not so much an archetype as an immediate reflection on the music.

Title page of the first published score of the B minor Mass.

MASS IN B MINOR, BWV 232

*T*he Mass in B minor stands as lofty in design, scope, and expression as anything written by the hand of man. It is one of several instances in the music of Bach of a piece created as an ideal type, rather than for practical use. As such it represents an attempt both to summarize the tradition of the mass in a single perfect specimen and to leave a statement on the nature of sacred music as a bequest to the future.

Most of the work's component parts date from various times in Bach's long residence in Leipzig; they were assembled to form a complete mass only near the end of his life. The earliest section is the Sanctus, from 1724. The Kyrie and Gloria are taken from a 1733 mass that Bach dedicated to the electoral court of Saxony at Dresden. The last major addition was the *Symbolum Nicenum*, or Credo; the keystone to the whole archlike structure, and itself a wonderfully symmetrical arch, it was written in 1748–49. Bach never heard the work in its entirety. Yet in spite of the fact that it represents a collection of movements in diverse styles, including some deliberately archaic elements, the Mass in B minor transcends the inconsistency of its origins. There is a powerful unity in its harmonic logic and overall plan, as well as compelling beauty in the music itself.

Following the model of the Neapolitan cantata mass, the score is divided like an opera into choral and solo numbers, 27 in all. The pillars of the work are the nine massive choruses of praise in D major, with their celebratory trumpets and drums. Between them Bach strings a variety of choruses, arias, and duets, some with obbligato instrumental solos. It is worth noting that as constructed, the B minor Mass lends itself neither to the standard Catholic liturgy nor to the Lutheran; as musicologist Karl Geiringer has pointed out, it reflects "a more ecumenical attitude."

The contrast of style and treatment Bach achieves

Singers in a small Baroque choir.

throughout the mass is as remarkable as the work's underlying expressive unity. In the second *"Kyrie eleison,"* for example, he harks back to the Netherlandish polyphony of the 16th century, while in the eight-part setting of *"Osanna in excelsis,"* the model is the Venetian double-choir style of the early 17th century. A motet-like *cantus firmus* technique is applied in the choral writing of the *"Credo in unum Deum"* and the *"Confiteor."* Serene diatonic harmony underscores the restful message of the *"Dona nobis pacem,"* while dissonance and intense chromaticism serve to convey the stabbing pain of the *"Crucifixus."*

The *"Crucifixus"* stands at the absolute center of the Credo and of the mass itself, just as the Crucifixion stands at the center of Christian faith. Its walking, chaconne-style bass line quite literally makes the sign of the cross 13 times on the page of music, going from the E below to the E above the middle line of the staff and then sinking by half-steps to B. But while this deep lament is the center of gravity in the mass, it is the "joyful noise" of the *"Et resurrexit"* chorus immediately following—where the singers often sound as if they are laughing in ecstasy—that marks the spiritual apogee of the work, and of Bach's entire life as a musician.

FOR MANY YEARS, *huge choruses were assembled to sing this music, compromising clarity of articulation and texture. More recently, interpreters have suggested the choral numbers be performed with one singer to a part. Bach would have expected the choral sections to be sung with three or four voices to a part. Conductor Robert Shaw put the one-to-a-part fallacy to rest with the observation that when three trumpets are playing, no one can hear the singers.*

 RECOMMENDED RECORDINGS

Monteverdi Choir, English Baroque Soloists/ John Eliot Gardiner.
Deutsche Grammophon Archiv 415 514-2 [2 CDs]

Arleen Augér, Ann Murray, Marjana Lipovšek, Peter Schreier, Anton Scharinger; Leipzig Radio Chorus, Staatskapelle Dresden/Peter Schreier.
Philips 432 972-2 [2 CDs]

Gardiner's account has all the virtues of a well-done period-instrument rendition—flow, clarity, color—yet conveys the grandeur and weight that are essential to Bach's conception, thereby combining the best of the new and the traditional. There is excellent choral work from the Monteverdi Choir, singing four or five to a part. The soloists, chosen from the ranks of the choir, have soft voices but are well blended and can always be distinguished over the chorus. The "*Christe eleison*" duet from Lynne Dawson and Carol Hall is particularly lovely. The 1985 recording is open, clear, and spacious.

The balance between chamber-sized detail and large-scale architecture is well gauged by Schreier, whose modern-instrument reading shows a firm grasp of period style. The approach is light and animated, and in the spirit of Karl Richter, Schreier gets chorus and soloists—of whom he is one—to soar through Bach's realm of text-made-sound with conviction and lucidity. The Dresden orchestra plays magnificently; the 1991 digital recording is solid and satisfyingly vivid.

LUDWIG VAN BEETHOVEN
MISSA SOLEMNIS IN D, OP. 123

Beethoven with Missa Solemnis *score, 1820 portrait by Stieler.*

*T*he compositional task Beethoven set himself in the *Missa Solemnis* was unusually far-reaching: to recapture the essence of the "true church music" of Palestrina and the Netherlandish polyphonists, and to combine its radiant spirituality with the expressive power of Classical symphonic argument, which Beethoven himself had raised to its greatest heights.

The influence of the old church style can be detected in Beethoven's harmonic language (the Credo's a cappella proclamation of "*Et resurrexit tertia die secundum Scripturas*" is a striking example) and in the continuity of the individual movements of the mass. Beyond this, Beethoven interjected a personal note into the liturgy by infusing his

ON A VISIT to
Beethoven in August
1819, Schindler heard "the
master singing parts of the
fugue in the Credo—sing-
ing, howling, stamping. . . .
[The] door opened and
Beethoven stood before us
with distorted features. He
looked as if he had been in
mortal combat with the whole
host of contrapuntists, his ev-
erlasting enemies. . . . Never,
it may be said, did so great a
work as the Missa Solemnis
see its creation under more
adverse circumstances."

setting with an unprecedented degree of dramatic
tension. The resulting work, completed in 1823,
is less a celebration of belief than a search for and
affirmation of faith, in the midst of suffering and
intellectual doubt.

This drama is already apparent in the Kyrie.
The solemn, broad, majestic opening is set in the
key of D major, as one would expect in a "festive
mass," and here the chorus has the principal role.
But with the words "*Christe eleison*" the entreaty
for mercy becomes more intimate. The harmony
shifts to B minor, the soloists take the lead, and
the writing grows agitated.

The Gloria is a movement of sheer magnificence
and enormous energy. Its structure resembles that
of a rondo—with the exultant music of the initial
"*Gloria in excelsis Deo*" punctuating the rest of the
setting as a sort of refrain—and it culminates with
a challenging and harmonically adventurous fugue.
The Credo, the longest movement of the score,
does the Gloria two better by climaxing with a
pair of *double* fugues on the words "*et vitam venturi*"
and "*Amen*," the first marked a manageable *Allegretto ma non troppo*, the second an all-but-
impossible *Allegro con moto*. The difficulty for the
chorus is an exhilarating one; the relief a singer
feels at just getting through such a fugue, and
coming out on the other side, is enormous. Beethoven had written that he wanted the *Missa
Solemnis* to be as much a sacrament for the musicians as for the audience, a re-creation of the
feeling and mystery at the heart of the Catholic
faith. Surely he had this in mind when he made
the end of the Credo so difficult, for the words
"*vitam venturi*" refer to the life of the world to
come, on "the other side" of our life on earth.

A climactic moment is reached with the elevation of the host in the Sanctus. Here Beethoven
inserts a subdued and darkly scored "Praeludium"
for the orchestra; in the course of 32 measures,
through a series of subtle modulations, the key
changes from D to G—an effect that is the musical

THIS MASS IS a culmi-
nation in Beethoven's
work. One can find in it
echoes of the eight symphonies that preceded it, of
the opera Fidelio, and
of the Hammerklavier
Sonata, along with ample
foreshadowings of the Ninth
Symphony, sketched at the
same time as the mass and
finished soon after it.

equivalent of transubstantiation. Then, as if from on high, a solo violin (representing the Holy Spirit) enters on the upper note of the G major chord, and the Benedictus begins.

From the standpoint of musical imagery, the most striking movement of the *Missa Solemnis* is the Agnus Dei. Beginning in the somber key of B minor, it opens conventionally with the threefold repetition of the prayer for mercy, "*Agnus Dei, qui tollis peccata mundi, miserere nobis.*" As the words change from "have mercy on us" to "give us peace," the key of A major is established and the darkness lifts. Beethoven writes above the score, "Prayer for inward and outward peace." His meaning soon becomes clear as the pastoral-sounding music is interrupted by the rumble of drums and the threatening éclat of trumpets. From afar a march is heard, bringing the tumult of war into the middle of the mass. As the soloists cry out in anguish, the setting takes on an operatic intensity. Following a calm interlude, the chorus hurls out its last "*Agnus Dei,*" in fortissimo, and the sweet music of peace again returns. There is a fleeting reminiscence of the martial threat, which is dispelled by the chorus's quiet repetition of "*pacem,*" and the mass ends—not triumphantly, but with a feeling of hopefulness.

John Eliot Gardiner brings period style and electricity to Beethoven's Missa Solemnis.

 RECOMMENDED RECORDINGS

Charlotte Margiono, Catherine Robbin, William Kendall, Alastair Miles; Monteverdi Choir, English Baroque Soloists/ John Eliot Gardiner.
Deutsche Grammophon Archiv 429 779-2

Edda Moser, Hanna Schwarz, René Kollo, Kurt Moll; Radio Chorus of the N.O.S., Hilversum, Royal Concertgebouw Orchestra/ Leonard Bernstein.
Deutsche Grammophon 413 780-2 [2 CDs]

A Good Buy

Herbert von Karajan's first Deutsche Grammophon (423 913-2) recording of the Missa Solemnis, dating from 1966, is a compelling one. The solo vocal quartet is one of the best ever assembled for this work and the playing of the Berlin Philharmonic is powerful. At budget price, and coupled with Mozart's Coronation Mass, K. 317, this is an attractive offering.

The outstanding recordings of the *Missa Solemnis* are from conductors who have given us distinguished accounts of Beethoven's symphonies as well. The exception is Gardiner, who has yet to record the symphonies. His interpretation of the *Missa Solemnis*, however, stands not only as the crowning accomplishment of his career to date, but as one of the most impressive achievements of the period-instrument revival. The concept is grand and powerful, lively though not unduly brisk. The execution is simply electrifying: Gardiner has the orchestra on the edge of their seats, the chorus going all-out, and sparks flying everywhere. Excellent singing from the soloists and a vivid recording complete the triumph.

Bernstein's reading of the score is spacious in design and effusive in sentiment, but with an assured sense of flow and connection. The playing of the Concertgebouw Orchestra is magnificent; never has the radiant sound-world of this score, virtually unique in Beethoven's oeuvre, been better conveyed. While vocalists Moser and Kollo, with the high parts, are under considerable strain, all four soloists deliver the goods. The choral singing is beautiful, as is the solo violin of Herman Krebbers in the Benedictus. The energy of a live performance and the warm ambience of the hall are captured in this potent analog recording.

HECTOR BERLIOZ

REQUIEM, OP. 5

Berlioz composed his *Grande messe des morts* as much with an eye toward visual impact as with an ear for sound. The score calls for a body of more than 100 strings, with wind and brass to match, and a chorus of 200. In a footnote, Berlioz suggests that the chorus can number as high as 800 in the larger movements. The 90-minute work was first performed on December 5, 1837, at a state funeral at the Cathédrale des Invalides in Paris for Count Damrémont, the governor-general of the French colonies in North Africa, who had lost his life in an attack on the Algerian city of Constantine two months earlier.

Berlioz's setting of the Latin Requiem is conceived on the grandest, most Romantic, and least liturgical of planes, in consideration of which George Bernard Shaw once remarked that it was "only a peg" for the composer to "hang his tremendous music on." And tremendous it is. There are passages that call for ten cymbal players and eight sets of timpani—musical lightning and thunder, if ever there was—and the work's most awesome moment, the onset of the *"Tuba mirum"* in the *Dies irae*, requires the coordinated entrance of four brass choirs that the score says are stationed "at the four corners of the large choral and instrumental mass."

But Berlioz also knows how to get effects of extraordinary delicacy from his gargantuan forces. In the Hostias, to symbolize the gulf between heaven and earth, he sets the groaning of eight trombones in their pedal register against dulcet chords in the three flutes. Later, in the Sanctus, he not only anticipates the ethereal string writing of his own *Roméo et Juliette* but previews some of the radiant orchestral sonorities Wagner will explore a few years hence in *Lohengrin*. Particularly arresting is the use of three pairs of cymbals, softly brushed, which musicologist David Cairns has described as an "audible equivalent of the swinging censers around God's throne."

The demands made on the chorus are monumental, from the sustained high A for the tenors just minutes into the opening *Requiem aeternam* to the blockbusting fortissimo passages of the *"Rex tremendae majestatis"* and the subdued pianissimo conclusion of the *"Quarens me,"* sung a cappella. At times the writing mimics the fugal manner of the Baroque, at other times it exhibits a rhythmic and harmonic boldness that will not be encountered again until the 20th century—all in an amazing range of color and emotion.

CONDUCTING *the Requiem's debut, François-Antoine Habeneck—at the precise moment in the "Tuba mirum"* when the four brass choirs had to be brought in—laid down his baton to take a pinch of snuff. Berlioz, seated a few steps away, bounded to the podium and took over the direction of the passage— thereby saving the piece from certain ruin, if we are to believe his* Memoirs.

Berlioz's Requiem, you will probably like his Te Deum *as well. The work is scored for large orchestra, triple chorus, and tenor solo, and includes a prominent part for antiphonal organ. Berlioz wrote that the organ and orchestra should be "like Pope and Emperor, speaking in dialog from opposite ends of the nave." For the work's first performance, the composer assembled 900 singers and instrumentalists.*

 RECOMMENDED RECORDINGS

Ronald Dowd;
Wandsworth School Boys' Choir,
London Symphony Orchestra & Chorus/
Sir Colin Davis.
Philips 416 283-2 [2 CDs; with Symphonie funèbre et triomphale]

John Aler;
Atlanta Symphony Orchestra & Chorus/
Robert Shaw.
Telarc CD 80109 [2 CDs; with Boito: Prologue to Mefistofele, *and Verdi:* Te Deum]

Davis's powerful account is one of the high points of his 1960s Berlioz cycle for Philips. In a reading notable as much for its attention to detail as for its sense of sweep, he builds grand climaxes with absolute sureness while showing an extraordinary ear for nuance and color. The playing of the London orchestra is ravishing, and the recording, made in Westminster Cathedral in 1969, is well focused and atmospheric.

Shaw's rendition of the Requiem is magnificently polished, with choral singing beyond compare. The drama is not quite as pronounced as with Davis, but the work's majestic architecture stands clearly revealed. For once, Telarc's thunderously bass-heavy pickup adds something to the sonic picture.

LEONARD BERNSTEIN

CHICHESTER PSALMS

*T*he town of Chichester in the south of England has had a cathedral since the 11th century. Since 1965, however, the cathedral, its choir, and the town itself have been known in musical circles thanks primarily to this work. Com-

Bernstein at work: praising God with the sound of the trumpet, and lots of percussion as well.

missioned by the Very Reverend Walter Hussey, dean of the cathedral, for the annual summer festival sponsored by the cathedrals of Chichester, Winchester, and Salisbury, *Chichester Psalms* is Bernstein's most important and most frequently performed sacred score.

Asked to compose a devotional work based on the Psalms, Bernstein chose six of his favorites and set them in Hebrew (he had set Hebrew texts before, most notably in his Symphonies Nos. 1 and 3). The psalms are grouped in pairs, so that the work is divided into three parts. The scoring calls for strings and brass, along with an enlarged percussion section and two harps. In the second psalm, Bernstein employs the unusual and very energetic meter of 7/4 throughout; the fifth has an even more unusual meter, 10/4, treated in a wonderfully flowing manner. There is an important part for boy alto in the third psalm, the famous Twenty-third, in which the soloist represents the shepherd boy David.

  RECOMMENDED RECORDING

John Paul Bogart; Camerata Singers, New York Philharmonic/Leonard Bernstein.
CBS Masterworks MK 44710 [with Poulenc: Gloria, *and Stravinsky:* Symphony of Psalms]

Bernstein's own 1965 recording is unsurpassed for its jazzy elan and sheer joy. The account is wild and rhythmically charged, if a little rough around the edges. The young alto Bogart is absolutely sure of himself, just like the young David. The coupling provides a good choice of repertory.

THE SOMBER opening subject of Denn alles Fleisch es ist wie Gras, *the second movement of A German Requiem, was recycled by Brahms from an abandoned sonata for two pianos that he sketched in 1854. The texts Brahms used in all seven movements go back as far as the Psalms of David. Two of them,* Wie lieblich sind deine Wohnungen *and* Selig sind die Toten, *had been set by Schütz in the 17th century.*

JOHANNES BRAHMS

A German Requiem, Op. 45

*T*he idea of composing a Requiem in the German language based on texts from the Lutheran Bible and the Apocrypha began to take shape in Brahms's mind in 1857, a year after the death of his friend and mentor Robert Schumann. But it was not until 1865, following the death of Brahms's mother, that he took up composition of the music in earnest. After another three years, the work stood complete—having grown from a choral piece into a cantata, and thence into a seven-movement Requiem for chorus, soloists, and orchestra. In the process, it became the central work of Brahms's career, the one that established him as a composer of major stature and linked two of the most important spheres of his lifelong musical endeavor, the vocal and the symphonic.

A northerner, Brahms was steeped in the traditions of Protestantism, though unlike Bach he remained unconvinced of man's afterlife. It was not his intention to pattern his Requiem after the Latin mass for the dead, nor to proclaim what he felt were false hopes for the resurrection. Instead, *Ein deutsches Requiem* is a work of consolation for those left behind.

The gentle opening movement, *Selig sind, die da Leid tragen* (*Blessed are they that mourn*), immediately marks the shift of emphasis away from the dead (the Latin Requiem begins with a plea for their eternal rest) and toward the living. The remaining movements touch on the subject of death from a variety of angles. The second, *Denn alles Fleisch es ist wie Gras* (*For all flesh is as grass*), a funeral march in B flat minor based on a sarabande-like subject, is the darkest part of the score. Yet it ends exultantly, in B flat major. The third movement, *Herr, lehre doch mich* (*Lord, make me to know mine end*), features a dialog between baritone solo

With Klemperer one feels the connection between Brahms and the tradition of Handel, Bach, and Schütz.

*THOSE WHO SANG
with or played in the
Philharmonia Orchestra during the 1950s and '60s
remember Wilhelm Pitz as
choral conductor without
peer on the London music
scene. Hired by Walter
Legge on the recommenda-
tion of Herbert von Karajan,
Pitz transformed the Philharmonia Chorus into one of
the best German choruses in
the world.*

and chorus with dramatic commentary from the
orchestra. At first urgent and hushed, the expression grows more turbulent—until the law is laid
down in a magnificent fugue, setting the words
"the souls of the righteous are in the hand of God."

The mood becomes pastoral with the flowing
3/4 meter and gentle, arpeggiated string figures
of the fourth movement, *Wie lieblich sind deine
Wohnungen* (*How amiable are thy tabernacles*). The
fifth movement, *Ihr habt nun Traurigkeit* (*And ye
now therefore have sorrow*), is a rhapsodic setting
for solo soprano and chorus that ends with the
words "I will see you again" gently repeated by
the soprano, while the chorus sings "I will comfort
you." Drama returns in the sixth movement, *Denn
wir haben hie keine bleibende Statt* (*For here we have
no continuing city*), as the baritone and chorus
preview the final judgment and the raising of the
dead; it, too, concludes with a fugue, symbolic of
immutable law. With *Selig sind die Toten* (*Blessed
are the dead*), the work ends on a note of untrou-
bled acceptance and resignation, in the pastoral
key of F major, far from the sting of death.

 RECOMMENDED RECORDINGS

**Elisabeth Schwarzkopf,
Dietrich Fischer-Dieskau;
Philharmonia Orchestra & Chorus/
Otto Klemperer.**
EMI Classics CDC 47238

**Elisabeth Schwarzkopf, Hans Hotter;
Vienna Singverein, Vienna Philharmonic/
Herbert von Karajan.**
EMI Classics CDH 61010

**Anna Tomowa-Sintow, José van Dam;
Vienna Singverein, Berlin Philharmonic/
Herbert von Karajan.**
EMI Classics CDM 69229

*The silver-toned Elisabeth
Schwarzkopf, whose solo work in*
A German Requiem *is aptly
devotional.*

AS PART OF HIS *effort to sign Herbert von Karajan to a recording contract in 1946, English producer Walter Legge presented the conductor with a bottle each of whiskey, gin, and sherry. It was a meaningful gesture in postwar Vienna, where everything was rationed, most things were unavailable, and little things mattered a great deal. With typical iron willpower, Karajan divided each bottle into 30 portions and stretched the gift over 90 days.*

Klemperer's account, recorded in 1961, remains unmatched among readings that emphasize the spirituality of the score. Drawing committed playing and singing from his forces, Klemperer opens the door to the beauties of the music without fuss or fanfare. Schwarzkopf's expressive portamento sounds a bit dated in style, but her singing is characterful nonetheless, while Fischer-Dieskau is a paragon of restrained expressiveness. The singing of the Philharmonia Chorus is especially beautiful. EMI has done a good job of remastering. Balances and tone quality are quite fine, and the Kingsway Hall ambience survives.

Although he tried several times, Karajan never surpassed his 1947 mono recording with the Vienna Philharmonic, a reading of fervent, postwar intensity. The closest he came in the stereo era was with his 1976 remake with the Berlin Philharmonic (and here again is the Vienna Singverein, which remained his favorite chorus over the years). The account is consistent with Karajan's view of the Brahms symphonies and with the earlier reading of the Requiem—a polished, firmly sculpted rendition with the conductor's usual grip, in spite of the fact that tempos are on the slow side. Van Dam sings with passion, and Tomowa-Sintow is radiant in *Ihr habt nun Traurigkeit.*

BENJAMIN BRITTEN

WAR REQUIEM, OP. 66

*W*ar was a deeply serious matter to Britten, who was a lifelong pacifist. With the tenor Peter Pears he left England for America in 1939, shortly before World War II broke out in Europe, and although he returned to England in 1942, he remained a conscientious objector to military service. During the war, Britten and Pears concertized frequently—one of the conditions for their exemption from the draft—and afterward Britten continued to examine the question of how

The pacifist and his War Requiem: *Benjamin Britten at his writing table.*

an individual of conscience deals with societal expectations in such works as the operas *Peter Grimes* and *Billy Budd* and the *War Requiem*.

Completed in 1961, the *War Requiem* received its first performance on May 30, 1962, at the dedication of the new Coventry Cathedral, built next to the ruins of the cathedral bombed out by the Luftwaffe in 1940. The score makes a profound statement about the value of human life; its text is a conflation of the Latin Requiem and the poignant, disturbing antiwar verse of the English poet Wilfred Owen, who died at the front during the final week of World War I. The performing forces are immense: full symphony orchestra, chamber orchestra, mixed chorus, boys' choir, organ, and soprano, tenor, and baritone soloists, plus two conductors. The two male soloists, accompanied by the chamber orchestra, are entrusted with the settings of Owen's poetry and represent soldiers from opposite sides of the conflict in which Owen perished. Britten's intent in these passages is to amplify the message of the mass and to move its focus from the abstract to the particular.

Musically, the *War Requiem* is a vast study of the tritone, the dissonant interval of an augmented fourth (spanning three whole tones), historically considered a symbol of the devil—to which Britten gives a haunting consonance and sonority, as if to show how attractive the beckoning of the horrible can be. The Latin text is treated with a spiritualized detachment in the settings for children's voices, which are to be heard as if at a distance (in many performances, the boys are placed in a choir loft or in the back of the hall, and they can indeed sound like angels). When the chorus or the solo soprano intones the Latin, it tends to become impersonally rigid and dogmatic, or airy and ironic. The *Dies irae*, mechanically sung and accompanied by frightful alarms in the brass and thundering reports of cannon in the percussion, is a vision of apocalyptic power, one of the most harrowing pieces of music ever writ-

War in Time of Mass

In bringing the imagery of war into a setting of the mass, Britten observed a precedent of long standing. Both Beethoven, in the Agnus Dei of his Missa Solemnis, and Haydn, in his Mass In Time of War, had used trumpets and drums to create a martial background to the chorus's plea for peace. During the Renaissance, a popular song called "L'homme armé" ("The Armed Man")—whose text probably refers to a crusade against the Turks—inspired no fewer than 31 masses by the likes of Dufay, Ockeghem, and Palestrina.

ten. The "*Recordare*," though sung as if in a trance, is almost unbearably beautiful.

The settings of Owen show Britten at his most piquant and plumb the depths of emotion. In the shadowy netherworld of death, the English soldier meets the German he killed the day before, who says to him:

> . . . Whatever hope is yours,
> Was my life also; I went hunting wild
> After the wildest beauty in the world.
>
> For by my glee might many men have laughed,
> And of my weeping something had been left,
> Which must die now. I mean the truth untold,
> The pity of war, the pity war distilled.

As the two soldiers sing "Let us sleep now," the soprano, the main chorus, and the children enter quietly with the final part of the *Libera me*, absorbing them into the larger voice of humanity. It is a moment of heartrending gentleness, the only possible end to a score whose visionary intensity places it on the same level as Picasso's *Guernica* and among the handful of indisputably great musical works from the second half of the 20th century.

 RECOMMENDED RECORDINGS

Galina Vishnevskaya, Peter Pears, Dietrich Fischer-Dieskau; Highgate School Choir, London Symphony Orchestra & Chorus/ Benjamin Britten.
London 414 383-2 [2 CDs]

Lorna Haywood, Anthony Rolfe Johnson, Benjamin Luxon; Atlanta Boy Choir, Atlanta Symphony Orchestra & Chorus/ Robert Shaw.
Telarc CD 80157 [2 CDs]

The composer's 1963 recording remains, after 30 years, the preferred account, unequaled in its scope and intensity. It brings together the three soloists for whom the work was written, chosen not only for their artistry but because they represented three of the nations most deeply scarred by World War II: the Soviet Union, England, and Germany. Britten holds the vast forces together, and the superbly engineered recording captures with chilling exactitude the power and the nuance of his ardent, visionary interpretation.

Only a conductor of Shaw's experience could hope to shed new light on a score the composer himself had so convincingly presented. The American finds a meditative gentleness in the music that is touching, and he imparts a distant, sad feeling to the climaxes that deepens their ambivalence. The solo singing is on a par with that of the original recording (the diction is in fact better), and the choral singing is suffused with Shaw's unique magic. Telarc's 1988 digital recording is a bona fide sonic spectacular.

GABRIEL FAURÉ

REQUIEM, OP. 48

Fauré late in life. He wanted sopranos who had known love to sing his Requiem.

French composer Fauré (1845–1924) held positions as church organist and choirmaster for 40 years, necessitating the production of a sizeable amount of sacred music. Yet he composed his setting of the Requiem, the work by which he is best known today, "purely for the pleasure of it." Although he completed a first version of the score in 1888, the piece was to grow and change for another decade, until the version most commonly performed today—in seven sections, for full orchestra, organ, chorus, and soprano and baritone soloists—was completed in 1900.

There is a warm, consoling quality to the music, with the emphasis from start to finish on rest and peace. The original version of the score, without

DURING THE 19TH *century, some of France's best composers found positions, and a measure of security, as organists in Parisian churches. In addition to Fauré, their number included Saint-Saëns, Franck, and Charles-Marie Widor. The chief 20th-century successor to this generation sustained by the king of instruments was Olivier Messiaen, who played at La Trinité from 1930 to 1992.*

the Offertory and the *Libera me*, made no mention at all of the Last Judgment; even in later versions, the terrors are quickly passed over. The soaring vocal lines of the Agnus Dei, particularly the opening part for tenors, are soothing, as is the remarkable violin solo in the Sanctus. The concluding *In Paradisum* echoes the feeling of beatitude that emerges in these pages. Fauré himself said he wanted bright, vigorous sopranos to sing this work, as opposed to "old goats who have never known love." Behind that comment is the same Mediterranean sensuality that characterizes the Requiem as a whole.

 RECOMMENDED RECORDINGS

Kiri Te Kanawa, Sherrill Milnes; Montreal Symphony Orchestra & Chorus/ Charles Dutoit.
London 421 440-2 [with Pelléas et Mélisande *Suite and* Pavane]

Judith Blegen, James Morris; Atlanta Symphony Orchestra & Chorus/ Robert Shaw.
Telarc CD 80135 [with Duruflé: Requiem]

Dutoit leads the full-orchestra version of the Requiem but holds the large forces back, giving the account ideal weight and balance. Appropriately French voicings are used on the organ, and women rather than boys in the chorus. Milnes is a bit wide of vibrato but sings with a suitably noble tone. Te Kanawa sounds covered and fruity, though hers is still a lovely voice. The 1987 recording takes full advantage of the presence and atmosphere of the cathedral of St. Eustache, and the coupling is the best available.

The chorus is at the center of Shaw's reading of the piece, presumably the more lightly scored 1893 version (Telarc does not specify). The account flows very well, and the work of both soloists

Kiri Te Kanawa adds vocal splendor to the Requiem.

is highly satisfying, particularly Blegen's airy soprano in *Pie Jesu*. The recording dates from 1985–86 and is one of Telarc's best, with excellent presence overall and real bass in the organ.

GEORGE FRIDERIC HANDEL

MESSIAH

Handel, sans wig, c. 1730 when he was at the height of his fame as an opera composer.

*H*andel was one of the greatest opera composers of the Baroque, but when he could no longer make money at it, he transferred his attention to the oratorio. By then, the oratorio had grown into something far removed from the church—a hybrid that clothed texts from the Bible, classical literature, epic poetry, and other sources in magnificent operatic trappings, intended not for edification but purely as entertainment. The genre had flourished in Italy since the middle of the 17th century; it did not exist in England at all until Handel established it in the 1730s. *Messiah* is Handel's greatest oratorio and by any measure the greatest choral work in English. It was composed at lightning speed between August 22 and September 14, 1741, and received its premiere in Dublin on April 13, 1742. The text, compiled by Charles Jennens, draws on both the Old and the New Testament to tell, in extremely compressed form, the story of the life of Christ.

The first act (Handel preferred "act" to "part") of *Messiah* establishes God's plan to redeem the world through a Savior and presents the story of the Nativity. It includes several of Handel's most evocative solo numbers and choruses. "O thou that tellest good tidings to Zion," which starts as an air for the alto soloist and brings in the chorus, is set to the lullaby-like rhythm of a siciliana. The brilliantly scored "For unto us a Child is born" unfolds as a jaunty march with exultant sixteenth-note roulades and, in an inspired touch, bracing unison proclamations of the words "Wonderful" and "Counselor." The pulsating string accompaniment to the soprano's recitatives "And lo! the angel of the Lord came upon them" and "And suddenly there was with the angel" lends a palpable excitement to the act's climactic visit of the heavenly host.

The theme of the second act is the victory of Christ over sin and the perpetuation of His kingdom on earth. This part of the score contains the alto air "He was despised," notable for its poignant chromaticism and the dying fall of its melodic lines; the aria's middle section, treating Christ's flagellation, is cast in the dark key of C minor. The chorus gets to do some scene painting of its own with "All we like sheep have gone astray," in which the choral sheep go "astray" by moving away from each other in contrary motion, and Handel plays on the word "turned" ("we have turned, ev'ry one to his own way") by setting it to long strings of "turns," ornamental figures that revolve around a single note. This part of *Messiah* ends with the famed "Hallelujah!" chorus, which Handel sets as a joyous, buoyant processional, trumpets and drums blazing in D major.

The final act turns to mankind itself and concerns the promise of redemption, resurrection, and eternal life. Opening the act is one of Handel's most moving creations, the air "I know that my Redeemer liveth." In the celestial key of E major, .this gracious sarabande for the soprano leaves one feeling absolutely certain that Handel believed his own message. The melodic line conveys calm ecstasy via recurrent upward leaps and long-sustained downbeats. Not for nothing is the opening phrase inscribed on Handel's memorial in Westminster Abbey. The oratorio's conclusion is a glorious triple choral number: "Worthy is the Lamb," sung wholly in unison and full of certitude; "Blessing and honour, glory and pow'r," in which imitative passages and powerful unisons are blended; and a concluding "Amen," treated as a fugue at magnificent length.

Something in *Messiah* commands the affection

USUALLY SUNG at Christmas, Messiah is thought of as a seasonal piece. Once the first part is over, however, it is the drama of Christ's sacrifice that becomes the focus of the work. In that sense, Messiah is as much a piece for Easter as for Christmas, a point surely not lost on the work's original Eastertide audience.

of English-speaking peoples in a way no other choral music does. Perhaps it is the way Handel taps into the feeling of his great story by keeping recitative to a minimum and emphasizing the direct, openly theatrical expression of the arias and choruses, in which the full persuasiveness of Baroque vocal art is brought to bear. Whatever the reason may be, Handel's deeply felt setting conveys the emotional tide of its story with almost miraculous insight, and has acquired a universality that is unique in the history of music.

RECOMMENDED RECORDINGS

Margaret Marshall, Catherine Robbin, Charles Brett, Anthony Rolfe Johnson, Robert Hale, Saul Quirke; Monteverdi Choir, English Baroque Soloists/ John Eliot Gardiner.
Philips 411 041-2 [3 CDs]

Heather Harper, Helen Watts, John Wakefield, John Shirley-Quirk; London Symphony Orchestra & Choir/ Sir Colin Davis.
Philips 420 865-2 [2 CDs]

Gardiner's is a highly musical and inspired account, featuring an excellent group of soloists and an outstanding period-instrument band. With dance rhythms athletically sprung and *da capo* arias tastefully ornamented, the performance generates consistent interest and is lively in spite of its length. There is splendid singing from the Monteverdi Choir—the ending of "All we like sheep" is quite potent—and wonderful work from the soloists. The recording, made in 1982, is impeccable.

The 1966 reading from Davis and the London Symphony is a classic. A compassionate interpretation, it represents a successful melding of the English oratorio tradition with the then-emerging

When he first heard the "Halle-lujah!" chorus, George II stood; everyone else had to as well.

notion of an authentic performance style emphasizing lightness of texture and firm rhythmic underpinning. At midprice on two CDs, it is an especially good bargain.

JOSEPH HAYDN

THE CREATION

Haydn's last public appearance at a performance of The Creation, *Vienna, 1808.*

*A*mong the most important byproducts of Haydn's two extended visits to London was his exposure to the oratorios of Handel. As luck would have it, during his second visit Haydn was offered an English libretto based on Milton's *Paradise Lost*, which had in fact been intended for Handel. It was from this that *Die Schöpfung* (*The Creation*) got its start. Haydn began to sketch the oratorio in London in 1794, but because he felt more comfortable working in German, upon his return to Vienna he had the libretto translated.

Completed in 1798, *The Creation* is in three parts. The first represents the first four days of Creation, the second part involves the fifth and sixth days, and the third part describes the blissful existence of Adam and Eve before the Fall. There are solo passages for the two of them, as well as for the angels Gabriel, Raphael, and Uriel. The chorus contributes to the narration and comments on the action.

The orchestral prologue is a magnificent portrayal of chaos. This harmonically nebulous fantasy points the way toward Romanticism with its focus on pure sound and urgent expression. But Haydn saves an even more dramatic effect for the first chorus. After Raphael has recited the lines "And darkness was upon the face of the deep . . . ," the chorus, in a hush, continues: "And the Spirit of God moved upon the face of the waters. And God said, Let there be light: And there was . . . LIGHT!" On the last word, the stillness is shattered as chorus and orchestra erupt with a *fortissimo* C

IF YOU LIKE THIS WORK, you will probably enjoy listening to its sequel. The Seasons, *which received its premiere in 1801, has an exuberance all its own and is full of deft touches of musical characterization. One unexpected delight is a reprise of the famous tune from the Andante of the* Surprise Symphony, *this time in a song about a farmer singing as he plows his fields in the spring.*

major chord, Haydn's musical equivalent of blinding light.

The second part of the oratorio carries the pictorialism further with portrayals of the animals as they are created. Haydn lets us hear the roaring lion in the brass, see the leaping tiger in the strings' rising scale passages, and follow the bounding stag through a thicket of dotted notes. The oxen in the meadows are represented by a little pastorale for flute, the insects by soft string tremolos, and the worm by a slowly turning half-step figure. With the oratorio's third part, Haydn reaches the work's highest level of inspiration. As he visits our "Grand Parents" in the Garden of Eden, the music fills with humanity and warmth, expressing the beauty of Creation and its fulfillment in the emotion of love.

RECOMMENDED RECORDINGS

Judith Blegen, Thomas Moser, Kurt Moll, Lucia Popp, Kurt Ollmann; Bavarian Radio Symphony Orchestra & Chorus/Leonard Bernstein.
Deutsche Grammophon 419 765-2 [2 CDs]

Agnes Giebel, Waldemar Kmentt, Gottlob Frick; Bavarian Radio Symphony Orchestra & Chorus/Eugen Jochum.
Philips 426 651-2 [2 CDs]

Barbara Bonney, Hans Peter Blochwitz, Jan Hendrik Rootering, Edith Wiens, Olaf Bär; South German Radio Chorus, Stuttgart Radio Symphony Orchestra/ Sir Neville Marriner.
EMI Classics CDCB 54038 [2 CDs]

Bernstein's is a broad symphonic statement, allowing the humor and humanity to shine through but emphasizing the profundity of the grand moments. And grand they are: in the introduction, one senses not only the dawn of Creation but the dawn of Romanticism as well. The work of chorus and soloists is good (though Blegen occasionally goes off-pitch), and the orchestral playing is inspired. The 1986 recording captures the live performance with exemplary detail.

Now somewhat outdated in style, Jochum's reading is exuberant and earthy. The soloists take a theatrical approach, and the chorus and orchestra speak with large gestures that have almost Brahmsian weight—but with a warmth and a conviction that carry the day. For Jochum, this is a Romantic opera about the Creation; he revels in its pictorialism and, as in everything he did, is full-throated in praise of God. Despite some tape hiss and a slight edge to the violins, the 1966 recording is open and natural in perspective. The winds are especially well captured, and the solo voices are properly balanced, not too far forward.

With a complement close to the original performing forces, Marriner is lighter, his manner graceful and endearing. The use of a fortepiano in the recitatives is a bit unnerving, since the instrument often sounds like a banjo or a cembalom. The singing is excellent, both among the soloists and in the chorus. In this 1989 recording, the orchestra sounds a touch recessed, though the ambience is fairly intimate.

LEOŠ JANÁČEK

SLAVONIC MASS

*W*hen in 1921 Janáček complained to an archbishop about the abysmal state of liturgical music in Czechoslovakia, the archbishop suggested that the composer himself do something about it. Five years later, Janáček answered the challenge with one of the most beautiful and powerful works of the sacred repertory, *Glagolská mše*, a setting of the Roman Catholic mass using a text in Church Slavonic, the language of the old

Janáček around the time he began work on his mass.

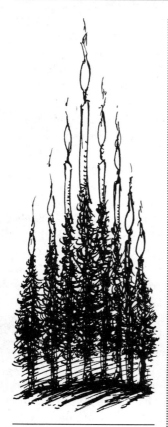

JANÁČEK WROTE
that while he was working
on the mass, he had in mind
"... the scent of the moist
Luhačovice forests—that was
the incense. I felt a cathedral
grow out of the giant ex-
panse of the woods and the
sky, its vault stretching into
the hazy distance. A flock of
sheep rang the bells. ...
The tall fir trees, their tips
lit by the stars, are the
candles ..."

Orthodox Christian service.

This *Slavonic Mass*, composed in the Moravian spa town of Luhačovice, takes the liturgy as the point of departure for an individualistic expression of pantheistic spirituality. The vitality of the setting makes it seem like the work of a young composer. Janáček was in fact past 70 when he wrote it, though still youthful—deeply in love with a young woman, full of the wonder of life, and more passionate about the world than he had ever been. The score is a testament, as Janáček himself put it, to the Czech nation's faith, "not on a religious basis but on a strong moral one which calls God to witness." It is also a wonderful celebration of the holiness of nature.

The work's architecture, like its music, is strikingly original. There are five large choral movements corresponding to the five main sections of the Latin mass: *Gospodi pomiluj* (Kyrie), *Slava* (Gloria), *Věruju* (Credo), *Svet* (Sanctus), and *Agneče Božij* (Agnus Dei). These movements are flanked by an orchestral introduction, an organ postlude, and a concluding orchestral *Intrada*. There is a pagan exuberance to the introduction and the *Intrada*, a haunting beauty in the quiet *Gospodi pomiluj* and the *Agneče Božij*, and towering splendor in the climaxes of the *Věruju* and the *Slava*. Janáček relies heavily on the chorus, saving the soloists for the most expressive moments in each setting. His unique manner of scoring is evident in the prominent string ostinatos and jubilant brass fanfares, the plaintive woodwind solos and growling trombone chords, and the long-breathed melodies in the violins.

 RECOMMENDED RECORDING

Elisabeth Söderström, Drahomíra Drobková, František Livora, Richard Novák; Prague Philharmonic Chorus, Czech Philharmonic/Sir Charles Mackerras.
Supraphon 10-3575-2

Mackerras conducts a performance that is urgent and impassioned, though polished and refined as well. The singers know their way around the music; the only foreigner among the soloists is the Swedish soprano Söderström, who is so good with the language she might as well be a Czech. The orchestra plays the music as only it can—here, too, an authentic accent is important. The recording, made in 1984, is spacious and well balanced.

WOLFGANG AMADEUS MOZART
REQUIEM IN D MINOR, K. 626

A Romantic image of Mozart on his deathbed, reading through the unfinished Requiem.

*C*ontrary to the image of the composer sinking irrevocably into poverty and despair—foisted on the public by the film *Amadeus* and generations of lazy biographers—the summer of 1791 found Mozart a busy, happy man. His financial situation, troubled though it had been, was beginning to stabilize—"at a relatively high level," according to the recent research of music historian Volkmar Braunbehrens. Best of all, opera commissions were coming in as fast as they could be handled.

A commission for a Requiem also arrived that summer. Its source was Count Franz Walsegg-Stuppach, a music-loving nobleman recently widowed who needed a suitable memorial for his wife. It was a generous commission, amounting to more than half of what Mozart might receive for an opera—and half of it was paid in advance. But work on other projects delayed Mozart, and he was unable to finish the Requiem before his final illness, most likely a recurrence of rheumatic fever, set in around November 20, 1791. Two weeks later, Mozart was dead. At that time, only the Introit and the Kyrie were complete. Five sections of the Sequence and both sections of the Offertory had been notated in outline.

Only after asking several more reputable composers to complete the piece did Mozart's widow, Constanze, turn to Franz Xaver Süssmayr, the composer's assistant. He finished some orchestrations and completed the "*Lacrimosa*," which Mozart had broken off after setting down the first eight bars. Presumably, Süssmayr composed the Sanctus, Benedictus, and Agnus Dei, although the quality of the music has led to speculation that at least some of the material is original; the Agnus Dei may indeed have been sketched in fairly detailed fashion by Mozart. Süssmayr finished the job in late 1792 and forged on the title page the inscription "*Requiem. di me W: A: Mozart mpr. 792*" ("Requiem, by me, W. A. Mozart, in my own hand, 1792"), perhaps to make it easier for Constanze to collect the remainder of the commission.

Considering the complex provenance of the score, it is something of a miracle that Mozart's spirit comes through so clearly. But the Requiem's mix of styles is distinctly Mozartean—no one but he could have fused the church style, opera (in the treatment of melody, texture, and scoring), and the Masonic ceremonial in quite the same way. The Masonic element is evident not only in the unusual gravity of utterance throughout the Requiem, but also in the work's dark-hued orchestration. The only woodwind color comes from two bassoons and two basset horns (whose plaintive sound Mozart had emphasized in his *Masonic Funeral Music* of 1785), while the flutes and oboes, with their brighter timbre, are eliminated altogether. The Requiem's overall structure, and the thematic and textural links between different sections of the score, reflect the symphonic approach Mozart employed in large-scale works, while the boldness and expressiveness of much of the harmony is typical of Mozart's late style. Certainly only Mozart could have devised the colorism in the "*Confutatis maledictis*," where tongues of flame (in the lower strings) lick at the souls of the damned, while from on high, the sopranos and altos intone the hopeful prayers of the contrite.

FIVE DAYS AFTER *Mozart's death, the Introit and the Kyrie were performed for the first time, at a service in his memory on December 10, 1791. The first performance of Süssmayr's completion of the Requiem took place on January 2, 1793, at a benefit for Constanze (above).*

Sir Colin Davis: a reading of Mozart's Requiem full of operatic grandeur.

 RECOMMENDED RECORDINGS

Angela Maria Blasi, Marjana Lipovšek, Uwe Heilmann, Jan Hendrik Rootering; Bavarian Radio Symphony Orchestra & Chorus/Sir Colin Davis.
RCA Red Seal 60599-2

Margaret Price, Trudeliese Schmidt, Francisco Araiza, Theo Adam; Leipzig Radio Chorus, Staatskapelle Dresden/Peter Schreier.
Philips 411 420-2

Rachel Yakar, Ortrun Wenkel, Kurt Equiluz, Robert Holl; Vienna State Opera Chorus, Concentus musicus Wien/ Nikolaus Harnoncourt.
Teldec 42756-ZK

The Davis account is a good place to start for those who like a big chorus, big orchestra, and big sound. A gloriously theatrical reading, it is forceful in the climaxes, warmly expressive in the softer pages. The wonderful solo vocal quartet, showcased to great effect in the "*Recordare*," seems to have just stepped off the opera stage. The 1990 recording offers closeup, sumptuous sound.

Presiding over modern forces, Schreier offers a conventional but stylistically informed interpretation in which the link between the Requiem and the great sacred works of the Baroque can be readily sensed. The reading combines seriousness of tone with an appealing sincerity of expression, and it gains much from the playing of the Dresden orchestra, which produces clear lines and translucent textures without surrendering its customary beauty of tone. The digital recording is satisfyingly balanced and captures the tonal richness of the performance.

Harnoncourt, using period instruments and Franz Beyer's 1972 rescoring of Süssmayr, directs a reading that is danceable, vivid, and surprising. The score's inner workings are clear, its sentiment intriguingly personalized by Harnoncourt's tendency to soften the tone from proclamatory to imploring. It is an individualistic view, and it is convincing. The recording places the chorus in the distance and is somewhat boomy.

CARL ORFF

CARMINA BURANA

BEST KNOWN for Carmina Burana, Carl Orff (above) probably had a greater impact on the music of this century as an educator than as a composer. Based on the concept that music should be taught in connection with physical movement, his method has won acceptance throughout the world. Only the Hungarian composer Zoltán Kodály has had a comparable influence in this century.

*C*armina Burana, best rendered in English as *Songs of Beuren,* was the title of a collection of medieval Latin and German lyrics published in 1847 by J. A. Schmeller, taken from a 13th-century manuscript then in the possession of the Benedictine abbey of Benediktbeuren, near Munich. To this day the original manuscript remains the richest source of secular poetry by the goliards—itinerant scholars and monks active in Europe from the late 10th to the early 13th century. In 1935 the German composer Orff (1895–1982) encountered Schmeller's collection and was immediately seized by the earthy, unbridled imagery of its material. He made use of some two dozen texts (though none of the melodies notated in the manuscript) to fashion one of the 20th century's most popular works for chorus and orchestra. The score, completed in 1936, received its premiere in Frankfurt on June 8, 1937.

Carmina Burana, like nearly all of Orff's work, manifests a preoccupation with music as spectacle. The writing invites performer and listener alike to participate in the hedonistic enjoyment of rhythmically catchy and frequently repeated tunes, as well as equally simple forms, consonant harmony, powerful singing, and colorful scoring marked by an unstinting use of percussion. The conception owes much to Stravinsky in its ritualistic repetition of rhythmic patterns, though Orff's treatment is considerably less sophisticated

Drinking Songs

Orff was not the first to celebrate the pleasures of carousing in music. There is a noble tradition of drinking songs in opera that includes Don Giovanni's "Fin ch'han dal vino" and Alfredo's "Libiamo ne'lieti calici" in La traviata, as well as memorable choruses in Verdi's Macbeth and Otello and Wagner's Der fliegende Holländer. Paeans to inebriation have been written by Mahler ("Der Trunkene im Frühling"), Berg (the concert aria Der Wein), and Schoenberg (the song "Moondrunk").

and more procedural, a quality that places him among the many grandfathers of modern minimalism. But the composer does show a remarkable ability to harness the energy of the standard goliardic stanza of 13 syllables, grouped as seven plus six, in which nearly all of the Latin parts of the text are written. His sensitivity to the mood of the poetry is equally noteworthy; not only does the music convey the exuberance and sarcastic bite of much of the text, it faithfully captures the tenderness that occasionally emerges in the midst of the bawdiness.

Among the most delightful settings are those from the section In taberna (In the Tavern). The funniest of all is "Olim lacus colueram" ("Once I Swam Upon the Lake"), also known as "The Ballad of the Roasted Swan," in which the swan sings about its former life while it turns on the spit. The tenor soloist delivers the swan's lament in falsetto over a shimmering accompaniment of muted strings and brass, while the men of the chorus interject expressions of sympathy for the bird as it cooks. "In taberna quando sumus" ("When We Are in the Tavern") concludes this section with a raucous drinking song straight out of a Munich beerhall in which, by the end, the men have drunk healths to all of medieval society.

 RECOMMENDED RECORDINGS

Jochum's picturesque account has a Germanness that is exactly on the mark. The orchestral playing is clean, characterful, and suggestive, the choral singing suitably lusty. No one has ever done the Bavarian beerhall bit any better, and the whole performance is fun from start to finish. Fischer-Dieskau brings the nuance and dramatic point of a Lieder artist to his solos, along with some barking in the upper range; Stolze, in spite of liberties with phrasing, proves unerringly comical. Janowitz is pleasing in everything but *"Dulcissime"* ("My Sweetest One"), where she squeezes down so hard she sounds like an organ pipe on the loose rather than a soprano. The analog recording has ample depth and good atmosphere.

The playing of the orchestra and London's fullbodied sound are reason enough to have the Blomstedt disc. The San Franciscans give a polished account, responsive to the letter as well as the spirit of the music. The choral singing is disciplined and well coached, though lightweight, and the soloists are fine except for McMillan, whose overwrought treatment is no asset. Blomstedt brings out details that escape notice in rougher performances of the piece.

GIUSEPPE VERDI

REQUIEM

*T*he *Messa da Requiem* by Verdi (1813–1901) is a monumental work of the imagination, not so much a statement of belief as a translation of the Latin text's rich dramatic possibilities into the language of opera. The work's unusual genesis links it to two of the greatest figures of 19thcentury Italy, the composer Gioacchino Rossini and the poet Alessandro Manzoni. On November 17, 1868, four days after Rossini's death, Verdi proposed that a Requiem in his memory, written in collaboration with Italy's leading composers, be

Verdi conducting the Requiem mass at La Scala, May 25, 1874.

✓ *IF YOU LIKE THIS WORK, you might want to investigate Verdi's* Quattro pezzi sacri *(Four Sacred Pieces). Published in 1898, when Verdi was 85, the four parts embrace a broad range of emotion, from the enigmatic musings of the opening "Ave Maria," for unaccompanied chorus, to the thunderous outbursts of soprano solo, double chorus, and full orchestra of the concluding Te Deum. Verdi felt so close to the latter that he asked to have the score buried with him when he died.*

performed on the first anniversary of his death. The idea was adopted, and Verdi contributed the final *Libera me*—though the planned performance of the *Messa per Rossini* never occurred. Five years later, the death of Manzoni, who for Verdi personified the spirit of Italian nationalism, spurred the composer to fashion a Requiem in his memory. In doing so, Verdi made use of the earlier *Libera me*. The finished work had its premiere at the Church of San Marco in Milan on May 22, 1874, the first anniversary of Manzoni's death.

Verdi was an agnostic all of his adult life, but he was a man of profound conscience and spirituality. In his Requiem, he projects the essentials of humanity—piety, emotion, agitation, and capacity for hope—as compassionately and dramatically as in any of the operas from his mature years. The opening *Requiem aeternam* and Kyrie are subdued in feeling but charged with expectation—a sentiment soon justified by the eruption of the *Dies irae*. This immense movement, nearly 40 minutes long, is the core of the work, presenting the listener with an overwhelming vision of the wrath, torment, and supplication of the Last Judgment. A more consoling tone is struck in the Offertory, which features the solo vocal quartet without the chorus; it concludes with a radiant prayer from the soprano, "*Fac eas de morte transire ad vitam*" ("Let them pass from death unto life"), which floats up to a high A flat on the word *vitam*. The ensuing Sanctus, a double fugue for double chorus, is thrillingly fast and brilliantly orchestrated, with scurrying passages in the strings that are transformed, at the end, into blazing chromatic runs in the full brass. The delicately scored Agnus Dei features a series of duets from soprano and mezzo soloists, answered by the chorus and orchestra. Verdi's scoring is similarly atmospheric in the *Lux aeterna*, which features the three lower soloists.

With the agitated opening recitative of the *Libera me*, Verdi returns to the world of *Aida*. This potent *scena* reprises material from the *Requiem aeternam* and *Dies irae*, summarizing and telescoping the entire drama of the Requiem before ending with a final plea for deliverance, marked *morendo* ("dying"), that trails off into silence.

 RECOMMENDED RECORDINGS

Elisabeth Schwarzkopf, Christa Ludwig, Nicolai Gedda, Nicolai Ghiaurov; Philharmonia Orchestra & Chorus/ Carlo Maria Giulini.
EMI CDCB 47257 [2 CDs; with Quattro pezzi sacri]

Susan Dunn, Diane Curry, Jerry Hadley, Paul Plishka; Atlanta Symphony Orchestra & Chorus/ Robert Shaw.
Telarc CD 80152 [2 CDs; with other works]

Giulini's broad but dramatic account from the mid-1960s brings the listener most convincingly into the operatic world of the score. What a performance it is, and what singing Giulini conjures from his soloists! Their heartfelt expression, the splendid singing of the Philharmonia Chorus, and the conductor's visionary insights into the music are the glories of this recording; the sound is not. Bass is deficient, and tape saturation in the loudest passages obscures detail and puts a glare on the brass.

Shaw learned from the master, Arturo Toscanini, and in his 1987 recording he managed to surpass him in some ways. Shaw is unerring in his staging of climaxes, and he draws phrasing and dynamics from the chorus that other conductors can only dream of. Points are made with exhilarating effect; the bass drum in the *Dies irae* is splendidly hammered, and the whooping brass in the "*Tuba mirum*" is breathtaking. Telarc's recording captures everything from the choral whispers to the crack of doom with impressive fidelity.

Opera conductor Carlo Maria Giulini leads the most beautifully sung Verdi Requiem on disc.

CHAPTER VI

OPERA

*L*ooked at one way, opera is indefensibly silly: where else do people stop in the middle of the most climactic moments of their lives and sing? Looked at another way, opera is the most powerful of all theatrical experiences, one where emotion, that most precious of human commodities, is distilled to purity, and character is crystallized in a few lines of music.

At the end of the 16th century, a group of Florentine musicians, poets, and scholars known as the Camerata tried to re-create the experience of ancient Greek theater by means of a new style of dramatic singing, called the *stile rappresentativo* or "theatrical style." The attempt failed, but opera was born. The first public opera house opened in Venice in 1637, and the growth of the art form was so rapid that by 1645 the English diarist John Evelyn wrote of the opera: "plays are represented in recitative music by the most excellent musicians, vocal and instrumental, with a variety of scenes painted and contrived, with . . . machines for flying in the air, and other wonderful notions; taken together, it is one of the most magnificent and expensive diversions the wit of man can invent."

Opera has changed drastically in the intervening 350 years,

though it is still a magnificent and expensive diversion. During the 1600s it developed from a courtly entertainment, in which the members of a noble household could even play a part, into a thoroughly commercial, public spectacle. Though it spread throughout Europe, opera remained the province of Italian poets and musicians. The division of opera into two main genres, the serious (opera seria) and the comic (opera buffa), led to a polarization of style, and endless debate, during the 18th century. The typical opera seria involved three pairs of lovers and a set of complications ultimately resolved in a happy ending. Its scene structure generally followed a three-act plan with 12 scenes to each act, the focal point of each scene being a *da capo* aria. Where opera seria sought to be edifying and spectacular, opera buffa proved merely to be entertaining. The buffa style emphasized short motifs and a disjunct line. It put a premium on a singer's acting ability, and allowed situations to develop more quickly and move in a more fluid way than was possible in opera seria.

Mozart contributed to the final flowering of serious opera with *Idomeneo, Rè di Creta* (1781) and *La clemenza di Tito* (1791). His greatest achievements, however, were in the comic genre, though he made of that genre something more serious and profound than any composer before him or, with the exception of Rossini and Verdi, since. The process so imaginatively revealed in his works, of blurring the divisions between styles and recombining their elements in new ways, was carried on by Rossini and others in the first decades of the 19th century. With the dawn of Romanticism came a new subjectivity and a renewed interest in social, moral, and political issues, amply reflected in the operas of the two giants of that era, Wagner and Verdi. Their works demanded playing of unprecedented expressive scope from the orchestra and required singers with voices of enormous power to be heard over it.

This tendency toward enlargement of sound and gesture continued into the 20th century. But the temptation to go to extremes proved so great that the history of contemporary opera has largely been one of retrenchment—centering on a new engagement with the text, plausible drama and telling musical characterization. Psychological realism has been the guiding principle of modern opera, though grandeur, humor, and irony have not been entirely lost.

The Count discovers Cherubino hiding in the Countess's boudoir in Le mariage de Figaro, *1780.*

WOLFGANG AMADEUS MOZART

*M*ore than anything else, what inspired Mozart was the act of characterization; for him, music *was* theater. Where other composers were content to reach into the grab-bag of stereotypes and come up with formula music and two-dimensional figures, Mozart sought to create living, breathing, three-dimensional characters who could, in effect, make the stage disappear. His own intense interest in humankind endowed him with an insight into personal relationships and an ability to see situations from different points of view, which enabled him to transcend operatic conventions.

Mozart's nose for the theater told him that Beaumarchais's 1781 sequel to *Le barbier de Séville*, entitled *La folle journée, ou le mariage de Figaro* (*The Madcap Day, or The Marriage of Figaro*), would make an excellent libretto. By the time he came across the play in 1784, the sharp, critical assessment of the social order that lurked between its lines had already caused performances to be banned throughout Europe. Mozart was aware that the controversy surrounding the *Figaro* play would make an operatic setting an exciting prospect for the public.

Fortunately, Mozart also had at hand the new court poet—and notorious free spirit—Lorenzo da Ponte, to make the play into a libretto. In order to fashion the complex action of the play into material suitable for singing, Da Ponte had to streamline the plot. While the satiric point of the comedy was marginally blunted by his modifications, the action was compressed and the pace quickened. Mozart played an active role in shaping the libretto, sending page after page back to Da Ponte for alterations as he worked out each scene's musical structure on paper and in his head. The premiere took place on May 1, 1786, at the Burgtheater in Vienna, with Mozart conducting from the keyboard.

Same scene with Frederica von Stade as Cherubino, c. 1986.

NVITED TO PRAGUE shortly after Figaro's *premiere there, Mozart found the populace already dancing to quadrilles and waltzes from the opera. "Here nothing is discussed but* Figaro," *Mozart wrote. "Nothing is played, blown, sung, or whistled but* Figaro. *No opera is succeeding like* Figaro. Figaro *and eternally* Figaro!"

Despite the public's enthusiasm for the score, which compelled the emperor to issue a decree after the third performance banning repetitions of ensemble numbers at court theaters, *Le nozze di Figaro* was not a success. It dropped out of the repertory after nine performances, thoroughly eclipsed by Vicente Martín y Soler's *Una cosa rara* (for which Mozart took friendly revenge in the finale of *Don Giovanni*, quoting one of its tunes as dinner music). Fortunately—for Mozart and for posterity—*Figaro* was produced in Prague in December 1786 and enjoyed an instant success.

With this work, Mozart carried the architecture of opera, and at the same time the art of characterization, into new realms. As music critic William Mann has pointed out, *Figaro* "is not just about comic tussles between master and servant, or between men and women, but about the interplay of real human beings." One reason it succeeds is that its arias are among the most brilliant crystallizations of mood in all of opera. Not only do they convey the unique essence of each principal character—Figaro's playful humor and panache, the Countess's bittersweet longing, the Count's vengeful pride, Cherubino's breathless infatuation, Susanna's deep, forgiving love—they also anchor the very structure of the opera itself. Still, *Figaro*'s real greatness lies in its ensemble numbers, to which Mozart gives hitherto unprecedented dramatic and comedic thrust. No matter how complex they become—and the Act III sextet is one of the most delectably complicated numbers in the repertory (according to both Michael Kelly, who created the role of Don Basilio, and Constanze Mozart, it was Mozart's favorite music)—they remain shapely and supple and never lose touch with the musical line. It is in these ensembles that the conversational style Mozart had perfected prior to *Figaro* comes to the fore . . . and in them as well that Susanna, the opera's true central figure, comes into her own.

One byproduct of *Figaro*'s success in Prague was a commission for a new opera, to be produced

MOZART and the librettist Da Ponte *(above) had met in 1783, shortly after Antonio Salieri had brought Da Ponte to Vienna. At first, Mozart was skeptical: "If he is in league with Salieri," he wrote, "I will never get anything out of him. But I would dearly love to show what I can do in an Italian opera." By the time Mozart broached the subject of* Figaro *to Da Ponte, he was even hungrier for the chance to show what he could do, and a good deal less suspicious of his collaborator. Da Ponte, aware of Mozart's ability, agreed at once.*

in the Bohemian capital the following autumn. Mozart again asked Da Ponte for a libretto, and the two agreed on the story of Don Juan. With time short and his hands full, Da Ponte needed a template; he found it in the libretto by Giovanni Bertati for Giuseppe Gazzaniga's one-act opera *Don Giovanni Tenorio o sia Il convitato di pietra*, which had just been premiered in Venice on February 5, 1787. Borrowing substantially from it, Da Ponte expanded the structure from one act to two, duplicating the layout of the first act when he fashioned the second.

This clever patchwork was handed over to Mozart, who began work on the score in the spring of 1787. Most of the opera was composed in Vienna that summer; on October 1, Mozart departed for Prague, with the overture, several numbers, and many of the recitatives as yet unwritten. The overture waited until the last moment: it may have been penned only two days before the first performance, which took place on October 29, 1787.

Il dissoluto punito o sia Il Don Giovanni (The Rake Punished, or Don Giovanni), the title Mozart and Da Ponte gave their creation, enjoyed a successful premiere in Prague but was less enthusiastically received when it was staged in Vienna half a year later. Since then, however, no other Mozart opera has been more widely performed. Theatrically, *Don Giovanni* is not nearly as tight a piece as *Figaro*, yet it is somehow more vivid on the stage because of the edge Mozart's music brings to its characters and situations. Mozart also goes further than he had in *Figaro* toward achieving a symphonic unity of key. For example, the overture and the opening numbers of the first act follow the harmonic plan of a full-scale symphony in D minor; the formal strength of the two finales is derived from much the same process.

The profile of Mozart's music is extraordinarily high throughout, and the characterization of the opera's principal figures—Don Giovanni, his servant Leporello, the two high-born ladies Donna

Joan Sutherland as the vengeful Donna Anna in Don Giovanni.

R AGE IS one of music's most frequently encountered emotions, usually brought on by what Shakespeare famously called "green-eyed jealousy." Donna Elvira's entrance aria in Don Giovanni, "Ah! chi mi dice mai," is a classic rage aria. The symphonic literature boasts several gripping treatments of the emotion, among them Dvořák's concert overture Othello (1892) and Janáček's Jealousy (1894). But the most telling portrait of rage in all of music is Verdi's Otello.

Anna and Donna Elvira, and the peasant girl Zerlina—is virtuosic. Don Giovanni, the chameleon, moves easily in both the highest and lowest circles, as the varied stylistic shading of his numbers makes clear. Leporello, who would like to be a cavalier, is good at mimicking the stations of others (as his catalog aria shows) and is ultimately more honest than his master. The discarded Elvira, easily wronged and a little absurd, has the most florid music in the opera, while Anna, the cold goddess of fury, conveys more masculine authority in her delivery than does her wimpish suitor, Don Ottavio. And there is a subtle polish to the rusticity of Zerlina; Mozart, in the duet "Là ci darem la mano," shows her playing on Don Giovanni's reflexes, allowing him to chase her until *she* catches *him*. The extraordinary detail Mozart finds in his characters contributes to the greatness of *Don Giovanni*, as does the way his music balances the comic and the serious, transcending the limits of genre.

On his return to Vienna following the premiere of *Don Giovanni*, Mozart heard the news that Gluck had just died. Three weeks later, Mozart was appointed by the emperor to succeed Gluck as court composer, at a salary of 800 gulden—less than half the 2,000 gulden Gluck had received. Mozart's finances, which had begun to deteriorate around the time he started work on *Don Giovanni*, remained severely straitened for several years. But by the end of 1790, things were looking up— and Mozart's fortunes improved dramatically in 1791 with the arrival of commissions for *La clemenza di Tito* and *Die Zauberflöte*.

The latter had come from his old friend, the actor-impresario Emanuel Schikaneder, a fellow Freemason who had settled in Vienna in 1789 to run the Theater auf der Wieden. Faced with an impending financial crisis and in need of a sure hit, he asked Mozart to collaborate on a *Zauberoper* ("magic opera") in German. *Die Zauberflöte* (*The Magic Flute*) belongs to the genre called *Singspiel* (similar to opera but with spoken dialog rather than recitatives). Notwithstanding its curious blend of fairy tale, Masonic ritual, and commedia dell'arte, the text fits firmly into the style and traditions of the popular Viennese theater of the day. The music, however, is of a profundity altogether outside of tradition.

The mock-solemn overture to *Die Zauberflöte* is one of the most brilliant instrumental movements Mozart ever fashioned. The numbers, ensembles, and set pieces that follow are extraordinary both in their variety and in the richness of their characterization, and they exhibit that uncanny finesse of Mozart's late style. The settings range from direct and folkish (as in Papageno's opening song) to ornately old-fashioned (the first-act rage aria of the Queen of the Night) to downright anachronistic (the *cantus firmus* duet for the Armed Men). But there is a strangely forward-looking Romanticism to the scoring and harmony in Tamino's "*Dies Bildnis ist bezaubernd schön*" ("This picture is bewitchingly lovely"), as well as a spirituality in the choruses of the priests that anticipates what will come in Wagner's *Parsifal*. Mozart dearly loved *Die Zauberflöte*, perhaps more than any of his other operatic creations. He could not have known that it would become the foundation of German Romantic opera, but he did know the value of what he had written. He died two months and a few days after the opera's first performance.

DOCTORS IN OPERA *are often portrayed as quacks or lechers. In* Così fan tutte *Mozart pokes fun at the theories of Franz Mesmer in the scene where the maid Despina masquerades as a doctor and "cures" the supposedly poisoned Ferrando and Guglielmo with a magnet. Doctor Bartolo, a character in both* The Barber of Seville *and* The Marriage of Figaro, *is a schemer lusting after his nubile ward in the former opera, and a blustering fool bent on revenge in the latter. In Donizetti's opera* L'Elisir d'amore, *Doctor Dulcamara is not above passing off a bottle of wine as the mysterious "elixir of love."*

 RECOMMENDED RECORDINGS

MOZART: *LE NOZZE DI FIGARO*

Samuel Ramey, Lucia Popp, Thomas Allen, Kiri Te Kanawa, Frederica von Stade; London Opera Chorus, London Philharmonic Orchestra/Sir George Solti.

London 410 150-2 [3 CDs; 1981]

Humorous period illustration of Papageno, the bird catcher in Die Zauberflöte.

MOZART: *DON GIOVANNI*

Eberhard Wächter, Joan Sutherland, Luigi Alva, Gottlob Frick, Elisabeth Schwarzkopf, Giuseppe Taddei, Piero Cappuccilli, Graziella Sciutti; Philharmonia Orchestra & Chorus/ Carlo Maria Giulini.

EMI CDCC 47260 [3 CDs; 1959]

MOZART: *DIE ZAUBERFLÖTE*

Peter Schreier, Anneliese Rothenberger, Walter Berry, Edda Moser, Kurt Moll; Chorus & Orchestra of the Bavarian State Opera/ Wolfgang Sawallisch.

EMI CDCB 47827 [2 CDs; 1972; special import]

BEETHOVEN & WEBER

*B*eethoven's only opera, *Fidelio* (1806), is a *Singspiel* like *Die Zauberflöte*, but it is a very different sort of work. Beethoven was not a man of the theater as Mozart was, but a man of ideas, of deep and passionately held convictions. Each character in *Fidelio*—which celebrates the courage and idealism of its heroine, Leonore, in the face of mortal danger—represents an ideal type, a far different approach from Mozart's emphasis on human complication. There is, for all that, great humanity in this music, but it is the ideas behind the drama—the message of brotherhood, the struggle for liberty and justice—that are most important to Beethoven. So important, in fact, that as themes they emerge again in the Ninth Symphony, where the composer finished what he had begun in *Fidelio*. The opera's only weakness is the sectional framework its libretto imposed on Beethoven's symphonically oriented sense of structure, though he made a virtue of the defect by giving most of the set pieces unique musical profiles, challenging himself to different compositional problems in each one.

Still, whereas Beethoven's symphonies, concertos, and chamber music cast a towering shadow over the 19th century, *Fidelio* had little impact in the sphere of opera. By contrast, it would be hard to overestimate the role played by his younger countryman Carl Maria von Weber (1786–1826) in the rise of German Romantic opera. Even if only one of Weber's works has held a place in the repertory, his influence on Wagner was clearly decisive. *Der Freischütz* touches on some of the grand themes of Romanticism: supernatural interference in the natural order, redemption through love, and the individual's transcendence of the social hierarchy. Weber's treatment of this material, particularly his evocative scoring and dramatic use of harmony, had tremendous impact not only on Wagner but also on Berlioz, Berg, and Richard Strauss.

 RECOMMENDED RECORDINGS

BEETHOVEN: *FIDELIO*

Christa Ludwig, Jon Vickers, Gottlob Frick, Walter Berry, Ingeborg Hallstein, Gerhard Unger; Philharmonia Orchestra & Chorus/Otto Klemperer.
EMI Studio CDMB 69324 [2 CDs]

Gundula Janowitz, René Kollo, Manfred Jungwirth, Hans Sotin, Lucia Popp, Adolf Dallapozza; Vienna State Opera Chorus, Vienna Philharmonic/ Leonard Bernstein.
Deutsche Grammophon 419 436-2 [2 CDs]

WEBER: *DER FREISCHÜTZ*

Karita Mattila, Francisco Araiza, Ekkehard Wlaschiha, Eva Lind, Kurt Moll; Leipzig Radio Chorus, Staatskapelle Dresden/Sir Colin Davis.
Philips 426 319-2 [2 CDs; 1990]

BEETHOVEN *based* Fidelio *on a rescue drama by J.-N. Bouilly entitled* Léonore, ou L'amour conjugal (Leonore, or The Triumph of Married Love), *a typical piece of Revolution-era literature. He originally called the opera* Leonore *(hence the name of the three overtures he composed for early productions), but later changed the title to* Fidelio—*the alias under which Leonore becomes a jailer in the prison where her husband Florestan is incarcerated.*

ROSSINI LIKED to say that he had cried only three times in his life: the night his earliest opera failed, the day he watched a truffled turkey go overboard at a boating party luncheon, and the first time he heard Paganini play the violin. He hated work, appreciated the good things in life, and always lived up to the maxim that "delight must be the aim and basis of music."

BEL CANTO & GRAND OPERA

The second decade of the 19th century saw the emergence of a new lion of the operatic stage, Gioacchino Rossini (1792–1868), whose comic gift was matched only by his prodigious capacity for work. In a mere 19 years (1810–29) he composed 39 operas, many of them works of the first order. He revitalized the buffa style, innovating as he went, and brought a sharpness to the art of characterization that rivaled Mozart's. *Il barbiere di Siviglia* (*The Barber of Seville*) was not Rossini's only masterpiece, but it is his best known work and one of the greatest comic operas ever written. It has held the stage continuously since its premiere in 1816, making it the oldest work never to have fallen out of the repertory. The libretto is among the finest Rossini set, and it inspired a score full of musical riches that remains as fresh today as on the day it was first heard. That Rossini was a week shy of his 24th birthday when that happened makes *The Barber of Seville* only that much more of a miracle.

Rossini's vocal writing, along with that of his near-contemporaries Gaetano Donizetti (1797–1848) and Vincenzo Bellini (1801–1835), exemplified the precepts of *bel canto* ("fine singing"), marked by a light, mellifluous tone and effortless delivery in florid passages. Donizetti's most frequently encountered opera, *Lucia di Lammermoor*, received its premiere in Naples in 1835. Composed to a skillful libretto by Salvatore Cammarano (based on Sir Walter Scott's novel *The Bride of Lammermoor*), it firmly established the composer's reputation and served as one of the cornerstones of Italian Romanticism. Its plot is a typically gothic affair involving a family feud, an arranged marriage, and a forged letter, leading to betrayal, murder, and madness. Its music stands at the crossroads between the decorative style of *bel canto* and the more sensational manner of the mid-19th century, soon to find its greatest exponent in

Verdi. Bellini contributed three masterpieces to the literature: *La sonnambula* (1831), *Norma* (1831), and *I puritani* (1835). *Norma*, his supreme accomplishment, is full of the long-breathed, often melancholy melodies for which the composer was celebrated, and its suggestive scoring shows what a sensitive ear Bellini possessed.

The French Revolution had marked the end of the world that brought opera into being, but scarcely the end of opera. In the wake of the great upheaval, there was a crystallization of social, moral, and political values that in fact gave opera, and the arts in general, a renewed vibrancy. Change became a value, as did resistance to change, and in much of Europe the revolutionary type and the bourgeois anti-type existed side by side. Opera found a new universe of ideas and situations to explore—and in Paris a new style of opera, called grand opera, developed directly out of the ferment. Grand opera's *spiritus rector* was the aptly named Eugène Scribe (1791–1861), an inexhaustible writer whose librettos worked endless variations on the same basic formula: the parade of history in five acts of pageantry and extravagance, central characters caught in the flux of religious or patriotic movements, huge tableaux involving the chorus, and awesome denouements.

Parisian grand opera was a business. Fortunes were spent on the decor and were made at the box office, and the so-called claque—whose caesar, Auguste Levasseur, was another aptly named figure—ruled triumphantly over docile audiences. One of the first grand operas was Rossini's 1829 extravaganza *Guillaume Tell* (*William Tell*), which relied for much of its effect on crowd scenes and pageantry. Rossini retired soon after its premiere, ceding the field to the German-born Giacomo Meyerbeer (1791–1864). Meyerbeer's greatest success came with *Les Huguenots* (1836), which portrays the St. Bartholomew's Day massacre of 1572 and was the first work to achieve 1,000 performances at the Paris Opéra.

Critics ever since the mid-19th century have

"What pleasures there are for a barber of quality," muses Figaro between shaves.

condemned grand opera as a dramatically shallow premise, a magnificent ship with an inadequate engine that went straight to the bottom as soon as it had been launched. But Parisian grand opera provided a blueprint for many of the finest works of Romanticism, as we shall see.

Cecilia Bartoli: a bright new star in the bel canto *firmament.*

A Word About Music

"Opera in English is, in the main, just about as sensible as baseball in Italian."
—H. L. Mencken

⊚ RECOMMENDED RECORDINGS

ROSSINI: *IL BARBIERE DI SIVIGLIA*
Leo Nucci, William Matteuzzi, Cecilia Bartoli, Paata Burchuladze; Chorus & Orchestra of the Teatro Comunale di Bologna/Giuseppe Patanè.
London 425 520-2 [3 CDs; 1988]

DONIZETTI: *LUCIA DI LAMMERMOOR*
Joan Sutherland, Luciano Pavarotti, Sherrill Milnes, Nicolai Ghiaurov; Chorus & Orchestra of the Royal Opera House, Covent Garden/Richard Bonynge.
London 410 193-2 [3 CDs; 1971]

BELLINI: *NORMA*
Joan Sutherland, Luciano Pavarotti, Montserrat Caballé, Samuel Ramey; Chorus & Orchestra of the Welsh National Opera/ Richard Bonynge.
London 414 476-2 [3 CDs; 1984]

ROSSINI: *GUILLAUME TELL*
Gabriel Bacquier, Montserrat Caballé, Nicolai Gedda, Mady Mesplé; Ambrosian Opera Chorus, Royal Philharmonic Orchestra/Lamberto Gardelli.
EMI Classics CDMD 69951 [4 CDs; 1973]

MEYERBEER: *LES HUGUENOTS*
Joan Sutherland, Anastasios Vrenios, Gabriel Bacquier, Martina Arroyo; Ambrosian Opera Chorus, New Philharmonia Orchestra/Richard Bonynge.
London 430 549-2 [4 CDs; 1969]

*WAGNER (above) be-
came, through talent,
hard work and ego, the most
prominent musician of his
era. As a young man, influenced by the writings of
anarchists and revolutionar-
ies, he espoused quite radical
views. As a result of his support for the Dresden uprising
of 1849, a warrant for his
arrest was issued in Ger-
many; he spent the next 14
years in exile, living mainly
in Switzerland.*

RICHARD WAGNER

*W*agner (1813–1882) was the consummate man of the theater and one of
the greatest opera composers in history. As an
intellectual he was a fascinating paradox of prag-
matism and idealism (had it not been for his
indisputable talent, he might easily have been
branded a crackpot), the living embodiment of
pride and prejudice. But as an artist he was gov-
erned by a visionary insight into the human
character and emotions, as well as by an unerring
instinct for what could be achieved on stage and
in musical sound. Wagner's early works carried
forward the precepts of German Romanticism
and grand opera, while boldly breaking new
ground. His mature music dramas changed the
course of music history; in them, Wagner developed a hauntingly sensuous musical language and
took harmony and orchestration to new realms.

His first distinctive work, *Der fliegende Holländer*
(*The Flying Dutchman*), has a revolutionary score
in which the sweep of Wagner's musical ideas and
the Teutonic power of his orchestration collide
head on with the melodic trappings and sectional
structure of grand opera. Here the dark side of
Romanticism, glimpsed briefly in Weber's *Der
Freischütz*, emerges with overwhelming force in
the person of the Dutchman, the legendary sailor
condemned to perpetually roam the seas in search
of a woman who will be faithful unto death. The
ominous subject matter excited Wagner's imagination to incandescence: the Dutchman's first-act
monolog is a masterpiece of psychological portraiture, and the musical effects that bring his
ghost ship to life are among the eeriest in opera.

Tannhäuser, which Wagner called a "grand Romantic opera," was composed between 1843 and
1845 and revised 15 years later for its Paris premiere. Its story is based on two legends that
originally had no connection with each other. In
one, the medieval knight Tannhäuser tires of the

A Viennese caricature of King Ludwig as Lohengrin. Wagner is the man in the moon.

Mad King Ludwig

Among the last and most generous of opera's princely patrons was the starstruck (some say neurotically obsessed) Ludwig II, King of Bavaria, through whose efforts Richard Wagner's Tristan und Isolde, Die Meistersinger, Das Rheingold, *and* Die Walküre *all received their premieres. During the 19 years of their acquaintance (1864–83), Ludwig lavished a total of 562,914 marks on Wagner. Ludwig's death, by drowning in the waters of the Starnbergersee near Munich, was most likely arranged by his own family to put an end to such excesses.*

affections of the goddess Venus and makes his way to Rome to seek the Pope's forgiveness for his life of ease and lust. In the other, the knight Heinrich von Ofterdingen receives demonic inspiration in a singing contest that takes place on the Wartburg. Wagner merged the characters of Heinrich and Tannhäuser, and he also created the figure of Elisabeth to serve as a foil to Venus, representing the pole of spiritual love as Venus represents that of physical love.

Tannhäuser, like the Flying Dutchman, is a doomed man who can be redeemed only by the self-sacrificing love of a woman. The trial of that love lies at the heart of the opera, where it is surrounded by the kind of spectacle one would expect to find in grand opera. The second act, which centers on the singing contest, opens with one of the finest set pieces in all of Wagner, Elisabeth's pulsating *"Dich, teure Halle,"* and it also includes a classic grand-opera processional.

Lohengrin (1850) marks a turning point in Wagner's development, a decisive step away from the conventions of grand opera toward the continuous music drama of *Tristan und Isolde* and the *Ring* cycle. Set pieces and numbers are abandoned as such, and the action unfolds more or less uninterrupted in lengthy scenes, with powerful climaxes based on confrontations between the central characters: Lohengrin, the mysterious knight from a "distant land" who appears, as if by magic, on a boat drawn by a swan; the gentle Elsa of Brabant, falsely accused of murdering her brother, whom the stranger champions and marries on the condition that she never ask his name; and the black-hearted Telramund and his sorceress wife, Ortrud, who attempt to undo Elsa by sowing doubt in her mind about Lohengrin. Wagner builds the opera to a potent climax in which good triumphs—without the good living happily ever after. His music for the final scene, prefigured in the opera's luminous orchestral prelude, is richly Romantic and has an emotive power quite new to the operatic sphere.

A Word About Music

"**W**agner has beautiful moments but awful quarter hours."
—Gioacchino Rossini

Placido Domingo, whose Lohengrin has the requisite strength along with Mediterranean warmth.

The largest undertaking of Wagner's career was *Der Ring des Nibelungen* (*The Ring of the Nibelung*), a four-work cycle that occupied him for a quarter century. No work of art has represented a greater investment on the part of its author, and few have had anything like the impact. The *Ring* is an allegory of the economic, political, and social conditions of Wagner's day. It also marks the zenith of 19th-century grand opera; the cycle's characters, situations, and complications, brilliantly treated as they are, emerge from the rich soil of that tradition, even if Wagner's musical architecture and his dramaturgy surpass anything that had previously been put on the stage. The theme of the *Ring* is one of redemption through love and death—a theme Wagner had touched on repeatedly, and explored most trenchantly in *Tristan und Isolde* (composed, perhaps out of necessity, with the *Ring* project in mid-course). A subsidiary theme involves the freedom of the individual to act outside the bounds of higher authority or law, and what the consequences for such actions are.

Wagner wrote the librettos of the four *Ring* operas in reverse order, starting in 1848 with *Götterdämmerung* (which he originally entitled *Siegfrieds Tod*), then drafting *Siegfried*, *Die Walküre*, and *Das Rheingold*. The four poems, as Wagner called them, took four years to write, and their texts were published in 1853 before a single note of the music had been set down. The following year, Wagner completed the score to *Das Rheingold* (which he called a *Vorabend* or "prologue"). He went on to compose the music for the three "evenings" of the cycle, in order: *Die Walküre* (1854–56), *Siegfried* (1856–71), and *Götterdämmerung* (1869–74). Wagner's work on *Siegfried* was broken off in 1857 and resumed in 1869; during that 12-year hiatus he composed *Tristan und Isolde* and *Die Meistersinger*.

Two-and-a-half hours long, *Das Rheingold* is short compared with the other *Ring* operas. Its opening scene takes place at the *bottom* of the

Rhine. During the orchestral introduction, the river's majestic ground tone (E flat) is sustained by the basses as the rest of the orchestra paints a spectacular portrait of the rolling current and shafts of sunlight piercing the depths, illuminating a lump of gold. The drama commences with the dwarf Alberich (the Nibelung of the tetralogy's title) and his theft of the gold from the Rhine Maidens, and it continues as Wotan, the chief of the gods, contracts out the building of Valhalla to a pair of giants. Possession of a ring formed from the gold confers unlimited power on Alberich, so Wotan must steal the ring, along with the horde of gold the dwarf has amassed. Before surrending the ring, Alberich lays a curse on it. The curse is quickly fulfilled when Fasolt and Fafner, the two giants (who have decided to be paid for their labor with the gold stolen from Alberich), fall to arguing over who will get the ring. Fafner kills Fasolt. The opera ends with the gods' emptily victorious march across a rainbow bridge into Valhalla.

The continuous musical structure of *Das Rheingold* is itself a gigantic achievement. Into this, with all the skill of a master builder, Wagner sets the main motifs of the cycle—which he calls leitmotifs and which identify various objects (Valhalla, the ring, the Rhine) as well as key concepts (brooding, the curse, the contract) and personages—preparing the listener for what is to come on the following evenings. Equally impressive is the suggestiveness of Wagner's score, conveying everything from the flow of a river to the flickering malevolence of fire, and even—with radiant brass, shimmering strings, and *six* offstage harps—the hues of a rainbow bridge.

In *Die Walküre*, the focus of Wagner's drama shifts from the gods to humans, specifically the warrior Siegmund and his twin sister Sieglinde, who will become the parents of the central figure of the *Ring* cycle, the hero Siegfried. There is another important relationship around which the final part of the opera revolves, that between

The dwarf Alberich steals the gold from the Rhine Maidens, and the rest—is opera, 15 hours of it.

The Valkyries as motorcycle molls, from Götz Friedrich's radical Ring *production at the Deutsche Oper Berlin.*

BEFORE SIEGFRIEDS Tod *became the* Ring, *Wagner intended to construct a temporary theater and give three performances of the opera as a one-shot deal, a sort of personal Woodstock. After the performances, which were to be free, the theater was to be torn down. Fortunately, the composer was too much the megalomaniac to stick with that plan for very long.*

Wotan and his disobedient but not disloyal daughter, the Valkyrie Brünnhilde. Ordered to see to Siegmund's death, Brünnhilde goes against her father's command, but very much with his deeper feelings—since Siegmund and Sieglinde, now pregnant, are both his children as well—and she spares the doomed man. For her rebellious act, Brünnhilde is sentenced to mortality: she will be left asleep on a rock surrounded by fire, until a hero dares the flames to awaken her. That hero, as yet unborn, will be Siegfried.

The most frequently performed of the *Ring* operas, *Die Walküre* is famous for its Act III prelude, "The Ride of the Valkyries" (used with great effect for Robert Duvall's helicopter attack in the film *Apocalypse Now*). The first act, which goes like a shot, ends with the impassioned love duet of Siegmund and Sieglinde. And there is nothing in opera to compare with the emotion of Wotan's farewell to Brünnhilde at the end of Act III, or with the "Magic Fire Music" of *Die Walküre*'s final pages.

With *Siegfried*, Wagner picks up the thread of his story after about 20 years have elapsed. The young Siegfried, raised in the forest by Alberich's brother Mime (without knowledge of his heroic origin), reforges the fragments of his father Siegmund's sword and puts it to immediate use. He kills Fafner, who has been sitting on the gold horde and the ring since the end of *Das Rheingold*; he then kills Mime, who was planning to kill him and get the gold; and he defiantly shatters Wotan's spear. The hero awakes the sleeping Brünnhilde, woos her, and wins her. *Siegfried* is often thought of as the scherzo of the *Ring* cycle—not only because it comes third, but because it is a rather upbeat piece of theater in spite of the carnage. The music of the final act, which finds Wagner at the peak of his powers, is sublime, exultant. The ecstasy of love is portrayed in a half-hour duet that only the composer of *Tristan und Isolde* could have written.

The complicated plot of *Götterdämmerung* is advanced by some of the greatest music Wagner wrote. Siegfried is brought into contact with the Gibichungs, Gunther and Gutrune, and into conflict with their half-brother Hagen, Alberich's son (just as Siegfried is a surrogate for Wotan, Hagen is for his father). Administered a magic potion, Siegfried loses all memory of Brünnhilde and forcibly woos her disguised as Gunther. Siegfried prepares to marry Gutrune, and against her will Brünnhilde is compelled to be Gunther's bride. In fury at her betrayal by Siegfried, the Valkyrie revenges herself by revealing his one weakness to Hagen. Hagen murders Siegfried, who in his dying moments returns to his senses. In the opera's mind-boggling denouement, Brünnhilde immolates herself on Siegfried's funeral pyre, sparks from which set Valhalla on fire; the Rhine overflows its banks and the Rhine Maidens get back the ring; the reign of the gods ends and the world is redeemed by love.

"Dawn and Siegfried's Rhine Journey" from the opera's Prologue and "Siegfried's Funeral March" from its third act are among the finest pages in all of Wagner. The power of the opening scene of the Prologue, in which the three Norns predict the end of the world, is breathtaking, as are the sweep of the second act and the tragic intensity of Brünnhilde's immolation. With this tumultuous scene, Wagner's *Ring*, the crowning glory of Romantic opera, fittingly comes to an end as well. The first performance of the complete *Ring* cycle took place in the summer of 1876, at the Festspielhaus in Bayreuth that the composer built especially for the occasion.

Between 1857 and 1867, Wagner turned his energies to two extraordinary projects—a love story of towering intensity based on a medieval epic by Gottfried von Strassburg, and a touchingly human comedy set in 16th-century Nuremberg. The love story was *Tristan und Isolde*, the comedy *Die Meistersinger von Nürnberg*. Both were huge works, and the latter also required immense per-

RICHARD *and Cosima Wagner, 1872 (above). Cosima (1837–1930) was the daughter of Franz Liszt and the Countess Marie d'Agoult. In 1857 she married Hans von Bülow, one of Liszt's most brilliant students, by whom she had two daughters. Her involvement with Wagner, whose music both her father and von Bülow had championed, began in 1863. Cosima and Wagner had three children—Isolde, Eva, and Siegfried—all born out of wedlock. They were married in 1870. The* Siegfried Idyll, *named for their son, was written as a birthday present for Cosima.*

THE FESTSPIELHAUS at Bayreuth (above) is made almost entirely of wood on the inside. The floor, ceiling, and benches are all wooden. Most importantly, the "black box" that surrounds the stage and the enormous pit which descends seven levels and 35 feet are also made from wood. For the floor of the pit Wagner found seasoned lumber 150 years old; that wood is now 250 years old, and it gives the theater the resonance of a fine old violin.

forming forces, calling for choruses in each act, a group of 17 principals, and hundreds of extras. Neither was geared to the musical or technical capabilities of the average 19th-century opera house. But each was necessary to Wagner as a study for the musical and dramatic situations that had arisen in his scheme for the *Ring*. Particularly important in this respect was *Tristan*, where Wagner explored the relationship of passion and free will in terms that prepared him for the completion of *Siegfried* and *Götterdämmerung*.

Tristan und Isolde is the mother of all fatal attractions, a story of two neurotic lovers undone yet ultimately transfigured by their love. The opera has only six principal roles (two of which are fairly small), a brief chorus (of men only) at the end of the first act, and a minimum of scenery. Its orchestra is also nearly normal in size, although the score does call at one point for 12 offstage horns. Yet the challenge of putting on *Tristan* was then, and has remained, one of the greatest in the theater. Wagner coined a new musical language when he wrote the work, entrusted the orchestra with a more important and more taxing part in the proceedings than it had ever had, and demanded of his two leading singers unprecedented endurance, compass, and vocal power. The harmonic syntax of *Tristan* is based on a degree of chromaticism never before attempted in tonal music, resulting in a fundamental change in the way harmonic implications and tensions are dealt with. Chords calling for resolution are allowed to stand, which produces in the listener a psychological yearning for resolution that mirrors the unsatisfied longings of the protagonists. The dysfunctional treatment of harmony, in which goals are implied but almost never reached, is masterfully sustained across nearly five hours of music, and with it Wagner opens up a whole new world of expression.

Since its first performance, in Munich in 1865, *Tristan* has held a place apart in the world of opera, standing as the litmus test of conductors, singers, directors, and houses. Wagner institutionalized Romanticism in this work, and with its score he turned the orchestra into the most powerful army in Europe. In imagining the seething confrontations of Tristan and Isolde in the first act, their voluptuous love music in the second, and most of all Tristan's feverish longings and Isolde's ecstatic *Liebestod* (or "love-death") in the finale, Wagner came as close as he ever would to the elusive goal of creating an ideal music drama.

The real hero of *Die Meistersinger von Nürnberg*, as the title makes clear, is not Walther von Stolzing, the young Franconian knight who becomes a mastersinger at the opera's end, but Hans Sachs, the cobbler-poet who has been one from its start. It is his yearning for what he cannot have—the hand of the beautiful but younger Eva, and the freedom to break the rules as Walther does—that gives the work its extraordinary psychological resonance and poignant, bittersweet air of nostalgia. The score is, along with *Tristan und Isolde*, the most autobiographical of Wagner's creations: a part of him resides in the character of Sachs, and a part in Walther, whose triumph over the odds and in spite of the railings of the critics is an allegory of Wagner's own.

It is Sachs, though, who has the opera's most moving and profound music, who sees more than the others, and feels more, and yet must do his best to make another man happy and triumphant. Sachs's two monologs—*"Was duftet doch der Flieder"* in the second act, and *"Wahn! Wahn! Überall Wahn!"* in the third—are among the finest pages in all of Wagner's output, and with their depth of feeling they are certainly the most human. They round out a work filled by big choruses and magnificent orchestral music, as well as warmth and good humor, a work whose C major conclusion is the most unambiguously optimistic gesture Wagner ever made.

Following the premiere of the *Ring* at Bayreuth,

Fischer-Dieskau as Sachs conveyed the humanity of Wagner's hero with the skill of a Lieder artist.

Adolf Menzel's drawing of Wagner during the Ring *rehearsal at Bayreuth, 1875.*

Wagner turned to what would be his last great project, *Parsifal*. The composer, who had sketched his first thoughts for its libretto way back in 1857, envisioned *Parsifal* as a work of consecration for the stage at Bayreuth. He intended it to be presented only there, and his wish was honored for a number of years after his death.

Wagner had touched on the character of Parsifal before, in his opera *Lohengrin*. In the final scene, Lohengrin announces that he is Parsifal's son and that his father presides over the knights of the Holy Grail. Perhaps the idea of telling Parsifal's own tale—how he was elevated to leadership of the knights—stayed with Wagner during the years that separated the two works. What changed, without any doubt, was Wagner's musical language. In *Parsifal*, the chromaticism of *Tristan* is applied with remarkable subtlety, and Wagner's use of leitmotif seems even more organic than it had been in the *Ring*. The scoring is extraordinarily refined and transparent, the music's long-breathed lines tailor-made for the acoustics at Bayreuth. The story of Parsifal, the "pure fool," is full of religious overtones, but Wagner handles them without the bombast that marked his philosophical writings on religion. His music, brilliantly evocative in the Act II portrayal of the evil Klingsor and his magic domain, rises to great heights of expressiveness in the final act, as Parsifal's acts of compassion win salvation for the suffering Amfortas, the humble Kundry, and the fellowship of the Holy Grail.

 RECOMMENDED RECORDINGS

WAGNER: *DER FLIEGENDE HOLLÄNDER*

José van Dam, Dunja Vejzović, Kurt Moll, Peter Hofmann; Vienna State Opera Chorus, Berlin Philharmonic/Herbert von Karajan.
EMI Classics CDMB 64650 [2 CDs; 1981–83]

WAGNER: *TANNHÄUSER*

**René Kollo, Helga Dernesch,
Christa Ludwig, Hans Sotin;
Vienna State Opera Chorus,
Vienna Philharmonic/Sir Georg Solti.**

London 414 581-2 [3 CDs; 1971]

WAGNER: *LOHENGRIN*

**Placido Domingo, Jessye Norman,
Eva Randová, Siegmund Nimsgern,
Hans Sotin; Vienna State Opera Chorus,
Vienna Philharmonic/Sir Georg Solti.**

London 421 053-2 [4 CDs; 1985–86]

Solti finished the 30-year job of recording Wagner's major operas with a stellar Lohengrin.

WAGNER: *DER RING DES NIBELUNGEN*

**Birgit Nilsson, Wolfgang Windgassen,
Theo Adam, Gustav Neidlinger, Kurt Böhme,
Josef Greindl, James King, Leonie Rysanek,
et al.; Chorus & Orchestra of the
Bayreuth Festival/Karl Böhm.**

Philips 420 325-2 [14 CDs; live, 1967]. Also available
separately: Das Rheingold [412 475-2; 2 CDs], Die
Walküre [412 478-2; 4 CDs], Siegfried [412 483-2;
4 CDs], and Götterdämmerung [412 488-2; 4 CDs]

WAGNER: *TRISTAN UND ISOLDE*

**Wolfgang Windgassen, Birgit Nilsson,
Christa Ludwig, Eberhard Wächter,
Martti Talvela; Chorus & Orchestra of the
Bayreuth Festival/Karl Böhm.**

Deutsche Grammophon 419 889-2 [3 CDs; live, 1966]

Furtwängler's visionary intensity makes for a gripping Tristan.

**Ludwig Suthaus, Kirsten Flagstad,
Blanche Thebom, Dietrich Fischer-Dieskau,
Josef Greindl; Chorus of the
Royal Opera House, Covent Garden,
Philharmonia Orchestra/
Wilhelm Furtwängler.**

EMI CDCD 47321 [4 CDs; 1952]

Wagner beating the drum for Parsifal, *his last opera.*

WAGNER: *DIE MEISTERSINGER VON NÜRNBERG*

Dietrich Fischer-Dieskau, Placido Domingo, Catarina Ligendza, Horst Laubenthal; Chorus & Orchestra of the Deutsche Oper Berlin/Eugen Jochum.

Deutsche Grammophon 415 278-2 [4 CDs]

WAGNER: *PARSIFAL*

Peter Hofmann, Kurt Moll, José van Dam, Siegmund Nimsgern, Dunja Vejzović; Chorus of the Deutsche Oper Berlin, Berlin Philharmonic/Herbert von Karajan.

Deutsche Grammophon 413 347-2 [4 CDs]

GIUSEPPE VERDI

*T*he preeminent figure in Italian opera during the second half of the 19th century, Verdi was perhaps the greatest dramatist the art of music has yet known. He reached the plateau of maturity with three back-to-back masterpieces, *Rigoletto*, *Il trovatore*, and *La traviata*, written between 1850 and 1853. These operas capped a long period of hard work, frequently mingled with frustration, to which Verdi referred as his years as a "galley slave." While at the oars he managed to turn out many good operas, and a couple of near-great ones in *Nabucco* (1842) and *Ernani* (1844). But it was with *Rigoletto* that he finally broke the shackles of convention and began to open the closed forms of Italian opera.

Part of *Rigoletto*'s success was due to its being based on a great play, Victor Hugo's *Le roi s'amuse*, which had premiered in 1832. Its volatile plot revolved around the amoral behavior of a ruler, which gave Verdi plenty of trouble with the censors. In the end, François I became the Duke of Mantua, who in Verdi's treatment emerges as a

THE BROAD, FERTILE Po valley seems to stimulate creativity. Verdi and Monteverdi, Italy's two greatest composers, were born in the Po valley, and the conductor Arturo Toscanini came from one of the region's hubs, the city of Parma.

Luciano Pavarotti captures the Duke's dangerous sophistication in Rigoletto.

complex, introspective character, shifting the emotional ground of the original somewhat. But the real focus of the opera remains the hunchback Rigoletto, whom Verdi treats as a tragic figure of commanding stature, willful yet noble in the vein of King Lear. Gilda, the daughter whom he tries to protect and ends up destroying, is also a substantial figure, one who reaches a new level of awareness as a result of her suffering. Her part, verging on the coloratura range, presents some unusual technical challenges.

Verdi's score is marvelously alive, though its music is often tough, at times almost brutal, as befits the subject. This was a revolutionary departure from the smoothness of *bel canto*, but Verdi was always more interested in elemental emotional intensity and the fury of the action than he was in pretty sound. Among the opera's highlights are its taut opening scene, which achieves a grand dramatic crescendo, and the final act's brilliantly evocative storm scene. Gilda's *"Caro nome"* and the Duke's *"La donna è mobile"* are justly celebrated arias, but it is with the quartet *"Bella figlia dell'amore"* that Verdi scales the heights of characterization by limning four personalities—those of Rigoletto, the Duke, Gilda, and Maddalena—simultaneously.

Il trovatore (1853) is dramatically less fine than either *Rigoletto* or *La traviata*, which did not prevent it from becoming one of the most popular operas of the 19th century—so popular that its "babies switched at birth" plot twist could be parodied by Gilbert and Sullivan in *The Gondoliers*, and the music itself by the Marx Brothers in *A Night at the Opera*. Here is a blood-and-thunder opera of the old style, with a libretto that relies more on passion and complication than it does on real character. But one still finds much great music in *Trovatore*, in addition to the famous Anvil Chorus. The gypsy Azucena's *"Stride la vampa,"* which follows that chorus, will always make people's hair stand on end, and Manrico's *"Di quella pira"* remains the finest exit aria Verdi ever wrote.

The real heart of the opera lies in its heroine Leonora's two great arias, *"Tacea la notte placida"* and *"D'amor sull'ali rosee."* In fact, there are enough great arias in the work to keep everyone happy, which is what inspired Enrico Caruso's memorable dictum that all *Trovatore* needs to be a success is the four greatest singers in the world.

La traviata, the most intimate of the three works that launched Verdi's middle period, is based on the play *La dame aux camélias* by Alexandre Dumas *fils*. It is the only one of Verdi's operas to take as its subject a story set in "the present day." From a dramatic standpoint, it reflects the composer's growing interest in social questions and their relation to characterization; from a musical standpoint, it shows him successfully injecting into the mold of Italian opera the new ideas that were transforming French music at mid-century.

The story was hot off the press when Verdi got it: Marie Duplessis, the real-life courtesan on whom the character Violetta Valéry is based, had died in 1847 at age 23. Dumas had written the novel *La dame aux camélias* in 1848, and he turned it into a play in 1852. By the time Verdi finished his setting of *La traviata* in 1853, he and the soprano Giuseppina Strepponi had been living together out of wedlock for six years, several of them in Paris. The similarities between their situation and that of Violetta and Alfredo Germont, the lovers at the heart of *La traviata*, was unmistakable, and certainly part of the reason Verdi responded so warmly to the story. He was intrigued as well by the complicated triangle, in which the father, Giorgio Germont, is the "other man." The opera is full of glorious intimate moments and conveys a telling insight into the uncertainty, fragility, and painful vulnerability of love. The characterization is deftly shaded, and Verdi builds each act's momentum using techniques perfected in *Rigoletto*. The whole work is a gripping emotional crescendo, and the character of Violetta, the consumptive young woman who sacrifices everything she has for her lover's sake,

Senator Verdi

Verdi was elected to the Italian parliament in 1874 and served as a senator for several years. Even today in Busseto, near Verdi's birthplace, the City Council chamber is dominated by a gilt-framed engraving of the composer in profile. Under that is a crucifix, and to one side, a good deal smaller, a framed color photo of the President of the Republic. Now that's clout!

Verdi conducts a performance of Aida *in Paris, 1876.*

is among Verdi's supreme achievements.

At the other end of Verdi's middle period are two works of extraordinary dramatic scope, *Don Carlo* and *Aida*, with which for many years he himself believed he had brought down the curtain on his career. *Don Carlo* was the second of Verdi's operas to be composed originally for the Paris Opéra (the other was *Les vêpres siciliennes*). Written in French and titled *Don Carlos*, it was first presented at the Opéra, in the customary five acts, in 1867. But it was destined to find its place in the repertory only after being translated into Italian and recast, first into four acts, then back into five, a process Verdi completed in 1886.

Verdi's second thoughts were always better than his first ones, and in its final incarnation *Don Carlo* is a work of astounding musical richness. Grand-opera elements survive in the larger-than-life trappings of the story, and they are particularly prominent in the Act II finale, a reenactment of an auto-da-fé that finds the principals and full chorus on stage and a radiant heavenly voice behind the scene proclaiming the salvation of those about to be set ablaze. But the focus remains firmly on the six principal characters and the issues of love, power, and betrayal that have brought them into conflict.

In spite of the opera's title, its central figure is Philip II, King of Spain, the father of Don Carlo, and a man torn between his devotion to the state, the responsibilities of his position, and the inflexible demands of authority—in this case, the Church, which is represented by the sightless yet terrifying Grand Inquisitor. Carlo is in love with Elisabeth of Valois, the French princess whose fate is to be married not to him, as she hopes, but to his father. Carlo and his friend Rodrigo, Marquis of Posa, support the insurgents in Flanders, which complicates their relationship with Philip. Also in orbit around Philip is the Princess Eboli, whose love for Carlo is unrequited and whose "fatal gift," her ravishing beauty, leaves the king enamored of her but unable to act on his feelings.

I N A QUIRK *of music history,* Don Carlo *treats the other side of the conflict portrayed in the drama* Egmont, *for which Beethoven wrote his celebrated incidental music. Where Beethoven had gone to Goethe for his inspiration, Verdi had chosen Schiller; and where Goethe had dealt with the Dutch resistance to Spain in the War of Spanish Succession, Schiller had concerned himself with the Spanish side and its Inquisition.*

Verdi's music rises to inspired heights in Philip's *"Ella giammai m'amò!"* ("She never loved me!") and Eboli's *"O don fatale"* ("O fatal gift"), and it imparts the usual sharp point to a series of dramatic duets: between Carlo and Elisabeth, Carlo and Rodrigo, Rodrigo and Philip, and most extraordinary of all, the memorable scene between Philip and Grand Inquisitor, its dark orchestral tones a chill reminder of the power of the Church to compel even a king.

By the 1870s Verdi was securely established as Italy's greatest composer. Famous throughout the world, and comfortably ensconced on his farm at Sant'Agata in the lush Parmesan countryside, he had no need to prove himself, or indeed to make a living by writing operas. But a generous commission from the Khedive of Egypt, the equivalent of at least $250,000 today, turned him to the composition of what has remained his most popular work, *Aida*. The Suez Canal had opened in 1869, and so had a new opera house in Cairo (with *Rigoletto*). Verdi had turned down the Khedive's request for an inaugural ode for the canal, but the idea of a lavish opera on an Egyptian subject, to celebrate the opening of the opera house, appealed to him.

Verdi, who as usual played an active role in the shaping of the libretto, unabashedly opted for a grand-opera design. The scenario that emerged is full of spectacle, ballets, and processions, peopled by victorious Egyptians and vanquished Ethiopians; while not as vast as that of *Don Carlo*, it is certainly more perfect. The Triumphal Scene of Act II (*"Gloria all'Egitto"*), with its huge choral proclamations, ballet interlude, and climactic sextet, is grand opera at its grandest.

But at its core, *Aida* is an opera about love and the impossibility of openly revealing it. One can imagine Verdi, in his study at Sant'Agata, licking his chops at the thought of a triangle involving two women and a man rather than two men and a woman. Both Aida, the enslaved Ethiopian princess, and her mistress Amneris, daughter of the

Regal yet vulnerable, with a voice of compelling richness, Leontyne Price is the great Aida of our time.

Egyptian king, are in love with Radamès, whose love for Aida and loyalty to Egypt put him in a difficult position. Aida's position is even more difficult, for she can neither openly express her love for Radamès nor reveal that her captive father, Amonasro, is the Ethiopian king. There was an autobiographical aspect to all this—Verdi at the time was developing feelings for the younger Austrian soprano Teresa Stolz, who would sing the opera's title role at its Italian premiere—and it got the engine of characterization going at full power. The emotional intensity Verdi generates in the confrontations of Aida and Amneris, Aida and Amonasro, and Aida and Radamès burns right through the trappings of convention and grips the listener from the moment the opera begins. By the opera's end, there is no real plot left to unfold. But it is in this final scene most of all—with the story over and Aida and Radamès being sealed alive in their tomb, at last able to share their love for each other—that Verdi shows just what he could do with music.

"And then one evening at La Scala in Milan the tremendous, dissonant opening chord of *Otello* came crashing out, that blow of a giant's fist. '*I am here still!*' Italian opera cried." The words are from Verdi author Franz Werfel. That evening in 1887 is one of the red-letter occasions in the history of opera, when Verdi stunned the world with the revelation that a full 15 years after *Aida* his powers remained unequaled.

In Shakespeare, Verdi had found the ideal inspiration, and in librettist Arrigo Boito the ideal collaborator for his unique genius. Shakespeare's familiar story of the jealous Moor elicited the most eloquent, powerful, and breathtakingly dramatic score Verdi was to write. From its explosive opening storm scene to the frenzied finale in Desdemona's chambers, *Otello* is a masterpiece of continuous development that encompasses traditional scenic and formal elements in a musical outpouring of overwhelming cumulative effect.

The interior of La Scala *in Milan, site of the* Otello *and* Falstaff *premieres.*

Piero Cappuccilli, whose burnished baritone made him a much sought-after Iago.

The characterization of Otello is gripping. He is a stunning presence on the stage (his opening *"Esultate!"* is one of the most commanding entrances in opera), whose music freezes one in fear every time he turns to threaten Desdemona or Iago. Yet his Act I love duet with Desdemona, *"Già nella notte densa,"* has a passion that mounts like a giant wave. Desdemona is sympathetically treated, and the villainous Iago is given huge stature by Verdi's music, most notably in his *"Credo in un Dio crudel"* and the Act II oath-swearing with Otello *("Sì, pel ciel")*, a carryover from the friendship duets of *bel canto* opera, ironically twisted as Iago changes the key on his commander.

But Verdi was not yet finished. In 1889 he took up a new Shakespeare project, again with Boito, this time the comedy *Falstaff*. The beauty of its language and the quick-hitting spontaneity of its dialog is matched by the scintillating musical textures with which Verdi propels the action to uproarious climaxes. The opera begins *in medias res*, literally in mid-musical sentence, and it ends, as comedy must, with marriage . . . and what may well be the most exhilarating fugue in all of music, as one by one the characters follow Falstaff in admitting that *"Tutto nel mondo è burla"* ("The whole world is crazy, and man is by nature a fool"). With *Falstaff*, Verdi completed a life work in which he proved, as Mozart had done, that the more important the drama is to the composer, the more effective his music becomes.

VERDI, CONCERNED about his advanced age and reluctant to draw his colleague Arrigo Boito away from his own opera Nerone, was barely able to disguise his excitement at the prospect of doing another Shakespeare opera. In a letter to Boito he wrote: "What a joy to be able to say to the public, 'HERE WE ARE AGAIN!! COME AND SEE US!' " To which Boito replied: "There is only one way to end your career more splendidly than with Otello, and that is to end it with Falstaff."

 RECOMMENDED RECORDINGS

VERDI: *RIGOLETTO*

Piero Cappuccilli, Ileana Cotrubas, Placido Domingo, Elena Obraztsova, Nicolai Ghiaurov, Kurt Moll; Vienna State Opera Chorus, Vienna Philharmonic/Carlo Maria Giulini.

Deutsche Grammophon 415 288-2 [2 CDs]

Domingo, Price, and Milnes are all in top form in Il trovatore.

VERDI: *IL TROVATORE*

Placido Domingo, Leontyne Price, Sherrill Milnes, Fiorenza Cossotto; Ambrosian Opera Chorus, New Philharmonia Orchestra/Zubin Mehta.

RCA Red Seal 6194-2 [2 CDs; 1969]

VERDI: *LA TRAVIATA*

Joan Sutherland, Luciano Pavarotti, Matteo Manuguerra; London Opera Chorus, National Philharmonic Orchestra/ Richard Bonynge.

London 430 491-2 [2 CDs; 1979]

VERDI: *DON CARLO*

Placido Domingo, Montserrat Caballé, Shirley Verrett, Ruggero Raimondi, Sherrill Milnes, Giovanni Foiani; Ambrosian Opera Chorus, Orchestra of the Royal Opera House, Covent Garden/Carlo Maria Giulini.

EMI CDCC 47701 [five-act version of 1886, in Italian; 3 CDs]

VERDI: *AIDA*

Mirella Freni, Agnes Baltsa, José Carreras, Piero Cappuccilli, Ruggero Raimondi; Chorus of the Vienna State Opera, Vienna Philharmonic/Herbert von Karajan.

EMI CDMC 69300 [3 CDs; 1979]

VERDI: *OTELLO*

Placido Domingo, Renata Scotto, Sherrill Milnes; Ambrosian Opera Chorus, National Philharmonic Orchestra/ James Levine.

RCA Red Seal RCD 2-2951 [2 CDs; 1978]

VERDI: *FALSTAFF*

Renato Bruson, Katia Ricciarelli, Leo Nucci, Barbara Hendricks; Los Angeles Master Chorale, Los Angeles Philharmonic/ Carlo Maria Giulini.

Deutsche Grammophon 410 503-2 [2 CDs]

Joan Sutherland never looked like the consumptive heroine of La traviata, *but on disc she is utterly convincing.*

Russian soprano Galina Vishnevskaya as Tatiana in Eugene Onegin.

L*OOK AT PUSHKIN'S works and you see nearly the whole of 19th-century Russian opera spread out in front of you.* Eugene Onegin, Boris Godunov, The Tale of Tsar Saltan, The Queen of Spades, The Golden Cockerel, Russlan and Ludmilla—*all are his tales. Look further, and you find* Rusalka, The Bronze Horseman, Mozart and Salieri, *and* The Miserly Knight, *with which Pushkin's influence spread beyond Russia, beyond opera, beyond the 19th century.*

RUSSIA, FRANCE & VERISMO

*M*ikhail Glinka's *A Life for the Czar* (1836) and *Russlan and Ludmilla* (1842)—the former rarely encountered outside Russia, the latter well known, though only for its overture—are the first important examples of Russian national opera. The elements of spectacle, myth, and history that figure in them were retained in the works of Glinka's successors, several of whom attempted a more profound psychological portraiture. Tchaikovsky's *Eugene Onegin* (1878), based like *Russlan and Ludmilla* on a tale by Pushkin, is an opera in which the whole sometimes adds up to less than the sum of its parts. Still, the character of Onegin—a jaded egotist at the beginning, a crumbling figure by the end—inspired some of the composer's best music. Mussorgsky's most important opera, *Boris Godunov* (1874), is, on one level at least, a free interpretation of grand opera. But Mussorgsky was far too quirky and individualistic to imitate anybody. In spite of his limited compositional technique, he had a profoundly original musical imagination, and his portrayal of the infanticidal 16th-century boyar Boris Godunov collapsing under the weight of guilt stands psychologically, and theatrically, as the first modern opera.

Bizet's *Carmen* (1874), another study of psychopathology, comes right behind it as the second. By far the most original and important voice in French opera at the close of the 19th century, Bizet transformed comic opera into a serious, passionate, and realistic genre. His treatment of the opera's central characters—Carmen, the freewheeling, fatalistic gypsy, and Don José, the obsessed and morally disintegrated soldier—remains one of the great achievements in all of opera. The score itself is among the most brilliantly orchestrated and melodically memorable compositions in history, an altogether remarkable accomplish-

AN ECONOMICAL or-
chestrator, Bizet was
nonetheless one of music's
great colorists. His sense for
the expressive character of
solo intruments was unsurpassed—never, for example,
has pastoral innocence been
more aptly evoked than by
the flute solo that opens the
prelude to Act III of Carmen—and he possessed a
gift for imaginative accompaniments and appealing
countermelodies.

ment considering Bizet was 36 when he finished.

Carmen proved to be an anticipation of the *verismo* style in opera, in which the stage is supposed to portray real life and real people. The finest embodiment of this style can be found in the forever-twinned operas of Pietro Mascagni (1863–1945) and Ruggero Leoncavallo (1857–1919): *Cavalleria rusticana* (1890) and *Pagliacci* (1892). The two works share the theme of murder committed by a jealous husband. In *Cavalleria rusticana*, the husband murders his wife's lover; in *Pagliacci*, he murders his wife, *then* her lover. Both also exhibit a two-act structure, though Mascagni linked the acts of *Cavalleria rusticana* with an intermezzo so that it would qualify in a competition for one-act operas, which it won.

 RECOMMENDED RECORDINGS

TCHAIKOVSKY: *EUGENE ONEGIN*

**Thomas Allen, Mirella Freni,
Anne Sofie von Otter, Neil Shicoff,
Paata Burchuladze; Leipzig Radio Chorus,
Staatskapelle Dresden/James Levine.**
Deutsche Grammophon 423 959-2 [2 CDs; 1987]

MUSSORGSKY: *BORIS GODUNOV*

**Ruggero Raimondi, Nicolai Gedda,
Paul Plishka, Kenneth Riegel,
Galina Vishnevskaya; Choral Arts Society
of Washington, Oratorio Society of
Washington, National Symphony Orchestra/
Mstislav Rostropovich.**
Erato 45418-2 [original orchestration; 3 CDs; 1987]

**Nicolai Ghiaurov, Aleksei Maslennikov,
Martti Talvela, Ludovic Spiess,
Galina Vishnevskaya; Sofia Radio Chorus,
Vienna State Opera Chorus,
Vienna Philharmonic/Herbert von Karajan.**
*London 411 862-2 [Rimsky-Korsakov orchestration;
3 CDs; 1970]*

*Nicolai Gedda: leading interpreter
of the tenor roles in Russian opera.*

BIZET: *CARMEN*
Agnes Baltsa, José Carreras, José van Dam, Katia Ricciarelli; Chorus of the Paris Opéra, Berlin Philharmonic/Herbert von Karajan.
Deutsche Grammophon 410 088-2 [3 CDs]

MASCAGNI: *CAVALLERIA RUSTICANA*
LEONCAVALLO: *PAGLIACCI*
Fiorenza Cossotto, Carlo Bergonzi, Joan Carlyle, Giuseppe Taddei; Chorus & Orchestra of the Teatro alla Scala/ Herbert von Karajan.
Deutsche Grammophon 419 257-2 [3 CDs; 1965; with intermezzos played by Berlin Philharmonic]

GIACOMO PUCCINI

Giacomo Puccini hailed from the walled town of Lucca, Tuscany.

he most successful figure in Italian opera in the century since Verdi stopped writing, Puccini (1858–1924) possessed outstanding theatrical instincts and a stupendous melodic gift (along with a tendency to plug his tunes in a way Verdi almost never did). He chose his subjects carefully, with an eye not just to how they would work on the stage, but to how they would look— and he was invariably attracted by exotic settings. Puccini's interest in putting striking imagery on the stage was matched by his extraordinary skill at combining harmonic language and orchestral color, chosen from an exceptionally rich palette. His best operas, which have become staples of the repertory, try to mimic reality (which is why Puccini is often considered a representative of the *verismo* style), and they manage to suspend the observer's disbelief as much through their use of detail as by the workings of plot.

The first opera to reveal Puccini's true genius was *La bohème* (1896). It is the composer's imaginative treatment of character and situation, his sure instinct for dramatic and comic effects, and above all his radiant, supremely expressive musical portraiture that have made *La bohème* one of the most popular operas. Based on Henri Murger's autobiographical novelette *Scènes de la vie de Bohème*, about the lives of a group of impoverished artists in mid-19th-century Paris, the opera possesses one of those delightful librettos that move at lightning pace and seem almost to have been written by the characters themselves. The music, in spite of the decidedly modern cast to Puccini's scoring and harmony, is similarly spontaneous.

La bohème straddles the divide between comedy and tragedy, and its music has a distinctive bittersweet quality. The plot revolves around two pairs of lovers: the poet Rodolfo and the seamstress Mimì are the central, more serious pair, while the painter Marcello and his flamboyant sweetheart Musetta provide a comic foil. Rodolfo's gently passionate nature expresses itself in his first meeting with Mimì, where he takes her hand in the dark and launches into *"Che gelida manina"* ("What a cold little hand"), one of the most gratifying of tenor arias. She responds to his advances with *"Mi chiamano Mimì"* ("I'm called Mimì"), a confession all tenderness and innocence that steals up on the listener, then subsides in a beautiful, expressive hush.

The second act of *La bohème* takes place outdoors at the Café Momus on Christmas eve, and in a good production it is an unforgettable experience: with hundreds of people on stage, Paris is re-created in front of one's eyes. The third act centers on a heart-melting duet (*"Addio, senza rancor"*) between Mimì and Rodolfo, which becomes a quartet with the arrival of Marcello and Musetta. In the finale, which returns to the garret setting of the first act, boisterous hi-jinks give way to pathos as Mimì's life ebbs away. Her death at first goes unnoticed by Rodolfo—but the moment he suspects something is wrong, a stabbing *fortissimo* issues from the brass. It is one of the great shocks in opera, and it brings the work to a grisly conclusion.

FAINT HEART *never won fair lady, but Mimì's "cold little hand" captures Rodolfo's heart in Act I of Puccini's* La bohème. *While a student at the Milan conservatory, Puccini himself had lived a fairly Bohemian existence. Dirt poor, he shared lodgings with his brother, a cousin, and fellow student Pietro Mascagni, the future composer of* Cavalleria rusticana, *who would not-so-chivalrously tell creditors Puccini was out while the future composer of* La bohème *hid in a closet.*

Maria Callas as Tosca. Her fiery interpretation was great theater as well as great singing.

Tosca (1900) is not an opera about Rome, though it manages to work several of that city's landmarks into its action (in no other locale could a prima donna leap to her death from as imposing an edifice as the Castel Sant'Angelo). Nor is it about Napoleon, though he is the unseen presence behind the action. *Tosca* is about passion, jealousy, betrayal, and revenge—all the usual elements of a good Italian opera—and it works because Puccini's music makes the emotions readily believable.

No matter where Puccini had chosen to set it, *Tosca* would still be a singers' opera, built around a handful of high-voltage scenes and arias. And it is ultimately on the singers in its three principal roles—as impressive a love triangle as one will ever find—that performances and recordings of *Tosca* rise or fall. On one side is Cavaradossi, the painter who, almost before his colors are mixed, plunges into the quickest-hitting tune in all of opera, "*Recondita armonia.*" On the other side is Scarpia, the chief of police, a menacing figure used to manipulating others. In the middle is Tosca, the celebrated diva, vulnerable and violent, whose "*Vissi d'arte*" literally stops the show in the second act. Her act-long confrontation with Scarpia (of which that aria is a part) ends badly for him, and is music drama at its finest.

Puccini's love of the exotic led him to compose operas set in times and places as strange as 13th-century Florence (*Gianni Schicchi*), legendary Peking (*Turandot*), and Gold Rush-era California (*La fanciulla del West*). It was clearly one of the factors that drew him to David Belasco's one-act play *Madame Butterfly*, about a young Japanese geisha who marries and is abandoned by an American naval officer, on which Puccini based what is clearly the better of his two Oriental operas. The scoring of *Madama Butterfly* (1904) is especially beautiful; whole scenes of the opera are suffused with a luminous, pastel glow that perfectly suggests the gentle, emotional world of the heroine. In "*Un bel dì, vedremo,*" the glow intensifies as

Mirella Freni and Placido Domingo embrace in the ecstatic finale to Act I of Madama Butterfly.

Butterfly radiantly affirms that her beloved will return. The opera's denouement is fierce and expertly gauged.

Despite its exotic atmosphere and the brilliance of its scoring, *Turandot,* left unfinished at Puccini's death in 1924, marks a falling off in taste and dramatic effectiveness. It remains popular with audiences in houses worldwide because the leading roles are star vehicles of the first magnitude, anchored by two of the highest-voltage arias ever written, Turandot's *"In questa reggia"* and Calaf's *"Nessun dorma."*

 RECOMMENDED RECORDINGS

PUCCINI: *LA BOHÈME*
Mirella Freni, Luciano Pavarotti, Rolando Panerai, Elizabeth Harwood; Chorus of the Deutsche Oper Berlin, Berlin Philharmonic/Herbert von Karajan.
London 421 049-2 [2 CDs; 1972]

Victoria de los Angeles, Jussi Björling, Robert Merrill, Lucine Amara; RCA Victor Symphony Orchestra & Chorus/ Sir Thomas Beecham.
EMI CDCB 47235 [2 CDs; 1956]

PUCCINI: *TOSCA*
Maria Callas, Giuseppe di Stefano, Tito Gobbi; Chorus & Orchestra of the Teatro alla Scala/Victor De Sabata.
EMI CDCB 47174 [2 CDs]

Montserrat Caballé, José Carreras, Ingvar Wixell; Chorus & Orchestra of the Royal Opera House, Covent Garden/ Sir Colin Davis.
Philips 412 885-2 [2 CDs; 1976]

PUCCINI: *MADAMA BUTTERFLY*

**Mirella Freni, Luciano Pavarotti,
Christa Ludwig, Robert Kerns;
Vienna State Opera Chorus,
Vienna Philharmonic/Herbert von Karajan.**
London 417 577-2 [3 CDs; 1974]

PUCCINI: *TURANDOT*

**Joan Sutherland, Luciano Pavarotti,
Montserrat Caballé, Nicolai Ghiaurov;
John Alldis Choir, Wandsworth School
Boys' Choir, London Philharmonic Orchestra/
Zubin Mehta.**
London 414 274-2 [2 CDs; 1972]

RICHARD STRAUSS

*Austrian baritone Bernd Weikl,
a steely, psychologically complex
Jochanaan in* Salome.

*T*he early years of the 20th century witnessed a deterioration in the fabric of European culture, and in its musical language, which the bourgeois composer Strauss was not afraid to deal with on the operatic stage. His *Salome* and *Elektra*, undertaken after the bulk of his symphonic poems had been written, are musically revolutionary studies of depravity. *Salome* (1905), a bombshell of an opera based on the play by Oscar Wilde, opens with an eerie run on the clarinet, ends with a bang, and in between contains some of the most virtuosic, suggestive, and complex music ever penned. Because of its graphic portrayal of sexual decadence and its prominent references to Christ, the opera was banned by the Viennese censors when Mahler tried to stage it there. But the premiere in Dresden was an overwhelming success, in spite of the difficulty of the music and the subject.

Strauss's supreme mastery of the orchestra is apparent on every page of *Salome*. His music is at its most febrile in portraying the distorted exoticism of Salome, the adolescent princess of Judea

Ljuba Welitsch as Salome: no singer has combined adolescent peevishness and sexual craving in quite the same way.

WHICH SHOULD come first in opera— the words or the music? The debate has absorbed composers and poets ever since Christoph Willibald Gluck weighed in with his reforms. A string of operas about opera followed, including Salieri's Prima la musica e poi le parole *and Mozart's* The Impresario. *More recently, Richard Strauss's* Capriccio (1942) *and John Corigliano's* The Ghosts of Versailles (1991) *have dealt with the question in intriguing ways.*

who covets the body of John the Baptist and becomes the Sphinx-like instrument of his fate when he refuses her advances. Her insatiable desire is conveyed in music that scales the heights of passion, while the lurid necrophilia of her deranged final moments calls forth an orchestral paroxysm of operatically unprecedented magnitude. Jochanaan (the Baptist's German name) is himself a disturbing mix of madness and evangelical fervor, his solo pronouncements a blend of German chorale and the sepulchral tones of the Commendatore in *Don Giovanni*. The hasty, fast-talking Herod, haunted by phantasms of guilt and desire, is portrayed in music of fawning opulence; his wife, the spiteful Herodias, in much harsher tones. The scene painting for which Strauss achieved celebrity in his symphonic poems is lifted to a new level in *Salome*, with passages like those representing Herod slipping in a pool of blood or describing a wind that feels "like the beating of vast wings" strewn throughout the score. The luxurious pages of "The Dance of the Seven Veils" set a new standard of symphonic eroticism, and Strauss goes out of his way to get the severing of the Baptist's head just right: the score calls for repeated muffled high B flats from a solo double bass, with the string pinched off by the thumb and forefinger so that the emerging sound, meant to represent the tendons of Jochanaan's neck being cut one by one, resembles "the suppressed, choked moaning of a woman."

By the time he wrote *Salome*, Strauss had already come across the talented Austrian poet Hugo von Hofmannsthal. Rarely have a composer and a librettist worked so closely together—for so many years on such a variety of subjects—and given birth to such a collection of top-flight works. The duo's fame rests chiefly upon their first two efforts, *Elektra*, premiered in Dresden in 1909, and *Der Rosenkavalier*. *Elektra*, like *Salome*, is in one continuous act, and shows an even fiercer compression than its sister work. The unseen presence behind the action is Agamemnon, the king of Mycenae, killed following his return from the Trojan War by his unfaithful wife Klytämnestra and her lover Aegisth. The opera opens with the orchestra (its complement specified by Strauss at 113 players) in full cry, shrieking the motive that represents Agamemnon's name—and taking us directly inside Elektra's haunted soul. Strauss's ravaged, bloodthirsty princess, fixated on avenging her father's murder, remains the focus of the entire opera, during which she is hardly ever off the stage.

Chrysothemis, her younger and more fearful sister, is a reflection of Elektra's own impotence, while Klytämnestra—in Strauss's treatment a neurotic Harpy tormented by nightmares and weighed down by talismans—serves as the distorted image of Elektra's guilt. In the end Orest, Elektra's brother, returns and does the deed Elektra herself is powerless to do. The scene in which sister recognizes disguised brother is one of the most powerful in Strauss's operas. Following the deaths of Klytämnestra and Aegisth, which are heard but not seen on the stage, Elektra loses her mind and dances herself to death.

All of the Strauss-Hofmannsthal operas from *Der Rosenkavalier* on are studies of love. What makes *Der Rosenkavalier*, composed between 1909 and 1910, especially remarkable is the way it succeeds in looking at love from three different viewpoints at once: those of the Marschallin, her impetuous young lover Octavian, and the bourgeois girl with whom Octavian ultimately falls in love, Sophie. A comic element is added by the boorish machinations of the Marschallin's kinsman, Baron Ochs. The backdrop to all this is Vienna of the 1740s, during the epoch of Maria Theresa—a period Strauss and Hofmannsthal sought to evoke in a fashion "half real and half imaginary," and to which the libretto and the music together impart a mix of mannered elegance, Romantic passion, and nostalgia. To provide the musical motif through which both the glamour and the bittersweet emotions of the story could

Rules at the Court Opera

"After the curtain has risen, members of the public are strictly enjoined to preserve their sense of illusion. To that end . . . the following measures will be taken: engaged couples, who are commonly prone to disturb their neighbors and distract attention from the stage by indulging in lively discussion, will be denied entry, and the doorkeepers will be instructed accordingly. Persons of both sexes entering in couples are required to furnish proof of their marital status. . . ."
—Vienna, 1897

Christa Ludwig as Octavian, bearing the silver rose—symbolizing a pledge of betrothal—from which Der Rosenkavalier *gets its name.*

be brought to life, Strauss turned to a dance that did not exist at the time in which the opera is set, though it came to be emblematic of Viennese life a century later: the waltz. Somehow, the incongruity of waltz music in Maria Theresa's Vienna is shunted aside by the radiance of Strauss's score and the utter fluency of his characterization.

Much of the opera is set in a conversational style, and the action seems to flow like that of a stage play. The curtain goes up to the boldest and most sensuous orchestral prologue—a no-holds-barred portrait of the Marschallin and Octavian in bed, climaxed by orgasmic whoops from the horns. In the remaining 516 pages of the score, Strauss generates a series of musical frissons and moves effortlessly between the serious and the burlesque. His orchestration is luminous and wonderfully imaginative, particularly in its shimmering depiction of the Silver Rose. And his assignment of the romantic leads to three female voices (Octavian is a pants role, written for mezzo soprano) allows him to indulge in some of his most beautiful love music, climaxed by the Act III trio in which the Marschallin lets go of Octavian. In spite of its theatricality, the sentiment of *Der Rosenkavalier* is delicate and genuine, and supremely well gauged.

In *Ariadne auf Naxos*, Strauss turned away from the lavish orchestration and profligate musical effect of his earlier operas and moved toward a more condensed, almost crystalline, idiom. *Ariadne* occupied Strauss and Hofmannsthal for the better part of six troubled years (1911–16), during which Europe went to war and Western music saw the collapse of traditional tonality. Hofmannsthal's original conception was to make *Ariadne* a pendant to Molière's *Le bourgeois gentilhomme*; a failure in that version, it reemerged after considerable reworking as an opera in one act. The plot is a convoluted one in which a "serious" drama—the mythical tale of Ariadne abandoned on the island of Naxos—and a "comic" entertainment coexist on the same stage. The opera consists of a Prologue, centering around the figure of the

Wartime Rationing

During World War I, Richard Strauss wrote for a reduced ensemble in his opera Ariadne auf Naxos and the related Bourgeois Gentleman Suite, the draft having decimated the theater orchestras of Germany. During the Second World War, Strauss sought alternately to escape through his music—in works such as the Symphony for Winds (Happy Workshop) and the Oboe Concerto—and to give voice to his grief, as in the Metamorphosen for 23 solo strings.

Strauss and his librettist, Hugo von Hofmannsthal: a remarkable collaboration.

Composer, and the Opera itself, in which the unfolding of the story about Ariadne is interrupted and commented upon by the participants in the entertainment, a raucous burlesque entourage borrowed from the commedia dell'arte.

Strauss composed *Ariadne* for an ensemble of only 37 players, a decision shaped equally by aesthetic considerations and wartime reductions in theater staffs. His scoring manages to achieve intimate expression without sacrificing sonority or richness of texture. In the part of Ariadne he exploited the huge range he considered a hallmark of the ideal soprano, while in Zerbinetta, the coquettish leader of the burlesque troupe, he created one of the great coloratura roles in opera, a delightful foil. Strauss saved some of his most poignant music for the part of the Composer, a Mozartean figure representing the artist as idealist, whose passionate longing for perfection is bound to be disappointed.

In their 23 years as a team (1906–29), Strauss and Hofmannsthal touched on a variety of subjects. But of their works after *Ariadne*, the only one to have established itself securely in the repertory is *Die Frau ohne Schatten* (1918), whose philosophical weight makes it heavy going in the theater and on recordings despite the extraordinary grandeur of much of Strauss's music.

RECOMMENDED RECORDINGS

STRAUSS: *SALOME*

Eva Martón, Heinz Zednik, Bernd Weikl, Brigitte Fassbaender; Berlin Philharmonic/Zubin Mehta.
Sony Classical S2K 46717 [2 CDs; 1990]

STRAUSS: *ELEKTRA*

Birgit Nilsson, Marie Collier, Regina Resnik, Tom Krause; Vienna Philharmonic/Sir Georg Solti.
London 417 345-2 [2 CDs]

STRAUSS: *DER ROSENKAVALIER*

Elisabeth Schwarzkopf, Christa Ludwig, Teresa Stich-Randall, Otto Edelmann; Philharmonia Orchestra & Chorus/ Herbert von Karajan.
EMI CDCC 49354 [3 CDs; 1956]

STRAUSS: *ARIADNE AUF NAXOS*

Jessye Norman, Julia Varady, Edita Gruberova, Paul Frey, Dietrich Fischer-Dieskau; Leipzig Gewandhaus Orchestra/Kurt Masur.
Philips 422 084-2 [2 CDs; 1988]

STRAUSS: *DIE FRAU OHNE SCHATTEN*

Julia Varady, Placido Domingo, Hildegard Behrens, José van Dam; Vienna State Opera Chorus, Vienna Boys Choir, Vienna Philharmonic/Sir Georg Solti.
London 436 243-2 [3 CDs; 1989 and 1991]

Willard White was a triumphant Porgy in the 1986 Glyndebourne production of Porgy and Bess.

THE 20TH CENTURY

Most 20th-century opera has had to deal one way or another with the enormous impact of Wagner and Verdi. Like the other French composers of his generation, Debussy fell under Wagner's spell in his youth, but unlike them, he was able to write a great opera that was not Wagnerian—even though *Pelléas et Mélisande* (1902) utilized leitmotifs, relied on short orchestral interludes to link scenes as *Parsifal* had done, and veered perilously close to the ecstasies of *Tristan* in its climactic scene. *Pelléas*, virtually a word-for-word setting of Maurice Maeterlinck's celebrated symbolist drama, is a work like no other—hardly an opera at all, but a drama of symbols transmuted into music.

In Berg's *Wozzeck* (1914–22) there is a similarly intimate connection between text and music. Based on Georg Büchner's play *Woyzeck* (1836, derived

Dishes Named for Musicians

"The opera ain't over 'til the fat lady sings" has become a maxim for underdogs everywhere. While not all opera singers have been fat, many have been gastronomes. The most celebrated was Gioacchino Rossini whose favorite dish (filet mignon) was dubbed **Tournedos Rossini.** Another famous Italian epicure was the gifted Luisa Tetrazzini, for whom the veal dish was named. The soprano Nellie Melba gave her name to **Peach Melba.**

from events that actually took place in 1821), it is a gripping, powerfully disturbing portrait of a soldier caught in the vortex of madness and despair. Following the example of Mussorgsky's *Boris Godunov*, the opera unfolds as a series of self-contained scenes that fade one into the next. Its elaborate symmetry—three acts, each in five scenes, with a confrontation between Wozzeck and his mistress Marie at the center (Act II, scene three)—is buttressed by Berg's use of conventional musical forms as structural devices, chosen for their dramatic point.

It is scarcely coincidental that the 20th century has seen a flowering of opera in English-speaking countries, where the achievements of Wagner and Verdi, and of their predecessors and successors, can be viewed with a certain detachment. Although it took the Metropolitan Opera 50 years to recognize it, Gershwin's *Porgy and Bess* (1935) is the great American opera, a fusion of an American subject with marvelously American music. And the operas of the English composer Britten have been among the most important of the century. *Peter Grimes* (1945), Britten's first masterpiece and the most popular of his operas, is a study of isolation, paranoia, and cruelty in which the relationship between the loner Grimes and a society determined to enforce its norms is insightfully probed. In *Grimes* and the equally fine *Billy Budd* (1951), Britten borrowed from the traditions of grand opera as a means of dealing with the underlying ambivalence of his dramatic material.

When Stravinsky did the same thing in *The Rake's Progress* (1951), the intention, as in so many of his works, was to create a parody of the past. Set to a libretto by W. H. Auden (based on a series of satirical engravings entitled *A Rake's Progress* that William Hogarth published in 1735), Stravinsky's virtuosic three-act comedy stands as the last work of a centuries-long tradition and the first work outside of it, a unique fusion of musical, theatrical, and social commentary.

RECOMMENDED RECORDINGS

DEBUSSY: *PELLÉAS ET MÉLISANDE*

Didier Henry, Colette Alliot-Lugaz, Gilles Cachemaille, Pierre Thau; Montreal Symphony Orchestra & Chorus/ Charles Dutoit.

London 430 502-2 [2 CDs; 1990]

BERG: *WOZZECK*

Dietrich Fischer-Dieskau, Evelyn Lear, Fritz Wunderlich, Gerhard Stolze; Chorus & Orchestra of the Deutsche Oper Berlin/ Karl Böhm.

Deutsche Grammophon 435 705-2 [3 CDs; 1965; with Lulu]

Böhm's insight and Fischer-Dieskau's dramatic urgency make this the best recording of Wozzeck.

GERSHWIN: *PORGY AND BESS*

Willard White, Leona Mitchell, McHenry Boatwright, Florence Quivar, Barbara Hendricks, François Clemmons; Cleveland Orchestra & Chorus/Lorin Maazel.

London 414 559-2 [3 CDs; 1975]

BRITTEN: *PETER GRIMES*

Peter Pears, Claire Watson, James Pease, David Kelly, Owen Brannigan, Jean Watson, Geraint Evans; Chorus & Orchestra of the Royal Opera House, Covent Garden/ Benjamin Britten.

London 414 577-2 [3 CDs; 1958]

Britten's Grimes *is one of the great opera recordings; the sound is miraculous.*

STRAVINSKY: *THE RAKE'S PROGRESS*

Don Garrard, Judith Raskin, Alexander Young, John Reardon, Regina Sarfaty; Sadler's Wells Opera Chorus, Royal Philharmonic Orchestra/ Igor Stravinsky.

Sony Classical SM2K 46299 [2 CDs; 1964]

INDEXES OF COMPOSERS AND PERFORMERS

INDEX OF COMPOSERS

B

BACH, JOHANN SEBASTIAN,
2, 4–5
Brandenburg Concertos, 3,
6–8
Cantatas *Nos. 140 and 147*,
403–6
Cello Suites, *BWV 1007–12*,
292–94
chamber music, 287, 290–94
Goldberg Variations,
BWV 988, 358–60
Mass in B minor, *BWV 232*,
5, 410–12
Orchestral Suites *Nos. 1–4*,
8–10
orchestral works, 4–10
sacred and choral music,
403–12
St. Matthew Passion,
BWV 244, 5, 406–9
solo keyboard works, 354,
356–60
violin concertos, 200–201
Violin Sonatas and Partitas,
BWV 1001–6, 290–92
The Well-Tempered Clavier,
BWV 846–893, 356–58
BARBER, SAMUEL:
Adagio for Strings, 10–11
*Essays Nos. 1–3 for
Orchestra*, 11
*Medea's Meditation and Dance
of Vengeance*, 11
BARTÓK, BÉLA, 12–14, 199,
202–5, 289, 355
Concerto for Orchestra, 12–14
*Music for Strings, Percussion,
and Celesta*, 12, 14
Piano Concerto *No. 3*,
12–13, 202–3, 265
String Quartets *Nos. 1–6*,
294–96
Violin Concerto *No. 2*,
204–5
BEETHOVEN, LUDWIG VAN,
15–16, 37, 38, 40
Cello Sonata in A, *Op. 69*,
298–99
chamber music, 288, 289,
296–309
concertos, 198–99,
206–14

Fidelio, 16, 448–49
Missa Solemnis in D, *Op. 123*,
16, 412–15
orchestral works, 3, 15–29
Piano Concerto *No. 3*,
in C minor, *Op. 37*,
206–7, 210–12
Piano Concerto *No. 4*,
in G, *Op. 58*, 207–8,
210–12
Piano Concerto *No. 5*,
in E flat, *Op. 73* (*Emperor*),
16, 209–12
Piano Sonata in C minor,
Op. 13 (*Pathétique*),
360–61, 369–70
Piano Sonata in C sharp
minor, *Op. 27*,
No. 2 (*Moonlight*),
362, 369–70
Piano Sonata in C, *Op. 53*
(*Waldstein*), 362–63,
370–71
Piano Sonata in F minor,
Op. 57 (*Appassionata*),
364, 370–71
Piano Sonata in E flat,
Op. 81a (*Les Adieux*),
364–65, 370–71
Piano Sonata in B flat,
Op. 106 (*Hammerklavier*),
366–67, 370–71
Piano Sonata in E, *Op. 109*,
368, 370–71
Piano Sonata in A flat,
Op. 110, 368–69,
370–71
Piano Sonata in C minor,
Op. 111, 369, 370–71
Piano Trio in B flat, *Op. 97*
(*Archduke*), 299–301
solo keyboard works, 355,
360–71
String Quartets, *Op. 18*,
301–3
String Quartets, *Op. 59*
(*Razumovsky*), 16, 304–6
String Quartet in C sharp
minor, *Op. 131*, 306–9
Symphonies *Nos. 1–9*
(complete cycles), 26–28
Symphonies *Nos. 1–9* (com-
plete cycles on period
instruments), 28–29

Symphony *No. 3*, in E flat,
Op. 55 (*Eroica*), 16, 17–19,
27, 29
Symphony *No. 5*, in C
minor, *Op. 67*, 16, 19–22,
24, 26–27, 28
Symphony *No. 6*, in F,
Op. 68 (*Pastorale*), 22–24,
27, 29
Symphony *No. 9*, in D
minor, *Op. 125* (*Choral*), 16,
24–26, 28, 29
Violin Concerto in D,
Op. 61, 212–14
Violin Sonata in A minor,
Op. 47 (*Kreutzer*),
296–98
BELLINI, VINCENZO, 450, 451
Norma, 451, 452
BERG, ALBAN, 199
Violin Concerto, 214–17
Wozzeck, 482–83, 484
BERLIOZ, HECTOR:
Corsaire Overture, 31
Requiem, *Op. 5*, 415–17
"Royal Hunt and Storm"
from *Les Troyens*, 31
Symphonie fantastique, 29–31
BERNSTEIN, LEONARD:
Chichester Psalms, 417–18
Overture *to Candide*, 32–33
Symphonic Dances from
West Side Story, 32–33
BIZET, GEORGES:
L'Arlésienne Suites
Nos. 1 and 2, 33–35
Carmen, 33, 471–72, 473
BORODIN, ALEXANDER:
String Quartet *No. 2*, in D,
309–11
BRAHMS, JOHANNES, 36–37
Cello Sonata in E minor,
Op. 38, 314–16
Cello Sonata in F, *Op. 99*,
314–16
chamber music, 289, 311–19
Clarinet Quintet in
B minor, *Op. 115*,
316, 317–19
Clarinet Sonatas, *Op. 120*,
316–17, 318–19
concertos, 199, 217–23
A German Requiem, Op. 45,
419–21

late piano works, 371–73
orchestral works, 36–49
Piano Concerto *No. 1*, in
D minor, *Op. 15*, 217–21
Piano Concerto *No. 2*, in
B flat, *Op. 83*, 217–21
Symphony *No. 1*, in
C minor, *Op. 68*, 37, 38,
39, 42–43
Symphony *No. 2*, in D,
Op. 73, 37, 39, 41, 42–43
Symphony *No. 3*, in F,
Op. 90, 37, 40–41, 42–43
Symphony *No. 4*, in E
minor, *Op. 98*, 37, 41–43
Violin Concerto in D,
Op. 77, 221–23
Violin Sonata in G, *Op. 78*,
311–14
Violin Sonata in A, *Op. 100*,
311–14
Violin Sonata in D minor,
Op. 108, 311–14
BRITTEN, BENJAMIN:
Billy Budd, 483, 484
"Four Sea Interludes" from
Peter Grimes, 44–45
Peter Grimes, 483, 484
War Requiem, *Op. 66*,
421–24
*The Young Person's Guide to
the Orchestra* (*Variations
and Fugue on a Theme of
Purcell*), 43–45, 134–35
BRUCH, MAX:
Violin Concerto *No. 1*, in
G minor, *Op. 26*, 223–26
BRUCKNER, ANTON, 45–49
Symphony *No. 7*, in E,
45–47
Symphony *No. 8*, in
C minor, 47–49

C

CHOPIN, FRÉDÉRIC, 198, 355,
373–78
ballades, 373–74, 377–78
nocturnes, 374–75, 377–78
Piano Concerto *No. 1*, in
E minor, *Op. 11*, 226–29
Piano Concerto *No. 2*, in
F minor, *Op. 21*, 226–29
polonaises and mazurkas,
375–76, 377–78
preludes, 375, 377–78
waltzes, 376–78

COPLAND, AARON, 49–52
Appalachian Spring, 50–52,
69–70
Billy the Kid, 51–52
Fanfare for the Common Man,
51–52, 69–70
Rodeo, 50, 51–52

D

DEBUSSY, CLAUDE, 289
Images, 380–82
La Mer, 54–57
orchestral works, 52–57
Pelléas et Mélisande, 53, 482,
484
*Prélude à l'après-midi d'un
faune*, 53–54, 56–57
Preludes, 381–82
Quartet in G minor, *Op. 10*,
320–21
solo keyboard works, 355,
379–82
Three Nocturnes, 52–53,
56–57
DONIZETTI, GAETANO:
Lucia di Lammermoor, 450,
452
DVOŘÁK, ANTONÍN:
Cello Concerto in
B minor, *Op. 104*,
229–32, 233
chamber music, 321–23
orchestral works, 57–60
Piano Quintet in A, *Op. 81*,
322–23
Sextet in A, *Op. 48*, 341
String Quartet in F, *Op. 96*
(*American*), 321, 323
Symphony *No. 7*, in D minor,
Op. 70, 57–58, 60
Symphony *No. 9*, in E minor,
Op. 95 (*From the New
World*), 59–60

E

ELGAR, EDWARD, 60–64
Cello Concerto in E minor,
Op. 85, 232–34
Pomp and Circumstance
Marches, 62–64
*Variations on an Original
Theme*, *Op. 36* (*Enigma*),
60–62, 63–64

F

FALLA, MANUEL DE:
Nights in the Gardens of Spain,
65, 234–35, 273–74
El sombrero de tres picos (*The
Three-Cornered Hat*), 64–66
FAURÉ, GABRIEL:
Requiem, *Op. 48*, 424–26
FRANCK, CÉSAR:
Psyché, 67–68
Symphony in D minor,
66–68
Violin Sonata in A, 324–26

G

GERSHWIN, GEORGE, 68–70
An American in Paris, 68–70
Porgy and Bess, 483, 484
Rhapsody in Blue, 68–70
GRIEG, EDVARD:
Peer Gynt, 70–71
Piano Concerto in A minor,
Op. 16, 235–37, 242, 280

H

HANDEL, GEORGE FRIDERIC,
72–73, 74–76
Messiah, 73, 426–29
Music for the Royal Fireworks,
75–76
Water Music, 3, 74–75, 76
HAYDN, JOSEPH, 77–78
chamber music, 287–88,
289, 326–29
The Creation, 429–31
orchestral works, 3, 77–86
String Quartets, *Op. 33*
(*Russian*), 326–27,
328–29
String Quartets, *Op. 76*
(*Erdödy*), 327–29
Symphony *No. 88*, in G,
79, 80–81
Symphony *No. 92*, in G
(*Oxford*), 79–81
Symphonies *Nos. 93–104*
(*London* or *Salomon*),
78, 81–86
Symphony *No. 94*, in G
(*Surprise*), 82, 85–86
Symphony *No. 100*, in G
(*Military*), 83, 85–86
Symphony *No. 101*, in D
(*The Clock*), 83, 85–86

Symphony *No. 102*, in B flat, 84, 85–86

Symphony *No. 103*, in E flat (*Drumroll*), 84, 85–86

Symphony *No. 104*, in D (*London*), 82, 84–86

Trumpet Concerto in E flat, 238–40

HINDEMITH, PAUL:
Symphonic Metamorphosis on Themes of Carl Maria von Weber, 88

Symphony *Mathis der Maler*, 87–88

HOLST, GUSTAV:
The Planets, Op. 32, 88–90

I · J · K · L

IVES, CHARLES:
Three Places in New England, 90–92

JANÁČEK, LEOŠ:
Sinfonietta, 92–94
Slavonic Mass, 431–33

KORNGOLD, ERICH WOLFGANG:
Sextet in D, *Op. 10*, 341

LEONCAVALLO, RUGGERO:
Pagliacci, 472, 473

LISZT, FRANZ, 198–99, 355
Piano Concerto *No. 1*, in E flat, 240–43, 280
Piano Sonata in B minor, 382–84
Les Préludes, 94–96

M

MAHLER, GUSTAV, 3, 97–107
Das Lied von der Erde (*The Song of the Earth*), 102–4, 105
Symphony *No. 2*, in C minor (*Resurrection*), 97–99
Symphony *No. 5*, in C sharp minor, 99–102
Symphony *No. 9*, in D, 104–7

MASCAGNI, PIETRO:
Cavalleria rusticana, 472, 473

MENDELSSOHN, FELIX, 107–10, 198–99, 289, 355
A Midsummer Night's Dream: Overture, *Op. 21*, and Incidental Music, *Op. 61*, 107–8, 109–10

Octet for Strings, in E flat, *Op. 20*, 329–30

Symphony *No. 4*, in A, *Op. 90* (*Italian*), 108–10

Violin Concerto in E minor, *Op. 64*, 243–46

MEYERBEER, GIACOMO:
Les Huguenots, 451, 452

MOZART, WOLFGANG AMADEUS, 111–12
chamber music, 288, 289, 331–38

Clarinet Concerto in A, *K. 622*, 259–62

Clarinet Quintet in A, *K. 581*, 336–38

concertos, 197–98, 246–62

Don Giovanni, 244, 248, 445–46, 448

Horn Concerto *No. 3*, in E flat, *K. 447*, 258–59

Eine kleine Nachtmusik (*A Little Night Music*), *K. 525*, 122–24

Le nozze di Figaro (*The Marriage of Figaro*), 443–44, 445, 447

operas, 442, 443–48

orchestral works, 3, 111–24

Piano Concerto *No. 9*, in E flat, *K. 271*, 246–47, 251–52

Piano Concerto *No. 20*, in D minor, *K. 466*, 247–48, 251–52

Piano Concerto *No. 21*, in C, *K. 467*, 249–50, 251–52

Piano Concerto *No. 24*, in C minor, *K. 491*, 250–52

piano sonatas, 355, 384–87

Posthorn Serenade, *No. 9*, *K. 320*, 123

Requiem in D minor, *K. 626*, 433–36

Sinfonia concertante in E flat for Violin and Viola, *K. 364*, 256–58

String Quartet in B flat, *K. 458* (*Hunt*), 331–33

String Quartet in C, *K. 465* (*Dissonance*), 331–33

String Quintet in C, *K. 515*, 333–36

String Quintet in G minor, *K. 516*, 333–36

Symphony *No. 29*, in A, *K. 201*, 113–15

Symphony *No. 38*, in D, *K. 504* (*Prague*), 112, 115–17

Symphony *No. 39*, in E flat, *K. 543*, 112, 117–18, 121–22

Symphony *No. 40*, in G minor, *K. 550*, 112, 118–19, 121–22

Symphony *No. 41*, in C, *K. 551* (*Jupiter*), 112, 119–22

Violin Concerto *No. 3*, in G, *K. 216*, 253–55

Violin Concerto *No. 5*, in A, *K. 219*, 253–55

Die Zauberflöte (*The Magic Flute*), 446–47, 448

MUSSORGSKY, MODEST, 124–27
Boris Godunov, 471, 472

A Night on Bald Mountain, 124–25, 126–27

Pictures at an Exhibition, 125–27

N · O · P

NIELSEN, CARL:
Symphony *No. 4*, *Op. 29* (*The Inextinguishable*), 127–29

Symphony *No. 5*, 129

ORFF, CARL:
Carmina Burana, 436–38

PROKOFIEV, SERGEI, 355
concertos, 262–67
orchestral works, 3, 129–35

Peter and the Wolf, Op. 67, 133–35

Piano Concerto *No. 3*, in C, *Op. 26*, 262–65

Symphony *No. 1*, in D, *Op. 25* (*Classical*), 129–30, 132–33

Symphony *No. 5*, in B flat, *Op. 100*, 130–33

Violin Concerto *No. 1*, in D, *Op. 19*, 265–67

PUCCINI, GIACOMO, 473–77
La bohème, 474–75, 476
Madama Butterfly, 475–76, 477
Tosca, 475, 476
Turandot, 475, 476, 477

R

RACHMANINOFF, SERGEI:
Piano Concerto *No. 2,* in
C minor, *Op. 18,* 267–68,
269–70
Piano Concerto *No. 3,*
264–65
*Rhapsody on a Theme of
Paganini, Op. 43,* 268–70
solo keyboard works, 355,
387–90
works for piano and
orchestra, 267–70
RAVEL, MAURICE, 135–39, 199,
289, 355
Boléro, 135, 138–39
Daphnis et Chloé, Suite *No. 2,*
137–39
Gaspard de la nuit, 390–92
orchestration of Mus-
sorgsky's *Pictures at an
Exhibition,* 125, 126, 127
Piano Concerto in D,
270–72
Piano Concerto in G,
270–72
Rapsodie espagnole, 136–37,
138–39
String Quartet in F, 320–21,
338–40
Le Tombeau de Couperin,
138–39
RESPIGHI, OTTORINO:
Fountains of Rome, 140–42
Pines of Rome, 140–42
RIMSKY-KORSAKOV, NIKOLAI:
orchestration of Mus-
sorgsky's *A Night on Bald
Mountain,* 124–25
Scheherazade, Op. 35, 142–44
RODRIGO, JOAQUÍN, 199
Concierto de Aranjuez, 272–74
ROSSINI, GIOACCHINO, 442
Il barbiere di Siviglia (*The
Barber of Seville*), 450, 452
Guillaume Tell (*William Tell*),
451, 452

S

SAINT-SAËNS, CAMILLE, 144–48
The Carnival of the Animals,
146–48
Symphony *No. 3,* in
C minor, *Op. 78* (*Organ*),
144–45, 147–48

SCARLATTI, DOMENICO:
keyboard sonatas, 392–94
SCHOENBERG, ARNOLD, 36
Verklärte Nacht (*Transfigured
Night*), *Op. 4,* 340–41
SCHUBERT, FRANZ:
chamber music, 289, 342–49
orchestral works, 148–53
Piano Quintet in A, *D. 667*
(*The Trout*), 342–44
piano sonatas, 394–97
Die schöne Müllerin, D. 795,
346–48
String Quintet in C, *D. 956,*
344–46
Symphony *No. 8,* in B minor,
D. 759 (*Unfinished*),
109–10, 148–51
Symphony *No. 9,* in C,
D. 944, 151–53
Winterreise, D. 911,
346–48
SCHUMANN, ROBERT, 198–99,
289
Carnaval, Op. 9, 398–99,
400
chamber music, 349–52
Dichterliebe, Op. 48, 350–52
Kreisleriana, Op. 16,
399–400
Piano Concerto in A minor,
Op. 54, 274–76
Piano Quintet in E flat,
Op. 44, 349–50
solo keyboard works, 355,
398–400
Symphonic Etudes, Op. 13,
399, 400
Symphony *No. 3,* in
E flat, *Op. 97* (*Rhenish*),
153–55
SHOSTAKOVICH, DMITRI, 3,
155–59
Symphony *No. 5,* in D minor,
Op. 47, 155–57
Symphony *No. 10,* in E
minor, *Op. 93,* 57–59
SIBELIUS, JEAN, 3, 160–65
Finlandia, 96
The Swan of Tuonela, 160,
164–65
Symphony *No. 2,* in D,
Op. 43, 160–62, 164
Symphony *No. 5,* in E flat,
Op. 82, 162–65
Violin Concerto in
D minor, *Op. 47,* 276–78

SMETANA, BEDŘICH:
String Quartet *No. 1,* in E
minor (*From My Life*), 311
Vltava (*The Moldau*), 165–66
STRAUSS, EDUARD, 166, 167,
168
STRAUSS, JOHANN I, 166–67,
168–69
STRAUSS, JOHANN II, 166, 167,
168–69
STRAUSS, JOSEF, 166, 167–69
STRAUSS, RICHARD:
*Also sprach Zarathustra,
Op. 30,* 172, 176
Ariadne auf Naxos, 480–81,
482
Death and Transfiguration,
171, 176–77
Don Juan, Op. 20, 169–70,
171
Don Quixote, Op. 35, 171,
173–74, 176–77
Elektra, 477, 478–79, 481
Die Frau ohne Schatten, 481,
482
Ein Heldenleben, Op. 40, 170,
171, 174–76
operas, 477–82
orchestral works, 169–77
Der Rosenkavalier, 170, 478,
479–80, 482
Salome, 477–78, 481
Till Eulenspiegel, Op. 28,
170–71
STRAVINSKY, IGOR, 177–83
The Firebird, 177–78, 182–83
Petrushka, 178–80, 182–83
The Rake's Progress, 483, 484
The Rite of Spring, 180–83

T · V · W

TCHAIKOVSKY, PIOTR ILYICH,
184–85
Capriccio italien, 96
concertos, 279–83
1812 Overture, 96
Eugene Onegin, 471, 472
Francesca da Rimini, 187
The Nutcracker Suite, Op. 71a,
185, 193–95
orchestral works, 184–95
Piano Concerto *No. 1,* in
B flat minor, *Op. 23,* 242,
270, 278–80
Romeo and Juliet, 184, 185,
186–87

Symphony *No. 4,* in
  F minor, *Op. 36,* 185,
  188–89, 192–93
Symphony *No. 6,* in B minor,
  Op. 74 (Pathétique), 185,
  187, 189–93
Violin Concerto in D,
  Op. 35, 281–83
VAUGHAN WILLIAMS, RALPH:
  A London Symphony,
  195–96
VERDI, GIUSEPPE, 442, 463–70
  Aida, 466, 467–68, 470
  Don Carlo, 466–67, 470
  Falstaff, 469, 470
  Otello, 468–69, 470
  Requiem, 438–40

Rigoletto, 463–64, 465,
  467, 469
La traviata, 463, 464,
  465–66, 470
Il trovatore, 463, 464–65,
  470
VILLA-LOBOS, HEITOR:
  guitar works, 273, 274
VIVALDI, ANTONIO:
  Concertos for Violin,
  Strings, and Continuo,
  *Op. 8, Nos. 1–4 (The
  Four Seasons),* 283–86
WAGNER, RICHARD, 442,
  453–63, 482
  *Der fliegende Holländer (The
  Flying Dutchman),* 453, 461

Götterdämmerung, 455,
  457–58, 459, 462
Lohengrin, 454, 461, 462
*Die Meistersinger von Nürn-
  berg,* 455, 458–59, 460, 463
Parsifal, 461, 463
Das Rheingold, 455–56, 462
*Der Ring des Nibelungen (The
  Ring of the Nibelung),* 454,
  455–58, 459, 462
Siegfried, 455, 457, 459, 462
Tannhäuser, 453–54, 462
Tristan und Isolde, 454, 455,
  458–60, 462
Die Walküre, 455, 456–57, 462
WEBER, CARL MARIA VON:
  Der Freischütz, 449, 453

INDEX OF PERFORMERS

A

Abbado, Claudio, 42–43, 245, 266–67, 282–83
Academy Chamber Ensemble, 330
Academy of Ancient Music:
 chamber music, 337–38
 concertos, 211–12, 261–62
 orchestral works, 10, 28–29, 85–86
Academy of London, 147–48
Academy of St. Martin-in-the-Fields:
 concertos, 225–26, 239, 257–58, 286
 orchestral works, 7, 76
Academy of St. Martin-in-the-Fields Chamber Ensemble, 123–24
Accardo, Salvatore, 286
Adam, Theo, 408–9, 435, 462
Alban Berg Quartet, 303, 336, 345–46
Aler, John, 417
Alexeev, Dmitri, 377–78, 389–90
John Alldis Choir, 477
Allen, Thomas, 447, 472
Alliot-Lugaz, Colette, 484
Alva, Luigi, 448
Amadeus Quartet, 319
Amara, Lucine, 476
Ambrosian Opera Chorus, 452, 470
Amsterdam Baroque Orchestra, 7–8, 201
Araiza, Francisco, 435, 449
Arrau, Claudio, 381–82
Arroyo, Martina, 452
Ashkenazy, Vladimir:
 chamber music, 297–98, 300–301, 313–14
 concertos, 264–65, 269–70
 orchestral works, 23–24, 67–68, 187
 solo keyboard works, 377–78, 391–92
Atlanta Boy Choir, 423–24

Atlanta Symphony Orchestra & Chorus, 417, 423–24, 425–26, 440
Augér, Arleen, 411–12
Ax, Emanuel, 315–16, 350

B

Bacquier, Gabriel, 452
Baker, Julius, 183
Baltsa, Agnes, 470, 473
Bär, Olaf, 352, 408–9, 430–31
Barbirolli, Sir John, 101–2, 164, 233–34
Barenboim, Daniel, 314, 315
Bartoli, Cecilia, 452
Battle, Kathleen, 99, 169
Bavarian Radio Symphony Orchestra, 237, 275–76, 287, 430–31, 435
Bavarian Radio Symphony Orchestra Chorus, 430–31, 435
Bavarian State Opera Chorus & Orchestra, 448
Bayreuth Festival Chorus & Orchestra, 462
BBC Symphony Orchestra, 237, 276
Beaux Arts Trio, 300–301, 350
Beecham, Sir Thomas, 31, 35, 143–44, 476
Behrens, Hildegard, 482
Bell, Joshua, 225–26
Bergonzi, Carlo, 473
Alban Berg Quartet, 303, 336, 345–46
Berlin Opera. *See* Deutsche Oper Berlin
Berlin Philharmonic:
 concertos, 220, 223, 228–29, 230–31, 255, 257–58
 opera, 461, 463, 473, 476, 481
 orchestral works, 27–28, 42–43, 96, 106, 109–10, 123–24, 132, 138–39, 147–48, 154–55, 164–65, 166, 168–69, 176–77, 192–93, 194–95
 sacred and choral music, 420–21
Berlin Radio Symphony Orchestra, 67–68
Bernasek, Vaclav, 341

Bernstein, Leonard:
 opera, 449
 orchestral works, 19, 25–26, 33, 42–43, 51–52, 69–70, 80–81, 99, 101, 150
 sacred and choral music, 414–15, 418, 430–31
Berry, Walter, 408–9, 448, 449
Bettelheim, Dolf, 350
Beyer, Franz, 335–36
Beznosiuk, Lisa, 10
Bishop-Kovacevich, Stephen, 237, 276
Björling, Jussi, 476
Blasi, Angela Maria, 435
Blegen, Judith, 425–26, 430–31
Blochwitz, Hans Peter, 430–31
Blomstedt, Herbert, 71, 88, 129, 437–38
Boatwright, McHenry, 484
Bogart, John Paul, 418
Böhm, Karl, 80–81, 257–58, 262, 462, 484
Böhme, Kurt, 462
Bonell, Carlos, 273–74
Bonney, Barbara, 408–9, 430–31
Bonynge, Richard, 452, 470
Borodin Quartet, 311
Boston Symphony Orchestra:
 concertos, 217, 242–43, 245–46
 orchestral works, 56–57, 92, 109–10, 138–39, 147, 150–51, 164
Boulez, Pierre, 182–83
Boult, Sir Adrian, 63, 89–90,
Brain, Dennis, 259
Brandis, Thomas, 257–58
Brannigan, Owen, 484
Brendel, Alfred, 347–48, 352, 384, 396–97
Brett, Charles, 428
Britten, Benjamin, 44–45, 252, 423–24, 484
Bronfman, Yefim, 325–26
Brown, Iona, 257–58
Bruson, Renato, 470
Büchner, Eberhard, 408–9
Budapest Festival Orchestra, 242–43
Burchuladze, Paata, 452, 472
Bury, Alison, 201

C

Caballé, Montserrat, 452, 470, 476, 477
Cachemaille, Gilles, 484
Callas, Maria, 476
Camerata Singers, 418
Cappone, Giusto, 257–58
Cappuccilli, Piero, 448, 469, 470
Carlyle, Joan, 473
Carreras, José, 470, 473, 476
Casadesus, Robert, 251–52
Casals, Pablo, 231–32
Chamber Ensemble, 337–38
Chamber Music Northwest, 318–19
Chamber Orchestra of Europe, 121–22
Chance, Michael, 405–6, 408–9
Chicago Symphony Orchestra:
  concertos, 217, 223, 225–26, 266–67, 270, 278, 283
  orchestral works, 14, 67–68, 126–27, 132–33, 176
Choral Arts Society of Washington, 472
Chung, Kyung Wha, 205, 217, 245, 266–67, 282–83, 325
Clemmons, François, 484
Cleveland Orchestra:
  concertos, 210–11, 220–21, 251–52
  opera, 484
  orchestral works, 26–27, 69–70, 155, 171, 182–83
Cleveland Orchestra Chorus, 484
Cleveland Quartet, 311, 350
Cliburn, Van, 270, 280, 372–73
Collier, Marie, 481
Columbia Symphony Orchestra:
  concertos, 251–52, 275–76
  orchestral works, 23–24, 26–27, 69–70, 98–99, 106–7, 121–22
Concentus musicus Wien, 435–36
Corp, Ronald, 134–35
Cossotto, Fiorenza, 470, 473
Cotrubas, Ileana, 469
Covent Garden. *See* Royal Opera House

Crook, Howard, 408–9
Curry, Diane, 440
Curzon, Sir Clifford, 252
Czech Philharmonic, 231–32, 432–33

D

Dallapozza, Adolf, 449
Daniecki, John, 437–38
Davis, Sir Colin:
  concertos, 237, 266–67, 275–76
  opera, 449, 476
  orchestral works, 31, 80–81, 85–86, 109–10, 164, 182–83
  sacred and choral music, 417, 428–29, 435
Dawson, Lynne, 412, 437–38
De Larrocha, Alicia, 235
De los Angeles, Victoria, 476
Dernesch, Helga, 462
De Sabata, Victor, 476
Detroit Symphony Orchestra, 14
Deutsche Oper Berlin Chorus, 437–38, 463, 476, 484
Deutsche Oper Berlin Orchestra, 437–38, 484
Di Stefano, Giuseppe, 476
Domingo, Placido, 462, 463, 469, 470, 482
Doráti, Antal, 14
Dowd, Ronald, 417
Dresden Staatskapelle. *See* Staatskapelle Dresden
Drobková, Drahomíra, 432–33
Drottningholm Baroque Ensemble, 286
Dunn, Susan, 440
Du Pré, Jacqueline, 233–34, 315
Dutoit, Charles:
  concertos, 245, 272, 273–74, 282–83
  opera, 484
  orchestral works, 56, 65, 89–90, 126–27, 132–33, 138–39, 141–42, 147–48, 182–83
  sacred and choral music, 425

E · F

Edelmann, Otto, 482
Egorov, Youri, 400
Emerson Quartet, 296, 323
English Baroque Soloists:
  orchestral works, 10, 114–15
  sacred and choral music, 405–6, 408–9, 411–12, 414–15, 428
English Chamber Orchestra, 201, 251–52, 255, 257–58
English Concert, 201
Equiluz, Kurt, 435–36
Evans, Geraint, 484
Fassbaender, Brigitte, 481
Ferrier, Kathleen, 104
Fischer, Adam, 203
Fischer, Iván, 242–43
Fischer-Dieskau, Dietrich:
  chamber music, 347–48, 352
  opera, 462, 463, 482, 484
  sacred and choral music, 405–6, 408–9, 420–21, 423–24, 437–38
Flagstad, Kirsten, 462
Fleisher, Leon, 210–11
Flor, Claus Peter, 159
Foiani, Giovanni, 470
Forrester, Maureen, 99
Fournier, Pierre, 176–77, 231, 294
French National Radio Orchestra, 31
Freni, Mirella, 470, 472, 476, 477
Frey, Paul, 482
Frick, Gottlob, 430–31, 448, 449
Frühbeck de Burgos, Rafael, 235
Furtwängler, Wilhelm, 21–22, 213–14, 462

G

Garcia, José Luis, 201
Gardiner, John Eliot:
  orchestral works, 10, 114–15
  sacred and choral music, 405–6, 408–9, 411–12, 414–15, 428
Garrand, Don, 484
Gedda, Nicolai, 408–9, 440, 452, 472

Ghiaurov, Nicolai, 440, 452, 469, 472, 477
Giebel, Agnes, 430–31
Gilels, Emil, 220, 370–71
Giulini, Carlo Maria, 213–14, 223, 440, 448, 469, 470
Gobbi, Tito, 476
Gothenburg Symphony Orchestra, 71
Gould, Glenn, 359–60, 372–73
Greer, Lowell, 76
Greindl, Josef, 462
Gruberova, Edita, 482
Grumiaux, Arthur, 255
Guarneri Quartet, 308–9, 320–21, 323, 339

H

Hadley, Jerry, 440
Haitink, Bernard, 56–57, 101, 157, 196, 210–11, 213–14
Hale, Robert, 428
Hall, Carol, 412
Hallstein, Ingeborg, 449
Hardenberger, Hakan, 239
Harnoncourt, Nikolaus, 121–22, 435–36
Harper, Heather, 428–29
Harrell, Lynn, 300
Harwood, Elizabeth, 476
Hauptmann, Cornelius, 408–9
Haywood, Lorna, 423–24
Heifetz, Jascha, 225, 245–46, 278, 283
Hellmann, Uwe, 435
Hendl, Walter, 278
Hendricks, Barbara, 470, 484
Henry, Didier, 484
Highgate School Choir, 423–24
Hobson, Ian, 389–90
Hofmann, Peter, 461, 462, 463
Hogwood, Christopher, 10, 28–29, 85–86, 211–12, 261–62
Holl, Robert, 408–9, 435–36
Holton, Ruth, 405–6
Horowitz, Vladimir, 393–94
Hotter, Hans, 420–21
Huggett, Monica, 201, 338
Hungarian State Orchestra, 203

I · J

Istomin, Eugene, 275–76
Jacobs, Paul, 183, 381–82
Janowitz, Gundula, 437–38, 449
Järvi, Neeme, 71, 157, 159
Jochum, Eugen, 150–51, 220, 430–31, 437–38, 463
John Alldis Choir, 477
Jungwirth, Manfred, 449

K

Karajan, Herbert von:
 concertos, 223, 230–31, 255, 259
 opera, 461, 463, 470, 472, 473, 476, 477, 482
 orchestral works, 27–28, 46–47, 49, 96, 106, 109–10, 123–24, 132, 138–39, 154–55, 164–65, 166, 168–69, 176–77, 192–93
 sacred and choral music, 420–21
Katchen, Julius, 313–14
Kavafian, Ani, 319
Kavafian, Ida, 319
Kelly, David, 484
Kempff, Wilhelm, 297–98, 369–70, 396–97
Kendall, William, 414–15
Kerns, Robert, 477
Kertész, István, 60, 141–42, 252
King, James, 462
Klemperer, Otto, 103–4, 408–9, 420–21, 449
Kmentt, Waldemar, 430–31
Kocsis, Zoltán, 242–43
Kollo, René, 414–15, 449, 462
Kondrashin, Kirill, 143–44, 270, 280
Koopman, Ton, 7–8, 201, 359–60
Krause, Tom, 481
Krebbers, Herman, 415
Kulka, Janos, 228–29

L

Laredo, Jaime, 257–58, 343–44
La Scala. *See* Teatro alla Scala
Laubenthal, Horst, 463
Lear, Evelyn, 484

Leipzig Gewandhaus Orchestra, 482
Leipzig Radio Chorus, 408–9, 411–12, 435, 449, 472
Leister, Karl, 319
Leningrad Philharmonic, 192
Leppard, Raymond, 239–40, 255, 257–58
Levine, James, 147–48, 470, 472
Levine, Julius, 343–44
Ligendza, Catarina, 463
Lin, Cho-Liang, 225–26, 255, 257–58, 278
Lind, Eva, 449
Lipovšek, Marjana, 408–9, 411–12, 435
Litton, Andrew, 273
Livora, František, 432–33
London Classical Players, 28–29, 150
London Opera Chorus, 447, 470
London Oratory Junior Choir, 408–9
London Philharmonic Orchestra:
 concertos, 205, 235, 265
 opera, 447, 477
 orchestral works, 63, 85–86, 89–90, 196
London Sinfonietta, 147–48
London Symphony Orchestra:
 concertos, 233–34, 235, 252, 255, 264–65, 266–67, 269–70
 orchestral works, 44–45, 60, 63, 65–66, 141–42
 sacred and choral music, 417, 423–24, 428–29
London Symphony Orchestra Choir, 428–29
London Symphony Orchestra Chorus, 417, 423–24
Los Angeles Master Chorale, 470
Los Angeles Philharmonic, 470
Loveday, Alan, 286
Lubin, Steven, 211–12
Ludwig, Christa, 104, 408–9, 440, 449, 462, 477, 482
Lupu, Radu, 325
Luxon, Benjamin, 423–24

M

Ma, Yo-Yo, 315–16
Maazel, Lorin, 69–70, 484
McGegan, Nicholas, 76
Mackerras, Sir Charles:
  opera, 432–33
  orchestral works, 94,
    114–15, 116–17, 123,
    153
McMillan, Kevin, 437–38
Manuguerra, Matteo,
  470
Margiono, Charlotte,
  414–15
Marriner, Sir Neville:
  concertos, 225–26, 233,
    239, 286
  orchestral works, 7, 76
  sacred and choral music,
    430–31
Marsalis, Wynton, 239–40
Marshall, Margaret, 428
Martón, Eva, 481
Maslennikov, Aleksei,
  472
Masur, Kurt, 482
Mathis, Edith, 405–6
Matteuzzi, William, 452
Mattila, Karita, 449
Mehta, Zubin, 470, 477,
  481
Melcher, Wilhelm, 336
Melos Quartet, 306, 333,
  335–36, 345–46
Menuhin, Sir Yehudi, 63–64,
  213–14, 297–98
Merrill, Robert, 476
Mesplé, Mady, 452
Miles, Alastair, 414–15
Milnes, Sherrill, 425, 452,
  470
Milstein, Nathan, 245, 282–83,
  292
Mintz, Shlomo, 266–67, 292,
  325–26
Mitchell, Leona, 484
Moll, Kurt:
  opera, 448, 449, 461,
    463, 469
  sacred and choral music,
    414–15, 430–31
Monoyios, Ann, 408–9
Monteux, Pierre, 67–68
Monteverdi Choir,
  405–6, 408–9, 411–12,
  414–15, 428

Montreal Symphony
  Orchestra:
  concertos, 245, 272, 273–74,
    282–83
  opera, 484
  orchestral works, 56, 65,
    89–90, 126–27, 132–33,
    138–39, 141–42, 147–48,
    182–83
  sacred and choral music,
    425
Montreal Symphony Orchestra
  Chorus, 425, 484
Moore, Gerald, 347–48
Moroney, Davitt, 357
Morris, James, 425–26
Moser, Edda, 414–15, 448
Moser, Thomas, 430–31
Mravinsky, Evgeny, 192
Munch, Charles, 56–57,
  138–39, 147, 245–46
Munich Bach Orchestra, 7–8,
  405–6
Munich Bach Orchestra
  Chorus, 405–6
Murray, Ann, 411–12
Muti, Riccardo, 96
Mutter, Anne-Sophie, 223, 255

N · O

Naegele, Philipp, 343–44
Najnar, Jiri, 341
National Philharmonic
  Orchestra, 35, 239–40, 470
National Symphony Orchestra,
  472
Neidlinger, Gustav, 462
New London Orchestra,
  134–35
New Philharmonia Orchestra,
  101–2, 452, 470
New Symphony Orchestra of
  London, 225, 228–29
New York Philharmonic:
  orchestral works, 33, 51–52,
    69–70, 99, 182–83
  sacred and choral music,
    418
Nilsson, Birgit, 462, 481
Nimsgern, Siegmund,
  462, 463
Norman, Jessye, 462, 482
Norrington, Roger, 28–29,
  150
Novák, Richard, 432–33
Nucci, Leo, 452, 470

Obraztsova, Elena, 469
Ollmann, Kurt, 430–31
Oratorio Society of
  Washington, 472
Orchestra New England, 92
Orchestra of the Age of
  Enlightenment, 153
Orlando Quartet, 320, 339
Otter, Anne Sofie von, 408–9,
  472
Ozawa, Seiji, 217, 242–43

P

Panerai, Rolando, 476
Paris Opera Chorus, 473
Parkening, Christopher, 273
Parnas, Leslie, 343–44
Parsons, Geoffrey, 352
Patanè, Giuseppe, 452
Pavarotti, Luciano, 452, 470,
  476, 477
Pay, Antony, 261–62, 337–38
Pears, Peter, 408–9, 423–24, 484
Pease, James, 484
Perahia, Murray, 210–11, 237,
  251–52, 275–76, 396–97
Perlman, Itzhak, 213–14, 217,
  223, 297–98, 300–301, 313–14
Philadelphia Orchestra, 96
Philharmonia Baroque
  Orchestra, 76
Philharmonia Orchestra:
  concertos, 213–14, 259,
    278
  opera, 462
  orchestral works, 23–24,
    103–4
  sacred and choral music,
    408–9, 420–21, 440, 448,
    449, 484
Philharmonia Orchestra
  Choir, 408–9
Philharmonia Orchestra
  Chorus, 420–21, 440, 448,
  449, 482
Pinnock, Trevor, 201
Plishka, Paul, 440, 472
Pludermacher, Georges, 386–87
Pogorelich, Ivo, 391–92
Pollini, Maurizio, 370–71, 400
Popp, Lucia, 408–9, 430–31,
  447, 449
Prague Chamber Orchestra,
  114–15, 116–17, 123
Prague Philharmonic Chorus,
  432–33

Previn, André:
    concertos, 264–65, 266–67, 269–70
    orchestral works, 44–45, 63–64, 109–10, 134–35
Price, Leontyne, 470
Price, Margaret, 435
Prinz, Alfred, 262
Puyana, Rafael, 393–94

Q · R

Quartetto Italiano, 303, 339–40
Quirke, Saul, 428
Quivar, Florence, 484
Radio Chorus of the N.O.S., Hilversum, 414–15
Raimondi, Ruggero, 470, 472
Ramey, Samuel, 447, 452
Randová, Eva, 462
Raphael Ensemble, 341
Raskin, Judith, 484
RCA Symphony Orchestra, 270, 280
RCA Victor Symphony Orchestra & Chorus, 476
Reardon, John, 484
Reiner, Fritz, 14, 176, 270, 283
Resnik, Regina, 481
Rhodes, Samuel, 350
Ricciarelli, Katia, 470, 473
Richter, Karl, 7–8, 405–6
Richter, Sviatoslav, 299
Riegel, Kenneth, 472
Robbin, Catherine, 414–15, 428
Rodriguez, Santiago, 242, 264–65, 280
Rogé, Pascal, 272
Rolfe Johnson, Anthony, 405–6, 408–9, 423–24, 428
Rootering, Jan Hendrik, 430–31, 435
Rosenberger, Carol, 65, 235, 318–19
Rostropovich, Mstislav, x–xiv, 176, 194–95, 230–31, 299, 345–46, 472
Rothenberger, Anneliese, 448

Royal Concertgebouw Orchestra:
    concertos, 210–11, 213–14
    orchestral works, 31, 56–57, 80–81, 85–86, 101, 143–44, 150, 157, 159, 182–83
    sacred and choral music, 414–15
Royal Opera House, Covent Garden, Chorus, 452, 462, 476, 484
Royal Opera House, Covent Garden, Orchestra, 452, 470, 476, 484
Royal Philharmonic Orchestra, 35, 44–45, 63–64, 134–35, 143–44, 164, 187, 273, 484
Rubinstein, Artur, 228–29, 323, 377–78, 400
Rysanek, Leonie, 462

S

Sadler's Wells Opera Chorus, 484
Saint Louis Symphony Orchestra, 11, 51–52, 99, 205
Salomon String Quartet, 333
Salonen, Esa-Pekka, 278
Sándor, György, 203
San Francisco Girls Chorus and Boys Chorus, 437–38
San Francisco Symphony Orchestra, 71, 88, 129, 437–38
San Francisco Symphony Orchestra Chorus, 437–38
Sängerknaben, Schöneberger, 437–38
Sarfaty, Regina, 484
Sargent, Sir Malcolm, 225
Sawallisch, Wolfgang, 448
Scharinger, Anton, 411–12
Schiff, András, 347–48, 357–58, 359, 360, 386–87, 393–94
Schiff, Heinrich, 233, 345–46
Schmidt, Andreas, 408–9
Schmidt, Trudeliese, 435
Schreier, Peter, 347–48, 405–6, 408–9, 411–12, 435, 448
Schwarz, Gerard, 65–66, 235
Schwarz, Hanna, 414–15
Schwarzkopf, Elisabeth, 408–9, 420–21, 440, 448, 482
Sciutti, Graziella, 448

Scottish National Orchestra, 157, 159
Scotto, Renata, 470
Semkow, Jerzy, 228–29
Serkin, Rudolf, 220–21, 343–44
Shaw, Robert, 417, 423–24, 425–26, 440
Shicoff, Neil, 472
Shifrin, David, 318–19
Shirley-Quirk, John, 428–29
Sinclair, James, 92
Sitkovetsky, Dmitry, 266–67
Skrowaczewski, Stanislaw, 228–29
Slatkin, Leonard, 11, 51–52, 99, 205, 225–26
Smetana Quartet, 306
Smithson String Quartet, 303
Söderström, Elisabeth, 432–33
Sofia Philharmonic Orchestra, 242, 264–65, 280
Sofia Radio Chorus, 472
Soloists of the International Festival of Naples, 286
Solti, Sir Georg:
    concertos, 205, 217, 265
    opera, 447, 462, 481, 482
    orchestral works, 85–86, 126–27, 132–33, 152–53
Sotin, Hans, 449, 462
South German Radio Chorus, 430–31
Sparf, Nils-Erik, 286
Spiess, Ludovic, 472
Staatskapelle Dresden, 233, 408–9, 411–12, 435, 449, 472
Stamp, Richard, 147–48
Standage, Simon, 201
Steinhardt, Arnold, 321
Stich-Randall, Teresa, 482
Stokowski, Leopold, 35
Stolze, Gerhard, 437–38, 484
Stravinsky, Igor, 484
Stuttgart Radio Symphony Orchestra, 430–31
Suk, Josef, 257–58, 313–14
Suthaus, Ludwig, 462
Sutherland, Joan, 448, 452, 470, 477
Symphony of the Air, 228–29
Szell, George, 26–27, 171, 210–11, 220–21, 231–32, 251–52
Szeryng, Henryk, 213–14

T

Tabakov, Emil, 242, 264–65, 280
Taddei, Giuseppe, 448, 473
Takács Quartet, 328–29
Talich, Václav, 231–32
Talich Quartet, 309, 341
Talvela, Martti, 462, 472
Tátrai Quartet, 328–29
Teatro alla Scala Chorus & Orchestra, 473, 476
Teatro Comunale di Bologna Chorus & Orchestra, 452
Te Kanawa, Kiri, 425, 447
Thau, Pierre, 484
Thebom, Blanche, 462
Thomas, Michael Tilson, 92
Tomowa-Sintow, Anna, 420–21

U · V

Unger, Gerhard, 449
Van Dam, José, 420–21, 461, 463, 473, 482
Varady, Julia, 482
Varcoe, Stephen, 405–6

Vásáry, Tamás, 228–29
Vejzović, Dunja, 461, 463
Verrett, Shirley, 470
Vickers, Jon, 449
Vienna Boys Choir, 482
Vienna Philharmonic:
    concertos, 245, 262, 282–83
    opera, 449, 462, 469, 470, 472, 477, 481
    orchestral works, 19, 21–22, 25–26, 42–43, 46–47, 49, 80–81, 94, 101, 103–4,106, 109–10, 152–53, 168–69
    sacred and choral music, 420–21
Vienna Singverein, 420–21
Vienna State Opera Chorus, 435–36, 449, 461, 462, 469, 470, 472, 477, 482
Vishnevskaya, Galina, 423–24, 472
Von Stade, Frederica, 447
Vrenios, Anastasios, 452

W · Y · Z

Wächter, Eberhard, 448, 462
Wakefield, John, 428–29

Wallenstein, Alfred, 228–29
Walter, Bruno, 23–24, 26–27, 98–99, 103–4, 106–7, 121–22, 275–76
Wandsworth School Boys' Choir, 417, 477
Watson, Claire, 484
Watson, Jean, 484
Watts, Helen, 428–29
Weikl, Bernd, 481
Welsh National Opera Chorus & Orchestra, 452
Wenkel, Ortrun, 435–36
White, Willard, 484
Wiens, Edith, 430–31
Wilcock, Elizabeth, 201
Windgassen, Wolfgang, 462
Wixell, Ingvar, 476
Wlaschiha, Ekkehard, 449
Wolf, Markus, 336
Wunderlich, Fritz, 104, 484
Yakar, Rachel, 435–36
Young, Alexander, 484
Zednik, Heinz, 481
Zimerman, Krystian, 242–43, 377–78, 384
Zukerman, Pinchas, 201, 205

PICTURE CREDITS

Wherever possible we have made every effort to find and credit the original source for each picture:

CHAPTER I

Pp. 6, 31, 38, 135, 159, 169, 171, 195: Library of Congress. **Pp. 8, 11, 17, 22, 52, 71, 84, 121, 125:** Performing Arts Research Center, New York Public Library at Lincoln Center. **P. 9:** Woodcut by Tobias Stimmer. **Pp. 12, 19, 32, 39, 43, 49, 56, 57, 62 B , 63, 64, 66, 88 A, 90, 99, 106, 110, 113–115, 127, 141, 142, 149, 151, 154, 156, 165, 167, 178:** Musical America. **Pp. 12 B, 58, 124, 127, 132, 158, 187, 189:** Eastfoto/ Sovfoto. **Pp. 17 B, 21, 50, 62 A, 69, 70, 145, 154, 166, 168, 192:** Culver Pictures. **P. 23:** Erich Salomon/Bildarchiv Preussischer Kulturbesitz. **P. 24:** Archiv/Photo Researchers. **Pp. 25, 29, 148, 161, 175:** AKG, Berlin. **P. 27:** German Information Center. **P. 30:** Bibliothèque Nationale, Paris. **Pp. 34, 48, 53, 85, 101, 103, 129, 160, 172, 180, 188, 193:** The Bettmann Archive. **Pp. 45, 88 B, 162:** Lim M. Lai Collection. **P. 51:** Arnold Eagle. **Pp. 55, 68, 190:** The Granger Collection. **P. 60:** Courtesy Decca. **P. 67:** Clive Barda/Musical America. **Pp. 74, 87:** Art Resource. **Pp. 75, 76, 80, 81:** The Mansell Collection. **P. 79:** Lauros-Giraudon. **P. 83:** Leo de Wys, Inc. **Pp. 86, 94:** Courtesy ICM Artists. **Pp. 92, 107:** Picture Collection, New York Public Library. **P. 95:** Photographie Bulloz. **P. 100:** Bild-Archiv der Österreichischen National-bibliothek, Wien. **P. 104:** Courtesy London Records. **P. 109:** Bodleian Library, Oxford. **P. 116:** Erich Auerbach/Courtesy Telarc. **P. 100:** F. Posselt/Courtesy Deutsche Grammophon. **P. 123:** Siegfried Lauterwasser/Courtesy Deutsche Grammophon. **Pp. 126, 196:** AP/Wide World. **P. 128:** Royal Danish Embassy. **P. 134:**

Courtesy Columbia Artists Management, Inc. **Pp. 139, 176:** Courtesy RCA/Gold Seal. **P. 140:** Italian Cultural Institute. **P. 144:** Novosti (London). **P. 147:** Private Collection. **P. 153:** Patrick Lichfield/Courtesy London Records. **P. 157:** A3 Studio/Courtesy Philips Classics Productions. **P. 164:** N. Zannini/ Musical America. **P. 177:** Paul Kolnick. **P. 182:** Ernst Haas/ Musical America. **P. 183:** J.-P. Leloir/Musical America.

CHAPTER II

Pp. 200, 220, 229, 234, 238, 242, 279: The Bettmann Archive. **P. 201:** Martha Swope/Courtesy Shirley Kirshbaum & Associates. **P. 202:** Interfoto-MTI-Budapest. **Pp. 204, 246, 251, 270, 274:** Musical America. **Pp. 207, 240:** German Information Center. **Pp. 209, 262:** Jean-Loup Charmet. **P. 210:** Don Huntstein/Courtesy Archives of the Cleveland Orchestra. **Pp. 211, 236:** Performing Arts Research Center, New York Public Library at Lincoln Center. **P. 213:** Hoenisch, Leipzig. **P. 214:** Ludwig Schirmer/ Courtesy Sony Classical. **P. 216:** Trude Fleischmann, Vienna. **P. 217:** Courtesy Angel/EMI. **Pp. 218, 222, 246 B, 253, 281, 286:** AKG, Berlin. **Pp. 224, 277:** Lim M. Lai Collection. **Pp. 225, 226, 244, 269:** Library of Congress. **P. 230:** Picture Collection, New York Public Library. **P. 231:** Courtesy, Elektra International Classics. **P. 233:** Richard Holt/Courtesy Philips Classics. **P. 235:** Fridmar Damm/Leo de Wys. **P. 237:** Private Collection. **P. 239, 276:** Tanja Niemann/Courtesy Sony Classical. **P. 243:** Susesch Bayat/Courtesy Deutsche Grammophon. **P. 245:** Siegfried Lauterwasser/Courtesy Deutsche Grammophon. **Pp. 249, 260:** Culver Pictures. **P. 250:** Royal College of Music. **P. 252:** Ramon

Scavelli. **P. 254:** From *Pre-Classic Dance Forms* by Louis Horst, Dance Horizons, Inc. **P. 255:** Courtesy Siegfried Lauterwasser. **P. 257 A:** The Metropolitan Museum of Art/Gift of Robert L. Crowell. **P. 257 B:** The Metropolitan Museum of Art. Gift of Dorothy and Robert Rosenbaum, 1979. **P. 258:** Paris, Musée de la Musique/Cliché Publimage. **P. 259:** George Maiteny, London. **P. 264:** Christian Steiner/Courtesy Elan. **P. 266:** Clive Barda/Performing Arts Library. **P. 267:** Sovfoto. **P. 272:** Daniel Aubry/Odyssey, Chicago. **P. 278:** Deborah Feingold/Courtesy Sony Classical. **P. 280:** Courtesy Van Cliburn International Piano Competition. **P. 282:** Walter H. Scott/Courtesy London Records. **P. 285:** Christian Steiner/Columbia Artists Management, Inc.

CHAPTER III

P. 290: The Collection of William H. Scheide, Princeton, New Jersey. **Pp. 291, 293:** From *Pre-Classic Dance Forms* by Louis Horst, Dance Horizons, Inc. **P. 292:** Martine Franck/Magnum. **Pp. 294, 316:** Lim M. Lai Collection. **P. 296:** Christian Steiner/ Courtesy IMG Artists. **P. 297:** Giraudon. **P. 298:** Malcolm Crowthers/Courtesy Columbia Artists Management, Inc. **Pp. 299, 315:** Courtesy EMI Classics. **P. 300:** Erich Lessing, from Art Resource. **P. 301:** Christian Steiner/Courtesy Columbia Artists Management, Inc. **P. 303:** Courtesy of the Smithsonian Institution. **P. 304:** The Granger Collection. **P. 306:** Paul Huf. **P. 309:** Dorothea van Haeften/ Courtesy Philips Classics Productions. **P. 310, 320, 331, 340:** The Bettmann Archive. **P. 311:** Culver Pictures. **P. 312:** Swiss National Tourist Office. **P. 315:** Clive Barda/Performing Arts Library. **P. 317:** The Met-ropolitan Museum of Art,